The CBT Handbook

The CBT Handbook

Edited by

Windy Dryden and Rhena Branch

Los Angeles | London | New Delhi
Singapore | Washington DC

First published 2012

SAGE Publications Ltd
1 Oliver's Yard
55 City Road
London EC1Y 1SP

SAGE Publications Inc.
2455 Teller Road
Thousand Oaks, California 91320

SAGE Publications India Pvt Ltd
B 1/I 1 Mohan Cooperative Industrial Area
Mathura Road
New Delhi 110 044

SAGE Publications Asia-Pacific Pte Ltd
33 Pekin Street #02-01
Far East Square
Singapore 048763

Library of Congress Control Number: 2011925515

British Library Cataloguing in Publication data

A catalogue record for this book is available from the British Library

ISBN 978-1-84920-551-1
ISBN 978-1-84920-552-8 (pbk)

Typeset by C&M Digitals (P) Ltd, Chennai, India
Printed by MPG Books Group, Bodmin, Cornwall
Printed on paper from sustainable resources

Contents

List of Figures and Tables

Editor and Contributor Biographies

Windy Dryden is Professor of Psychotherapeutic Studies, Goldsmiths, University of London. He is a Fellow of the British Psychological Society and of the British Association for Counselling and Psychotherapy. He began his training in REBT in 1977 and became the first Briton to be accredited as an REBT therapist by the Albert Ellis Institute. In 1981, Windy spent a six month sabbatical at the Center for Cognitive Therapy, University of Pennsylvania, one of the first British psychologists to do an extended training in Cognitive Therapy. He is a Fellow of the Albert Ellis Institute and a Founding Fellow of the Academy of Cognitive Therapy.

Rhena Branch is a CBT therapist accredited with the BABCP and UKCP and a member of the AREBT. She is also a qualified supervisor. Rhena has her own private practice in North London. In the past she has worked in a variety of settings including alcohol and drug rehabilitation centres, NHS settings and with the Priory Hospital. Rhena teaches and supervises on the Masters course at Goldsmiths, University of London. Co-authored publications to date include: *CBT for Dummies*, *Self-esteem for Dummies*, *CBT Workbook for Dummies*, *The Fundamentals of Rational Emotive Behaviour Therapy*, *The Cognitive Behaviour Counseling Primer*.

Geoff Baxter works as a CBT therapist in private practice and at the Priory Hospital and is performance therapist at Trinity College of Music. He is also a supervisor on the Rational-Emotive and Cognitive Behaviour Therapy MSc course at Goldsmiths, University of London. Geoff originally trained as a musician and while working as a freelance trombonist became interested in the psychology of performing. After completing a Masters Degree in Psychology for Musicians he started working as a therapist specialising in the treatment of performers. His initial therapeutic training was in clinical hypnotherapy and he has a Masters Degree in Rational-Emotive and Cognitive Behaviour Therapy.

Tim Bond is Professor and Head of the Graduate School of Education at the University of Bristol, where he uses counselling skills both therapeutically and to support problem-solving in currently challenging times for universities, teachers and the public sector. He researches and writes extensively on ethical and legal issues for counselling and psychotherapy including *Standards and Ethics for Counselling in Action*, Third Edition (Sage, 2009).

Paul Farrand is based within the Mood Disorders Centre at the University of Exeter, UK. Here he is the clinical teaching lead for the Improving Access to Psychological Therapies low intensity CBT training programme, teaches and supervises on the high-intensity CBT programme and leads an undergraduate module in CBT. He is a leading editor of the *Oxford Guide to Low Intensity CBT Interventions*, which is the first internationally edited textbook on low-intensity CBT. He is a trustee of the BABCP and an accredited CBT therapist.

Kevin Gournay is Emeritus Professor at The Institute of Psychiatry, King's College London. He originally trained as a Nurse Behaviour Therapist with Isaac Marks in the 1970s and subsequently undertook further education and training and is now a Registered Psychologist. His PhD was on the cognitive behavioural treatment of agoraphobia. He has very wide-ranging clinical, research and training experience. He was appointed CBE in the New Year's Honours 1999. He is a Fellow of the Academy of Medical Sciences, a Fellow of the Royal College of Nursing and an Honorary Fellow of the Royal College of Psychiatrists.

Beverly Haarhoff is a Senior Lecturer, School of Psychology, Massey University, Auckland, New Zealand where she coordinates the Post Graduate Diploma in CBT. Beverly is a registered clinical psychologist. In the past she has worked in a variety of mental health settings both public and private. Currently her time is divided between teaching, supervision, clinical practice, and research. Her research focus is the transfer of key CBT competencies acquired in training to practice and the role of self-practice/self-reflection in the improvement and consolidation of CBT competencies.

Ken Laidlaw is a Senior Lecturer at Edinburgh University and works with NHS Lothian as a Consultant Clinical Psychologist/Clinical Lead for the older adults psychology service, Edinburgh. He has worked under Professor A.T. Beck at the University of Philadelphia, USA (the father of CBT), and has a long and productive association with Professors Larry W. Thompson and Dolores Gallagher-Thompson at Stanford University, California, USA and Professor Bob Knight at the University of Southern California in Los Angeles. He has published widely, including an RCT of CBT for late life depression and a number of journal articles and book chapters on CBT with older people. He is also the co-author of three books: *CBT with Older People* (2003), John Wiley & Sons Ltd, *The Handbook of Emotional Disorders in Later Life* (2008), Oxford University Press, and *The Casebook of Clinical Geropsychology* (2010), Oxford University Press. Ken regularly provides workshops on CBT with older people in the UK and internationally. He is a Board member of the International Psychogeriatric Association.

Margot Levinson is currently Programme Leader for the MSc CBP (Children and Adolescents) at Derby University. She is also a Cognitive Behavioural Psychotherapist in Derbyshire CAMHS. Her background is in Psychiatric Social Work with children and families. She has been a practitioner for over 30 years in social care and mental health in a wide variety of settings. Margot is also an experienced trainer in both the voluntary and independent sector. Her research interests are the political context of children's mental health, diversity, ethics and all aspects of child CBP.

William R. Lindsay is Consultant Clinical Psychologist and Lead Clinician in Scotland for Castlebeck Care. He was previously Head of Psychology (LD) and Consultant Clinical Psychologist with The State Hospital, Carstairs. He is Professor of Learning Disabilities and Forensic Psychology at the University of Abertay, Dundee and Visiting Professor at Northumbria University. He has published over 200 research articles, books and book chapters and given numerous conference presentations and workshops on cognitive therapy and the assessment and treatment of people with intellectual and developmental disabilities.

Warren Mansell is a Reader at the University of Manchester, a clinical psychologist and an accredited cognitive behavioural therapist. He has been the co-chair of the annual conference of the British Association of Behavioural and Cognitive Psychotherapies (BABCP) since 2008 and has authored over 80 publications. In 2011 he received the May Davidson Award from the British Psychological Society for outstanding contribution to clinical psychology in the 10 years since qualifying. His books include: *Cognitive Behavioural Processes across Psychological Disorders: A Transdiagnostic Approach to Research and Treatment*; *The Oxford Guide to*

Metaphors in CBT; *Coping with Fears and Phobias: A Step-by-Step Guide to Understanding and Facing Your Anxieties*; and *The Bluffer's Guide to Psychology.*

Gladeana McMahon is a Behavioural Coach and a BACP Accredited Counsellor and Counselling Supervisor. She is a fellow of the British Association for Counselling and Psychotherapy, International Stress Management Association, Institute of Management Studies, Royal Society of Arts and Association for Coaching. An internationally published author with some 20 books of an academic and self-help nature to her name, she has written extensively on issues related to private practice. Gladeana is Co-Director of the Centre for Stress Management and Centre for Coaching.

Stirling Moorey is a consultant psychiatrist in Cognitive Behaviour Therapy and honorary senior lecturer at the Institute of Psychiatry. He has been involved with cognitive therapy since spending his medical student elective at Beck's Center for Cognitive Therapy in Philadelphia in 1979. He teaches and supervises trainee therapists in the new Improving Access to Psychological Therapies services. His research interests are in psycho-oncology and he is co-author with Dr Steven Greer of *Cognitive Behaviour Therapy for People with Cancer*.

Michael Neenan is Associate Director of the Centre for Stress Management, Blackheath, London. He is an accredited (with the BABCP) cognitive behavioural therapist. He also works as a coach helping executives to improve their performance and runs courses for companies on developing resilience. He is the author of *Developing Resilience: A Cognitive Behavioural Approach* (2009) published by Routledge.

Michael J. Scott is a Consultant Psychologist and author of eight books on CBT, most recently *Simply Effective Group Cognitive Behaviour Therapy*, *Simply Effective Cognitive Behaviour Therapy* and *Moving on after Trauma*. He has a special interest in trauma and is currently writing *CBT for Common Trauma Responses*, Sage Publications. Dr Scott's other main interests are: the wider dissemination of CBT by keeping it simple, faithful to empirically supported treatment yet with the flexibility to easily address the needs of clients in routine practice with more than one disorder; the use of self-help materials and group work.

John L. Taylor is Professor of Clinical Psychology, Northumbria University and Consultant Clinical Psychologist with Northumberland, Tyne & Wear NHS Foundation Trust. He is currently Past President of the British Association for Behavioural and Cognitive Psychotherapies (BABCP). He has published work related to his clinical research interests on the assessment and cognitive-behavioural treatment of mental health, emotional and behavioural problems experienced by people with intellectual and developmental disabilities in a range of research journals, books and professional publications.

Peter Trower is Honorary Professor of Clinical Psychology, University of Birmingham, Fellow of the BPS, Associate Fellow of the Albert Ellis Institute, Diplomate of the Academy of Cognitive Therapy and Associate Director of the Centre for REBT at the University of Birmingham. One of his research specialities has been the development of REBT and CBT for people with psychosis. His most recent practitioner book is *Cognitive Behavioural Counselling in Action*, Second Edition.

Gillian Waldron is a Consultant Psychiatrist in Adult General Psychiatry, currently working in private practice at The Priory Hospital North London. She was previously a consultant in community psychiatry to the Royal London Hospital, where she was responsible for the organisation and delivery of an innovative multidisciplinary Crisis Intervention Service in Tower Hamlets. She has had research and clinical interests in the psychiatric conditions associated with childbirth and the results of sexual trauma.

Chris Williams is Professor of Psychosocial Psychiatry and Honorary Consultant Psychiatrist at the University of Glasgow. His main clinical and research interest is in the development and evaluation of self-help approaches that provide wider access to cognitive behavioural therapy (CBT) approaches. He is a Past President of the British Association for Behavioural and Cognitive Psychotherapies – the lead body for CBT (www.babcp.com) – and is a Patron of Anxiety UK (www.anxietyuk.org.uk) and of Triumph over Phobia (www.topuk.org).

Frank Wills is an independent CB therapist, trainer and author, living in Bristol. He comes originally from the Wirral and supports Tranmere Rovers FC and the England cricket team – activities that have made him so skilled in dealing with anxiety and depression.

Rob Willson is a cognitive behaviour therapist in private practice in North London. He has previously been therapy services manager in an acute psychiatric hospital, and has worked in both primary and secondary care settings. Rob taught and supervised at Goldsmiths, University of London for seven years before moving to the Institute of Psychiatry to conduct research and study for a PhD. Rob has co-authored several CBT self-help texts including *CBT for Dummies* and *Overcoming Obsessive Compulsive Disorder*.

Trevor Withers manages a team in Solihull working with children and adolescents with emotional, social and behavioural difficulties. He works in mainstream and special schools and has delivered training nationally both in schools and to a range of professionals. As a BABCP accredited Cognitive Behaviour Therapist he undertakes CBT work for Solihull CAMHS.

Dichelle Wong MBChB(Hons), BSc(Hons), MRCPsych(UK), Specialty Registrar in Old Age Psychiatry, NHS Lothian, was trained in Edinburgh and worked for two years as a Senior House Officer, treating patients on medical wards, many of whom are older people. She then pursued General Psychiatry and has now subspecialised in Old Age Psychiatry. She has provided CBT, Interpersonal Therapy and Psychodynamic Psychotherapy for patients. Her current research interest is functional magnetic resonance imaging in those with memory impairment. Recent publications include 'A novel therapy for a well-known problem' (Interpersonal Therapy case report), accepted for publication in *Contemporary Psychotherapy;* 'Eating disorders: Bulimia nervosa' and 'Anorexia Nervosa' peer reviewed articles published on *Behind the Medical Headlines* website produced by the Royal College of Physicians of Edinburgh and Royal College of Physicians and Surgeons of Glasgow; Falls Audit of Risk Assessments and Checklists in the *NHS Lothian Clinical Governance Newsletter.*

Wendy Wood is a senior lecturer within the Faculty of Education Health and Sciences at the University of Derby. She has been involved in counselling and psychotherapy training for 13 years and has been a therapist for over 20 years.

Editors' Introduction

Cognitive Behaviour Therapy (CBT), in our view, is a therapeutic tradition which comprises a growing number of specific approaches (Dryden 2012)[1]. This handbook is aimed at the growing number of Cognitive Behaviour Therapy (CBT) professionals and students within this tradition, who are working and training in the United Kingdom. It is also aimed at those professionals and students outside of the CBT tradition who want an authoritative, practical guide to CBT.

The handbook is divided into five parts. Part 1 is devoted to the nature and theoretical development of CBT: what it is, what it isn't and how it is typically misunderstood. Part 2 is devoted to CBT practice, and shows the growing range of practical issues that CBT therapists are likely to encounter. Part 3 discusses the clinical challenges that arise during the course of CBT treatment. Part 4 shows the applicability of CBT to a range of populations and details a number of clinical settings in which it is practised. Finally, Part 5 addresses the major professional issues present in the field today.

As editors we endeavoured to invoke the collaborative spirit of CBT by negotiating with contributors their chapter structure, focus and content. We hope you agree that the result of our collaboration has made for a comprehensive, accessible and highly relevant volume. We would like to thank all the contributors for their hard work. We would also like to thank Alec Grant and Michael Townend for their contribution to the development of this project. Finally, we credit Susannah Trefgarne and the editorial team at SAGE for their support, encouragement and professionalism.

Windy Dryden
Rhena Branch

[1]Dryden, W. (ed.) (2012) *Cognitive Behaviour Therapies.* London: Sage.

PART ONE

CBT: Practice

ONE What Is CBT and What Isn't CBT?

WARREN MANSELL AND
JOHN L. TAYLOR

Introduction

This chapter provides an overview of CBT and its current application within health and social care services in the UK. The defining features of CBT are described in terms of its underpinning principles. A multilevel definition of CBT is set out that incorporates its theoretical underpinnings, the evidence base, treatment techniques and paradigms, therapist competencies and practice, and service delivery and contexts. How CBT can be distinguished from non-CBT interventions is then considered. Finally, some of the future challenges and directions for the development of CBT are outlined.

What is CBT?

> 'We are what we think. All that we are arises with our thoughts. With our thoughts we make the world.'
>
> *Buddha (Hindu Prince Gautama Siddharta, the founder of Buddhism, 563–483 BC)*

> 'Man is not moved by things but by the view that he takes of them'
>
> *Epictetus (The Enchiridion, AD 135)*

It can be seen in the quotes above that the conceptual roots of CBT can be traced to philosophies from both Western and Eastern origins (Gilbert, 2010). Yet, the term Cognitive Behaviour Therapy (CBT) only came in to being during the 1970s (e.g. Taylor & Marshall, 1977). Figure 1.1 illustrates the development of CBT since its inception.

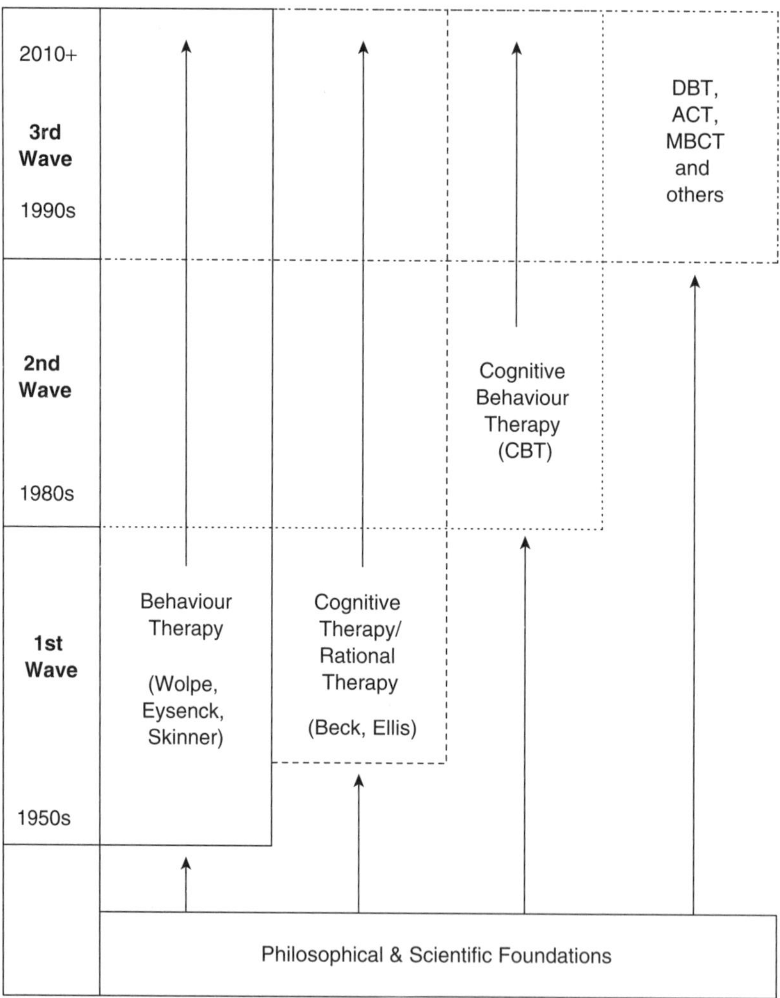

Figure 1.1 A simplified diagram of the development of CBT (for a more elaborate diagram, see Mansell, 2008a). The vertical column on the left represents a timeline from 1950s at the bottom to the present day, with the timings of the 1st, 2nd and 3rd waves of CBT demarcated. The extent to which each new wave builds on, and coexists together with the previous waves, is demonstrated by the overlapping blocks. The continuing revisiting of philosophical and scientific influences is illustrated by the upward arrows.

The movement began in the 1950s, when the scientific bases of cognitive therapy and behaviour therapy were developed - commonly known as the 'first wave' (Rachman, 1997). The key figures in the development of behaviour therapy are commonly regarded as the psychologists Joseph Wolpe, Hans Eysenck and B.F. Skinner (e.g. Wolpe, 1958). Behaviour therapy based its approach around theories of how learning new 'associations' between experiences (classical conditioning) and between experiences and behaviour (operant conditioning) could be reproduced in patients with psychological problems who have had learned counterproductive behaviours after a history of aversive or traumatic experiences. At around the same time, two psychoanalysts - Aaron T. Beck (a psychiatrist) and Albert Ellis (a psychologist) - were developing cognitive therapy and rational therapy, respectively (Beck, 1963; Ellis, 1962). Both approaches identified the role of biases in current thinking styles (e.g. catastrophising; following 'must' rules) that developed from earlier experiences and which contribute to current psychological distress. They brought in methods to address them based on a collaborative relationship, open questioning and testing beliefs against the real world (which will be elaborated later).

After a decade or so of these approaches developing separately, the 'second wave' led to their fusion as CBT that took prominence in the 1980s. According to Rachman (1997), this resulted from the increasing common ground between the two approaches - behaviour therapists became increasingly aware of the limitations of pure learning theory and the advantages of cognitive science; cognitive therapists incorporated the behavioural emphasis on empiricism into their evaluation of the therapy through objective and statistical methods. Arguably, the classic example of this integration within CBT is the *behavioural experiment* (Bennett-Levy et al., 2004) - a method whereby a controlled situation is created in which the client tries out a new way of behaving and then collects evidence to see whether their beliefs are found to be supported or disconfirmed. One example is a client with panic disorder who is afraid of having a heart attack and so sits down whenever he feels exerted. In the behavioural experiment, the client tries out standing up rather than sitting down and discovers that he does not have a heart attack - this intervention combines the precision of a behavioural account with a locus of change - a 'belief' about imminent danger - that is cognitive.

During the time that the second wave was gaining momentum, the seeds of a 'third wave' were sown. Now, since the 1990s, we have seen the development of this third wave of CBT, for example Dialectical Behaviour Therapy (DBT; Linehan, 1993), Mindfulness-Based Cognitive Therapy (MBCT; Segal et al., 2002), and Acceptance and Commitment Therapy (ACT; Hayes et al., 1999). These third wave therapies have been developed by revisiting and integrating diverse theoretical and therapeutic and philosophical influences such as attachment theory, meditation and radical behaviourism (Mansell, 2008b). The third wave approaches differ from one another to some degree, yet arguably share an emphasis on a 'mindful states of awareness', which we shall discuss later. Potentially, this results in CBT lacking coherence in its theories, principles and techniques because all three waves of CBT now coexist in services (Mansell, 2008a). The newer forms of CBT can appear on the face of it somewhat different as they use a diverse range of new terms, tools and techniques. In the following section we illustrate that, despite these differences, CBT can still be clearly distinguished as an entity in three distinct if overlapping ways:

- Through the underpinning principles of CBT (the collaborative relationship, prioritising the present, empiricism and rationalism) that are shared across its various forms.
- Through a multilevel definition of CBT that incorporates principles, theory, evidence, service delivery and context, therapist competencies and practice, tools and techniques, and the present moment during therapy itself.
- Through what a CBT client would experience in therapy sessions.

The Principles of CBT

CBT can be most clearly distinguished in terms of its core principles which remain relatively constant across the wide range of behavioural and cognitive therapies that are available. The principles of CBT are evident in the way that it is practised rather than in any specific technique, or indeed any specific psychological theory. These principles include the following.

The Collaborative Relationship. In many non-CBT therapies, the relationship between client and therapist is seen as the main agent of change. In CBT, the client and therapist working together is seen as an essential *necessary* condition to practise CBT. However it is *not* generally regarded as *sufficient* to bring about change in most cases. The collaborative relationship in CBT involves the client and therapist working together to try to understand the client's problems and the process of recovery. This approach has also been termed 'guided discovery'. Both therapist and client bring essential information to the session – the client brings their experiences and insights, and the therapist brings their therapeutic skills and their scientific-practitioner approach. CBT does not utilise the kind of expert–patient relationship that characterises many other interactions between patients and health professionals. For example, in behavioural therapy for a specific phobia, the therapist and client work together to produce a step-by-step 'graded hierarchy' for the client to face his or her fears. The first step on the hierarchy would be chosen by the client. For example, a bird phobic may choose to look at a photograph of a bird as a first step. Even in third-wave CBT, the development of a collaborative therapeutic relationship remains central.

Prioritising the Present. CBT is focused on working with the client on his or her present problems. Some CBT therapies acknowledge the importance of understanding how past experiences shape present beliefs, behaviours and thinking. Good practice requires, and the competencies of CBT therapists include, the ability to undertake a careful personal history, including significant previous experiences and events, with the aim of helping the client to focus on present concerns and how they can be more effectively managed. The importance of the present moment is clear in techniques such as 'thought catching', in which the client is helped to notice the thoughts that pass through their mind as they occur. Also, when clients are confronting their fears in therapy, the focus is on the current feelings of anxiety, in order to help them to tolerate them better and to illustrate how the intensity of the emotion reduces over time. Within third-wave therapies, for example MBCT, the client learns to focus on their breathing as it is occurring and the thoughts that appear in the present moment.

Empiricism. This is the view that personal beliefs are based on evidence gathered from our senses. This philosophy is often considered to mark the beginning of the culture of scientific thinking in the seventeenth century. Famously, Sir Francis Bacon told a parable about a long argument between two friars over the number of teeth in a horse's mouth. This was settled eventually by the use of direct evidence – actually counting the teeth. Arguably, CBT empowers clients to use an empirical approach for themselves; to test for evidence against their long-held beliefs and assumptions (e.g. 'I need to please other people all the time to be worthwhile') rather than to simply accept them as true. The principle of empiricism in CBT also guides the way that clients are encouraged to test out their beliefs and the effects of their thinking styles and behaviours in the real world. Classically, this is achieved through 'behavioural experiments' (Bennett-Levy et al., 2004). A behavioural experiment can be used not only to test the evidence for a particular belief, but to evaluate the effects (advantages *vs*. disadvantages) of any cognitive or behavioural process utilised in the light of evidence. This metacognitive aspect of therapy underpins many contemporary innovations in CBT (e.g. Wells, 2000; Watkins, 2008). CBT also utilises empiricism in evaluating its own effectiveness. The therapist monitors the outcomes in individual clients; services evaluate their outcomes across multiple clients; and the theories underpinning CBT are tested against evidence in research studies.

Rationalism. This refers to the notion that one's feelings have an origin in one's thinking. This is often mistaken for a view that being 'rational' is a virtue in itself, and that we need to train people to be logical thinkers. This is not quite accurate. Rationalism is based on a philosophy in which the explanation for one's feelings and behaviour lies in one's thinking. It is because one *believes* something to be true - whether or not it is in fact true - that affects one, rather than there being some unknown cause. The philosophical roots of rationalism are longstanding - going back, for example, to the Stoic movement of Ancient Greece, stated at the start of the chapter in the quote by Epictetus. This principle can be seen clearly in most CBT approaches. For example, CBT for panic disorder helps people to understand that it is their beliefs about the harmful effects of their bodily sensations (e.g. believing that an increased heart rate signals a heart attack) that is driving a panic attack. Within ACT (e.g. Hayes et al., 1999) the client learns to see how he is equating a thought about an event (e.g. 'I might hit my baby') with the event itself, and is helped to 'defuse' thoughts from events using a variety of techniques.

A Multilevel Definition of CBT

In addition to the core principles of CBT described above, there are other levels at which we can conceptualise CBT. Table 1.1 describes these levels and gives examples that are CBT and non-CBT. Importantly, if a psychological therapy is provided that is not consistent with the features of CBT at one of these levels, it seriously compromises the extent to which that therapy can be labelled CBT. This is an issue that deserves consideration in the present climate in which the term 'CBT' has become so widespread - much more widespread than the valid practice of CBT.

The levels are described in further detail here:

Principles of CBT. This level of definition is arguably the most consistent, as described above.

Theoretical underpinnings. The British Association of Behavioural and Cognitive Psychotherapies (BABCP) defines CBT as follows: 'The term "Cognitive-Behavioural Therapy" (CBT) is variously used to refer to behaviour therapy, cognitive therapy, and to therapy based on the pragmatic combination of principles of behavioural and cognitive theories.' (BABCP, 2005). While the principles described above are shared among nearly all forms of CBT, they do differ in terms of the psychological theories underpinning them. Generally, the underpinning theories are

Table 1.1 A Multilevel Definition of CBT

Level of Conceptualisation of CBT	Examples from CBT	Examples that are not CBT
Principles	Empiricism; Rationalism; Collaboration; Guided Discovery	Catharsis; Expert Opinion; Pragmatic Eclecticism
Theoretical Underpinnings	Cognitive and/or behavioural theories, e.g. Beck (1967); Mowrer (1939); Wells & Matthews (1994)	Theories that do not involve cognition and/or behaviour (e.g. biological lesion model of OCD)
Evidence Base	Therapy is (designed to be*) validated through empirical tests of core mechanisms, controlled trials and pragmatic evaluation in the setting where it is being delivered (Salkovskis, 2002)	The key mechanisms of the therapy are not (designed to be*) validated in empirical research, and the therapy is not designed to be validated by controlled studies and a pragmatic evaluation in the current setting.
Service Pathways Delivery & Context	Clients choose to come to therapy; collaborative working with service users; mental health problems seen by professionals in the service as being maintained by thinking styles and behaviour	Clients are persuaded to attend; therapy is seen as a superficial way of coping with a 'medical illness'; therapy is designed to increase medication adherence
Therapists' Competence and Practice	Agenda setting; Questioning; Formulation; Client provides therapist with feedback; Regular evaluation of cognitive change	Therapist assumes the problems to be discussed; information is presented as fact, not for discussion; no evidence for change is collected; 'debating' with client
Therapeutic Tools & Techniques	Socratic Questioning; Downward Arrow Questioning; Thought Diary; Activity Schedule; Vicious Cycles; Behavioural Experiments	CBT tools are provided without a rationale or formulation, or with the impression they are the full treatment; non-CBT techniques (e.g. free association; listening and reflection only)
The Present Moment	Client is de-centering from thoughts; client is willingly approaching feared experiences; client is questioning herself; client and therapist feel like they are working on the problems together as a team	Client is feeling criticised when questioned so that collaboration breaks down; client is persuasively encouraged to avoid facing fears; client consistently makes over-generalised statements (e.g. "I am stupid") without being queried about them; dialogue dwells on past or speculates on the future to the expense of the present problem

*CBT is designed for these forms of evaluation but may be in the process of validation through these multiple stages at the time of use.

behavioural or cognitive in nature, but it is accepted that even these theories have origins in a range of sources including attachment theory, developmental psychology, and social psychology (Mansell, 2008b). With the advent of third wave therapies, there has been further importation of theoretical frameworks, many of which have their grounding in behavioural and cognitive approaches. Thus, while the principles of CBT are clear and relatively consistent across all forms of CBT, the theoretical underpinnings are diverse and require a consensual framework that integrates the principles and practice of CBT.

Evidence base. Much has been written and said about the evidence base supporting the effectiveness of CBT for mental health problems. It is important to consider the different elements of a robust evidence base. First, the scientific support for CBT involves reciprocal links between theory, practice, clinical observations and research (Salkovskis, 2002). This involves a wide range of empirical studies testing the theories that underpin CBT including experimental studies, diary studies, interviews, and longitudinal studies exploring the long-term impact of interventions. Without this, it is impossible to be sure that a therapy works through the mechanisms proposed by the theory. Second, the real proof of the impact of CBT has emerged in its use in routine clinical settings, and more specifically by the individual clinician who uses the empirical method to evaluate his or her own CBT practice. Third, if CBT has a stronger evidence base than therapy *x*, this does not mean that CBT is more effective than therapy *x*. It simply means that there is more evidence available for CBT. There needs to be a range of studies directly comparing CBT with therapy *x* to show that CBT is significantly more effective than therapy *x*. Finally, there are many ways to evaluate the impact of CBT, one of which is symptom change after a fixed number of sessions. Other potentially valid outcome indicators include improvements in functioning (e.g. getting back to work, improved relationships), the duration of recovery, and the cost-benefits of delivering the therapy in practice. Applying these standards, CBT emerges well in terms of its evidence base, although there is significant room for improvement in developing the evidence base (see later).

Service pathways, delivery and context. The knowledge and attitudes of health professionals can have a significant impact on clients' access to safe and effective treatment for mental health problems. For example, some health professionals may view the prescription of long-term medication as the treatment of choice for mental health problems such as severe anxiety disorder. In recent years the National Institute for Health and Clinical Excellence (NICE) has been established as an independent organisation in England to provide guidance on the promotion of good health and the prevention and treatment of ill health (www.nice.org.uk).

NICE has now provided 'clinical guidelines' for a range of common mental health problems including anxiety disorders (including panic disorder and generalised anxiety disorder), depression (mild, moderate and severe), post-traumatic stress disorder, obsessive-compulsive disorder, and body dysmorphic disorder. (Guidelines are also available on schizophrenia, eating disorders, bipolar disorder, personality disorders and a range of other severe and complex mental health problems.) NICE guidelines are developed following a careful scrutiny of the research evidence available in the literature and using the expertise of healthcare professionals, patients and carers, academics and other stakeholders. They specify which interventions are indicated for which disorders.

A summary of cognitive behavioural therapy interventions recommended by NICE in the treatment of common mental health problems can be found on its website. For example, it is recommended that people with generalised anxiety disorder should receive 16–20 hours of high-intensity CBT which is usually delivered in the form of weekly sessions of 1–2 hours over a 4-month period.

The nature and effectiveness of psychological therapies are affected by the ways in which people can access treatment, referral pathways, how it is explained, and how it is offered. Historically referral and service pathways have been varied and variable in terms of quality. NICE has published guidelines on commissioning services to provide CBT for common mental health problems which aim to prevent the risk of deterioration to more severe forms of their condition, reduce dependence on medication, improve choice and reduce inequality, help with coping strategies and return to work. NICE recommends that key components of services providing CBT for common mental health problems are:

- Recognising and diagnosing common mental health problems – identification and accurate diagnosis of clients' problems are essential to them receiving the most effective intervention.
- Use of a 'stepped care' model – stepped care provides a framework so that services can be organised to help patients to quickly access the most effective, but least intrusive, intervention appropriate to their needs.
- Development of high quality services providing CBT – this has been done through very significant government investment in the Improving Access to Psychological Therapies (IAPT) programme. IAPT is focussed on the implementation of NICE guidelines for common mental health problems and expanding the psychological therapy workforce and service in England (www.iapt.nhs.uk). Between its inception in 2008 and 2009, IAPT employed 1,500 therapists

(including 800 trainees) and in the first nine months of operation the initial 35 sites treated 73,000 people. The goal is to treat 900,000 people in the first three years.

Therapists' competence and practice. Within the NHS, a wide range of health professionals deliver psychological therapies, including CBT. Most of these practitioners have a primary professional qualification (e.g. nurse, psychologist, psychiatrist) but the nature and quality of their CBT training is variable. In its guidelines on commissioning CBT services, NICE recommends commissioners to ensure that therapists are 'competent' to deliver CBT to a high standard.

The Cognitive Therapy Scale (CTS-R; Young & Beck, 1980; Blackburn et al., 1981) is widely accepted as the standard for assessing the competence of cognitive behavioural therapists. It is used to assess a range of competencies of CBT therapists in training including interpersonal effectiveness, collaboration, eliciting cognitions and behaviours, and guided discovery. The available evidence suggests that competence improves during training (Milne et al., 1999) and that competence is at least moderately related to patient outcome (Shaw et al., 1999). CBT therapists reaching criterion on the CTS-R demonstrate the required competencies and have been rated by patients as having higher interpersonal and active listening skills than other types of therapists (Keijsers et al., 2000).

The BABCP is the body responsible for accrediting CBT therapists and CBT training courses in the UK. The BABCP accreditation criteria set out the competencies CBT therapists must have and be able to demonstrate and the Association provides a register of accredited CBT therapists to help service users locate therapists in their locality who practise in accordance with its 'Standards of Conduct, Performance and Ethics in the Practice of Behavioural and Cognitive Psychotherapies' (www.cbtregisteruk.com). IAPT service users can learn what skills they can expect their CBT therapists to have by referring to specific advice provided by the Department of Health (Roth & Pilling, 2007)

Tools and techniques. This is the level of definition that can often lead to confusion and myths about the nature of CBT. There are many styles of interviewing and enquiry (e.g. Socratic questioning), written tools and materials (e.g. thought diaries; graded hierarchies) and skills training techniques (e.g. role-play, *in vitro* imaginal rehearsal) that are used in CBT. Use of one or more of these techniques does not constitute CBT. CBT will often involve the use of a range of techniques sequentially so that they become integrated during the therapy process and practised *in vivo* between sessions. However, irrespective of the specific tools and techniques that are used, CBT will always have a coherent underpinning theory and will adhere to the guiding principles of CBT described earlier.

BABCP (2005) describes different levels of CBT-based intervention that involve the application of tools and techniques and require different levels of training and skills.

- Cognitive behavioural psychotherapy – this is a formulation based form of psychotherapy for clients with more severe mental problems such that they cannot help themselves and have sought help from an expert therapist who has trained to a level that makes them eligible for specialist accreditation.
- CBT interventions that can be described by protocol – this involves the use of circumscribed interventions by practitioners who received training in the application of specific interventions for specific problems under the supervision of a CBT psychotherapist.
- Guided self-help – this can involve access to computerised CBT (cCBT), self-help materials, and awareness training groups supported by a health worker trained in assisting and signposting services and resources for clients with common mental health problems.
- Self-help – use of books, audio and video materials that individuals access for themselves without support from health care workers.

There is evidence for the effectiveness of interventions at each level, although in some areas such as guided self-help this is at an early stage of development.

The present moment. It could be argued that at any particular moment during a session, the nature of the therapeutic relationship determines whether CBT is going on. If, for example, the therapist takes an expert stance and does not invite contributions from the client, the spirit of collaborative empiricism is lost. CBT fosters an approach to relating to one's thoughts that aids recovery. Rather than seeing their thoughts as facts about the world, clients begin to see their thoughts as possible hypotheses about the world that can be observed in the mind's eye. Aaron T. Beck (Beck et al., 1979) called this process 'decentring', and it has since been described as adapting a 'mindful', or a 'metacognitive' stance (Segal et al., 2002; Wells, 2000).

Within the third-wave CBT, mindfulness has become more prominent, with a range of techniques (e.g. meditation; seeing thoughts as clouds; the 'two-chair' technique) designed to help clients relate to their own thinking processes in a more decentred, here-and-now manner.

The Client's Perspective of CBT

How would a client know that they were receiving CBT as opposed to another form of psychological therapy? The following is one example of a client's experience of CBT provided by one of our clients anonymously:

> 'CBT can offer you support and is tailored to your needs. Talking to the therapist made me feel understood and both the therapist and I worked together in a team to find ways to cope. I learned how to relax and be in a calm state of mindfulness – a revelation to me. I can now choose with better care the activities I am involved in and their intensity as well as the activities that are not appropriate at certain other times. I can now manage things better by charting my mood, any symptoms and factors that trigger problems. I am now on my own but the therapy has made me aware that I am in the position to combat problems by understanding myself better. Finally, CBT has been of great help for me in starting to build my self-esteem and feel valued and satisfied rather than feeling the need to please others constantly.'

The first thing a client would notice is that the therapist would want him or her to say what the problem is that they have come to talk about. Often this becomes an explicit 'agenda' for the session, or a 'problem list' that the client puts together to work on with the therapist.

The second thing a client would notice is that he or she is being asked questions about thoughts, feelings, bodily changes, behaviour, and responses from other people. These are things that the client may have only been fleetingly aware of in the situation they are talking about. The questions are designed to help the client to become more aware of these automatic processes, to understand, together with the therapist, how they fit together. This helps to build a 'formulation' – a map of how these elements link together to make a problem worse, or better. Some of the questions are used to try to help the client to describe the personal meanings they attach to their experience – e.g. 'What is the worst that could happen in this situation?'; 'What would it mean about you as a person if you were to do this?'

Third, the therapist would use questions, and other techniques, to help the client to try out different ways of thinking and behaving, and to test the effects. This is the empirical focus of CBT that helps clients to think scientifically about their own thoughts and beliefs and build up ways of approaching their problems that work for them.

The client would also be asked to assess their symptoms, to evaluate their progress in therapy and to rate their thoughts, feelings and beliefs at regular intervals during therapy. This ongoing assessment provides material for the therapist and client to work on in treatment sessions, and helps to signal improvement or to take appropriate steps should there be any deterioration.

During CBT, these stages would be repeated and would feed into reformulations of need as the client comes up with new goals to work on and new problems to understand. The ultimate aim is that the client eventually manages their own problems independently from the therapist, although they may come back for 'booster' sessions in the future.

What is Not CBT

A therapy that does not adhere to the principles of CBT; a therapy that deviates significantly on one of the multiple levels of definition provided; or a therapy that a client would not recognise as CBT is not CBT. Table 1.2 uses an example of therapy dialogue to illustrate, from the client's perspective, typical responses from the therapist that are consistent with CBT and contrasts these with responses not consistent with CBT.

As illustrated in Table 1.1, true CBT comprises multiple levels that are integrated to form a coherent system. It would not be valid for a therapy to be described as CBT if it fits one or two of these levels of definition. For example, a thought diary is a tool used in CBT. However, it needs to be used according to CBT principles - within an agreed formulation framework, as a collaborative approach to collecting evidence. Without this scaffold it is not CBT, but use of a technique often used in CBT.

According to rumour, Beck once quipped, tongue-in-cheek - 'If it works, it's cognitive therapy!' Putting this *bon mot* to one side, there are arguably a range of therapies that are not considered as forms of CBT because their proponents do not consider them to be CBT for a number of reasons. However, on closer inspection, they share many CBT principles, practices or techniques. For example, 'reframing' in motivational interviewing resembles reality testing, and 'dilemmas' in Cognitive Analytic Therapy resemble all-or-none thinking within CBT. These shared features are encouraging because they provide some evidence of convergent validity. That is, if interventions from different traditions share some basic treatment techniques and paradigms they are likely to be focussing on common processes or mechanisms involved in causing psychological distress. Such similarities also point towards the potential of a more integrative approach that considers CBT alongside, rather than separately to other evidence-based and theory-driven psychotherapies (Higginson et al., 2011).

Conclusions

In this chapter we have attempted to set out the principles, defining characteristics and patient experience of CBT. Figure 1.2 provides a simple integrative model of how the components of CBT fit together. It sets the key elements of the therapy session itself within a context

Table 1.2 A Hypothetical Therapeutic Dialogue Illustrating Examples of What is CBT and What Is Not CBT

Client Statement	CBT	Not CBT
"I find it really hard to breathe when I am in a panic attack."	*Downward Arrow Question* "What do you think is going to happen when you find it hard to breathe?"	*Psycho-education given as reassurance* "Don't worry, you will always be able to breathe during a panic attack."
"I think I am going to suffocate."	*Downward Arrow Question* "When you say suffocate, what is the worst that you think will happen?"	*Advice* "Why don't you just tell yourself – I will not suffocate?"
"I am afraid that I will die because everything starts to feel unreal."	*Asking about behaviour* "What is it that you do when you are convinced you will die?"	*Reflective statement* "You are afraid you will die."
"I have to breathe a lot more to catch my breath."	*Socratic Question* "Have you ever tried just breathing at a normal rate when this happens?"	*Vague technique without rationale* "I suggest that you try to think more positively."
"Yes… actually I didn't get that unreal feeling that time."	*Eliciting a reappraisal* "What do you make of that?"	*Forcing reappraisal with implicit criticism* "This means it is your fault making yourself ill by breathing too fast."
"Maybe I am making things worse by breathing too quickly? Do you think I could make myself feel unreal by breathing faster?"	*Suggesting a Behavioural Experiment* "Let's see. What do you think of trying to change our breathing together, to see if you are right about that?"	*Avoidance of testing fear beliefs* "I don't think you should try that just in case it makes things worse."

Table 1.2 (Continued)

Client Statement	CBT	Not CBT
"I will try it but only if you go first!"	*Collaboration; Assessing the nature of the evidence* "OK, and you will go after? So, how will you know if it has had an effect? Shall I just tell you?"	*Lack of collaboration* "Really, you need to do these things yourself."
[both try out breathing faster as an experiment and reporting how it feels] "So this is just a strange feeling that goes away when I slow down my breathing again!"	*Psycho-education in the spirit of guided discovery* "It seems so, and that's what most people experience. Do you want to know any more about how this feeling comes about?"	*Offering information in an inaccessible manner* "You are hyperventilating which causes alkalosis of the blood."
[explained the effects of hyperventilation] "This makes sense, but I am still worried about panicking in the future."	*Normalising and goal setting* "That's understandable given how long you have been having them. Do you want to talk about your worries about having the panic attacks next?"	*Forcing a historical interpretation* "I am not surprised because I find that most clients need to fully express their anger towards their parents before their panic attacks will stop."

of the underpinning theory, the reflective practice that drives training and improved practice, and the overall empirical evaluation of theory and practice. We have also indicated what isn't CBT – although some distinctions are more perceived than real and point to the potential for the development of more integrative approaches in future.

In recent years the development of CBT services has accelerated as a result of NICE recommendations and the government's investment in IAPT services. This has resulted in the rapid training of a large number of mental health practitioners to deliver evidence-based psychological therapies, predominantly CBT, to increasing numbers of people experiencing common mental health problems. The longer-term impact and effect of this programme on the psychological well-being of communities and on the professional practice of psychological therapy are yet to be determined.

The key to this unprecedented investment in psychological therapies has been the plethora of research providing support for the effectiveness of CBT. It has a strong evidence base across a wide range of presenting problems, not only demonstrated in hundreds of controlled trials (Butler et al., 2006) but also within a range of service contexts (e.g. Gillespie et al., 2002; Morrison et al., 2004). Its effectiveness is not restricted to measures of symptom improvement, but has also been demonstrated in long-term improvements in quality of life (e.g. Sharpe et al., 1996) and in service user feedback research (e.g. Knight et al., 2006). The principles of CBT have been developed to form a range of 'low-intensity' formats that make it simpler to access and easier to deliver, such as self-help books and computerised CBT (Richards et al., 2003). There are many examples of treatment trials in which CBT has been shown to be superior to other psychological therapies (e.g. Bryant et al., 2003; Giesen-Bloo et al., 2007).

On the other hand, there are considerable challenges to CBT (Mansell, 2008a). There is a persuasive case that across trials and settings as a whole, CBT does not lead to consistently better outcomes than other *bona fide* (typically theory-based) psychological therapies (Wampold et al., 2002). A recent meta-analytic review of 1,981 patients revealed that when looking more closely at different types of *bona fide* treatments, CBT is superior in outcome to psychodynamic therapy for treating anxiety, depression and general functioning, but not evidently superior to interpersonal and supportive therapies (Tolin, 2010). The effects of CBT within serious mental health problems are currently modest (Lynch et al., 2010). Finally, there is evidence that in certain settings such as primary care, other modalities of therapy may be more efficient and cost effective (Ward et al., 2000). Thus, the empirical strengths of CBT are met by significant challenges that cannot be ignored. On the basis of historical precedence, CBT practitioners and

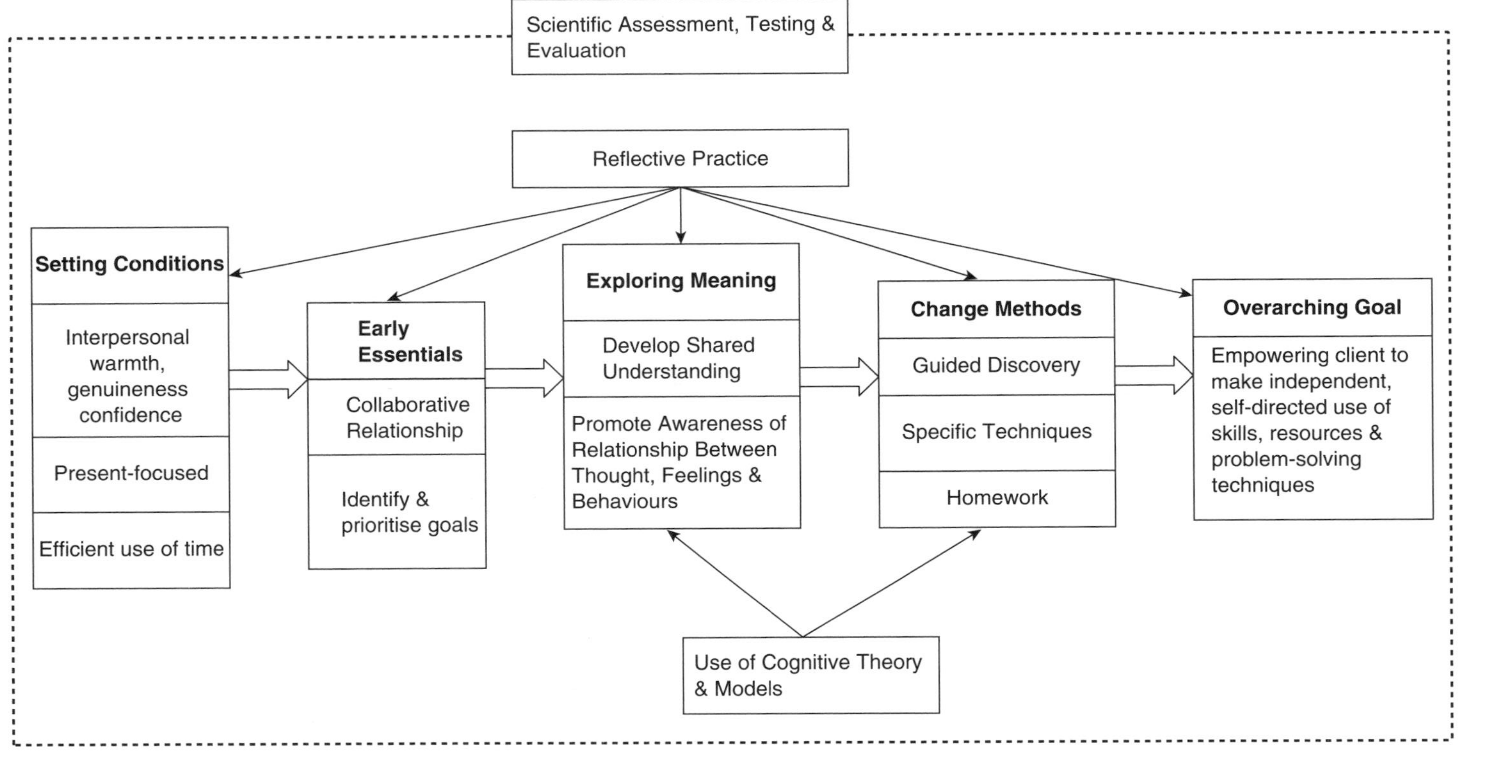

Figure 1.2 A model of the core components of CBT. Reproduced from Mansell (2008a) with permission from Cambridge University Press.

researchers are likely to address these challenges ahead in a direct and fruitful manner.

Further Reading and Resources

A historical introduction to CBT is provided by Rachman (1997). Two companion articles to this chapter are Mansell (2008a,b), in which the dilemmas relating to the definition of CBT are explored, myths about CBT are addressed, and its future developments are indicated.

The following websites are also relevant to the material covered here:

- British Association of Behavioural and Cognitive Psychotherapies - www.babcp.com
- Association of Behavioral and Cognitive Therapies - www.abct.org
- National Institute for Heath and Clinical Excellence - www.nice.org.uk
- Improving Access to Psychological Therapies - www.iapt.nhs.uk

References

BABCP (2005). *What Are Cognitive and/or Behavioural Psychotherapies?* Retrieved from www.babcp.com/public/what-is-cognitive-behaviour-therapy on 17 May 2010.

Beck, A.T. (1963). 'Thinking and depression: I. Idiosyncratic content and cognitive disortions', *Archives of General Psychiatry*, 9: 324–33.

Beck, A.T (1967). *Depression: Chinical, Experimental and Theoretical Aspects.* New York: Harper & Row.

Beck, A.T., Rush, A.J., Shaw, B.F. and Emery, G. (1979). *Cognitive Therapy of Depression.* New York: Guilford Press.

Bennett-Levy, J., Butler, G., Fennell, M., Hackmann, A., Mueller, M., Rouf, K. and Westbrook, D. (2004). *Oxford Guide to Behavioural Experiments in Cognitive Therapy.* Oxford: Oxford University Press.

Blackburn, I.M., James, I.A., Milne, D.L. and Reichelt, F.K. (1981). *Cognitive Therapy Scale Revised (CTS-R).* Newcastle upon Tyne: Unpublished Manuscript.

Bryant, R.A., Moulds, M.L. and Nixon, R.V.D. (2003). 'Cognitive behaviour therapy of acute stress disorder: A four year follow-up', *Behaviour Research and Therapy*, 41: 489–94.

Butler, A.C., Chapman, J.E., Forman, E.M. and Beck, A.T. (2006). 'The empirical status of cognitive-behavioural therapy: A review of meta-analyses', *Clinical Psychology Review*, 26: 17–31.

Ellis, A. (1962). *Reason and Emotion in Psychotherapy.* Secaucus, NJ: Citadel Press.

Epictetus (135AD). *The Enchiridion*. Translated by Elizabeth Carter. Retrieved from www.davemckay.co.uk/philosophy/epictetus on 17 May 2010.

Giesen-Bloo, J., van Dyck, R., Spinhoven, P., van Tilburg, W., Dirksen, C., van Asselt, T. et al. (2007). 'Outpatient psychotherapy for borderline personality disorder: Randomized trial of schema-focused therapy vs transference-focused psychotherapy', *Archives of General Psychiatry*, 63: 649–58.

Gilbert, P. (2010). *The Compassionate Mind*. Constable: London.

Gillespie, K., Duffy, M., Hackmann, A. and Clark, D.M. (2002) 'Community based cognitive therapy in the treatment of post-traumatic stress disorder following the Omagh bomb', *Behaviour Research and Therapy*, 40: 345–57.

Hayes, S.C., Strosahl, K.D. and Wilson, K.G. (1999). *Acceptance and Commitment Therapy: An Experiential Approach to Behavior Change*. New York: Guilford Press.

Higginson, S., Mansell, W. and Wood, A.M. (2011). 'An integrative mechanistic account of psychological distress, therapeutic change and recovery: the Perceptual Control Theory approach', *Clinical Psychology Review*, 31: 249–59. doi:10.1016/j.cpr.2010.01.005

Keijsers, G.P., Schaap, C.P.D.R. and Hoogduin, C.A.L. (2000). 'The impact of interpersonal patient and therapist behavior on outcome in cognitive-behavior therapy: A review of empirical studies', *Behavior Modification*, 24: 264–97.

Knight, M.T.D., Wykes, T. and Hayward, P. (2006). 'Group treatment of stigmatisation and self-esteem in schizophrenia: a waiting list trial of efficacy', *Behavioural and Cognitive Psychotherapy*, 35: 304–18.

Linehan, M. (1993). *Cognitive-behavioral Treatment of Borderline Personality Disorder*. New York: Guilford Press.

Lynch, D., Laws, K.R. and McKenna, P.J. (2010). 'Cognitive behavioural therapy for major psychiatric disorder: does it really work? A meta-analytical review of well-controlled trials', *Psychological Medicine*, 40: 9–24.

Mansell, W. (2008a). 'The seven Cs of CBT: A consideration of the future challenges for cognitive behavioural therapy', *Behavioural and Cognitive Psychotherapy*, 36: 641–49.

Mansell, W. (2008b). 'What is CBT *really* and how can we enhance the impact of effective psychotherapies such as CBT?', in R. House and D. Loewenthal, *Against and For CBT: Towards a Constructive Dialogue*. Ross-on-Wye: PCCS Publications Ltd.

Milne, D.L., Baker, C., Blackburn, I., James, I. and Reichelt, F.K. (1999). 'Effectiveness of cognitive therapy training', *Journal of Behavior Therapy and Experimental Psychiatry*, 30: 81–92.

Morrison, A.P., Renton, J.C., Williams, S., Dunn, H., Knight, A., Kreutz, M. et al. (2004). 'Delivering cognitive therapy to people with psychosis in a community mental health setting: An effectiveness study', *Acta Psychiatrica Scandinavica*, 110: 36–44.

Mowrer, A.H. (1939). 'Stimulus response theory of anxiety', *Psychological Review*, 46: 553–65.

National Institute for Heath and Clinical Excellence (NICE). *Summary of Cognitive Behavioural Therapy Interventions Recommended by NICE*. Retrieved from www.nice.org.uk/usingguidance/commissioningguides/cognitivebehaviouraltherapyservice/summarycbtinterventions.jsp on 19 May 2011.

Rachman, S. J. (1997). 'The evolution of Cognitive Behaviour Therapy', in D.M. Clark and C.G. Fairburn (eds), *Science and Practice of Cognitive Behaviour Therapy*, Oxford: Oxford University Press, pp. 3–26.

Richards, D.A., Lovell, K. and McEvoy, P. (2003). 'Access and effectiveness in psychological therapies: self-help as a routine health technology', *Health and Social Care in the Community*, 11: 175–82.

Roth, A.D. and Pilling, S. (2007). *Cognitive and Behavioural Therapy (CBT) for People with Depression and Anxiety: What Skills Can Service Users Expect Their Therapists to Have?* London: DoH.

Salkovskis, P.M. (2002). 'Empirically grounded clinical interventions: Cognitive behavioural therapy progresses through a multi-dimensional approach to clinical science', *Behavioural and Cognitive Psychotherapy*, 30: 3–9.

Segal, Z.V., Williams, J.M.G. and Teasdale, J.D. (2002). *Mindfulness-based Cognitive Therapy for Depression: A New Approach to Preventing Relapse.* New York: Guilford Press.

Sharpe, M., Hawton, K., Simkin, S., Surawy, C., Hackmann, A., Klimes, I. et al. (1996). 'Cognitive behaviour therapy for the chronic fatigue syndrome: A randomised controlled trial', *British Medical Journal*, 312: 22–6.

Shaw, B.F., Elkin, I., Yamaguchi, J., Olmsted, M., Vallis, T.M., Dobson, K.S. et al. (1999). 'Therapist competence ratings in relation to clinical outcome in cognitive therapy for depression', *Journal of Consulting and Clinical Psychology*, 67: 837–46.

Taylor, F.G. and Marshall, W.L. (1977). 'Experimental analysis of a cognitive-behavioral therapy for depression', *Behavioral Science*, 1: 59–72.

Tolin, D.F. (2010). 'Is cognitive-behavioral therapy more effective than other therapies? A meta-analytic review', *Clinical Psychology Review*, 30: 710–20.

Wampold, B.E., Minami, T., Baskin, T.W. and Tierney, S.C. (2002). 'A meta-(re)analysis of the effects of cognitive therapy versus "other therapies" for depression', *Journal of Affective Disorders*, 68: 159–65.

Ward, E., King, M., Lloyd, M., Bower, P., Sibbald, B., Farrelly, S. et al. (2000). 'Randomised controlled trial of non-directive counselling, Cognitive-Behaviour Therapy, and usual general practitioner care for patients with depression. I: Clinical effectiveness', *British Medical Journal*, 321: 1383–8.

Watkins, E.R. (2008). 'Constructive and unconstructive repetitive thought', *Psychological Bulletin*, 134: 163–206.

Wells, A. (2000). *Emotional Disorders and Metacognition: Innovative Cognitive Therapy.* Chichester, UK: John Wiley & Sons, Ltd.

Wells, A. and Matthews, G. (1994). *Attention and Emotion: A Clinical Perspective*. Hove: Lawrence Erlbaum.

Wolpe, J. (1958). *Psychotherapy by Reciprocal Inhibition.* Pala Alto, CA: Stanford University Press.

Young, J.E. and Beck, A.T. (1980). *Cognitive Therapy Scale.* Unpublished manuscript. Philadelphia, PA: University of Pennsylvania.

TWO CBT Theory

PETER TROWER

Introduction

Does the Practitioner Need to Understand The Theory?

The assertion is sometimes made that the Cognitive Behaviour Therapy (CBT) practitioner does not really need to be familiar with the theoretical basis of CBT in order to practise. Some might argue that the theory may be important for the academic and researcher, but hardly for the therapist, who only needs to know what works (the evidence base) and how to work it (the procedures). Indeed a hard line empiricist might argue that theory is not needed at all – the famous behaviourist B.F. Skinner made such an argument (Skinner, 1950).

The view in, and rationale for, the present chapter is that it is indeed important, probably essential, for the CBT practitioner to understand CBT theory, for at least two reasons. One is that theory guides the therapist in the continuous creative process of assessing, formulating and treating clients. To misquote the philosopher Kant, empiricism without theory is blind – it is difficult to know where one is going without it (Kant, 1964/1787). The second point is that, as we shall show when discussing CBT in detail, the client's problems have a great deal to do with the client's own 'lay theories' about his plight, and part of the therapy will be to help the client understand his problem in a new way that CBT theory provides. CBT theory should, after all, show the pathway to recovery.

Theoretical Confusion in CBT?

Having made a case for the importance of understanding CBT theory, we then need to ask: what is *the* CBT theory? Unfortunately there isn't an easy answer to this. As Mansell (2008) points out, CBT lacks clarity as a therapeutic system, with diverse and imprecise terminology and little agreement as to the features that would identify it and distinguish it from other therapies.

One of the problems relevant to this chapter is the lack of coherence to one theory. There appears to be little in common between classic behavioural approaches, early cognitive therapy and the more recent surge of multilevel, hierarchical models and variants which draw on an eclectic mix of theories: 'to our colleagues and clients, the arena of CBT can appear as a confusing mixture of ideas' (Mansell, 2008: 643). Mansell identifies the challenges of this 'family of related therapies' and calls for a number of improvements, one of which is the focus of this chapter, namely theoretical coherence.

Clarifying the Developmental Stages of CBT Theory

In order to attempt to bring some clarity to the theoretical coherence issue, this chapter will be structured around the developmental stages of CBT theory through one revolution (namely the cognitive revolution) from behaviour therapy and modification to CBT, and several evolutions from CBT to the more recently developed 'third wave' multilevel models and variants. Each development was spurred by dissatisfaction with the previous theory, so I will select and describe the key theories, the critiques of these theories, and the consequent new or modified theories, showing how the new differed from the old. The aim here is not to critically and endlessly review the validity of the theories, the critiques and the subsequent rejoinders and rebuttals, but to show the thinking that lay behind and spurred new thinking and theorising. Since the volume of theories, therapies, critiques and rebuttals is enormous, this chapter will not be a comprehensive but a selective review of developments that have most influenced CBT practice. Since most contemporary CBT practice is increasingly eclectic, the chapter will conclude with a discussion of selected present and future trends that provide and promise to provide much needed theoretical integration.

The Behavioural Approach and its Critics

The application of learning theory to the development of behavioural therapies in the 1950s and 1960s was so successful that the approach became widely recognised as a major breakthrough in the psychological treatment of mental health problems. Yet within 20 years or so, these relatively new behavioural approaches were being rapidly overtaken in popularity by a cognitive approach which was so different in theory (though not in key aspects of methodology) that it was characterised as a revolution in terms of the Kuhnian concept of a paradigm shift (Kuhn, 1962; Mahoney, 1974). What was this difference? To understand CBT theory and its impact, it is helpful to look at the two theories and these fundamental differences.

Behavioural Science and the Behavioural Therapies

The behavioural therapies were based on the behavioural science paradigm which rejected 'mental events' as unscientific because unobservable, and asserted that cognitive constructs are epiphenomena that play no role in explaining, predicting, or describing human behaviour. They therefore looked for observable learned relationships between stimulus and response in classical conditioning, and between a behavioural 'operant' and a consequent reinforcement in operant conditioning.

Behaviour Therapy (BT), for example, is based largely on the classical conditioning theory of fear acquisition, in which neutral stimuli that are associated with a fear-producing state of affairs develop fearful qualities and become conditioned fear stimuli, automatically producing a conditioned fear and avoidance response. Once established, these classically conditioned fear responses are maintained through operant conditioning (i.e. reinforcement) of avoidance behaviour (Mowrer, 1939). One approach to classical conditioning-based therapy then is to break this conditioned stimulus-response connection and to establish a new, nonfearful response to that stimulus. One of the main behaviour therapies designed to achieve this 'counter-conditioning' was systematic desensitisation (Wolpe, 1958).

Critiques of Behavioural Theories

Despite considerable successes, particularly in the anxiety disorders, a number of critiques were published during the 1970s, concerning various issues including empirical limitations shown in outcome studies, limited applicability to major areas of mental health such as depression, and the failure of the theory to explain key psychological phenomena (e.g. Rachman, 1977).

However Mahoney (1974) called for a more radical 'revolutionary' rather than evolutionary paradigm shift from behaviourism largely because it was a deterministic theory, with its model of the person as a 'passive organism' totally under the control of external causes, and this model did not fit or explain many of the key aspects of human functioning.

Beck (1976) similarly argued that behaviour therapy shared with neuropsychiatry and psychoanalysis an assumption 'that the emotionally disturbed person is victimised by concealed forces over which he has no control' (Beck, 1976: 2). Indeed there was a widely shared dissatisfaction among cognitive-oriented therapists with the notion that people were entirely at the mercy of their conditioning history and that individual differences in the interpretation of a feared situation, in perceived control, or in the ability to formulate plans and goals had no role to play either in generating the problems or on the outcome of treatment (Brewin et al., 1996).

The Cognitive Behavioural Approach and its Critiques

The Cognitive Revolution

Mahoney (1974) assembled convincing evidence that a 'cognitive revolution' based on a cognitive learning model was well under way in clinical psychology as well as psychology generally by the early 1970s. This model was 'revolutionary' rather than evolutionary because it placed cognitive mediation between the stimulus and the response, a radical switch from the person as a passive organism conditioned by external forces to an active agent who is goal-seeking, information-processing and problem-solving. The foremost CBT approaches at the time of Beck (later to be the most influential developer of CBT) and Ellis (the first developer of a CBT approach) fitted well into the new paradigm. For example Beck's Cognitive Therapy (CT) model emphasised cognitive mediation in human learning, in which 'man has the key to understanding and solving his psychological disturbance within the scope of his own awareness' (Beck 1976: 3). A similar model of the person was expressed by Ellis (1962, 1994) in Rational Emotive Behaviour Therapy (REBT). He asserted that it was the person's irrational beliefs about adversities (stimuli) that mainly led to their emotional and behavioural reactions (responses) rather than the adversities directly. In each case the focus of CBT in mental health problems was primarily aimed at modifying the mediating belief system rather than the stimulus conditions or behavioural reinforcement contingencies.

CBT Theory, General Version

Even though the cognitive paradigm clearly places the 'causal' role mainly in the mediating cognitive process rather than environmental contingencies, is it possible to identify a clear and coherent CBT theory for the 'family of related therapies' that Mansell (2008) calls for? In other words can we identify a general version of CBT theory? Kazdin (1978) put forward a definition of cognitive behaviour modification as a set of treatments that 'attempt to change overt behaviour by altering thoughts, interpretations, assumptions, and strategies of responding' (p. 337). This definition has reasonably stood the test of time. A more elaborated definition of CBT theory has been proposed by Dobson and his colleagues (Dobson & Dozois, 2010) in the form of three fundamental propositions:

1 Cognitive activity affects behaviour
2 Cognitive activity may be monitored and altered
3 Desired behaviour change may be effected through cognitive change

1. Cognitive activity affects behaviour. This is a restatement of the basic mediational model (Mahoney, 1974). Dobson and Dozois (2010) report that there is now overwhelming evidence that cognitive appraisals of events can affect the response to those events, and that there is clinical value in modifying the content of these appraisals.

2. Cognitive activity may be monitored and altered. The assumption is that cognitions are knowable and assessable, though there may be biases in cognitive reports, and further validation of cognitive reports is needed. Also most cognitive assessment has emphasised content rather than cognitive process, although this is rapidly changing with the influence of the third wave approaches.

3. Desired behaviour change may be effected through cognitive change. Dobson and Dozois (2010) state that though this proposition is generally accepted, it is extremely difficult to document the further assumption that changes in cognition mediate behaviour change. Tests of cognitive mediation are often less than methodologically adequate, and many fail to produce compelling results.

CBT Theory, Standard Version

While the family of related CBT therapies may have in common the three fundamental propositions of the general theory, they are also quite distinct from each other in most other respects. A review of the specific theories underpinning the whole range of cognitive-based therapies is beyond the remit of this chapter, but one of these has now become the standard approach, certainly in the United Kingdom, and has been adopted as the approach for the British Government's Improving Access to Psychological Therapies (IAPT) programme of training and service provision and the approach most recommended in the UK National Institute for Health and Clinical Excellence (NICE) guidelines. This is Beck's Cognitive Therapy (CT) (e.g. A.T. Beck, 1967, 1976; Beck et al., 1979; J. Beck, 1995) and the closely allied later developments (e.g. Clark et al., 1997), particularly in behavioural applications (Bennett-Levy et al., 2004), which are now generally referred to as CBT.

Beck's CT theory

In his 40-year retrospective since his first article on the cognitive approach (Beck, 1963) Beck (2005) states that the cognitive model of psychopathology stipulates that the processing of external events or internal stimuli is biased and therefore systematically distorts the individual's construction of his or her experiences, leading to a variety of cognitive errors, e.g. overgeneralisation, selective abstraction, and personalisation. Underlying these distorted interpretations, referred to as negative automatic thoughts (NATs) are dysfunctional assumptions (DAs) and core beliefs incorporated into relatively enduring cognitive structures or schemas. When these schemas are activated by external events, drugs, or endocrine factors, they tend to bias the information processing and produce the typical cognitive content of a specific disorder.

Cognitive specificity

A distinctive feature of Beck's CT theory is the cognitive specificity hypothesis, which proposes a distinct cognitive profile for each psychiatric disorder. Broadly speaking depression is characterised by beliefs concerned with loss and defeat. Anxiety disorders are characterised by danger-oriented beliefs. Specific cognitive profiles have been demonstrated in a wide variety of disorders, including anorexia nervosa, obsessive-compulsive disorder, panic disorder, generalised anxiety disorder, body dysmorphic disorder, social anxiety disorder, post-traumatic stress disorder, and more recently schizophrenia and subtypes such as persecutory delusion. Each of the personality disorders has also been differentiated on the basis of its distinctive set of dysfunctional core beliefs.

Cognitive vulnerability

Another feature of the theory is the notion that certain beliefs constitute a vulnerability to a disorder (stress diathesis model). Beck (2005) proposed that the predisposing beliefs could be differentiated according to whether the patient's personality was primarily autonomous or sociotropic. Autonomous individuals were more likely to become depressed following an autonomous event (e.g. a failure) than following a sociotropic event (e.g. loss of a relationship), and the reverse was true of sociotropic individuals.

A number of cognitive vulnerabilities for the anxiety disorders have been proposed by other authors. For example McNally (2002) proposed that Anxiety Sensitivity is a dispositional variable marked by fears about the harmfulness of anxiety-related sensations, and is especially elevated in people with panic disorder.

Adaptations of Beck's theory

Later adaptations of Beck's basic theory by a number of researchers, particularly Clark and his colleagues (Clark, 2004), have added to the power and generalisability of the theory in explaining the maintenance of disorders. One of the first developments was a shift of emphasis from a linear to a circular model of causality, shown most clearly by Clark's seminal paper on the cognitive approach to panic disorder (Clark, 1986) (though circular causality was also previously proposed by both Beck and Ellis). In this model, bodily sensations initially trigger catastrophic misinterpretations (e.g. prediction of an imminent heart attack) which 'cause' feelings of panic and exacerbation of the initial sensations, which in turn trigger yet more catastrophic beliefs leading to yet more symptoms, in a continuing vicious cycle. In a second theoretical development that built on the circular model, Salkovskis et al. (1996) show that in order to prevent the predicted catastrophic outcome the person would employ in-situation safety-seeking behaviours, but in so doing would prevent disconfirmation of their groundless belief, thereby maintaining rather than resolving the problem. Exposure planned as a belief disconfirmation strategy accompanied by dropping of safety-seeking behaviours is significantly more effective than habituation based exposure therapy (Salkovskiset al., 2006). This development of the theory brought to greater prominence the importance of behavioural experiments of this kind - the B in CBT.

Other key adaptations, such as the work of Ann Hackmann and her colleagues on the role of distressing imagery and memories in emotional processing in anxiety and depression (e.g. Hackmann et al., 1998; Hackmann et al., 2011) are reviewed by Clark (2004).

Critiques of Cognitive Behavioural Theories

As with the critiques of behavioural approaches, there are numerous critiques of Beck's cognitive approach, and numerous rejoinders and rebuttals. However, the focus here is on those critiques that represent the critical thinking that has mainly given rise to 'third wave' and multilevel approaches, to be discussed in the final section of the chapter.

Hayes' Critique

Hayes (2004) identifies three 'empirical anomalies' in the CBT outcome literature. First, he asserts that component analyses do not show that cognitive interventions provide added value to the therapy. Second, CBT treatment is often associated with a rapid, early improvement in symptoms that most likely occurs before the implementation of any distinctive cognitive techniques. Third, measured changes in cognitions do not seem to precede changes in symptoms.

In a review of component studies Longmore and Worrall (2007) find little evidence that specific cognitive interventions significantly increase the effectiveness of the therapy. There is little empirical support for the role of cognitive change as causal in the symptomatic improvements achieved in CBT. However, Longmore and Worrell equate 'cognitive' with the specific features (e.g. negative automatic thoughts) and techniques (e.g. thought challenging) of CT; but in the wider scientific literature 'cognitive' has a much broader meaning, relating to how internal mental representations drive and mediate action. In this sense, the evidence is that psychological change is cognitively mediated.

Teasdale's Critique

Teasdale (1993) points out five problems with CT theory. First, a number of therapies (including antidepressant medication) that do not target negative thinking, nonetheless reduce most measures of negative thinking to an extent similar to CT. The changes in negative thinking may be a *consequence* of the reduction in depression rather than antecedent to it.

Second, the cognitive model suggests that vulnerability to depression depends on individuals possessing underlying dysfunctional assumptions and attitudes. There has been a conspicuous failure to demonstrate the predicted presence of these attitudes in vulnerable individuals once their depression has remitted; the evidence suggests such attitudes are often mood-state dependent, rather than enduring characteristics of vulnerable individuals.

Third, it is a common clinical observation that patients can experience emotional reactions without being able to identify negative automatic thoughts.

Fourth, 'rational' argument or 'corrective' information is frequently ineffective in changing emotional response, even when the client 'intellectually' believes the logical power of the evidence. Beck's cognitive model recognises only one level of meaning, and for that reason has considerable difficulties with the distinction between 'intellectual' and 'emotional' belief, or, more generally, between 'cold' and 'hot' cognition. Many clinicians regard 'emotional' belief as qualitatively distinct from 'intellectual' belief, and functionally more important.

Finally, Teasdale observed that conventional cognitive therapy for depression focusing on negative automatic thoughts, is frequently ineffective. In response, treatment procedures have been imported wholesale on an ad hoc basis from other therapy traditions based on quite different underlying rationales.

Critique of the Disorder-Specific Approach

One of the key features of Beck's cognitive therapy is the specificity hypothesis and the diagnosis-specific approach that this generated with considerable success. However, as a number of authors point out (e.g. Taylor and Clark, 2009; Harvey et al., 2004), there are a number of difficulties with this approach. A theoretical problem is that patients commonly present with two or more disorders. Such comorbidity is typically not explained by disorder-specific theories. Comorbidity also implies that many disorders may have etiologic factors in common.

As Harvey et al. (2004) point out, the DSM (Diagnostic and Statistical Manual of Mental Disorders) syndromal approach is a key driving force to the 'disorder-focus' that characterises CT and most CBT. This is a categorical rather than a dimensional system that defines each disorder as a distinct entity, distinct not only from other disorders but from normal behaviour. This does not reflect clinical reality, often minimises the complexity of the clinical picture and thereby misses important information, but can lead to patients feeling stigmatised as 'mentally ill', which in itself can cause further anxiety and depression (Birchwood et al., 2006).

Third Wave Theories and Alternative Approaches

Decentring

Beck (1976) described decentring as the ability of a person to examine his automatic thoughts as psychological phenomena rather than as identical to reality. Decentring involves being able to make the distinction between 'I believe' and 'I know'. 'The ability to make this distinction is of critical importance in modifying those sectors of the patient's reactions that are subject to distortion' (Beck, 1976: 243).

Despite their criticism of Beck's Cognitive Therapy, John Teasdale and colleagues and Steven Hayes and colleagues, and other theorists identified as 'third wave', nonetheless recognise the concept of decentring as key to the third wave approach. Indeed, although emerging from different theoretical frameworks, the third wave therapies tend to follow a final common pathway, of which decentring is a key concept and the first step in the process. But after this essential first step, these approaches depart markedly from the traditional Beckian approach.

Interacting Cognitive Subsystems (ICS) and Mindfulness

Segal et al. (2002) point out that the traditional cognitive therapy approach to depression had its effects through changing the *content* of depressive thinking, but 'we realised that it was equally possible that when successful, this treatment led implicitly to changes in patients' *relationships* to their negative thoughts and feelings' (Segal et al., 2002: 38). They noticed patients switched to a perspective within which thoughts and feelings could be seen as passing events in the mind. This insight led to a fundamental shift in approach. Rather than seeing decentring as one of a number of things going on in cognitive therapy, it was now seen as central. This shift could protect people with a history of depressive relapse from future depression.

The theoretical explanation for the importance of this fundamental shift is provided by the Interacting Cognitive Subsystems (ICS) model (Teasdale and Barnard, 1993). In this model the mind is composed of information processing subsystems, one of which represents propositional meaning, as in verbal concepts, another of which represents a higher order implicational level of meaning, which includes intuitive, holistic, 'felt senses'. Only implicational meaning has the capacity to generate emotion. It is the continued interaction between propositional and implicational meanings related to the self that maintain depressive disorders.

Central to this account is the notion of depressive interlock, which is that information processing of depressogenic themes in these two subsystems becomes 'stuck' in continuous ruminative cycles. Prevention of this depressive interlock can be achieved by teaching 'mind management' skills that enable the person to disengage from 'central engine' modes that support depressive interlock. This model led to the development of mindfulness-based cognitive therapy (MBCT; Segal et al., 2002). It was adopted from a method developed by Kabat-Zinn (1990) as the method by which patients would be taught how to decentre from their negative thoughts, to see them simply as thoughts, freeing them from the distorted reality they created and which led to depressive relapse.

But how do people with recurrent depression get cognitively stuck in the first place? The theory that explains this aspect is Teasdale's Differential Activation Hypothesis (DAH; Teasdale, 1988). Teasdale asserts that firstly depressed mood negatively biases information processing, thereby increasing the accessibility of depressogenic interpretations of experience. Secondly, as a result of these mood effects on cognitive processing, increased negative interpretations of events produces further depression. Therefore, if a depressive state activates negatively biased interpretations of experience, this can precipitate further negatively biased, self-referent information processing which leads to a downward spiral of depression. MBCT enables the individual to radically change the relationship with, rather than content of, negative thoughts and feelings. The nonjudgmental, present moment, focus of mindfulness enables disengagement from dysfunctional mind states.

S-REF Theory and Metacognitive Therapy (MCT)

Like MBCT, Metacognitive Therapy (MCT; Wells, 2009) does not advocate challenging the content of negative automatic thoughts or traditional schemas. In contrast, the metacognitive approach focuses on mental processes of thinking style, attending and controlling cognition. Adrian Wells, the founder of MCT states 'in CBT disorder is caused by the content of cognition but in MCT disorder is caused by the way thinking processes are controlled and the style they take. Content *is* important in MCT but it is the content of metacognition rather than the content of cognition that counts' (Wells, 2000: 651).

The theoretical grounding of MCT is the Self-Regulatory Executive Function model (S-REF: Wells & Matthews, 1994). The authors propose that a thinking style called the Cognitive Attentional Syndrome (CAS) is a universal feature of disorder and is responsible for prolonging and intensifying distressing emotions. The CAS consists of: (1) worry and rumination; (2) threat monitoring; and (3) coping behaviours that are maladaptive because they impair flexible self-control or prevent corrective learning experiences.

Treatment is focused at the metacognitive level without the need to challenge the content of negative automatic thoughts or schemas. Patients are helped to know both what to do in response to threat and negative thoughts (i.e. reduce the CAS); and also how best to do it. Metacognitive programs or 'how-to' knowledge are shaped through experiencing different types of relationships with cognition and through manipulating cognitive processes such as the control of attention and worry. MCT therefore incorporates techniques such as attention training, which is one type of detached and situational attentional refocusing to modify and develop the necessary procedural or 'how-to' (i.e. experiential) metacognitions (Wells & Matthews, 1994; Wells, 2009)

Relational Frame Theory (RFT) and Acceptance and Commitment Therapy (ACT)

Acceptance and Commitment Therapy (ACT; Hayes et al., 1999) follows a similar final common pathway to the other third wave approaches, particularly the employment of mindful acceptance. However ACT is derived from a fundamentally different and earlier heritage than the other third wave therapies, namely radical behaviourism.

According to Relational Frame Theory all language and thought are dependent on deriving relations among events, namely relational frames. The environment will seemingly 'contain' stimulus functions that are dependent on relational frames, such that, for example, the fearful person who constructs a fearful environment will act is if that fearsomeness has been discovered, not constructed. RFT provides a third wave alternative to CBT, based on changing the contexts that support a thought ~ action or emotion ~action relation.

ACT (derived from RFT) therefore differs from traditional CBT in that rather than trying to teach people to control their thoughts, feelings, sensations, memories and other private events, people are taught to 'just notice', accept, and embrace their private events, especially previously unwanted ones. ACT helps the individual get in contact with a transcendent sense of self known as 'self-as-context' or the conceptual 'I' — the 'I' that is always there observing and experiencing and yet distinct from one's thoughts, feelings, sensations, and memories. ACT commonly employs six core principles to help clients develop psychological flexibility:

1 Cognitive defusion: Learning to perceive thoughts, images, emotions, and memories as what they are, not what they appear to be.
2 Acceptance: Allowing them to come and go without struggling with them.
3 Contact with the present moment: Awareness of the here and now, experienced with openness, interest, and receptiveness.
4 Observing the self: Accessing a transcendent sense of self, a continuity of consciousness which is changing.

5 Values: Discovering what is most important to one's true self.
6 Committed action: Setting goals according to values and carrying them out responsibly.

Transdiagnostic Approach

In contrast to Beck's disorder-specific approach, Harvey et al. (2004) identify empirically five cognitive and behavioural domains of processes, present across a wide range of disorders, in others words they are 'transdiagnostic' rather than specific to any one disorder. They provide a detailed review of the psychological literature of each process and evaluate whether the process is significant across a wide range of axis 1 disorders specified in DSM-IV. For example, they take one of these disorders, social phobia, and show that there is a role for all five of these processes. The processes they identify, and apply in social phobia, are:

- attentional processes, particularly self focused attention;
- memory processes, including selective retrieval of past failures;
- reasoning processes, such as the interpretative bias evident on leaving a social situation;
- thought processes, particularly rumination;
- behavioural processes, in the form of avoidance and safety behaviours.

Mansell et al. (2009) identify several advantages to the transdiagnostic approach, including less time spent on selecting the right therapy, no problem with comorbidity in an individual, avoidance of the stigma attached to a diagnostic label like 'schizophrenia' or 'personality disorder', and fostering a more idiographic approach to treatment. The authors do point out, however, that the transdiagnostic approach can complement, rather than compete with, a disorder-specific approach, in any one service.

Rational Emotive Behaviour Therapy (REBT) Theoretical Concepts

Although not a third wave theory - indeed it is the original CBT - Rational Emotive Behaviour Therapy contains several of the concepts prominent in these developments. First, Ellis (1962) proposed a metacognitive explanation for disturbance, namely the idea that clients had a 'demanding' as opposed to a 'preferential' philosophy which was largely out of conscious awareness, but from which they derived their self condemning and other irrational evaluative beliefs. Secondly, he proposed that it was only these 'hot' evaluative beliefs and not the inferences that they drew about events that led to emotional disturbance – a precursor of emotional processing. Thirdly, Ellis proposed discomfort tolerance (as opposed to discomfort intolerance) as an evaluative belief clients could develop in response to adversities – a precursor of mindful acceptance. However, Harrington and Pickles (2009) argue that pure nonjudgmental mindful acceptance of adversity is unrealistic compared to an attitude of tolerance in which the adversity is fully evaluated. Fourthly, Ellis advocated a concept of self as 'unrateable', as having no essence but only existence as alive and fallibly human – arguably a precursor of Hayes's 'contextual self'. Fifthly, as Taylor and Clark (2009) point out, Ellis (1962) was among the earliest CBT practitioners to develop transdiagnostic theory and treatment. 'Ellis's CBT, particularly his group treatment, was truly transdiagnostic; group members could have any of a variety of emotional problems and were all treated in much the same way with Ellis's form of CBT' (Taylor & Clark, 2009: 4).

Theoretical Integration

The initial 'revolution' and subsequent evolution of theory, critique, new theory, further critique, and further new theory would be straightforward if only each new theory had neatly superseded the previous one, which could then be discarded, as characterises genuine scientific revolutions and paradigm shifts, conceptualised so famously by Kuhn (1962). However, the continuing cycle of theory-building, critique, rejoinder and reassertion of the validity of the earlier theories means we still have today adherents to each and all of them, from the early behavioural to the latest third wave models, if modified in the process. This adds up to a confusing picture as Mansell (2008) points out. Should we draw the Dodo Bird verdict that they are all winners and all shall win prizes? Or is the more accurate picture the ancient parable of the Blind Men and the Elephant, namely that people tend to understand only a portion of Reality and then extrapolate from that to the whole, each claiming *his* is the only correct version?

The more complex multilevel theories, including the third wave models, are reaching for an emergent if slightly fuzzy picture of the whole elephant – or most of it. In addition to ICS (Teasdale & Barnard, 1993), MCT (Wells, 2009) and ACT (Hayes et al., 1999) just described, there is the Schematic, Propositional, Associative, and Analogical Representation Systems (SPAARS) model (Power & Dalgleish, 1997); Dual Representation Theory (Brewin, 1989; Brewin et al., 1996), Schema Therapy (Young et al.,

2003), the evolutionary psychology-based Social Mentality Theory and Compassion-Focused Therapy derived from it (Gilbert, 1989, 2005) and most recently the resurgence of Perceptual Control Theory Approach and the Method of Levels therapy (Powers, 1973; Higginson et al., 2011).

These accounts provide a rich variety of frameworks for an integration of the apparently disparate earlier theories. These approaches have core principles in common but also important differences. Rather than attempt a review of these models, I will select one that specifically integrates the behavioural and cognitive approaches, is currently widely accepted and has been and remains influential in generating CBT interventions: this is Brewin's Dual Representation Theory.

Dual Representation Theory – A Current Integrative Theory

Despite the cognitive revolution, the behavioural approach, with its exposure based treatments and the conditioning mechanisms of behaviour change, remains a lively and fertile area of scientific development (Moscovitch et al. (2009). Current empirical studies continue to show conditioning effects in a variety of psychological problems, but mostly alongside, rather than instead of, cognitive change.

Brewin et al. (1996) observed that the lack of theoretical overlap between the two approaches (i.e. the absence of an explicit role for conditioning in cognitive therapies and the absence of a role for verbal mediation in behaviour therapies) led to a prolonged period of mutual denunciation and largely fruitless argument between the two groups of practitioners.

Cognitive and social psychologists have long proposed the existence of two cognitive systems with different functions and properties, one that is automatic and outside of awareness and involves large-scale parallel information processing, and one that is more effortful and involves conscious experience.

Most automatic processing has the potential to include a large amount of information and takes place rapidly and outside of awareness, although we can become aware of its products, for example, in the forms of thoughts and images. This kind of processing is influenced by previous learning, and new stimuli tend to elicit routinised responses in a relatively inflexible way. In contrast, conscious processing is slow and deliberate, operates on a fraction of the information available but is highly adaptable and responsive to new information, which allows for great flexibility in behaviour. These two types of processing are represented in separate memory systems, one nondeclarative (implicit), the other declarative (explicit), the former not consciously accessible.

Brewin (1989) and Brewin et al. (1996) proposed dual representations in memory of emotional experiences as the minimum cognitive architecture within which the complex relationship between emotion and cognition could be understood. One was knowledge gained through the unconscious parallel processing of their responses to aversive situations, stored in situationally accessible memories (SAMs), the other knowledge is gained through the more limited conscious experience of such situations, and stored in verbally accessible memories (VAMs). Whereas verbally accessible knowledge can in principle be deliberately interrogated and retrieved, situationally accessible knowledge can only be retrieved automatically when environmental input matches features of the stored memories. In this dual representation theory, both kinds of knowledge can give rise to maladaptive emotions and behaviour.

Dual representation theory and the other multilevel theories of this type (e.g. SPAARS, ICS) have been influential in *integrating* conditioning-based approaches to learning and therapy (as in flashbacks in PTSD) and cognitive-based approaches (as in cognitive restructuring of 'hotspots' in flashbacks in PTSD), in the conduct of CBT interventions. Trauma and trauma-type images encoded in SAMs are accessed via re-experiencing and then modified by and re-introduced following conventional cognitive therapy. This approach, first developed for PTSD and generally referred to as imagery rescripting, is now being widely applied to other anxiety disorders and depression and is one of the most vigorous growth areas of CBT currently (e.g. Butler et al., 2008; Grey, 2009; Hackmann et al, 2011; Stopa, 2009).

Concluding Question

Although the third wave and multilevel theories have important commonalities that have the potential to facilitate integration, they also have substantial differences and incompatibilities, strengths and weaknesses, but tend to be promoted as complete and comprehensive therapeutic systems for purposes of research evaluation, therapy and training. The problem is there is theoretical coherence within but not between the theories, and from an integration perspective, confusion remains. Perhaps what is still required for future developments is not so much an evolution of yet new theories but the development of a metatheory – a true further paradigm shift, just as behaviourism and cognitivism were paradigm shifts in their time. One such proposed metatheory has already existed alongside the others, though has been further developed recently. This is Perceptual Control Theory, which is a model of general functioning and therefore is not only transdiagnostic but also in a sense 'trans-theoretical'. Perceptual Control Theory is fully explained, and the case made for its adoption as a truly integrative metatheory, in Chapter 8. Could this theory be a candidate for the integrative model that we seek?

References

Beck, A.T. (1963). 'Thinking and depression: idiosyncratic content and cognitive distortions', *Archives of General Psychiatry*, 9: 324–33.

Beck, A.T. (1967). *Depression: Clinical, Experimental and Theoretical Aspects*. New York: Harper & Row.

Beck, A.T. (1976). *Cognitive Therapy and the Emotional Disorders*. London: Penguin.

Beck. A.T. (2005). 'Current state of cognitive therapy: a 40-year retrospective', *Archives of General Psychiatry*, 62: 953–9.

Beck, A.T., Rush, A.J., Shaw, B.F. and Emery, G. (1979). *Cognitive Therapy of Depression*. New York: Guilford.

Beck, J. (1995). *Cognitive Therapy: Basics and Beyond*. New York: Guilford.

Bennett-Levy, J., Butler, G., Fennell, M., Hackmann, A., Mueller, M. and Westbrook, D. (2004). *Oxford Guide to Behavioural Experiments in Cognitive Therapy*. Oxford: Oxford University Press.

Birchwood, M., Trower, P., Brunet, K., Gilbert, P., Iqbal, Z. and Jackson, C. (2006). 'Social anxiety and the shame of psychosis: a study in first episode psychosis', *Behaviour Research and Therapy*, 45: 1025–37.

Brewin, C.R. (1989). 'Cognitive change processes in psychotherapy', *Psychological Review*, 96: 379–94.

Brewin, C.R., Dalgleish, T. and Joseph. S.A. (1996). 'Dual representation theory of posttraumatic stress disorder', *Psychological Review*, 103: 670–86.

Butler, G., Fennell, M. and Hackmann, A. (2008). *Cognitive Behavioural Therapy for Anxiety Disorders*. New York: Guilford.

Chadwick, P. (2006). *Person-Based Cognitive Therapy for Distressing Psychosis*. Chichester: John Wiley & Sons, Ltd.

Clark, D.M. (1986). 'A cognitive approach to panic', *Behaviour Research and Therapy*, 24: 461–70.

Clark, D.M. (2004). 'Developing new treatments: on the interplay between theories, experimental science and clinical innovation', *Behaviour Research and Therapy*, 42: 1089–1104.

Clark, D.M. and Fairburn, C.G. (eds) (1997). *The Science and Practice of Cognitive Behavioural Therapy*. Oxford: Oxford University Press.

Dobson, K.S. and Dozois, D.J.A. (2010). 'Historical and philosophical bases of the cognitive-behavorial therapies', in K.S. Dobson (ed.), *Handbook of Cognitive-Behavioral Therapies*. New York. Guilford Press.

Ellis, A. (1962). *Reason and Emotion in Psycho-therapy*. New York: Lyle Stuart.

Ellis, A. (1994). *Reason and Emotion in Psycho-therapy*, Revised and Updated. New York: Birch Lane Press.

Gilbert, P. (1989). *Human Nature and Suffering*. Hove: Lawrence Erlbaum.

Gilbert, P. (2005). *Compassion: Conceptualisations, Research and Use in Psychotherapy*. Hove: Routledge.

Grey, N. (ed.) (2009). A *Casebook of Cognitive Therapy for Traumatic Stress Reactions*. Hove: Routledge.

Hackmann, A., Surawy, C. and Clark, D.M. (1998). 'Seeing yourself through others' eyes: a study of spontaneously occurring images in social phobia', *Behavioural and Cognitive Psychotherapy*, 26: 3–12.

Hackmann, A., Bennett-Levy, J. and Holmes, E.A. (2011). *Oxford Guide to Imagery in Cognitive Therapy*. Oxford: Oxford University Press.

Harrington, N. and Pickles, C. (2009). 'Mindfulness and cognitive behavioral therapy: are they compatible concepts?', *Journal of Cognitive Psychotherapy*, 23: 315–23.

Harvey, A., Watkins, E., Mansell, W. and Shafran, R. (2004). *Cognitive Behavioural Processes across Psychological Disorders: A Transdiagnostic Approach to Research and Treatment*. Oxford: Oxford University Press.

Hayes, S.C. (2004). 'Acceptance and commitment therapy, relational frame theory, and the third wave of behavior therapy', *Behavior Therapy*, 35: 639–65.

Hayes, S.C., Strosahl, K.D. and Wilson, K.G. (1999). *Acceptance and Commitment Therapy: An Experiential Approach to Behavior Change*. New York: Guilford Press.

Higginson, S., Mansell, W. and Wood, A.M. (2011). An integrative mechanistic account of psychological distress, therapeutic change and recovery: the perceptual control theory approach', *Clinical Psychology Review*, 31: 249–59.

Kabat-Zinn, J. (1990). *Full Catastrophe Living: Using the Wisdom of your Body and Mind to Face Stress, Pain, and Illness*. New York: Dell.

Kant, I. (1964/1787). *Critique of Pure Reason*. London: Macmillan.

Kazdin, A.E. (1978). *History of Behavior Modification: Experimental Foundations of Contemporary Research*. Baltimore: University Park Press.

Kuhn, T.S. (1962). *The Structure of Scientific Revolutions*. Chicago: University of Chicago Press.

Longmore, R.J., and Worrall, M. (2007). 'Do we need to challenge thoughts in Cognitive Behaviour Therapy?', *Clinical Psychology Review*, 27: 173–87.

McNally, R.J. (2002). 'Anxiety sensitivity and panic disorder', *Society of Biological Psychiatry*, 52: 938–46.

Mahoney, M.J. (1974). *Cognition and Behavior Modification*. Cambridge, MA: Ballinger.

Mansell, W. (2008). 'The seven c's of CBT: a consideration of the future challenges for Cognitive Behaviour Therapy', *Behavioural and Cognitive Psychotherapy*, 36: 641–9.

Mansell, W., Harvey, A., Watkins, E. and Shafran, R. (2009). 'Conceptual foundations of the transdiagnostic approach to CBT', *Journal of Cognitive Psychotherapy: An International Quarterly*, 23: 6–19.

Moscovitch, D.A., Antony, M.M. and Swinson, R.P. (2009). 'Exposure-based treatments for anxiety disorders: theory and process', in M. Antony and M.B. Stein (eds), *Oxford Handbook of Anxiety and Related Disorders*. Oxford: Oxford University Press.

Mowrer, O.H. (1939). 'Stimulus response theory of anxiety', *Psychological Review*, 46: 553–65.

Power, M. and Dalgleish, T. (1997). *Cognition and Emotion: From Order to Disorder*. Hove: Lawrence Erlbaum.

Powers, W.T. (1973). *Behaviour: The Control of Perception*. Chicago: Aldine Publishing Co.

Rachman, S. (1977). 'The conditioning theory of fear acquisition: a critical examination', *Behaviour Research and Therapy*, 15: 375–87.

Salkovskis, P.M., Clark, D.M. and Gelder, M. (1996). 'Cognition-behaviour links in the persistence of panic', *Behaviour Research and Therapy*, 34: 453–8.

Salkovskis, P.M., Clark, D.M., Hackmann, A., Wells, A. and Gelder, M. (1999) 'An experimental investigation of the role of safety-seeking behaviours in the maintenance of panic disorder with agoraphobia', *Behaviour Research and Therapy*, 37: 559–74.

Salkovskis, P.M., Hackmann, A., Wells, A., Gelder, M.G. and Clark, D.M. (2006). 'Belief disconfirmation versus habituation approaches to situational exposure in panic disorder with agoraphobia: A pilot study', *Behaviour Research and Therapy*, 45: 877–85.

Segal, Z.V., Williams, J.M.G. and Teasdale, J.D. (2002). *Mindfulness Based Cognitive Therapy for Depression: A New Approach to Preventing Relapse*. New York: Guilford Press.

Skinner, B.F. (1950). 'Are theories of learning necessary?', *Psychological Review*, 57: 193–216.

Stopa, L. (ed.) (2009). *Imagery and the Threatened Self*. Hove: Routledge.

Taylor, S. and Clark, D.A. (2009). 'Transdiagnostic cognitive-behavioral treatments for mood and anxiety disorders: introduction to the special issue', *Journal of Cognitive Psychotherapy*, 23: 3–5.

Teasdale, J.D. (1988). 'Cognitive vulnerability to persistent depression', *Cognition and Emotion*, 2: 247–74.

Teasdale, J.D. (1993). 'Emotion and two kinds of meaning: cognitive therapy and applied cognitive science', *Behaviour Research and Therapy*, 31: 339–54.

Teasdale, J.D. and Barnard, P.J. (1993). *Affect, Cognition and Change*. Hove: Lawrence Earlbaum.

Wells, A. (2000). *Emotional Disorders and Metacognition: Innovative Cognitive Therapy.* Chichester: John Wiley & Sons Ltd.

Wells, A. (2009). *Metacognitive Therapy for Anxiety and Depression.* New York: Guilford Press.

Wells, A. and Matthews, G. (1994). *Attention and Emotion: A Clinical Perspective.* Hove: Lawrence Erlbaum.

Westbrook, D., Kennerley, H. and Kirk, J. (2007). *An Introduction to Cognitive Behavioural Therapy*. London: Sage.

Wolpe, J. (1958). *Psychotherapy by Reciprocal Inhibition.* Palo Alto, CA: Stanford University Press.

Young, J.E., Klosko, J.S. and Weishaar, M.E. (2003). *Schema Therapy: A Practitioner's Guide.* New York: Guilford.

THREE CBT: Past, Present and Future

STIRLING MOOREY

The Ancient Origins of CBT

We are what we think
All that we are arises with our thoughts
With our thoughts we make the world

Thus begins the Dhammapada (Byrom, 1993), a collection of scriptures ascribed to the Buddha, which places the origins of cognitive therapy at least 2,500 years before it became a brand name. The Buddha's teachings described how intentions and actions have consequences that promote either well-being and happiness or discontent and suffering, and he laid out a sophisticated programme for developing healthy thinking and behaviour. This allows us to become aware of what is happening as it happens so that we can make wise decisions about what to do in a given situation that will lead to well-being for ourselves and others. Although the Buddha may have been the first cognitive therapist, the Eastern spiritual context of his psychology meant that it did not have a direct influence on the development of Cognitive Behaviour Therapy, but as we shall see recent innovations in CBT have drawn on this tradition by modifying it for a Western secular audience.

The Western philosophical underpinnings of cognitive therapy are often associated with Stoic philosophy, beginning with Zeno in the third century BC, who taught in the colonnades (or Stoa) of the Athenian marketplace. Stoicism reached its zenith in the first century under the Greek Epictetus, and Roman writers such as Marcus Aurelius and Seneca. Epictetus is perhaps most well known for the quotation that succinctly defines the principles behind all cognitive behavioural therapies:

> *Man is disturbed not by things, but by the views he takes of them.' (Ench. 5)* (Long, 1995)

The Stoics believed that reason could overcome our baser instincts and emotions, and help us to find equanimity in the face of life's vicissitudes. Since we have relatively little control over much that happens to us, we should attend to what we can control – our reactions to external events. Our predicament is like that of a dog tied to a cart: if the dog resists it will be pulled along anyway and injured, but if it runs alongside the cart it will be unharmed. So the wise person aligns him or herself with necessity. Albert Ellis, one of the pioneers of CBT, acknowledged Stoicism as a major influence on the 'rational humanist' philosophy that informed his Rational Emotive Behaviour Therapy (Ellis, 1962). Other varieties of CBT have a less explicit philosophical base but nonetheless recognise their debt to Epictetus and his fellow Stoics.

Behaviour Therapy – the First Wave of CBT

The legacy of the Stoics can be seen in philosophical and everyday notions about reason and emotion down the ages, but our story now moves on to the twentieth century and the opposing movements of behaviourism and psychoanalysis. To some degree they kept the 'C' out of 'CBT' when the man in the street would have readily accepted that what we think is a major factor in determining how we feel and act. Psychoanalysis on the one hand played down the significance of conscious thought, because it believed that it was the underlying unconscious motivations that determined how we behaved. Behaviourism on the other hand, in its attempt to create a 'scientific' psychology only allowed for observable phenomena, i.e. behaviour to be counted as a legitimate subject for study. Thoughts were far too unreliable because their study depended on the reporting of subjective experience which was inherently unreliable. The basic principles of learning theory, both classical conditioning (Pavlov) and operant conditioning (Watson & Rayner, 1920) were established.

While mental health was dominated by behaviourism and psychoanalysis through much of the early twentieth century there were some proponents of the role of conscious mental processes. Emile Coué (1857–1926), a psychologist and pharmacist used techniques of autosuggestion to treat patients with a range of physical and mental conditions. He believed that whatever the mind concentrated on habitually tended to be realised. He was the inventor of the positive self-statement '*Tous les jours à tous points de vue je vais de mieux en mieux*' (Every day in every way I am getting better and better) which his patients were expected to repeat to themselves on a regular basis. Coué's naïve optimism was a crude attempt at cognitive change, but the advice of Dale Carnegie (1888–1955) in his 1948 self-help book *How to Stop Worrying and Start Living* (Carnegie, 1948) is very similar to that of the modern cognitive therapist. He describes how to develop effective problem-solving, how to decatastrophise by asking 'What is the worst that can possibly happen if I can't solve my problem?' and preparing for the worst eventuality, and recommends moving from a future-oriented worry focus to taking one day at a time.

Towards the middle of the century some voices within American psychoanalysis such as Alfred Adler (1927) and Karen Horney (1937) began to develop theories that placed more emphasis on patients' beliefs and attitudes. For instance, Horney (1937) wrote about the 'tyranny of the shoulds', a phrase that could just as easily have been coined by a cognitive therapist. It was in this context of Neo-Freudian thinking that two therapists, Ellis (1962) and Beck (1963, 1964) independently began to investigate the role of beliefs and thoughts in neurosis. Another lone voice of cognitivism at this time was that of George Kelly (1955) who was interested in how we understand our world through dichotomous constructs (Personal Construct Theory). In the 1950s and '60s, however, these early cognitive therapists were still considered fairly eccentric, because learning theory had found an intervention that was both scientifically acceptable and effective: behaviour therapy.

Joseph Wolpe (1958) applied classical learning theory concepts to the treatment of neurosis. He proposed that a phobia could be understood as a conditioned neurosis, and therefore might be deconditioned. His systematic desensitisation was based on the principle of reciprocal inhibition. He suggested that if a person with a phobia was exposed to the phobic stimulus and their anxiety was inhibited, this would break the associative learning linking the stimulus with the fear response. In practice this was done by asking the subject to imagine the stimulus then engage in a relaxation technique until the fear reduced. The patient imagined increasingly anxiety provoking images moving up the fear hierarchy until their phobia was overcome. Over the next decade these methods were refined and the fundamentals of effective exposure were defined. Exposure in real life was found to be more effective than exposure in imagination; it was discovered that relaxation was not essential for successful exposure; and it was found that the speed of habituation was proportional to the amount of time the patient was exposed to the feared stimulus. Simple phobias (Watson & Marks, 1971) and agoraphobia (Mathews et al., 1981) could now all be treated with behaviour therapy, and obsessive compulsive disorder, previously thought to be an intractable condition, also responded to exposure with response prevention (Marks et al., 1975). The behavioural revolution had taken place.

Cognitive Behaviour Therapy – the Second Wave

During the 1970s and '80s the relevance of cognitive processes to human behaviour and experience became accepted in academic psychology. At the same time clinicians began to challenge the hegemony of behaviour therapy and to demonstrate that attention to thoughts and beliefs in therapy could produce positive change (Mahoney & Arnkoff, 1978). Mainstream psychology was still wedded to learning theory and so cognition was often conceptualised as a form of covert behaviour that could be conditioned like any other. The difference now was that the person rather than the therapist could take control of this process by manipulating environmental contingencies to increase or decrease the frequency of unhelpful thoughts or emotions – 'self-control theory' (see Mahoney & Arnkoff, 1978). Bandura (1977) expanded learning theory to encompass the social realm and introduced the concept of self-efficacy, defined as 'the belief in one's capabilities to organise and execute the courses of action required to manage prospective situations' (Bandura, 1995: 2). Thus one of the fundamental principles of modern Cognitive Behaviour Therapy was established: that a person can exert control over their own life and can learn to become their own therapist. Other key figures during this phase of the cognitive revolution were Donald Meichenbaum (1977) who developed cognitive behaviour modification and stress inoculation training and Arnold Lazarus (1976) who developed multimodal behaviour therapy which seeks to integrate behaviour, physiology, cognition, interpersonal relationships, sensation, imagery, and affect in assessment and therapy.

With this renewed interest in conscious mental activity, the work of Ellis and Beck now became respectable. Ellis (1913–2007) can be considered the father of Cognitive Behaviour Therapy. He trained in psychoanalysis in the 1940s but became increasingly disillusioned. He proposed a radically new approach to mental distress influenced by Stoic philosophy, the American Neo-Freudians, the General Semantics of Alfred Korzybski (Korzybski, 1994), and his own personal experience. Like Epictetus he considered that it is not things themselves that cause our suffering but the beliefs we hold about them. His classic ABC analysis states that an Activating event is evaluated in a particular way through our Beliefs which produce an emotional, behavioural and cognitive Consequence. We tend to demand that the world is different from how it is (Demandingness), 'awfulise' about it (Awfulising) and believe we cannot tolerate it (Low Frustration Tolerance).

A fourth factor is the human predisposition to rate and evaluate ourselves and others. Through education and disputation with our self-defeating beliefs we can reduce our suffering by approaching life more rationally. Ellis called this new approach Rational Therapy, but in order to emphasise its multimodal nature he later renamed it Rational-Emotive Therapy and finally Rational Emotive Behaviour Therapy (REBT). Ellis's influence has been enormous and REBT is one of the most widely practised forms of CBT worldwide.

Beck's Cognitive Therapy

Undoubtedly the most influential living figure in CBT is Aaron Beck: a psychiatrist who was originally trained as a psychoanalyst. Beck built up a substantial body of research into depression and suicide and through this formed the view that cognition was at the centre of depression (Beck 1967). He first 'discovered' negative automatic thoughts while he was conducting psychoanalysis with depressed patients. His analysands reported that as they were lying on the couch attempting to free associate, they had a running commentary in their minds. They would think things like 'He's bored with me. I'm not an interesting case. I'm not doing this right.' Beck noticed that the themes of these spontaneous intrusions were similar for all his depressed patients. They were organised around negative views of the self (e.g. I'm boring), the world (e.g. My therapist isn't interested in me) and the future (e.g. Nothing will ever get better). The therapy that arose from Beck's cognitive model focused on teaching patients to learn to identify and modify their thinking. At the heart of Beckian CBT is the 'Dysfunctional Thought Record'. The patient is asked to keep a diary of changes in their mood, writing down the situation that may have triggered the mood shift, the automatic thoughts about the situation and the emotional reaction. This self-monitoring often helps the person to *distance* and *decentre* (Beck, 1976) themselves from their negative thinking.

Once they are able to recognise their automatic thoughts the next step is to evaluate them and write an alternative or 'rational' response. Patients are taught to ask themselves questions to test the validity of the thoughts ('What's the evidence?'), to explore other perspectives ('Is there an alternative way of looking at this? What would I say to a friend in the same situation?'), and to assess the helpfulness of their reaction ('What's the effect of thinking this way?'). With practice patients become adept at recognising and evaluating these habitual thought patterns.

In line with his research interests, Beck first applied the therapy to depression (Beck et al., 1979). He incorporated some of the techniques from behavioural approaches to depression such as scheduling activities that gave a sense of pleasure and achievement, and setting graded tasks, which are particularly helpful for patients with more severe depression. But in keeping with his cognitive approach, these were presented as experiments to test negative beliefs, e.g the belief 'I can't enjoy anything' can be tested by asking the patient to rate how much pleasure she gets from activities over the week (using an activity schedule: Beck et al., 1979), and scheduling activities she used to enjoy. This often leads to the discovery that it is still possible to get some pleasure even when you are depressed, which can instil hope and undermine negative thinking.

In Beck's model, vulnerability to a particular psychological disorder comes from underlying dysfunctional assumptions or schemas. Schemas help us to select and organise, experience and predict what is going to happen next. Beck suggested that adverse life events interact with beliefs to activate schemas and produce depression. For instance, a person with a belief such as 'I can only be happy if I am liked by everybody' may become depressed if they suffer a significant rejection. This is an aspect of the theory that was present at the beginning (Beck et al., 1979) but has been developed considerably over the last 30 years (Beck et al., 1990; J.S. Beck, 1995) as we shall see later. Cognitive therapy for depression consists of three phases: an initial phase of behavioural activation; a core phase of identifying and testing negative thinking; and a final phase of relapse prevention and evaluating underlying assumptions.

Beck's approach differs from Ellis's in a number of ways. Beck is a pragmatist and has developed theories for specific disorders rather than an overarching philosophy. From an REBT perspective, Cognitive Therapy goes for less 'elegant' solutions because it focuses so much on distorted interpretations or inferences, rather than immediately targeting irrational beliefs. Ellis favoured a direct assault on beliefs through disputation, whereas Beck preferred to use guided discovery (or Socratic Questioning) to lead the patient to a recognition of the unhelpfulness of their beliefs. Finally, as a psychiatrist and researcher, Beck has always been interested in evaluating therapy and Cognitive Therapy has fitted well into the world of psychiatric classification and drug trials in a way that REBT with its broader philosophical perspective has not.

Focusing Down and Opening Out: Developments in CBT in the Last Three Decades

Over the last 30 years Cognitive Behaviour Therapy has been applied to an ever-widening range of problems. It has moved beyond mood and anxiety disorders to behavioural disorders such as eating disorders and addictions, to somatoform disorders such as chronic fatigue, and even into the area of psychosis. CBT has been applied in a range of formats in addition to individual therapy, so we now have interventions delivered for groups, couples and families. The client group has also been extended beyond adults of working age to cover children and adolescents, older adults, forensic patients and people with learning difficulties. It is not possible to review its application in all these fields, so the discussion will focus on some examples that illustrate how research and clinical practice have evolved in recent years.

Cognitive Therapy for Depression

Prior to the first trial of cognitive therapy for depression (Rush et al., 1977) the idea that a psychological treatment might be as effective as antidepressant medication was virtually unthinkable. The CBT project in depression research has tended to keep the intervention constant, one might even say frozen with the 1979 manual of *Cognitive Therapy for Depression*, while refining the methodology of studies. Over the subsequent decades randomised controlled trials have confirmed that in mild-moderate depression Beck's cognitive therapy is as effective as antidepressant medication, that in severe and chronic depression it can add to the effectiveness of antidepressants (Scott et al., 2000), and that it has a definite relapse prevention effect (Evans et al., 1992; Hollon et al., 2005). See Whisman (2008) for a consideration of how cognitive therapy is being adapted to manage complexity and comorbidity in the increasingly challenging caseloads of therapists. The evidence is strong enough that CBT is recommended by the National Institute for Health and Clinical Excellence (NICE) at every step of the care pathway: computerised CBT for mild depression, CBT as one of the treatments of choice for moderate depression, CBT in combination with anitdepressants as the treatment for severe depression, and CBT and Mindfulness Based Cognitive Therapy as recommended treatments to prevent relapse.

Refining the Model: the Example of Anxiety Disorders

The approach in anxiety disorders has been somewhat different from depression. The work of Clark and colleagues exemplifies a particular paradigm: they select a specific anxiety disorder, investigate the factors maintaining it in close detail, and then devise a treatment programme to address these. Clark began this with panic disorder (Clark, 1996). He took the generic cognitive model of anxiety (Beck et al., 1985) and began to ask what might be unique about the cognitive components of panic. He identified the presence of catastrophic cognitions regarding impending death, collapse or loss of control and so drew out what is now the classic panic cycle (Clark, 1986). Physical symptoms (usually from autonomic nervous system arousal) are misinterpreted as signs of impending danger, which leads to anxiety and further physical symptoms, thus spiralling from anxiety to panic. A significant refinement came with the introduction of the concept of safety-seeking behaviours (Salkovskis, 1991). These are subtle forms of avoidance which can be seen as perfectly reasonable responses given the person's beliefs about the situation, but actually maintain the disorder. For instance, if you feel breathless and believe you are going to suffocate it makes sense to open a window, or if you have a chest pain and believe you are having a heart attack it is rational to sit down and avoid exertion. Unfortunately, these safety behaviours prevent you from testing the negative belief and so the next time you face the same situation you will have the same reaction. Agoraphobic symptoms arise out of more overt avoidance of situations where panics have occurred, and are linked to both the core panic cognitions, but also fear of social embarrassment. Clark has carried out a number of carefully designed experiments that support the various elements of his model of panic (Clark, 1996).

The key difference between the anxiety disorders is the nature of the perceived threat. In panic the focus is on physical symptoms that foreshadow *immediate* catastrophe, whereas in health anxiety the focus is on physical symptoms that predict some danger in the future (Warwick & Salkovskis, 1989). This differentiates between the acute symptoms seen in panic and the more chronic symptoms of hypochondriasis. In social phobia the threat is from judgement and rejection, and the focus is on an internal image of a shamed self (Clark & Wells, 1995), while in obsessive compulsive disorder (OCD) it is the intrusive, obsessional thoughts themselves that are threatening because they are unacceptable (Salkovskis, 1985). Some forms of safety-seeking behaviours are specific to particular disorders, e.g. neutralising rituals in OCD, while others may occur in various disorders, e.g. reassurance seeking in OCD and health anxiety. More complex models have been developed for post-traumatic stress disorder and generalised anxiety disorder (Ehlers & Clark, 2000). These refinements of the cognitive model of anxiety have led to effective treatments for the specific anxiety disorders. Therapy involves establishing a shared understanding of the problem and the alternative conceptualisation offered by the model (often comparing the old understanding as Theory A and the new hypothesis as Theory B), questioning beliefs through verbal discussion in the session, and then collaboratively agreeing a behavioural experiment to test the belief. In panic, for instance, this might involve a hyperventilation exercise in the session to demonstrate that although you *feel* like you are going to faint you do not. There is much less emphasis on thought records than in the standard form of cognitive therapy as used in depression, because although cognitive restructuring alone can change beliefs at an intellectual level, it usually requires an experiment while anxiety is activated to change them at an emotional level. This work has led to a greater interest in behavioural experiments as a key technique in the treatment of all disorders, not just anxiety (Bennet-Levy et al., 2004).

Treating the Untreatable: the Example of Psychosis

CBT for psychosis has shown how the model can be applied to conditions previously thought to be beyond the bounds of psychological approaches. Following the landmark work of Kingdon and Turkington (1994), there has been a growing interest in the application of cognitive techniques in psychosis as an adjunct to antipsychotic medication. The therapy needs to be more flexible than standard cognitive therapy. A shared model of the problems is developed, gradually building up alternative explanations for symptoms the patient assumes are based on reality. The story of how the symptoms first appeared and what they meant to the patient is elaborated, and it is often possible to see that the first psychotic experiences occurred in states of altered consciousness through the impact of stress, sleep disturbance or drugs (Kingdon & Turkington, 1994). If symptoms can be reconceptualised as stress reactions, the patient is then more willing to consider examining them and testing the validity of their beliefs. Delusional beliefs and beliefs about hallucinations are gently challenged and behavioural experiments devised. In addition, most of these treatment packages also teach coping strategies, challenge negative self-concepts and work on social disability and relapse.

Psychosis is just one example of the many challenging areas where CBT is now being applied. Another example is the application of CBT with people in a palliative care setting. A recent study demonstrated that home care nurses could learn CBT techniques to use in their generic work with dying patients, and that these skills had a significant impact on the anxiety the patients experienced (Moorey et al., 2009).

Deepening the Model: CBT for Personality Disorders

As cognitive behaviour therapists have begun to work with more complex, comorbid disorders, particularly personality disorders, CBT has needed to construct a more sophisticated theory of how beliefs develop in response to childhood adversity, and how they influence relationships in the present. If we have a stable, supportive family upbringing, we tend to see ourselves as basically worthwhile and competent, we see others as potentially supportive and well inclined, and we see the world as a generally benign place. We acquire *positive schemas*. If on the other hand we have aversive experiences in childhood, we may see ourselves as worthless or incompetent, others as critical or abusive, and the world as dangerous or hostile. We all have some positive and some negative core beliefs, but the negative beliefs are usually dormant and when triggered are often temporary and mitigated by our positive beliefs. We sometimes prevent these core negative beliefs from being activated by developing conditional assumptions about the world. These 'if-then' beliefs predicate self-worth on the world being a certain way. We may believe that if we succeed we are worthwhile, or that if we get people's approval it means we are OK. Adverse life events activate these assumptions and the core beliefs associated with them. For instance, someone who has a rigid belief he has to succeed to be worthwhile may react badly to failing an exam. This may awaken core doubts about his competence, intelligence and worth and so lead to a depressive episode.

Understanding these beliefs becomes important when working with recurrent or chronic problems. In people with personality disorders the negative core beliefs are on the surface much of the time and the associated conditional beliefs and compensatory strategies are only partially effective. People with borderline personality disorder, for example, believe they are fundamentally bad and incompetent, that other people may be abusive, and that the world is a hostile, dangerous and unpredictable place. They hold these beliefs very strongly and so standard methods of cognitive restructuring are often ineffective – 'I know all you're showing me about the good things I do for people, but I still *know* I'm bad!' CBT for personality disorder therefore needs a longer time frame than CBT for Axis I disorders and has to employ a greater range of techniques. More emotion based and even Gestalt techniques have been adapted within a cognitive framework (Young et al., 2003) in order to produce cognitive change at a more experiential level. There is more emphasis on past history and on developing new ways of behaving and thinking (Davidson, 2007; Beck et al., 1990; Young et al., 2003). Finally, because so many of the person's self-defeating beliefs and behaviours are in the interpersonal sphere, CBT for personality disorder needs to pay attention to the therapeutic relationship far more than in other conditions (Moorey, 2010a).

Transdiagnostic Processes

So far we have looked at the developments in CBT for particular conditions. Adrian Wells was the first to propose a *metacognitive model* that spanned a range of disorders (Wells, 2000). He proposed that processes such as worry and rumination were driven by underlying positive beliefs about the benefits of ruminating and negative beliefs about the consequences. Harvey et al. (2004) proposed a transdiagnostic approach to research and treatment. They reviewed the evidence for the roles of attention, memory, reasoning, thoughts and behaviour in maintaining psychological disorders and suggested therapeutic techniques arising from the research. Another promising vein is the use of imagery in CBT. Imagery rescripting has been found to be helpful in PTSD, social phobia, depression and personality disorders (Holmes et al., 2007).

Rationalism and Constructivism

Alongside the expansion and development of CBT as described so far, there has been a second strand of broadly cognitive thought that could be seen to have begun with the publication of 'Cognitive Processes and Emotional Disorders' (Guidano & Liotti, 1983). Constructivist theories emphasise the organism's active role in creating perceptions of reality through its interaction with the world, for humans primarily the social world. In this context this includes writers such as Michael Mahoney, one of the pioneers of the cognitive revolution in behaviour therapy (Mahoney, 1995a), Vittorio Guidano, Safran and Segal (Safran & Segal, 1990), and the more cognitively oriented personal construct therapists such as Robert Neimeyer.

Mahoney (Mahoney, 1995b) summarised the supposed differences between rationalist and constructivist theories:

> Rationalist thought is said to be characterised by three related assumptions (a) that irrationality is the primary source of neurotic psychopathology, (b) that explicit beliefs and logical actions can easily overpower and guide emotions and behavioural actions and (c) that the core process in effective psychotherapy is the substitution of rational for irrational thinking patterns ...
>
> Constructive metatheory, on the other hand, (a) adopts a more proactive (vs reactive and representational) view of cognition and the organism, (b) emphasises tacit (unconscious) core ordering processes and (c) promotes a complex systems model in which thought, feeling, and behaviour are interdependent expressions of a life span developmental unfolding of interactions between self and (primarily social) systems.

The debate between rationalist and constructivist models was active during the 1990s but seems to have quietened considerably in the last decade. Looking at Mahoney's distinction helps us to understand how cognitive therapy has progressed over the last three decades. The rationalist label may well have applied to early CBT and REBT, but both therapies now have a much more sophisticated understanding of human experience and behaviour. In fact, CBT appears to have absorbed some of the ideas of constructivism without losing its focus, empiricism or comprehensibility (a criticism that can be made of some of the constructivist theorists). The importance of tacit processes is recognised in post-traumatic stress disorder (Ehlers & Clark, 2000) and in Beck's revised cognitive model of 'modes' (Beck, 1996). In personality disorder an understanding of how schemas develop over the lifecycle is vital (Young et al., 2003; Moorey, 2010a). At a clinical level, Christine Padesky's approach is explicitly constructivist in the sense that rather than challenging negative beliefs she helps the patient create alternative, helpful beliefs which can be tested through experience. Salkovskis' Theory A and Theory B is another example of constructing an alternative model which can be tested, as opposed to the 'rationalist' approach of disconfirming dysfunctional beliefs. Finally, work with people with physical illness often requires a collaborative approach to exploring alternative possibilities of seeing the world (Moorey, 1996; Moorey & Greer, 2002; Sage et al., 2008).

From Content to Context – the Third Wave of CBT

The term third wave therapy refers to a group of therapies including Dialectical Behaviour Therapy (DBT: Linehan, 1993), Acceptance and Commitment Therapy (ACT: Hayes et al., 1999), Behavioural Activation (BA: Jacobson et al., 2001), and Functional Analytic Psychotherapy (FAP: Kohlenberg et al., 2009). These therapies share a foundation in radical behaviourism and an interest in the *function* of problematic behaviours, thoughts, emotions and physical sensations rather than their *content* (Hayes, 2004). According to Hayes they emphasise 'contextual and experiential change strategies rather than direct and didactic ones'. Their difference from traditional 'second wave' CBT is most obvious in their approach to cognition. Rather than challenge negative thoughts, patients are helped to acknowledge the thoughts without engaging with them. This is done through experiential exercises (ACT) or mindfulness practice (DBT). The behavioural component of therapy may involve a functional analysis of unhelpful behaviours (FAP) or identifying behaviours that help you work towards your life values (ACT). Another feature is an emphasis on directly experiencing negative emotions without engaging in ruminations or avoidance behaviour. Mindfulness Based Cognitive Therapy (MBCT: Segal et al., 2002) is often included in this group, although it is not based on Skinnerian learning theory. MBCT has been developed to treat recurrent depression. It teaches mindfulness meditation, a secular application of Buddhist meditation practice. This develops the skill of being able to accept whatever we are experiencing in the moment without trying to fix or change it. By learning to be aware of what is happening to us here and now we can make skilful choices about how we act so that we do not get caught up in depressive ruminations or unhelpful behavioural patterns.

Where Exactly are We Now and Where are We Going?

As we have seen, there have been enormous developments in CBT since behaviour therapy first countenanced cognition. Cognitive behaviour therapy today is a broad church. It encompasses some old-style behaviourists and new 'third wave' behaviourists, as well as many who practise an eclectic combination of cognitive and behavioural techniques. It includes therapists working within a 'rationalist' framework who challenge irrational beliefs and therapists who see themselves as co-constructing a therapeutic reality with their clients. It includes therapists who practise short-term therapy, only focus on maintenance processes and eschew core beliefs, and also therapists who focus entirely on early maladaptive schemas and see patients twice a week for three years. Why hasn't CBT fractured and split in the way that psychoanalytic schools have fragmented? There are probably three reasons:

1 Cognitive behaviour therapists all sign up to the necessity of putting their models and methods under empirical scrutiny, whether this is through randomised controlled trials (RCTs) or well-designed single case studies. This has led to some treatments, e.g. thought stopping being abandoned when they are found to be ineffective.
2 Despite their differences there is an agreement that thoughts and behaviours are the locus of explanation and interest, and an agreement that learning theory (whether behavioural or social) is an underlying principle.
3 There is a respectful and collaborative attitude towards the client or patient. Cognitive behavioural models tend to normalise and not pathologise – the default position is 'you and I are doing our best given what we have learned and how we see the world. It is my job as therapist to work with you to help you find the most helpful ways to think and act in your present situation.' Cognitive behavioural therapies place a lot of emphasis on giving the therapy away so that the client can learn to become his own therapist.

In Britain, the strength of the evidence base for CBT has significantly influenced the NICE guidelines and as a result it has become the dominant psychological therapy in the NHS. This is in no small part due to the Improving Access to Psychological Therapies (IAPT) programme which will greatly increase the number of CBT therapists in primary care. All patients are given outcome measures at each session, so there is a likelihood that there will be 90% data capture making IAPT the largest naturalistic trial of CBT for anxiety and depression ever undertaken. One of the criticisms of CBT and the NICE guidelines approach has been that too much emphasis is placed on the findings from randomised controlled trials which may not be applicable to the complexity, chronicity and comorbidity seen in clinical services. The IAPT enterprise will help to establish how much these findings can be generalised. We are at the beginning of this next phase in CBT research: moving from efficacy studies which show the treatment works in controlled settings to effectiveness studies which assess its place in the 'real world'. Now that they have been established as efficacious, cognitive behavioural approaches to anxiety, depression and psychosis will all be subject to more service-based evaluations.

How will CBT evolve over the next 30 years? There will be an incremental progression as we further refine our models of specific disorders, and identify the active ingredients of treatment – the most promising area is the specific anxiety disorders where the paradigm of Clark and colleagues continues to produce more focused cost-effective treatments. Whether this can be applied to generalised anxiety disorder and depression is an interesting question. These disorders are more likely to interface with interpersonal and personality factors, i.e. core beliefs about vulnerability, competence and worth than some of the specific anxiety disorders. So far models of GAD have proven quite complex, needing to incorporate perceived general threat, perceived inability to cope, intolerance of uncertainty, worry and meta-worry. It has not been possible to identify a core focus in depression in the way Clark and colleagues have done with anxiety disorders, and it has also not been possible to extract subtypes of depression that can be conceptualised in a way that leads to new therapies. Developments in the field of depression have in fact come from the new third wave therapies such as behavioural activation, which with its stripped down protocol threatens to take the 'C' out of 'CBT', and from transdiagnostic approaches such as CBT for ruminations. Holding the Beck protocol for depression constant has had benefits for exploring the application of this model, but it has not grown and refined itself in the way that therapy for anxiety has done over the last 20 years. Given that only 60% of patients recover with a course of cognitive therapy and the placebo response is around 30% there is scope for improvement.

In CBT for psychosis and bipolar disorder the effect sizes are considerably lower than in anxiety and depression. Will it be possible to improve outcomes further? Personality disorder research is still in its infancy, and there is a long way to go before we understand the core features of these disorders. Do we need a deeper understanding of developmental processes so that we can improve the longer-term schema therapies? Or might it be possible to bypass content and work with context and process on a shorter timescale?

Cognitive behaviour therapy has made considerable progress by producing cognitive models and treatments for these different disorders, but it is possible that the way forward does not lie with condition specific interventions at all, but with a better understanding of the maintenance processes that are common to all disorders. Most of the cognitive models include an explanation of how selective attention, cognitive and memory bias, repetitive thoughts and behavioural processes (such as avoidance, safety behaviours and maladaptive interpersonal behaviours) operate to confirm self-defeating beliefs.

Applying what we know from experimental research on these processes could lead to more effective transdiagnostic interventions (Harvey et al., 2004). Rather than a DSM-IV diagnosis determining the formulation there could be much more emphasis on assessing the role of various cognitive processes (through standard questionnaire measures or measures of the processes themselves). Each patient might have a 'cognitive behavioural profile' which outlines the relative contribution of different maintenance factors and so informs choice of interventions. An example of this is the 'six cycles model' (Moorey, 2010b) which separates the relative contribution of cognitive bias, rumination and self-attacking, emotion, avoidance, active unhelpful behaviours and physical factors. Although initially developed for depression these six domains may be of relevance across a range of disorders. Mathews (2006) has pointed out that although clinicians have adopted the language of cognitive science, until recently there has been relatively little from experimental psychology they could draw on to inform their clinical work. This is changing and the future is likely to see a much closer interaction between cognitive science and cognitive therapy.

An even more ambitious approach is to design and track treatments on the basis of the *biological mechanisms* underlying disorders. This is still a highly speculative project but Siegle and colleagues (Siegle et al., 2007) reviewed the evidence for so-called 'neurobehavioural' therapies, and described 'cognitive control training' which uses computer based tasks to improve prefrontal cortical function and so relieve depression. Even if linking psychological with biological processes at this level does not develop further, biological science is likely to be more closely linked with therapy. This is already happening in the field of neuroimaging where CBT and other therapies have been shown to change brain function (Siegle et al., 2007). A more exciting possibility is the use of medication to enhance CBT. We know that a combination of CBT and antidepressants in depression can be more effective than each alone, but this is a very nonspecific sort of interaction. More sophisticated neuropharmacology will develop in the next few years. For instance, D-cycloserine has been shown to facilitate extinction learning in both animals and humans (Hofmann, 2007). So in the future we may carry out more effective behavioural experiments with D-cycloserine augmentation.

Finally, there is likely to be increasing interest in the interpersonal and social context in which CBT is delivered. Because it originated as an intrapersonal theory, cognitive therapy has sometimes found it difficult to embrace interpersonal behaviour. The new behaviour therapies describe the interpersonal context of problems and therapy much more explicitly (see for instance Kohlenberg et al., 2009) and mainstream CBT will probably integrate some of these ideas to enrich the model. Psychoanalysis became part of the twentieth century zeitgeist. Almost imperceptibly, the importance of our beliefs and our thinking, and our capacity to change them, is becoming part of our everyday discourse. Will Cognitive Behaviour Therapy be a defining theory for twenty-first-century experience?

So, CBT in the next 30 years will seek to demonstrate its effectiveness in the broader health economy, will refine its techniques to make them even more effective, and will integrate them with biological, psychological and social science. In doing this it seems to be rediscovering its behavioural roots, and reaching even further back to incorporate 2500 year old meditation practices. The future may hold yet more rediscoveries from our psychological and philosophical tradition.

All intelligent thoughts have already been thought. What is necessary is only to try to think them again.

Johann Wolfgang von Goethe

References

Adler, A. (1927). *The Practice and Theory of Individual Psychology*. New York: Harcourt Brace.

Bandura, A. (1977). 'Self-efficacy: Toward a unifying theory of behavioral change', *Psychological Review*, 84; 191–215.

Bandura, A. (1995). *Self-Efficacy in Changing Societies*. Cambridge: Cambridge University Press.

Beck, A.T. (1963). 'Thinking and depression: 1. Idiosyncratic content and cognitive distortions', *Archives of General Psychiatry*, 9: 324–33.

Beck, A.T. (1964). 'Thinking and depression: 2. Theory and therapy', *Archives of General Psychiatry*, 10: 561–71.

Beck, A.T. (1967). *Depression: Clinical, Experimental and Theoretical Aspects*. New York: Hoeber.

Beck, A.T. (1976). *Cognitive Therapy and the Emotional Disorders*. New York: International Universities Press.

Beck, A.T. (1996). 'Beyond belief: a theory of modes, personality and psychopathology', in P.M. Salkovskis (ed.), *Frontiers of Cognitive Therapy*. New York: Guilford Press.

Beck, A.T., Rush, J.L., Shaw, B.E. and Emery, G. (1979). *The Cognitive Therapy of Depression*. New York: Guilford Press.

Beck A.T., Emery, G. and Greenberg R.L. (1985). *Anxiety Disorders and Phobias: a Cognitive Perspective*. New York: Basic Books.

Beck, A.T., Freeman, A. et al. (1990). *Cognitive Therapy of Personality Disorders*. New York: Guilford Press.

Beck, J.S. (1995). *Cognitive Therapy: Basics and Beyond*. New York: Guilford Press.

Bennet-Levy, J., Butler, G., Fennel, M., Hackmann, A., Mueller, M., and Westbrook, D. (eds) (2004). *Oxford Guide to Behavioural Experiments in Cognitive Therapy*. Oxford: Oxford University Press.

Byrom, T. (1993/1976). *Dhammapada: the sayings of the Buddha: a Rendering by Thomas Byrom*. Boston & London: Shambhala.

Carnegie, D. (1948). *How to Stop Worrying and Start Living*. Suffolk: The Chaucer Press.

Clark, D.M. (1986). 'A cognitive approach to panic', *Behaviour Research and Therapy*, 24: 461–70.

Clark, D.M. (1996). 'Panic disorder: from theory to therapy', in P. Salkovskis (ed.), *Frontiers of Cognitive Therapy*. London: Guilford Press, pp. 318–44.

Clark, D.M. and Wells, P.A. (1995). 'A cognitive model of social phobia', in R.G. Heimberg, M.R. Liebowitz, D.A. Hope and S.A. Schneier (eds), *Social Phobia: Diagnosis, Assessment and Treatment*. New York: Guilford Press, pp. 69–93.

Davidson, K.M. (2007). *Cognitive Therapy for Personality Disorders: A Guide for Clinicians*, 2nd edn. Hove: Routledge.

Ehlers, A. and Clark, D.M. (2000). 'A cognitive model of posttraumatic stress disorder', *Behaviour Research and Therapy*, 38: 319–45.

Ellis, A. (1962). *Reason and Emotion in Psychotherapy*. Secaucus, NJ: Lyle Stuart.

Evans, M.D., Hollon, S.D., DeRubeis, R.J., Piasecki, J.M., Grove, W.M., Garvey, M.J. and Tuason, V.B. (1992). 'Differential relapse following therapy and pharmacotherapy for depression', *Archives of General Psychiatry*, 49: 802–8.

Guidano, V.F. and Liotti, G. (1983). *Cognitive Processes and the Emotional Disorders*. New York: Guilford Press.

Harvey, A., Watkins, E., Mansell, W. and Shafran, R. (2004). *Cognitive Behavioural Processes across Psychological Disorders: A Transdiagnostic Approach*. Oxford: Oxford University Press.

Hayes, S.C. (2004). 'Acceptance and commitment therapy and the new behavior therapies: Mindfulness, acceptance and relationship', in S.C. Hayes, V.M. Follette and M. Linehan (eds), *Mindfulness and Acceptance: Expanding the Cognitive Behavioral Tradition*. New York: Guilford Press, pp. 1–29.

Hayes, S.C., Strosahl, K.D. and Wilson, K.G. (1999). *Acceptance and Commitment Therapy: An Experiential Approach to Behavior Change*. New York: Guilford Press.

Hofmann, S.G. (2007). 'Enhancing exposure-based therapy from a translational research perspective', *Behaviour Research and Therapy*, 45: 1987–2001.

Hollon, S.D., DeRubeis, R.J., Shelton, R.C., Amsterdam, J.D. et al. (2005). 'Prevention of relapse following cognitive therapy vs medication in moderate to severe depression', *Archives of General Psychiatry*, 62: 417–22.

Holmes, E.A., Arntz, A. and Smucker, R. (2007). 'Imagery rescripting in Cognitive Behaviour Therapy: images, treatment techniques and outcomes', *Journal of Behavior Therapy and Experimental Psychiatry*, 38: 297–305.

Horney, K. (1937). *The Neurotic Personality of our Time*. New York: Norton.

Jacobson, N.S., Martell, C.R. and Dimidjian, S. (2001). 'Behavioral activation therapy for depression: Returning to contextual roots', *Clinical Psychology: Science and Practice*, 8 (3): 255–70.

Kelly, G. (1955). *The Psychology of Personal Constructs*, Vols I and 2. New York: Norton.

Kingdon, D.G. and Turkington, D. (1994). *Cognitive Behaviour Therapy of Schizophrenia*. Hove: Lawrence Erlbaum.

Kohlenberg, R.J., Tsai, M. and Kanter, J.W. (2009). *A Guide to Functional Analytic Psychotherapy: Awareness, Courage, Love, and Behaviorism*. New York: Springer.

Korzybski, A. (1994). *Science and Sanity An Introduction to Non-Aristotelian Systems and General Semantics*, 5th edition. Englewood, NJ: Institute of General Semantics.

Lazarus, A. (1976). *Multimodal Behaviour Therapy*. New York: Springer.

Linehan, M.M. (1993). *Cognitive-behavioural Treatment of Borderline Personality Disorder*. London: Guilford Press.

Long, G. (1995). *Enchiridion by Epictetus*. New York: Prometheus Books.

Mahoney, M.J. (1995a). *Constructive Psychotherapy*. New York: Guilford Press.

Mahoney, M.J. (1995b). 'Theoretical developments in the cognitive psychotherapies', in M.J. Mahoney (ed.), *Cognitive and Constructive Psychotherapy*. New York: Springer, p. 8.

Mahoney, M.J. and Arnkoff, D.B. (1978). 'Cognitive and self-control therapies', in S.L. Garfield and A.E. Bergin (eds), *Handbook of Psychotherapy and Behaviour Change*, 2nd edition. New York: John Wiley & Sons, Inc.

Marks, I.M., Hodgson, R. and Rachman, S. (1975). 'Treatment of chronic OCD 2 years after in vivo exposure', *British Journal of Psychiatry*, 127: 349–64.

Mathews, A.M. (2006). 'Towards an experimental cognitive science of CBT', *Behavior Therapy*, 37: 314–18.

Mathews, A.M., Gelder, M.G. and Johnstone, D.W. (1981). *Agoraphobia: Nature and Treatment*. Tavistock, London.

Meichenbaum, D. (1977). *Cognitive Behaviour Modification: An Integrative Approach*. New York: Springer.

Moorey, S. (1996). 'When bad things happen to rational people', in P.M. Salkovskis (ed.), *Frontiers of Cognitive Therapy*. New York: Guilford Press.

Moorey, S. and Greer, S. (2002) *Cognitive Behaviour Therapy for People with Cancer*. Oxford: Oxford University Press.

Moorey, S., Cort, E., Kapari, M. et al. (2009). 'A cluster randomised controlled trial of Cognitive Behaviour Therapy for common mental disorders in patients with advanced cancer', *Psychological Medicine*, 39: 713–23.

Moorey, S. (2010a). 'CBT and psychoanalysis', in A. Lemma and M. Patrick (eds), *Off the Couch*. London: Routledge.

Moorey, S. (2010b). 'The six cycles model: Growing a "vicious flower" for depression', *Behavioural and Cognitive Psychotherapy*, 38: 173–84.

Rush, A.J., Beck, A.T., Kovacs, M. and Hollon, S. (1977). 'Comparative efficacy of cognitive therapy and pharmacotherapy in the treatment of depressed outpatients', *Cognitive Therapy and Research*, 1: 17–37.

Safran, J.D. and Segal, Z.V. (1990). *Interpersonal Process in Cognitive Therapy*. New York: Basic Books.

Sage, N., Sowden, M. and Chorlton, E. (2008). *CBT for Chronic Illness and Palliative Care: A Workbook and Toolkit*. London: John Wiley & Sons, Ltd.

Salkovskis, P.M. (1985). 'Obsessive-compulsive problems: a cognitive-behavioural analysis', *Behaviour Research and Therapy*, 23: 571–83.

Salkovskis, P.M. (1991) 'The importance of behaviour in the maintenance of anxiety and panic: a cognitive account', *Behavioural Psychotherapy*, 19: 6–19.

Scott, J., Teasdale, J.D., Paykel, E.S., Johnson, A.L., Abbott, R., Hayhurst, H., Moore, R. and Garland, A. (2000). 'Effects of cognitive therapy on psychological symptoms and social functioning in residual depression', *British Journal of Psychiatry*, 177: 440–46.

Segal, Z.V., Williams, J.M.G. and Teasdale, J.D. (2002). *Mindfulness-Based Cognitive Therapy for Depression: A New Approach to Preventing Relapse*. New York: Guilford Press.

Siegle, G.J., Ghinassi, F. and Thase, M.E. (2007). 'Neurobehavioral therapies in the 21st century: summary of an emerging field and an extended example of cognitive control training for depression', *Cognitive Therapy and Research*, 31: 235–62.

Warwick, H.M.C. and Salkovskis, P.M. (1989). 'Hypochondriasis', in J. Scott, J.M.G. Williams and A.T. Beck (eds), *Cognitive Therapy in Clinical Practice*. London: Croom Helm.

Watson, J.B. and Rayner, R. (1920). 'Conditioned emotional reactions', *Journal of Experimental Psychology*, 3: 1–14.

Watson, J.P. and Marks, I.M. (1971). 'Relevant and irrelevant fear in flooding – a crossover study in phobic patients', *Behavior Therapy*, 2: 275–93.

Wells, A. (2000). *Emotional Disorders and Metacognition: Innovative Cognitive Therapy*. Chichester: John Wiley & Sons, Ltd.

Whisman, M.A. (ed.) (2008). *Adapting Cognitive Therapy for Depression: Managing Complexity and Comorbidity*. New York: Guilford Press.

Wolpe, J. (1958). *Psychotherapy by Reciprocal Inhibition*. Palo Alto, CA: Stanford University Press.

Young, J.E., Klosko, J.S. and Weishaar, M.E. (2003). *Schema Therapy: A Practitioner's Guide*. New York: Guilford Press.

FOUR Common Myths and Misconceptions about CBT

MICHAEL NEENAN

Introduction

CBT is a generic term for a range of cognitive behavioural approaches but the term is most strongly linked to Aaron Beck's cognitive therapy (CT), so myths about CBT are really aimed at his approach. Dictionary definitions of myths and misconceptions refer to holding false beliefs. However, myths and misconceptions can have some elements of truth embedded within them and, if found, will be acknowledged. Attempting to debunk myths about CBT has only limited success because, from my teaching experience, some non-CBT practitioners are more interested in perpetuating them which then helps, in their mind, to elevate the importance and effectiveness of their own approach. Some CB therapists also engage in mythmaking by overestimating the efficacy of CBT and its applicability to almost any problem (Dobson & Dobson, 2009). Within the CBT field, disagreements can emerge between alternative approaches, e.g. the debate between CT and rational emotive behaviour therapy (REBT) regarding empirical versus philosophical approaches to psychotherapy, which I also discuss.

Some Common Myths about CBT

1. CBT Focuses on Thinking and Excludes Feeling

Clients come to therapy usually complaining about how they feel rather than what they think; therefore emotions are usually the entry point for exploration. Teaching clients the link between thinking and feeling helps them to see that by modifying their unhelpful thoughts this also moderates the intensity of their negative feelings. If CBT is merely a dry discussion of ideas, the client is likely to leave therapy perhaps intellectually stimulated but still emotionally stuck. Clients' emotions need to be activated in the session if the therapist is to gain access to key 'hot' cognitions (emotionally charged thinking) and to make a start on examining them. Therapists should be skilled at drawing out clients' feelings if they don't reveal them, e.g. 'By what you've told me, could you be feeling ashamed about what you did?'; if cognitive behavioural therapists are not able to elicit, understand, explore and help change emotional states, then therapy will never get off the ground. As Clark observes: 'The success of CT is in part judged by reductions in negative emotional responses like sadness and fear, as well as concomitant increases in positive emotions' (1995: 160).

2. CBT Focuses on Symptoms, Not Underlying Causes

Only dealing with the symptoms of a problem leaves its hypothesised roots intact (e.g. in early childhood experiences or unconscious conflicts) thereby continuing to be the source of new symptoms – known as symptom substitution by psychodynamic therapists. Unless these deep roots are directly targeted, therapy remains superficial (not depth centred). CBT's focus is largely on clients' present problems and how these problems are being maintained rather than how they were acquired or developed. Good outcomes are achieved by showing clients how to identify and change these maintaining processes (beliefs and behaviours) to overcome their problems such as in social anxiety where clients test their catastrophic predictions (e.g. 'I'll make a fool of myself') by entering previously avoided situations in order to develop more realistic viewpoints and constructive behaviours. If CBT's supposed superficiality promotes symptom substitution and impairs real change, Dobson and Dobson ask:

> Then why are the research outcomes [for CBT] so positive? Why do some studies show that relapse rates are lower compared to medications? Generally,

> clients have a risk of relapse; however, the same, rather than different, problems tend to recur. There is no evidence for symptom substitution and ample evidence to oppose this viewpoint. Consequently, this myth has no substance at all (2009: 251).

For the record, CBT usually explores and modifies three levels of thinking and examines how they are interlinked:

a Negative automatic thoughts (NATS), e.g. 'I didn't impress my boss with the report. He probably thinks I shouldn't have been promoted' (these are related to a particular situation);
b Cross-situational rules for living (also known as conditional beliefs), e.g. 'If I don't please others then I will be criticised and rejected' (this rule applies to a range of situations, not just at work. How will he see himself if he is criticised and rejected?); and
c Core beliefs about oneself, others and/or the world, e.g. 'I'm a failure' (the client's attempts to please others in order to prevent the activation of his core belief actually maintains and strengthens the belief rather than changes it in any helpful way).

CBT usually starts at the level of the clients' NATS as they are readily accessible for inspection and the easiest to change in order to bring symptom reduction before moving on to, if clinically justified, uncovering the deeper beliefs that predispose individuals to experience their problems. However, in working with personality disorders, the therapist's primary focus will be on modifying clients' longstanding core dysfunctional beliefs (e.g. 'I'm bad') and behaviours (e.g. self-punishment) if change is to be achieved (Davidson, 2008).

3. CBT is Just Positive Thinking

If your partner leaves you, don't worry because you'll find another one soon. If you are criticised by your manager, just put it down to her bad mood. Some therapists might believe that positive thinking will automatically lead to positive feelings. Leahy (2003) warns against the therapist becoming a cheerleader for positive thinking. How does the therapist know the client will find another partner soon or the manager did not mean her criticism? Clients are likely to become frustrated with the therapist's sunny reassurance.

CBT is not based on positive thinking but on realistic thinking whereby 'the main thrust is on *gathering accurate information to pinpoint and counteract distortions ... in order to make adaptive decisions*' (Beck et al., 1979: 299; original italics). So using one of the above examples, it is true that the manager meant her criticism of some of the client's work but the distortion he has introduced is that he believed her criticism applied to *all* of his work; by changing his focus to what has been actually criticised leads to the next step of deciding how he wants to respond to the criticism. Therapists would also examine the usefulness of holding on to thoughts and beliefs that interfere with goal-achievement, e.g. 'How does believing that all criticism is destructive help you to learn that some criticism is constructively meant and a valuable aid in improving your performance?'

4. Only Intelligent Clients Can Really Benefit from CBT

There appears to be a lot to do in CBT: clients are expected to provide detailed information about their problems; fill out various inventories to obtain baseline measures of the severity of their problems; detect their maladaptive thinking and link it to their emotional and behavioural reactions; fill in forms to detect and distinguish between situations, thoughts and feelings; use reason and reality-testing to challenge distorted thinking; carry out and review homework tasks; and provide feedback on their experiences of therapy. Therefore, it seems that CBT is a highly intellectual endeavour suited only to the intelligent and articulate. However, as Beck et al. (1979) observe, high intelligence is not required from either the therapist or client. The important point is to adapt CBT to the intellectual and verbal abilities of each client. In the following clinical vignette, the therapist uses a visual representation of the thought-feeling link as the client struggles to understand the concept just through discussion:

Therapist: My left hand is the situation which, in your case, is making mistakes. My right hand is your belief about making mistakes which is ...?

Client: That I'm an idiot.

Therapist: Now when you bring the left and right hand together, what happens to your mood?

Client: It goes down.

Therapist: [drops hands] Down it goes.

Client: So should I keep the right hand away from the left hand?

Therapist: Not quite. The right hand, so to speak, needs to come up with a new belief that doesn't involve putting you down, so when you do make mistakes the focus is on correcting them, not condemning yourself for making them. The hands come together in a compassionate way.

Client: I need a nicer right hand to try and stop my mood going down when I make a mistake.

Therapist: Exactly.

This 'left hand–right hand' understanding of the cognitive model helped the client to change his viewpoint regarding making mistakes and other difficulties he had without requiring intellectual rigour on his part. CBT has been adapted for working with, among others, older people (Laidlaw et al., 2003), learning disabilities (Taylor, 2007), and children and young people (Stallard, 2002).

5. CBT is Not Interested in the Social Context of Clients' Problems

This misconception assumes that CBT takes the purely cognitive view that distorted thinking alone creates a person's emotional distress irrespective of life circumstances (Gilbert, 2000). Not so. CBT is 'directed at correcting the combination of psychological and situational factors which may be contributing to the patient's distress' (Blackburn & Davidson, 1995). Therapists investigate the internal and external worlds of the client and examine how they interact. For example, a client who wants to leave an abusive relationship stops herself from doing so each time because she feels pity for her partner's anguish at 'being abandoned' and guilty for having 'caused' his distress. As Hauck observes: 'Don't let the sufferings of others turn you away from what you consider your best interests' (1974: 88); so the client needs to develop in this situation what might be called an 'empathy block' towards her partner. Additionally, to ease her guilt feelings, it is important for her to realise that his anguish is self-induced, not caused by her. If she can internalise this viewpoint she can be free of him and experience an improvement in her circumstances.

Another example. The fashion/beauty industry presents what might be regarded as pernicious propaganda: doing its best to instil/build-on people's discontent with their appearance while presenting them with ideal images of looks, weight and body shape which most would be unable to achieve (and those who do achieve it, having to undertake a gruelling regime to maintain it). While it is important to discuss with the client fashion/beauty industry dictates and why she feels compelled to follow them, it is outside of her control (as well as the therapist's) to change these messages but within her control to start changing her mind about her own appearance thereby beginning to free herself from the tyranny of size zero thinking, 'You have to be thin to be attractive. Do I still want to believe that?'

Cognitive behavioural therapists are aware that practical help can sometimes be the best help in improving a client's environmental circumstances that hours of talk may not deliver, e.g. writing letters of support for a client's social housing application or entry into a drug rehabilitation centre (Neenan and Dryden, 2004).

Reflection Point

What might be the effect on the client if you continually tell him that the focus of therapy is only on his faulty thinking and that the wider culture plays no part in his problems?

6. CBT Ignores the Unconscious

It does in regard to the Freudian psychoanalytic view that 'attributes an individual's neurosis to unconscious psychological factors: The unconscious elements are sealed off by psychological barriers that can only be penetrated by psychoanalytic interpretations' (Beck, 1976: 2). Beck (1976) suggested that people have the ability to understand and deal with their psychological problems within the scope of their own awareness. CBT does use the concept of preconscious (Weishaar, 1993) which means that a client's thoughts are often outside his current awareness but are accessible through reflection, questioning, exposure to avoided situations or feelings. For example, a client is worried about revealing sensitive personal information to close friends but is not sure why he feels this way. Through using a process known as Socratic questioning – the therapist asks questions to stimulate thought and increase awareness – the client is able to understand the deeper meaning of his worry:

Therapist: What would be worrying about revealing sensitive information to close friends?

Client: Well, if I told them that I had some panic attacks a few years ago, I can't take it back. My weakness is out there for all to see.

Therapist: What would be worrying about your weakness being out there for all to see and you can't take it back?

Client: Then others have got something over me, to use my weakness against me particularly if I fell out with them.

Therapist: And if you did fall out with them and they used it against you?

Client: I'd be angry with them but also with myself.

Therapist: Would the anger towards them and yourself be as equally strong?

Client: No, stronger with myself.

Therapist: Because ...?

Client: Because I shouldn't have revealed that information about myself in the first place to now become a laughing stock.

Therapist: But as you did reveal this information about yourself resulting in these consequences?

Client: [quietly] I'd never be able to forgive myself for my stupidity in doing it. It would always be with me what I'd done.
Therapist: Is that what you're most worried about in opening up to your close friends?
Client: Yes, it might backfire on me.

Socratic questioning enables the client to provide his own answers to the therapist's questions rather than rely on the interpretations that might be offered by the therapist which can put the client 'in a compromising position - in that it is simpler to agree than to disagree, or to seem ungrateful or difficult' (Blackburn & Twaddle, 1996: 8–9). Clients are shown ways to detect, examine and change their problem-perpetuating thinking as part of the skills they need to develop to become their own therapist.

7. CBT Downgrades the Importance of the Therapeutic Relationship

The standard view of the therapeutic relationship in CBT is that it is necessary to help promote client change but not sufficient to produce optimum change - this is achieved through the execution of cognitive and behavioural techniques (Beck et al., 1979). These techniques are applied to the client's problems that occur outside of therapy, and only applied to the relationship itself when difficulties within it prevent the successful implementation of these techniques (these difficulties were called by Beck et al. (1979) 'technical problems'). Later developments in CBT viewed 'the relationship ... as an intervention tool in itself' (Blackburn and Twaddle, 1996: 7), e.g. clients with personality disorders can use the relationship as a safe arena to examine their existing core beliefs such as 'No one can be trusted' and test new ones, 'Some people can be trusted sometimes.'

Dobson and Dobson state that the importance of the therapeutic relationship has been emphasised throughout CBT's development and 'this emphasis on interpersonal process (within CBT) has become more sophisticated over time' (2009: 254) citing, as examples, dealing with resistance (Leahy, 2001), and developing an interpersonal model (Safran & Segal, 1990) which shows, for example, how to repair ruptures in the relationship through metacommunication, i.e. the therapist and client stepping outside of the strained relationship in order to comment upon it in a non-blaming spirit of collaborative inquiry. While there is much discussion in the research literature over the relative importance assigned to the relationship or treatment techniques, Leahy suggests 'that assuring the use of cognitive therapy techniques and improving the therapeutic alliance may provide the optimal treatment' (2008: 770).

Reflection Point

Therapists can overvalue the importance of the relationship and fail to see that some clients are more interested in action plans for change than developing an empathic bond with the therapist. Have you made this error?

8. CBT Does Not Delve Into the Client's Past

CBT's main focus is on how to overcome present problems rather than speculate on why they occurred. Westbrook et al. (2007) advance several key reasons for this present-centred focus:

a Processes that maintain a problem are not usually the same processes that started the problem, e.g. a client who begins drinking heavily when she loses her job finds several years later that she cannot function in her daily life without a drink. Dealing with her current alcohol dependency is the primary focus, not exploring her feelings and behaviour at the time of the job loss as this will be of little, if any, help now in weaning her off the alcohol with all its physical and psychological complications.

b It is easier to get clearer evidence about maintaining processes than original causes, e.g. a client who complains of social isolation avoids making friends or finding partners in case he is rejected as 'not good enough' which can be targeted for change through experiments with new beliefs and behaviours rather than trawling through family dynamics thirty years earlier trying to make speculative causative connections between events then in order to explain his problems now.

c Present maintaining processes can be altered whereas past processes cannot be as they are in the unalterable past but they can be better understood in terms of why the client continues to upset herself about past events, e.g. the therapist explains that 'although past events like your father favouring your older sister over you may have made a considerable contribution to your past distress in seeing yourself as second best, unfortunately these past events continue to have an undesirable effect upon you today because you *still* see yourself as second best; so it's your current thinking about past events, not past events themselves, that we need to work on. Does that make any sense?'

However, clinical attention

> shifts to the past in three circumstances: when the patient expresses a strong predilection to do so; when work directed toward current problems produces little or no cognitive, behavioral, and emotional change; or when the therapist judges that it is important to understand how and when important dysfunctional ideas originated and how these ideas affect the patient today (Beck, 1995: 7).

For example, with the last circumstance, a client who saw himself as unloveable and ascribed this 'fact' to the failure of his adult relationships traced the childhood origins of this belief to not being kissed and cuddled by his mother and spending lots of time alone in his room 'as she didn't want to be with me'. However, in discussing his mother's temperament it emerged that she wasn't physically demonstrative – she displayed the same lack of physical affection towards her grandson – and this helped him to understand that he did not push his mother away because of his intrinsic unloveability, she kept her distance for her own reasons. He could see how the past continued to operate in the present through his longstanding 'I'm unloveable' core belief.

Reflection Point

If a client wants to examine her past, what criteria would you use to determine if the examination is useful from a CBT perspective?

9. CBT is Just Technique Oriented

This misconception assumes that cognitive behavioural therapists simply consult their treatment manuals for particular disorders (e.g. panic, obsessive compulsive disorder) and apply the recommended evidence-based techniques to bring amelioration of clients' symptoms. The application of techniques comes after a case formulation (or conceptualisation) of the client's presenting problems has been developed collaboratively. A case formulation is a highly individualised understanding of a client's problem in terms of its development (e.g. the client was terrified when she got lost for several hours driving to Liverpool for the first time), what circumstances activate it (e.g. anticipating or actually getting lost when travelling to new destinations) and how it is being maintained (e.g. avoid going to new places or trying to be absolutely certain that the travel directions are correct in every respect). The case formulation guides treatment and the choice of which techniques are likely to be helpful in this particular case such as embarking on a series of graduated 'getting lost' experiments to new places to demonstrate that being lost is often unavoidable but time-limited rather than being lost indefinitely, trapped in a traveller's limbo, which was her central fear which had emerged from the conceptualisation.

Without a case formulation to guide therapy, techniques are likely to be used in a scattershot fashion and the focus of therapy endlessly shifting to what appears to be interesting at any given moment (Blackburn and Twaddle, 1996). Anticipating point 10, Butler et al. (2008) state that one of the three central principles guiding the development of a case formulation is keeping it as parsimonious (simple) as possible: 'The more complex the formulation ... the harder it will be to remember, and the harder it will be to use (for the patient as well as for the therapist)' (p. 49).

10. CBT Seems Simplistic

This means viewing complex or difficult issues as simpler than they really are. CBT follows the law of parsimony or Ockham's razor: 'If you can explain something adequately without introducing further complexity, then the simple explanation is the best explanation' (Warburton, 2007: 107). For example, in panic disorder the central maintaining feature which results in panic attacks is clients' catastrophic misinterpretations of certain bodily sensations which means they are in imminent danger – e.g. 'My heart's racing. I'm going to have a heart attack'; 'I'm feeling dizzy. I'm going to faint' (Clark, 1996). Through education about panic attacks, exposure to the feared sensations and behavioural experiments to test out catastrophic cognitions, clients learn that these sensations are harmless, not harmful. CBT is a highly effective, evidence-based treatment for panic disorder with a majority of clients being panic free at the end of therapy (12–16 sessions or less) and treatment gains being maintained at follow-up (Clark, 1996). The cognitive model of panic is easy to understand and effective in its application.

Now, if another therapy asserts, for example, that panic disorder is just a symptom of a deeper problem or trauma – further complexity has been introduced – then the onus is on that therapy to provide evidence, not conjecture, of these deeper causes and that better outcomes, both short- and long-term, can be demonstrated through their methods (if equal outcomes with CBT can be demonstrated but the other therapy is more clinically intrusive and longer then why bother subjecting clients to it unless they want that particular approach?). Even when complex explanations are justified, CBT's use of Ockham's razor still applies:

> While we favor simple explanations, it should be noted that the law of parsimony specifies the simplest *sufficient* explanation for a stated purpose. Thus, there is nothing inconsistent within a multifactor explanation for a set of clinical issues if they produce a better outcome than a simpler but less effective outcome (Naugle and Follette, 1998: 67; original emphasis).

For example, a client may blame all her current life dissatisfactions and difficulties (e.g. bored with her job, heavy drinking, frequent rows with her husband, falling out with her neighbours) on a recent car accident. While it is true that experiencing intrusive images of the accident and being fearful of another accident deters her from driving, to blame all her current problems solely on the accident would be too parsimonious thereby becoming a simplistic understanding of events. Careful questioning and history-taking reveals that some of her dissatisfactions and difficulties existed *before* the accident, which have been exacerbated by the accident but not caused by it. This multifactor explanation is sufficient to account for the range of her current problems and therefore a wider problem-solving focus is required from her rather than the simplistic solution, which she initially chose, that being able to drive again would resolve all of her problems. In assessing clients' problems, the therapist can walk a fine line in trying to distinguish between simple and simplistic explanations of events.

11. CBT is Just Common Sense

This means that CBT simply encourages clients to think realistically about their problems (e.g. 'Things are rarely as bad as they seem') instead of blowing them out of proportion (e.g. 'It's the end of my happiness'); once common sense prevails, then emotional relief will be achieved. In Beck's book *Cognitive Therapy and the Emotional Disorders* (1976) there is a chapter entitled 'Common Sense and Beyond' in which he says that each person 'by virtue of his personal experience, emulation of others, and formal education ... learns how to use the tools of common sense: forming and testing hunches, making discriminations, and reasoning' (1976: 12–13). The therapist can encourage her clients to draw on their common sense in helping to tackle their problems.

However, the application of common sense has its limits and fails 'to provide plausible and useful explanations for the emotional disorders' (Beck, 1976: 14). For example, a client may have had hundreds of panic attacks over the years and believed that his pounding heart signalled an imminent heart attack but, on each occasion, no attack has occurred. The client has accumulated a tremendous amount of evidence to disconfirm his perennial catastrophic prediction but no such disconfirmation has taken place. Why has his common sense failed him so many times on this issue? Also, common-sense advice from family and friends fails to reassure him (e.g. 'If you were going to have a heart attack, you would have had one by now, so there's nothing to worry about, is there?'). To find the answer to this puzzle requires the uncommon sense of the therapist-as-detective in trying to pinpoint blocks to change:

Therapist: You've had hundreds of false alarms, so to speak, but you're still terrified that it might happen next time. Is that right?
Client: Yes.
Therapist: What do you do during your panic attacks?
Client: I sit down to take the strain off my heart.
Therapist: And that helps you in what way?
Client: By taking the strain off my heart I'm less likely to have a heart attack.
Therapist: So sitting down each time you have a panic attack protects you from having a heart attack.
Client: Seems that way.
Therapist: And if you didn't sit down?
Client: Something very bad would happen. I don't want to take the risk.
Therapist: Can you see that by sitting down each time, sometimes called a safety behaviour [Salkovskis, 1991], you never get the opportunity to test out your panic belief and show that it might be false [there is nothing wrong with his heart according to the client's doctor]. So sitting down averts the feared imminent catastrophe but what does it do in the longer-term?
Client: Still keeps me frightened of having a heart attack because I just managed to escape that one. It was a close shave.
Therapist: Sitting down is actually part of the problem rather than the solution to dealing with these panic attacks.

By agreeing to drop his safety behaviours and engage in experiments like continuing to exercise when he feels panicky – experiments initially carried out in the therapist's office but gradually transferred to doing them at home alone – the client learns to draw new and nondangerous conclusions about his heart when it is under pressure, 'It's fine.' The client may reflect that what he has learnt in therapy now seems like common sense: 'How are you going to know if your heart is okay if you don't jump up and down and run around?', but it did not seem like common sense before he learnt it as he was fearful about dropping his safety behaviours and wondered if the therapist was mad by suggesting it to him.

CT and REBT: Uneasy Bedfellows

As well as dealing with misconceptions about CBT from non-CBT therapists, practitioners from different CBT approaches can also have their disagreements. One such disagreement exists between Beck's cognitive therapy (CT) and Albert Ellis's rational emotive behaviour therapy (REBT), launched in 1955, several years before Beck's approach emerged. Unlike CT's disorder-specific case formulation approach, REBT's general approach asserts that rigid and extreme thinking is likely to be found in all emotional disorders such as social anxiety, e.g. 'I must [rigid] not let my hand shake in front of others because if it does I will appear weak and pathetic [an extreme evaluation of the self based on a feared event occurring].'

A recent bone of contention was the claim made by Padesky and Beck (2003) that CT is primarily an evidence-based psychotherapy while REBT is primarily a philosophically based psychotherapy (among his philosophical sources, Ellis drew heavily on the writings of the Stoic philosophers in developing REBT). Ellis replied that this characterisation of his therapy was only partly true 'because both systems are philosophically *and* empirically based as, in all probability, are all systems of therapy' (2005: 183; original emphasis). He pointed out that while he was developing REBT, he was reading philosophy, personally experimenting with different therapy methods trying to find what worked and paying attention to many experimental outcome studies, so 'they [Padesky and Beck] fail to note that empirically based scientific thinking and philosophical based thinking also interact' (Ellis, 2005: 184). He concedes that REBT outcome studies are much fewer and of poorer quality than those for CT.

Padesky and Beck (2005) make distinctions between the terms philosophical (which all therapies are to some extent) and philosophically based (offering precepts for dealing with life's challenges), and empirically responsive (paying more attention to undertaking research as REBT is belatedly doing) and empirically based (research is the driving force of the therapy as in CT). They point out the extensive research CT has carried out as well as the continually evolving cognitive conceptualisations of disorders and their treatment that are often quite different now than they were 25 years ago and state the 'gold standard' of an empirically based psychotherapy: 'a commitment to empirically examine every tenet of the therapy and follow the data, wherever they may lead' (2005: 188). The true scientist is committed to basing her judgements on what the research evidence shows.

If I was to offer some judgements on the above discussion, I would support Padesky and Beck's terminological distinctions and their assertion that REBT is primarily a philosophically based psychotherapy. Since its inception in 1955, REBT has been more interested in promulgating its approach than being overly troubled by the need to develop an evidence base in order to support its hypotheses. As Dobson and Dozois observe: 'The theory and practice of REBT have not undergone any major reformulations since their introduction. Thus Ellis's original conceptualisation of RE[B]T, as outlined in his book *Reason and Emotion in Psychotherapy* (1962), remains a primary reference for this approach' (2001: 14).

However, if philosophy is, in the popular sense, the search for wisdom, and REBT believes it has philosophical wisdom to impart such as helping clients to develop a flexible and non-extreme outlook, then it seems odd for REBT to seek scientific support to give itself legitimacy when the client's subjective sense of well-being or enlightenment should be the main criterion by which to judge its effectiveness. Some of these criticisms from CT can be countered by stating that science has no monopoly on truth or meaning when seeking ways to help people tackle their psychological problems.

Reflection Point

Is there room for a philosophically based psychotherapy in this era of evidence-based treatments and can effectiveness be measured in terms of usefulness to the client rather than how the therapy performs in clinical trials?

Conclusion

In this chapter, I have examined some of the common myths about CBT (i.e. Beck's CT). As this is a CBT book, debunking myths is likely to be endorsed by the intended readership; the greater task is to respond to and correct misleading information from outside the CBT community. Some of the myths discussed in this chapter I first heard when I started CBT training in the 1980s which indicates their durability. Nevertheless, it is only when myths have been dispelled and misconceptions corrected that a balanced and accurate discussion of CBT's strengths and limitations can be better conducted.

Further Reading

Weishaar, M. E. (1993). *Aaron T. Beck*. London: Sage.

Chapter 4: Extensive examination of criticisms of CBT and the rebuttals of them have led, through lively debate with CBT's detractors, to further refinements of the cognitive model.

Dobson, D. and Dobson, K.S. (2009). *Evidence-Based Practice of Cognitive-Behavioral Therapy*. New York: Guilford Press.
Chapter 12: Excellent discussion of myths about CBT including pinpointing any grains of truth that might be present in each myth.

References

Beck, A.T. (1976). *Cognitive Therapy and the Emotional Disorders*. New York: International Universities Press.

Beck, A.T., Rush, A.J., Shaw, B.F. and Emery, G. (1979). *Cognitive Therapy of Depression*. New York: Guilford Press.

Beck, J.S. (1995). *Cognitive Therapy: Basics and Beyond*. New York: Guilford Press.

Blackburn, I.V. and Davidson, K. (1995). *Cognitive Therapy for Depression and Anxiety*, 2nd edn. Oxford: Blackwell Scientific Publications.

Blackburn, I.V. and Twaddle, V. (1996). *Cognitive Therapy in Action*. London: Souvenir Press.

Butler, G., Fennell, M. and Hackman, A. (2008). *Cognitive-Behavioral Therapy for Anxiety Disorders*. New York: Guilford Press.

Clark, D.A. (1995). 'Perceived limitations of standard cognitive therapy: a consideration of efforts to revise Beck's theory and therapy', *Journal of Cognitive Psychotherapy*, 9 (3): 153–72.

Clark, D.M. (1996). 'Panic disorder: from theory to therapy', in P.M. Salkovskis (ed.), *Frontiers of Cognitive Therapy*. New York: Guilford Press.

Davidson, K. (2008). *Cognitive Therapy for Personality Disorders: A Guide for Clinicians*, 2nd edn. Hove: Routledge.

Dobson, D. and Dobson, K.S. (2009). *Evidence-Based Practice of Cognitive-Behavioral Therapy*. New York: Guilford Press.

Dobson, K.S. and Dozois, D.J.A. (2001). 'Historical and philosophical bases of the cognitive-behavioral therapies', in K.S. Dobson (ed.), *Handbook of Cognitive-Behavioral Therapies*, 2nd edn. New York: Guilford Press.

Ellis, A. (1962). *Reason and Emotion in Psychotherapy*. New York: Lyle Stuart.

Ellis, A. (2005). 'Discussion of Christine A. Padesky and Aaron T. Beck, "Science and philosophy: comparison of cognitive therapy and rational emotive behavior therapy"', *Journal of Cognitive Psychotherapy*, 19 (2): 181–85.

Gilbert, P. (2000). *Counselling for Depression*, 2nd edn. London: Sage.

Hauck, P. (1974). *Depression*. London: Sheldon Press.

Laidlaw, K., Thompson, L.W., Dick-Siskin, L. and Gallagher-Thompson, D. (2003). *Cognitive Behaviour Therapy with Older People*. Chichester: John Wiley & Sons, Ltd.

Leahy, R.L. (2001). *Overcoming Resistance in Cognitive Therapy*. New York: Guilford Press.

Leahy, R.L. (2003). *Cognitive Therapy Techniques: A Practitioner's Guide*. New York: Guilford Press.

Leahy, R.L. (2008). 'The therapeutic relationship in cognitive-behavioral therapy', *Behavioural and Cognitive Psychotherapy*, 36 (6): 769–77.

Naugle, A.E. and Follette, W.C. (1998). 'A functional analysis of trauma symptoms', in V.M. Follette, J.I. Ruzek and F.R. Abueg (eds), *Cognitive-Behavioral Therapies for Trauma*. New York: Guilford Press.

Neenan, M. and Dryden, W. (2004). *Cognitive Therapy: 100 Key Points and Techniques*. Hove: Brunner-Routledge.

Padesky, C.A. and Beck, A.T. (2003). 'Science and philosophy: comparison of cognitive therapy and rational emotive behavior therapy', *Journal of Cognitive Psychotherapy*, 17(3): 211–24.

Padesky, C.A. and Beck, A.T. (2005). 'Response to Ellis' discussion of "Science and philosophy: comparison of cognitive therapy and rational emotive behaviour therapy"', *Journal of Cognitive Psychotherapy*, 19 (2): 187–9.

Safran, J.D. and Segal, Z.V. (1990). *Interpersonal Process in Cognitive Therapy*. New York: Basic Books.

Salkovskis, P.M. (1991). 'The importance of behaviour in the maintenance of anxiety and panic: a cognitive account', *Behavioural Psychotherapy*, 19: 6–19.

Stallard, P. (2002). *Think Good-Feel Good: A Cognitive Behaviour Therapy Workbook for Children and Young People*. Chichester: John Wiley & Sons, Ltd.

Taylor, J.L. (2007). *Cognitive ability, skills and remediation in CBT for people with intellectual disabilities*. Paper presented at the BABCP 35th Annual Conference, Sussex University, Brighton, September.

Warburton, N. (2007). *Thinking from A to Z*, 3rd edn. London: Routledge.

Weishaar, M. E. (1993). *Aaron T. Beck*. London: Sage.

Westbrook, D., Kennerley, H. and Kirk, J. (2007). *An Introduction to Cognitive Behaviour Therapy: Skills and Applications*. London: Sage.

PART TWO

CBT: Practice

FIVE The Therapeutic Relationship in CBT

WINDY DRYDEN

Introduction

In this chapter, I will consider the therapeutic relationship in CBT.[1] In order to put this into historical context, I will begin by outlining the early views of three founding fathers of CBT - Joseph Wolpe, Albert Ellis and Aaron T. Beck - concerning the place of the therapeutic relationship in this therapeutic tradition. I will do so by considering their views on the subject as expressed in their early seminal books on Behaviour Therapy (BT), Rational Emotive Behaviour Therapy (REBT) and Cognitive Therapy (CT) respectively. I will then discuss more modern ideas on this subject using Bordin's (1979) ideas of the working alliance theory as an organising framework.

The Therapeutic Relationship in CBT: Historical Context

It is useful to place the therapeutic relationship in CBT in historical context to see how much the views of key figures have influenced the field on this issue.

[1]In this chapter, I am following the convention adopted in this Handbook of using CBT to refer to the therapeutic tradition and not a specific therapeutic approach.

Joseph Wolpe

> All that the patient says is accepted without question or criticism. He is given the feeling that the therapist is unreservedly on his side. This happens not because the therapist is expressly trying to appear sympathetic, but as the natural outcome of a completely nonmoralizing approach to the behaviour of human organisms (Wolpe, 1958: 106)

Apart from the old-fashioned use of the term 'human organisms', this quote from Joseph Wolpe's (1958) *Psychotherapy by Reciprocal Inhibition* – a seminal work on the treatment of anxiety by systematic desensitisation, at the time the pioneering method in the nascent field known as 'behaviour therapy' – is remarkably up-to-date concerning the therapist's contribution to the therapeutic relationship in CBT. The therapist shows that he[2] respects the client in three ways: (1) by accepting without question or criticism what the patient says; (2) by showing the patient that he is unreservedly on the latter's side; and (3) by adopting a 'completely nonmoralising approach' to his behaviour. Wolpe (1958: 106) goes on to say: 'In so far as this kind of expression of an attitude by the therapist can free the patient from unadaptive anxieties, it must be regarded as psychotherapeutic.'

So right from the inception of behaviour therapy, we have one of its founding fathers pointing to important ingredients of the therapeutic relationship. However, this point needs to be viewed in context. The above references to the importance of the therapeutic relationship in behaviour therapy are the only times that this relationship is mentioned in a book that was mainly devoted to the theory of reciprocal inhibition and to the treatment of anxieties largely by systematic desensitisation.

Albert Ellis

In the same year as Wolpe's book was published, Albert Ellis – the founder of what is now known as rational emotive behaviour therapy (REBT) – gave a paper at a workshop on psychotherapy held by the American Academy of Psychotherapists in Madison, Wisconsin, critiquing Rogers's (1957) paper on the necessary and sufficient conditions for therapeutic personality change. In this paper, which was later published

[2]I am using 'he' here because Wolpe (1958), in the above quote, referred to the therapist as 'he'. In the rest of the chapter, I will refer to the therapist as 'she' and the patient/client as 'he'. This was determined by the toss of a coin.

in his seminal work on REBT entitled *Reason and Emotion in Psychotherapy*, Ellis (1962) advanced the argument that the conditions articulated by Rogers in his 1957 paper - three of which have come to be known as the 'core conditions' in the field of counselling and psychotherapy (empathy, respect and genuineness) - may well be desirable, but are not necessary for therapeutic change to occur. He went on to outline, in his book, that what the effective [REBT] therapist needs to do, in addition to providing these desirable core conditions, is to adopt a highly active-directive stance and encourage clients to identify, challenge and change the irrational ideas which lie at the source of their psychological disturbances and to act and think in accord with their alternative rational ideas. While the language may have changed and softened over the years, this accurately encapsulates Ellis's view up to the time of his death in 2007, with one exception.

This exception concerns therapist warmth. Ellis's position on the place of therapist warmth in psychotherapy - and not just in REBT - was that while clients appear to value this condition, it may serve to reinforce their dire needs for approval and lead them to become more rather than less anxious about the possible future loss of approval, not only from their therapist, but from others in general (see Ellis & Dryden, 1985). A study carried out by DiGiuseppe et al. (1993) discovered that Ellis did, in fact, practise as he preached on this point. The researchers found that clients of Ellis perceived him as less warm and intimate than did clients of other REBT therapists. In other words, Ellis de-emphasised being warm with his clients while other REBT therapists did not do this with their own clients. This latter point is a salutary lesson to those who think that all REBT therapists develop relationships with their clients in the manner of Albert Ellis.

Aaron T. Beck

Twenty-one years after the publication of Wolpe's (1958) groundbreaking book, Aaron T. Beck - the founder of cognitive therapy (CT) published his seminal text on this approach entitled *Cognitive Therapy of Depression* (Beck et al., 1979). This book had a significant impact on the field of psychotherapy as Wolpe's and Ellis's books had done about twenty years earlier, but instead of an isolated quote or two on the importance of the therapeutic relationship (in Wolpe's case) and a critique of Rogers's 'necessary and sufficient' hypothesis (in Ellis's case), Beck et al. devoted an entire chapter to the role of the therapeutic relationship in CT.

Beck et al. began by outlining three desirable characteristics for the cognitive therapist and in doing so acknowledged their debt to Rogers

(1957). These characteristics are: warmth, accurate empathy and genuineness. They continue by arguing that effective cognitive therapists develop and maintain a basic sense of trust in the therapeutic relationship and create rapport with the patient. Then, they stressed the importance of engaging the patient in what they call a 'therapeutic alliance of collaboration' (Beck et al., 1979: 54). This sense of collaboration is linked to the basic tasks of the therapeutic dyad which are to co-investigate the empirical status of the patient's cognitions as they are manifest in his depressive reactions. This linkage between style of relating and therapeutic tasks came to be known as 'collaborative empiricism' and has been a cornerstone of Beck's cognitive therapy ever since. Beck et al. concluded their discussion of the therapeutic relationship in cognitive therapy by briefly considering a number of 'transference' and 'counter-transference' reactions that, if unchecked, will disrupt the collaborative nature of the relationship. While Beck et al. argue that the therapist needs to investigate negative client reactions collaboratively with the client, their only advice to the therapist who has a negative view of the depressed patient is 'to remind himself the patient's views are only cognitions and beliefs; i.e., they should be tested and either confirmed or disconfirmed' (Beck et al., 1979: 59).

Beck et al. (1979: 27–8) also provided a warning to the novice therapist not to neglect the therapeutic relationship in their zeal to learn the techniques of the therapy and alerted trainees to the heightened interpersonal sensitivity of depressed patients to 'any action statement that might be construed as rejection, indifference or discouragement'. Without specifically saying so here, Beck et al. alluded to this dynamic occurring in the therapeutic relationship and provided a formal space for this to be discussed in the feedback at the end of the session which has become a standard feature of Beck's cognitive therapy and which enhances the collaborative nature of the therapeutic relationship.

In summary, while Beck et al. (1979) echoed Wolpe's views on the importance of the therapeutic relationship in CBT they extended his position by stressing that this importance is not only defined by desirable therapist characteristics, but by the collaborative nature of that relationship. Furthermore, Beck et al. provided a contrast to Ellis concerning the nature of therapeutic partnership in their respective approaches. Whereas Ellis urged therapists to adopt a highly active-directive stance and challenge their patients' irrational ideas, Beck et al. encouraged CT therapists to develop a more collaborative style and to work with their patients in examining or investigating their patients' negative cognitions. Indeed, by and large, Beck discourages the use of therapist challenge in CT. In a contribution to the Academy of Cognitive Therapy Listserve Beck (2002) states:

> I notice that many of you have used the word 'challenge' in response to investigating patients' automatic thoughts, beliefs, and hallucinations. I wonder if this is really the appropriate word since it sounds confrontational. In practice, we all approach these phenomena with an investigative spirit (e.g., guided discovery, collaborative empiricism). In other words, we do not imply that a patient's particular verbal production is wrong (as implied by the word 'challenge'), but we examine, evaluate, test, etc.

While disagreeing with Ellis about therapist style, Beck et al. (1979) do agree with him that the core conditions are not sufficient for therapeutic change to occur. However, while Ellis (1962) argued that these conditions are 'desirable, but neither necessary nor sufficient', Beck et al.'s (1979) views were that they were 'necessary, but not sufficient', a position currently to be found on the website of the British Association for Behavioural and Cognitive Psychotherapies (BABCP). In discussing the key factors influencing the delivery of CBT, Grazebrook and Garland (2005: 2) say that: a 'therapeutic relationship – a trusting, safe therapeutic alliance is essential, but not sufficient for successful CBT'.

The current view of the role of the therapeutic relationship in cognitive therapy reflects the necessary but not sufficient position to be found in Beck et al. (1979). Thus, in CT, the therapeutic relationship, on its own, may not contribute to the potency of treatment, but its absence means that even an accurate cognitive-behavioural conceptualisation and the use of empirically supported treatment techniques based on this conceptualisation will not bring about meaningful change. So, in effective cognitive therapy, relevant techniques based on an accurate cognitive-behavioural conceptualisation are rooted in a collaborative therapeutic relationship. In short, the collaborative relationship permeates effective cognitive therapy and it is this that gives the techniques of assessment and treatment their power.

While making the case for a collaborative therapeutic relationship in cognitive therapy, Beck et al. (1979) did not provide a comprehensive discussion of the threats to this relationship and how these need to be managed, despite alluding to this issue. As we shall see, later theorists and practitioners have done this.

Gilbert and Leahy (2007)

Almost fifty years after Wolpe's book was published and almost 30 years after the publication of Beck et al.'s seminal work, an entire book appeared that was devoted to the therapeutic relationship in CBT (Gilbert & Leahy, 2007). This edited book, which in my view will also become seminal in future years, contained chapters on the following issues:

- emotion in the therapeutic relationship;
- transference;
- dealing with ruptures in the therapeutic relationship;
- compassion in the therapeutic relationship;
- internal working models of attachment in the therapeutic relationship;
- using the therapeutic relationship with difficult-to-engage clients;
- schematic mismatch in the therapeutic relationship;
- self and self-reflection in the therapeutic relationship.

I will pick up on some of these themes in what follows. While the understanding of the role of the therapeutic relationship in CBT has grown increasingly sophisticated over the years, this complex understanding is still based on the idea that effective cognitive therapists are both technically proficient and proficient in developing and maintaining the collaborative nature of the relationship that allows their technical skill to have its full effect.

Working Alliance Theory (Bordin, 1979)

In the same year as Beck et al. (1979) published *Cognitive Therapy of Depression*, a paper by Ed Bordin (1979) was published in the journal *Psychotherapy: Theory, Research and Practice*. This article served to alert therapists across the psychotherapeutic spectrum to the importance of the working alliance in the practice of psychotherapy. Broader than the concept of the therapeutic relationship, the working alliance, as conceptualised by Bordin in his 1979 paper, was comprised of three components: bonds, goals and tasks. Almost twenty years later, I added a fourth component which I call 'views' (Dryden, 2008). Table 5.1 provides brief definitions of these four components. In what follows I will attempt to show how these components illuminate important aspects of the therapeutic relationship in CBT. Before I do, I wish to stress that while I will be discussing these components separately, they are, in fact, very much interrelated.

Table 5.1 Brief Definitions of the Four Components of the Working Alliance

- *Bonds* refer to the interpersonal connectedness between the therapist and client
- *Views* refer to the understandings that both participants have on salient issues
- *Goals* refer to the purpose of the therapeutic meetings
- *Tasks* refer to the procedures carried out by both therapist and client in the service of the latter's goals

Bonds

When the bond between CBT therapist and client becomes a focus for consideration, certain concepts become salient.

The Core Conditions

I have already discussed the concept of the core conditions in discussing the early views of Ellis and Beck. The current predominant view is that such therapist-offered conditions as empathy, respect and genuineness are necessary but not sufficient for the successful practice of CBT (Grazebrook & Garland, 2005). From a working alliance perspective, a more complicated picture is found that reflects recent research on the issue (Beutler et al., 2004) and which shows that such core conditions are often important for most but not all clients. The implications for the CBT therapist are that she needs to emphasise certain conditions with some clients and to de-emphasise other conditions with other clients in order to establish the most productive and idiosyncratic therapeutic bond with each individual client. An example of this is shown in the following case study.

Case Study 5.1

Morrie felt very uncomfortable when his therapist showed empathy delivered warmly. His CBT therapist noticed this and brought this up at the end of one of their sessions. Morrie admitted that when his therapist showed warmth he cringed and really didn't like it. The therapist took this issue to supervision and discussed two options with her supervisor: to explore this cringing response with Morrie or to deliver empathy in a more matter-of-fact manner. The therapist decided to raise these two possible strategies with the client and be guided by his decision. Morrie did not want to explore his cringing response to his therapist's warmth. He did not like it and that was that. His therapist decided to implement the matter-of-fact form of empathy and in subsequent feedback sessions, Morrie reported that he had noticed this change and found it more helpful.

This vignette shows a number of important points:

1 The therapist uses her observational skills to identify a possible area of client interpersonal discomfort.
2 She raises it with the client in the feedback section at the end of the session to find out more about it.

3 She discusses two ways forward with the client (after discussing it with her supervisor) and goes along with the client's decision on this matter. If she had favoured the other approach, she would have given a rationale for it, but still abided by the client's ultimate decision after discussion. To do otherwise would be to pose a threat to the working alliance.
4 The feedback section of CBT therapy sessions emerged from CT and is discussed in Beck et al.'s (1979) seminal text. It is an aspect of what I call the 'reflection process' (Dryden, 1990) where the therapist and client stand back from the 'therapeutic action' to reflect on it. This standing back involves both therapist and client entering into an 'observing ego' state of mind. When they are fully involved in that action, they are in an 'experiencing ego' state of mind.

Interpersonal Style

The second area relevant to the therapeutic bond concerns work that has been done on the interpersonal styles of both client and counsellor. Here the focus is more interactive than in the previous area. The line of reasoning that has emerged from such work is that the counselling bond can be enhanced when the 'fit' between the interpersonal styles of counsellor and client is good and threatened when such a fit is poor. In CT, the preferred style is where the two participants are actively collaborating in working with the cognitive-behavioural elements of the client's problems. However, not all clients can collaborate with the CT therapist or find this collaboration helpful as shown in the following case study.

Case Study 5.2

Teresa sought cognitive therapy for depression, but had a real issue working in a collaborative way with her therapist. She felt that her therapist knew what she should do, so he should just come out and say it rather than 'pussyfooting' around with all this Socratic questioning and 'teamwork approach'. Teresa did not wait for her CBT therapist to raise this as an issue. She told him straight that she wanted him to tell her what was on his mind rather than him working gently to find out what was on hers. Her therapist discussed this in supervision and adjusted his style accordingly, stopped using Socratic questioning and was more declarative in his statements. Teresa found this 'up-front' approach much more to her liking and was able to put into practice much of what her therapist told her to do. She openly rubbished his other suggestions, but he accepted such statements as Teresa's preferences for bluntness in relationships.

DiGiuseppe (1991) has discussed a number of therapist styles that can be employed in disputing or examining clients' irrational beliefs or dysfunctional schemas.[3] Socratic questioning is the preferred style in both CT and REBT, but there are times when this questioning style does not yield therapeutic benefit for the client. As DiGiuseppe (1991: 183) notes 'Some clients of limited intelligence, limited creativity or extreme emotional disturbance may not come up with an appropriate answer to a Socratic question.' He goes on to say that letting them suffer because they do not respond well to this interpersonal style of questioning may not be ethical. CBT therapists should persist with a particular style for a reasonable amount of time before switching to another style of questioning. DiGiuseppe (1991) outlines the following alternatives to Socratic questioning:

- *A didactic style*. Here points are made declaratively and the therapist then checks the client's understanding of and response to the point made.
- *A metaphorical style*. Here points are made with reference to a metaphor, story, analogy or parable. The main advantage of this style is that it increases the memorability of the point if the client can resonate to the method used (Blenkiron, 2010). Again the therapist needs to check the client's understanding and response to the point expressed in the method used.
- *A humorous style*. Much has been written on the role of humour in psychotherapy (e.g. Lemma, 1999). With certain patients, humour can facilitate the working alliance and helps them to take themselves seriously, but not too seriously, and thus encourages them to put their life situation into a healthier perspective (Ellis, 1977). However, with other patients, humour may either increase their tendency to defend themselves against psychological pain by the use of minimisation or leave them with the sense that the therapist is ridiculing them. Getting client feedback on the therapist's use of humour is, therefore, critical.

To DiGiuseppe's list, I would add:

- *A self-disclosing style.* While psychodynamic therapists strive to be neutral and anonymous in their encounters with most patients, CBT therapists are more prepared to reveal personal information about themselves. Thus, self-disclosure may be a powerful way of encouraging clients to re-evaluate dysfunctional schema or irrational beliefs and provide one way of dealing with their problems (Dryden, 1990).

[3]While the grammatically correct plural of the word schema is 'schemata', I will observe custom and use the term 'schemas'.

> For example, I sometimes use a personal example of how I overcame my anxiety about stammering in public. I disclose that I used to believe 'I must not stammer.' I stress that this belief increased rather than diminished my anxiety. I then show how I questioned this irrational belief by proving to myself that there was no evidence to support it, then changed it to the following rational belief: 'There is no reason why I must not stammer. If I stammer, I stammer. That's unfortunate, but hardly awful.' I then describe how I pushed myself to put this rational belief into practice while speaking in public and finally outline the productive effects that I experienced by doing so.

The above is an example of the coping model of therapist self-disclosure where the therapist says, in effect, 'I used to have this problem, but this is what I did to overcome it'. This contrasts with a mastery model of therapist self-disclosure where the therapist discloses that she has never experienced a problem similar to her client's because she has always had functional thoughts about the issue at hand. The mastery model tends to accentuate the differences between the therapist and her client and, in my experience, is less productive than the coping model in encouraging clients to re-evaluate their own dysfunctional beliefs. However, some clients will not find either model useful. If this is the case, it is best to avoid self-disclosure as a questioning style – use another style instead. As elsewhere, gaining client feedback on the use of therapist self-disclosure is crucial.

This section on interpersonal style shows the importance of the therapist demonstrating interpersonal flexibility in CBT. However, this needs to be done genuinely and putting on an act for a client may not be immediately noticed, but it will be discerned eventually with deleterious effects on the working alliance. Arnold Lazarus (1981) has argued elegantly that an effective therapist needs to be an 'authentic chameleon'. In this context, being able to modify one's interpersonal style from patient to patient, but to do so authentically.

Another slightly different way of looking at the counsellor–client interactive bond has emerged from social psychology (e.g. Dorn, 1984). Here, the focus has been on clients' expectations for therapist participation and therapists' use of a power base particularly in the early stage of therapy. This topic falls outside of the scope of a single chapter on the therapeutic relationship in CBT, but I refer the interested reader to Schaap et al. (1993) for a full discussion of this issue with reference to behavioural psychotherapy.

Transference and Counter-transference

The final area which is relevant to the bond between CBT therapist and client relates to the concepts of transference and counter-transference.

Although these concepts have been derived from psychoanalytic approaches to psychotherapy (see Jacobs, 2004) and their very mention has a negative effect on many CBT therapists, my position is that it is the phenomena to which the terms point that are more crucial than the use of terms themselves. The terms point to the fact that both clients and therapists bring to the counselling relationship tendencies to perceive, feel and act towards another person which are influenced by their prior interaction with significant others. These tendencies can and often do have a profound influence on the development and maintenance of the therapeutic alliance. Working with transference in CBT is considered by Miranda and Andersen (2007) among others and the issue of counter-transference in CBT has been discussed by Ellis (2002) and Leahy (2007).

Miranda and Andersen (2007) present a social-cognitive model of transference and suggest CBT therapists deal with this issue as follows. First, ask patients to name and describe significant others with special reference to facets of their interpersonal relating. Once these representations have been identified the therapist can see when these are activated in the therapeutic relationship and patients can be helped to see the link between the present response to the therapist and the representations of significant others. Particular cues in the therapist's behaviour need to be identified with the help of the patient. My own recommendation to the therapist is to apologise for any unintended sensitivity since this does promote the use of the reflection process so necessary when transferential experiences are processed with patients.

Ellis (2002) and Leahy (2007) both identify unhelpful therapist schemas which render CBT therapists vulnerable to experiencing an unhelpful counter-transference response (e.g. need for approval, intolerance and emotional inhibition). Self-acceptance, self-compassion and humility are important if therapists are to acknowledge anti-therapeutic reactions to patients and the dysfunctional schemas on which they are based. Therapists are particularly vulnerable to feeling ashamed of having such reactions (which lead them not to admit their existence even to themselves) particularly if they have dysfunctional schemas about being a therapist (e.g. 'Because I am a CBT therapist, I really should not have negative reactions to my patients'). Dealing with such issues raises the question concerning the place of personal therapy for CBT therapists and the nature of this therapy.

Views

The second component of the expanded model of the therapeutic alliance is called 'views' (Dryden, 2006). These concern the views held by therapists and clients on such relevant issues as:

- The nature of clients' psychological problems;
- How clients' problems can best be addressed;
- The practical aspects of therapy.

The Views of the Therapist

CBT therapists are obviously influenced by CBT theory when they come to understand the nature of their clients' problems. However, there are a number of different approaches within the CBT tradition and these approaches may emphasise different aspects of cognition, for example, in clients' problems. Thus, in REBT the role of irrational beliefs is emphasised in psychological disturbance and these irrational beliefs are formulated in precise ways (i.e. rigid beliefs, awfulising beliefs, discomfort tolerance beliefs and depreciation beliefs) with the same irrational beliefs being deemed to be present across diagnoses (Dryden, 2009). In Beck's cognitive therapy, when underyling cognitive structures are deemed to underpin psychological disturbance, they are known as schemas and the wording of these schemas arises out of the collaborative formulation of a client's problems rather than being determined by theory. Thus, a client's dysfunctional underlying cognitive structure may differ according to the specific approach adopted by the CBT therapist. In may be assumed that two different therapists working within the same CBT approach may have the same views of a client's problem. However, this is not necessarily the case. Albert Ellis (the founder of REBT) and the author of this chapter, Windy Dryden (as a leading proponent of REBT), formulated the same client's problem differently in a single-session intervention with that client (see Robb, 2011).

CBT therapists also differ concerning their views of how to help clients with their problems based, in large part, on how they conceptualise these problems. This becomes particularly salient when it comes to how to help clients with their dysfunctional cognitions. While CT and REBT therapists, for example, may encourage clients to stand back and investigate the empirical status of such cognitions,[4] practitioners of Acceptance and Commitment Therapy (ACT), a so-called third wave CBT approach will more likely help their clients to 'accept' the existence of such cognitions without investigating them and thence to commit themselves to value-based activity.

The Views of the Client

Clients are also likely to come to CBT with some idea of what determines their problems and how best their therapist can help them. Such

[4]REBT therapists will also encourage their clients to investigate the logical status of such cognitions while CT therapists will do so, but with less frequency.

ideas may be well informed and accurate as in the case of a person who has read about a particular CBT approach, has sought a practitioner of that approach because she (in this case) has resonated with it and has a clear idea of what to expect. Thus, a number of people have read a self-help book on REBT that I have written and have sought me out because the ideas that I expressed in that book 'spoke' to them personally and they wanted therapy from me.

On the other hand, the ideas that potential clients may have about CBT may be inaccurate. This often happens when they have been unilaterally referred by a GP (for example) for CBT and have been told very little about what CBT is. When this is the case, therapists need to address the issue, explain clearly what CBT is and respond to any misconceptions that clients have about it (see Chapter 4).

Effective Therapy Occurs When the Client's Views are Similar to the Therapist's

Working alliance theory holds that when clients' views are similar to their therapists' on the above issues then therapy is more likely to be effective than when such views are different. When they are different these differences need to be acknowledged and openly discussed. Effective CBT therapists are good at explaining CBT in a way that resonates with clients and, in particular, elicit instances when clients have changed unhelpful thoughts in other areas of their life with positive effect. Helping such clients to see that they have, in fact, used the principles of CBT in their own lives encourages them to see the relevance of CBT to their own problems and facilitates their engagement with CBT.

However, some potential clients are steadfast in their opposition to CBT and these clients should be referred to other therapies that better match their views on what determines their problems and how these can best be addressed, as shown in the following case study.

Case Study 5.3

Sonya was hospitalised for severe depression and after being stabilised on medication she was referred by her psychiatrist to join the hospital's CBT group. She had vaguely heard of CBT and the psychology assistant who assessed her for the group explained more about it. Sonya strongly disagreed with the CBT formulation of her depression. She held strongly to the idea that her depression had strong roots in her past relationship with her mother and

(Continued)

(Continued)

only an in-depth analysis of this relationship could help her to address effectively her issues. She did agree to give the group a try, but could not engage with the CBT ideas and methods expressed in the group. She was then referred to an ongoing psychodynamic group with which she could engage and claimed later that this group helped her 'get to the bottom of her depression'.

While CBT is a major tradition within psychotherapy it is not the only tradition and some clients will not resonate with the approach no matter how hard therapists try to deal with their opposition to CBT.

Goals

The third component of the working alliance – goals – pertains to the objectives both client and counsellor have for coming together. They are therefore the raison d'être of therapy. Perhaps more than in any other therapeutic tradition, CBT therapists are goal focussed and deal explicitly when clients' goal-setting is not self-evident as in the following.

1 When clients express goals in vague terms, CBT therapists help them to specify their goals as clearly as possible so that they are achievable.
2 When clients may express goals that involve changes in other people or life events, CBT therapists renegotiate these goals so that their achievement falls within the client's power.
3 Clients may express goals that are based on their disturbed feelings, attitudes or behaviour (for example, an anorexic client who wishes to lose more weight). CBT therapists will provide a rationale so that the client's disturbance is dealt with first before setting concrete goals.
4 Clients' goals change during the therapeutic process and thus CBT therapists will update themselves on the current status of their clients' goals during the reflection process and more formally in specific review sessions.

Goals and the Working Alliance

Bordin (1979) argued that a good therapeutic outcome is facilitated when the therapist and client agree what the client's goals are, and agree to work towards the fulfilment of these goals. Thus, Bordin was concerned basically with outcome goals. The working alliance is threatened when either explicitly, or perhaps more commonly implicitly, the therapist and client have different outcome goals in mind for the client. These threats are minimised in CBT because goal-setting is made explicit.

In a general text on counselling (Dryden, 2011), I argued that from a working alliance perspective, counsellors increase their chances of helping clients to reach their goals when both agree to pursue goals that are:

- within clients' direct control to achieve;
- realistic and achievable;
- set by your clients' themselves;
- positively stated;
- clearly stated;
- uncontaminated by psychological disturbance;
- based on the present state of clients (an overcoming-disturbance goal when clients are disturbed; a personal development goal when they are not);
- set to reflect the amount of effort clients are prepared to make to achieve the goals.

It is my contention that effective CBT therapists help their clients do all these things as a matter of course.

Tasks

The final component in this view of the working alliance pertains to tasks - activities carried out by both CBT therapist and client that are goal-directed in nature. CBT as a therapy tradition is rich in its use of techniques. However, when an alliance perspective on tasks is taken, the slant is different from one which emphasises the content of such tasks and several questions become salient. From this perspective effective CBT occurs when:

1 the client understands the nature of the therapeutic tasks that he is being called upon to execute;
2 the client sees the instrumental value of carrying out these tasks i.e. that doing so will help him to achieve his outcome goals;
3 the client has the ability to carry out the therapeutic tasks required of him;
4 the client has the confidence to execute the task;
5 the task has sufficient therapeutic potency to facilitate goal achievement; the CBT research literature is replete with such tasks;

6 the client understands the nature of his CBT therapist's tasks and how these relate to his own;
7 the CBT therapist has sufficient skill in implementing her tasks and in ensuring that the client can carry out his tasks as detailed above.

The Four Components of the Working Alliance are Interrelated

So far I have dealt with the four components of the working alliance in CBT - bonds, views, goals and tasks - as if they were separate. In reality, however, they are interrelated. Let me close by exemplifying this point.

1 Successful structuring of therapist and client task behaviour in the therapy process can help to strengthen the initial bond between counsellor and client and serve to clarify the client's goals.
2 Skilful responding to a client's early test of trust in the therapy relationship can free the client to engage more deeply in the therapy process and will help to deepen the bond between therapist and client. It will also enable the client to concentrate on his own task behaviour.
3 Sensitive and effective handling of client reluctance will increase the likelihood that the 'reluctant' client will commit himself to the therapy process and set goals that are relevant to himself rather than to any coercive third party.
4 Selecting tasks that meet a client's predominant pattern of dealing with the world encourages the therapist to speak the client's 'language' and serves to strengthen the therapeutic bond by helping the client feel understood in the task domain of the alliance.
5 Meeting a client's expectations for therapy early in the relationship helps to establish a solid relationship (bond) into which appropriate challenges (tasks) can be introduced in the middle stages of the work to facilitate client change.
6 Becoming aware and handling sensitively so-called transference phenomena militates against the development of self- and relationship-defeating patterns in therapy process and helps clients achieve their goals more effectively.
7 Skilful handling of the termination process and the client's attempts to terminate therapy prematurely consolidates the client's progress towards goal attainment and helps to bring the bond to a mutually satisfying end.

Reflection Points

- What is your view of the role of the therapeutic relationship in CBT?
- How do you respond when it is clear that your client does not share your view of a salient aspect of CBT?
- How would you describe the styles in which you interact with your clients?
- What is your view of the role of humour in CBT?
- What particular therapeutic tasks do you most frequently use in CBT? What is the reason for your choice?

References

Beck, A.T. (2002). 'The word "challenge"', *Posting on the Listserve of the Academy of Cognitive Therapy,* 4 June.

Beck, A.T., Rush, A.J., Shaw, B.F. and Emery, G. (1979). *Cognitive Therapy of Depression*. New York: Guilford Press.

Beutler, L.E., Malik, M., Alimohamed, S., Harwood, T.M., Talebi, H., Noble, S. and Wong, E. (2004). 'Therapist variables', in M.J. Lambert (eds), *Bergin and Garfield's Handbook of Psychotherapy and Behavior Change,* 5th edn. New York: John Wiley & Sons, Inc., pp. 227–306.

Blenkiron, P. (2010). *Stories and Analogies in Cognitive Behaviour Therapy*. Chichester: John Wiley & Sons, Ltd.

Bordin, E.S. (1979). 'The generalizability of the psychoanalytic concept of the working alliance', *Psychotherapy: Theory, Research and Practice*, 16: 252–60.

DiGiuseppe, R. (1991). 'Comprehensive cognitive disputing in RET', in M.E. Bernard (ed.), *Using Rational-Emotive Therapy Effectively: A Practitioner's Guide*. New York: Plenum, pp. 173–95.

DiGiuseppe, R., Leaf, R. and Linscott, J. (1993). 'The therapeutic relationship in rational-emotive therapy: Some preliminary data', *Journal of Rational-Emotive and Cognitive-BehaviorTherapy*, 11: 223–33.

Dorn, F.J. (ed.) (1984). *The Social Influence Process in Counseling and Psychotherapy*. Springfield, IL: Charles C. Thomas.

Dryden, W. (1989). 'The therapeutic alliance as an integrating framework', in W. Dryden (ed.), *Key Issues for Counselling in Action.* London: Sage, pp. 1–15.

Dryden, W. (1990). 'Self-disclosure in rational-emotive therapy', in G. Stricker and M.N. Fisher (eds), *Self-disclosure in the Therapeutic Relationship.* New York: Plenum, pp. 61–74.

Dryden, W. (2006). *Counselling in a Nutshell.* London: Sage

Dryden, W. (2008). 'The therapeutic alliance as an integrating framework', in W. Dryden and A. Reeves (eds), *Key Issues for Counselling in Action,* 2nd edn, London: Sage, pp. 1–17.

Dryden, W. (2009). *Rational Emotive Behaviour Therapy: Distinctive Features*. Hove: Routledge.

Dryden, W. (2011). *Counselling in a Nutshell*, 2nd edn. London: Sage.

Ellis, A. (1962). *Reason and Emotion in Psychotherapy*. New York: Lyle Stuart.

Ellis, A. (1977). 'Fun as psychotherapy', *Rational Living*, 12(1): 2–6.

Ellis, A. (2002). *Overcoming Resistance: A Rational Emotive Behavior Therapy Integrated Approach*, 2nd edn. New York: Springer Publishing Co.

Ellis, A. and Dryden, W. (1985). 'Dilemmas in giving warmth or love to clients: An interview with Albert Ellis', in W. Dryden, *Therapists' Dilemmas*. London: Harper & Row, pp. 5–16.

Gilbert, P. and Leahy, R.L. (eds) (2007). *The Therapeutic Relationship in the Cognitive Behavioral Psychotherapies*. Hove: Routledge.

Grazebrook, K. and Garland, A. (2005). *What is CBT?*. Paper prepared for a UKCP/BABCP mapping exercise. Bury: BABCP.

Jacobs, M. (2004). *Psychodynamic Counselling in Action*, 3rd edn. London: Sage

Lazarus, A.A. (1981). *The Practice of Multimodal Therapy*. New York: McGraw-Hill.

Leahy, R.L. (2007). 'Schematic mismatch in the therapeutic relationship: A social-cognitive model', in P. Gilbert and R.L. Leahy (eds), *The Therapeutic Relationship in the Cognitive Behavioral Psychotherapies*. Hove: Routledge, pp. 229–54.

Lemma, A. (1999). *Humour on the Couch: Exploring Humour in Psychotherapy and in Everyday Life*. London: Whurr.

Miranda, R. and Andersen, S.M. (2007). 'The therapeutic relationship: Implications from social cognition and transference', in P. Gilbert and R.L. Leahy (eds), *The Therapeutic Relationship in the Cognitive Behavioral Psychotherapies*. Hove: Routledge, pp. 63–89.

Robb, H. (2011) 'Two REBT therapists and one client: A comparison', *Journal of Rational-Emotive and Cognitive-Behavior Therapy*, 28: 141–4.

Rogers, C.R. (1957). 'The necessary and sufficient conditions of therapeutic personality change', *Journal of Consulting Psychology*, 21: 95–103.

Schaap, C., Bennun, I., Schindler, L. and Hoogduin, K. (1993). *The Therapeutic Relationship in Behavioural Psychotherapy*. Chichester, John Wiley & Sons, Ltd.

Wolpe, J. (1958). *Psychotherapy by Reciprocal Inhibition*. Palo Alto, CA: Stanford University Press.

SIX Assessment and Formulation in CBT

FRANK WILLS

Introduction

Mutual appraisal characterises much human interaction. When therapists first meet clients, they seek to appraise the nature and extent of the problems clients bring (assessment); to understand the mechanisms that drive the problems (formulation) before seeking to ameliorate those problems (treatment). Assessment and formulation may be regarded as part of the 'pre-treatment phase' (Persons, 2008) though healing can begin at any time – e.g. a good initial telephone call may set up a therapeutic bond and lead to symptom relief as the client is 're-moralised' (Howard et al., 1993). The pre-treatment period usually lasts between 2–4 sessions. After that, there is a marked shift towards the more formal interventions that constitute 'treatment'.

This chapter will focus on key aspects of assessment and formulation and the relationship between them.[1] Some other aspects of 'pre-treatment' however need to be discussed first in order to clarify the whole context in which assessment and formulation take place.

Firstly, CBT sets particular store on a collaborative therapeutic relationship (Wills, 2009). Collaboration includes ensuring that CBT is 'suitable' for this client with this problem at this time. Collaboration

---

[1]Many points are further illustrated by a case study at the end of the chapter.

also means that CB therapists may be less concerned with the absolute accuracy of assessment and formulation than with their helpfulness to clients. The chapter will therefore discuss helpful and 're-moralising' ways to communicate assessment and formulation data to clients.

Secondly, the 'pre-treatment' phase culminates in drawing up collaborative treatment goals to which the client is invited to give informed consent. The client therefore needs to understand the rationale for each step of therapy. Persons (2008) recommends that clients, even when keen to give immediate consent, should be given time to reflect on whether they really do want to 'sign up' for treatment. Therapists should for example describe what will be required of clients and refer to any potential downsides of treatment. While we are now rightly keen to 'increase access to psychological therapy' we also need to promote real engagement with treatment. It is important to bear these factors in mind because the tone of treatment is set during assessment and formulation and momentum for 'negotiating motivation' usually shifts away from therapists once clients start therapy.

Assessment

Clients may arrive with a diagnosis that CB therapists, even if sceptical of the diagnostic paradigm, will often review to determine if it can be safely accepted or whether other aspects may be significant. This might be termed a 'first client suitability check' – is a client with this problem a reasonable bet for CBT? As CBT is now widely applied and there is usually literature for CBT even with clients who have uncommon mental health problems, this does not necessarily rule that many clients out. Most therapists are therefore likely to conduct a 'second suitability check' on whether CBT will help this particular client as a structured part of early assessment.

Rogerian styles of therapy are wary of structured assessment (Tolan, 2006) and tend to receive clients 'where they are' by inviting them to 'tell their story' in their own way.[2] CBT is usually regarded as a more formal approach and indeed CB therapists may well be following a predetermined structure for assessment. There are for example structured interview schedules relating to DSM-diagnoses (Structured Clinical Interview for Diagnosis, SCID). Other general schedules such as the Adult Intake Questionnaire (Persons, 2008) or problem specific ones – e.g. OCD questionnaire (Rachman, 2003) can also be used. Such

[2]Thorne (1992, p. 21) tells the fascinating story of the experience in therapy that led Rogers to this view.

schedules can be augmented by brief symptom measures such as the Beck Depression Inventory (BDI, Beck & Steer, 1993). Formal methods may, however, not fit with either therapist style or client need. I once tried to administer a ten-page questionnaire to an OCD client three times without ever getting past the first page! I have, however, observed an IAPT triage worker ask a preset list of questions by telephone with great sensitivity and skill, simultaneously typing the answers directly into a database. Compromise between closed and open assessment can be achieved by using a semi-structured list of one's own making. The following list of question areas (Figure 6.1) and assessment-orientated Socratic questions (Figure 6.2) may be adapted to the particular needs of therapists or clients. In the same IAPT office, I was pleased to see the questions in Figure 6.2 typed as a crib sheet next to the telephones.

Assessment – Current Problem

Collecting detail about client difficulties can feel relentless. There are, however, good reasons to persevere, within reason. Firstly, detail can become relevant later in therapy when the therapist needs to know, for example, how long it is since the client had a close relationship because it forms evidence on the negative belief, 'I am unlovable.' Secondly, it can be difficult to return to items that clients are likely to assume that therapists know – it can raise the suspicion that therapists have not been listening. Thirdly, detail on symptoms can be crucial in determining how they are best managed in treatment. Some anxiety symptoms must be tolerated for some time before any countervailing technique is likely to be worth trying (Clark & Beck, 2010). Acceptance of symptoms is therefore likely to be a helpful part in overcoming anxiety (Roemer & Orsillo, 2009). Knowing the intensity, frequency and duration of symptoms is important for any planned intervention. Such details establish a 'baseline' without which it is not possible to pick up the first signs of small improvement that often typifies psychological change (Wills, 2008).

Client Suitability

CBT suitability criteria often include items such as 'ability to access thoughts and feelings' and 'readily make a therapeutic relationship'. Such criteria, however, often resemble those of psychologically healthy people, perhaps giving us cause to wonder if we may only be ministering to the 'worried well'. Perhaps these criteria do give reasonable predictions

1. Current problem:

What is the problem? Give a recent, detailed example, collecting information on:

* Triggers to problem (internal/external)
* Thoughts
* Feelings
* Physical factors
* Behaviour
* Environment/context

On-going symptoms: frequency, duration, intensity.

2. What keeps the problem going now?:

What makes things worse? What makes it better?
Safety behaviours and unhelpful coping strategies:

* Avoidance
* Checking symptoms/danger
* Reassurance-seeking
* Rituals
* Suppressing thoughts/emotion
* Hopelessness/lack of belief in change
* Other people's negative behaviour
* Lack of/dependency on social support
* Life events/stresses
* Worry/rumination/obsession

3. How did the problem develop?

History of the problem
What was going on in the client's life at the time?
Main life events and stresses
What started it in the first place?
Is it life-long or recurring?
Key themes in the individual's or family's life
Ideas about underlying assumptions and rules:

4. Developmental history:

Early life history, educational and occupational background:
Family and relationships:
Significant life events:
Themes within the family:
Medical and psychiatric history:
Previous experience of therapy:

5. General health issues:

Medication:
Prescribed or non-prescribed drugs:
Alcohol, smoking:
History of dependency:

6. Interpersonal assessment:

How does the client respond to the therapist and therapy?

7. Expectations of and goals for therapy:

Hopes and fears about therapy:
Problem list:
Main goals for therapy:

Figure 6.1 Assessment information for CBT (adapted from Wills, 2008).

What went through your mind when that happened?
What happened just before you...?
What happened just after you...?
What conclusions did you draw when ...?
What did you mean when you said ___?
What is the evidence that x is true? What is the evidence against x being true?
What is the worst that could happen?
What leads you to think that might happen?
If that happened, what then? What might you do? How would you cope?
In similar situations in the past, how did you cope?
How does thinking that way make you feel?
Were you aware of any body sensations when__ ?
What would you say to a friend who said/thought/felt/did that?
What are the advantages and disadvantages of thinking that?
Is there an alternative way of seeing that?
What would it mean to see things differently?
Is there something else that you could tell yourself about it that would make things better for you?
How would you like things to be different?
What would you like to do?
What would have to happen to make that change possible?

Figure 6.2 Socratic questions for assessment (Wills, 2008).

about who will do well with CBT, but they may not be able to tell us much about who *could* do well with CBT. We may only start to get a feel for that after several sessions (Wills, 2008). Ilardi and Craighead (1994) suggest that it is possible to make good predictions on the outcome of therapy from what happens in the first 4–6 sessions.

The Importance of Specific Examples

Specific examples of recent problematic functioning sharpen assessment and increase the chances of therapeutic impact in early contact – a factor known to improve the likelihood of good outcome generally (Persons, 2008). Such examples are usually uppermost in clients' minds although not usually considered in detail. Exploring specific examples helps to establish typical response patterns to difficult events – typically in the form of a vicious cycle of thoughts, feelings and behaviours (see Figure 6.3).

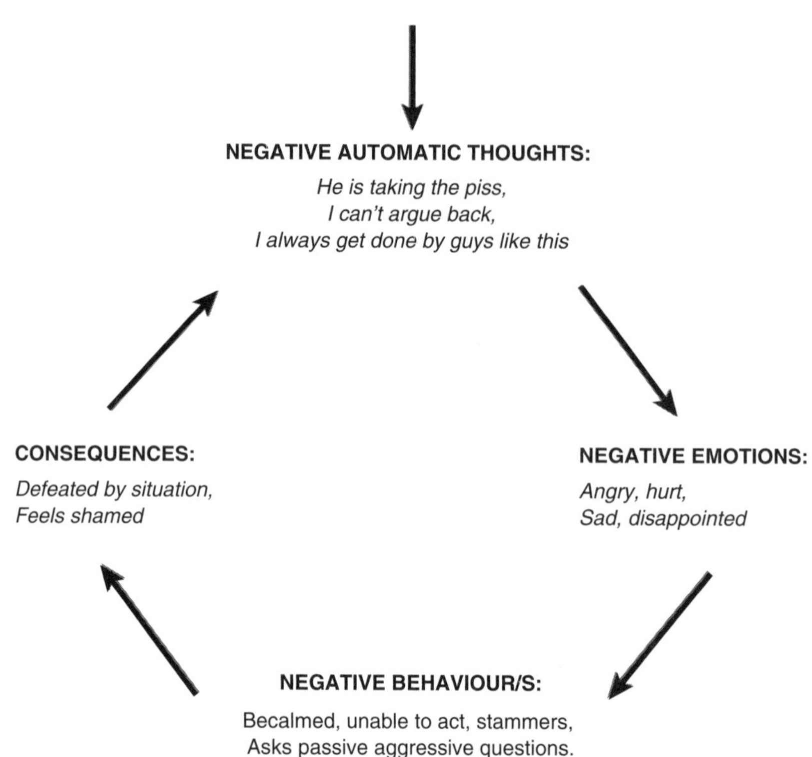

Figure 6.3 Vicious cycle (Alec).

These patterns are intrinsically interesting and we can note how vicious cycles slot into our formulation (see Figure 6.4).

Use of specific examples is a good way of *bringing client issues live into the therapy room* as clients can start to feel distressed as they relate them. The presence of some distress can be helpful because it means that the information will be highly salient in understanding the client's general distress. Distress also opens up the possibility of emotional processing and healing even at this early stage. The therapist can facilitate these possibilities by getting the client (Alec) to relate the incident in *first-person, present-tense language,* as illustrated in the following example:

The therapist has asked the client to use the present tense to describe his experience of anxiety while dealing with a car mechanic:

Therapist: So you're there ... what are you wearing?
Client: I'm wearing my office clothes ... quite smart ... I'm not feeling my best ... I am feeling tense and headachy ...

EARLY EXPERIENCE:

Father had alcohol problems and left the family home. The paternal role was taken over by Alec's older brother who tended/tends to interfere in Alec's education, career, lifestyle and accommodation. Mother is/was passive. She supported Alec when doing so did not contradict his father. Alec's sister was also undermined by father and has since had significant psychiatric problems including severe bulimia.

CORE BELIEFS/SCHEMAS:
I am incompetent
I have to do what father says
I could end up a loonie like my dad and sister

UNHELPFUL ASSUMPTIONS:
If I can be competent with people then I can get along and not be like my dad

TRIGGER/S:
Situations where I appear not to be able to be competent with people (specific example: garage mechanic 'doing' me)

NEGATIVE AUTOMATIC THOUGHTS:
He is taking the piss, I can't argue back,
I always get done by guys like this

NEGATIVE EMOTIONS:
Angry, hurt,
Sad, disappointed

CONSEQUENCES:
Defeated by situation,
Feels shamed

NEGATIVE BEHAVIOUR/S:
Becalmed, unable to act,
stammers, asks passive aggressive questions.

Figure 6.4 Longitudinal formulation (Alec).

Therapist: What can you see in front of you?

Client: The mechanic wiping his hands – looking defiant ... his hands are all oily – he's a skilled manual worker not some office dude in a tie like me. He knows what he is doing but I feel a fool ...

The client's NATs emerge quickly and we get the sense that he really is *back there* as he talks – the emotional immediacy suggests that his description of the incident is germane to his main problems.

Discussing the Client's Developmental History in CBT

New therapies tend to develop in opposition to prevailing orthodoxies. Both humanistic and cognitive-behavioural approaches developed in contradistinction to psychodynamic models. This was especially true in relation to how they saw the role of early experience in shaping later functioning – although Beck initially saw cognitive therapy as a new emphasis in psychodynamic therapy (Wills, 2009). CB therapists have, however, tended to show uncertainty, even guilt (McGinn et al., 1995) about being *snared* into unproductive exploration of past experience. I will firstly look at positive ways of engaging with client histories, and secondly, discuss some less productive ways.

CB therapists are inevitably interested in clients' learning histories. They conjecture that negative thoughts revealed in vicious cycles are influenced by other deeper assumptions and beliefs that relate to both early and later learning experiences. During his videotaped interview with 'Richard' (Psychological and Educational Films, 1986) Beck asks about the client's childhood and Richard reveals much early disturbance. Beck then simply asks, 'Oftentimes when people have those sorts of experiences they reach certain conclusions about life, what conclusions did you draw?' The client replies by giving near verbatim reports on his core beliefs and assumptions. This seems like a perfect move in assessment – the client is engaged, the experiences reveal themselves as salient and material for formulation duly emerges. Such experiences might be explored with more detail and emotion later in therapy – and then by conscious choice with deliberate therapeutic purpose. On the whole, my experience has been that there are actually few clients for whom their history does not become relevant in at least one stage of CBT.

Exploring past experience does, however, have the potential to derail therapy, especially when CB therapists are drawn into being *amateur psychoanalysts*. Hypotheses about the effects of childhood experience are usually speculative and complex. The exchanges of therapy can, however, turn them into over-generalisations – e.g. *I am anxious because my mother was overprotective of me.* Actually there is evidence that parenting styles do influence later propensity to anxiety but they are neither monocausal nor invariant (Salkovskis et al., 1998). Believing this *can* help the client - especially as an alternative to thinking *I am anxious because I am a weak person.* The danger is not so much that the client holds to an oversimplistic formulation but that the therapist might do so. On the whole, it seems best for therapists to remember that all formulations are socially constructed and therefore best held with a light touch. Problems can also arise when oversimplified formulations play straight into the clients' negative patterns. Clients may carry fears that their problems arise from a central flaw that is 'in' them. This negative belief can be particularly strong when there is a family history of psychiatric illness. This is yet another reason to hold historical hypotheses lightly. This problem has been well addressed by 'new behavioural' writing on depression and behavioural activation (Martell et al., 2001) with its emphasis on 'context'. Gilbert (2009) powerfully argues that if any of us had been born into a drug culture, the chances of us having professional careers would have been greatly reduced. The therapists should understand the clients' histories but must counterbalance this by understanding the nitty-gritty of their everyday lives in the environments in which they live.

Feeding Back Assessment Information to the Client

CB therapists are committed to giving and receiving feedback about therapy on an ongoing basis (Wills, 2009). Ethical practice increasingly demands transparency from practitioners. I have, however, observed trainee therapists who have spent so long giving rationales for procedures that they were left with too little time to carry out those procedures. How then can we achieve a reasonable balance between giving the client information about assessment and overburdening them with too much information? An obvious place to start is to ascertain what the client would like to know. In my experience, this usually concerns three main questions:

- What is wrong with me?
- How much change can I reasonably hope for?
- How long will it take?

These are reasonable questions and therapists should give reasonable answers to them. They are of course difficult questions and our replies need to be appropriately general – '... with other clients, I have found that ... but I can't completely know that for you yet ...' It is also necessary to be appropriately humble and provisional – "This seems to be what it is ... but we might find other things as we go along the way...' It is often helpful to have some kind of review every six or so sessions during which assessment and the 'problem list' are revisited and revised accordingly.

Ending Assessment and Establishing the Problem List

Assessment is a continuous and provisional process but clearly assessment activities eventually dovetail into treatment proper. The construction of a problem list (Persons, 2008) marks the transition between these phases. Problems emerge with greater clarity as the assessment proceeds. Assessment should cover not only clients' problems but also their motivation and priorities: all these three elements come together in the problem list. The list aims to include all the problems that are likely to be addressed during the therapy, usually in order of priority. It functions as an action template that in conjunction with the formulation template both drives therapy and acts as a reference point for review. The problem list forms during assessment, crystallises in formulation and is periodically reviewed during treatment. The most serviceable problem lists have the following features:

1 they are agreed with the client;
2 they have clear, unambiguous problems that can be addressed by interventions with known efficacy for them;
3 they have problems that are measurable in valid and reliable ways so that progress can be monitored;
4 they are prioritised in a way that allows reasonable hope of progress within the limits of the amount of therapy available.

I will mention but one of the many variations of these requirements. Therapist and client may not agree the exact nature and priority of all problems. Lack of agreement is not, however, a complete barrier to treatment. For example, substance abuse may not be immediately apparent and some clients show a marked reluctance to acknowledge it. This can be difficult if a therapist concludes that it is a central mechanism that maintains the actual referred problem and that progress is unlikely unless it is addressed. While client and therapist can 'agree to differ' for a time, this can only lead to more problems later – e.g. a feeling of 'abandonment' if the therapist decides that therapy is not viable. There are no easy solutions to such dilemmas but conscious clinical decision-making skills and supervision clearly can help, especially when therapists produce clear assessments and formulations.

Formulation

Information from assessment feeds the formulation process like data collection feeds data analysis in formal research – data is collated and categorised using different orders of categories. Information from the client's history is matched with higher order categories such as schematic functioning, core beliefs and assumptions. 'Here and now' material is matched with lower order categories such as 'vicious' and 'maintenance cycles'. In formulation there are also many 'middle order' categories such as environmental and contextual factors. Formulation can seem daunting to aspiring CB therapists so that it makes sense to allow a formulation to build up organically by a piecemeal approach.

Formulation: A Piece-By-Piece Approach

Though formulation is usually described as a process of building what is known about the client into a serviceable overall plan, it may also be regarded as an excellent way of establishing what is *not* known – *yet*. Formulations vary in content – from quite long narratives (Johnstone & Dallos, 2008) to short narratives (Persons, 2008) and longitudinal diagrams (Beck, 1995). Whatever the format is, we can leave gaps – in narratives and in diagrams – for things we don't yet know. Trainees who castigate themselves for being so 'incompetent' as to have incomplete formulations (Worthless et al., 2002) should challenge these negative cognitions by reminding themselves that all formulations are provisional and therefore incomplete and that spotting a gap is a useful reminder about what next to ask the client (Wills, 2008).

Piecemeal processes are, however, well served by a systematic way of scrutinising the pieces. Here I chose to start from the literal bottom of a longitudinal formulation and work my way up.

At The Level of Vicious Cycle of Thoughts – Feelings – Behaviour – Physiology and Environmental Factors

CB therapists look for typical response patterns to common problem situations. Standard CBT theory suggests that responses to trigger situations are mediated through cognitions, hence the position of negative automatic thoughts (NATs) in this diagram – interposing between the trigger/s and the emotional and behavioural responses. This inevitably oversimplifies such responses and may make it difficult for clients to understand especially when they are not aware of any negative thoughts. This lack of awareness may be due to the fact that the brain finds it functional to process emotions more quickly than thoughts (Le Doux, 1998). Such an explanation may be difficult for clients to grasp yet a more pragmatic view of it is hardly any less scientific – 'let's see if we can experiment with different ways of thinking about this and see what happens'. The vicious cycle is probably most helpful when it has a lot of intuitive 'fit' for client and therapist. Most people feel anxious if they have thoughts like, 'I am so boring. No one could find me interesting.' When Alec had that thought at a party, like many others would do, he made an excuse and left.

The process of testing the 'fit' of elements in the cycle also helps to generate empathy between therapist and client and clients' empathy for themselves. Therapists do need, however, to allow for idiosyncratic appraisals. I once saw two clients within the same day, both of whom were feeling anxious about starting work with a new boss. One thought, 'I won't be able to make a good impression on the boss' and the other thought, 'I'll make a good impression on the boss but the others will see me as a goody-goody.'

Some care should also be taken to work through a range of possible emotional responses. Despite reporting anxiety, the client who fears his colleagues' reaction to how he gets on with a new boss, may report 'anger' as his emotional response. This is interesting and may take us into whole new vicious cycles – 'they should not treat me like a *keener* – like the people who bullied me at school'. At assessment and formulation these variations are noted with interest but once in treatment clinical decision-making has to be used to decide what to target and how to target it. Here, for example, we might stay with challenging the original anxiety making NAT with a thought record, or seek to change how the client's different behavioural responses are reinforced at work. If we have the full picture, either or both interventions become possible. Similarly careful tracing of the behavioural responses helps to clarify how their consequences may maintain the overall cycle. Like other anxious clients Alec often tried too hard to be inconspicuous – with the ironic consequence of drawing unwanted attention (Wells, 1997).

Understanding Triggers

While many triggers may seem conceptually straightforward, it is useful to be aware of some variations. Firstly, there are distal (relatively distant in time or space) triggers and proximal (relatively near) triggers. For some people, for example, trying to make relationship is a distal cue that triggers a historical reaction of mistrust. A more proximal set of triggers with the same theme may include those involved in an attempt to relate to a particularly aloof person from a higher social class with an audience of colleagues at an office party. We notice that the first trigger is a general one but the second set of triggers is far more specific. As argued earlier specific examples enhance understanding and increase the possibility of therapeutic processing. It is often helpful to ask questions about the specific moment that the negative cycle began. Knowing the specific moment often helps therapists to get closer to the meaning driving the distress of clients. For example, a client may report being upset by phone calls from an ex-partner as a general trigger but may be helped to find a more specific moment such as when the ex-partner called without realising that it was the client's birthday – leading the client to conclude, 'It really is all over now, I will never find anyone to love again.' Therapists may find questions such as 'What was happening when the hurt really kicked in?' and 'What did that mean to you when that happened?' helpful in finding a specific moment of pain.

Adding in Schematic Functioning: Unhelpful Assumptions and Core Beliefs

We do not have space here for a full exposition on the different levels of cognition and how they build into the formulation. Useful descriptions of these can be found in Sanders and Wills (2005). It is, however, useful to scrutinise possible core beliefs and unhelpful assumptions and to assess the degree of 'fit' that they have with each other and with other aspects of the developing formulation. Assumptions are often, for example, rules of living in 'if... then' form: Alec for example has the assumption *If I can please, placate or avoid difficult people, then I'll be okay*. This assumption may 'work' as a strategy for managing his subjugation schema but is an accident waiting to happen – because it will probably create anxiety about the extent to which he is placating people and also set up 'disaster' when placation fails. As Albert Ellis might have said, this assumption offers an *inelegant* solution (Dryden, 1991). If Alec had an incompetence schema, a different fit between that and his assumption would need to be elicited.

We can slot beliefs and assumptions into our formulation as they become apparent, maintaining the slight scepticism towards client history that I advocated for assessment and also continuing to scrutinise fit – now between all types of cognitions – NATs, unhelpful assumptions, core beliefs and schemas. Construct validity and reliability for interpreting similar data across therapists have been found to be much lower for this level of the formulation than for the vicious cycle elements (Kuyken, 2006).

Formulating Acceptance and Mindfulness

CBT was the last of the major current models to come into the mainstream therapy field. It is now, however, quite far from being the 'new kid on the block' and seems to be entering an expansive middle age. One feature of this stage is that the model has been parenting a growing family of variant CBT-related approaches. This is testament to CBT's vitality but may lead to difficulty in integrating an increasing number of new concepts from approaches such as Schema Focused Therapy (SFT), Acceptance and Commitment Therapy (ACT) and Mindfulness-based Cognitive Therapy (MBCT) – to name but a few of the alphabetically challenging models. Wells (2006) offers some interesting ideas on how to combine the simplicity of foundational concepts with newer and more idiographic elements, at least in relation to formulating anxiety disorders. Jacobson and Christenson (1996) developed an early model that gives a particularly clear illustration of the usefulness of formulating acceptance. They designed an acceptance-based Integrated Couples Therapy (ICT) model as an extension of their earlier Behavioural Couples Therapy (Jacobson & Margolin, 1979). The earlier model was based largely on 'behavioural exchange': couples would negotiate changing some aspect of their behaviour in exchange for a similar response from the other. Subsequent research, however, suggested that even when couples did this the resolution was subject to high levels of relapse in subsequent years. Jacobson and Christenson (1996) reformulated relationship difficulties as frequently stemming from the partners attempting to change each other's aversive behaviours – resulting in a 'mutual trap' where both partners merely dug their heels in more deeply. When partners were able to be more accepting of the other's aversive behaviours, however, the atmosphere in the relationship improved and paradoxically truly consensual mutual change was more likely. An abbreviated short narrative ICT formulation is shown in the following case study:

Case Study 6.1

Delia and Len came from very different families of origin. Len came from a naval family with a 'clipped' and unemotional communication style. Delia came from a warm but argumentative family who believed in always showing emotions. For Len and Delia this difference became a highly problematic incompatibility that prevented them from discussing and resolving many important issues. They fell into a mutual trap wherein Delia tried to make Len reveal his emotions and Len tried to get Delia to be more rational. The more they tried to change each other the more they stuck to and deepened their original positions, bringing the relationship perilously close to foundering on the rocks.

Therapy based on this formulation aimed to promote Len's empathic acceptance of Delia's emotional nature and Delia's of Len's rationality – an interesting breakthrough came when it emerged that his rationality and her emotionality had initially been attractions to the other – but 'reinforcement erosion' had occurred. A formulation based on the older 'behavioural exchange' concept would probably have focused on skill deficits in each partner, perhaps even unwittingly reinforcing the 'mutual trap' that was now hypothesised as maintaining the conflict.

A range of approaches to formulation of mindfulness interventions is developing (Baer, 2006). Overall the formulation of mindfulness is based on the idea of bringing mindful attention to view negative functioning so that this functioning is experienced from 'standing in a different place' (Segal et al., 2002) – mostly informed by a specific model of the client group's main psychological problem (Teasdale et al., 2006). Attempts to integrate mindfulness and acceptance elements into a more traditional CBT-based and individual notion of formulation are now emerging in these approaches (Roemer & Orsillo, 2009).

Putting It Together for the Client: Sharing What You Know and What You Don't Know

If therapy has been proceeding in a collaborative fashion, there should be no real surprises when the formulation emerges. Many CB therapists make regular use of whiteboards to build up longitudinal diagram formulations in the piecemeal way described above. It may be useful to remember, however, that a diagram is in shorthand – the client is perhaps less likely to disagree because the use of arrows underspecifies the actual hypothesised relationship between elements in a diagram.[3] For this reason, I have developed the practice of having both a longitudinal diagram and a short narrative formulation, both given to the client. I have not found long narrative formulations particularly helpful though occasionally a longer short narrative is necessary! The process of combining a diagram and short narrative is illustrated in Alec's case study in the author's website link (www.sagepub.co.uk/wills).

> When Alec first looked at the formulation map, he pointed out that the arrow between his early experience and his subjugation schema did not explain what the link was. He defined this link as 'I so don't want to be like my brother that I keep my anger too buttoned down and this makes me agitated and anxious.' This idea was discussed and then added into the short narrative formulation.

Testing Assessment and Formulation

We have noted that there are varying degrees of interrater reliability for the different aspects of the formulation. It is unsurprising that this is so for the historical elements and we have already argued for cautionary and light touch use of these elements. Historical hypotheses are in any case very difficult to test. Though therapist agreement on formulating the more current level of symptoms is better, even here the results are not so overwhelmingly good to suggest less cautious use. Questions that test the formulation can therefore pay dividends:

1 To what extent does the client agree with the formulation?
2 Is this formulation more convincing than rival explanations?

---

[3]Kelly is said to have first conceptualised 'personal construct' theory by looking at a stimulus -> response diagram and asking himself, *What does the arrow symbolise?*

3 What significant issues in the client's situation does the formulation not explain?
4 Does the formulation fit with other available information: measures, clinical reports etc.? (Adapted from Kuyken, 2006).

Conclusion: Taking Assessment and Formulation into the Treatment Stage

Using Assessment and Formulation in Goal-Setting Supported By Clinical Decision-Making and Evidence From ESTs

We noted earlier that the problem list solidifies as formal assessment finishes and is amended as the preliminary formulation emerges. The problem list often suggests the probable goals for therapy because goals are often the 'flipside' of problems (Egan, 2002). Discussions on goal agreement are based on the key principle of collaboration and problem-focused therapy. Besides a degree of primacy afforded to the client's view the therapist uses clinical wisdom and decision-making, and, knowledge of the evidence for empirically supported interventions known to promote good outcome in the types of areas identified (Persons, 2008) to steer the therapy. These are complex and interactive factors and a brief illustration of how they operate at this stage is offered in Table 6.1 wherein the relationship elements in problem definition, goal refinement and targeted interventions can be traced across the columns of the table.

The next step is the development of a treatment plan based on all that has emerged in pre-treatment. This involves considering how the many interventions in the CBT armamentarium - described throughout the rest of this book - may be brought to bear on the problems on the list. Therapists may sometimes not make sufficient allowance for other treatment elements, already or potentially impacting on the client's situation. A 'rogue intervention' element in Alec's case appeared in the form of a charismatic hypnotherapist (see case study). Additionally, I once attended a case conference that identified that the client - a problem drinker - was engaged with at least 20 'helping agents': including three therapists as well as doctors, social workers, community justice workers etc. The group suggested that the therapist presenting the case should withdraw from direct contact with the client and focus on helping the other 'treating agents' to liaise with each other. This surprising yet sound outcome

Table 6.1 Goal-setting using various sources of information (Alec)

Assessment/formulation	Client Factors	Technical interventions/ESTs
Nature/frequency/intensity/duration of symptoms Attitude to self Functional analysis of specific situations Nature/frequency/intensity/duration of symptoms Client history Interpersonal behaviour in sessions Response to therapist instructions Response to marker events in therapy – e.g., reviews	**Problem List:** 1 Lack of assertiveness 2 Low self esteem 3 Anxiety symptoms 4 Depressive symptoms	Cognitive restructuring/ Beck's CT Fennell's application of CT to LSE/ Compassion focused therapy (Gilbert) Assertiveness training/CBT Anxiety management/exposure treatment
	Underlying mechanism/s: As Alec was brought up he had to cope with massive and unhelpful over-involvement by his brother. His mother was sympathetic but could not stand up to his brother to help Alec. Alec's confidence was undermined, especially when he needed to assert his wants and needs. The mechanism is continued today by his brother's behaviour and by any situations that remind Alec of the issues he faces with his brother.	Schema focused interventions Emotional processing of traumatic memories Imagery restructuring Narrative therapy.
GOAL-SETTING:	1 To produce more effective responses based on assertiveness to trigger situations.	Use behavioural rehearsal and role-play to practice handing difficult assertiveness situations.
	2 To build a more positive image of self.	Review new learning, use cognitive restructuring and compassion-based therapy to build self-concept.
	3 To use CBT to reduce anxiety score by at least 50%. 4 To use CBT skills to reduce depression score by at least 50%.	Use thought records and behavioural experiments to reinforce efforts to manage anxiety and depression better.

became more possible when assessment and formulation considered all the psychological and environmental factors impacting on the client's wider social field.

Case Study 6.2: Assessment and formulation for the client 'Alec'

Referral and first contacts

Alec obtained my name from a therapist website and called to refer himself. He said that he had been feeling 'down' and had experienced 'some issues with various relationships' – he had just broken up with a girlfriend – and wanted to try CBT to sort them out. We had a longish and useful conversation. Alec seemed very keen to check me out but we made arrangements to meet without any real difficulty.

Most salient features of assessment

Current problem focus: Alec was a 32-year-old single man who worked in a large-scale construction office. He was pleased that he had taken the initiative to finish the relationship with his girlfriend because he felt that it 'wasn't going anywhere' and he felt reasonably confident that he would find another partner in due course. His main relationship problem was with his brother, who he said had 'undermined my self-confidence ever since I was a young lad'. Alec felt that this had made him lack self-esteem and consequently he frequently got anxious and lacked assertiveness in many social situations. These situations cropped up at work sometimes where he was involved in a stressful project, but felt that things would get better when the project was completed – this proved to be a correct estimate. The difficulties cropped up much more with his brother who still tended to 'interfere' in his life, and with other people, mainly men, who reminded him of his brother.

Alec scored 7 (no depression) on the BDI and 9 (no anxiety) on the BAI. He estimated that these scores would have shot up into the 40s (severe) at the time of trigger events and for a period after. Low scoring probably indicated strong emotional and cognitive avoidance strategies that Alec used, including 'people-pleasing', but also, however, did indicate a genuinely situation-specific element to his problems. Thereafter we did keep weekly BDI/BAI scores but adapted them to measure his response to and after specific events. He tended to score quite highly – 30–40 –severe range – in both. He kept a record of the frequency of provocative trigger events and found that they happened about 6–8 times per month, mostly in highly specific and anticipatable events. His

(Continued)

(Continued)

sleep tended to suffer at these times. He would not have met the criteria for any DSM anxiety disorder so we defined his diagnosis as 'situation-specific anxiety'.

Assessment of problem development: Alec's father had drinking problems and left the family when Alec was six years old. He reported not feeling abandoned and being glad when he went because the house became initially more peaceful. Alec had a brother who was ten years older than him and a sister who was six years older. He said his mother was 'nice but weak' and soon his 'bombastic' brother 'rose to power' and took on the role of bullying father towards Alec and Alec's mother was too weak to intervene. The 'bullying' was emotional rather than physical and consisted mainly of constant criticism and undermining Alec's confidence. To some extent this type of relationship had continued up to the present: his brother lived quite nearby and often arrived unannounced and subjected Alec to much unwanted advice and criticism. The situation had recently been complicated by the fact that Alec's house had serious problems. His brother was a builder and would do jobs for him cheaply. Unfortunately in order to have this work done Alec had to pay a 'high price' in terms of inner turmoil and upset.

Interpersonal assessment: Alec showed much self-consciousness during our early meetings. He was inclined to criticise himself and was very sensitive to any comment from the therapist that might be interpreted as critical.

(Ex-post facto note: These sensitivities probably led to a breakdown in communication during our third session. When I reflected on what had happened, however, I realised that I had been under the weather during that session and this caused me to be less careful in my interaction than usual. In the following session, we reviewed this incident. While noting his sensitivity I also acknowledged and made a reparatory gesture (i.e. retrospectively reducing the fee for the previous session). Both therapist and client felt that this 'repair' to the working relationship did much to set up an improved therapeutic relationship and the eventual success of the therapy).

Problem list

1 Inability to manage anxiety symptoms in certain quite specific 'red flag' situations – in which Alec was dependent on help/collaboration/service from people (mainly men) who might take advantage of his vulnerability – his brother, some work colleagues, people offering services where value/cost was hard for him to estimate – builders, mechanics, some shops and stores.
2 Inability to articulate his wants and needs by using appropriate assertiveness skills.
3 Inability to reformulate his relationship with his brother in adulthood so that he was no longer the 'hopeless young kid brother'.

Short narrative formulation of maintenance cycle and underlying mechanism (short narrative format)

Alec's upbringing lacked good sources of positive reinforcement for the development of positive self-concept. Key figures, such as his father and brother, were actively undermining in their behaviour towards him. His way of coping was to be passive; arguments would only egg his brother on to greater heights of meanness. His mother was quite supportive but was only a weak source of reinforcement as she slowly lost control of various household resources to her older son. Alec was more able than his brother in school and this allowed him to build an area of self-confidence that he built on by getting good qualifications and a lower management job. His main tactic at work was to keep his 'anger buttoned down' and be very nice to people and because he had quite good interpersonal skills, this did allow some achievement and promotion at work. He did, however, continue to have regular ongoing problems with assertiveness and anxiety difficulties in some specific social situations – though these were not frequent enough to stimulate an ongoing anxiety disorder. The situation had changed during the last 6–12 months due to a collection of difficult precipitants – see below.

Precipitating factors

- **Distal:** Long term relationship difficulties with brother.
- **Proximal:** (a) Dependence on brother's help with major building problems in his house; (b) long-running, difficult project at work; (c) ending of relationship with girlfriend.

Treatment goals

1 To respond more effectively to trigger situations where assertiveness was required.
2 To reduce current anxiety responses to trigger situations by at least 50%.
3 To reduce depression scores (BDI) by at least 50%.
4 To build a more confident self-image as shown by an at least 20% increase in the Rosenberg self-esteem measure.

Treatment plan

1 To facilitate Alec in the use of behavioural rehearsal and the principles of assertiveness to practise responses to situations requiring assertiveness both in-session and in vivo homework assignments.
2 To facilitate Alec in the use of cognitive restructuring, acceptance and behavioural experiments to handle situations that induce anxiety and/or depression better.
3 To facilitate Alec in the use of continua, positive data log, historical test and imagery restructuring to modify unhelpful schemas, core beliefs and assumptions related to self-concept.

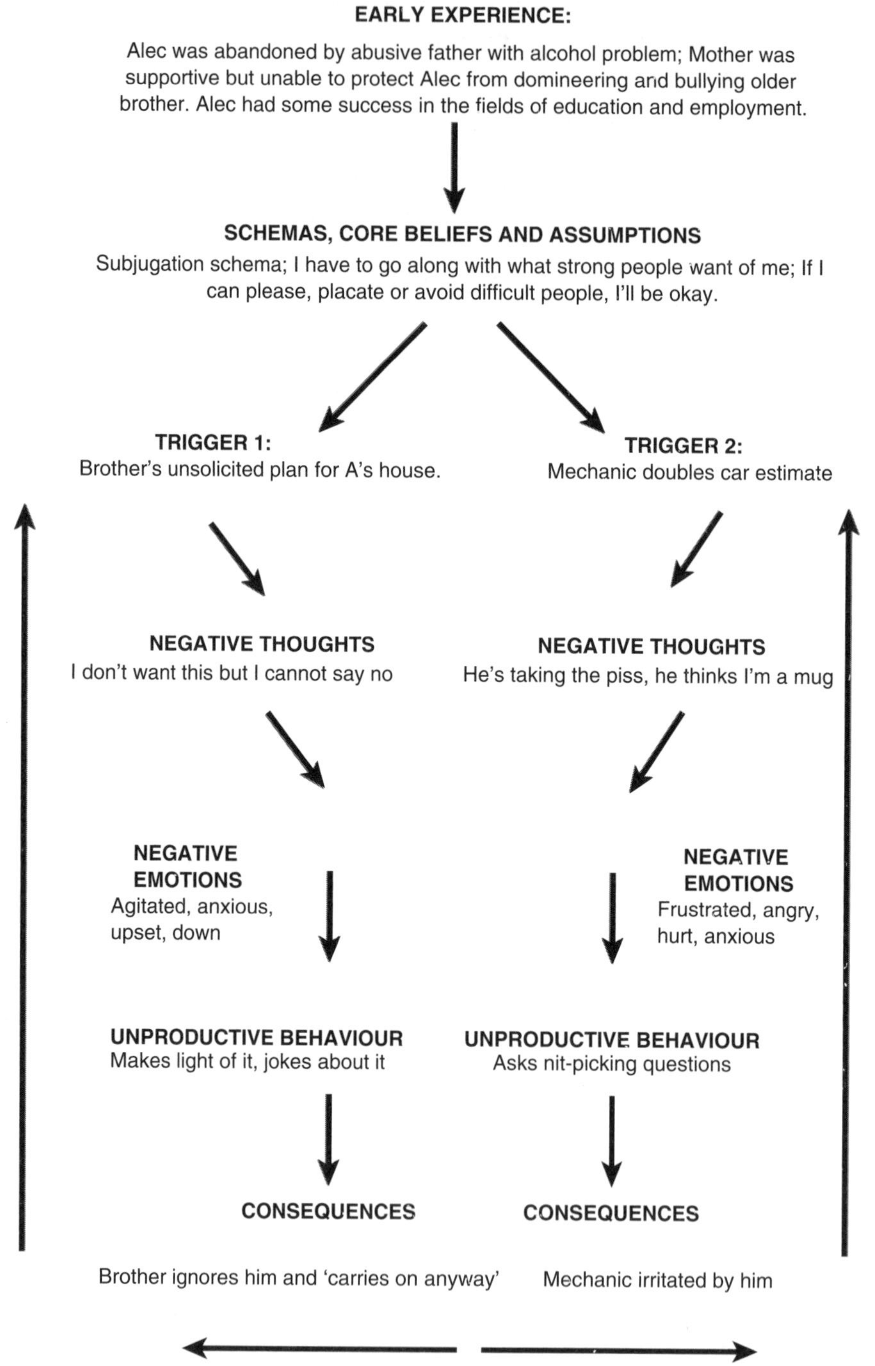

Figure 6.5 Longitudinal diagram formulation: Alec.

References

Baer, R.A (2006). *Mindfulness-Based Treatment Approaches: Clinician's Guide to Evidence Base and Applications*. Burlington, MA: Academic Press.

Beck, A.T. and Steer, R.A. (1993). *Manual for the Revised Beck Depression Inventory: User's Guide.* San Antonio, TX: Psychological Corporation.

Beck, J. (1995). *Cognitive Therapy: Basics and Beyond.* New York: Guilford.

Clark, D.A. and Beck, A.T. (2010). *Cognitive Therapy of Anxiety Disorders: Science and Practice*. New York: Guilford.

Dryden, W. (1991). *A Dialogue with Albert Ellis: Against Dogmas.* Buckingham: Open University Press.

Egan, G. (2002). *The Skilled Helper: A Problem-management and Opportunity-development Approach to Helping* (7th edn). Pacific Grove, CA: Brooks Cole.

Gilbert, P. (2009). *The Compassionate Mind: A New Approach to Life's Challenges*. London: Constable and Robinson.

Howard, K.I., Lueger, R.J., Maling, M.S. and Martinovich, Z. (1993). 'A phase model of psychotherapy outcome: Causal mediation of change', *Journal of Consulting and Clinical Psychology*, 61: 678–85.

Ilardi, S.S. and Craighead, E.W. (1994). 'The role of non-specific factors in Cognitive Behaviour Therapy for depression', *Clinical Psychology: Science and Practice*, 1 (2): 138–55.

Jacobson, N.S. and Margolin, G. (1979). *Marital Therapy: Strategies Based on Social Learning and Behavior Change Principles*. New York: Brunner Mazel.

Jacobson, N.S. and Christenson, A. (1996). *Integrative Couple Therapy.* New York: W.H. Norton.

Johnstone, L. and Dallos, R. (2008). *Formulation in Psychology and Psychotherapy: Making Sense of People's Problems*. London: Routledge.

Kuyken, W. (2006). 'Evidence based formulation: is the emperor clothed?', in N. Tarrier (ed.), *Case Formulation in Cognitive Behaviour Therapy*, Chichester: John Wiley & Sons, Ltd, pp. 12–35.

Le Doux, J. (1998). *The Emotional Brain: The Mysterious Underpinnings of Emotional Life.* New York: Simon & Schuster.

McGinn, R.K., Young, J.E. and Sanderson, W.C. (1995). 'When and how not to feel guilty', *Cognitive Behavioural Practice*, 2: 187–212.

Martell, C.R., Addis, M.E. and Jacobson, N.S. (2001). *Depression in Context: Strategies for Guided Action*. New York and London: W.W. Norton.

Persons, J.B. (2008). *The Case Formulation Approach to Cognitive Behaviour Therapy*. New York: Guilford.

Psychological and Educational Films (1986). *Three Approaches to Psychotherapy: Richard*. Corona Del Mar: Psychological and Educational Films.

Rachman, J. (2003). *The Treatment of Obsessions*. Oxford: Oxford University Press.

Roemer, L. and Orsillo, S.M. (2009). *Mindfulness and Acceptance-Based Behavioral Therapies in Practice.* New York: Guilford.

Salkovskis, P.M., Forrester, E., Richards, H.C. and Morrison, N. (1998). 'The devil is in the detail: Conceptualising and treating obsessional problems', in N. Tarrier (ed.), *Treating Complex Cases: The Cognitive Behavioural Approach.* Chichester: John Wiley and Sons, pp. 46–60.

Sanders, D. and Wills, F. (2005). *Cognitive Therapy: An Introduction.* London: Sage.

Segal, Z.V., Williams, J.M.G. and Teasdale, J.D. (2002). *Mindfulness-based Cognitive Therapy: A New Approach to Preventing Relapse.* New York: Guilford.

Teasdale, J.D., Segal, Z.V. and Williams, J.M.G. (2006). 'Mindfulness training and problem formulation', *Clinical Psychology: Science and Practice,* 10 (2): 157–60.

Thorne, B. (1992). *Carl Rogers.* London: Sage.

Tolan, J. (2006). *Skills for Person-centred Counselling and Psychotherapy.* London: Sage.

Wells, A. (1997). *Cognitive Therapy of Anxiety Disorders.* Chichester: John Wiley and Sons.

Wells, A. (2006). 'Cognitive therapy case formulation in anxiety disorders', in N. Tarrier (ed.), *Case Formulation in Cognitive Behaviour Therapy.* Hove: Routledge, pp. 52–80.

Wills, F. (2006). 'CBT: Can counsellors fill the gap?', *Healthcare Counselling and Psychotherapy Journal,* 3: 6–9.

Wills, F. (2008). *Skills for Cognitive Behaviour Therapy and Counselling.* London: Sage.

Wills, F. (2009). *Beck's Cognitive Therapy: Distinctive Features.* London and New York: Routledge.

Worthless, I.M., Competent, U.R. and Lemonde-Terrible, O. (2002). 'And finally ... Cognitive Therapy Training Stress Disorder: a cognitive perspective', *Behavioural and Cognitive Psychotherapy,* 30: 365–74.

SEVEN CBT Skills

FRANK WILLS

Introduction

The CBT approach is a family of like-minded therapies that took on its characteristic theoretical and practical form with the cognitively oriented contributions of Albert Ellis (Dryden, 2009) and Aaron Beck (Wills, 2009), both of whom incorporated the principles of behaviour change into their work. Behaviour therapy is often considered to be the 'first wave' of CBT, cognitive therapy the second, while what might be termed an 'acceptance and mindfulness' wave is emerging as the third.

There is no completely satisfactory definition of skills in the context of therapy though most definitions stress their discrete, behavioural nature and see them as being implemented smoothly and often sequentially. They are located in a context of relevant knowledge. CBT has a useful skill measure, the Cognitive Therapy Scale (CTS, Young & Beck, 1980, 1988; Milne et al., 2001) that is subdivided into 'general therapy' and 'cognitive behavioural' skills. General therapy skills include the listening and communication micro-skills – such as reflection of feeling and summarising – common to all therapy models (Ivey & Ivey, 2006). This chapter will focus on micro-skills specific to CBT.

Nelson-Jones (2008) suggests that therapeutic skills can be divided into communication and understanding skills so that a wide perspective on CBT skills would include assessment, formulation, alliance building, strategies and interventions. As many of these areas are covered elsewhere in this volume, this chapter will focus on cognitive and behavioural intervention skills. Cognitive interventions will be described as frequently using a generic communication skill – Guided Discovery through Socratic

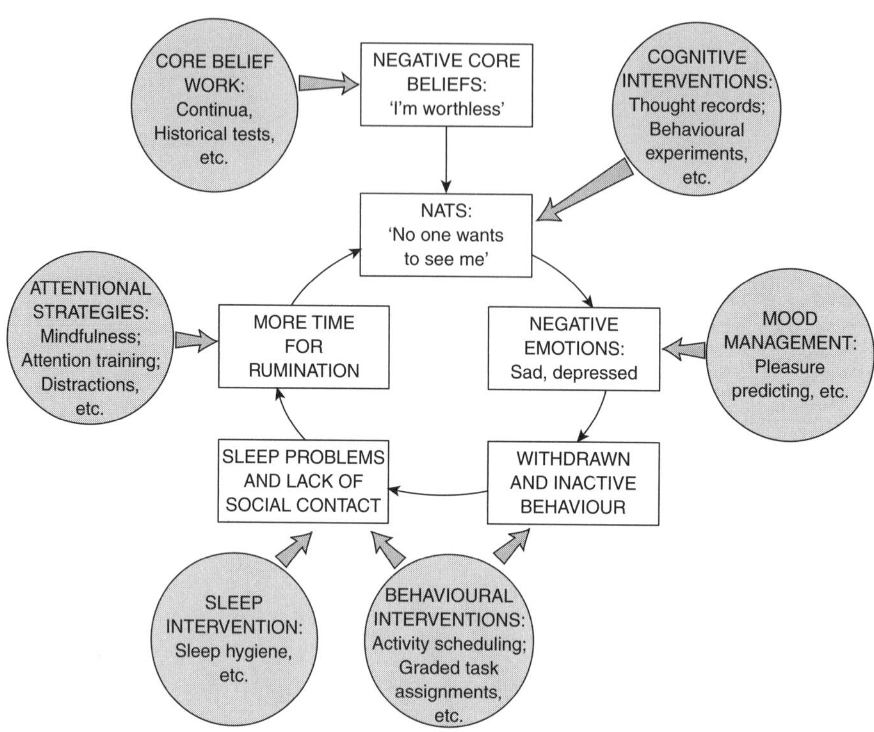

Figure 7.1 'Vicious cycle' formulation map with therapeutic targets.

Dialogue[1] (GD/SD) – that is applied to different types and levels of therapeutic work. Behavioural interventions will be described as using GD/SD skills in the service of functional analysis and allied therapeutic work.

Context Of CBT Skill Use

CBT is often criticised as being technique-driven and mechanical (Sanders & Wills, 2005). Two main counter-arguments may be made: firstly, CBT should be 'formulation-driven' (Wells, 1997: 23), and secondly, the format of CBT should be adapted to the interpersonal style and needs of the client (Wills, 2008). It is important to remember therefore that the intervention skills described in this chapter should be seen as focusing on targets identified by a formulation map such as is shown in Figure 7.1.

Skill use will be illustrated by vignettes throughout the chapter and will include some discussion of some of the main interpersonal issues that arise during their use.

[1]Carey & Mullan (2004) entertainingly describe some of the confusions regarding terminology in relation to Socratic questioning.

Cognitive Intervention Skills

Cognitive interventions may focus on the content of negative thoughts and beliefs or on processes connected with them - such as the way we pay attention to them - or on both. Discussion here will focus mainly on the use of GD/SD in relation to the content of negative thoughts.

Guided Discovery

Guided Discovery can be regarded as an overarching strategy that underpins much skill use in CBT. It refers to the way CB therapists seek to facilitate clients' movement from less towards more functional patterns of thinking, feeling and doing. The therapist uses various types of questions and prompts to facilitate an experimental frame of mind whereby clients may consider new ways of thinking and behaving and 'try them on for size'. Guided Discovery may oscillate between the two poles of therapist guidance and client self-discovery and the interpersonal art of GD/SD may lie in finding the individual client's best balance between being guided and discovering for oneself.

Guided Discovery Through Socratic Dialogue (GD/SD)

GD/SD is usually understood as an inductive process because it bypasses deductions drawn from clients' negative beliefs by encouraging more objective and inductive examination of everyday experiences. Inductive reasoning is regarded as less powerful than deductive reasoning (Skyrms, 2000) - because an emerging generalisation can be destroyed by the discovery of a single contradictory example - but is probably closer to the way most people reason in their everyday lives.

GD/SD usually proceeds in a series of questions and prompts that are designed to help clients retrieve information that is relevant to their concerns but may lie 'outside the box' of their currently biased negative processing style. Overholser (1993) uses analysis from Bloom's taxonomy (Bloom, 1956) to suggest that certain types of question - analytic, evaluative and synthesising - are particularly good at stimulating higher order cognitive processes associated with GD/SD. Analytic questions (AQ) typically encourage clients to unpack problems by exploring relationships between their component parts. Evaluative questions (EQ) explore the meanings that clients give to various factors associated with their problems – often leading to 'repacking' the issues under a new definition. Therapists can then use summaries (S) and synthesising questions (SQ) to gather in and inter-link emerging material so that clients are prompted to draw new conclusions.

GD/SD may proceed in different ways but Padesky and Greenberger (1996) identify a common and helpful format. The therapist:

1 asks analytic and evaluative questions to uncover relevant information that is currently outside the client's awareness;
2 uses accurate listening and reflection;
3 summarises the information gathered;
4 asks a synthesising question inviting the client to apply the new information to his or her original belief.

Sage et al. (2008) capture the dual nature of GD/SD by pointing out that typical questions are both open yet directional. Wells (1997) suggests that the GD/SD pattern is an interaction between asking open-ended questions that invite the client to expand on their views and probing questions that dig below the surface of them.

The various types of GD/SD question are illustrated in linked case studies slowing a series of dialogues between a CBT therapist and a 35-year-old client who is suffering from anxiety and depression following a relationship break-up. The dialogues come from successively later sessions:

Case Study 7.1: GD/SD 1

C1.1[2]: (Despondent) I have no real friends.

T1.1: (Surprised) Really? So, for you, a real friend is ...? (AQ)

C1.2: ... someone you can have fun with ... and you can say what you both really feel.

T1.2: You said you went to the cricket with some friends ... how do they measure on these things? (EQ)

C1.3: You know blokes ... fun but it was all piss-taking!

T1.3: With all of them, all the time? (AQ)

C1.4: ... in fact, Terry told me about his break-up – said he was devastated actually... like me ... actually it isn't that I don't have real friends ... I just don't have a girlfriend.

T1.4: And that's one of our goals – to increase your chances of meeting someone but we shouldn't forget what you do have – some good mates by the sound of it.

[2]In the dialogues, C stands for client and T for therapist.

In response to the AQ T1.1, C1.2 yields two criteria that allow an EQ, T1.2, and a further AQ, T1.3. Collectively the questions facilitate inductive movement from the cold world of 'no real friends' to the warmer world of 'no girlfriend ... but some good mates'. It is not yet clear where this will lead but by looking at actual friends, the dialogue is now about more specific and concrete matters that can be more easily explored and evaluated. Evaluation is often a fertile area in therapy because, as Ellis has pointed out, evaluation often degenerates into relatively meaningless categories of 'good' and 'bad' whereas important life issues are rarely this black and white (Dryden, 1991). 'Black and white' thinking is also a frequently encountered cognitive distortion (Burns, 1999) – a variant of the overgeneralisation often targeted in GD/SD.

The ground gained in Dialogue 1 is developed in a later session with the same client:

Case Study 7.2: GD/SD 2

C2.1: (discussing his drinking) I sometimes think it doesn't agree with me. My mates seem to knock it back ... but I can't keep up – and then it messes with my sleep ... I don't understand why I keep getting drawn into it.

T2.1: So what do you think keeps drawing you in? (AQ)

C2.2: I guess it is the fear of standing out. You'd get called a wimp – it is only piss-taking but can be hard to take.

T2.2: So that makes it hard to take the healthy option? (EQ)

C2.3: Yes ... and that makes me sound like a wimp for not standing up to my mates and being my own person!

T2.3: Being your own person ... sounds important. What would that be like? (EQ)

C2.4: Funnily enough, it makes me think of going out with Brenda. She liked the theatre – which I do. We went to a play and the boys were like – *His bird's making him go to the theatre.* I could hide behind that – I didn't have to say *I* liked the theatre.

T2.4: So you are a bit trapped between your mates, your more intellectual interests and having a girlfriend (S). How does all that fit together? (SQ)

C2.5: I end up not getting what I want. (T: Which is?) I want a girlfriend, a cultural life and some time with my mates (T: Sounds reasonable).

The analytic, evaluative and synthesising questions act as thought stimulators and some further new and unexpected ground is gained. We can notice that the client is racing on now so that some of his linkmaking thoughts – for example, those leading to C2.4 – are unreported. As we move to our final vignette, it is important to note that frequent summaries help to conserve and organise what is being gained in developing dialogue. Padesky (1993) suggests that a lack of summaries is often what most inhibits successful GD/SD.

Case Study 7.3: GD/SD 3

C3.1: (talking about a new woman in his office) ... she seemed keen to speak to me ... because she's new, not so posh ... I think she sees me as the same ... probably feels sorry for me.
T3.1: What tells you that? (AQ)
C3.2: You know my luck!
T3.2: OK – so that's how it feels. Is there any other evidence? (AQ)
C3.3: She has asked me to go on a bike rally against Climate Change ... but I'm supposed to go to football with the lads. Imagine telling them I was doing that!
T3.3: OK let's gather that in: There's a woman who might be interested in you. She might not meet your mates' criteria but you say you want to be your own person – what about your criteria? First of all, bikes? (EQ)
C3.4: Well, yes ... I used to be keen on bikes when I was younger ... went to youth hostels and all that. (T: Climate Change?)
C3.5: Well, I have not been involved before but I am interested in politics ... and she seems lovely ... so yes, it does meet my criteria, doesn't it? (laughing) That would be being my own person, I reckon!

Analysing skill use often shows how the therapist's and client's tasks parallel each other. In GD/SD the therapist's questions are often matched by the client's internal questions and here the client's summary at C3.5 matches the therapist's at T3.3.

I chose these three actual dialogues from separate sessions spaced over several weeks because they emphasise the fact that GD/SD often takes time to develop. This should help us to refrain from being overly persuasive at any one moment in time. Rather than trying to force a 'Damascus' moment we might seek to 'catch the prevailing wind' of the client's mind.

GD/SD: a Generic Method Across Various Areas of Cognitive Intervention

Sometimes it is helpful to reinforce GD/SD with written methods. These range from merely writing a negative thought on a whiteboard and 'contemplating' it with the client, to the more formal steps of a thought record (Padesky & Greenberger, 1996). A thought record can strengthen the structuring of GD/SD, especially when questions are included in its format. A thought record also seems to mimic the steps of normal and healthy problem-solving (Wills, 2009). An important therapeutic rationale for modifying negative thoughts may be the balancing of emotional and cognitive tracks in the brain (Epstein, 1998; Le Doux, 1997). As Dryden (1995) observes, cognitive change needs to be both intellectually and emotionally convincing. CB therapists therefore need to be just as comfortable on the client's emotional and interpersonal terrain as any other type of therapist.

Other cognitive interventions, such as working with the meaning embedded in clients' images and working with core beliefs and schemas through continua (Padesky & Greenberger, 1996) are focused on less immediately accessible cognitions but still often rely on GD/SDs to generate the relevant material, as shown in the following dialogue with a 52-year-old woman suffering from depression following a job redundancy:

Case Study 7.4: GD/SD in imagery work

C4.1: (Talking about having internal images of rejection while contemplating a job application) ... I could see myself struggling and the interviewers giving me a real hard time.
T4.1: How were they doing that? (AQ)
C4.2: They were looking at my forms and shaking their heads ... and then looking at me with contempt.
T4.2: And what did them doing that mean to you? (EQ)
C4.3: That I was wasting their time and I should not have even applied.
T4.3: You said that before Ted left you, you felt more confident about work but now when you even think of working you get these negative images (S). What's happened, do you think? (SQ)
C4.4: I'm just so lacking in confidence ... and I feel so hopeless ... like I am infected with pessimism.
T4.4: May be we could heal this infection?
C4.5: That would be nice!

In this dialogue, the questions and summaries help to 'unpack' (Hackman & Holmes, 2004) the negative image and 'repack' it by analysing and evaluating the underlying material. The analogy of 'infection' and the metaphor of 'healing' are examples of how meta-meaning devices can help to prepare the client to access the higher order cognitive processes necessary for rethinking. The following dialogue illustrates intervention aimed at schema level as the therapist explores the client's 'incompetence schema'.

0% competent	50%	100% competent
Gets 0% things right	50% things right	100% things right
	40% James –50% Client –60% Jane –90% Brian	
Not at all popular	Quite popular	Very popular
Earns no money	Earns average money	Earns a lot of money

NB: Continuum chart shown as completed to the point illustrated in the dialogue.

Figure 7.2 Example of criteria continuum line.

Case Study 7.5: GD/SD in continua work

T5.1: (Introducing the 'criteria method' - Wills, 2008 - to examine an incompetence schema) Let's have a look at what competence is made of. In your field of work, what would a person do to be competent? (AQ/EQ)

C5.1: He would ... get nearly everything right ... be very popular ... and earn a lot of money.

T5.2: Taking the first one, in your firm who gets the most things right? (C: Brian) And where would you put him on our continuum line? (C: There – *indicating 90%)* Where would you be? (C: Here - *indicating 50%)* Who would be below you? (C: James - *indicating 40%)* Anyone else? (C: Jane would be here - *indicating 60%)* (EQs) OK so far it looks like Brian is an outlier. You are in the middle of the rest. (S) How does that fit with being incompetent? (SQ)

C5.2: Well, Brian is a legend in our field. The rest of us are just 'also rans' actually.

In this example, asking analytic and evaluative questions deconstructs 'competence' and 'getting things right' leading to more productive and workable ground: focusing on the more specific and solvable problem of 'working alongside a legend' as against the less clear problem of 'being incompetent'. From this small beginning, the client went on to a more radical paradigm shift: comparing 'old world competence' – which stresses 'achievement' and money-making – to 'new earth competence' – which stresses ethical living.

It emerged that this client spent much time observing and ruminating over Brian. These factors might have led to an attention focused approach which increasingly might use interventions such as the metacognitive and/or mindful strategies of Wells (1997), Hayes et al. (2004) or Williams et al. (2007). The reader may learn more of these strategies by reading these works but will find that GD/SD skills continue to figure there too.

GD/SD – Interpersonal Attunement: How Guided? How Discovery-based?

If there is a continuum between 'light touch' and 'directional' GD/SD we might expect to find Padesky (1993) and Teasdale (1996) at the former end and Ellis (1962) at the other. Padesky (1993) argues that GD/SD should not seek to 'change minds' and should try to proceed without any preconceived direction. Teasdale (1996) argues that directional GD/SD is likely to focus on propositional meaning rather than the more salient implicational meaning associated with therapeutic change. While much GD/SD can proceed in this way, it seems difficult to think that therapists work with no awareness of how previous similar work has gone – indeed the notion of any 'expertise' would be located there. Wells (1997) takes a more pragmatic view, suggesting that very open exploration is likely to involve more time than is usually available in everyday clinical work.

There may also, however, be a further argument that more forceful GD/SD may be appropriate in some cases. Ellis (Dryden, 1991) has argued that psychopathology is not 'polite' and will not merely go away when nicely invited to. In my practice, I have found that clients troubled by strong hostility and anger seem very wedded to righteous anger and rarely respond to light touch GD/SD. I have found the more philosophically based and forceful approach of REBT (Ellis & Tafrate, 1997; Hauck, 1980) more effective with these clients. Still & Dryden (2003) stress the influence of Epictetus in REBT and it is interesting that the meagre records we have of Epictetus' dialogues are mainly in the form of exhortations – though they may not have been actually conducted in this way. Sherman (2005) also points out that Epictetus' discussion of grief shows a philosophy less austere than is sometimes imagined. In summary, it seems unlikely that there is only one true way of doing GD/SD and it may be better to conceive of a continuum of GD/SD styles adaptable to the needs of individual clients.

Beck (1976) describes how his discovery of 'automatic thoughts' came when, during a session, a client reported negative thoughts about him and the therapy process. It is obvious that such thoughts must occur frequently and form a kind of 'undergrowth' beneath the formal content of therapy. Such thoughts often seem to focus on issues like when clients feel 'pushed around' by therapists or by the structure of therapy (Beutler et al., 1994) – thus confirming the plausibility of the case for light touch work. There may, however, be situations – and I have encountered them – when a client is thinking, 'I wish this therapist would be more forceful with me.' The client's formulation may often be a good guide on what client thoughts and beliefs may be played out in the therapeutic relationship but the therapist still needs the skill and courage to explore what is going on between him and the client in the 'here and now' by using the skill of immediacy (Wills, 2008). Such an approach to CBT can ensure that it is delivered in a flexible and interpersonally sensitive way.

Behavioural Interventions

After decades of relative disfavour among therapists,[3] there has been a revival of interest in behavioural methods. The 'cognitive revolution' of the 1970s and '80s overshadowed the behavioural model. Many behaviourists took on the 'CBT' mantel but continued to develop purely behavioural methods, especially in the anxiety problems where exposure treatment proved effective.

Behavioural Activation (BA)

The scope of behaviour therapy was expanded particularly by behavioural activation (BA) (Jacobson & Hollon, 1999; Martell et al., 2001) in the treatment of depression. Beck et al. (1979) had incorporated 'activity scheduling' into cognitive therapy of depression. Activity scheduling aims to increase the rate of engagement in behavioural and pleasurable activity. Jacobson and his colleagues extended this work by putting more emphasis on the context and meaning of such activities, especially on how interpersonally rewarding they were. Their research found that relatively simple interventions based on these principles were often highly effective without the need for further therapy. This research has led to an interesting debate about whether cognitive interventions add value to behavioural activation. CB therapists may consider that for some clients behavioural interventions will prove most effective whereas for others they may be usefully augmented with cognitive interventions. There is no obvious reason why both aims cannot coexist.

Much behavioural work is underpinned by the theory and practice of functional analysis (Ramnero & Torneke, 2008). Functional analysis has adapted the user-friendly label of ABC[4] (Antecedent-Behaviour-Consequences). The concept essentially combines Pavlovian classical

[3]Behavioural therapists have not been given fair recognition for providing many of the first nonmedical approaches in mental health (Bruch & Bond, 1998) nor for their continuing robust opposition to the medical model (Martell et al., 2001).

[4]This should not be confused with the ABC model of REBT – see Dryden (1995).

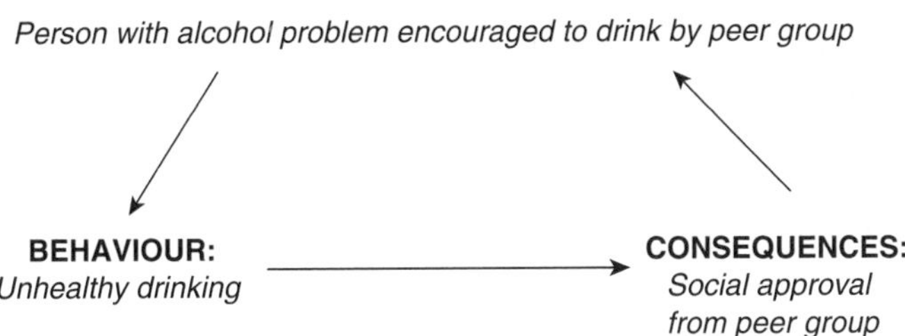

Figure 7.3 Behavioural ABC model (example).

learning theory with Skinnerian operant conditioning theory by suggesting that many key behaviours are both triggered by antecedent events and maintained by consequent rewards in the environment. A simple example is given in Figure 7.3.

Figure 7.1 established that negative behaviour is intimately associated with the maintenance of negative thoughts and feelings. Clients are frequently seeking help to change negative patterns, crucially including behaviour. They often want to change not only their thoughts and feelings but also the way they respond to certain events. Using the ABC model, a therapist can help clients to (i) identify triggers for unwanted responses, and, (ii) experiment with different behavioural responses to see if they result in any more helpful consequences. There follows a case study and a series of further related vignettes illustrating the use of communication skills to implement an ABC-based intervention, in this case, BA.

Case Study 7.6: Doreen

Doreen, an Afro-Caribbean mother in her 40s, was depressed following separation from her husband. She was assigned a relatively inexperienced 'low-intensity' IAPT worker for behavioural activation. She had been previously active in religious and charitable activities in her local community. Her worker reasonably thought that she would be positively mobilised by re-engagement in such work. Doreen's lack of interest in doing this was interpreted as due to her depression. Supervision from a more experienced colleague, however, led to reassessment and reformulation. It turned out that Doreen had moved to her husband's neighbourhood when they got married. His relatives, many of who lived locally, blamed her for the failure of the marriage. They also were active in the same local activities and this made it purgatorial for Doreen to participate. This new understanding helped to refocus the intervention towards re-engagement with similar activities elsewhere.

Earlier behaviourists defined antecedents of behaviour only in observable, and concrete terms. A useful advance came when the cognitive behavioural perspective showed that internal events, including thoughts and feelings, could trigger behaviour. It is also important to note that the effect of antecedent events may depend on how they are appraised – i.e. they are cognitively mediated. The first vignette illustrates the identification of triggers in Doreen's situation:

Case Study 7.7: BA 1 – identifying the A->B link

T6.1: (looking over Doreen's activity schedule) So Tuesday afternoon and evening seem to have been difficult – what was happening? (AQ)

C6.1: I was short of food but I didn't have the energy to go to the supermarket but when I thought of going to the corner shop I got the 'horrors'.

T6.2: The 'horrors' – what are they? (AQ)

C6.2: I just kept thinking that I'd see his sister there ... and she'd give me her evil stare – I can't stand it!

T6.3: And what would be so bad about her evil stare? (EQ)

C6.3: (Shuddering) It's like I am to blame, it's all my fault – I am an official 'bad person'!

The antecedent event may be seen as an internal one – the negative thoughts and images that come into Doreen's mind when she thinks about going to her local shop. A case may also be made, however, for more external factors evident in this situation. Doreen is actually alone at home and has identified what she probably regarded as a shortcoming in her housekeeping and mothering duties – being short of food at a time when her children were due home from school. The therapist should not ignore the possibility that had she considered going to the shop at a different time and in a different place, where supportive others were, she may not have had this reaction. Such considerations could influence ideas about what to change in her response. Before considering a response intervention, however, the therapist should complete the ABC analysis:

Case Study 7.8: BA 2 – identifying the B->C link

T7.1: So what happened next? (AQ)

C7.1: I tried to force myself to go out but I just kept on putting on my coat and then taking it off again ... in the end I fooled about so much that the children got back before I got out. I knew what Delroy was thinking ...

(T: What?) He's been getting mad that I don't look after them and was thinking 'Oh no food again!' I snapped at him and then we were arguing again.

T7.2: How did you feel about that? (EQ)

C7.2: Oh so bad ... He stood his ground – really shouted at me and I ran away and hid in my room. So eventually he had to go out and get some tea from the shop. I didn't have to see that bitch but I ended up feeling even worse about myself.

T7.3: So it seems like there was a short-term fix but a longer term cost. (S) It seems like you often think of going to do something but then get waylaid. Is there a way of thinking about doing things like this without ending up so paralysed?

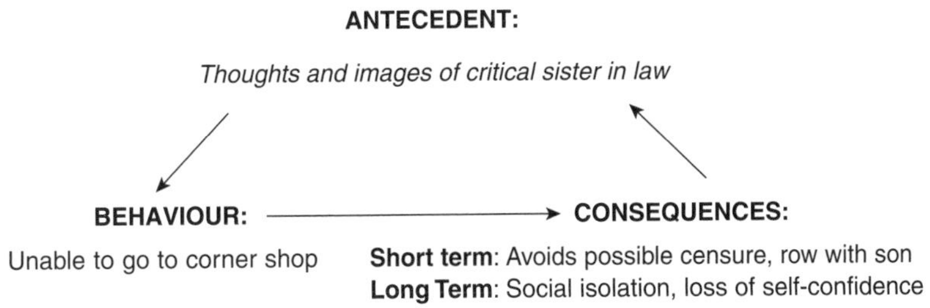

ANTECEDENT:

Thoughts and images of critical sister in law

BEHAVIOUR: → **CONSEQUENCES:**

Unable to go to corner shop

Short term: Avoids possible censure, row with son
Long Term: Social isolation, loss of self-confidence

Figure 7.4 ABC Model for 'Doreen'.

Subsequent discussion established that there were indeed times when Doreen had been able to go to the shop and that certain failures such as these could be linked to particularly 'bad moments' – when she was alone and/or had been ruminating in a negative fashion. She needed therefore to have a 'bad moment strategy' backed up by an 'emergency moment strategy':

Case Study 7.9: BA 3 – experimenting with new behaviour

C8.1: Last time we discussed how it's hard for me to ask for help ... but I think that I just have to accept that right now I can't do it all myself. If I can phone someone and just tell her that I am having the horrors she might help me out.

T8.1: How might they do that? (AQ)

C8.2: They could just talk me up a bit so I could work up my courage and get out to the shop, or maybe go to the shop for me if I am absolutely stuck.

Further discussion and planning on implementing new behaviours is usually necessary but the parameters of new responses have been laid in this ABC discussion. It is also interesting to note that the therapist could have suggested running this as a 'behavioural experiment' (Bennett-Levy et al. (2004) to test the negative thought that 'I can't face my sister in law' or 'I have to solve this problem on my own.' Either way a new coping behaviour would likely have been similar to that being shaped in BA 3 above. Readers will also observe the way the same types of question pattern described as cognition interventions earlier also do service in support of behavioural interventions here. During the course of sessions Doreen revealed strong beliefs about the need to 'get things right' and 'look after her own problems'. This sometimes made it difficult to accept help from the therapist and others. It was therefore helpful for the therapist to remain sensitive to this interpersonal style and to define trying new behavioural responses as adding to her 'self-efficacy' (Bandura, 1997).

Concluding Discussion: Developing CBT Skills

For an empirically supported treatment, there has been remarkably little systematic research on skill use in CBT. For reasons described elsewhere (Wills, 2010) I am not hopeful that such research is likely to emerge soon. By presenting, in this necessarily short chapter, some detailed analysis of the use of key CBT skills, I aim to offer a modest practitioner-led attempt to highlight how CBT skills might be developed in a similar way to those of the 'micro-skills' perspective in counselling practice (Ivey & Ivey, 2006). CBT courses and research projects have accumulated quite large banks of data on practice in the form of practice tapes and transcripts, assessed or otherwise. Such materials could be archived and made available for process analysis and research. Rogers (1980) paints a graphic picture of his team's excitement when they analysed the first proper recordings of therapy and as they began to see which therapist skills produced which client responses. Some of that spirit and method would be a breath of fresh air and could help to bridge what can be seen as a current 'skills gap' in CBT.

References

Bandura, A. (1997). *Self-efficacy: The Exercise of Self-control.* New York: Freeman.

Beck, A.T. (1976). *Cognitive Therapy and the Emotional Disorders.* Harmondsworth: Penguin.

Beck, A.T., Shaw, B.E., Rush, A.J. and Emery, G. (1979). *Cognitive Therapy of Depression.* New York: Guilford.

Bennett-Levy, J., Butler, G., Fennell, M., Hackman, A., Mueller, M. and Westbrook, D. (2004). *Oxford Guide to Behavioural Experiments.* Oxford: Oxford University Press.

Beutler, L.E., Machado, P., Neufeldt, S.A. (1994). 'Therapist variables', in A.E. Bergin and S.L. Garfield (eds), *Handbook of Psychotherapy and Behaviour Change*, 4th edn. Oxford: Wiley, pp. 229–69.

Blackburn, I-M., James, I.A., Milne, D.L., Baler, C., Standart, S., Garland, A. and Reichelt, F.K. (2001). 'The Revised Cognitive Therapy Scale (CTS-R): Psychometric properties', *Behavioural and Cognitive Psychotherapy*, 29: 431–46.

Bloom, B.S. (ed.) (1956). *Taxonomy of Educational Objectives: The Classification of Educational Goals. Handbook 1: The Cognitive Domain.* New York: McKay.

Bruch, M. and Bond, F.W. (1998). *Beyond Diagnosis: Case Formulation Approaches in CBT.* Chichester: John Wiley & Sons, Ltd.

Burns, D.D. (1999). *The Feeling Good Handbook*, rev. edn. New York: Penguin.

Carey, T.A. and Mullan, R.J. (2004). 'What is Socratic questioning?', *Psychotherapy*, 41 (3): 217–26.

Dryden, W. (1991). *Against Dogma: A Dialogue with Albert Ellis.* Milton Keynes: Open University Press.

Dryden, W. (1995). *Brief Rational Emotive Behaviour Therapy.* Chichester: John Wiley & Sons, Ltd.

Dryden, W. (2009). *Rational Emotive Behaviour Therapy: Distinctive Features.* Hove: Routledge.

Ellis, A. (1962). *Reason and Emotion in Psychotherapy.* Syracuse, NJ: Citadel.

Ellis, A. and Tafrate, R.C. (1997). *How to Control Your Anger before It Controls You.* New York: Citadel/Kensington.

Epstein, S. (1998). *Constructive Thinking: The Key to Emotional Intelligence.* Westport, CT: Praeger.

Hackman, A. and Holmes, E.A. (2004). 'Reflections on imagery: A clinical perspective and review of the special edition of Memory on using imagery in psychotherapy', *Memory*, 12 (4): 389–402.

Hauck, P. (1980). *Calm Down: How to Cope with Frustration and Anger.* London: Sheldon.

Hayes, S.C., Strohsal, K.D. and Wilson, K.D. (2004). *Acceptance and Commitment Therapy: an Experiential Guide.* New York: Guilford Press.

Ivey, A.E. and Ivey, M.B. (2006). *Intentional Interviewing and Counseling: Facilitating Client Development in a Multi-Cultural Society*, 6th edn. Monterey: Brooks Cole.

Jacobson, N.S. and Hollon, S.D. (1999). 'Cognitive therapy versus pharmacology: Now the jury has returned its verdict, it is time for the rest of the evidence', *Journal for Consulting and Clinical Psychology*, 64: 104–8.

Le Doux, J.E. (1997). *The Emotional Brain: The Mysterious Underpinnings of Emotional Life.* New York: Simon & Schuster.

Martell, C.R., Martell, M.E. and Jacobson, N.S. (2001). *Depression in Context: Strategies for Guided Action.* New York: Norton.

Milne, D.L., Claydon, T., Blackburn, I-M., James, I. and Sheikh, A. (2001). 'Rationale for a new measure of competence in therapy', *Behavioural and Cognitive Psychotherapies*, 29: 21–33.

Nelson-Jones, R. (2008). *Introduction to Counselling Skills: Text and Activites.* London: Sage.

Overholser, J. (1993). 'Elements of Socratic method: I: Systematic questioning; II: Inductive reasoning', *Psychotherapy*, 30 (1): 67–74; 75–85.

Padesky, C. (1993). Socratic questioning: changing minds or guiding discovery?', *Keynote address* at the European Congress of Behavioural and Cognitive Therapies, London, 24 September 1993; www.padesky.com (accessed, 19 May 2011).

Padesky, C. and Greenberger, D. (1996). *A Clinician's Guide to Mind over Mood.* New York: Guilford.

Ramnero, J. and Torneke, N. (2008). *The ABCs of Human Behaviour: Behavioural Principles of the Practicing Clinician.* Oakland, CA: New Harbinger.

Rogers, C.R. (1980). *A Way of Being.* Boston, MA: Houghton-Mifflin.

Sage, N., Sowden, M., Chorlton, E. and Edeleanu, A. (2008) *CBT for Chronic Illness and Palliative Care.* Chichester: John Wiley & Sons, Ltd.

Sanders, D. and Wills, F. (2005). *Cognitive Therapy: An Introduction.* London: Sage.

Sherman, N. (2005). *Stoic Warriors: The Ancient Philosophy behind the Military Mind.* Oxford: Oxford University Press.

Skyrms, B. (2000). *Choice and Chance: An Introduction to Inductive Logic.* Belmont, CA: Wandsworth/ Thompson Learning.

Still, A. and Dryden, W. (2003). 'Ellis and Epictetus: Dialogue vs. Method in psychotherapy', *Journal of Rational-Emotive and Cognitive Behavioural Therapy*, 21 (1): 39–55.

Teasdale, J. (1996). 'Clinically relevant theory: Integrating clinical insight with cognitive science', in P. Salkovskis (ed.), *Frontiers of Cognitive Therapy.* New York: Guilford, pp. 26–47.

Wells, A. (1997). *Cognitive Therapy of Anxiety Disorders.* Chichester: John Wiley & Sons, Ltd.

Williams, J.M.G., Teasdale, J., Segal, Z.D. and Kabat-Zinn, J. (2007). *The Mindful Way through Depression.* New York: Guilford Press.

Wills, F. (2008). *Skills of Cognitive Behaviour Counselling and Psychotherapy.* London: Sage.

Wills, F. (2009). *Beck's Cognitive Therapy: Distinctive Features.* Hove: Routledge.

Wills, F. (2010). 'Yada, yada, yada – the missing bit of CBT: A call for practitioner process research on CBT skills'. Paper given at BABCP Annual Conference, July 2010.

Young, J.E. and Beck, A.T. (1980). *The Cognitive Therapy Scale Rating Manual.* Unpublished manuscript, University of Pennsylvania, Philadelphia, PA.

Young, J.E. and Beck, A.T. (1988). *The Cognitive Therapy Scale.* Unpublished manuscript, University of Pennsylvania, Philadelphia, PA.

EIGHT Working with Comorbidity in CBT

WARREN MANSELL

Overview

Comorbidity refers to the situation in which an individual qualifies for the diagnosis of more than one disorder, either across their lifecourse (lifetime comorbidity) or at present (current comorbidity). In many services, comorbidity of psychological disorders is the norm rather than the exception. In this chapter, the common experience of comorbid problems is described and the literature on the treatment of comorbidity using CBT is briefly reviewed. A transdiagnostic model of psychological distress is introduced that unifies across different cognitive, behavioural and interpersonal processes – proposing that they each involve *control* as a process. A simple model for formulation is introduced that allows therapists to model clients' conflicting attempts to control their internal experiences, and the underlying personal goals that drive these processes. Several cases are introduced to illustrate how a CBT approach can be based around a theory of hierarchical control and conflict. The approach is designed to guide and sustain clients' present moment awareness on the higher order goals and values that drive their experience and allow them to shift perspectives and reprioritise in a way that gains a greater overall level of control and purpose in their lives. A newly formed version of cognitive therapy called Method of Levels is proposed as the most efficient technique, yet its aims are consistent with many familiar methods in CBT. The chapter finishes with key points for discussion in relation to diagnosis, its utility, and the future of the transdiagnostic approach.

Comorbidity and the Impact of CBT

Most therapists treat a diverse range of people and their problems appear to vary widely in severity, duration and complexity. The epidemiological evidence tells us that comorbidity is common, with up to a third of people with a psychological disorder qualifying for another disorder within the last year, and lifetime comorbidity rates of around 50% in the USA National Comorbidity Survey (Kessler et al., 2005). To an epidemiologist, this co-occurrence might look like bad luck, but to the therapist, it illustrates the shared features of different psychological disorders. For example, the process of worry is highly prevalent in a range of psychological disorders. The National Comorbidity Survey further revealed that it was around a sixth of the population who had several concurrent disorders, associated with greater severity, chronicity and impairment. Yet only a minority of these ever received a professional treatment for their problems.

Generally, the evidence suggests that the presence of comorbidity is nearly always associated with a more severe and enduring presentation, yet there is equivocal evidence of whether comorbidity significantly impacts on the outcomes from CBT in terms of the degree of change that is achieved. In a review of this question within panic disorder (Mennin & Heimberg, 2000), it was concluded that comorbid depression does not have a clear detrimental effect on the positive effects of CBT for panic disorder across studies. In some cases the patients did, however, seek greater levels of additional treatment after the therapy.

Even in the domain of comorbid personality disorders, the effects are not always clear cut. For example, Sanderson et al. (1994) found equal benefits on the depression and anxiety in patients with or without personality disorders, but those with personality disorders were more likely to drop out of treatment. There are a range of recent studies that explicitly target populations with comorbid presentations, yet find benefits from CBT, for example within eating disorders (Fairburn, et al., 2009), PTSD (Gillespie et al., 2002) and schizophrenia (Barrowclough et al., 2001). In particular there is an increasing recognition and evidence base that comorbid anxiety disorders and depression can be treated using CBT in clients with a psychotic disorder (Tarrier, 2005). Where substance abuse is the comorbid disorder, there is a recognition that CBT can be complemented by Motivational Interviewing, which helps clients to manage their ambivalence towards making changes before embarking on a more directive therapeutic method (e.g. Barrowclough et al., 2001).

The above overview indicates that while the presence of comorbidity is often a marker for greater severity and chronicity, it does not necessarily have a negative impact on the benefits from CBT, as long as one accepts that people with comorbid disorders typically start from a lower baseline of functioning, and that they may be more likely to disengage from treatment. Therefore, therapists should normally expect to work with comorbid presentations for longer if they and their clients have the goal of full and lasting recovery, and be more willing to adapt to maintain engagement. Yet the evidence does suggest that CBT, as it stands at present, can be used fruitfully. But, how currently should one proceed in clinical practice, given these potentially promising findings?

An Overview of the Treatment Approach to Comorbid Disorders in CBT

In an illuminating article, MacManus et al. (2010) clarified three approaches to working with comorbidity in CBT for anxiety disorders: (a) treat one disorder only and evaluate the impact on comorbid disorders; (b) treat each comorbid disorder one at a time and (c) provide a therapy that targets shared maintenance processes (e.g. worry; safety-seeking behaviours).

In their review, McManus et al. (2010) found that between 17% to 67% of cases experienced remission of their comorbid disorder when their primary disorder was treated successfully. While this is encouraging, they point out that many clients continue to have a disorder and that significant risk of relapse remains. The default way of approaching clients with more than one presenting problem is to work on them each separately, using a specific model of each. Through discussing the problem list with the client, the problem that the client wants to work on first can be chosen. There may be some discussion between the therapist and client if the therapist believes that their skills would make a particular problem more achievable first, or of greater urgency. Maybe surprisingly, several studies that have combined therapies for different diagnoses in people with comorbidity have shown poorer effects than focusing on one disorder alone (McManus et al., 2010). It is possible that by exploring the process of how the choice of problem to work on is made in therapy, we can understand better how to combine treatment approaches.

Comorbidity, Appraisal of Problems, and Engagement with Therapy

How do people choose what problems to work on in therapy? To begin to analyse this question it is important to enquire how people decide that they have a psychological problem in the first place. Many people do not attend therapy, or do so erratically because of how they appraise their problems and how to cope with them. There are a number of factors that prevent people accessing therapy (e.g. Vogel et al., 2007). Principal reasons include that the person: (a) may not believe they have a problem, (b) may not believe they can be helped, (c) is too afraid or ashamed to engage with and divulge their feelings, or (d) has such severe and multiple problems they find it hard to even access psychological help. Paradoxically, these same psychological factors (e.g. denial, poor social support, emotion suppression, lack of engagement) are most often those that are regarded *within therapy* as maintaining psychological distress. Taken to its logical extreme, it begs the question – 'Who are the people we see in therapy?' They must be drawing on other strengths that allow them to actually seek psychological help despite these tendencies to avoid thinking about their problems. This in turn implies that *ambivalence* is common, or even ubiquitous: people have goals to both avoid thinking and avoid talking about their emotional problems *and* they have goals to try to think about them in order to solve them or express them to another person.

Taking the above view, it would seem that part of developing a successful CBT for people with multiple presenting problems is to make their access to therapy as easy as possible, to be flexible with the 'moving target' as presenting problems shift over time, and to be aware of clients' core ambivalence about making changes. The following sections consider these issues within a new transdiagnostic approach to CBT for comorbid psychological disorders.

Transdiagnostic Approaches to CBT

In their review, McManus and colleagues proposed targeting common maintenance processes across disorders as their third form of transdiagnostic intervention. Readers are referred to an earlier article that provides a conceptual overview of the many transdiagnostic forms of CBT that are now available, including metacognitive therapy, mindfulness-based CBT and rumination-focused CBT (Mansell et al., 2009).

Here, the focus is to introduce a theory that has the capacity to inform us about the issues raised earlier concerning control and ambivalence, and has the capacity to simplify comorbid problems into a unified, transdiagnostic (or more accurately a 'nondiagnostic') account. The theory, called Perceptual Control Theory (PCT; Powers, 1973/2005) was developed by an American control systems engineer during the 1950s and '60s. It is a theory of how living systems control, which has applications throughout the life sciences, social sciences and humanities (see pctweb.org), yet has made its most recent influence on the field of CBT (Carey, 2008; Mansell, 2005). In essence, I will suggest that it is critical to understand the process of control, its tendency to cause conflict, and the way that conflicting attempts to control the same experience are 'reorganised' (Mansell & Carey, 2009). Within this approach, the process of bringing distressing experiences into awareness and exploring their related personal goals forms one of the most critical interventions for long-term recovery, even in severe and comorbid mental health problems (Higginson et al., 2011). Cognitive therapy techniques that have this property, as well as those from other disciplines, are proposed to be the main facilitators of change.

Perceptual Control Theory

During the nineteenth century, a range of eminent psychologists viewed their field as the study of purpose and self-regulation (e.g. James, 1890; Morell, 1853). This approach waned during the behaviourist years of the mid twentieth century, where the focus was on controlling and predicting the observable behaviour of others. However, throughout the second half of the twentieth century, control theories, inspired by cybernetics (Wiener, 1948), heralded the return of an understanding of purpose and control to psychology (Mansell & Carey, 2009). Arguably, PCT represents the most systematic control theory described to date. A PCT approach to CBT involves making certain, focused assumptions about the nature of psychological functioning and distress. These are the following:

1 'Control' is a fundamental feature of a functioning individual. Control can be defined as maintaining a specified variable (or variables) within a limited range despite external disturbances.
2 In the same way as our brain controls physiological variables such as body temperature, arousal and hormone levels, it also controls a wide range of perceptual variables such as light intensity and proximity to safety.

3 Behaviours, including any outputs such as emotional and physiological reactions, *are* the control of perception; in other words, all behaviours are the variable means to the fixed ends specified by the individual (cf. James, 1890).
4 Lower order control systems receive their reference values (their goals) from the outputs of higher level systems, which in turn receive their references from higher systems. Thus, experience is seen to be controlled by multiple layers of systems that are arranged as hierarchies. Higher level systems are specified in detail within PCT, but can be approximated to 'deeper' cognitive structures that are familiar from cognitive theory: coping strategies, through dysfunctional attitudes, to core beliefs or self-standards (Higginson et al., 2011). See Figure 8.1 for an everyday example.
5 Conflict occurs when two systems have different reference values for the same perceptual variable (e.g. very close vs very far from home). Conflict is seen as a normal consequence of having multiple goals and is resolved through *reorganisation* – a form of trial-and-error learning that changes the properties of control systems to reduce their conflict.
6 Chronic instability in the control of 'intrinsic variables' (e.g. food intake, arousal levels) due to conflict reflects psychological dysfunction and the feeling of 'losing control'.
7 Owing to the fact that control systems receive their standards from higher level systems, long-term change needs to occur in the higher level system that is setting the standards for the conflicted systems.
8 Psychological therapy and natural recovery work by encouraging reorganisation of higher level systems that are setting incompatible standards for lower level processes. This is seen to occur automatically as a person's present awareness is focused and sustained on this level of control.

The full details of PCT are well beyond these summary principles, including the mathematical and biological specification of how control systems work, and how they can be configured to model social interaction, automaticity, memory recall, mental imagery and planning (see Powers, 1973/2005). However, the above principles can suffice for the present purpose.

Within this approach, the client is regarded as a sophisticated living control system who is striving to regulate his or her everyday experiences. People come to therapy because they have lost control of their lives. Arguably, active states such as anxiety reflect fluctuating loss of control caused by ongoing conflict (e.g. approach vs avoidance), whereas inactive states such as depression reflect the certainty of loss of control as previous goals are disengaged, leading to a sense of

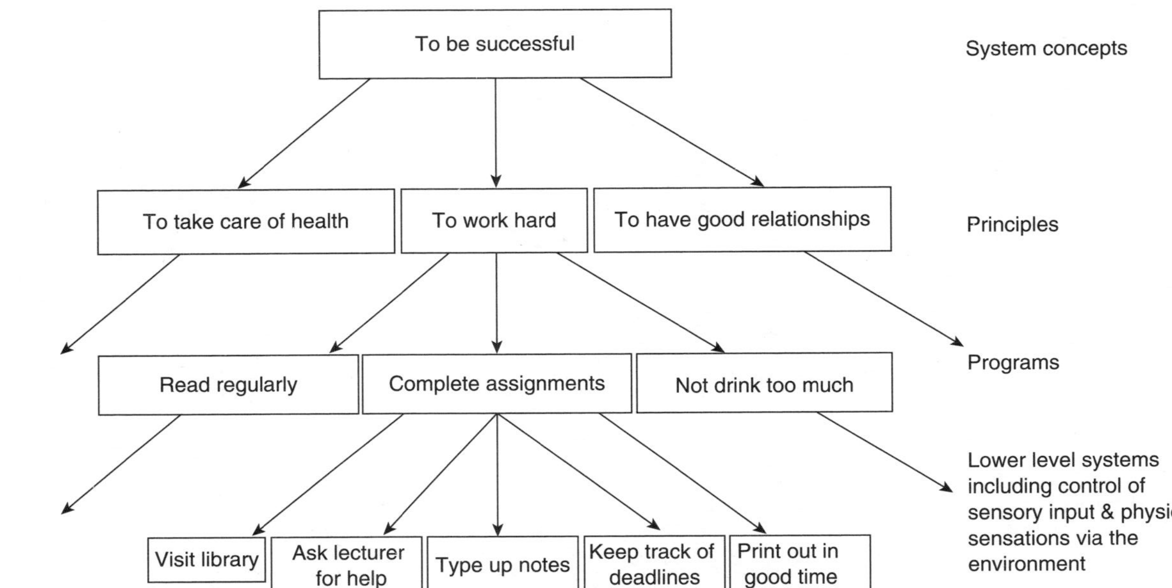

Figure 8.1 An example of a control system hierarchy.

hopelessness and lack of purpose (cf Mineka & Kelly, 1989). According to PCT, a successful therapist asks questions to try to help the client notice this process of control, where it succeeds and where it is blocked, and facilitate the client's own attempts to solve his or her problems. What we call 'shifting perspectives', 'insight', or 'reappraisal' would each be regarded as indications of *reorganisation* of higher level systems - a self-generated shift in the way that the client represents, targets and pursues their goals to improve their life in the domain that is being discussed, and often in order to pursue greater overall control of their lives.

The evidence for a PCT-guided transdiagnostic approach to psychological distress is emerging from a variety of sources. First, the principles of PCT itself have been tested robustly through computer models that match the modelled system to a high level of precision (see Mansell & Carey, 2009). Second, independent components of the theory as applied to psychological distress have empirical validation. For example, the relationship between conflict in high level goals and psychological distress has support from a wide range of empirical literature (Kelly et al., 2012), and there is evidence that perseveration at low levels of control (as opposed to being aware of higher order goals driving one's action) is associated with psychopathology (Serpell et al., 2009). Third, qualitative and quantitative studies have reported a process of recovery from psychological disorders that fits the predictions of PCT (for a review, see Higginson et al., 2011). Finally, Method of Levels, a cognitive therapy developed from PCT has an emerging evidence base as a transdiagnostic therapy (Carey, 2008).

Arbitrary Control: The Core Maintenance Process in PCT

PCT suggests that the key problem with the maintenance processes that have been identified in various fields of CBT is that they involve *arbitrary control*. This is the most common cause of goal conflict. It occurs when the person tries to control an experience that is also being controlled by a second goal of which the person is either unaware or unconvinced of its relative importance. This can happen either *between* (e.g. trying to control other people without considering their needs) or *within* individuals. It may be an important ability when used appropriately - for example we need to inhibit our own, or other people's, day-to-day goals when there is an immediate, serious threat (cf. Gray, 1982). However, it is where arbitrary control is used chronically by a person because of the higher order goal it is attempting to achieve (e.g. 'to be completely calm') that problems arise. For a person to engage in arbitrary control, they would not be aware, at that moment, of the important goal they are inhibiting. This inhibited goal may be:

- a cherished personal goal that they do not want to admit to themselves and others (e.g. to be famous; to have power and influence over others; to be cared for);
- a bodily system that is biologically essential (an 'intrinsic variable' - see earlier), such as the need to eat, to be close to others, and to reproduce;
- the need to experience *change* in itself - to reorganise higher level goals - which may involve feelings of loss of control as change is happening, alongside certain unpleasant emotions.

It is proposed that a range of familiar maintenance processes are seen as dysfunctional *only* when they are forms of chronic arbitrary control (see also Mansell, 2005):

- *Avoidance behaviour* is a problem when it conflicts with important approach tendencies towards the same situation (e.g. want to go to a job interview but avoiding it).
- *Attentional avoidance* is a problem when it conflicts with the tendency to need to be vigilant to the same thing (e.g. avoiding eye contact with other people but wanting to be connected to others).
- *Emotion suppression* is a problem when it involves chronically limiting emotional experiences that are necessary for normal functioning (e.g. trying to never feel anxious even though it is part of a normal reaction to a threat).
- *Thought suppression* is a problem when the person also needs to consider the thoughts that are being suppressed (e.g. pushing thoughts of attacking someone out of one's mind but also wanting to be vigilant to these thoughts just in case one acts on them).
- *Criticism and hostility* by the self or others are a problem when they conflict with the normal process of maintaining self-esteem and safety (e.g. calling oneself names to perform better at work).
- *Safety behaviours and overprotectiveness* are a problem when they conflict with other goals (e.g. tensing muscles to not appear nervous which makes it harder to be oneself in front of others).
- *Worry and rumination* are a problem when carrying them out conflicts with what is needed to solve the problem (e.g. saying 'why me?' over and over after a trauma which suppresses the memories that are needed to be recalled to gain a genuine understanding of what happened).

- *Automaticity and lack of mindfulness* are a problem when the routine one is following conflicts with one's goals but there is little awareness of this at the time (e.g. smoking to relieve stress but leading to health problems in the long term).

By understanding arbitrary control, we gain a better insight as to when client control and therapist control, and their relative balance, are helpful versus unhelpful, in therapy. While PCT assumes that control is a fundamental aspect of life, control is not always successful, or without its drawbacks, as it may inhibit other important goals. Thus, on the one hand, we should allow clients to take control over aspects of their care that may prove fruitful wherever possible. One simple example is to allow them the choice of their appointment time and number of sessions (Carey & Spratt, 2009). On the other hand, it is the therapist's goal to help the client to question any decision, with the view that exploring it in more detail and looking at the personal motives behind it, will reduce the experience of conflicts in the future. It also recognises the potential for conflict and disengagement if therapists take control over their client's decisions or dominate a therapeutic session with advice. Sometimes this will happen, because all therapists are human, and it is not irreversible, but neither is being 'controlling' a legitimate long-term stance for therapy to take.

A Transdiagnostic Control Theory Model (TCTM) Based on PCT

The transdiagnostic model for formulation is shown in Figure 8.2 (cf. Carey, 2006; Mansell, 2005; Powers, 1973/2005). Essentially, the formulation involves using questioning to help reveal an experience that is being controlled in opposing ways, either within the mind or body of the client, or via the social and physical environment, or both. In the model, it is the degree and duration of conflict, and its escalation through arbitrary control, that maintains psychological distress, rather than any specific process, such as worry or safety behaviours – their detrimental impact is caused by the extent to which they constantly inhibit personally important goals. In therapy, the higher order goals, rules and values that drive this conflict are then explored using further questions. Method of Levels is recommended as a specific technique designed to sustain the client's awareness on their higher order goals. Readers are referred to therapy manuals on this technique (Carey, 2006, 2008). However, familiar techniques can have a similar function: Socratic questioning, downward arrow techniques and identification of 'hot cognitions' are examples. When complete, the

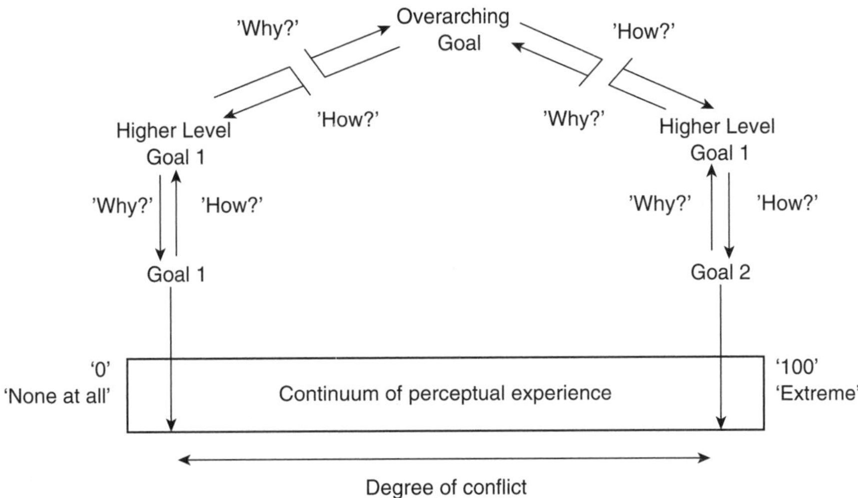

Figure 8.2 A transdiagnostic control theory model for CBT.

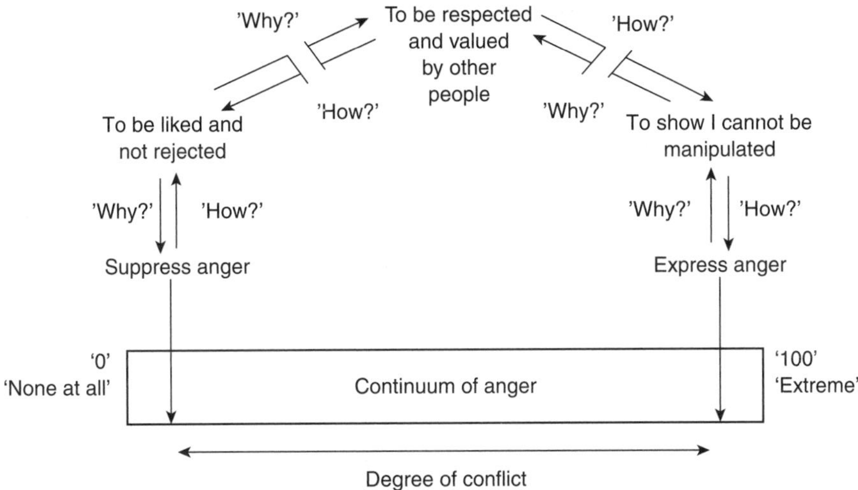

Figure 8.3 Client conceptualisation using the TCTM.

TCTM model should reveal both higher order conflicting motives and an overarching purpose, which is often an ideal sense of self in the world, which paradoxically drives both conflicting lower order goals (see Figure 8.2).

Figure 8.3 provides a case illustration of a client (described later) who is ambivalent towards expressing anger. The formulation illustrates his conflicting reasons for both expressing and suppressing his anger, and their shared overarching goal. Further clinical examples are given in Table 8.1.

Table 8.1 Examples of perceptual experiences that are under conflicting control across three different clients with comorbid problems.

Age, sex of client and presenting problems	*Possible diagnoses*	*Conflict Examples: enhancing vs suppressing current perception of…*	*High level control of enhancement*	*High level control of suppression*	*Overarching goal*
32M – depressed; fear of sweating; perfectionistic; highly restrictive diet	Major depressive episode; social phobia; specific phobia	Taste and texture of food	To consume a healthy range of foods	To not be sick in public	To be respected and valued by other people
		Images and feelings when performing in public	To become more confident with senior people	To not make a fool of oneself	To be respected and valued by other people
35F – depressed; worried; anger problems; high moods; trauma	Bipolar disorder; PTSD; GAD	Feelings of excitement and energy	To save other people from danger	To prevent being traumatised again	To live in a caring world
		Intrusive memories	To get everything 'off my chest'	To not dissociate	To have a coherent sense of self
18M – excessive worry; fear of dentists; spontaneous panic attacks; fear of vomit	Panic disorder; GAD; specific phobia	Arousal and imagery when at dentists	To get teeth treated	To not vomit; to not look mad	To be normal

The key components of the therapy are described below:

1 *Selecting a problem to discuss.* The first step in therapy following from this model is to select a problem to discuss, much as in traditional agenda-setting. This is critical as the theory regards people as self-regulating entities who work via the setting and monitoring of their own goals.
2 *Exploration and focus on the problem.* The second step is to explore this problem in detail; this may sometimes resemble the information gathering for a CBT formulation. In particular the therapist is interested in the process of *present-moment perceptual control* in relation to the problem – What are you trying to experience? What does it look like? How do you know when it is working? What is stopping it working? When does it stop and start? Does the problem happen suddenly or unfold gradually? This line of questioning can help to build a simple formulation of the conflicting process. Sometimes, even at this stage, the client can realise that thinking about and talking about their experiences is not as bad as they had feared. This is essentially an informal behavioural experiment in which the client exposes themselves to previously avoided experiences ('I usually try to push these feelings/memories/thoughts to the back of my mind'), and allows their re-evaluation ('This sounds sensible/ridiculous/not quite right'). Also, the client may spontaneously notice their arbitrary control – 'I am fighting with myself!' – for example, they may be rigidly controlling something (e.g. suppressing feelings) that they have good reasons not to control (e.g. it is a normal emotion). On occasions, the client may describe a metaphor of their problem, and this can be explored to similar effect (see Stott et al., 2010).
3 *Going 'up levels'.* Subsequent questioning then allows the discussion of the higher level goals that are driving this conflict (e.g. 'What makes doing this so important for you?'). It is at this level that the client can be helped to question their existing rules and form new rules or values that are less conflicted. When this promotes change, the client often describes 'changing their priorities in life', or 'seeing the world in a different way'. Often it is disruptions in speech and nonverbal behaviour that signal thoughts about the higher level goals (Carey, 2006). Asking questions to expand on this can help bring these relatively automatic thoughts from the background to the fore – 'What made you smile just then?'; 'When you move your eyes like that, what are you noticing?'
4 *Addressing Misbalances in Control.* There will be occasions when the above procedure does not lead to the expected change, or the clients are unhappy with the process itself. On these occasions, the therapist may need to go back to steps 1 to 3 and further clarify the problem. If this does not make a difference, then there may be a problem in the balance of control in the session, which is covered in the next section.

Considering the Client's Degree of Control During the Session

According to this model, effective transdiagnostic CBT helps the client to decide what to bring into mind and explore at this moment in time. Over the course of therapy, attending to and sustaining awareness on deeper problems, whatever their nature or terms of reference (e.g. strong emotions; deeply held beliefs; schemata; cherished goals; recurrent habits; distressing imagery) should help the client to evaluate how to manage their own problems. Within this approach, it is the change which accompanies addressing the deeper problems as they are manifested in the present moment, alongside the associated feelings, that is critical to long-term recovery. Nevertheless, clients need to navigate towards this point in a way that allows them to feel in overall control, and it is this process of the client understanding their process of change that maintains their engagement in therapy or other forms of help.

In essence, the methods that the therapist uses to try to help the client explore their problem will naturally vary in how much they compromise each client's own ability to control their experiences at that moment. For example, an anxious client may feel pushed into thinking of 'the worst thing that could happen' through the downward arrow technique and therefore feel out of control. An emotionally distant client being questioned in the same way may answer it with a prerehearsed answer that fails to get them to consider what they are really worried will happen and therefore feel that they have too much control over the session to learn anything from it. Thus, it seems that effective therapy involves keeping the client in a zone where they feel sufficiently in control to feel safe, but sufficiently uncertain, to begin to consider their problem (cf. Grawe, 2006). These issues are illustrated using a case study, alongside an example of a TCTM formulation.

Case study 8.1: case conceptualisation example

Background

Jeremy was 30 years of age and worked as a banking clerk. He had a fear of eating since the age of eight, to the degree that he only ate five different processed foods and no fresh fruit, vegetables, fish or meat. He was critical of himself and often embarrassed at his severe eating fears which limited his social activities. Jeremy also experienced social phobia about situations *not* involving food. At work meetings he feared rejection and humiliation, being convinced that he looked like a nervous wreck, sweating and trembling. He also reported being a perfectionist, always trying '110%' at work, fearful of not being the model employee and impressing his employers at every opportunity. He linked this back to his parents' controlling style of relating to him and his sister; they told him that he would die unless he ate properly and that he would be responsible for his younger sister gaining weight and dying early too. On the surface, it appeared that he was engaging in arbitrary control across a wide range of domains that had its roots in early relationships.

Jeremy came to therapy after an extended period at work in which his manager was becoming increasingly controlling, critical and setting unrealistic demands that compromised Jeremy's ability to do his job well. He felt increasingly angry about his manager but feared saying anything about it. Instead, he lost motivation in his work, procrastinated and delayed tasks, experienced panic attacks over his fears of failure and began to hide away from colleagues in the workplace. He eventually received sick leave for the anxiety and depression that were interfering with his ability to work. Importantly, Jeremy had received two previous therapies, both of which he considered as detrimental. First, he had been given a form of hypnotherapy in which he had experienced a forceful attempt by the therapist to admit he had been abused as a child, based on the evidence of some fragmented memories Jeremy had reported. Second, he saw a CBT therapist, whose enthusiastic attempts to help Jeremy set a graded hierarchy for facing his food fears led him to disengage within a small number of sessions. It appeared that Jeremy was particularly concerned about being controlled by others in the context of his fears and this could compromise engagement unless the therapy progressed in a truly client-centred manner.

Overview of therapy

The therapy largely followed Method of Levels, but occasionally used CBT techniques at focused points. From the start of therapy it was clear that there could be many potential targets. Jeremy was encouraged to talk about whichever problem he considered most relevant at present. He chose to postpone facing his eating fears even though he saw them as at the root of his problems. He felt that to start with, he needed to understand what had culminated in his work stress and he needed to reduce his current feelings of depression. During the initial sessions of MOL, Jeremy described his 'scared side' which was the side of himself that feared being a failure and would do anything to avoid it, including not doing any activity that committed himself, not facing his eating fears, and not asserting himself towards his family or his employers. He described how sometimes his scared side was in control, but at other times, his 'real self' was in control. For him, overcoming his depression involved two goals – building up his own confidence through activities which helped him feel stronger in the face of the scared side – and challenging or ignoring what the scared side told him. A TCTM approach considered his scared side as that which exercised control in often arbitrary and therefore counterproductive ways, in contrast to his real self that 'took a step back' and considered his own (higher order) goals in challenging

(Continued)

(Continued)

situations. He appeared to build on his real self over the course of therapy as MOL helped him to access this broader perspective on a variety of different problems.

One example of several formulations used is illustrated in Figure 8.4. On the one hand Jeremy knew that he needed to express his anger to stop himself from being manipulated by his parents, but on the other hand he was afraid of losing their approval. Ultimately, both of these goals were led by the understandable need to be respected and valued by other people. When Jeremy chose to discuss the early memories relating to this concern, the possibility of sustaining awareness on this experience and exploring the higher order goals within imagery was suggested (cf. Holmes et al., 2007). Within this memory, Jeremy was encouraged to revisit his past interactions with his parents during dinner times as an adult and explain what he would want to say to his child self; he made this choice – 'You don't have to believe what they tell you; you will be OK when you grow up, just like me'. Later on in therapy, he was still struggling to accept his own anger, and so some simple information was given explaining that anger is a normal result of experiencing a blocked personal goal. This explanation was based on control theory, and was presented to help him consider broadening his goal of 'no anger at all' to 'some anger' within conflict situations. On the following session, Jeremy had confronted his manager in an appropriate, assertive manner; he also spontaneously described how he was now using this information to gain perspective on his anger – he would visualise himself as a footballer with multiple goals on the pitch in front of him, each with a different amount of 'blockage'. When he felt angry, he now saw this as a useful signal to consider whether he could (a) reduce the blockage, (b) widen the goal, or (c) look for another goal. MOL questioning was used to help him reflect on how and when he could use this metaphor, across his many concerns.

Outcomes

Jeremy showed reductions in depression and anxiety over the early sessions of therapy which were maintained and built upon over less regular sessions over two years. He expanded his range of foods that he could eat, and made a career choice to abandon the 'rat race' and its related demand for perfectionism. Instead, he pursued work that helped him to fulfil his personal goals of being close to nature, getting exercise, and helping other people.

Points for Discussion

Why do different comorbid disorders present differently? Challenging the artefact of psychiatric classification

Harvey et al. (2004) proposed three explanations for why psychological disorders present so differently despite sharing the same maintenance processes. They found no evidence of processes that were specific to one disorder, and some evidence that the levels of a process differential disorders – for example, self-reports of worry are typically higher in GAD than other anxiety disorders (Fresco et al., 2003). However, Harvey et al. (2004) concluded that the most convincing explanation is that people with different disorder labels are differentiated by their different current concerns (Klinger, 1996). These are the same range of concerns that differentiate people in the general population. This raises the possibility, illustrated by Figure 8.4, that the psychiatric classification system, despite its ability to discriminate between disorders, is an *artefact* of individual differences in the general population. A transdiagnostic approach, on the other hand, attempts to understand the core processes that contribute to a greater degree of dysfunction and distress regardless of disorder category (the y-axis in Figure 8.4). Comorbidity may emerge from a combination of several current concerns in the same individual that conflict because they pursue them through arbitrary control rather than balancing them in the light of their higher order goals. This intriguing hypothesis remains to be tested.

What is the Future of the Transdiagnostic Approach To CBT?

There seem to be good reasons to expect the transdiagnostic approach to flourish and transform our mental health system – *and* good reasons to expect it to dwindle as an idealistic pipe dream. The methods of classifying disorders and treating them according to their diagnosis are very much established within the way our services are organised, especially secondary and tertiary care. There is also good evidence that disorder-based CBT is highly effective for a well-defined population, even in the presence of comorbidity and in real-world (nontrial) settings (e.g. Gillespie et al., 2000). The transdiagnostic approach does not generally claim a more efficacious treatment. It typically claims a greater flexibility for complex cases and more efficient training and delivery without the need for extended assessment sessions. Whether these important advantages outweigh the advantages of maintaining the current diagnostic method (including limiting the upheaval of systemic change in the mental health system) is an open question that only future generations will be able to answer.

Conclusion

This chapter has reviewed the impact of comorbidity on clinical practice, in particular the challenges to a disorder-based form of CBT. The

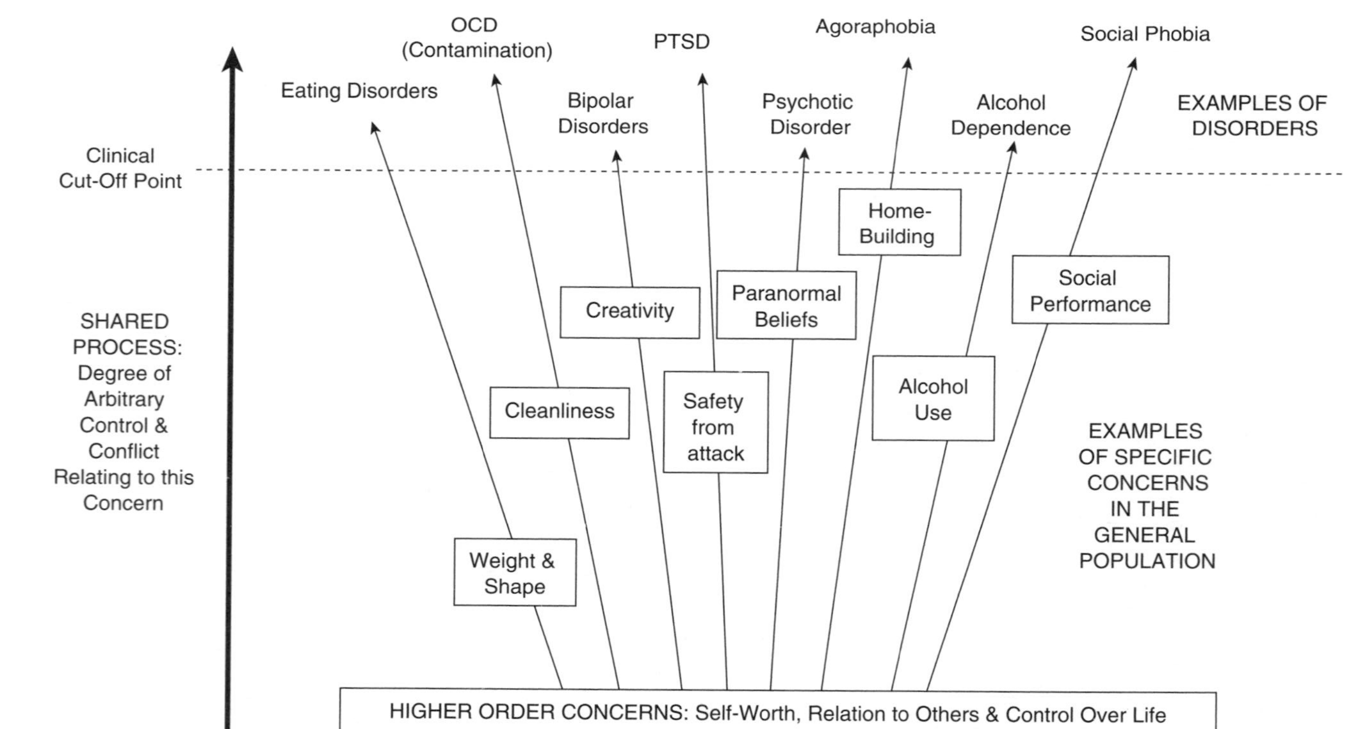

Figure 8.4 An illustration of how psychiatric classification may have emerged as an artefact of the variation in concerns within the general population.

later sections of the chapter provide the first introduction to using a formulation based on control theory, and how to use an understanding of control to guide decision-making during therapy. Future research will be necessary to test the hypothesis that such an approach has at least equivalent outcomes, and more efficient methods of delivery and training, compared to alternative approaches.

Further Reading and Resources

Harvey et al. (2004) provide a systematic review of the research literature which supports a transdiagnostic account.

The website www.pctweb.org contains an accessible introduction to PCT and its empirical basis across a wide range of disciplines.

The following special issues of journals complement this chapter:

- *Journal of Cognitive Psychotherapy*, Volume 23, Issue 1
- *International Journal of Cognitive Therapy*, Volume 1, Issue 3
- *The Cognitive Behaviour Therapist*, Volume 2, Issue 3
- *Clinical Psychology Review*, Volume 31, Issue 2

References

Barrowclough, C., Haddock, G., Tarrier, N., Lewis, S.W., Moring, J., O'Brien, R. et al. (2001). 'Randomized controlled trial of motivational interviewing, cognitive behavior therapy, and family intervention for patients with comorbid schizophrenia and substance use disorders', *American Journal of Psychiatry*, 158: 1706–13.

Carey, T.A. (2006). *Method of Levels: How to Do Psychotherapy without Getting in the Way.* Hayward, CA: Living Control Systems Publishing.

Carey, T.A. (2008). 'Perceptual control theory and the Method of Levels: Further contributions to a transdiagnostic perspective', *International Journal of Cognitive Therapy*, 1: 237–55.

Carey, T.A. and Spratt, M.B. (2009). 'When is enough enough? Structuring the organization of treatment to maximise patient choice and control', *The Cognitive Behaviour Therapist*, 2: 211–26.

Fairburn, C.G., Cooper, Z., Doll, H.A., O'Connor, M.E., Bohn, K., Hawker, D.M. et al. (2009) 'Transdiagnostic cognitive behavioral therapy for patients with eating disorders: A two-site trial with 60-week follow-up', *American Journal of Psychiatry*, 166: 311–19. doi: 10.1176/appi.ajp.2008.08040608.

Fresco, D.M., Mennin, D.S., Heimberg, R.G. and Turk, C.L. (2003). 'Using the Penn State Worry Questionnaire to identify individuals with generalized anxiety disorder: A receiver operating characteristic analysis', *Journal of Behaviour Therapy and Experimental Psychiatry*, 34: 283–91.

Gillespie, K., Duffy, M., Hackmann, A. and Clark, D.M. (2002). 'Community based cognitive therapy in the treatment of post-traumatic stress disorder following the Omagh bomb', *Behaviour Research and Therapy*, 40: 345–57.

Grawe, K. (2006). *Neuropsychotherapy: How the Neurosciences Inform Effective Psychotherapy*. Hove: Lawrence Erlbaum.

Gray, J.A. (1982). *The Neuropsychology of Anxiety: An Enquiry into the Functions of the Septo-Hippocampal System.* Oxford: Oxford University Press.

Harvey, A.G., Watkins, E.R., Mansell, W. and Shafran, R. (2004). *Cognitive Behavioural Processes Across Psychological Disorders: A Transdiagnostic Approach to Research and Treatment.* Oxford: Oxford University Press.

Higginson, S., Mansell, W. and Wood, A.M. (2011) 'An integrative mechanistic account of psychological distress, therapeutic change and recovery: the Perceptual Control Theory approach', *Clinical Psychology Review*, 31: 249–59.

Holmes, E.A., Arntz, A. and Smucker, M. (2007). 'Imagery rescripting in Cognitive Behaviour Therapy: Images, treatment techniques and outcomes', *Journal of Behaviour Therapy and Experimental Psychiatry*, 38: 297–305.

James, W. (1890). *The Principles of Psychology.* New York: Dover.

Kelly, R.E., Wood, A.M. and Mansell, W. (2012). 'Goal conflict and psychological distress: A review in the context of a hierarchical model'. Manuscript submitted.

Kessler, R.C., Chiu, W.T., Demler, O. and Walters, E. (2005). 'Prevalence, severity, and comorbidity of 12-month DSM-IV disorders in the National Comorbidity Survey Replication', *Archives of General Psychiatry*, 62: 617–27.

Klinger, E. (1996). 'Emotional influences on cognitive processing, with implications for theories of both', in P.M. Gollwitzer and J.A. Bargh (eds), *The Psychology of Action: Linking Cognition and Motivation to Behaviour.* New York: Guilford Press, pp. 168–89.

McManus, F., Shafran, R. and Cooper, Z. (2010). 'What does a "transdiagnostic" approach have to offer the treatment of anxiety disorders?', *British Journal of Clinical Psychology*, 49: 491–505.

Mansell, W. (2005). 'Control theory and psychopathology: An integrative approach', *Psychology and Psychotherapy: Theory, Research and Practice*, 78: 141–78.

Mansell, W. and Carey, T.A. (2009). 'A century of psychology and psychotherapy: Is an understanding of "control" the missing link between theory, research, and practice?', *Psychology and Psychotherapy: Theory Research and Practice*, 82: 337–53.

Mansell, W., Harvey, A.G., Watkins, E.R. and Shafran, R. (2009). 'Conceptual foundations of the transdiagnostic approach', *Journal of Cognitive Psychotherapy*, 23: 6–19.

Mennin, D.S. and Heimberg, R.G. (2000). 'The impact of comorbid mood and personality disorders in the cognitive-behavioral treatment of panic disorder', *Clinical Psychology Review*, 20: 339–57.

Mineka, S. and Kelly, K.A. (1989). 'The relationship between anxiety, lack of control and loss of control', in A. Steptoe et al. (eds), *Stress, Personal Control and Health.* Chichester: John Wiley & Sons, Ltd., pp. 163–91.

Morell, J.D. (1853). *Elements of Psychology*. London: Pickering.

Powers, W.T. (1973/2005). *Behavior: The Control of Perception.* Escondido, CA: Benchmark Publications.

Sanderson, W.C., Beck, A.T. and McGinn, L.K. (1994). 'Cognitive therapy for Generalised Anxiety Disorder: Significance of comorbid personality disorders', in R.L. Leahy and E.T. Dowd (eds), *Clinical Advances in Cognitive Psychotherapy: Theory and Application.* New York: Springer Publishing, pp. 287–93.

Serpell, L., Waller, G., Fearon, R.M.P. and Meyer, C. (2009). 'The roles of persistence and perseveration in psychopathology', *Behavior Therapy*, 40: 260–71.

Stott, R., Mansell, W., Salkovskis, P. M., Lavender, A. and Cartwright-Hatton, S. (2010). *The Oxford Guide to Using Metaphors in CBT: Building Cognitive Bridges.* Oxford: Oxford University Press.

Tarrier, N. (2005). 'Co-morbidity and associated clinical problems in schizophrenia: Their nature and implications for comprehensive cognitive–behavioural treatment'. *Behaviour Change*, 22: 125–42.

Vogel, D.L., Wester, S.R. and Larson, L.M. (2007). 'Avoidance of counselling: Psychological factors that inhibit seeking help', *Journal of Counseling and Development,* 85: 410–22.

Wiener, N. (1948). *Cybernetics: Control and Communication in the Animal and the Machine*. Cambridge, MA: MIT Press.

NINE Working with 'Diversity' in CBT

MARGOT LEVINSON

Introduction

There is a very well documented legacy of racism and inertia in relation to the mental health needs of Black and Minority Ethnic (BME) clients in the UK (Fernando, 2003; Cooper et al., 2008; DoH, 2003). There is also a clear political history which offers an explanatory context for this. For this reason the chapter will concentrate on CBT with BME clients although many of the points made are equally applicable to other disadvantaged client groups who fall under the 'Diversity' umbrella. This chapter challenges a perceived complacency about 'Diversity' practice in CBT with BME clients. This sort of critical analysis has been largely absent from CBT literature in the UK.

The first objective is to promote a better informed and ethically proactive stance towards 'Diversity' in CBT. By briefly highlighting some of the historical political issues and detailing BME disadvantage, it is hoped readers may be influenced to commit to an ethic of social justice. The author aims to raise the consciousness (Friere, 1970) of therapists at a personal level because they 'act out ', in a real sense, the politics of mental health and CBT. The second objective is to critically appraise CBT service delivery and training. The third objective is to improve CBT 'Diversity' practice using lessons learned from generic mental health practice with BME clients and the findings of CBT studies.

This chapter will address background issues, policy, service delivery, training and finally clinical practice. The rationale for this order is that the background material will explain some reasons why BME clients haven't received good mental health services. Policy, service delivery and training control what, how and where CBT is practised. Thus, for practice to change other things must change first.

CBT has, through Improving Access to Psychological Therapies (IAPT), taken centre stage nationally. An explicit IAPT objective is to reduce benefit claims and help the claimants to return to work (London School of Economics and Political Science. The Centre for Economic Performance's Mental Health Policy Group, 2006) not just restore their mental health. For BME clients who are over represented in the statistics on unemployment, low paid employment and ill health, 'Universalist' services like IAPT may not be a benign initiative.

'Universalist' services presume all peoples' problems can be understood using 'standard ideas' and their similarities are more important than their differences when it comes to clinical practice (Falicov, 1995). 'Universalist' services in CBT are those where all clients receive the recommended assessment, prescribed evidence-based treatment plan (based on Random Controlled Trials, RCTs) and prescribed number of sessions i.e. a 'one size fits all' approach (Bell et al., 2009). 'Universalism' leads to a view that cultural training is, at best, irrelevant.

The starting premise is that the presentation of CBT as politically neutral and 'Diversity' as just a descriptive label is inaccurate.

Racism – A Political Undercurrent in British Politics

Britain has a history of inviting immigration and struggling with the political consequences of it. Successive waves of immigration, particularly from former colonies have, at times, been seen as a threat to social cohesion and stability. One of the most infamous expressions of this fear was Enoch Powell's 'Rivers of Blood' speech (Powell, 1968). A decade later in 1978, Margaret Thatcher as Prime Minister, echoed his sentiments in an interview where she claimed that

> people are really rather afraid that this country might be rather swamped by people with a different culture (World in Action, 1978).

The 1980s saw political unrest expressed in 'race riots' as a response to emerging evidence of overt racial discrimination and immigration policy. Black children were more likely to be taken into 'care' and stay there longer. Black adults were more likely to be 'sectioned' into psychiatric care or be subject to police powers to 'stop and search' on the street and arrested for criminal offences (Mclaughlin, 2005).

The Scarman Report (Scarman, 1981) commissioned by the Home Secretary following the riots concluded there was 'racial disadvantage that is a fact of British life'. Nearly 20 years later the Stephen Lawrence Inquiry concluded the police were institutionally racist (Macpherson, 1999).

Labels 'Frame' How We See Things

'Diversity'

'Diversity' is the latest in a long line of descriptions of 'difference' which have been used to denote BME groups within the population. The term 'Diversity' adroitly circumvents emotionally and politically charged terminology like class, racism, homophobia, sexism and ageism.

In the 1970s social work education had moved from seeing clients as 'individual problems' to seeing them as victims of structural inequality, in effect a Marxist analysis. By the 1990s, following more race riots, many social workers identified racism as a manifestation of that social inequality.

For the Central Council for Education and Training in Social Work (CCETSW), racism became a central 'wrong' to be 'righted' in the name of social justice. CCETSW published the controversial paper 30:

> *Rules and Requirements for the Diploma in Social Work (Paper 30)(Second Edition)*
>
> racism is endemic in the values, attitudes and structures of British society including that of social services and social work education. CCETSW recognises that the effects of racism on black people are incompatible with the values of social work and therefore seeks to combat racist practices in all areas of its responsibilities (CCETSW, 1991: 6).

The government, alarmed at the overtly political stance of social work education, intervened and removed 'antiracist' social work from the curriculum. 'Anti-oppressive' practice replaced it, spreading the notion of oppression to include sexuality, learning difficulties, older adults, women, physical disabilities, developmental difficulties and children.

Oppression as a direct outcome of racism had disappeared. 'Celebrating Diversity' tacitly promotes the idea one can create social cohesion without addressing underlying structural inequalities.

NHS policies mirror this optimism. Delivering Race Equality in Mental Health Care (DRE) is an action plan for eliminating discrimination and achieving equality in mental health care for all people of BME status (DoH, 2005).

Psychology and Psychiatry

A substantial academic literature supports the view that racism has been historically embedded in psychology and psychiatry (Richards, 1997; Fernando, 2003; Cooper et al., 2008; Jun, 2010). This includes a vigorous debate about whether psychiatry is institutionally racist (Lau, 2008) and the interrelationship of racism with other aspects of poverty and disadvantage (McKenzie, 2008). McKenzie (2008) argues change requires modifying service structures; data collection; commissioning; clinical training and practice; health promotion and adopting a more integrated approach including social care, voluntary sector and other agencies.

The Facts of BME Disadvantage

One could be forgiven for concluding little has changed since the 1980s other than the list of the groups experiencing discrimination and inequality has grown and the statistics verifying their disadvantage have accumulated. BME communities still experience poor housing, poor education, high unemployment or badly paid and insecure employment; arguably attributable to continuing but increasingly subtle discrimination (Khan, 2008).

ONS (2004) provides clear positive correlations between poverty and disadvantage and greater incidence of mental ill health. Inequality of access to health resources is a continuing part of the mosaic of disadvantage that affects BME communities (Nazroo and Karlsen, 2001). The government endorses this view (DoH, 2003) This is manifested for BME clients in higher rates of compulsory detention, greater use of secure settings; more accessing mental health resources via the criminal justice system and longer hospital admissions. These statistics run alongside less access to talking therapies, greater use of medication and multiple reports of negative experiences of the mental health services. The DoH is frank in its evaluation that these factors increase the likelihood that BME clients are going to receive a substandard service because their needs may not be properly identified and assessed.

Relevant Theory

Multiculturalism

'Diversity' fits neatly with the notion of multiculturalism. British society is demographically multicultural (ONS, 2001). However, multiculturalism is also a political philosophy which views all cultures as of equal value eschewing the history of racism and class disadvantage. Multiculturalism presumes minorities live in closed ethnic groups, have a single set of values and beliefs to which all members subscribe equally and that group membership is the most important defining aspect of individual identity. A consequence of multicultural philosophy is a view that individuals are best served by political solutions aimed at their ethnic group rather than any other factor.

Racial and Ethnic Identity

How an individual positions themselves in relation to their racial and ethnic identity is a complex and dynamic process. Berry and Kim (1988) suggest four positions of 'acculturation'. An individual may occupy different positions at different times. Assimilation is where the host/dominant culture is seen as better than the original culture, separation is where the opposite holds true, marginalisation is where both host and original culture are seen as low value and integration is where both are seen as high value.

The definitions of race, ethnicity and culture are also complex. In the Race Relations (Amendment) Act 2000, a racial group is defined by their race, colour, nationality (including citizenship), or ethnic or national origins. Jews, Sikhs, Gypsies and Irish Travellers have been recognised by the courts as racial groups for the purpose of the Act (HMSO, 2000). This legal definition highlights the definitional difficulties. The categories in the legislation are ill defined, overlap and intersect. Jews exemplify this confusion – not a race, have multiple ethnicities, cultures, colours and nationalities, many are self identified as secular: but all are Jews. Culture and ethnicity are fluid and subtle, being redefined continually both for groups and individuals and across generations. There are no undisputed definitions for these terms.

A Practice Definition of Ethnicity

Nazroo and Karlsen (2001) suggest an applied definition of ethnicity based on self-description. Does the individual consider themselves traditional in relation to values, beliefs and practices, the degree to which they participate in the ethnic community, and the degree of identification with a specific racial group? They propose that ethnicity is associated with social disadvantage which is economically based and has extra dimensions of experiences of exclusion, racial harassment and discrimination.

Empirically Supported Therapies (ESTs)

There is a lack of research about psychotherapies' effectiveness with ethnic populations or how to modify psychotherapies for them (Bhui and Morgan, 2007; Hall, 2001). ESTs, of which CBT is the most prominent, have been developed on random controlled studies (RCTs) evidence. RCTs rarely control adequately for race, ethnicity and class variables (Smith, 2008) but are used to produce prescriptive advice on how to assess and treat specific mental health disorders (La Roche & Christopher, 2008). 'Universalist' services (Bhui & Morgan, 2007) adopt this 'one size fits all' approach (Bell et al., 2009). The measures used may not have cross cultural validity and the workers are unlikely to have training in working cross-culturally as it is not prescribed in the curriculum (DH/Mental Health Programme/Improving Access to Psychological Therapies, 2008).

Cultural competence requires workers to communicate effectively across cultures, make and sustain a therapeutic relationship with clients from other cultures and to know when and how to adapt diagnosis and treatment (Qureshi et al., 2008). The interrelationships between class, ethnicity and disadvantage in mental health remain under researched (Smith, 2008).

Culturally Sensitive Therapy (CST)

Research evidence does not support ESTs as being particularly effective for BME clients (Sue et al., 1999). There is a lack of research and existing research fails to take account of relevant variables (Hall, 2001). Equally, there is no evidence that CSTs are more effective with BME clients although there is some evidence BME clients prefer them and that they aid engagement and retention (Jackson, 2009).

Cardemil (2008) describes three separate models of CST. The first concerns therapists' attitudes and behaviours including cultural knowledge, understanding of power issues and the capacity to engage and maintain a therapeutic relationship. The second involves adapted ESTs, which, though they reflect dominant values, may use culturally specific measures and recognise culturally relevant issues such as community pressures. The third includes developing new therapies which use culturally specific attributions of the meaning of symptoms, behaviours and illnesses and traditional responses as well as tackling social inequalities. A synthesis of these models and evaluative research may produce a way forward.

If an EST is modified for a better BME fit, it is no longer an EST. The realistic solution would be to make modifications to ESTs and compare the outcomes with standard ESTs. Hall (2001) describes how this might be achieved. However, this is not necessarily a panacea and Bell et al. (2009) point out CSTs cannot, by definition, be universal and suggests practitioners will still have to learn when to generalise and when to tailor things individually.

Change

Changing Service Delivery

One could take the view that, given the persistence of the problem of BME disadvantage, in the face of legislation, policies, guidance and directives there is something about the nature of the problem which makes it irrevocably insoluble. Alternatively, one could assume that the fault lies with the way that the problem has been constituted leading to inappropriate or incomplete attempts at resolution. Policies designed to improve mental health services may remain ineffective unless an attempt is made to transform the structures which propagate and maintain those inequalities (Prilleltensky & Nelson, 1997; Vera, 2003).

Positive change would involve moving CBT services further into local BME communities, collaboration in community specific health promotion initiatives and identifying accessible, acceptable venues. A drive to train and deploy BME staff would also be helpful. Collecting accurate data on race, ethnicity, engagement and outcomes related to particular interventions is needed alongside service user feedback around cultural and racial issues and expectations and procedures of therapy (Lau, 2008). Lau is scathing in her view that primary care needs to value process and client experience not just throughput and outcomes. It is also important to track dropout rates from BME clients and the reasons for this. Bhui and Morgan (2007) argue that refugees are often bewildered and worried by the CBT approach. Commissioners could prioritise 'Diversity' training and put extra resources into areas with high BME populations.

Changing CBT Training

Professional training in CBT does not specify a 'Diversity' curriculum nor how competence in it should be calibrated and assessed.

There is a view in professional CBT training that 'Diversity' issues should be embedded in all aspects of the curriculum. The rationale is that it shouldn't be an optional add on but an integral part of the way we think about and practise CBT. The 'downside' of this is that it makes it difficult to evaluate its quality or outcomes.

An evidence-based approach would describe and quantify changes in the clinician's practice and evaluate service user satisfaction and outcomes following 'Diversity' training (Bhui et al., 2007). Minimum training requirements and standards for CBT could be revised. Programmes could be required to teach some of the history of 'Diversity' and disadvantage and critiques of psychology, psychiatry and social policy. Students can be exposed to the existing research on working with BME mental health clients. Students need to work with some BME and/or disadvantaged clients and show how their assessment, engagement, formulation and treatment addresses 'Diversity' issues. CBT programmes could insist students gain service user feedback incorporating cultural competency and sensitivity (Jackson, 2009) on their assessed casework. Clinical supervisors could routinely explore 'Diversity' issues and address these in the supervisor's reports.

BME service user views should be on the curriculum and service user groups can be involved in interviewing and teaching. Bhui et al. (2007) suggest using role-plays; video feedback and video materials; case discussion; literature, art and films to improve awareness, understanding and skills. Programme Leaders can devise a 'Diversity' syllabus, e.g. trauma and refugees; how to adapt CBT for a cultural fit; how CBT can accommodate faith beliefs. This could be delivered through seminars and casework presentations which encourage dialogue and challenge (Lim et al., 2008). There is a pressing need to discover with some accuracy what kind of training enhances the BME client's qualitative experience of CBT and its outcomes.

Changing Assessment

Exploring race and ethnicity may require extra assessment sessions. Clinicians should always ask about race/ethnicity and not make assumptions as it may not be obvious from the referral or the client's appearance (Cardemil and Battle, 2003). A client's language and literacy capabilities need assessing. As well as considering whether interpreters are desirable it will help the therapist think about how the client will cope with written materials and whether the standard CBT practice will need adaptation. CBT therapists are advised to avoid metaphors and idiomatic language. Certain techniques like computerised CBT or bibliotherapy might not be feasible.

For recent immigrants or refugees the clinician should check if the client has had access difficulties, their understanding of the agency and how the problem might be affecting family relationships and what this means to the client (McKenzie, 2008). Cardemil and Battle (2003) suggest clinicians start talking about race and ethnicity early in therapy explaining to clients that it will give the therapist a better understanding of the client and asking if the client feels comfortable discussing these issues.

Asking the client where they stand in relation to their community, its apparent values, beliefs and practices and how, if at all, they think this is relevant to the problem is important. The clinician might also ask if the client's views have changed over time and why. Therapists can also ask the client whether they feel comfortable with the clinician's race/ethnicity and invite them to suggest how any doubts or worries are best handled. Exploring expectations may reveal issues like expectations of concrete and direct advice from 'the expert' (Tsui & Schultz, 1985).

Therapists can convey an accepting stance to disclosure of exclusion, discrimination or prejudice and ask whether this is part of the clinical problem and its maintenance or an environmental stressor (Nazroo & Karlsen, 2001). If the client does not want to engage on these issues the therapist should respect this but leave the invitation open. Cross-culturally validated and appropriate measures should be used.

Changing Formulation

Formulation with BME clients requires a more holistic and environmentally aware approach. If the issues above are relevant they can be included in the formulation and a collaborative attempt made to work out how they influence the problem, its maintenance and proposed interventions. Client beliefs about mental health, therapy and its purpose can also be included along with environmental supports and stressors. Exploring whether the client experiences their cultural group as supportive, hostile or indifferent may be relevant. Poor housing and poverty may need consideration because they may affect attendance and between-session work. Culturally specific traditions for understanding and dealing with the client's symptoms or behaviours need consideration. Can they be incorporated or are they in direct conflict with a CBT approach? If the latter is the case then this will need to be discussed seeking a mutually acceptable solution. Client strengths need matching to possible interventions. It may be helpful to involve the family more than a standard CBT approach would, even if just to offer psycho-education and reassurance about mental health problems and the prognosis.

Changing Treatment

Workers have to decide how much modification of standard CBT protocols is necessary. Recent research using a multi centre RCT found a six-session CBT intervention, to improve insight to psychosis, was more effective for white service users. For the BME clients the treatment was less effective and the dropout rate was higher (Rathod et al., 2005). A subsequent qualitative study with BME service users, lay members from BME community groups and professionals working with the service users experiencing psychosis supports the idea that CBT can be acceptable to BME groups if it is modified to address patients culturally shaped understandings of psychosis and the access pathways to treatment are reconsidered (Rathod et al., 2010).

Practitioners need to recognise when ESTs embed practices, assumptions and ideas that do not have universal application, e.g. that CBT is understandable and acceptable to BME clients; that individual independence is a universally desirable goal; that work with individuals is the optimum approach; that what the community think about you doesn't really matter. Equally, CSTs may need individual tailoring for a specific client, taking account of their ethnicity, beliefs and practices. Therapists in 'universalist' services need to be more aware because of their adherence to manualised and protocol driven, disorder models of treatment.

Clients should not have their responses to poverty, poor housing or racism clinically pathologised. Resolution of these problems is likely to be environmental or community based. CBT could, like psychology, adopt an ethical principle of promoting social justice (Brown, 1997; Vera, 2003) and be prepared to intervene and advocate with and for clients. Particular interventions will need consideration of whether they are culturally acceptable and ecologically coherent to the client, e.g. changing elements of traditional gender roles, encouraging independent living and decision-making within a family oriented culture.

Change in Working with Interpreters

There is no statutory duty on the NHS to provide interpreters. CBT relies on negotiating clear and collaborative expectations of therapy with clients and uses dialogue in the form of guided discovery as a central intervention.

BME clients may get a better service with an interpreter even if they can speak English. Using family members, friends or untrained community contacts can breach confidentiality, inhibit disclosure of family issues, maintain abusive power structures, prevent disclosure of domestic violence or sexual abuse and interfere with the sharing of information (Phelan & Parkman, 1995).

Professional interpreters need to understand the exact language spoken; the CBT model; how the clinician works; the information sought; the purpose, length and nature of the interview; how to introduce CBT and manage difficulties. Empathy doesn't carry well across languages and cultures and both interpreters and therapists may need training in cross language empathy and translation (Pugh & Vetere, 2009).

Changing Group Work

Kohn et al. (2002) report on a 16-session depression group for African American women using an adapted manualised CBT programme. In theoretical terms this is an adapted EST (Cardemil, 2008). The changes made were to make the group ethnically specific and closed; incorporate some meditative experiential work; institute an end of group ritual and change the language used to describe CBT techniques, for example renaming homework as 'therapeutic exercises'. Additional content included a session on creating healthy relationships; a session on spirituality; a session on African American family issues and a session on African American female identity. They also used culturally specific African American anecdotes to illustrate ideas. This offers a model to think about how a CBT team might adapt a CBT EST manual for a British BME group.

Changing CBT Child and Adolescent Mental Health Services (CAMHS) Practice

Bradby et al. (2007) found in a qualitative study with British Asian families using CAMHS, that major disincentives were the stigma of mental illness and fear of gossip in their communities. Families who had children with complex problems said that professionals' discriminatory attitudes and behaviour exacerbated childrens' problems. Families where children had serious and enduring mental health problems felt they had no option but to tolerate culturally insensitive services. The vignette shows how some of the themes raised in the study are relevant. It also exemplifies how good CBT 'Diversity' practice addresses (see comments in brackets) language competency; expectations of therapy style; financial status; cultural beliefs/values around mental illness; power relationships/structures in the family and community;

preferred biological explanations for psychological phenomena and environmental issues in the assessment and formulation. These factors have a direct bearing on engagement; collaboration; empathy and the process and outcomes of treatment. Although the following case study is CAMHS based the issues are also pertinent to adult CBT.

Case Study 9.1: Practice vignette

Jaswinder and her mum, Jaswant were referred to CAMHS because of the onset of OCD symptoms in Jaswinder. Assessment revealed Jaswant was a lone, low-income parent who lost her home after her husband left them (loss of status in the community). While she identified as Sikh, this was more a cultural than religious affiliation. Jaswant felt marginalised by the community because of her low status as a divorced woman. Jaswant did, however, subscribe to community values: placing a high value on education, respect for elders and 'respectable' social behaviour for Jaswinder in relation to her choice of friends and activities (community norms). She expected Jaswinder to marry within the community and worried about her marriage prospects (community values and expectations). Jaswant lived in her brother's house (financial dependency) and had little control (community norms and pressures). She feared upsetting her family and was aware that in the Sikh community Jaswinder's problems could be seen as 'madness' and shameful (stigmatising, marginalising beliefs about mental health problems) and affect the wider family's standing in the community (community power structures) and damage Jaswinder's future marriage prospects (community norms, status and pressures). CBT sessions addressed how best to deal with the family's fear of stigma and loss of status. Jaswant was given materials to take home for the family (all fluent and literate in English) normalising OCD. An invitation to meet the family at home or elsewhere was made. Organic/biological theories (more acceptable to some South Asian communities) as well as psychological theories were offered about the causes of OCD. Jaswant was reassured by the good recovery rates cited in research (countering fears of mental illness and intergenerational problems). She was also reassured that OCD would be unlikely to affect Jaswinder's college and job prospects. Appointments were outside working hours as Jaswant couldn't afford to miss work regularly (class and income adaptations). Assessment revealed that Jaswant wanted and expected an 'expert stance' (Tsui & Schultz, 1985) (cultural norms and expectations) and a fairly 'directive approach'. Jaswant's wishes and expectations were discussed and accommodated so that Jaswant was offered expert 'knowledge' (from research) but interventions were designed collaboratively.

Jaswinder disclosed psychological bullying at school with a 'racist' component (environmental issue). Jaswinder had not revealed this before because she worried about upsetting Jaswant. Jaswant felt able to broach this issue in school and contact was facilitated with a BME education advocacy group (local BME agencies)

(Continued)

(Continued)

who were willing to take it up with the school (identifying social and community issues and taking a proactive social justice stance). Jaswant and Jaswinder were able to discuss their difficulties living with the extended family and develop some coping strategies. They also talked about how to deal with racist comments and texts. Feedback was elicited and both commented positively on the accommodation of ethnicity, cultural and racial issues in the therapy.

What this vignette would look like without a 'Diversity' approach and an ethic of social justice

Standard CBT asks 'what is the problem': (5 Ws; FINDS; modulating variables; coping strategies; personal history, onset and development of the problem; activating event; antecedent, behaviour, consequences (situational, behavioural, emotional, physiological and interpersonal); motivation; expectations of therapy; medication use; previous experiences of treatment; mental status and risk. Culturally competent and sensitive (CCS) CBT also asks 'how does the person with the problem identify themselves and what does the problem mean to them?' Standard CBT would have identified OCD but would not have fully uncovered the meanings, impact of the problem and actual and potential consequences for the family in relation to the Sikh community (see bracketed information in the vignette).

The lack of CCS in a standard CBT assessment would have undermined engagement and cultural empathy and may have resulted in 'drop out'. The family would have been unlikely to trust the therapist enough to disclose their insecurity and unhappiness with their living arrangements; Jaswinder's experience of racism; their worries about stigma and a hostile response from the Sikh community and the ramifications of this. The CCS approach strengthened engagement and collaboration by working with the family to deal with these problems as well as the OCD.

Standard CBT presumes clients want psychological explanations for problems and that an 'expert and directive' stance is undesirable but using a CCS CBT approach (Malek, 2004) showed this is not what the client expected or wanted. Failure to clarify this would have undermined collaboration, confidence in and compliance with treatment.

Standard adult CBT assumes an individual focus so the conflicts in the household and their impact may have been missed, even though these were generating enough anxiety to be considered maintenance factors. CCS CBT practice included them in the formulation and treatment.

Standard CBT looks at the environment around the problem rather than around the person who has the problem. The issues of low-paid work, financial dependency on relatives, difficulty getting time off for appointments, and racist bullying in school may have been missed in assessment and omitted from treatment. Standard CBT without an ethic of social justice can easily collude with the client's disadvantage. CBT practice with an ethic of social justice actively explored the 'class' and 'race' factors and adapted the CBT to include them in treatment.

Conclusion

CBT has become the main therapy of choice for the government evidenced by the NICE guidelines and the investment in IAPT. Being a 'political handmaiden' carries responsibilities for CBT in respect of 'Diversity'. There is an uncontested history of inequality for BME clients in both access to mental health care and the quality of the care offered. CBT literature has paid scant attention to this in relation to services, policy, training, theory and practice representing itself as apolitical. This chapter set out to challenge this stance and to reveal possible ways of redressing established inequalities. It has argued that change requires CBT to integrate CSS and adopt an ethical principle of promoting social justice.

Resources

Patient Voices (www.patientvoices.org.uk) – three-minute 'digital stories' of healthcare including those from BME mental health service users. Free to use in education and training.

Fernando, S. (2003). *Cultural Diversity, Mental Health and Psychiatry: The Struggle Against Racism*. London: Brunner Routledge – seminal text.

Malek, M. and Joughin, C. (eds) (2004) *Mental Health Services for Minority Ethnic Children and Adolescents*. London: Jessica Kingsley Press – source text for child and family clinicians.

www.jrf.org.uk – Joseph Rowntree Foundation.

www.bmementalhealth.org.uk – BME voluntary organisation.

References

Bell, C.C., Wells, S.J. and Merritt, L.M. (2009). 'Integrating cultural competency and empirically-based practices in child welfare services: A model based on community psychiatry field principles of health', *Children and Youth Services Review*, 31: 1206–13.

Berry, J.W. and Kim, U. (1988). 'Acculturation and mental health', in P.R. Dasen, J.W. Berry and N. Sartorius (eds), *Health and Cross-cultural Psychology*. Cross-cultural Research and Methodology Series:10. London: Sage, pp. 207–36.

Bhui, K. and Morgan, N. (2007). 'Effective psychotherapy in a racially and culturally diverse society', *Advances in Psychiatric Treatment* 13: 187–193; doi: 10.1192/apt.bp.106.002295 (accessed 17/04/2010).

Bhui, K., Warfa, N., Edonya, P., McKenzie, K. and Bhugra, D. (2007). 'Cultural competence in mental health care: A review of model evaluations', *BMC*

Health Services Research, 7: 15; doi:10.1186/1472-6963-7-15 (accessed 17/04/2010).

Bradby, H., Varyani, M., Oglethorpe, R., Raine, W., White, I. and Helen, M. (2007). 'British Asian families and the use of child and adolescent mental health services: a qualitative study of a hard to reach group', *Social Science and Medicine*, December, vol./is. 65/12(2413-24), 0277-9536 (accessed 17/04/2010).

Brown, L.S. (1997). 'Ethics in psychology: Cui bono', in D. Fox and I. Prilleltensky (eds), *Critical Psychology: An Introduction*. London: Sage.

Cardemil, E.V. (2008). 'Commentary: Culturally sensitive treatments: Need for an organizing framework', *Culture and Psychology*, 14: 357–67.

Cardemil, E.V. and Battle, C.L. (2003). 'Guess who's coming to therapy? Getting comfortable with conversations about race and ethnicity in psychotherapy', *Professional Psychology: Research and Practice*, 34 (3): 278–86.

CCETSW (1989). Central Council for Education and Training in Social Work's Rules and Requirements for the Diploma in Social Work (Paper 30). CCETSW.

CCETSW (1991). Rules and Regulations for the Diploma in Social Work, 2nd edn (Paper 30). CCETSW.

Cooper, C., Morgan, C., Byrne, M., Dazzan, P., Morgan, K., Hutchinson, G., Doody, G.A., Harrison, G., Leff, J., Jones, P., Ismail, K., Murray, R., Bebbington, P.E. and Fearon, P. (2008). 'Perceptions of disadvantage, ethnicity and psychosis', *British Journal of Psychiatry,* 192: 185–90. doi: 10.1192/bjp.bp.107.042291 (accessed 17/04/2010).

Department of Health (2003). Delivering Race Equality: A Framework for Action. Mental Health Services: Consultation Document. London: DoH.

Department of Health (2005). Delivering Race Equality in Mental Health Care: A Summary. An Action Plan for Services – A Model for Reform. London: DoH.

DH/Mental Health Programme/Improving Access to Psychological Therapies (2008). IAPT Implementation Plan: National Guidelines for Regional Delivery Implementation Plan: Curriculum for high-intensity therapies workers. http://psychology.iop.kcl.ac.uk/cbtcourse/images/DoH_IAPT_HighIntensity.pdf (accessed 17/04/2010).

Falicov, C.J. (1995). 'Training to think culturally: a multidimensional comparative framework', *Family Process*, 34: 373–88.

Fernando, S. (2003). *Cultural Diversity, Mental Health and Psychiatry: The Struggle Against Racism*. London: Brunner, Routledge.

Friere, P. (1970). *Pedagogy of the Oppressed*. Harmondsworth: Penguin.

Hall, G.C.N. (2001). 'Psychotherapy research with ethnic minorities empirical, ethical, and conceptual issues', *Journal of Consulting and Clinical Psychology*, 69 (3): 502–10.

HMSO (2000). Race Relations (Amendment) Act 2000 www.legislation.gov.uk/ukpga/2000/34/notes/contents.

Jackson, K.F. (2009). 'Building cultural competence: A systematic evaluation of the effectiveness of culturally sensitive interventions with ethnic minority youth', *Children and Youth Services Review*, 31: 1192–8.

Jun, H. (2010). *Social Justice, Multicultural Counseling and Practice: Beyond a Conventional Approach*. Thousand Oaks, CA: Sage.

Khan, O. (2008). *Financial Inclusion and Ethnicity. An Agenda for Research and Policy Action*. The Runnymede Trust.

Kohn, L.P., Oden, T., Muñoz., R.F., Robinson, A. and Daria Leavitt, B.A. (2002). 'Adapted cognitive behavioral group therapy for depressed low-income African American women', *Community Mental Health Journal*, 38 (6): 497–504.

La Roche, M. and Christopher, M.S. (2008). 'Culture and empirically supported treatments: On the road to a collision?', *Culture and Psychology*, 14 (3): 333–56; http://cap.sagepub.com/cgi/content/abstract/14/3/333 (accessed 19/10/2008).

Lau, A. (2008). 'Delivering race equality in mental health services', *Advances in Psychiatric Treatment*, 14: 326–329, doi: 10.1192/apt.bp.107.004986 (accessed 10/04/2010).

Lim, R.F., Luo, J.S., Suo, S. and Hales, R.E. (2008). 'Diversity initiatives in academic psychiatry: Applying cultural competence', *Academic Psychiatry*, 32: 283–90.

London School of Economics and Political Science. The Centre for Economic Performance's Mental Health Policy Group (2006). *The Depression Report. A New Deal for Depression and Anxiety Disorders*. London: LSE.

McKenzie, K. (2008). 'Improving mental healthcare for ethnic minorities', *Advances in Psychiatric Treatment*, 14: 285–91; doi: 10.1192/apt.bp.107.004366 (accessed 10/04/2010).

Mclaughlin, K. (2005). 'From ridicule to institutionalization: Anti-oppression, the state and social work', *Critical Social Policy*, 25 (3): 283–305; doi: 10.1177/0261018305054072 (accessed 10/04/2010).

Macpherson, W. (1999). *The Stephen Lawrence Inquiry*. London: Home Office.

Malek, M. (2004). 'Meeting the needs of minority ethnic groups in the UK', in M. Malek and C. Joughin (eds), *Mental Health Services for Minority Ethnic Children and Adolescents*. London: Jessica Kingsley Press.

Nazroo, J. and Karlsen, S. (2001). *Ethnic Inequalities in Health: Social Class, Racism and Identity*. Lancaster University: ESRC Report.

Office of National Statistics (2001). *Census 2001 – Ethnicity and Religion in England and Wales*. www.statistics.gov.uk/census2001/profiles/commentaries/ethnicity.asp#ethnic (accessed 19 May 2011).

Office of National Statistics (2004). *Mental Health of Children and Young People in Great Britain*. Summary Report. London: ONS.

Phelan, M. and Parkman, S. (1995). 'Education and debate. How to do it: Work with an interpreter', *British Medical Journal*, 311: 555–7.

Platt, L. (2007). Poverty and ethnicity in the UK. www.jrf.org.uk/publications/poverty-and-ethnicity-uk (accessed 06/01/10).

Powell, E. (1968) 'Rivers of Blood' speech, Midland Hotel Birmingham, 20 April 1968 www.freebase.com/view/en/rivers_of_blood_speech (accessed 10/04/2010).

Prilleltensky, I. and Nelson, G. (1997). 'Community psychology: Reclaiming social justice', in D. Fox and I. Prilleltensky (eds), *Critical Psychology: An Introduction*. London: Sage.

Pugh, M.A. and Vetere, A. (2009). 'Lost in translation: An interpretative phenomenological analysis of mental health professionals' experiences of empathy in clinical work with an interpreter', *Psychology and Psychotherapy*, September, vol./is. 82/Pt 3(305-21), 1476-0835 (accessed 10/04/2010).

Qureshi, A., Collazos, F., Ramos, M. and Casas, M. (2008). 'Cultural competency training in psychiatry', *European Psychiatry*, January, 49–58.

Rathod, S., Kingdon, D., Smith, P. et al. (2005). 'Insight into schizophrenia: The effects of cognitive behaviorial therapy on the components of insight and association with sociodemographics - data on a previously published randomised controlled trial', *Schizophrenia Research*, 74: 211–19.

Rathod, S., Kingdon, D., Phiri, P. and Gobbi, M. (2010). 'Developing culturally sensitive cognitive behaviour therapy for psychosis for ethnic minority patients by exploration and incorporation of service users' and health professionals' views and opinions', *Behavioural and Cognitive Psychotherapy*, 38: 511–33.

Richards, G. (1997). *Race, Racism and Psychology towards a Reflexive History*. London: Routledge.

Scarman, L.G. (1981). *The Scarman Report, the Brixton Disorders, 10–12 April*. London: HMSO.

Smith, L (2008). 'Positioning classism within counseling psychology's social justice agenda', *The Counseling Psychologist*, 36: 895; doi: 10.1177/0011000007309861 (accessed 18/10/08).

Sue, D.W., Bingham, R.P., Porche-Burke, L. and Vasquez, M. (1999). 'The diversification of psychology: A multicultural revolution', *American Psychologist*, 54: 1061–9.

Tsui, P. and Schultz, G.L. (1985). 'Failure of rapport: Why psychotherapeutic engagement fails in the treatment of Asian clients', *American Journal of Orthopsychiatry*, 55: 561–69.

Vera, E.M. (2003). 'Multicultural competence, social justice, and counselling psychology: Expanding our roles', *The Counseling Psychologist*, 31 (3): 253–72.

World in Action (1978) Interview for Granada TV. Margaret Thatcher with journalist Gordon Burns (27 January 1978).

TEN Levels of Therapist Involvement in CBT

CHRIS WILLIAMS

Introduction

CBT has changed the face of psychotherapy over the last 60 years. First developed in the early 1950s by Aaron Beck and others, the model was established and refined during the next 20 years (Beck, 1952). *Cognitive Therapy of Depression* (Beck et al., 1979) allowed the approach to be delivered in a consistent (manualised) way. This rapidly accelerated further research into the approach, and crucially meant that training could be disseminated widely through the increasing number of CBT training courses.

From 1979 to 2000 the dual strengths of a credible and growing research base and burgeoning training courses resulted in CBT being identified as a treatment of choice for depression and anxiety. In the UK, demand for CBT grew rapidly and was further encouraged in the first decade of the new millennium by influential reviews by the National Institute for Health and Clinical Excellence that confirmed CBT's place as an evidence-based and cost-effective form of psychotherapy (e.g. NICE, 2004, 2006, 2009). The result has been a mismatch of demand and supply where far more people could potentially benefit from CBT than there are practitioners able to deliver it, with resulting waiting lists as a consequence (Shapiro et al., 2003).

Time for New Solutions

An unintended consequence of developing waiting lists is that many CBT services understandably tightened their entry criteria for CBT. By opting to focus treatment on more complex cases, with significant comorbidity, paradoxically this meant that the very people most likely to benefit from CBT (i.e. those facing mild to moderate anxiety and depression) were least likely to receive it.

A pivotal paper, published in 2000 by Karina Lovell and David Richards, two highly respected nurse researchers, trainers and therapists, led the call for change in the delivery of CBT (Lovell & Richards, 2000). They identified the lack of access to CBT, the challenge of waiting lists and the resulting inequity of access, and came to a new conclusion. Instead of arguing that more practitioners were needed in more services, they asked a very basic question of CBT: '*Is there clear evidence showing that CBT is best offered as a one-to-one therapy over 12–16 weeks?*' This questioned the very basis of the then default one-to-one delivery by specialist CBT services. They concluded there was evidence for existing ways of delivering treatment - but also for a range of other ways of delivering CBT. For example, multiple systematic reviews had already shown that CBT self-help could be effective, and also that shortened/focused forms of CBT such as behavioural activation for depression (e.g. Dimidjian et al., 2006) and exposure and response prevention for phobias and OCD (e.g. Lovell et al., 2006), could also be equally effective yet required far fewer and sometimes shorter sessions. This work built on other work in the USA, Australia and the UK and was rapidly seized upon by service commissioners.

In England, change has accelerated rapidly as a result of the influential position paper by the health economist Lord Richard Layard (Layard, 2006) which summarised persuasively the arguments for widening access to CBT approaches on grounds of not only benefit to the individual patient, but also that the costs of services could be more than paid for by the cost-savings of helping people back to work. This has led in England to the Increasing Access to Psychological Therapies (IAPT) initiative which aims to significantly increase access to CBT as delivered through multiple new teams (www.iapt.nhs.uk/). In Scotland, the so-called Doing Well by People with depression programme had also focused on increasing the capacity of teams to deliver evidence-based therapies (www.scotland.gov.uk/Publications/2005/07/2994711/47119). The latter project has emphasised working with the existing workforce (in contrast to IAPT which has focused on training and introducing new teams and new types of workers such as PWPs – psychological well-being practitioners). Doing Well has more recently led to the Widening Self-help (WISH) programme where CBT self-help resources and linked training are being widely disseminated across five large health board areas in Scotland.

New Ways of Working

For more than the last decade, health services across the world have been looking to restructure and address waiting lists. Many of these changes have incorporated new ways of delivering CBT. These new ways of working include the offer of so-called low-intensity (LI) ways of delivering CBT – in addition to the classic one-hour sessions for 12–20 weeks (termed high-intensity working – HI). A definition of low-intensity working is given in Box 10.1.

Box 10.1: Low-intensity interventions (reproduced from Bennett-Levy et al., 2010)

The primary purpose of low-intensity CBT interventions is to increase access to evidence-based psychological therapies in order to enhance mental health and well-being on a community-wide basis, using the minimum level of intervention necessary to create the maximum gain. Low-intensity CBT interventions have been mainly developed in the context of patients with mild to moderate psychological disorders, enabling high-intensity CBT to be reserved for patients with more severe disorders. Therefore, compared with high-intensity CBT, low-intensity interventions:

- reduce the amount of time the practitioner is in contact with individual patients – whether this is reduced through seeing more than one patient at the same time (i.e. group CBT); *or* seeing them for fewer/shorter sessions (i.e. advice clinics); *or* supporting their use of self-help materials (i.e. self-help books, internet-based CBT interventions); *or* facilitating their engagement with community and voluntary resources; *and/or*
- use practitioners specifically trained to deliver low-intensity CBT, who may not have formal health professional or high-intensity CBT qualifications, e.g. paraprofessionals, peer supporters, voluntary sector; *and/or*
- use CBT resources whose content is often less intense (self-paced, own time, bite-size pieces); *and/or*
- provide more rapid access to early intervention and preventive CBT programs.

Low-intensity CBT interventions aim to communicate key CBT principles in accessible ways, and to deliver content in a variety of flexible forms – face-to-face, email, groups, phone-based – which maximise the opportunity for patient choice.

(Continued)

(Continued)

Typically, low CBT intensity interventions are simple and brief. They focus on the use of CBT self-help materials and techniques, emphasise the value of between-session homework, and assess, monitor and evaluate progress as an intrinsic part of the intervention. The content may constitute a treatment intervention in itself (e.g. behavioural activation, internet-based therapy, guided CBT), may support or promote an intervention (e.g. motivational enhancement, '10 minute CBT' GP consultations, advice clinics), or may be preventive of treatment interventions (preventive/educational programs). Compared with traditional services for patients with mental health problems, low-intensity CBT interventions increase:

- access and/or speed of access to treatment;
- the total number of people who can access evidence-based treatments;
- service flexibility, responsiveness, and capacity;
- patient choice;
- cost-effectiveness of services.

LI working is underpinned by some key concepts. It has an evidence base with national treatment recommendations supporting the use of CBT self-help (book-based and computerised CBT, e.g. NICE, 2009). Crucially the impact of CBT self-help is significantly improved by the addition of support in the use of the approach by a practitioner. There is clear evidence that supported CBT self-help is more effective than unsupported self-help (Gellatly et al., 2007). This support can include face-to-face, telephone, Skype/video-conference, email, groups and online live chat among the possible options. Of course, reviews like Gellatly et al. focus on clinical populations and grouped data. There will always be individuals who are motivated and able to use CBT self-help resources alone. However, on average, over many people with depression, there are added advantages of providing support. The benefits of support now appear clear for many with depression. However, it is as yet unclear whether the support can be provided by the package itself - and some new resources (e.g. www.llttf.com) include automated emails that intelligently (i.e. refer specifically to progress, use and make appropriate support recommendations) encourage the use of the package. As always, more research will be needed.

Why is CBT so Suited to LI and HI Ways of Working?

One way of conceptualising CBT is that, however offered, it is fundamentally a self-help form of psychotherapy (Williams, 2003: 175). It aims to teach people how to 'become their own therapist'. It is therefore highly educational, but is crucially different from psycho-education alone in that it also teaches skills of self-assessment, self-monitoring and self-change as well as purely providing information about the symptoms and available treatments for various disorders. The CBT techniques that are taught have been evaluated in research, and shown to be applicable in specific clinical disorders such as depression, panic and other disorders.

In CBT, the practitioner teaches people to learn techniques they can then apply in their own lives. These skills focus on identifying and then changing unhelpful patterns of thinking and reacting that otherwise worsen how the person feels. In many ways it mimics what happens in educational settings. A teacher (therapist) acts to assess prior learning and understanding, helps the person identify what skills and knowledge they need to learn, provides them with learning resources (handouts, worksheets, books), supports them in applying this in their own lives, and then helps the person reflect on progress (through homework tasks and in session). There are strong parallels therefore between CBT as a form of psychotherapy, and CBT as an adult educational model (Williams & Morrison, 2010). In one (clinical work) we use terms such as therapist or counsellor, in the other (education) we use words like teacher, trainer, or mentor, yet both share goals in common.

Learning can also occur in a number of ways. There can be a direct didactic style teaching, small group learning (for example in classes or group therapy), interactive tutorials (for example the one-hour traditional therapy session), and a blend of one-to-one teaching coupled with the use of coursework and use of course resources such as books, online resources, DVDs and other teaching resources (as is used in CBT self-help settings). This can focus on using just one resource, or be an example of so-called *blended learning* where different ways of learning are mixed together (blended) to aid learning and application (Williams & Morrison, 2010).

The emphasis in LI working is on the practitioner encouraging and supporting the person to use CBT self-help resources – and the resources themselves deliver the CBT model. In contrast, in HI working the focus for teaching the CBT is through the sequencing of questions and provision of information and skills-teaching provided by the expert practitioner. There may still be a use of CBT self-help – or the use of other resources (e.g. worksheets and other 'homework' resources) to help structure the application of what has been learned. The difference in ways of working also has implications for training. Because the way of working in LI and HI working is very different, the competencies required for LI working are therefore also different from those required for HI working (see later).

The Range of CBT Self-help Resources

A variety of CBT self-help resources can be used to suit the preferred learning style and reading abilities of the individual client.

Resources include:

- Written handouts, workbooks, booklets and books – also termed '*bibliotherapy*'. These may be in printed form, or available to read online (for example the four free books at www.fiveareasonline.com).
- Audiovisual resources – such as relaxation resources and DVDs (e.g. the free online TV course at www.livinglifetothefull.com/www.llttf.com).
- Computerised CBT (cCBT), e.g. Beating the Blues (www.beatingtheblues.co.uk), FearFighter (www.fearfighter.com) and Living Life to the Full Interactive (www.llttfi.com).
- Classes/groups, e.g. June Brown's Confidence classes (Brown et al., 2004), Jim White's Stress Control Classes (White et al., 1992; White 1998), and the Living Life to the Full Classes (Williams & Chellingsworth, 2010).

CBT self-help resources provide a structured and consistent way of delivering CBT. They do this by utilising a CBT structure that communicates the CBT model through that structure – thereby achieving fidelity to the model.

The Evidence Base for CBT Self-help

Clinical treatment guidelines by NICE (2009) and SIGN (2010) for depression, NICE for anxiety (2006) and Cochrane for bulimia (Schmidt et al., 2006) have identified CBT self-help as being an effective treatment. However, there are some areas where CBT self-help does not appear to be effective (e.g. post-traumatic stress disorder – PTSD – Ehlers et al., 2003) and anorexia (Schmidt et al., 2006). It should not be assumed therefore that CBT self-help is automatically an appropriate choice.

Choosing CBT Self-help Resources

The NICE (2006, but now withdrawn) technology appraisal of computerised CBT (cCBT) for anxiety and depression introduced an emphasis on the use of cCBT which implicitly emphasised it above other CBT self-help approaches. This appraisal was kept separate from the then depression guidance (NICE, 2004) and it's recommendations meant that the introduction of cCBT was mandatory within the health service in England. However, quite quickly reviews such as Gellatly et al. (2007) reported that the clinical effect of computers and written resources are equivalent. Perhaps this is not surprising as they aim to deliver the same evidence-based CBT model. This argument of a class-effect for CBT self-help was subsequently accepted by NICE, which withdrew the 2006 cCBT appraisal and incorporated recommendations concerning CBT into the updated depression guidelines (NICE, 2009). The current situation therefore in England (as informed by NICE) and Scotland (as informed by the SIGN guidelines - SIGN, 2010; Integrated Care Pathway for depression (www.icptoolkit.org/condition-specific-care/depression) and Matrix of Psychological therapies (www.scotland.gov.uk/Topics/Health/health/mental-health/servicespolicy/matrixfeb2009)) is that both book- and computer-based CBT can be used for treatment in mild to moderate depression. Such resources should be supported (guided) by a practitioner.

Perhaps the best way of seeing such a range of self-help resources is to consider 'how do you want to learn'. For example, while some people love to read books, others don't have a single book in their house - but do have a large flat screen television and DVD player. Similarly, for some people computers are a first point of call to seek information (e.g. Google) and support (e.g. social networking), whereas others are scared of computers, or lack the confidence or money to access them. So, for example, we know that access to computers is reduced when people are unemployed (Ottens, 2006).

In choosing CBT self-help resources, the following are key principles to bear in mind so as to achieve both a communication of the evidence-based CBT model, but in an accessible and usable form. Thus, the resources should address a disorder for which CBT has an evidence base (e.g. depression, generalised anxiety, panic, bulimia) and be based on a proven disorder-specific model. The CBT ideas and concepts should be communicated clearly and accessibly (Martinez et al., 2008). For example, the traditional language of CBT results in reading ages that around one in five users will struggle to read - equating to many millions of UK adults. To put this in context, 16% of adults struggle to read at reading age 11. Almost all CBT self-help resources have higher reading ages than this - some substantially higher. It asks a lot of people to have to learn a complex language before they can begin to apply it.

How materials are laid out and presented on the page also matters. Text can be broken down into manageable blocks with significant white space (i.e. gaps) between paragraphs. Other factors that can help include using short sentences and paragraphs, illustrative case examples and an accessible writing style. Resources (even books) should also be interactive so that users don't just read them neutrally but are asked to apply what they learn to their own life. It may also be that non-specific (common) factors such as encouragement, and a positive tone by the author also predicts outcome (Richardson et al., 2008).

Finally, to increase accessibility, the same resources can be made available in a range of different formats so that book, DVD and online methods can be combined (blended) to maximise learning (Williams & Morrison, 2010).

Different Models for Delivering Supported Self-help

CBT self-help can be used in various ways – to supplement one-to-one expert HI working, and also as a LI intervention. For example, we know that >90% of accredited CBT practitioners – most of whom work in HI settings, use CBT self-help resources (Keeley et al., 2002; Whitfield & Williams, 2004). Research to date instead indicates that people with more severe symptoms can also make use of CBT self-help. For the most part, however, the widening introduction of CBT self-help into services is currently being led by a wish to widen access to treatment and by providing rapid early and local access to self-help support.

Different models of delivery have been described including the following.

Stepped Care

Here, approaches such as CBT self-help are offered at a particular stage in the clinical service (e.g. Step 2 within IAPT) and is usually offered before access to specialist one-to-one HI CBT treatments. The rationale for the stepped approach is summarised by Bower and Gilbody (2005). An issue currently being debated is whether everyone must undergo treatment with the initial steps (for example behavioural activation, group treatments or guided CBT approaches) before they are 'stepped up' to other steps. This might mean that someone is required to undergo a low intensity based treatment when in fact their preference and need is for a high-intensity therapy.

Matched Care

This concept emphasises that the intervention, type and extent of support is matched to the needs of the patient (Williams and Chellingsworth, 2010). The matching is based on patient preference as well as complexity rather than on simple measures such as mood severity. Preference informs the modality of treatment and the type of support (e.g. face-to-face, telephone or e-support). The complexity of problem determines the frequency and length of support. NICE (2009) recommends that complexity includes the presence of risk, co-morbid mental health problems, complex social problems and past treatment history.

The matching is done based on an assessment that encompasses complexity to judge what treatment options are appropriate, and also addresses the question 'how do you want to work?' (see below).

Choosing Who Does Well/Badly

A range of people can make use of CBT self-help. It is important therefore not to equate CBT self-help with treatment solely of mild to moderate symptoms. Fitting with the matched care approach we recommend the use of three questions when deciding on the use of guided CBT:

- Is CBT self-help or other low intensity intervention appropriate?
- Can the person work in this way? How do they like to learn?
- Does the person want to work in this way?

Offering *Structured Support* Using the Plan, Do, Review Model

Clinical outcomes are significantly more impactful when the support for use of self-help is structured and protocolised. In HI CBT goals are often described in terms of SMART Objectives (Doran, 1981). These address goals that are:

- <u>S</u>pecific
- <u>M</u>easurable
- <u>A</u>ttainable
- <u>R</u>ealistic
- <u>T</u>ime-bound

However, our unpublished work in Glasgow shows that many practitioners, even when very experienced, fail to routinely structure their planning of using self-help approaches with a clear SMART structure. A colourful and easily used way of protocolising the SMART way of working is the use of Planner and Review sheets (Williams, 2009b) which are available for free download from www.fiveareas.com and www.fiveareasonline.com. The content of the Planner sheet is summarised below.

Planner Sheet:

Planner Sheet (Williams, 2009b)
My Notes **Date**

Which workbook/module will I work on next?

Plan to take things forwards

1). **What** am I going to do?

2). **When** am I going to do it?

Is my planned task one that:

Q). Will be useful for understanding or changing how I am? Yes☐ No ☐
Q). Is a specific task so that I will know when I have done it? Yes☐ No ☐
Q). Is realistic: is it practical and achievable? Yes☐ No ☐

3). What problems/difficulties could arise, and how can I overcome this?

Mood rating score: **(date)**

My next contact time ....

Re-arrangement details: Remember – if you know in advance you can't make the session, please let us know by contacting your local support worker

PLEASE NOTE: If you are struggling/feel worse, or if at any time you feel suicidal please visit your doctor/go to A+E/Phone NHS 24/Direct

Protocolised Support

Many practitioners like to think of therapy as an exciting roller-coaster of creatively working together with a client to personalise therapy and work to overcome a range of target problems. However, the history of recommendations for CBT in treatment guidelines has seen a significant move towards delivery using manualised and operationalised delivery. For example, for HI CBT there has been a tightening of the NICE recommendations for delivery between the 2004 and 2009 reviews. The same is true in the delivery of CBT self-help. Initially CBT self-help was offered with or without support. More recently Gellatly et al. (2007) have clearly shown the benefits of support for improved outcome at least for the treatment of depression with CBT self-help.

The NICE 2009 guideline for depression reinforces this with a strong recommendation about the need for support. Our own research has shown marked differences in outcome depending on how protocolised the support is. For example working with clear goals (e.g. a Plan, Do, Review model) and the use of telephone or face-to-face support protocols can improve the reliability of the delivery of therapy and make sure that a range of key topics are covered when engaging, planning targets and reviewing progress. There are many benefits therefore of working to a protocol in supporting CBT self-help. Such protocols can be either highly detailed (e.g. a whole script is read out) or consist of checklists to ensure key topics/points are covered. Examples of both types of script are available at www.livinglifetothefull.com and in Williams and Chellingsworth (2010).

Groups and Classes

Many services have initially focused upon supporting the use of CBT self-help using one-to-one support by a practitioner delivered face-to-face or over the phone. An alternative way of providing support in using CBT self-help is to deliver this in a group or classroom setting. Here again the focus is on the use of self-help resources rather than delivering formal group psychotherapy. CBT self-help classes therefore focus on using books or other resources to teach the key CBT skills, but also make use of the added benefits that classes offer. For example, classes allow individuals to recognise they are not alone. Discussion and role-play allow the perspective, hopes, fears and practical advice from others to be learned. Classes can help build social confidence and connections between people. Examples of current classes that focus on facilitating CBT self-help are June Brown's confidence classes (e.g. Brown et al., 2004). These focus on a widely used CBT-based confidence book (Fennell, 2009). Similarly, the charity Triumph over Phobia runs classes led by people who themselves have often experienced anxiety, phobias or obsessive compulsive problems. Their course focuses on a book by Marks (2005). A further example is the Living Life to the Full classes which focus on the so-called little CBT books written by CW. This 8 session class focuses on teaching CBT-based life skills and addresses a wide range of problems experienced during times of low mood and anxiety. The course content is also available for free to view on line at www.llttf.com.

NICE CG90 (NICE, 2009) highlights that the evidence base is strongest for CBT classes/courses that run with smaller numbers of participants rather than larger numbers, and are best led by two practitioners. Large class versions of delivery – often attractive to commissioners – are not specifically recommended by NICE as an effective delivery model.

Monitoring Outcomes

Low-intensity ways of working such as CBT self-help require new models of monitoring outcomes. In IAPT, the so-called minimum data set includes a battery of short mood (depression and anxiety), social functioning and employment questionnaires (www.iaptmds.co.uk and select the appropriate link). They are completed at every contact with the patient. Risk is also enquired of at every contact. Risk can be monitored either by clinically checking risk (again at every contact), or by using valid and reliable questionnaires that identify when a full risk assessment is required by a trained health worker. This can be operationalised using online case management software (below) which tackles head-on the dilemma that older HI models of supervision fail when an individual LI worker has 40–60 people on their caseload. In other words, LI working requires LI supervision (and record keeping) as well.

Low-intensity Case Management

Because the clinical caseloads of low-intensity workers are far higher than for HI practitioners, new ways of offering 'supervision' are also required. In IAPT, for example, the term supervision is not used in a low intensity context and instead the term case management is used.

In case management, there are several key principles:

- Every patient is discussed at key time points; baseline, after 4 sessions (usually at one month) and at final session.
- In addition, patients are reviewed with a senior clinician if they deteriorate, or show active risk to themselves or others, or fail to attend/drop-out. This allows a problem-focused intervention and sign-posting to other appropriate services as needed.
- In IAPT, there is often a focus on technology to facilitate and organise the case management approach – as there is an assumption that

with large clinical caseloads (a typical LI worker might have a caseload of 60 and a typical IAPT team receives more than 10,000 referrals per annum) mistakes and omissions will inevitably occur. Because of this, the case management approach can be automated by an online clinical resource such as PC-MIS which raises alerts when patients miss appointments, or deteriorate, and flags up the need for routine regular review at set time points (www.pc-mis.co.uk).

Practitioner and Public Attitudes Towards LI Working

Surveys of CBT self-help shows that practitioners often rate CBT self-help resources as being less effective than seeing a practitioner for one-to-one work (e.g. Keeley et al., 2002; Whitfield & Williams, 2004; Macleod et al., 2008). In contrast, public attitude surveys shows that self-help approaches are endorsed positively (Jorm et al., 2004).

In fact, overall HI working is not obviously offering a better delivery profile than LI working. For example, both LI and HI CBT can have low take-up rates and significant drop-out seen in many services (Clark et al., 2009). It is also by no means clear that CBT self-help is any less effective than one-to-one specialist CBT. A recent high quality review has strongly suggested that LI and HI CBT provide equivalent results, with a short-term greater improvement in favour of CBT self-help (Cuijpers et al., 2010). Overall, it seems likely instead that a key element is *'how do you like to learn?'*, i.e. individual preference about how the person wants to work on their difficulties. Some will want one-to-one expert longer sessions or will require this, whereas others will try hard to avoid this for a variety of reasons such as shame, anxiety and more. However, the findings reinforce suggestions that most people with non-complex presentations be offered guided CBT (self-help) in the first instance unless they don't wish to work in this way.

One potential problem is that patient attitudes are not always fully informed. So, for example, in clinical team settings, unpublished work by Mark Kenwright has found that many patients given the choice of written or online/CCBT opt for written resources although this may change with time as people become more used to reading text via computers and handheld devices. Perhaps this is not too surprising as many will not have a clear idea of what cCBT entails. Support for this is seen in the study by Mitchell and Gordon (2007) which found a significant rise in the proportion of people willing to accept the offer of cCBT for depression once they had had the opportunity to see what a computerised package actually looked like. It may well be that as services offer cCBT, the approach will become more familiar and therefore more immediately acceptable.

Implications for Training/Supervision

The skills and competencies required to introduce and support guided (LI) CBT are different from those needed to deliver HI CBT. These different competencies are highlighted by the varying skills sets identified by skills for health in HI working (see www.ucl.ac.uk/clinical-psychology/CORE/CBT_Competences/CBT_Competences_Map.pdf for an overview) and LI working (www.ucl.ac.uk/clinical-psychology/CORE/CBT_Competences/Problem_Specific_Competences/Guided_Self_Help.pdf).

A model of training and teaching in the use of CBT self-help is described in Williams et al. (2011). There are several key features. The course focuses on helping patients plan, implement and review progress using the Plan, Do, Review model. A problem-solving stance and a clear structure of overcoming blocks to use is taught. Semi-structured scripts, role-play and use of reflective practice/application in the practitioner's own life is emphasised. Applied learning with logbooks and regular plans to apply the approach lead to a focus on Practice Review at the start of each session. Finally, skills-based assessments such as objective structured clinical assessments (OSCEs) can provide an objective assessment of key skills such as how to feed back an initial assessment/formulation, introduce and then review use of CBT self-help. Key elements of the training are summarised within Williams and Chellingsworth (2010) and at www.fiveareastraining.com.

Major bodies such as the British Psychological Society (BPS) and the British Association for Behavioural and Cognitive Psychotherapies (www.babcp.com) are now accrediting low-intensity practitioners such as Psychological Wellbeing Practitioners (PWPs) in England. A clear differentiation should be made however between LI and HI working. In the first, the supporter encourages use of the CBT self-help resources – and it is the resources that deliver the fidelity to the CBT model. In contrast, in HI working, the therapist has internalised the structure of the CBT model, and is responsible for the delivery of the model in a flexible way based on an individual case formulation. This difference means there can be a larger focus on use of semi-structured scripts and checklists in low-intensity working, however a key challenge for workers is how to communicate relationship and engagement while using such tools.

Implications for Service Design and Who Delivers Interventions

Two divergent models have developed in England and Scotland. In England, NICE has driven the development of low-intensity working including CBT self-help and behavioural activation. This has a focus for the LI and HI work delivered within IAPT and significant funding has gone into the establishment of new IAPT teams, consisting of both LI and HI workers. Specialist training courses have been developed in a range of universities and a new type of worker - the PWP (psychological wellbeing practitioner) - developed. Outcomes have been very good and roughly equivalent for HI and LI interventions (Clark et al., 2009). Unpublished data suggest that the IAPT teams that achieve the best results offer a balance of both LI and HI working.

In contrast, in Scotland, funding has tended to focus on structural changes within the existing workforce. LI training courses in Scotland include the Dundee/Stirling Psychological therapy in Primary Care course and the SPIRIT LI training in Glasgow. These also have been driven by key strategic documents and reviews including the SIGN non-pharmaceutical treatments of depression review (SIGN, 2010). Also, the Integrated Care Pathway for depression (www.icptoolkit.org/) has emphasised regular outcome monitoring and the use of CBT self-help for mild to moderate depression.

The approach in both countries bring strengths and weaknesses. It is possible in IAPT to create new teams - but at large cost, and there are ongoing issues as to how the new ways of working integrate with existing working and other treatment approaches. The advantages of building on existing working in Scotland is that this approach allows greater immediate integration, but with the possibility that workers do not embrace or work using established protocols. In both, it is clear that wider roll-out can include delivery and support offered by non-mental health specialists (e.g. Pittaway et al., 2009).

This offers the possibility for public health and other workers such as teachers, condition management/back-to-work practitioners, primary care staff and others to offer support for CBT self-help approaches. It also means that work can be delivered via colleagues based in the voluntary sector to provide a non-NHS way for people to seek help as an alternative to traditional NHS pathways.

Conclusions

CBT self-help approaches can be effective and offer a radically new way of organising services. Central to the approach is a patient-centred assessment that includes a learning assessment ('how do you want to work') as well as an assessment of depression and other clinical problems particularly focusing on the presence of complexity. The use of the term guided CBT offers many advantages for describing the use of CBT self-help - as it avoids any confusion about what the term self-help means to patients, referrers and others. Guided CBT is more effective when accompanied by 'structured support' (Williams and Chellingsworth, 2010) - which significantly improves outcome. At present with widespread moves to implementation, the delivery of a wide range of ways of delivering and supporting such CBT interventions has sometimes run ahead of practical delivery models in many services. The challenge of new ways of working offers exciting prospects for the delivery of mental health services in the twenty-first century.

References

Beck, A.T. (1952). 'Successful outpatient psychotherapy of a chronic schizophrenic with a delusion based on borrowed guilt', *Psychiatry*, 15: 305–12.

Beck, A.T., Rush, A.J., Shaw, B.F. and Emery, G. (1979). *Cognitive Therapy of Depression*. New York: Guildford Press.

Bennett-Levy, J., Richards, D.A., Farrand, P., Christensen, H., Griffiths, K., Kavanagh, D., Klein, B., Lau, M., Proudfoot, J., White, J. and Williams, C. (eds) (2010). *The Oxford Guide to Low Intensity CBT Interventions* Oxford: Oxford University Press.

Bower, P. and Gilbody, S. (2005). 'Stepped care in psychological therapies: access, effectiveness and efficiency', *British Journal of Psychiatry*, 186: 11–17.

Brown, J.S.L., Elliott, S.A., Boardman, J., Ferns, J. and Morrison, J. (2004). 'Meeting the unmet need for depression services with psychoeducational self-confidence workshops: preliminary report', *The British Journal of Psychiatry*, 185: 511–15.

Clark, D.M., Layard, R. Smithies, R., Richards, D.A., Suckling, R. and Wright, B. (2009). 'Improving access to psychological therapy: initial evaluation of two UK demonstration sites', *Behavioural Research and Therapy*, 47: 910–20.

Cuijpers, P., Donker, T., van Straten, A., Li, J. and Andersson, G. (2010). 'Is guided self-help as effective as face-to-face psychotherapy for depression and anxiety disorders? A systematic review and meta-analysis of comparative outcome studies', *Psychological Medicine*, 40 (12): 1943–57.

Dimidjian, S., Hollon, S., Dobson, K., Schmanling, K.B., Kohlenberg, R.J., Addis, M., Gallop, R., McGlinchey, J., Markley, D., Gollan, J.K., Atkins, D.C., Dunner, D.L., and Jacobson, N.S. (2006). 'Randomised controlled trial of behavioural activation, cognitive therapy and antidepressant medication in the acute treatment of adults with major depression', *Journal of Consulting and Clinical Psychology*, 74: 658–70.

Doran, G.T. (1981) 'There's a S.M.A.R.T. way to write management's goals and objectives', *Management Review*, 70 (11).

Ehlers, A., Clark, D.M., Hackmann, A., McManus, F. and Fennell, M. (2003). 'A randomized controlled trial of cognitive therapy, self-help and repeated assessments as early interventions for posttraumatic stress disorder', *Archives of General Psychiatry*, 60 (10): 1024–32.

Fennell, M. (2009). *Overcoming Low Self-esteem.* London: Constable Robinson.

Gellatly, J., Bower, P., Hennessy, S., Richards, D., Gilbody, S. and Lovell, K. (2007). 'What makes self-help interventions effective in the management of depressive symptoms? Meta-analysis and meta-regression', *Psychological Medicine,* 37: 1217–28.

Jorm, A.G., Griffiths, K.M., Christensen, H., Korten A.E., Parslow, R.A. and Rodgers, B. (2004). 'Actions taken to cope with depression at different levels of severity: a community survey', *Psychological Medicine*, 34: 293–9.

Keeley, H., Williams, C.J. and Shapiro, D. (2002). 'A United Kingdom survey of accredited cognitive behaviour therapists' attitudes towards and use of structured self-help materials', *Behavioural and Cognitive Psychotherapy*, 30: 191–201.

Layard, R. (2006). 'The case for psychological treatment centres', *British Medical Journal*, 332: 1030–2.

Lovell, K. and Richards, D. (2000). 'Multiple Access Points and Levels of Entry (MAPLE): ensuring choice, accessibility and equity for CBT services'. *Behavioural and Cognitive Psychotherapy,* 28: 379–91.

Lovell, K., Cox, D., Haddock, G., Jones, C., Raines, D., Garvey, R., Roberts, C. and Hadley S. (2006). 'Telephone administered Cognitive Behaviour Therapy for treatment of obsessive compulsive disorder: randomised controlled non-inferiority trial', *British Medical Journal*, Oct. 28: 333(7574): 883.

Macleod, M., Martinez, R. and Williams, C.J. (2008). 'Cognitive Behaviour Therapy self-help: who does it help and what are its drawbacks?', *Behavioural and Cognitive Psychotherapy*, 37: 61–72.

Marks, I. (2005). *Living with Fear.* London: McGraw Hill Higher Education.

Martinez, R., Whitfield, G., Dafters, R. and Williams, C.J. (2008). 'Can people read self-help manuals for depression? A challenge for the stepped care model and book prescription schemes', *Behavioural and Cognitive Psychotherapy*, 36: 89–97.

Miller, A.F. and Cunningham, J.A. (1981). 'How to avoid costly job mismatches', *Management Review,* Nov, 70: 11.

Mitchell, N. and Gordon, P.K. (2007). 'Attitudes towards computerized CBT for depression amongst a student population', *Behavioural and Cognitive Psychotherapy*, 35: 421–30.

NICE (2004). *Depression: Management of Depression in Primary and Secondary Care.* CG23. London: National Institute for Clinical Excellence.

NICE (2006). *Depression and Anxiety: Computerised Cognitive Behaviour Therapy for Depression and Anxiety* (Review of Technology Appraisal 51). London: National Institute for Clinical Excellence.

NICE (2009). *Depression: Management of Depression in Primary and Secondary Care.* CG90. London: National Institute for Clinical Excellence.

Ottens, M. (2006). 'Use of the internet among individuals and enterprises', *Eurostat: Statistics in Focus,* 12: 1–7.

Pittaway, S., Cupitt, C., Palmer, D., Arowobusoye, N., Milne, R., Holttum, S., Pezet, R. and Patrick, H. (2009). 'Comparative, clinical feasibility study of three tools for delivery of cognitive behavioural therapy for mild to moderate depression and anxiety provided on a self-help basis', *Mental Health in Family Medicine*, 2009 (6): 145–54.

Richardson, R., Richards D.A. and Barkham, M.B. (2008). 'Self-help books for people with depression: a scoping review', *Journal of Mental Health*, 17: 543–52.

Schmidt, U., Murphy, R., Perkins, S. and Williams, C. (2006). *Cochrane Review. Self Help and Guided Self Help for Eating Disorders. Systematic peer review*. Cochrane collaboration. www.cochrane.org/reviews/en/ab004191.html (accessed, 19 May 2011).

Shapiro, D.L., Cavanagh, K. and Lomas, H. (2003). 'Geographic inequity in the availability of cognitive behavioural therapy in England and Wales', *Behavioural and Cognitive Psychotherapy*, 31, 185–92.

SIGN (2010). Guideline 114: *Non-pharmaceutical Treatment of Depression in Adults: A National Clinical Guideline.* www.sign.ac.uk/pdf/sign114.pdf (accessed, 19 May 2011).

Swan, J., Sorrell, E., MacVicar, B., Durham, R. and Mathews, K. (2004). '"Coping with depression": an open study of the efficacy of a group psycho-educational intervention in chronic, treatment-refractory depression', *Journal of Affective Disorders*, 82 (1): 125–9.

White, J. (1998) '"Stress Control" large group therapy for generalised anxiety disorder: two year follow-up', *Behavioural and Cognitive Psychotherapy*, 26: 237–45.

White, J., Keenan, M. and Brooks, N. (1992). 'Stress Control: a controlled comparative investigation of large group therapy for generalised anxiety disorder', *Behavioural Psychotherapy*, 20: 97–114.

Whitfield, G. and Williams, C.J. (2004). 'If the evidence is so good why doesn't anyone use them? Current uses of computer-based self-help packages', *Behavioural and Cognitive Psychotherapy*, 32 (1): 57–65.

Williams, C. (2003). 'New technologies in self-help: another effective way to get better?', *European Eating Disorders Review*, 11: 170–82.

Williams, C. (2009a). *Living Life to the Full Class*. Available online at www.llttf.com and www.fiveareas.com/resourcearea/index.php?_a=viewProd&productId=85.

Williams C. (2009b). Planner and Review sheet. Available for free download from www.fiveareasonline.com (accessed 19 May 2011).

Williams C. and Chellingsworth, M. (2010). *CBT: A Clinician's Guide to Using the Five Areas Approach*. London: Hodder Education.

Williams C., and Morrison, J. (2010). 'A new language for CBT', in J. Bennett-Levy, D. Richards, P. Farrand et al. (eds) (2010). *Oxford Guide to Low Intensity CBT Interventions (Oxford Guides in Cognitive Behavioural Therapy)*. Oxford: Oxford University Press.

Williams, C., Dafters, R., Ronald, L., Martinez, R. and Garland A. (2011). 'Training practitioners in cognitive behavioural self-help – the SPIRIT (Structured Psychosocial InteRventions in Teams) project', *Behavioural and Cognitive Psychotherapy*, 39: 139–49. Also see www.fiveareastraining.com

ELEVEN Multidisciplinary Working in CBT Practice

GILLIAN WALDRON AND ROB WILLSON

This chapter aims to describe the most likely types of, and settings for, multidisciplinary work (MDW) which the CBT therapist is likely to encounter. It will examine the advantages and pitfalls of working with other mental health professionals, and the particular professional requirements this imposes. It highlights the different challenges of MDW posed by different settings and different professional mixes. It is not a list of instructions or a predetermined formula, but seeks to point out key aspects of MDW work, which merit consideration and discussion. It is drawn from our own experience of years working within mixed disciplinary groups in a number of different roles, and not from evidence-based research (since none is hugely relevant to this subject). In the spirit of multiple disciplines, and therefore multiple perspectives on the person 'receiving' care, we have deliberately chosen to use the terms 'client' and 'patient' interchangeably.

The traditional view of the CBT therapist working one-to-one with clients (or patients) is in some ways at odds with the notion of working as part of a team. However, in reality CBT therapists working within the health professions frequently form part of multidisciplinary (sometimes called interdisciplinary) teams of varying formality. At the most informal end, treatment views may be discussed over a cup of coffee with colleagues. Such informality can foster multidisciplinary confidence and encourage a frank exchange of therapeutic opinions. At the other end of the scale, it is a legal requirement for disciplines to work formally together in a highly efficient and productive way. An example of formal multidisciplinary work is where the safety and welfare of minors are concerned. Hence therapists, care workers and other mental health professionals may all be present at a Child Protection Conference.

At workshops Aaron Beck has often been heard to give the ultimate in pragmatic responses to the question 'What exactly is cognitive therapy?' His response would usually be something along the lines of: 'Whatever helps the patient get from problem to goal' or 'Anything that works.' Placing this definition of cognitive therapy at the heart of your practice speaks directly to working with other professionals to help your client move towards his or her goals.

Effective working within a multidisciplinary team (MDT) is more difficult than it sounds. There are hierarchical differences to be considered, many of them unspoken, unacknowledged or only dimly recognised by some professionals. Among any group of professionals there are also differences in training, orientation and experience, different understanding of the aims and goals for any given problem, language and style variations, diverse responsibilities and differences in levels of skill. Specific personality types sometimes select specific professions; some are therefore more comfortable working within a team than others.

It is, in practice, unusual for a CBT therapist to work entirely alone with a client. Of course in private practice a client may refer himself for individual treatment and not wish the general practitioner or any other health professional to be contacted. However, more often referrals will come from another professional such as a GP or psychiatrist, or treatment will take place in situations where other disciplines are already involved. Most users of mental health services are engaged with two or three professional types at any one time (Burns, 2004).

MDW in Different Settings

Traditionally, CBT training focuses upon the specific treatment of a clients' practical and emotional difficulties and clinical disorders. More rarely does training attend to the setting in which treatment may actually occur. Treatment settings are discussed elsewhere in this book (see Part 4) and of course have a great impact on MDW. We shall only briefly discuss different settings with regard to MDW here.

Primary Care Settings

Primary care (including GP practices, health centres and polyclinics) has many different disciplines working within it: doctors, practice nurses, district nurses and midwives, health visitors, physiotherapists, occupational therapists, dieticians, chiropodists, specialist nurse-practitioners (for example in diabetic or asthma care) counsellors and psychologists. Other professionals will visit sporadically, for example physicians or psychiatrists consulting about particular patients or holding clinics. The CBT therapist in a primary care setting may receive clinical input from any of these - depending on the needs of the patient/client, and may gain information, more or less formally, about other family members which impact on the treatment decisions and outcomes for the client.

What are the principles that underpin these inputs and contacts?

Nature of the Position

The therapist may be working entirely in this setting, or visiting only to treat a specific client. S/he may be the only mental health worker in this environment or part of a team of other CBT therapists or of other mental health professionals. Referrals may be made formally at case discussion meetings, or by GPs via the phone or referral slip, informally by self-referral, or bookings made by a receptionist or other nonclinical member of staff.

'Contract' with Client

The contract is an agreement between the client and therapist outlining the nature of the relationship, and the tasks to be undertaken by each party. This may constitute a single assessment prior to a recommendation for other specific treatment, such as being placed on a waiting list for CBT or computerised treatment. It may be a contract for a specific number of sessions to do a specific piece of work, perhaps after an assessment/referral from a senior colleague.

Planned Interaction with Other Disciplines

This may include supervision, individually or in a group, case discussions with other mental health workers, e.g. community psychiatric nurse, meetings with GPs and other professionals in wider case management meetings.

Unplanned Interaction with Other Disciplines

This may arise because of urgent changes in the clinical situation, whereby a case management decision has to be made quickly. An example may be increased risk of self-harm or suicide. Impromptu meetings are essential and helpful in such instances. Relatively unhelpful or inappropriate interaction with professionals from other disciplines can also occur. For example, chance encounters in the corridor resulting in something of the ilk: 'tell me, how are you getting on with Mrs Soandso?' Such informal transactions and requests for information or clinical updates have to be managed professionally by the CBT therapist. For example, the therapist may need to ensure that confidentiality can be maintained in the environment, or have to agree to communicate at another time, or in writing.

Differences in Goal

You may be working with Mrs Soandso to help her overcome her anxiety disorder. The GP may be worried about how to control her demand for appointments and investigations while the diabetic nurse is trying to teach her to monitor her blood glucose level more consistently. Moreover, the dietician is focused on helping Mrs Soandso to lose weight and yet another GP is debating contacting Social Services to assess whether her daughter is properly caring for Mrs S's grandson ... potentially confusing stuff. These differences in goal may not be explicit, or not sufficiently so, and are common when working in a kind of 'one-stop shop' for health problems. Managing such differences in goals should form part of an agreed care plan, ideally agreed in writing by all involved clinicians and the patient.

Confidentiality

What is the arrangement for information sharing and note taking in this setting? Primary care information, either digital or in written or spoken form, is inevitably available to nonclinical staff. This is often necessary to promote efficient administration meaning that efforts to maintain confidentiality cannot be entirely successful. How is the balance between communication and confidentiality maintained in any particular setting, and to what extent is this explicit, or assumed? Can it be changed by a professional to meet the particular needs of an individual case? There should be a policy about whose responsibility it is to teach the principles of confidentiality to nonclinical staff who may not have experience of this in previous employment; the way that notes and data access are managed should be monitored. The policy should include a plan for dealing with particular problems of confidentiality, such as a patient relative of a staff member, or a patient in the public eye.

Secondary Care Settings

These may include general mental health services, outpatient clinics, community mental health centres or inpatient wards. They may provide population specific services for adults of working age, older/elderly adults, families or children and adolescents. The CBT therapist in secondary care settings is likely to be part of a team which will include psychiatrists, psychiatric nurses, psychologists, social workers and occupational therapists, who will come together in specific forums for case discussions. Forums typically include ward rounds and case conferences. These may be fluid and flexible, or formal and rigid, depending in part on their history and evolution in any particular setting. Statutory meetings are also likely to take place, especially for the Care Planning Approach (CPA) system. The CPA is a strategy to improve service delivery to certain groups of vulnerable people with mental health problems in the community. It is, since its review in 2008, specifically applied to those at greatest risk, or those whose care needs require input from a wide range of services. It is a statutory obligation for trusts to provide a system of CPA meetings, where key workers, called Care Coordinators, are appointed to oversee the continuing treatment and support of the vulnerable service user, especially in the transition from hospital to community care.

Many of the principles outlined for primary care settings will apply here, but there are some differences.

- *More specific and shared goal* Unlike in primary care, the overt goals for a client/patient are more likely to be commonly shared between CB therapist and other members of the team. This makes communication easier, but increases scrutiny, accountability and the opportunity for informed criticism.

- *Hierarchy* There is likely to be a clear hierarchy of responsibility and decision-making in this type of multidisciplinary setting, headed usually (but not always) by the consultant psychiatrist, psychologist or senior nurse. The hierarchy may also be determined in part by length of service, status and personality factors, and its details may not be immediately apparent to the new worker in the team. There may also be personal alliances and discords that undermine effective MDW and communication, in this or indeed, any other setting. If this is the case it will generally be best to try and bring them out into the open in a nonconfrontational manner and discuss the best way forward. Keeping the care of the patient and the pragmatic delivery of treatment at the heart of such conversations will often provide enough common ground to keep things productive.

Tertiary Care Settings

These are likely to be CBT therapist positions in specialist treatment centres where patients are referred for specific treatment for different groups of conditions. In mental health they may be forensic units, specialist units for refractory affective disorders or difficult to treat OCD, for example. They may be medical units - specialist gastroenterology departments, oncology departments or pain clinics, or obstetric infertility units. They may be mixed medical/surgical superspecialisms such as transplant units or post-traumatic plastic surgery departments. CBT may have a role in any or all of these units and this is increasingly the case. However, in medical or surgical units, this role is inevitably a junior one, as an adjunct to the main task of the team. Less enlightened senior surgeons, for example, may not share the language or the confidence in psychological treatments that the CBT therapist does. In contrast however, in some specialist mental health units therapists are likely to take a leading role.

- *Working 'on the front line'* The type of unit mentioned above may be very much at the forefront of work in a given field - with a reputation to make or maintain and a keen interest in research. This may sometimes cause tension and conflict with the clinical demands on the team. Conversely, these factors can make for a cohesive and highly functioning team, but there may be strong charismatic personalities involved that need to be negotiated and managed. It can be difficult, for instance, to maintain confidence in one's professional ability in such a team, which may be rigorously critical and have exacting and possibly unrealistic standards of outcomes. More positively, however, such settings are likely also to be facilitating and nurturing of new talent and are exciting places to learn and practise new skills.

- *Interaction with other units* Most tertiary care units will be a small department in a larger hospital and there may be all sorts of complications such as professional jealousy, misunderstanding, competition for resources and space when interacting with disciplines of nearby or related units. There may also be legitimate criticism and increased scrutiny, especially if, for example, the funding is from a grant or charitable body. These considerations will not usually be the concern of the CBT therapist or anyone not in a managerial role, but they may be an influence on working relationships within and without the care-providing group. It may be important to be aware of the pressure of deadlines, assessment visits and research difficulties for example, which may conflict with the primary treatment purpose of the unit. All workers in the team need to be aware of maintaining their focus on the task, and their professional approach, regardless of the tensions that may develop.

Styles of Multidisciplinary Interaction

Let us now look at different patterns of working together between disciplines and examine the particular requirements and constraints that may be involved.

'Low-level' MDW

Examples of low-level MDW are primary or secondary care settings where your client may be receiving care from several professionals, one of whom refers the client to you for disorder specific CBT treatment. The referral is usually made by letter or memo. There are no opportunities for any round-table discussions. Although there may be some telephone contact to review progress, generally there is no interprofessional contact for weeks at a time.

Note-keeping and Record-taking

In this setting, there will be no shared notes. You will keep your own personal session notes and records of your treatment plan/recorded outcomes, filed and organised within your own department. It remains important to record details of contact with the referrer and any other disciplines, but there will be no automatic requirement to share case files.

Communication with Referrer

Ideally, the referrer's original letter should be replied to after the client has been seen and assessed, with an opinion and a treatment plan. Consent from the client will be needed, in writing and dated. If other nonreferring professionals, such as the client's GP, are to be written to as well, client consent must be obtained for each person to be contacted. It is good practice to copy correspondence automatically to the client unless there are specific reasons not to, which should be noted. There may be some conflict about sharing difficult diagnoses with the patient, and it would be inappropriate for one team member to make a decision to divulge this until the conflict is resolved, or there may be doubt about whether the client has control over his own post. In any event, all letters and notes about a client must be written in a professional and considered manner such that you would be comfortable with your client reading them.

It is important to consider where your correspondence will be kept. Will it be scanned digitally into GP notes or other primary care records? Or will it be part of a case file held in an inpatient on a psychiatric unit? These considerations may determine the degree of detail you go into about a particular case. Very sensitive past historical information, especially involving third parties, for example, may be inappropriate details to include in a letter to a GP since such details are likely to be released should further referrals be made in the future. It is, however, important to record significant aspects of history and treatment which are relevant to the client and may have future implications - if for example, you discover a previously unknown needle phobia in a patient who requires surgery sometime in the future - but not details of the client's abusive past relationship with their father who is also registered with the practice and friendly with one of the receptionists.

'Mid-level' Intensity MDW

Mid-level MDW involves working together in a loosely constructed team, where case referrals are made through mutual discussion, and progress and outcomes are monitored in a similar way. It may be a community mental health team, a psychiatric inpatient unit, a GP practice with psychologically minded GP principals, or a specialist unit of some kind (for example a transplant unit), which values CBT input.

Note-keeping and Communication

Here the referral will be noted as an outcome of a meeting and there will be no formal referral letter, and probably no requirement for correspondence between the members of the team. There will, however, be different requirements about note-keeping, and these will be specific to each unit. Probably there will be some shared notes and records where client/patient contact, treatment plan and outcomes, risk assessments and so on will be recorded. The CBT therapist will also keep independent session notes, often in a separate area of the unit. As usual, the CBT therapist records details of assessment, treatment progress and other information relevant to overall client care. CBT session notes may also, however, contain sensitive client information (current or historical) not relevant to the overall treatment plan that may needlessly jeopardise confidentiality if stored in the general file. Usually, in mid-level MDW settings, all notes are collated and jointly filed when treatment of the client/patient comes to an end.

The Multidisciplinary Meeting

This is the forum in which most MDW difficulties occur. The CBT therapist may be a relatively junior member of the team, and there may be participants in the meeting who do not have sympathy with or understanding of the therapy. There may be genuine professional differences and conflicting views about the significance of a CBT contribution to a particular case, and there may be prejudices or unrealistic expectations from all participants.

Some of the unspoken influences in such a meeting might be difficult initially to detect and only become clear over time - for example, stereotypes and prejudices between individuals or disciplines, autocratic or weak leadership, disagreements about what constitutes commitment and a professional approach. Others' influences may be immediately obvious - for example, individuals claiming the position of the most dedicated or skilled, others being habitually negative about any treatment approach and those who are typically either too ready, or not ready enough, to take on a case.

Good MDW respects all the disciplines involved but recognises that they are not of equal value all of the time. For example, one case may require treatment to be 90% CBT and 10% non-CBT, while for another case it may be vice versa. An effective MDW team will discuss input balance for a case, allowing all views to be expressed, before a conclusion is reached, generally by consensus. There will be differences in experiences and responsibility, both within and between the disciplines involved, which ideally must be valued too.

A risk inherent to MDW – as opposed to working alone, is that your estimate of the value of CBT to the patient/client may not necessarily be shared by others involved in a given client case. MDW therefore requires you to be confident about your knowledge of CBT theory and its clinical applications as well as the intricacies of each individual case. The CBT therapist fresh from training will often be the most junior member of a MDW team. Being the most junior member does not invalidate your opinion but, as already mentioned, you need to be prepared to be disagreed with by other professionals. It is important that you are given, and that you take, a chance to express your opinions. If this does not happen, it begs the question why you are included in discussion forums if your input is not deemed necessary or significant. If this occurs, then one should question this preferably in a private session with one's supervisor or a senior member of the team.

The MDW team can be a very rewarding place in which to work. At best it is supportive, educational and facilitates a way of working with your client, which uses the best available skills to maximise the possibility of a good outcome.

'High-level' MDW

High-level MDW means working almost all the time across disciplines and is most common in super-specialist units. The CBT therapist for example, might work together with a physiotherapist in a Chronic Fatigue unit or in a Trauma rehabilitation unit. S/he may also work with a social worker in a child psychotherapy unit, or with a training psychiatrist running groups in a psychogeriatric day hospital.

Note-keeping

In this setting, all the notes are kept together and any team member may add progress notes equally. These notes may be kept as a whole separately from traditional 'medical' notes in a 'parent' department of which this unit is a part.

Maintaining Discipline Boundaries

It can be difficult in MDW settings to maintain the boundaries of your discipline, and in working practice, these can sometimes get lost. If you work together intensively and for a long time with one or more partners, there is an inevitable tendency for a congruence of approach and belief to develop, which may challenge and be at some variance from your original approach. It may be important in light of this to establish some external supervision and/or support network to ensure individual skills and knowledge are preserved for the benefit of the client.

The Role of the Cognitive Behavioural Therapist in MDW Settings

The role of the cognitive behavioural therapist within a multidisciplinary team will vary greatly (Fernando & Keating, 2008). CBT therapists can come from a range of professional backgrounds and this will of course affect their role in a team. A consultant psychiatrist who is also trained in CBT will likely have very differing roles and responsibilities than a recently qualified CBT-trained psychotherapist. The therapist may or may not be acting as the patient's 'keyworker' within a service, and may or may not be viewed as part of the 'psychiatric care team' or other group of which the patient has prior experience. Differing roles are likely to have an impact on the nature of the therapeutic relationship. As far as possible it is of course desirable to limit your role to 'therapist' with a given client, but we recognise that this is frequently impractical. The job of the CBT therapist is to be aware of the effect of dual roles on therapy with a particular client and to raise these with the client and other members of the team. It may be possible to address these complexities by asking another member of the MDT to assume one of your roles for you, or it may be sufficient to make non-CBT items part of your agenda, or to set separate meetings for other issues. If you find that your CBT training has not necessarily equipped you well to deal with issues such as medication or housing problems, and as such these are dominating therapy sessions in a way that is counterproductive, then discussing how best to address such factors with the MDT is a natural way forward.

A Cognitive Behavioural View of Multidisciplinary Working

A cornerstone of cognitive therapy is *collaboration*. In the therapy office you might have a perspective of collaborating with your client to test out certain target cognitions. Consider working with other professionals as an extension of your ability to collaborate and form an effective working alliance with others. Far from interfering with or 'diluting' your carefully constructed cognitive-behavioural treatment, workers from other disciplines can be an incredible resource. Interacting and communicating with your MDT need not be just a 'chore' or seen only as a necessary legal requirement. Consider some of the following advantages:

- increased professional support;
- possible resource for behavioural experiments (e.g. normalising);
- knowledge of other resources available to the patient;
- sounding board for your own ideas;
- a resource of personal and professional experiences;
- alternative professional disciplines will often have ideas/strategies that would not have occurred to you;
- perspectives can align giving a greater sense of confidence in testing out a formulation of a client's difficulties.

A cognitive-behavioural therapist can consider the assessment that informs the multidisciplinary team as a *hypothesis* on the nature of the patient's difficulties and the treatment plan as an *experiment*. You may wish to try and agree with other members of the MDT on how you will measure the success or otherwise of the plan (or the outcome of the experiment).

Using a CBT Formulation in MDW

Good CBT is usually driven by a cognitive-behavioural 'formulation' or 'conceptualisation'. Sharing this with a client to help them make sense of their problems and understand where to start to make changes is common practice. Sharing this conceptualisation with other members of the MDT will help them to understand your perspective on the client's problems and your treatment plan. You may in fact be able to use a cognitive-behavioural formulation to draw together different aspects of the skills and interventions provided by the MDT into a coherent plan. A model for understanding five aspects of a patient's life and building a cognitive-behavioural formulation is the 'hot cross bun' (Greenberger & Padesky, 1995). The five aspects represented include: 'cognition', 'physiology', 'moods', 'behaviour' and 'environment' (see Figure 11.1).

As shown in the image below, 'cognition', 'physiology', 'moods' and 'behaviour' interact. Equally, they occur within, and are influenced by, the environment. Using the hot cross bun as a template can be helpful

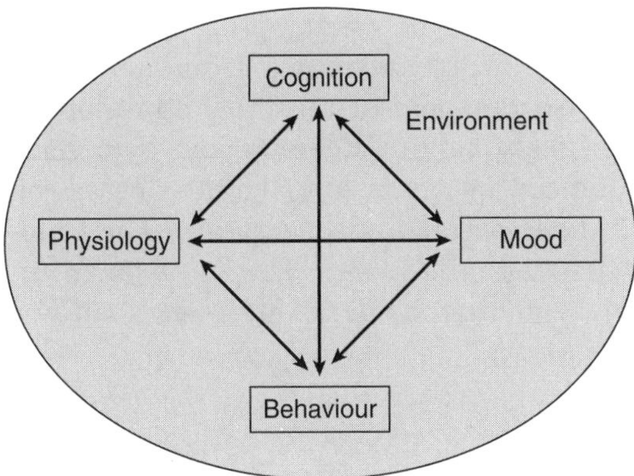

Figure 11.1 The 'hot cross bun'.

in defining where a client's problems primarily lie and where to target interventions. It can then be agreed who is going to be responsible for different elements of the overall care plan. The hot cross bun helps to identify different areas or 'zones' of care.

For example the psychiatrist or GP may be responsible for medication and blood tests in the physical 'zone'. However, both the CBT therapist and the GP might encourage better sleep pattern, which also falls within the same zone. The CBT therapist might target aspects of behaviour to help the client tackle his or her environment (such as getting on top of paperwork) and a social worker may try and aid in a longer-term change in housing.

Keeping Things Going in the Right Directions

Identifying what professional values underpin your therapeutic practice, and acting consistently with these values can be helpful in a number of ways. It can be helpful in fostering a sense of being a 'good enough' therapist even when the going is tough with a patient or patients. It can also be very helpful to stay focussed upon your values when you feel that the 'system' or another clinician within the team is failing the patient. Most professionals working in mental health will have had training in one or more forms of psychotherapy and will be keen to practise their skills. While different members of the MDT have skills specific to their own training, some overlap is inevitable in mental health work. Negotiating through differing views, power dynamics, and sometimes complex personalities can be challenging. A good relationship with another professional or professionals from a different professional background can also be some of the most stimulating and rewarding aspects of your professional life. Keeping your own values as a therapist clear in your mind can help you to make the process of MDW rewarding rather than undermining and frustrating. The following are examples of core CBT therapeutic values. The list is far from exhaustive and we strongly urge you to consider your own healthy and productive values to bring to MDW.

Respect and Optimism for the Person for Whom the Team is Providing Care

At times you may find yourself being the only person who has a resolutely optimistic view of a patient and who refuses to write them off as a 'PD' (personality disorder). It is sadly still possible to encounter this pejorative use of Axis II diagnosis within healthcare. A CBT therapist can bring the attitude that people are likely to respond better if you think the best of them. Labelling and endless rediagnosing is rarely constructive, and it can be argued that people are far more likely to recover if they build on their strengths rather than being confronted solely with their 'weaknesses'.

Respect and Openness to Other Clinicians/Workers

Remember that other professionals do not necessarily 'buy' the CBT model, and may have very good reasons for viewing patients' difficulties in other ways. A particular client's care should never be seen as an opportunity to 'convert' other professionals. Keep focussed on the purpose of collaboration and do not allow yourself to be sidetracked by very old and tired debates about the merits or otherwise of CBT.

Remain Focussed on Moving From Problem to Goal

As discussed earlier, this active, change-focussed perspective is a central tenet of CBT. As a CBT therapist this is a focus that you can bring not only to your work with clients, but to communication and interaction with others involved in his or her care. Keeping this in mind will help you remain steadfastly constructive during case discussion forums and hopefully influence others to do the same.

Respect for the Patient's Uniqueness as a Person

Bear in mind that the aim of psychological treatment is to help a unique individual function better. As a CBT therapist your task is to consider the *function* of patient's behaviour within a given context, avoiding value judgments about what is 'normal' or 'appropriate'. For example in one person's situation it may help them to build stronger connections with their parents, yet in another it may be far more therapeutic to help them avoid contact with their parents without feeling guilty.

The Patient has the Capacity to be Resourceful, Creative and Carry Responsibility for His/Her Own Recovery

'Homework' or 'self-directed therapy' is of course central to the success of CBT. It is therefore implicit in our client vision that they themselves are the key ingredient to treatment success, no matter how many skilled professionals are involved. Communicating this CBT perspective can be a key dimension of participating within an MDT. Many excellent MDT's encourage patient input and consultation wherever practical, and readily consider how the patient may be able to act or advocate for his or her self. However, at times, such as when a patient is very dependent or has longstanding difficulties, this level of autonomy can be lost. Dependency issues may well need to be a target for change and addressed not only with the patient but also with those providing care.

Communicating Effectively

It might seem reasonable to assume that therapists, almost by definition, are good communicators. Our experience has shown us that this is not wholly true. Even excellent therapists have their communication blind spots, whether it's because they are too hurried, too slow, too arrogant, too shy, too brief, too expansive and so on. Try to be aware of your own tendencies and correct for them. A common problem for many clinicians, who rightly put the patient at the centre of the system, is to over-rely on the patient as a conduit for information. This is both unfair on the patient, and can lead to incomplete or inaccurate information being passed along. The patient needs to know enough, but should not be overloaded.

Keep Things Clear and Simple

Avoid CBT-jargon and stick to plain English or generic psychiatric terminology. Your job as a team member is to carry out your own roles and responsibilities and to communicate these effectively to other members of the team. If you cannot explain your treatment plan and rationale in clear and simple language, then you probably need to check your own understanding with your supervisor.

Keep a Sense of Perspective of Your Own Importance in the Team

Having managed and collaborated with numerous CBT therapists and other clinicians over many years we are aware that one of the greatest challenges to MDW working is the personalities of the team members. This is of course unsurprising given that the 'workers' are first and foremost human beings. It is essential to be self-aware and consider certain elements of your own personality that being part of an MDT may activate. One example of a problematic personality trait is a tendency towards 'all-or-nothing' thinking. Given the growing evidence base for CBT efficacy, a therapist with this trait could easily fall into the trap of 'CBT right–other perspectives wrong' (and yes, we have encountered this rather a lot in practice ...). An overly dogmatic position is rarely productive in any discussion and if this is a tendency for you then you might need to actively practise humility, flexibility and diplomacy. The mainstay in mental health treatment is very much 'horses for courses'. Additionally, if you are the kind of individual who tends to minimise your own skill or expertise then you may need to strengthen your own appreciation of the importance of your contribution. Personality complications and professional attitude problems can be addressed and ultimately resolved through regular supervision.

Conclusion

It is almost certain that your client will be involved with other health-related professionals in some way. You are therefore not working alone with your client, and it is important to keep aware of this, particularly when encountering problems. It is very important to maintain professional contact and communication with the other professionals who share responsibility, even if you never physically meet together. Actively participating in MDW in a constructive fashion will make your work more effective and more rewarding.

Summary of Points

- Multidisciplinary work is an essential tool of coordinated care in health and Social Services.
- There are many different models for MDW.
- Each member of a multidisciplinary team will have an essential role, the importance of which will vary according to the case.
- Working well with other people requires courtesy and respect for differences while standing firmly by one's own professional principles.
- Skills in MDW are best acquired by experience and maximising the opportunity to learn from others.

This chapter has endeavoured to give some pointers towards effective and rewarding joint working in multidisciplinary contexts. Being a CBT therapist within a MD setting can be challenging. It is not something that can be generalised in traditional research because it is so dependent on the individual personalities involved; such literature as there is tends to be specific to particular settings.

References

Burns, T. (2004). *Community Mental Health Teams: A Guide to Current Practices*. Oxford: Oxford University Press.

Fernando, S. and Keating, F. (2008). *Mental Health in a Multi-Ethnic Society: A Multidisciplinary Handbook*. London: Routledge.

Greenberger, D. and Padesky, C.A. (1995). *Mind Over Mood: Change How You Feel by Changing the Way You Think*. New York: Guilford Press.

TWELVE Adapting CBT to a Broad Clientele

WINDY DRYDEN

Introduction

I will be discussing in this chapter how to adapt your approach to CBT when working with a range of different clients. The relevant issues will be considered and I will summarise my own views with regard to them. By summarising my position I do not wish to propose it as a model for good practice. Instead, it is intended to provide an illustration of one approach among many. The fundamental aim of this chapter is to explore a number of issues and allow you to reflect upon them.

'Bespoke therapy' was a term coined by Lazarus (1989) to identify an approach towards therapy based on the idea of 'tailoring'. The term 'bespoke' was used to focus on a customised approach to clinical work in contrast to a more fixed 'off-the-peg' style of therapy in which CBT is practised in an identical form, irrespective of who your client might be. In 'bespoke therapy', on the other hand, the approach is adjusted to fit the client and is developed out of an assessment of the particular variables in respect to your client. Later in this chapter I will examine a number of these variables.

Why Your Approach Should be Varied

In North American universities the first year 'Introduction to Psychology' courses (informally termed Psychology 101) usually commence by stating what appears to be obvious - that 'people are different!' If we apply this to CBT we can see clearly that all CBT approaches are based on the idea that clients are different. In fact, all CBT approaches encourage practitioners to treat each one of their clients as a unique individual. It therefore follows that as clients differ from each other and should be treated individually, you should respond as a therapist in a way that is most appropriate to each of your clients and that this should apply regardless of the particular form of CBT you practise.

What Should You Vary?

Assuming that you accept that you should give different responses to different clients as their therapist, regardless of what form of CBT you practise, what exactly will you be varying? In the following I will be responding to this question. As I have suggested above, my approach should be regarded as that of one CBT practitioner and I hope you will find your thinking stimulated in relation to your own practice on this issue.

I will be dealing with the following three major areas where customising your approach is important:

- customising CBT to fit your client's suitability for different therapeutic arenas;
- customising CBT to fit your client's stage of change on a problem;
- customising CBT to fit your client's relational style.

But first I will examine how the context in which you work may affect your CBT practice and I will begin by highlighting the fact that therapy does not occur in a vacuum.

How Your Work Context May Affect Your Clinical Decisions

Many therapists may consider that they have high levels of independence and initiative. They do, but only within the framework and limits of their work context. This is clearly the case if you work in a clinic practice where several constraints may well be placed on CBT service delivery.

Case Study 12.1

Alan works in the CBT-based voluntary sector. In the organisation in which he works, CBT is limited to eight sessions. Alan has to work within a strict set of exclusion criteria. The guidelines make it clear to whom he can and cannot offer CBT, but less clear for whom the service may be offered. Unfortunately, his is the only CBT-based service in the area. As a result, while on some occasions Alan offers eight-session CBT to clients with problems amenable to such short-term intervention, he often has to decide whether to offer this service to clients who need much longer intervention but who do not meet the exclusion criteria. Because he knows that if he turns away these clients, it is quite likely that they will receive no therapy of any kind, he offers them the service, which is a stance that affects his decisions regarding what they can usefully work on during the time they have together.

Even if you are in private practice, where to all intents and purposes you are self-employed, it probably means that constraints are set on your clinical decision-making when it comes to making any changes to your practice. In my case, although I work part-time in private practice, my office is not sufficiently large to allow me to run groups, so when a patient is referred to me whom I regard as most suited to a group therapy environment, I have to refer them to a CBT therapist who runs groups or to non-CBT group therapy, as I am not logistically able to run groups in my practice.

There is one further sense in which your work context may impinge on your work, and that is in relation to the process by which a client comes to see you in that setting. They may contact you and ask to be allocated specifically to you, but otherwise, if they have no preferences, how does a client get to see a particular CBT therapist? Some clients get assigned to a therapist according to the time both client and therapist have available for appointments; other clients may be allocated on the basis of what they have disclosed about themselves to a receptionist who decides on the allocation. To illustrate this, the following comes from a receptionist at the Albert Ellis Institute in New York:

'It should go without saying that when I do a telephone intake, I attempt to accommodate a potential client as best as I am able. If they request a specific therapist, time and/or day, fee or sex of therapist, I, naturally, comply with these wishes when possible.

'When a potential client who does not have specific requests calls, I generally begin by giving them my brief REBT and Institute monologue. I have found that this is not only a constructive introduction for them, but it is also an opportunity for me to solicit reactions which are often indicative of who they will best work with. It seems to me that productive therapy (like productive learning) is likely to occur when the parties involved like and understand one another. So, as we (humans) tend to like and understand those people who are similar to ourselves, I will often endeavour to place a potential client with a therapist who might give me similar reactions to the REBT monologue as the client does. I do not mean with respect to what they say, but how they say it, what sort of accent they have, what sort of questions they ask.

'On the other hand, there are times when a client calls up and immediately it is evident that there is a specific problem. For instance, they are obviously stressed out and angry, a good candidate for stress and low frustration tolerance management or they are particularly passive and thus, a good candidate for assertiveness training. In a case like this, I throw what I have advocated in the previous paragraph out of the window and try to steer them in the direction of a therapist who works specifically in the given area.

'When all else fails, and I feel that it would not be inappropriate, I ask for a specific issue with which the client needs to deal and then try to match them with a therapist who works in this area. Incidentally, I do have a list which details therapists' specialisms. However, I seldom have to resort to this for some clients will immediately "spill their guts" to me, while most I am able to place without having to pry. On the very rare occasion when a person is extremely hesitant to comment or is simply scared out of their minds, the priority becomes getting them here, at least once, to see anybody.

'Of course, I wish that all telephone intakes ran as smoothly as I make them out on paper. However, these are the basic guidelines that I use for myself and so far, most intakes work out pretty well.'

Which Therapeutic Environments Best Suit Clients in CBT Therapy?

Now that a client has been referred to a CBT therapist, the best therapeutic environment for the therapy has to be decided. A therapeutic environment or arena is the interpersonal context in which therapy can ensue. The most common are: individual, couple, family and group. Ignoring the empirical issue concerning the effectiveness of different arenas for different client problems as it is too complicated to consider here, I would like to focus, in this section, on a number of criteria you may want to bear in mind when recommending a specific arena to a specific client.

I will start by providing the relevant criteria recommended by Albert Ellis, one of the originators of CBT:

> In regard to your question about placing people in individual, marital, family, or group therapy, I usually let them select the form of therapy they personally want to begin with. If one tries to push clients into a form of therapy they do not want or are afraid of, this frequently will not work out. So I generally start them where they want to start. If they begin in individual therapy and they are the kind of individuals who I think would benefit from group, I recommend this either quickly after we begin or sometime later. People who benefit most from group are generally those who are shy, retiring, and afraid to take risks. And if I can induce them to go into a group, they will likely benefit more from that than the less risky situation of individual therapy. On the other hand, a few people who want to start with group but who seem to be too disorganised or too disruptive, are recommended for individual sessions until they become sufficiently organised to benefit from a group.
>
> Most people who come for marital or family therapy actually come alone and I frequently have a few sessions with them and then strongly recommend their mates also be included. On the other hand, some people who come together are not able to benefit from joint sessions, since they mainly argue during these sessions and we get nowhere. Therefore sometimes I recommend that they have individual sessions in addition to or instead of the conjoint sessions. There are many factors, some of them unique, which would induce me to recommend that people have individual rather than joint sessions. For example, one of the partners in a marriage may seem to be having an affair on the side and will not be able to talk about this in conjoint sessions and therefore I would try to see this partner individually. Or one of the partners may very much want to continue with the marriage while the other very much wants to stop it. Again, I would then recommend they be seen individually. I usually try to see the people I see in conjoint sessions at least for one or a few individual sessions to discover if there are things they will say during the individual sessions that they would refuse to bring out during the conjoint sessions.
>
> On the whole, however, I am usually able to go along with the basic desire of any clients who want individual, marital, family or group psychotherapy. It is only in relatively few cases that I talk them into taking a form of therapy they are at first loathe to try. (Ellis, personal communication)

As this chapter chiefly concerns individual CBT, I will now provide a set of indications and contraindications for this particular arena. Before doing so, I would like to emphasise the fact that these decisions once made are not set in stone and may be changed during the course of CBT.

Nine Indications for Individual CBT

I will outline in this section indications for working with clients in the arena of individual CBT.

1 By its very nature, individual CBT offers clients more confidentiality than other therapeutic arenas. It is therefore preferable when clients need to reveal things about themselves in privacy without being anxious that others may use this information to their detriment. Some clients worry how other people might react to such disclosures – which might occur for instance in group counselling – and this kind of fear may prevent them from participating productively. Similarly, clients who would otherwise not reveal 'secrets' will find individual CBT the most appropriate therapy. However, as in other situations, transferring to other types of therapy, such as group or family therapy, may be more suitable later when these clients are more able and/or prepared to reveal themselves to others.

2 Because of its one-to-one nature, individual CBT affords an opportunity for a closer relationship to develop between therapist and client than may otherwise exist when other clients are present. This may be especially important for those clients who have not developed close relationships in their lives and who may initially find group therapy, for instance, too threatening.

3 One-to-one CBT can be performed in tandem with the client's pace of learning. It works particularly well therefore with those clients who, because of their present mental state or learning speed, need the full undivided attention of their therapist. This is particularly vital with clients who may be confused and might be distracted by the complex interactions that can sometimes occur in other therapeutic environments.

4 Similarly, if clients are feeling despairing and suicidal, they may benefit more from individual therapy by having the therapist's full attention: such sessions can allow the therapist to focus interventions more dynamically upon helping the client to emerge from suicidal crisis. It should be noted, however, that therapists are responsible for protecting the welfare of suicidal clients who may be at risk of self-harm. In some situations this responsibility may preclude individual outpatient CBT, such as when recommending psychiatric hospitalisation seems advisable.

5 Individual CBT is required when the major problems clients face concern their relationship with themselves rather than with others.

6 Individual CBT may be required for clients who wish for individual therapy separate from others; for instance, those who have decided to leave a relationship and wish to deal with the individual problems that ensue. In this case, however, some sessions in tandem with the partner may also be useful, particularly if it concerns conciliation (Gurman et al., 1986).

7 It can be useful for CBT therapists to vary their style of therapy with clients and thus minimise the risk of perpetuating the client's problems by responding in such a way that an inappropriate interactive

style ensues. Individual CBT offers therapists an opportunity to vary their interactive styles with clients without having to worry that such variation may have an adverse effect on other clients who may be present.

8 Individual CBT is particularly useful with clients who have deep problems regarding sharing therapeutic time with other clients.
9 Individual CBT may also be necessary for negative reasons. Clients may participate in individual CBT who may not benefit from having therapy in other arenas. Thus, clients who may monopolise a CBT therapy group or be too withdrawn within it to benefit from the therapy, or who are considered too vulnerable to benefit from family counselling, are often seen individually in CBT.

Four Contraindications for Individual CBT

In this section I outline contraindications for working with clients in individual CBT.

1 Clients who are likely to become overly dependent on the therapist, particularly when such a dependency becomes so intense that it leads to client deterioration, should not be given individual therapy. These clients may be more appropriately helped in group CBT where this kind of intense dependency is less likely to develop because the therapist has to relate to several other people.
2 Because individual CBT can be a close interpersonal encounter for the client, it is less likely to be indicated for clients who may find such a degree of intimacy, or the prospect of such intimacy, unduly threatening.
3 Individual CBT may not be considered appropriate for clients who find it too comfortable. Based on the assumption that personal change is often best effected in situations where there is a high level of stimulus, individual CBT may not challenge these clients sufficiently. In addition, Ravid (1969) noted that it may not be productive to offer individual therapy to clients who have already had a lot of previous individual therapy but who still require further therapeutic help.
4 Individual CBT may not be appropriate for clients for whom other types of therapy might be considered more beneficial. For instance, clients who are particularly withdrawn, shy and reluctant to take risks are more prone to benefit from group CBT (if they can be persuaded to participate) than from the less risky situation of individual CBT. Furthermore, partners who can use the conjoint situation of CBT couples therapy productively often benefit more from this

arena than from individual CBT. This is especially the case when they have, to a major extent, conquered their disturbed feelings about their unproductive relationship and are dealing with issues relating to enhancing relationship satisfaction, which would particularly require their joint participation.

Tailoring CBT to Fit the 'Stages of Change' Model

Jim Prochaska and Carlo DiClemente made a highly significant contribution to substance abuse therapy a number of years ago (e.g. Prochaska & DiClemente, 1983) by arguing that people with substance abuse problems differ in relation to their 'stage of change' and any interventions should be tailored with this in mind. Before I describe the stages of change and show how I employ them to tailor interventions in a bespoke way with my clients, I would like to make the following general points.

Different Interventions for Different Stages

The stages of change model chiefly indicates that you need to use different interventions with your clients depending on their stage of change. I discuss in the following how I use this principle in action. Clients may resist change because their CBT therapists are using interventions which are inappropriate for their stage of change, although appropriate for a different stage of change. CBT therapists may then make the mistake of assuming that their clients are either in a more advanced stage or less advanced stage than is actually the case.

Different Stages for Different Problems

When clients come to CBT for help with more than one problem, it is important to understand that they may be in different stages of change for different problems (see Chapter 15). From this it should be appreciated that a client is only in a certain stage of change for a specific problem, not for all of her problems.

The Stages of Change

There are a number of versions of the 'stages of change' model. Here, I will present the one that informs my thinking and will show how it helps me to tailor my approach to different clients.

The Pre-contemplation Stage of Change

If your client is in the 'pre-contemplation' stage of change, she is denying that she has a problem. The person may have been told or even ordered to come for CBT; or alternatively a referring agent - who has not taken time to explore whether the person actually wants CBT - may have sent her for help. From a technical point of view, this person would not be regarded as a client until she has given informed consent to proceed with CBT (see Chapter 22).

It is important with such clients not to have a judgmental view but to help them understand why they have attended the session and why other people consider they require CBT. While some types of CBT are essentially more persuasive than others, it is important to adopt a non-persuasive approach in helping the client in this stage of change to become involved in a discussion on why other people consider she requires help. In this context, motivational interviewing strategies can be helpful. These are strategies based on the 'spirit of motivational interviewing', as Rollnick and Miller (1995) called them. Such a spirit is characterised by the following ideas:

- 'Motivation to change is elicited from the client, and not imposed from without ...
- 'It is the client's task, not the therapist's, to articulate and resolve his or her ambivalence ...
- 'The therapeutic style is generally a quiet and eliciting one ...
- 'The therapist is directive in helping the client to examine and resolve ambivalence ...
- 'The therapist respects the client's autonomy and freedom of choice (and consequences) regarding his or her own behaviour.'

(Rollnick & Miller, 1995: 325)

As a consequence of this form of enquiry, the person may reach the decision that she does not have any kind of problem for which CBT could help her, or she may realise that she does have a problem and may start to think about whether or not she is prepared to address this issue. In the latter case, she has entered a stage of change which is called contemplation.

The Contemplation Stage of Change

Clients in the contemplation stage of change start to realise that they have a problem, but they are in two minds about making any kind of change. In such cases, it is important for the therapist to accept this ambivalence and to encourage the client to accept it likewise as an overture to exploring the costs and benefits of the existing problem and any goals the client might be considering.

Most of my interventions at this stage are governed by cost-benefit analysis where I encourage the client to reflect on their situation in terms of a 2 × 2 × 2 matrix (see Figure 12.1) and to think about the costs and benefits of the problem and the goal, both to themselves and to relevant others, from (a) a short-term perspective and (b) a long-term perspective.

I generally invite clients either to assess these factors in a structured way (with written sheets) or in a less structured manner through dialogue but in such a way that their assessment is still being viewed against the matrix. Unless there is a good reason not to, I usually accept their preferences.

The Preparation Stage of Change

When clients have reached the preparation stage of change, they have decided to change and are making plans to do so. At this stage I will explain the CBT model of change and the tasks that both the client and I will need to undertake during the necessary CBT therapy towards fulfilling her goals (Dryden, 2001, 2006). If the client indicates that she has a basic understanding of the CBT model and wishes to proceed on this basis, she may be considered to have given her informed consent to undertake the action stage of change.

Benefits				Costs			
Short-Term		Long-Term		Short-Term		Long-Term	
Self	Others	Self	Others	Self	Others	Self	Others

Figure 12.1 Cost-benefit analysis grid

The Action Stage of Change

It is only when a client has reached the action stage of change that I begin what is most commonly understood as CBT therapy. It is at this point that I help the client to understand, question and change the dysfunctional attitudes and schemas underlying her problem. I can now assist her not only to formulate alternative functional schemas that will allow her to achieve her goals but also to undertake a variety of thinking, behavioural and emotive assignments to strengthen her conviction in these functional schemas. The way in which I do this will depend on other factors (as discussed below), but this is the stage of change at which this is to be done.

The Maintenance Stage of Change

Having reached the maintenance stage of change the client has achieved her goal or has made considerable progress towards it and is ready to consider how to maintain this change. At this point I help her identify vulnerability factors in order that she can deal with them; ideally, this will prevent lapses in progress (it would perhaps be best to regard these as hiccups in the process of change). I also help her manage the lapses that are bound to occur. I do this by encouraging her to accept herself for lapsing and from this to identify the factors which led to her lapse. By doing this, I will help her plan how to deal with these factors more effectively.

The Relapse Stage of Change

A relapse is different from a lapse because it involves clients returning fully to older pre-CBT disturbed patterns of response. It tends to happen when a client has either ignored a series of lapses or not learned sufficiently from them. I consider my main tasks at this stage to be as follows:

- to encourage clients to accept themselves for relapsing;
- to respond to them therapeutically in such a way as to respect their *current* stage of change;
- to help them understand and learn from those factors that led to their relapse;
- to encourage them to work actively in the maintenance stage of change when they are in that stage.

Tailoring CBT to Fit Clients' Relational Styles and Interpersonal Preferences

If you were going to meet your MP for the first time it is most unlikely that your behaviour towards them would be the same as with your friends at the pub. We vary the way in which we relate to people depending on whom we are relating to and the context framing our interactions. Lazarus (1989) advises CBT therapists to vary their style of relating with different clients according to those particular clients' style of relating. This, he suggests, should be done in a genuine way and he comments that effective CBT therapists in this sense can be regarded as 'authentic chameleons'. In applying this concept to my own CBT work, I will now briefly discuss how I tailor my relational style to match three aspects of client relational functioning:

1 formal/informal relational style;
2 influence preferences;
3 degree of reactance and dependence.

Formality/Informality in Relational Style

CBT may be practised in different styles. To demonstrate these style variations, I have chosen the relational style of formality and informality.

- With clients who tend to be informal in their style of relating, I prefer to adopt an informal style of practising CBT. This may involve, for instance, the use of humour and even self-disclosure in my interventions.
- With clients who are formal in their style of relating, I prefer to emphasise a formal style of practising CBT. In this case I would use more formal language, be more businesslike and ensure that humour and self-disclosure are kept to a minimum.

Varying the Foundation of My Influence

Some theorists (e.g. Dorn, 1984) regard CBT as a process of influence. From this point of view, the effectiveness of a therapist can largely be ascribed to the degree of benign influence they have on their clients. As to the issue of whom they might be most influenced by, different clients have different interpersonal preferences:

- Some clients are more influenced by me if I emphasise my expertise and will then listen, interact and be influenced by me. In such cases, I emphasise my qualifications, refer to my books and articles, and draw on my long, varied career in the field.
- Other clients, on the other hand, are completely unimpressed by my expertise and qualifications but if they like me, they are more likely to listen to, interact with and be influenced by me. With such clients, I emphasise my more likeable qualities, varying these like a good 'authentic chameleon' according to those qualities my clients find likeable.

Varying How I Relate to Clients According to Degrees of Reactance and Dependence

Relating style and response to attempts to influence the client is brought into a single focus if we consider a client's degree of reactance and degree of dependence. I will begin by dealing with clients who are highly reactant.

Highly Reactant Clients

When a client is high in reactance, she (in this case) will tend to regard others' attempts to influence her as being attempts to control her or curb her freedom (see Beutler, 1983). She will respond to this by asserting her freedom in ways that demonstrate to herself and the others that she is free and cannot be controlled. As I practise an active-directive therapy (i.e. CBT), I am careful to avoid anything that highly reactant clients might view as a threat to their freedom. I will do so in the following ways:

- I will be as specific as possible about what I am aiming to do in CBT and to seek their permission in so doing;
- I will emphasise the idea that they may choose to believe whatever they wish to believe;
- I will refer to therapy as being self-therapy and describe myself as being a consultant in that process.

Once the client herself can see that negative thoughts and dysfunctional schemas underlie her problems and that realistic thoughts and functional schemas are healthy alternatives which will lead to her stated goals, they will work towards changing her negative thoughts and dysfunctional schemas, provided she is confident that she has reached her own conclusions independently and that her decision to pursue such realistic thoughts and functional schemas has not been influenced by me.

Highly Dependent Clients

Generally, conducting therapy with low-reactance clients does not tend to be problematic unless they are highly dependent. These clients are likely to want their CBT therapists to do their work for them and to agree with everything that their therapist says. In the beginning, it might appear gratifying to work with highly dependent clients - who are often complimentary - but it may well soon become obvious that they are not actually changing and that their true goal is to maintain the therapeutic relationship in order that they can depend on their CBT therapist for ongoing emotional support and decision-making. In customising CBT to such clients, I tend to do the following:

- If the question they put to me is one they can easily answer themselves, I encourage them to do so.
- I refuse to accept 'I don't know' for an answer, particularly when delivered as a knee-jerk response. Dependent clients, by instantly saying 'I don't know', stop themselves from thinking for themselves and by so doing, they are relying on their CBT therapists to think for them.
- I will help them identify, challenge and act against the underlying schemas that govern their dependency (for instance: 'I'm not strong enough to take care of myself'; 'It is easier to ask others to sort out my problems than for me to sort them out myself'). Since dependent clients are well known to be poor at completing homework assignments (or if they do complete them, they do it to please their CBT therapists), I spend considerable time working with them to commit themselves to carrying out these assignments and whenever they don't do them I will challenge them about this, unless their reasons for not completing the task are quite reasonable. My approach to CBT approach with such clients is based on the assumption that they are quite capable of taking the initiative to look after and help themselves.

How to Decide What to Vary

If you agree to the idea that it is important to vary your CBT approach with different clients, you may well have asked yourself how to decide what to vary. My own position is to follow George Kelly's famous principle: 'If you want to know anything, ask the client, he might just tell you.' The following are a few of the questions I ask clients to help me determine how best to customise my CBT approach with them in the areas discussed in this book.

General Questions

- What have you found helpful in past therapeutic relationships - and why?
- What things could I do that would be particularly helpful to you - and why?
- Tell me about people in your past who have been helpful to you. What did they do that was particularly helpful to you?

Arena Question

- Which therapeutic arena (individual, group, couple or family CBT) would be most helpful to you - and why?

Stages of Change Questions

- Who suggested that you come for CBT and why? If it was someone else's idea, what do you think of that idea?
- To what extent are you clear about which problems you need to tackle in CBT?
- How ready are you to address your problems?
- What reservations, if any, do you have about coming for CBT?

Relational-Style Questions

- Would you prefer it if I was relatively formal or informal in my interactions with you - and why?
- Would it help you or not if I told you things about my life experience that were relevant to your problems and how best to deal with them - and why?

- Do you think CBT therapists should show a sense of humour in CBT sessions or not - and why?
- How do you react when you feel that others are trying to influence you, even when you can see that they have your interests at heart?
- Would you rather someone else solved your problems for you or would you rather help yourself - and why?

Referral

I hope this has helped you see the value of varying your CBT approach with different clients. But supposing you decide that no matter how much you vary it you are just not the right person to help a client? I would like to end this chapter by discussing a subject that is seldom examined in the CBT literature, which is referral.

Both trained and trainee CBT therapists frequently find themselves pressured into seeing a client, even if for different reasons. If you are a trained therapist with a practice then your livelihood may be at risk if you keep referring clients to other CBT therapists. As a trainee therapist, you may be required to put in a certain number of CBT hours and this kind of pressure means that for every client you refer to someone else, you will be losing precious CBT hours needed to fulfil course requirements.

Now that I have made this point, it is still important for you to remember that your primary concern is to ensure that your client receives the best help available. If you decide that you are not the right person for your client, no matter which elements you vary, then you are required to refer the person to another practitioner who can better offer bespoke therapy, or, to put it another way:

'You may be a great tailor for most clients, but for other clients sometimes other tailors may make a better suit!'

To illustrate this, many years ago when I worked in Birmingham, a man rang me and asked if I practised an approach to therapy known as RT. The therapy I practise, which is known as Rational Emotive Behaviour Therapy (REBT), was originally called Rational Therapy (RT) and I decided that this man must be referring to REBT, though in its earliest form. On that assumption, I agreed to see him. After I had outlined the basics of REBT, he gave me a puzzled look and then said that he hadn't heard such intellectualised twaddle in a long while.

As it turned out, what he was actually seeking was Reichian Therapy (RT), a body-work oriented therapy which is completely different from REBT! Never forget that not all clients want or will benefit from CBT.

Reflection Points

- If you object to the idea that you should vary your CBT approach with different clients, what are your precise objections to or reservations about this idea?
- If you are in favour of this idea, how do you currently vary your approach?
- What inclusion and exclusion criteria do *you* use for seeing clients in individual CBT?
- How do you vary your relational style with different clients and what leads to your decision to make such variations?
- How do you vary your CBT approach to work effectively with clients in different stages of change?

References

Beutler, L.E. (1983). *Eclectic Psychotherapy: A Systematic Approach*. New York: Pergamon.

Dorn, F.J. (ed.) (1984). *The Social Influence Process in Counseling and Psychotherapy*. Springfield, IL: Charles C. Thomas.

Dryden, W. (2001). *Reason to Change: A Rational Emotive Behaviour Therapy (CBT) Workbook*. Hove, East Sussex: Brunner-Routledge.

Dryden, W. (2006). *Getting Started with CBT: A Concise Guide for Clients*. Hove, East Sussex: Routledge.

Gurman, A.S., Kniskern, D.P. and Pinsof, W.M. (1986). 'Research on the process and outcome of marital and family therapy', in S.L. Garfield and A.E. Bergin (eds), *Handbook of Psychotherapy and Behavior Change*, 3rd edn. New York: John Wiley & Sons, Inc.

Lazarus, A.A. (1989). *The Practice of Multimodal Therapy*. Baltimore, MD: Johns Hopkins University Press.

Prochaska, J.O. and DiClemente, C.C. (1983). 'Stages and processes of self-change of smoking: Toward an integrative model of change', *Journal of Consulting and Clinical Psychology*, 51: 390–5.

Ravid, R. (1969). 'Effect of group therapy on long-term individual therapy', *Dissertation Abstracts International*, 30: 2427B.

Rollnick S. and Miller, W.R. (1995). 'What is motivational interviewing?', *Behavioural and Cognitive Psychotherapy*, 23: 325–34.

PART THREE

CBT: Common Challenges

THIRTEEN Challenges in the CBT Client–Therapist Relationship

RHENA BRANCH

The Cognitive Behaviour Therapy (CBT) position on the therapeutic alliance (including classical Rogerian components as well as Bordin's tasks, bonds and goals) is comprehensively covered in Chapter 5 of this book. Therefore this chapter will focus primarily on challenges within CBT practice to creating a working alliance. Therapist factors contributing to alliance ruptures and preventative/repair strategies will be introduced. There are, of course, a myriad of client factors that also impact on the successful development of a working alliance within CBT. However, due to the brevity of this chapter only therapist factors are considered here.

The therapeutic alliance is a large and important subject in any psychotherapeutic orientation and no less so in CBT, despite popular misconception. There are several cogent texts written on the subject for the interested reader to investigate (Gilbert & Leahy, 2007; Safran & Muran, 2000; Safran & Segal, 1996). Increasingly, more attention is being given to the therapeutic relationship in CBT literature and on training courses. This is an invaluable addition since CBT is an *active-directive, collaborative* treatment approach. It may not be essential to prize each and every client - nor for all clients to feel exceedingly warm towards the CBT therapist. However, since CBT treatment involves much 'two-way traffic', a solid working relationship is likely to facilitate client compliance and hence treatment efficacy. After all, the chances of getting a client to do something uncomfortable are surely increased if they generally think well of you and trust that you are acting in their best interest.

Laying Solid Alliance Foundations

Throughout a course of CBT treatment it is likely that some form of relationship fracture will occur - though they will vary greatly in terms of severity. Rather than alliance problems equalling treatment failure, research has indicated that alliance ratings going from high to low, then back to high (following active resolution) correlated with good outcomes (Kivlighan & Shaughnessy, 2000; Stiles et al., 2004).

This suggests that the effectiveness of treatment need not be impeded, providing relationship fractures are promptly addressed and repaired. A skilled therapist and a willing client can potentially repair even the most serious of alliance ruptures. However, most alliance ructions are relatively minor and often spontaneously resolve without need for direct discussion. Moreover, although ruptures can be mended and need not irrevocably damage overall treatment, they are not an essential part of treatment either. Ideally the alliance will be soundly established early on and fractures successfully avoided throughout the course of treatment. The following general points outline a few ways in which CBT therapists may expedite alliance formation and minimise the risk of ruptures in early treatment:

- being professionally reliable and upholding boundaries i.e. good timekeeping, providing reassurance regarding confidentiality;
- eliciting client expectations from CBT during the first session and dealing with any doubts, misconceptions or confusion;
- being open to client questions;
- adapting interaction style to suit the client while remaining genuine, i.e. using colloquial or formal language appropriately, using humour and irreverence with suitable clients;
- admitting confusion readily and asking for client clarification;
- taking legitimate responsibility for 'getting things wrong', i.e. forgetting details, explaining concepts incorrectly or poorly, misrepresenting something the client has related etc.;

- allowing the client space and time to acclimatise to being in treatment;
- looking like a professional, i.e. dressing to suit the setting in which you are practising.

These points, and perhaps the last in particular, lead into a further consideration regarding alliance issues. The CBT therapeutic alliance is in essence a *professional working relationship;* it is commonplace rather than magical – functional rather than curative. Ultimately the patient/client is paying the CBT therapist to perform a specific 'job'. While the therapeutic alliance is undoubtedly a powerful, perhaps even pivotal, treatment component, it bears remembering that this is at base level a service user–service provider interchange. Hence, first impressions do count when it comes to laying down the bedrock for a sound working alliance. In order to inspire confidence in your clients you need to be perceived rapidly as credible, interested and approachable. These three components can be broken down as such:

Credible – conveying that you know what you are doing in *general*, i.e. sound theoretical base, clinical experience, knowledge of the client's presenting problem, confidence in your abilities.

Interested – conveying that you *specifically* understand the individual client you are treating, i.e. attention to symptoms, empathy with the negative impact of the problem on your client's life, asking pertinent questions and attending to responses, creating an accurate problem formulation.

Approachable – conveying that you are professional, nonjudgmental and *accepting*, i.e. registering neither undue shock nor horror at client information, openly answering questions (when appropriate), adapting to your client's style of interaction, being respectful, yet direct, when asking potentially uncomfortable or embarrassing questions.

Therapist Beliefs and the Alliance

As CBT therapists we spend a lot of time unearthing the dysfunctional core attitudes that cause our clients to perpetuate their disturbance. More rarely, perhaps, do we scrutinise our own with respect to building therapeutic relationships. Therapists of all experience levels may hold problematic beliefs or 'demands' that can potentially rupture the alliance and/or prevent timely and effective repair of ruptures. Such beliefs often include the following:

- 'My client must not question my qualifications, level of experience or knowledge of his problem/disorder.'
- 'My client must not find fault with my methods nor expose gaps in my skills.'

- 'My client must be compliant. (He must agree with my problem formulation, homework ideas and CBT principles in general.)'
- 'My client must respond positively to my suggestions at all times.'
- 'My client must like me.'
- 'My client must get better under my care.'
- 'My client must be deferential to my superior knowledge of psychology and psychotherapeutic interventions.'
- 'My client must feel comfortable at all times.'
- 'My client must not confront me on the basis of my humanity/human fallibility' (i.e. 'He must not question me on a personal level about whether or not I employ the strategies I recommend').
- 'I must be able to "figure out" my client quickly and easily.'
- 'I must like my client in order to help him.'
- 'I must impress my client (and/or the referrer who sent him to me).'
- 'I must not upset or offend my client.'
- 'I must feel comfortable with my client at all times.'
- 'I must see evidence that my client is improving quickly.'
- 'I must not make errors with regard to conceptualisation or intervention.'

Although the above list may appear rather extensive, other therapist beliefs not mentioned here can equally cause alliance problems. Be honest with yourself about your own rigid thinking when wrestling with therapeutic impasse and relationship problems.

Reflection Points

Despite being trained CBT therapists, our own rigid and irrational thinking can cause fractures within an existing therapeutic alliance or impede its initial development. Take a second look at the previous list and take note of any beliefs that resonate with you. Ask yourself these questions:

- Do I 'bump up against' any of the listed beliefs when striving to establish a working relationship with my clients?
- Do I hold other specific beliefs or demands that may pose obstacles to forming or maintaining a working alliance with my clients?
- Do I accept myself as a competent CBT therapist even while recognising my own rigid thinking?
- Am I prepared to challenge my own faulty thinking in the interest of best serving my clients and developing as a CBT therapist?
- Am I prepared to share my reflections about the previous points with my clinical supervisor?

Common Challenges to Establishing/ Safeguarding the Therapeutic Alliance

There are many types of mistakes therapists can make, which ultimately may impact negatively on the alliance (Leahy, 2003; Gilbert & Leahy, 2007). Most can be addressed through further training, experience, adequate supervision and reflective practice.

Some of the more common pitfalls are outlined briefly below:

Inadequate Socialisation to the Model

Some clients will have basic knowledge of CBT before arriving at your office; others will have none at all. It is important to ask about previous therapy including what was useful (and what was not) in the client's opinion. Preparing clients for the active-directive nature of CBT is essential; a client who expects a more person-centred style may be shocked or put off otherwise. It is worth clarifying client expectations of therapy straight away to eliminate any confusion or potential of working at cross-purposes. Clients new to CBT need proper introduction to the role of homework in treatment as well.

Lack of Skill and/or Experience

The only remedy for lack of experience is continued practice. Skill deficits can be remedied via competent supervision, autodidacticism, specialist training and continued professional development. Despite your best efforts to self-educate and seek supervision, some clients will doubt your ability to treat them effectively. In such cases the alliance will generally fail to take root and/or thrive; typically you will lose the client. Though losing a client can be discouraging and perhaps lead to self-doubt, you can also choose to view it as part of a learning curve and as a natural stage in your professional development. Provided you are willing and able to accept yourself as a therapist in the nascence of your career, there need be no shame attached to alliance ruptures arising from want of skill and experience. The crucial point is to be self-accepting and resist ego-defensive behaviour. The two case vignettes included in this chapter exemplify this point further.

Poor Collaboration

Although CBT is a collaborative process, the ratio of therapist to client input will change as treatment progresses. For example the ratio may be 90–10 in favour of the therapist during the first few sessions, 70–30 in middle sessions and 60–40 in pre-termination sessions. Pitching the collaboration ration correctly contributes to building and maintaining the alliance. Expecting too much input from your clients too early on may leave them feeling overwhelmed and unsupported. Alternatively, being overly directive may threaten client autonomy and possibly impede CBT skills acquisition. It is important to recognise how much input you can realistically expect from each individual client, some inevitably will be more able to take responsibility for establishing goals, devising homework and transferring learning from problem to problem (and so on) than others.

Insufficient Assessment/Inaccurate Assessment

Because CBT is often billed as a treatment with a 'here-and-now' emphasis, trainees and novices may unwittingly neglect important historical information during assessment. Although it is true that CBT uses past experiences to better understand how psychological problems are perpetuated and reinforced in the present, early childhood/adulthood events merit significant attention. Failure to adequately enquire about (or view seriously) historical client factors such as parental relationships, schooling issues, past traumas and so on may convey to your client that you are not interested in them as a whole person. Without thorough investigation into relevant factors from your client's past you will also find it difficult to build a complete conceptualisation. Inception of personal core schemata typically takes place during early developmental years or adolescence. For example, a client who was bullied throughout primary school may understandably continue to harbour dysfunctional beliefs about rejection.

Inaccurate assessment may also pose an alliance rupture risk. Your clients will expect you to *correctly* understand them and the nature of their difficulties. Should you decide unilaterally that your assessment is correct, without seeking client verification, you run the risk of both getting it wrong and damaging the burgeoning therapeutic relationship. Offering your hypotheses to your client during assessment for them to either concur with or amend, introduces the collaborative nature of

CBT. The spirit of working together also ideally engenders a mutual respect. You, as therapist, are a CBT expert – yet you recognise that your client is the expert on *himself*.

Arrogance/Ego-Defensiveness

Beliefs such as those listed earlier on in this chapter account for much of the arrogance and ego-defensiveness occasionally displayed by CBT therapists. Therapist 'narcissism', as it is sometimes called, is perhaps one of the most common and pernicious tripwires to establishing and safeguarding the therapeutic alliance. This is by no means a hazard only to the newly qualified; in fact seasoned practitioners may be more likely to fall prey to ego-sensitivity and react defensively to client resistance or challenges. The best possible solutions to ego-protective arrogance on the part of the CBT therapist are searching self-reflection and accompanying supervision. In some cases a course of personal therapy to address irrational beliefs about 'needing to be seen as right at all times by your client' for example, may also be constructive remedial action. The second case vignette included in this chapter neatly illustrates the *opposite* of therapist arrogance in response to a challenging client.

Forcing the Relationship (Trying Too Hard)

The therapeutic alliance, as discussed in Chapter 5, is a desirable and important aspect of overall CBT treatment. It requires a degree of deliberate effort on the part of the CBT therapist to establish; however, there is an element of organic development to consider also. As with any professional relationship (or nonprofessional one for that matter), mutual understanding and trust tends to deepen over time. CBT is somewhat unique in its position on the therapeutic alliance (again refer to Chapter 5 for more in-depth information on the alliance itself), as it is not considered the sole or most significant mediator of change. Therefore the CBT therapist can 'afford' to lay the foundations for a sound working alliance and then give it space and time to grow. Trying *too hard* to engender a 'shoulder-to-shoulder' relationship with your client in the first few sessions can have a paradoxical effect. You may inadvertently scare the client off by pushing for a premature level of intimacy and familiarity, or simply appear insincere. Students and supervisees are often advised that earnestly engaging with your client in the first few sessions, with a view to understanding their problems and planning treatment, is perhaps the best first step in building a working alliance.

Failing to Take Environmental Factors into Account

Your clients exist outside of the consulting room just as we therapists do. Failing to adequately enquire about and include environmental factors in your overall conceptualisation can limit your understanding of your client and thereby destabilise the alliance. Environmental conditions can include financial stress, job security and satisfaction, relationships with significant others, sexuality, physical health, living conditions and general lifestyle.

Poorly Timed Interventions/Poorly Executed Interventions

Almost every CBT therapist will time an intervention badly and/or execute an intervention incorrectly *at least once* during his career. Chances are that this will happen during training or soon thereafter although practitioners at any level of experience can make such mistakes. Challenging a client's dysfunctional belief too early on and without sufficient preparation is perhaps a more commonly mistimed intervention. Instead of helping the client to see for himself the faulty nature of his thinking through Socratic questioning and dispute, the client perceives personal criticism or even attack. Needless to say, the alliance takes a hefty knock in such an instance. Other examples of bad timing may include between-session assignments that the client lacks the skills to execute, e.g. asking a client to complete a cost-benefit analysis (CBA form) or daily thought record (DTR) without sufficient preliminary guidance. Clients may perceive lack of therapist support or experience a crisis of confidence when faced with tasks they do not understand adequately nor possess the skills to complete. While employing a given intervention prematurely can undermine client confidence and create confusion, leaving an intervention too late may lead the client to conclude progress is at halt or, in fact, in retrograde. Again, good supervision combined with self-reflection should bring problems regarding the proper timing and execution of interventions to the CBT therapist's attention. It is incumbent upon the therapist to own up to mistakes regarding the timing of interventions and plainly 'doing them incorrectly'. The majority of clients will respond well to an explanation and appropriate apology from a well-meaning therapist, and thus the alliance can be salvaged.

Failing to Recognise Client Limitations (Pushing the Client Too Hard or Too Far)

It can be frustrating when your client is unable or unwilling to make the changes that you as a mental health professional truly believe are in his best interest. The temptation may be to force your client to go the extra mile; however, this can be counterproductive. At best your client may close down and refuse – or at worst he may suddenly leave treatment. Either way, being too rigid about your own goals for your client does the alliance no favours. Ultimately it is up to the client to what degree he wishes to overcome his difficulties and though you can point out the potential benefits of pushing through discomfort, you need to accept your client's decision on the matter.

Insufficiently Focused and Specific Treatment

A shared understanding of realistic therapeutic goals is the best measure for keeping treatment focused from session to session. Therapeutic goals are typically agreed upon in early sessions but also merit regular ongoing review. Goals inform the types of between-session tasks devised and ideally foster client motivation for change. Since goals are specifically tailored to address your client's individual emotional problems and/or diagnosed disorders, keeping them at the forefront of your mind prevents treatment from becoming nebulous and vague. Considering that the majority of clients do want to see a return on their therapeutic dollar, therapist specificity coupled with evidence of progress reliably promotes a sound working relationship. The alliance can wane when the client perceives treatment is adrift and that no one is at the helm of the ship. Despite CBT being a collaborative therapy, it is the therapist's duty to keep sessions focused and goal-directed.

Sticking Rigidly to an Unproductive Intervention

Failing to notice that an intervention is falling flat and persisting with it session after session can shake your client's faith in treatment.

There are many possible reasons for a given intervention failing to work, for example: the client may not be ready or willing to embrace it at this stage; it may not be quite the right tool for the job; you may be lacking the knowledge and skill needed to explain it properly. There is little point in continuing to flog a dead horse. Using creative thinking and being flexible about adapting interventions is a way out of this cul-de-sac. With supervisory guidance and self-directed learning, there is no reason to fear deviating somewhat from treatment protocol.

Being Overly Wedded to Therapeutic Orientation

Although CBT may be the only form of therapy in which you are qualified, it can sometimes be advantageous to adopt techniques more usually associated with other orientations, such as the 'empty chair' Gestalt technique or more ubiquitous ones like progressive relaxation (PR). CBT practitioners are perhaps more likely to borrow interventions from neighbouring cognitive therapies such as mindfulness based CBT, acceptance and commitment therapy (ACT), Rational-Emotive Behaviour Therapy (REBT) or dialectic behaviour therapy (DBT) – to list but four possibilities.

Theoretically consistent eclecticism means adhering to the core principles underpinning CBT while freely using whichever interventions are most likely to be helpful to your client. Sticking too rigidly to conventional CBT techniques may deprive your client of valuable learning and limit your own skills base. While it is advisable to work with 'what you know best', in the interest of the alliance it is equally valid to explore other interventions that may benefit and appeal to your client. Regular supervision generally safeguards hygienic CBT practice and can help ensure that you are employing alternative techniques properly and appropriately.

Providing Too Much Information

There are two main ways in which CBT therapists may give their clients more information than is needed or useful; the first is via self-disclosure and the second through psycho-education. Self-disclosure is allowable in CBT (whereas it is often strongly discouraged in other therapeutic traditions) and many therapists use it to good effect. Prudent and timely self-disclosure can instil hope, normalise symptoms and experiences, provide 'role model'-esque examples and humanise the therapist thereby strengthening the alliance. However, any disclosure on the therapist's part must be purely in the interest of serving the patient; there must be a bona fide therapeutic reason behind it. Often personal information is offered in response to a direct client question; this is ethically sound provided the client is not at risk of being damaged by the information. For example, in some instances the client may compare himself negatively to the therapist based on information disclosed. Therapist self-disclosure can be a grey area and if there is any doubt about the effect sharing personal information may have on a given client, it is best avoided. Offering information that shakes the client's faith in your credibility as a professional can decimate a working alliance, e.g. telling a client about someone committing suicide while under your care. Equally, imparting personal information that is at odds with your client's most cherished values may produce alliance ruptures. If your client strongly values fidelity for example, discussing your seven-year affair is clearly ill advised. In rare circumstances the therapist may get carried away and, although not imparting counter-therapeutic information per se, may end up turning treatment into a 'two-way' chat.

Psycho-education is a basic part of early-mid CBT treatment. Some therapists, however, alienate, confuse and often *bore* their patients by overdoing it. Remember that your client only needs to understand theoretical principles relevant to overcoming his particular difficulties; he is not a student or trainee. CBT does purport to aid patients in 'becoming their own therapists' of course, but this does not mean actually training them up as qualified CBT practitioners. Ideally keep didactic psycho-educational interventions brief and wherever possible, highly idiosyncratic.

The following two case studies are entirely fictional although they have been created to represent as realistically as possible alliance challenges CBT therapists may encounter. In both vignettes the therapists successfully address alliance ruptures through direct discussion with the client. The first scenario presents a less severe alliance fissure but one that could have widened had the therapist demurred from broaching the subject with his client. The second scenario depicts a more challenging alliance rupture; the client is more confrontational and requires skilful handling. These examples show 'ideal' therapist responses to alliance problems; in real life the dialogue would in all probability flow less smoothly and seamlessly.

Case Study 13.1

Joe is an experienced CBT therapist (six years post qualification) working out of a GP surgery. His long-term patient Madge suffers from chronic depression compounded by low self-esteem. On one occasion, Madge arrived for her regular appointment only to find that the reception area was being refurbished. Unable to find Joe immediately, Madge left assuming that the surgery was closed for business and that Joe had neglected to inform her. Joe asked the receptionist to contact Madge regarding her absence and to apologise for any confusion the refurbishment may have caused. The receptionist informed Madge that the surgery had in fact been open despite appearances and booked her another appointment. The next week Madge arrived as usual. Based on his understanding of Madge and her sensitivity to dismissive behaviour from others, Joe thought it best to clarify what had happened the week previous before continuing with normal therapy.

Joe: I'm sorry about the confusion last week, Madge, I hadn't been made aware that the reception area would be so disrupted, I'm sorry you had a wasted journey. Did you ask the workmen if the surgery was closed by the way?

Madge: Actually no I didn't, I just left. I suppose it would have made sense to ask but I jumped to conclusions I guess.

Joe: Can you tell me what conclusions you jumped to?

Madge: It's rather embarrassing – but my first thought was that you no longer wanted to treat me and therefore you hadn't told me that the surgery was closed.

Joe: Really? And did you also draw conclusions about why I would no longer wish to treat you?

Madge: I assumed you thought I was a hopeless case, wasting your time and boring you from week to week.

Joe: I see. I can imagine those thoughts were very upsetting. May I assure you Madge, that isn't the case at all? If I did think you weren't benefiting from CBT any longer – I would address that with you directly. Do you believe that now?

Madge: Yes I do, but at the time those were my thoughts. Silly really.

Joe: Well you certainly formed some pretty drastic inferences based on the actual circumstances. But let's be clear that though your immediate thoughts may have been silly – you, however, as a person, are not.

Madge: Yes OK, I guess so.

Joe: Hmmm, you could have said that with a little more conviction but I'll let you off the hook for now. (*Madge laughs lightly.*) Can we look at this as an example Madge? Do you think you make similar inferences in different situations involving other people?

Madge: Definitely.

Joe: Can you give me another similar example perhaps?

Madge: Uh let me think ... yes. My son had booked me up to babysit my five-year-old grandson last month. He and my daughter-in-law were going to a dinner party out of town and wanted to stay the night in a bed and breakfast. At the last minute though, he rang and cancelled saying that my grandson had been invited to sleep over at his class-mate's and my services were not needed after all.

Joe: OK. And what conclusions did you make about that situation?

Madge: I decided that he and his wife didn't trust me to look after my grand-son properly. Maybe they felt I was too depressed and miserable to entertain him adequately. I did manage to challenge those thoughts and review the evidence as we've been working on. Not being needed for childcare isn't tantamount to utter rejection as a grand-parent. But I did feel cut to the quick for about an hour after my son's call.

Joe: So if I understand you correctly, your automatic thoughts led you to feel depressed because you interpreted your son's change of mind as a rejection. Is that right?

Madge: Absolutely. But I worked myself out of it pretty quickly.

Joe: And that's progress indeed. What about last week with our appoint-ment? How long did your disturbed feelings last exactly?

Madge: Again, I got things into a more realistic and rational perspective fairly quickly. Before the receptionist rang, I think.

Joe: So you'd managed to challenge your beliefs about being rejected by me – prior to the situation being made clear by my receptionist. Is that right?

Madge: Yes. In the main anyway.

Joe: Well, again, that sounds to me like significant progress, Madge.

Madge: I suppose it is. In the past I could have been plagued with negative thoughts and depression for days in response to both events. I may have not even come back to see you.

Joe: Well, I'm glad you did and that we've talked about all this today.

Madge: I am as well. I think it's important.

Joe: Incidentally Madge, I do apologise for not making myself aware of the level of chaos hitting the surgery last week and failing to warn you in advance. This experience may have given us useful stuff to work through, but I am sorry for my contribution to your distress.

Madge: Thanks, Joe, I appreciate that.

Joe: Now perhaps we can look more closely at the beliefs you hold about yourself that give rise to the sort of inferences you made in these two examples ...

Summary of therapist interventions

Based on his knowledge of Madge's emotional problems and related beliefs, Joe follows his intuition regarding how she might be likely to respond to the

(Continued)

(Continued)

appointment confusion. Rather than glossing over the issue, Joe raises it directly with his patient and offers appropriate reassurance. Joe is neither defensive nor overly conciliatory when Madge relates her automatic thoughts about the event; he remains direct and therapeutically inquisitive. Joe then uses the information Madge offers to make thematic links with other events in her life. By doing so, Joe makes sound clinical use of the missed appointment experience and indirectly underlines the principle of emotional responsibility. To clarify, Joe urges Madge towards understanding that her core beliefs give rise to faulty inferences (automatic thoughts) about specific events and lead her to feel emotionally disturbed. He also rather casually comments on progress that Madge has made thereby contradicting her earlier assertion that she is a 'hopeless case'. Finally Joe takes legitimate responsibility for his part in the appointment confusion and apologises.

Although Madge reports challenging her inferences prior to attending the session cited, a less advanced or more severely disturbed CBT patient may not have done so; therefore the alliance may have been at more risk of rupture. Failing to address a situation such as the one in the example directly and openly may not only deprive client and therapist of rich therapeutic material, but may also create avoidable tension within the working relationship.

Case Study 13.2

Zara completed her CBT training 18 months ago. She now works full-time in an NHS hospital seeing an average of 15 patients each week. One of her patients called Stuart, a man in his late fifties, is a complex case. Stuart is diagnosed with Narcissistic Personality Disorder (NPD) and experiences frequent bouts of low mood as well as anger problems. He has seen several different therapists over the years from various traditions – although Zara is his first CBT therapist. Stuart can be challenging and confrontational in sessions. However, in a relatively short period of time, Zara has managed to establish a reasonably good relationship with him. Stuart arrived to his fourth session with Zara in an uncommunicative frame of mind. He seemed angry and defensive from the outset. Although Zara felt daunted by Stuart's demeanour she decided to address his apparent disgruntled mood with him directly.

Zara: Before we review your homework Stuart, can I check in on your current mood? You seem to me to be a bit out of sorts.

Stuart: What do you mean?

Zara: Well, to be frank, you seem angry. Has something happened prior to you arriving here today?

Stuart: No that's not it.

Zara: Oh. What is bothering you, Stuart?

Stuart: You don't want to know.

Zara: Well, it's going to be difficult for us to get much out of today's sessions I think, unless I do know what's bothering you. Don't you think?

Stuart: Look, I've been coming here for four weeks now and I don't think this CBT business is going to work for me.

Zara: Can you tell me more about why you think that, Stuart?

Stuart: I'm not convinced you've got enough experience to help me. My problems are really complicated. Also I come early to my appointments and I see people leaving your office just before I come in, you can't possibly be able to remember all the people you see. You're too busy. Maybe I should see someone more experienced and more my age.

Zara: Well, you're right that I am pretty busy but I do remember our work together from session to session, at least I think I do! I keep case notes that I refer to as a reminder as well. Is there anything in particular that I've forgotten or overlooked that you feel angry about?

Stuart: No. Not that I can think of particularly.

Zara: And although, as you know, I have been qualified for almost two years – it's not an eternity, I accept. Are there specific concerns you have about my ability to understand and help you with your problems? Please be honest with me, Stuart.

Stuart: Well, every week you seem to suggest the same exercises. Like socialising more and activity scheduling. It just doesn't seem like enough to get me out of this bloody mess I'm in with work relationships and losing my temper with my family.

Zara: Hmm. You may have a point there, Stuart. I may have been sticking too rigidly to homework assignments designed to ideally lift your mood. I may have been overlooking the other work and family problems you have as a result. I do urge you to remember, though, that this is only our fourth session and we do have time to address your other difficulties too.

Stuart: Yes well, if I end up getting fired and my wife takes the kids and runs off then I'll have even more time to fritter away in therapy! Won't I?

Zara: Right, well obviously we need to do whatever we can to prevent those events from happening, don't we? Look Stuart, I take your concerns about CBT treatment generally, and with me specifically, seriously.

Stuart: So what do you propose? I mean, I do think you may simply be too 'green' for someone with my severity of problems. Like I said, you're quite young.

Zara: OK. Regrettably there's nothing I can do about my age, Stuart, I'm sure you'll agree. However, you're clearly an intelligent determined man, Stuart, and I see no reason why you won't be able to get *something* out of CBT treatment if you choose to give it an adequate chance. For my part, with your permission I'd like to take your case to my clinical

(Continued)

(Continued)

supervisor this week and discuss the best treatment protocol for you. My supervisor is a very experienced and well-respected psychologist and CBT practitioner. I'm confident that he will direct me appropriately in terms of your treatment, if I'm neglecting certain techniques and so on – he'll tell me.

Stuart: Perhaps your supervisor is the person I should be seeing.

Zara: That's an option we can keep open. If after two more sessions you still feel that I'm not the right therapist for you, then I will refer you to him. I can also inform him of your concerns about treatment with me this week during my supervision, if that's OK with you. He may not be able to take you on himself, Stuart, since he's pretty booked up, but he is likely to be able to recommend someone else older and more experienced. What do you think?

Stuart: Yes well, as I'm here today I suppose we may as well make use of the time. I think I'm just feeling frustrated and impatient today. For the past couple of days in fact. I may not be being fair to you, Zara, my anger may be getting the better of me again.

Zara: Thank you for clarifying that, Stuart. What do think of my proposed plan regarding my supervisor? Do I have your permission to discuss the complexities of your case in-depth with him?

Stuart: Yes of course. Perhaps you and I can work effectively together. Shall we see?

Zara: That would certainly be my preference. I would like the chance to offer you the best CBT treatment I can, Stuart. However, I am prepared to refer you on as discussed if it becomes evident that doing so is in your best interest.

Stuart: That's great. Thanks. Shall I tell you about my week and how the activity scheduling worked out then?

Zara: Excellent idea. Let's see if we can also grapple with some of your home and work problems this session as well ...

Summary of therapist interventions

Firstly, Zara correctly and appropriately directs questions to Stuart about his current mood state. Ignoring his obvious displeasure almost certainly would have exacerbated his ill-humour, prevented any useful therapeutic work from taking place and probably driven a final nail into the therapeutic alliance coffin.

Stuart is a patient who has a vested interest in being a 'complex case' and to some degree 'unfixable'. He also seems to believe that he is so different to other patients that he needs a 'top of the field' expert or specialist to help him. Zara is quick to pick up on this; she neither disagrees nor explicitly colludes with Stuart's self-diagnosis. Stuart brusquely answers Zara's carefully measured questions and she remains professionally composed throughout. She does not allow herself to become defensive, combative or apologetic when

Stuart levies criticism at her clinical capabilities and degree of experience. Instead, Zara addresses his complaints in turn, puts forward her own ideas and counter-arguments courteously, acknowledges grains of truth and proposes possible solutions. To an extent, Zara plays to Stuart's irrationality (specifically his need to be seen as an exceptional case) by deliberately mentioning the complexity of his problems and agreeing to consider referring him to her supervisor. She also gently challenges his negative predictions about CBT through commenting on his intelligence and determination. Zara thus manages to soothe Stuart's ego without being excessively warm or insincere. Refusing to dance attendance to his irrational beliefs at this stage would have been counter-productive with regard to rescuing the alliance. Chances are that Stuart would have become more resistant and more invested in proving that Zara lacks the wherewithal to help him.

Zara's agreement to consider Stuart's request for a more experienced older therapist conveys neither personal offence nor does it imply that Zara wholly concurs with Stuart's assertion that she can not handle his problems. Rather she gives Stuart the message that she takes his concerns seriously and that she is not rejecting him for confronting her about her abilities. This intervention successfully takes some of the fire out of Stuart's defiance.

Conclusion

Alliance issues have historically been somewhat overlooked or under-appreciated on CBT training courses. This is probably in part due to heavy emphasis on amassing knowledge of theory, formulaic strategies and treatment protocols. It may also be due to the distinction frequently made between CBT and other psychotherapy approaches on therapeutic alliance grounds. As Chapter 5 discusses (in contrast to person-centred therapy for instance) the Rogerian core conditions of empathy, congruence and positive regard are considered desirable in CBT yet neither necessary nor sufficient to produce positive change. Therefore being attentive to relational factors may be viewed as decidedly *un*-CBT. Realistically, in any patient–practitioner situation, the quality of the relationship is likely to impact on client satisfaction and on actual (or perceived) treatment outcomes. It therefore stands to reason that existing CBT training can be augmented with more emphasis on effective alliance development and maintenance.

Though this chapter has touched on therapist factors involved in alliance formation, much more remains to be said on the subject. Also, as mentioned in the introduction, contributing client factors – the depth and breadth of which are not to be underestimated – have been excluded from this chapter. Recommended further reading includes those texts cited in the bibliography.

Bibliography

Gilbert, P. and Leahy, R.L. (eds) (2007). *The Therapeutic Relationship in the Cognitive Behavioural Psychotherapies*. Hove, East Sussex: Routledge.

Kivlighan, D.M. and Shaughnessy, P. (2000). 'Patterns of the working alliance development: A typology of client's working alliance ratings'. *Journal of Counseling Psychology,* 47: 362–71.

Leahy, R.L. (ed.) (2003). *Roadblocks in Cognitive-Behavioural Therapy: Transforming Challenges into Opportunities for Change*. New York: Guilford Press.

Safran, J.D. and Muran, J.C. (2000). *Negotiating the Therapeutic Alliance: A Relational Treatment Guide*. New York: Guilford Press.

Safran, J.D. and Segal, Z. (1996). *Interpersonal Processes in Cognitive Therapy*. Maryland: Aronson, Rowman and Littlefield Publishers.

Stiles, W.B., Glick, M.J., Osatuke K., Hardy, G.E., Shapiro, D.A., Agnew-Davies, R., Rees, A. and Barkham, M. (2004). 'Patterns of alliance development and rupture-repair hypothesis: Are productive relationships U-shaped or V-shaped?', *Journal of Counseling Psychology*, 51: 81–91.

FOURTEEN Challenges with Homework in CBT

RHENA BRANCH

The efficacy of CBT treatment for a variety of common psychiatric disorders has been evidenced in several research studies. The National Institute of Clinical Excellence (NICE) cites CBT as the psychotherapeutic treatment of choice for anxiety and depressive disorders, post-traumatic stress disorder (PTSD), obsessive-compulsive disorder (OCD), addiction, eating disorders and many others. A possible contributing factor to the success of CBT during actual treatment – and its continued efficacy post treatment, is the routine use of between-session 'homework' assignments. Research seems to indicate that compliance with, and completion of, CBT homework assignments correlates with better treatment outcomes (Rees et al., 2005; Thase & Callan, 2006). A meta-analysis conducted by Kazantzis et al. (2000) examined the role of homework in CBT treatment. Where positive outcome could not be better attributed to other variables such as therapist competency, client motivation and commitment, disorder severity or alliance factors, homework seems a powerful treatment lynchpin.

Through various forms of between-session tasks, clients become adept at applying therapeutic insight, new skills and adaptive strategies to everyday life situations. In-session collaborative homework devising is part and parcel of the CBT emphasis on assisting clients to become 'their own therapists' in the future.

An in-depth investigation of the numerous types of homework assignments typically employed by CBT practitioners is beyond the scope of this chapter. However, the relevance and appropriate implementation of homework in CBT will be discussed. Common challenges that CBT therapists (of all levels of training and experience) encounter when devising, monitoring and reviewing homework will also be addressed.

The Therapeutic Purpose of Homework

Each therapy session lasts an average of 50 minutes and most clients will have one session of CBT per week. Considering that each week contains 168 hours, one hour devoted to therapy is hardly tantamount to intensive treatment. In fact, it could be legitimately regarded as 'a mere drop in the ocean', especially with respect to more severe and complicated presentations. In order to maximise therapeutic impact and promote continued progress between weekly sessions, CBT practitioners collaborate with their clients to devise pertinent homework.

Homework is reviewed during the following session, usually at the beginning, and any learning points, obstacles or resistance to its completion are openly discussed. Conscientiously reviewing homework conveys genuine therapist interest to the client, thereby strengthening the alliance, and reinforces the importance of continued goal-orientated action between sessions. A cardinal sin (as it were) for the CBT therapist is to spend time thoughtfully setting a patient's 'between-session task' in one session, then completely forgetting to review it in the next. If you expect your client to take homework seriously, then you as therapist are compelled to do the same. Suggestions for recording and reviewing homework are offered later in this chapter.

In addition to the points mentioned above, homework also helps clients to resolve what is often referred to as the 'head–heart' or 'head–gut' issue (Dryden & Branch, 2008). Frequently clients will make a cognitive shift yet report that, although they *know intellectually* that the new belief is true and sensible, they don't *feel* its truth in their heart or 'gut'. Regular practice of acting in accordance with a new belief helps to turn intellectual insight into emotional insight. To clarify, thoughtful and intelligent behavioural homework helps to translate cognitive change into emotional change. Typically, cognitive and behavioural modifications are precursors to experiential emotional improvement. Therefore homework plays a vital role in consolidating core philosophical or inferential restructuring and

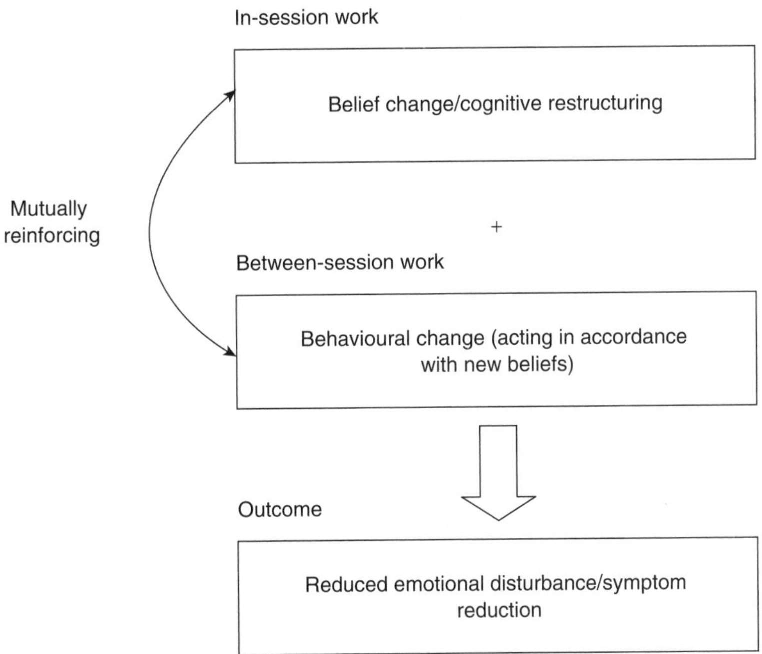

Figure 14.1 Reinforcement of in-session learning via between-session tasks.

appreciable reduction in emotional disturbance. Figure 14.1 illustrates this point.

As already mentioned, when agreed homework is not completed or fails to produce desirable therapeutic results, possible reasons are mutually investigated. Such investigation can unearth other environmental, behavioural and secondary emotional factors previously unbeknownst to the therapist. In this respect, homework also serves to further initial assessment.

Many experienced CBT practitioners report that patients who work diligently on overcoming their problems between sessions tend to experience mood lift, gain confidence in their ability to employ useful strategies, recover readily from lapses, improve more quickly in general and experience a greater sense of self-accomplishment. Bearing these points in mind and remembering that a primary aim of CBT is to equip the client with the skills needed to combat psychological disturbance post treatment, homework is considered an essential ingredient of sustained therapeutic success (Neimeyer & Feixas, 1990). Moreover, the act of carrying out therapeutically prescribed behaviours and reinforcing associated cognitive changes between actual sessions promotes client independence. Although the client is, in all likelihood, *reliant* on the CBT therapist for expert guidance and input initially, collaborative homework setting helps to avoid fostering *dependence* on the therapist.

Terminology

Certain patients do not respond well to the term 'homework'. For some the term may seem patronising or evoke unpleasant associations with school days. Clients who are highly autonomous, independent or strongly value their self-sufficiency may be more likely to balk at being 'told what to do' by the therapist. They may also be more particular about the label given to their CBT homework. In such cases it is prudent to play to the individual's strengths and invite frank co-devising of homework, allowing the patient to choose what to call therapeutic assignments. Other individuals suffering from work-related stress, anxiety problems, depression or simply leading busy lives might hear the word 'homework' and feel overwhelmed or pressured. It can seem like 'just another thing to do' and loom darkly in their already crowded minds. It is important to be aware of this and take extra care to devise highly relevant homework that can ideally be incorporated into the client's everyday life. Equally important, is striking a delicate balance between stretching the client and overwhelming him (Dryden & Branch, 2008). Too much homework (or overly ambitious assignments) may put the client off CBT altogether, not enough homework (or insufficiently challenging assignments) can mean that treatment arrives at a cul-de-sac.

Generally, informed clients will come to their first session of CBT expecting between-session assignments. The majority will not take umbrage to the term 'homework' in which case, it is advisable to use it for the sake of simplicity. For those who *do* reject the homework label, some alternatives include:

- between-session tasks;
- continued therapeutic practice;
- weekly targets;
- positive change exercises;
- therapeutic objectives;
- change work;
- goal-orientated practice;
- skill acquisition practice;
- treatment tasks.

Essentially any term that is palatable to the patient can be applied to CBT homework. The term chosen will ideally inspire the client to do the work and remind him of the therapeutic rationale behind doing so.

Types of CBT Homework

It is common for trainee and novice CBT therapists to struggle over setting appropriate homework assignments. A rule of thumb is that the homework should follow logically from the work done in session (Dryden & Branch, 2008). Effective CBT homework is tailored specifically to the individual and targets his particular difficulties. A plethora of potentially useful homework assignments are available to the creative and imaginative practitioner (Shelton & Ackerman, 1974; Kazantzis et al., 2005; Branch & Willson, 2007). However, as with many CBT skills, good homework setting takes practice and experience. This section outlines typical types of homework assignments and their appropriate application.

Bibliotherapy

Frequently, trainees feel compelled to give the client *something* to do from one session to the next and default to bibliotherapy. While this is not usually counter-productive, it is not always the most relevant assignment. Depressed patients, for example, often benefit more from a behavioural task than a reading assignment. Certain patients who are prone to unhelpful self-analysis may already have a stack of psychology books on the bedside table. In such cases, it is often best practice to encourage the client to read less rather than more. Trainees should also be wary of using bibliotherapy as a substitute for providing psycho-education themselves. Such information is often better delivered directly so that questions and misunderstandings may be addressed immediately. Also, theoretical explanation and psycho-education is unavoidable in CBT practice; therefore it is wise to get 'stuck in' and practise accessible delivery from the start of your training. The following are general guidelines for bibliotherapy assignments:

- Keep reading assignments relatively brief. A chapter is usually a manageable amount for most patients to absorb and review in the following session.
- Ensure that you have read the information recently yourself to facilitate intelligent discussion with the client.
- Choose disorder specific and/or highly idiosyncratic literature. For example, there is little utility or justification in recommending a chapter on intrusive thoughts associated with OCD to a client with social phobia. At best the material will fail to resonate meaningfully with the client and at worst it may lead to further confusion and

disturbance. The patient may also doubt your understanding of his difficulties, which may damage the working alliance.
- Intersperse reading homework with other relevant types of assignments.
- Keep yourself informed of research outcomes and changes to treatment protocols. Update your personal library regularly to ensure you have the most recent resources to hand.

Tip

- Subscribe to CBT journals and other psychiatric journals – and make time to actually *read* them. Use some of your supervision time to discuss theoretical advances and new clinical developments in CBT. Attend plenty of CPD (continued professional development) events including workshops, conferences and lectures.
- Be sensitive to client limitations such as English as a second language, dyslexia and literacy issues.

Written Homework

The previous points regarding the use of bibliotherapy also pertain to written homework assignments. The majority of written homework in CBT will be completed on forms designed for a particular therapeutic purpose. Rather than urging clients to simply record their thoughts and feelings in a free-style diary fashion, CBT practitioners use specialised forms, worksheets and questionnaires to accurately elicit the information needed to help clients overcome their particular problems. Such written assignments are also used to introduce or reinforce key theoretical principles and underscore therapeutic learning. Forms are very frequently used both within and between sessions. More common forms include: ABC forms, cost-benefit analysis forms (CBA), daily thought records (DTRs), activity schedules, behavioural experiment records, the zigzag, rational portfolios, and various self-monitoring forms. Countless other CBT forms also exist. Open any CBT book, especially self-help materials, and you are sure to find a bevy of forms within. Forms can be very useful therapeutic tools; however, like bibliotherapy, they should ideally be used with consideration and precision. Handing your client a form or worksheet for the sake of it is unlikely to yield any therapeutically relevant information. Clients may also be disinclined to complete poorly conceived written tasks or do so incorrectly, becoming bored and frustrated. Having a clear rationale for using a given form ensures both client and therapist understand what information is relevant to record. The various purposes of using forms typically include the following:

- socialising clients to the model;
- continuing assessment;
- increasing client awareness of negative automatic thoughts (NATs) and related trigger situations/events;
- increasing client awareness of the impact specific behaviours have on their mood;
- helping clients to understand the link between specific thoughts/ beliefs and emotions;
- eliciting safety behaviours that perpetuate and maintain disorders (i.e. excessive checking, reassurance seeking, avoidance and hypervigilance);
- monitoring the frequency, intensity and duration of problematic emotions;
- recording the emotional and/or practical benefits of specific behavioural and cognitive changes;
- reinforcing conviction in new adaptive beliefs;
- eliciting and refreshing commitment to therapeutic goals;
- testing out the validity of negative predictions;
- consolidating therapeutic learning;
- planning and preparation (i.e. relapse prevention).

Caution

For certain clients, written homework is contraindicated. Clients who are overly self-analytical, for example, may be 'thinking themselves' deeper into their own disturbance. These types of clients are already likely to be avid writers of diaries; thus a simple ABC form may be returned completely wedged with script. In this case, either help the client to streamline what he writes or do not give written assignments at all. Severely depressed clients often benefit from focusing *less* on their thoughts and feelings initially. Using a daily thought record (DTR) for instance may unwittingly encourage depressive rumination and be unhelpful at best or damaging at worst. If in doubt about the appropriateness of a written assignment (or any homework task for that matter) with a specific client or client population, speak to your supervisor.

Imagery Exercises

Imagery or visualisation exercises can be very useful in preparing a client to move on to behavioural assignments. Generally it works best to practise imagery exercises in session and then recommend that your client do the same as homework. Some clients are more willing and able than others to use imagery work effectively. A proportion of clients may be embarrassed by the idea of closing their eyes and imagining a scenario. You can sometimes casually lead into visualisation, thereby relaxing an embarrassed or reluctant client successfully. The following example illustrates how you can gently introduce visualisation without needing to make a big production of it:

Therapist: OK, Ted. To help you overcome your anger problem, would you try to conjure up the image of your girlfriend nagging you about fixing the toilet right now?

Ted: What, like remember what she was saying to me when I lost my rag?

Therapist: That's right, just try to remember the whole event vividly. Close your eyes if you think that'll help or keep them open if you prefer.

Ted: OK.

Therapist: Good. Have you got the image in your mind?

Ted: Yes.

Therapist: OK, can you remember what you were thinking and feeling at the time?

Ted: Yeah, I can feel my blood pressure rising.

Therapist: Great, that's what we want. Now can you try to change your thoughts about her nagging to those that we've been working on? Take your time. Just try to imagine being in the same situation but thinking rationally about her nagging.

Ted: OK, I'm getting there but I still feel angry.

Therapist: That's OK. Now I'd like you to try and imagine changing the outcome of that situation. Could you try imagining that you're still annoyed but instead of totally losing it, you talk to her calmly?

Ted: Uh, yeah. I can sort of see myself being cross but not hurling abuse at her.

Therapist: Great. Can you also clearly imagine how you're thinking differently in order to achieve that calmer response? Again, take a bit of time to really see and feel it ...

Ted may then go on to practise the same type of imagery assignment between sessions and also practise thinking/behaving like his imagined adaptive self in real situations.

Assignments with Behavioural and Cognitive Elements

These are perhaps the most common type of CBT homework tasks. The basis is to combine a cognitive shift (new adaptive belief) with a corresponding behavioural change. As depicted in the diagram earlier in this chapter, behavioural changes help to reinforce cognitive changes - and the two in conjunction will often precede emotional improvement. An example may be helping your client adopt the belief 'I want to be successful at work but I don't absolutely have to be at all times. I can learn from mistakes and it doesn't mean that I'm a total failure should I make errors.' While holding this belief your client may offer new ideas during meetings whereas previously he would have held his tongue for fear of criticism.

Behavioural Experiments

These homework tasks involve urging your client to test out negative predictions in real life by behaving in a prescribed fashion (Bennett-Levy et al., 2004). For example, a client who is convinced that if he smiles at people in social situations he will invariably be snubbed and rejected may test this prediction out in real life, recording how often he is snubbed versus how often a smile is returned.

They can also be used to help a client see and experience the ways in which changes to behaviour and lifestyle impact on mood. A client may be encouraged to abandon alcohol for a week to see if it improves his overall mood and energy for example. Or a depressed client may try being more socially active plus exercising twice a week to see if his mood lifts as a result.

Exposure and Response Prevention (ERP)

These assignments are most often used to treat phobias, OCD and other anxiety disorders. It is also arguably true that the bulk of work with anorexic clients involves exposure and response prevention. Clients are helped to confront their feared situation or object while resisting engaging in neutralising rituals and/or safety behaviours. The theory behind ERP is that rituals or safety behaviours provide temporary relief of anxiety and discomfort but serve to ultimately reinforce the erroneous belief that a specific event, situation, action or object is implicitly dangerous.

Homework Devised to Further Assessment

In the earlier stages of treatment, homework assignments may be used to gather more information to further problem conceptualisation. You may for example, ask your client to record how often he uses checking behaviour in OCD treatment. You may urge a body dysmorphic client (BDD) to time precisely how long he spends in front of the mirror checking his appearance each day. Or you may ask your anorexic client to compile a list of forbidden foods, safe foods and eating rituals. A client with generalised anxiety disorder (GAD) may be asked to record anxiety spikes and corresponding situations/thoughts/memories etc. It is also not unusual for CBT practitioners to use assessment-driven homework in later stages of treatment when progress has reached a standstill or other types of homework are no longer being completed (Tompkins, 2004). Information gathering assignments can be very helpful in resolving therapeutic impasse and unearthing secondary gain or metapsychological problems.

This list of typical types of CBT homework is not exhaustive by any means. Nor do the brief descriptions provided here adequately explain how to properly conduct more sophisticated homework such as ERP and behavioural experiments. It is advisable to read further (see the reference list at the end of the chapter) and ask for specific supervision on homework setting.

Frequently homework assignments overlap and combine various elements. Do not be afraid to be creative and inventive when negotiating between-session tasks with your client. One of the rewarding aspects of collaborative work is that your client may come up with a highly relevant task that you would not have considered on your own.

Collaborative Devising

Because CBT is a collaborative approach, it stands to reason that homework should be co-devised and mutually agreed upon. As therapist, you are likely to have superior knowledge about the types of assignments most likely to aid your client in overcoming his problems. Your client, however, knows more about his personal circumstances, routine and time constraints. It may be tempting to 'tell your client what to do' in order to save time and effort. However, doing so can undermine the alliance, create client resistance and runs counter to helping the client to become his own therapist in future. Though you may be confident that you know what task will most benefit your client, it is best practice to always offer suggestions tentatively and encourage client input. Chances are you will need to 'tweak' client homework suggestions to keep them in line with received treatment protocol. You will probably also need to urge your client to push himself beyond his comfort zone to increase the therapeutic benefit of homework. This should ideally be done in a frank, explanatory and inclusive manner.

Once homework has been devised it is advisable to elicit doubts, reservations or fears your client may be quietly harbouring about completing the task. This helps to ensure that your client truly understands the reason for doing the task, believes to an adequate extent that it will help him, possesses the skills required and is truly willing to do the between-session work.

Therapist Input and 'Kick Starting' the Patient

Despite the best of intentions, clients may fail to do their homework because they lack the confidence to 'fly solo' in the first instance. Sometimes a client may need to see you complete a task first before they are ready and willing to do it on their own. For example, you might hold a snake before encouraging your client to do so in the case of snake phobia. Or you may lock your car without double-checking the doors in OCD (obsessive-compulsive disorder) treatment. Other times you may need to devote a session or more to carrying out behavioural assignments alongside your client – travelling with him on the tube or using a lift together, for example. Eating disordered clients often need a lot of encouragement and monitoring so you may either eat together in session or go out for meals. While it is important to avoid promoting dependence on the therapist, it is frequently useful to participate in behavioural assignments with clients just to get them started. Doing so can ensure future compliance, strengthen the alliance and provide opportunity to observe your client in action. You may notice safety behaviours unknown to the client that are complicating treatment.

Recording and Reviewing Homework

Forms for recording homework can be useful and you may wish to devise one of your own. The main points to adhere to when recording homework are:

- Clearly identify when, where, how often and with whom the task is to be carried out. For examples of this refer to the case vignette.
- Check that homework has been accurately recorded and all necessary steps are outlined.

- Keep a record of the homework assignment with your case notes. (Keeping clear homework records on file also affords you a degree of professional safety in the unlikely event that a client alleges you recommended an illegal or immoral action.)
- Homework is typically best reviewed at or near the start of each session. This underlines the message that homework is an important aspect of treatment, keeps treatment focused and conveys therapist interest and competency. Often the bulk of CBT sessions in mid to late treatment phases will be comprised of homework review. A lot of useful information arises from homework review whether it has been completed successfully, gone awry in some way or not been done at all.

Below are some pointers for effective homework review:

- Ensure that you consult your copy of the homework task prior to session thereby refreshing your memory.
- Investigate possible psychological, emotional and environmental reasons for homework either left undone or producing poor outcomes.
- With regard to behavioural tasks, including ERP (exposure and response prevention), ask your client to 'walk you through' everything he did. This helps you check that the homework has been done correctly and that all relevant steps have been fully carried out.
- Pay close attention to detail when reviewing any type of homework task. Subtle disorder maintaining behaviours and cognitive strategies can go undetected without deliberate inspection. For example, clients may unintentionally use self-reassurance, distraction or mental neutralising rituals during exposure-based tasks.
- When your client reports that a homework assignment has been successful, it is important to investigate to what he attributes the success. Ideally this will be a positive change in thinking and behaviour. Therapists often mistakenly assume that this is the case and neglect to double-check. It is possible that homework has 'gone well' because the client is still employing a safety behaviour or some element of avoidance, or that a negative triggering event or prediction failed to occur. While the client may be pleased that the homework has been executed with limited emotional discomfort, true therapeutic learning is likely to be limited or entirely negated. It is incumbent upon you, as therapist, to sensitively point this out and make appropriate amendments to future homework.
- Manage your own expectations and beliefs about homework results and client compliance.

Case Study 14.1

The following is a representational account of the type of homework that may be given throughout 13 sessions of CBT for a client suffering from social anxiety.

Alexis is 23 years old and has suffered with social anxiety since her early teens. She worries constantly about what others think of her and whether they find her likable and interesting. Alexis avoids large social gatherings where she doesn't know everyone present and one-to-one interaction with people she doesn't know very well. During social interaction, Alexis monitors other people's reactions to her, prepares conversation in her head before speaking, avoids prolonged eye contact and keeps her opinions to herself. Afterwards, she replays the interaction in her mind over and over, looking for any evidence that she's said something stupid or offensive.

1 Week 1 – Monitor and record safety behaviours and avoidance strategies in social environments (playing with phone, sitting in corners, avoiding alcohol for fear of losing control, sticking to 'safe' subjects, keeping head down etc.)
2 Week 2 – Write out at least five good arguments for why it's *desirable* to be liked by others but not absolutely *essential* at all times. (Remind yourself how believing these arguments will help you overcome your anxiety.)
3 Week 3 – Go out for drinks after work on Friday. Drop safety behaviours; make at least two spontaneous comments; be mindful of the belief 'I want others to like me but I don't absolutely *have* to be liked by everyone.'
4 Week 4 – Practise the same points from last week in these situations: pub quiz on Monday, lunch with work acquaintance on Wednesday, after work drinks on Friday. (Resist mentally reviewing your performance by distracting yourself with chores, TV or reading.)
5 Week 5 – Repeat homework from previous week but also offer your opinion on any issue at least once in each situation. Maintain eye contact.
6 Week 6 – Sit next to the guy you fancy from accounts during after work drinks on Friday. Allow yourself to talk spontaneously and hold eye contact. Be mindful of the belief 'I want others to like me but I don't absolutely *have* to be liked by everyone.'
7 Week 7 – Review your list of arguments from week 2 and re-rate your conviction in their validity. Double-check that you aren't resorting to old safety behaviours in social situations; if you are, drop them. Combine and repeat homework from weeks 4–6.
8 Week 8 – Friend's wedding on Saturday. Strike up a conversation with another guest that you don't know very well. (Remember that you can tolerate awkward silences without needing to fill them.)
9 Week 9 – Deliberately and respectfully disagree with something a friend or work colleague says (however superficial) and don't back down. Aim to do this on at least two occasions.

(Continued)

(Continued)

10 Week 10 – Agree to go out for dinner with the guy from accounts. Resist using safety behaviours and strongly *prefer* but don't *demand* that the date goes smoothly.
11 Week 11 – Lunch with friends on Wednesday. After work drinks on Friday. Do most of the talking during lunch and talk a lot during drinks on Friday. Bear the discomfort of possibly boring others and taking up too much 'air time'.
12 Week 12 – Fill in relapse prevention form. Include most useful strategies and ideas derived from treatment. Record possible difficulties that may arise in future and strategies to surmount them.
13 Week 13 – Continue to practise diligently and build on previous homework tasks.

Common Obstacles to Homework Compliance and Ways of Overcoming Them

Although the vast majority of clients truly wish to feel better and wholly overcome their psychological disturbance, many will falter when it comes to homework. There are several possible reasons for homework noncompliance and the more common ones are outlined as follows.

The Client Does Not Understand the Rationale Behind the Homework

Homework needs to have a clear therapeutic purpose that both the therapist and client fully understand. It is the therapist's job to explain the rationale for specific assignments, ensure the client understands, elicit and address doubts or reservations and promote compliance and commitment to doing between-session practice. Unless the client really believes that a given assignment is likely to help him overcome his problems, he is unlikely to put himself through the effort and potential discomfort of completing it.

The Homework is Overwhelming

Assignments need to strike a careful balance between being challenging enough to be of therapeutic benefit and set within the range of what the client is currently able to manage. Setting overly ambitious assignments early on may put the client off CBT altogether. Additionally, homework that is too difficult may erode your client's confidence and feed into feelings of hopelessness thereby impeding therapeutic progress. It is therefore important to agree with your client on what is realistic. Graded hierarchies are often used in CBT to move clients steadily through increasingly challenging tasks without overwhelming them.

The Homework is Not Specific

Vague assignments that fail to make clear exactly *what* is to be done *when* and *why* are easily forgotten or avoided. The client can become confused about the purpose of the homework and may do it incorrectly, partially or not at all. Refer to Case study 14.1 for examples of specificity in homework setting.

The Client Lacks The Skills to Do the Homework

It can be easy to take for granted that your client has the basic skills needed to complete homework. For example, filling out an ABC form, behaving assertively, dropping safety behaviours or making an activity schedule may seem relatively straightforward to the CBT therapist but may be less so to the client. Clients may be reluctant to ask for guidance and help developing core CBT skills or life skills due to embarrassment or shame. Check with your client about his skill set prior to sending him off to complete a task. Devoting a portion of session time to skills development is often necessary.

The Homework is Overly Complicated

When the steps involved in a homework assignment are too complicated the client may lose motivation. For example, the situation in which practice is meant to take place may be difficult to orchestrate or the assignment may require too much time and interfere unduly with the client's normal schedule. Ideally strive to give your client clear and simple task orientated instructions. Additionally, be aware of creating assignments that your client will find relatively easy to contrive in his actual daily life.

The Client's Primary Problems Interfere with Homework Completion

It is not uncommon for CBT therapists at any level of experience to encounter clients who simply seem unable to get on with between-session tasks. In some cases the therapist may overestimate the client's skills and/or motivation. In other cases, however, the therapist may underestimate the debilitating effect of the client's primary problem. In cases of severe depression, for example, clients may be unable to sustain motivation to do even the simplest behavioural activation task once the session is over. You may need to discuss medication with your client's referring GP or psychiatrist as your first intervention. Some degree of mood lift is often needed before a very depressed client is able to engage with between-session tasks. Highly anxious patients may also lack the 'discomfort tolerance' necessary to execute homework. They may understand and accept the rationale behind assignments but when it comes to actually doing them, they doubt their ability to cope with the discomfort involved. In these cases you will need to work on increasing your client's tolerance for effort, discomfort and unpleasant emotions or physical sensations. It can help to emphasise why it is worth it to do uncomfortable tasks, i.e. what stands to be gained and also introduce 'short-term pain for long-term gain' concepts.

Homework has Not Been Recorded

The risk that homework will be forgotten or left undone increases when the therapist, client or both fail to record it adequately. Recording homework helps jog the client's memory, increases motivation to complete the assignment and underscores the message that homework is an important part of CBT treatment. Guidelines for recording CBT assignments are included in the previous section.

Safety and Sense

It may seem to be stating the obvious but it is important to ensure that you never put your client at risk. Use your common sense when devising homework with your client. While most clients will object should you suggest potentially dangerous tasks, others may not. Overly compliant clients may assume that you know best and fail to exercise their own judgement. For general guidance, do not advise your client to do things that you would not be prepared to do yourself. Also use your imagination; certain homework tasks may have hidden risks either due to your client's physical health or environmental circumstances.

Possible assignments that carry inherent risk may include:

- Advocating assertive behaviour with a physically violent partner. Although your client may lack assertion, an unpredictable or volatile person is not a suitable practice target.
- Participating in extreme sports. Your client may choose to sky-dive or go rock-climbing in a bid to overcome fear of heights for example. Such extreme measures are not necessary in the main, however, and you are best leaving such choices to your client's discretion.
- Using alcohol to excess. (Even moderate consumption can be dangerous for people with certain health conditions and those unaccustomed to drinking alcohol.) Alcohol can also lower inhibitions and act as a depressant. In general, be extremely cautious about suggesting alcohol use.
- Doing exposure/behavioural assignments in 'rough' areas. Even making eye contact in certain situations may carry a risk to safety. Use your common sense when advocating increased social interaction.
- Any assignment that, should your client 'fail', may increase suicidal ideation. With clients who are a real suicide risk, it is best to devise assignments where they are virtually guaranteed positive outcomes. Examples may include self-care routines such as cleaning their living area or buying some healthy and appealing food.

It is not always possible to anticipate every possible risk when creating between-session practices. However, it is recommended that you err on the side of caution should you be in any doubt about the safety of a specific assignment.

Conclusion

Homework is an integral part of CBT treatment for virtually any kind of psychiatric or emotional disorder. Intelligent, creative and idiosyncratic between-session assignments can aid the recovery process greatly and give clients skills to help them remain disorder free long into the future. The points discussed throughout this chapter, and those included below, will hopefully guide CBT practitioners (from novice to expert) towards sensible and effective use of homework.

Reflection Points

- Am I relying too heavily on homework assignments that I feel comfortable using? You may feel comfortable with a type of homework but it may not be the most useful one for your client's particular difficulties. Consult CBT literature, speak to other practitioners and seek supervision about disorder specific assignments. Be prepared to take educated risks and stretch your homework repertoire.
- Do I believe in the efficacy of the assignment devised? If you are not convinced that a task is going to help, your scepticism will probably be conveyed to your client. Try homework out for yourself. Ensure that you only recommend between-session practices that you truly believe are useful.
- Do I fully understand the steps involved in the assignment and the rationale behind it? You may have learnt about a homework assignment via listening to other practitioners or through independent reading. While this is a normal way of developing as a therapist, you may need to put in extra effort to fully grasp the theory behind a given exercise. Often there are crucial steps involved in a seemingly straightforward assignment that, if misunderstood, confound therapeutic outcome. Take care to learn the steps yourself before suggesting an assignment to your client.
- Am I regularly and thoroughly reviewing homework with my client? Homework loses impact if you fail to review it according to the points outlined previously in this chapter. Future homework is often based on what has been learnt and achieved from past homework. Without conscientious review, such treatment continuity is lost.
- Am I letting my client off the proverbial 'hook'? You may avoid confronting your client about failure to complete tasks because you fear damaging the alliance. Provided you are respectful and genuinely interested in your clients' recovery, the alliance is unlikely to rupture. In fact, your interest in their improvement may be highlighted by your refusal to accept excuses for avoiding assignments, thereby strengthening the alliance. Remember also that CBT is an active-directive therapeutic approach; hence challenging your client is quite unavoidable.

References

Bennett-Levy, J., Butler, G., Fennell, M., Hackmann, A., Mueller, M. and Westbrook, D. (eds) (2004). *Oxford Guide to Behavioural Experiments in Cognitive Therapy*. Oxford: Oxford University Press.

Branch, R. and Willson, R. (2007). *Cognitive Behavioural Workbook for Dummies*. Chichester: John Wiley & Sons, Ltd.

Dryden, W. and Branch, R. (2008). *The Fundamentals of Rational Emotive Behaviour Therapy*, 2nd edn. Chichester: John Wiley & Sons, Ltd.

Kazantzis, N., Deane, F.P. and Ronan, K.R. (2000). 'Homework assignments in cognitive and behavioural therapy: A meta-analysis', *Clinical Psychology: Science and Practice*, 7 (2): 189–202.

Kazantzis, N., Deane, F.P., Ronan, K.R. and L'Abate, L. (eds) (2005). *Using Homework Assignments in Cognitive Behaviour Therapy*. New York: Routledge.

Neimeyer, R.A. and Feixas, G. (1990). 'The role of homework and skill acquisition in the outcome of group cognitive therapy for depression', *Behaviour Therapy*, 21 (3): 281–92.

Rees, C., McEvoy, P. and Nathan, P. (2005). 'Relationship between homework completion and outcome in Cognitive Behaviour Therapy', *Cognitive Behaviour Therapy*, 34: 242–7.

Shelton, J.L. and Ackerman, J.M. (1974). *Homework in Counselling and Psychotherapy (Examples of Systemic Assignments for Therapeutic Use by Mental Health Professionals)*. Illinois: Charles C. Thomas Publisher.

Thase, M.E. and Callan, J.A. (2006). 'The role of homework in Cognitive Behaviour Therapy of depression', *Journal of Psychotherapy Integration*, 16 (2): 162–77.

Tompkins, M.A. (2004). *Using Homework in Psychotherapy*. New York: Guilford Press.

FIFTEEN Challenges with Maintenance and Change in CBT

WENDY WOOD

Grazebrook and Garland (2005) describe the outcome and goal of CBT as:

> The acquisition and utilisation of such skills is seen as the main goal, and the active component in promoting change with an emphasis on putting what has been learned into practice between sessions (homework). Thus the overall aim is for the individual to attribute improvement in their problems to their own efforts, in collaboration with the psychotherapist.

These fundamental aims provide the key to both analysis and potential resolution of some of the challenges faced by the therapist and client as they work through the process of CBT. This chapter will examine and address various challenges to maintenance and change throughout the therapy process while bearing the aforementioned aims in mind.

Challenges to maintaining change can occur at any point in the therapeutic process; challenges can be viewed from the perspective of the client and therapist's processes.

One of the most influential models of change has been the transtheoretical model (TTM) (Prochaska & DiClemente, 1983). Since its first inception 'there has been a considerable amount of work done in applying the model to a range of patient populations and client settings'

Table 15.1 Summary of Revised Stages of Change (adapted from Freeman and Dolan, 2001)

Stage	Key features
Noncontemplation	Not considering or even thinking about change (p227)
Anticontemplation	'Actively opposed to change'(p227)
Precontemplation	'Thinking about thinking about change' (p228)
Contemplation	'Directly and actively considering change' (p228)
Action Planning	Collaborative development of treatment plan
Action	'Behavioral progress towards change' (p228)
Prelapse	'Overwhelming cognitions related to the reversal of the changed behavior' (p229)
Lapse	'Skills needed to maintain the change decrease or are ignored'(p229)
Relapse	'Return to the behaviors that were the cause of the original referral' (p230)
Maintenance	'Final stage in the continuous process of maintaining and developing the skills of the previous stages' (p230)

(Freeman & Dolan, 2001: 225). Freeman and Dolan (2001) modified Prochaska and DiClemente's original model in light of their clinical experience. They proposed that the modification is 'consistent with a cognitive-behavioural orientation that is highly specific and prescriptive' (p. 226). It is Freeman and Dolan's (2001) version that will be applied here (see Table 15.1).

Beginnings

Despite our best efforts to 'reduce distress' going to see a therapist can be very anxiety provoking. Some clients may perceive the experience as threatening and undermining (Leahy, 2001). Ignoring these issues will result in therapeutic impasse, passivity, withdrawal, premature termination, and other notable failures in the therapeutic process (Leahy, 2003).

Paying close attention to developing a good collaborative relationship from the beginning helps lay down firm therapeutic foundations that may help to circumvent (or at least reduce) the impact of any future challenges, or in Leahy's (2003) terminology, 'roadblocks' in the change process. For example, paying attention to the immediate cognitive and or emotional responses exhibited by both client and therapist during initial contact can help deepen mutual understanding of CBT treatment and promote therapeutic progress.

Case Study 15.1

Julie came to the first session following a self-referral. Her boyfriend suggested it might be a good idea as he had previously experienced a positive outcome from CBT. Julie reported she was feeling low and lacking in energy. As the assessment progressed the therapist began to wonder if Julie really thought there was a problem, if she was motivated to change and whether Julie was coming simply to assuage her boyfriend's concerns. The therapist shared her thoughts with Julie.

Julie stated that she was not really sure whether there was a problem. She had been working long hours and revising for forthcoming exams and she wondered if her mood and energy would return once the exams were over. At the same time she could appreciate her boyfriend's concerns and wondered if CBT could help her manage her workload better.

This transparency allowed the therapist and Julie to devise an appropriate way forward. Julie was given some bibliotherapy and a session was booked for the following week to further assess her mood. At the next session, Julie reported feeling more confident about her coping strategies. She had used the reading to help her implement new strategies. A follow-up session was booked after Julie's exams and at this appointment she reported sustained improvement.

This case provides a good example of someone who is not certain that they have a problem nor if they need CBT treatment, but considers it worthwhile to investigate the matter further with a therapist before making a decision.

Freeman and Dolan (2001) expand on Prochaska and DiClemente's (1983) model suggesting the addition of a 'noncontemplation' stage. This is where the individual is not deliberately thinking about change. Importantly 'patients at this point are not actively avoiding, resisting, or opposing change. They simply have not considered it, and may be willing to work on change when it is made manifest or obvious by the therapist' (p. 227).

With regard to the therapist, there is potential here for what Freeman and McCloskey (2003) describe as various examples of 'therapeutic narcissism'. There may be a temptation to continue with traditional assessment thus neglecting to assess Julie's stage of change. Therapists 'may expect that the patient in all instances should implement his or her suggestions without ever being challenged. This can easily lead to a sense of powerlessness and resentment on the part of the client' (p. 33).

Freeman and Dolan (2001) suggest yet a further addition to Prochaska and DiClemente's (1983) model. They suggest an 'anticontemplation' stage. 'Anticontemplation involves the process of becoming reactive and violently opposed to change. This is a response often seen in individuals mandated for therapy by the courts, or required to come to therapy by family or significant others' (p. 227). Where coercion is apparent it is important to examine the nature of the client's opposition to change.

Case Study 15.2

Ian came to therapy because his girlfriend threatened to leave him if he did not do something about his temper. He accepted that he did 'have a short temper' and acknowledged that this had led to physical fights between himself and his girlfriend. However, he stated: 'If she didn't keep on winding me up things would be fine. She knows how to get to me and she keeps on pushing until I lose it. It's her that needs sorting. I don't know what you think you can do for me.'

Ian's example illustrates the anticontemplation stage which is characterised by poor insight with regard to personal responsibility and an absence of motivation to change. Angry clients are perhaps more frequently in the anticontemplation stage when they commence treatment than clients with other emotional disorders. Tafrate and Kassinove (2003) make an important point that 'it seems certain that a subset of angry adults does exist who voluntarily seek treatment and who possess a high level of motivation to actively engage in change strategies. Thus we do not wish to portray all angry adults as unmotivated' (p. 305).

In order to increase motivation when dealing with angry clients Tafrate and Kassinove recommend 'refraining from the traditional active-directive presentation style of the cognitive behavioral therapist in favor of a motivational interviewing format as outlined by Miller and Rollnick (1991: 305)'.

In terms of the therapist factors in this case, an issue identified by Freeman and McCloskey (2003) is establishing a sound working alliance: 'Working with patients who have been adjudicated for therapy or otherwise against their will, the collaboration must be built slowly' (p. 32). DiGuiseppe and Tafrate (2007) in their comprehensive book *Understanding Anger Disorders* conclude:

> The biggest mistake that we see practitioners make in treating anger is moving too quickly into active changes strategies. Without adequately preparing clients for treatment, initial attempts to change anger will often be met with resistance or, worse yet, anger at the therapist. A variety of strategies can be used in the preparatory phase of treatment. A good starting point almost always involves the deliberate use of empathy. (p. 335)

Other presenting problems that may be referred at this stage of change include:

- health anxiety;
- obsessive compulsive disorders;
- eating disorders;
- substance misuse/abuse.

Patients are also frequently in the 'Precontemplation' stage at presentation and during the early stages of therapy. Precontemplation is where 'a person begins to consider the consequences, purpose and the possibility of change. A metacognitive state wherein the patient is thinking about thinking about change.' Freeman and Dolan (2001: 228). In the example below, Joy illustrates the precontemplation stage in that she is prepared to consider the possibility of change, but is not yet entirely convinced.

Case Study 15.3

Joy was referred by her GP following extensive physical investigations which failed to provide any explanation for her symptoms, including: breathing difficulties, excessive sweating, palpitations and sleep disturbance. At the first CBT session she stated, 'I really thought my doctor was missing something, but I probably ought to give this a try.'

It is common for people experiencing health anxiety to have doubts about the possibility of a psychological explanation for their symptoms, and indeed to become angry at the thought that people are judging them as being 'neurotic' or imagining things. It may also be more culturally acceptable to seek help for physical rather than psychological symptoms (Leahy, 2001).

As with anticontemplators, a motivational interviewing format may be beneficial here. It is again incumbent upon the therapist to build collaboration through challenging pre-existent dysfunctional beliefs and ideas sensitively. It is important to work at the client's pace initially, thereby fostering a sound therapeutic alliance. For example, Ledley et al. (2005) point out that:

> it is important to gauge clients' levels of understanding. For the client who catches on to concepts quickly, it is appropriate to move a little more quickly through introductory material and get on with the 'meat' of the therapy ... In some cases, you will be concerned that the client does not understand the core concepts, yet still expresses a desire to move on. This is tricky. Some clients will understand the concepts best by *doing*; for these clients, progressing

> on to a more active part of therapy is fine. However, we always want to ensure that clients understand the rationale for *why* we do certain things. They do not need to *believe* the rationale (e.g., if you stop doing compulsions during OCD treatment, feared outcomes are unlikely to occur), but they need to understand the purpose of each therapy technique (e.g. refraining from compulsions should help me whether or not my feared consequences will occur) and be open to trying them. (p. 131)

Middle

The middle phase of therapy is most often associated with the implementation of the treatment plan.

One of the more common challenges during the middle phase of CBT treatment is the client and/or the therapist becoming 'stuck' – experiencing an impasse. Hill and Knox (2009) discuss the results of research into impasse:

> Hill, Nutt Williams, Heaton, Thompson, and Rhodes (1996) qualitatively investigated the experiences of 11 seasoned therapists about a therapeutic impasse (i.e., a deadlock or stalemate) that resulted in the termination of therapy with a client. In these impasses, there was general disagreement between the therapist and client about the goals and tasks of therapy, and often there were power struggles over how therapy should be conducted. Therapists reported that they and the clients were angry, frustrated, hurt, disappointed, and upset about the lack of progress. (p. 19)

Case Study 15.4

Jim referred himself to a private CBT therapist. He was a successful businessman with his own company that he had built up over several years. Over recent months he described feeling disinterested in his usual activities and very low in mood. The only thing that had helped was alcohol, and he had begun to drink every day. He recognised that drinking excessively was not good for his health. Nor did it fit with his beliefs about maintaining physical fitness. Jim attended two sessions of CBT, then failed to attend his third appointment and did not respond to a follow-up letter.

In terms of stages of change (Freeman & Dolan, 2001), Jim had started therapy in the contemplation phase or state of readiness to change. 'Contemplation is that point in the change process when the patient has reached a point of readiness to engage in the change process' (p. 228).

Potential reasons for Jim dropping out of therapy as articulated by Freeman and McCloskey (2003) may include the following.

Fear of Changing One's Actions, Thoughts or Feelings

This attitude is best expressed as, 'The devil that you know is better than the devil that you don't know.' Some individuals are unhappy, disappointed or depressed about their circumstances but see any other alternative as a black void that might swallow them up. They wonder what it would be like to be different, how being different would feel, how others would view their being different, and what would happen if they did not like the difference. Could they go back to their old ways? (Freeman & McCloskey, 2003: 28)

In terms of the therapist factors that may influence this case Freeman and McCloskey (2003) suggest the following:

- *'Lack of experience or skill on the part of the therapist'* (p. 31) – Skilled clinical supervision and further training can remedy this. However, remedial action is dependent on the therapist's ability to accept their clinical limitations. Willingness to address skills issues precludes therapeutic narcissism as discussed earlier.
- *'Poor socialization of patient to the CBT treatment model'* (p. 31) – Other health professionals, clients' families and friends may hold unhelpful or erroneous views about CBT and psychotherapy in general. Inadequate early socialisation can also be due to the therapist's lack of skill, as discussed above. To overcome or prevent this, it is important that time is taken to explain CBT in general as well as the specifics of the treatment plan, regardless of assumptions the therapist may make about the client's knowledge. It is always worth practising (rehearsing in role-play with a clinical supervisor or with fellow trainees) ways to psycho-educate clients. Also reviewing any literature that may assist verbal explanation is valuable. As mentioned previously, paying attention to the client's immediate cognitive/emotional responses and checking their understanding in a nonpatronising way will assist in assessing client understanding.
- *'Poor timing of intervention'* (p. 33) – This can be the result of the therapist's lack of experience, but there can also be other reasons. Therapists may feel pressured by time-limited therapy to move clients through the process before they are ready. Clearly this is false economy if the intervention is unsuccessful. In such cases, it is useful for the therapist to develop their skills of reflective practice. Schön (1983) suggested that there are two types of reflection:

1 'Reflection *on* action' – is reviewing what has occurred after an event.
2 'Reflection *in* action' – which Smith (2001) described as 'thinking on our feet. It involves looking to our experiences, connecting with our feelings, and attending to our theories in use. It entails building new understandings to inform our actions in the situation that is unfolding.'

> The practitioner allows himself to experience surprise, puzzlement, or confusion in a situation which he finds uncertain or unique. He reflects on the phenomenon before him, and on the prior understandings which have been implicit in his behavior. He carries out an experiment which serves to generate both a new understanding of the phenomenon and a change in the situation. (Schön, 1983: 68)

By developing these skills the therapist may more effectively recognise untimely interventions and be able to explore them within clinical supervision.

As a result of the possible complicating factors noted above, Jim may not re-engage with therapy at this point. However it is possible that he will return to therapy in the future. If he did return it would be beneficial to explore the stages of change with Jim and attempt to identify what went wrong last time. Looking at earlier problems in some detail enables both the therapist and client to learn from the experience.

Another stage of change seen in the middle phase of treatment is the 'action planning' stage. 'The therapeutic process has begun and the patient is beginning to make plans on how change will occur' (Freeman & Dolan, 2001: 228).

Case Study 15.5

Tim was a 32-year-old man who worked in a busy office environment. His occupational health department referred him for CBT after he returned to work following several weeks of sick leave. Following assessment (and development of a CBT formulation) Tim and his therapist began developing a treatment plan, about which Tim appeared motivated and enthusiastic initially. However, Tim cancelled his second appointment leaving a message saying that, due to work commitments, he was not able to attend. A further appointment was made, and Tim missed that appointment as well because he had problems with his car. Tim attended the next session but arrived fifteen minutes late.

There are several reasons clients may miss appointments including those illustrated above. Ledley et al. (2005) suggest that 'missing sessions and coming late can also be seen as self-handicapping strategies. If clients do not do the work of therapy, they cannot feel bad about themselves if it does not work effectively for them.' They go on to suggest some useful questions, which can help uncover the reasons behind nonattendance and persistent lateness:

> Why are you late/did you miss the session?
> Were you nervous about what was supposed to be happening in the session that day?
> Did you have a negative experience in the previous session?
> Do you think your thoughts about treatment or about your ability to make positive changes got in the way? For example, are you worried that the treatment is not going to help you?
> Is your lateness part of the problems you are looking for help with?
> For example, is it difficult to come to the session because you are concerned about being judged by colleagues or managers about your productivity?
>
> (Ledley et al., 2005: 172)

The therapist factors that may be involved here include any of the above issues, but also the possibility of what Freeman and McCloskey (2003) describe as 'lack of flexibility and creativity in treatment planning ... These qualities allow the treatment plan to be more fluid and individually tailored to the client's needs' (p. 35). So it is necessary for the therapist to develop creativity, which may be aided through effective use of clinical supervision, self-reflection, peer supervision and professional development activities.

Yet another stage associated with the middle phase of therapy is what Freeman and Dolan (2001) describe as the 'action' stage. 'Patients at this point are actively working at implementing change' (p. 229).

Case Study 15.6

Jan is a 26-year-old office worker. She was referred for CBT by her GP. She explained that following a road traffic accident she had been avoiding the place where the accident occurred. This had resulted in Jan having to make an extensive detour in her journey to work every morning. Jan had researched CBT on the internet and spoken to friends. She concluded that CBT would help her to get over her PTSD symptoms. Initially things appeared to be going well and Jan was receptive to the formulation and the treatment plan. However, during her fourth session Jan stated that she had tried to travel on the road where the accident occurred, but found that she became tearful immediately and felt really anxious about having to do this again.

Further exploration of Jan's account revealed that she believed she needed to be completely free of negative feelings to judge the exposure intervention as successful.

Using the Leahy Emotional Schema Scale (Leahy, 2003) may help identify client's emotional schemata and allow the opportunity for client and therapist to mutually explore pertinent beliefs. Jan's scenario above exemplifies Leahy's model of the *schema of controllability*. He suggests the following intervention:

> Do you think that you have to control your feelings and get rid of the 'negative' feelings? What do you think would happen if you couldn't get rid of that feeling entirely? Is it possible that trying to get rid of a feeling completely makes that feeling too important to you? Are you afraid that having a strong feeling is a sign of something worse? Going crazy? Losing complete control? Isn't there a difference between controlling your actions and controlling your feelings? (p. 105)

Potential therapist issues that may create problems here include 'unstated, unrealistic or vague therapy goals' (p. 34). It is vitally important to plan exposure sessions carefully:

- Be clear about the purpose of the exposure.
- Define the parameters of the exposure - clearly and accurately.
- Identify automatic thoughts about the exposure, dispute them and come up with a more constructive realistic response to take with them into the exposure.
- Set some realistic and achievable goals.
- Use a handout to guide the client through the exposure.
- Set up a telephone check in, email contact or ask clients to take notes for the next session soon after the exposure. This supports the client in processing the exposure effectively, rather than falling back into familiar but unhelpful thinking patterns. This can also be a chance to 'troubleshoot' in case the exposure did not go according to plan.

Endings

The next stage to be explored is labelled 'prelapse' (Freeman & Dolan, 2001). 'Prelapse is a point in the change process characterized by active and often overwhelming cognitions related to the reversal of the changed behavior. There has not, to this point, been an active reversal of behavior' (p. 229).

Case Study 15.7

Ken was referred for CBT by his GP after being diagnosed with depression. Having worked well with his therapist on the cognitive and behavioural elements maintaining his depression, Ken's mood improved to the point where he was able to return to work. Ken worked well at monitoring and challenging his unhelpful thoughts. He had learned to assert himself with family and friends. He reviewed his diet and started eating healthily and instigated a fitness regimen. Ken later attended a monthly follow-up session. He reported that although things were still going well, he was aware that he was experiencing thoughts such as 'It's all very well making an effort with diet and exercise when there is no work stress to get in the way, but it's really hard keeping it going when I'm under extra pressure.'

From the client's perspective it is possible that environmental factors (in Ken's case the work environment) may have an impact on overall confidence about maintaining positive changes made via CBT. To preempt and overcome such potential loss of confidence, it is important to explore possible barriers to maintaining change *before* the client goes back to work, and think about how to problem-solve if things appear to be slipping. It is also important for the therapist to consider using booster sessions where possible and/or tapering sessions slowly over a period of months. Tapering sessions is often part of a relapse prevention plan. Rowa et al. (2005) suggest 'motivational enhancement sessions' for depressed clients based on Westra and Phoenix's (2003) work on anxiety:

> motivational enhancement sessions could include (1) education about the stages of change and identification of the client's current stage; (2) listing the pros and cons of both the *status quo* and changing it (i.e., accomplishing some valued goals); (3) brainstorming other problems for which the client was able to make important changes and borrowing ideas and inspiration from those experiences; (4) having the therapist and the client switch roles (i.e., have the client take a pro-change role stance with the therapist playing the devil's advocate, forcing the client to think of strong arguments for change); and (5) having the client elaborate on the most important personal costs of depression. For the latter strategy, it would be important to ensure that clients know that if they wish, many of these consequences may be averted with successful treatment.
>
> (Rowa et al., 2005: 217–18)

The final two stages associated with the end phase of therapy identified by Freeman and Dolan (2001) are lapse and relapse. Lapse is a stage described as 'the skills needed to maintain the action stage decrease or are ignored and the changes developed in therapy begin to decrease. Although there has not been a full return to pre-treatment behavior and affect' (p. 229).

> Relapse is a return to the behaviours that were the cause of the original referral and were, ideally, altered in the action stage ... Patients at this point are actively working to overcome relapse. (Freeman & Dolan, 2001: 230)

Case Study 15.8

Sally, a 24-year-old office worker, was referred to a CBT therapist for social anxiety. She responded well to exposure-based interventions; however, there ensued a three-week break in therapy as a result of Sally's being ill and the therapist going on leave. When Sally returned to treatment she reported that she had noticed that she had begun to make excuses for not going out with colleagues. This bothered her because she thought she was 'sliding back'.

The above case provides an example of lapse rather than relapse because there is not a full return to the pre-treatment behaviours and affect. However, there is evidence that Sally is neglecting the skills needed to maintain change; she is making excuses and avoiding going out with colleagues at times. However, Sally is aware of the potential consequences of her complacency and raises her concerns about 'sliding back'.

Case Study 15.9

Connor, a 36-year-old nurse, returned to therapy after experiencing a relapse. He had completed 16 sessions of CBT and attended two six-monthly follow-up sessions, having successfully maintained therapeutic gains. However, during the following year, he began experiencing anxiety and depression again – to the extent that he suddenly left work in tears three weeks prior to being re-referred to his original CBT therapist. Connor said, 'I'm so angry with myself, I let this happen – I knew from our work that it was possible to lapse or even relapse, and I still let it happen!'

Recent research seems to suggest that about half of patients who respond to cognitive therapy for major depressive disorders will relapse within two years (Vittengl et al., 2011). With this in mind, it is important to note that regarding depression (and any other disorders for that matter) relapse prevention is an ongoing consideration throughout treatment and beyond. Helping clients to become their own therapists is the aim of CBT. However, for many clients this requires careful planning and consideration to achieve. It is good CBT practice, for example, to begin tapering sessions as the treatment plan comes to an end. So session frequency may gradually (and appropriately) reduce from weekly to biweekly and eventually six–ten monthly. This allows both client and therapist to monitor any lapse situations while still allowing the client to understand that he/she has recovered beyond the need for weekly treatment.

Another possible strategy for working with lapse and relapse is to consider the use of a cognitive-behavioural model of relapse such as Relapse Prevention Therapy (RPT) (Marlatt et al., 2002).

RPT is a cognitive-behavioural approach to treating addictive behaviours that specifically addresses the nature of the relapse process and suggests coping strategies useful in maintaining change (Marlatt & Gordon, 1985; Parks et al., 2001). It is based on the idea that addictive behaviours are acquired, over-learned habits with biological, psychological, and social determinants and consequences. Engaging in an addictive behaviour typically provides immediate rewards that increase pleasure and/or decrease pain. In other words, people engage in addictive behaviours to 'feel good' (enhanced pleasure) or to 'feel better' (self medication of pain) - although both motives can exist at the same time. The immediate rewards derived from engaging in addictive behaviours serve to maintain the addiction, despite delayed negative consequences that can be quite severe and long lasting.

RPT is based on a cognitive-behavioural model of the relapse process developed over the past 30 years by Marlatt and his colleagues (Marlatt & Gordon, 1985; Parks et al., 2001; Marlatt et al., 2002) identify several key questions about relapse both as a process and as an event:

1 Are there specific situational events that serve as triggers for relapse?
2 Are the determinants of the first lapse the same as those that cause a total relapse to occur, if not, how can they be distinguished from one another?
3 How does an individual react to and conceptualise the events preceding and following a lapse and how do these reactions affect the person's subsequent behaviour regarding the probability of full-blown relapse?
4 Is it possible for an individual to covertly plan a relapse by setting up a situation in which it is virtually impossible to resist temptation?
5 At which points in the relapse process is it possible to intervene and alter the course of events so as to prevent a return to the addictive habit pattern?

6 Is it possible to prepare individuals during treatment to anticipate the likelihood of relapse and to teach them coping behaviours that might reduce the likelihood of lapses and the probability of subsequent relapse?

(Marlatt et al., 2002: 6)

Although the above questions are developed within the field of addictions, it is certainly worth considering the utility of some of these questions with other presenting problems. The questions could be utilised with the client in session and by the therapist during clinical supervision to add clarity to formulation.

The final stage of change identified within the cycle is 'maintenance'.

> Maintenance is the final stage in the continuous process of maintaining and developing the skills of the previous stages. The goals are to (a) fine-tune and adjust changes (b) support growth (c) encourage stability and (d) help the patient to be his or her own therapist. (Freeman & Dolan, 2001: 230)

Case Study 15.10

Jade, aged 42, had been receiving CBT for obsessive compulsive disorder (OCD). She worked very well with Exposure-Response Prevention (ERP). Marks (1997) suggests: 'With ERP, sufferers are persuaded to 1) expose themselves daily to cues they avoid because they induce discomfort and rituals, and 2) stay in contact with those cues during the ensuing discomfort and not ritualize for at least an hour or until the discomfort slowly subsides' (p. 1021).

Jade learned to manage any lapses well. At the end of the therapy she reported that she felt 'completely liberated after what felt like a lifetime of being trapped in a bubble of checking'. However, despite this purported success she appeared sad. She stated that she wished she had sought help years earlier because there was so much that she had missed out on as a result of the OCD which had 'kept her trapped'.

Franklin et al. (2005) discuss this process of 'recovery and subsequent regret', commenting:

> It was important clinically to allow the patient to grieve for these significant losses ... yet at the same time it was important to make sure that the patient did not focus on what could no longer be accomplished but instead considered what could still be done. Accordingly, the therapist and the patient constructed an extensive list of things that the patient could work on now that would be fulfilling and meaningful (e.g., spending more time with her children) that could provide a more balanced focus against what was no longer deemed feasible. (p. 163)

The above quote also reflects one of the six core processes in Acceptance and Commitment Therapy (ACT) (Hayes et al., 2006), regarding values.

> Values are chosen qualities of purposive action that can never be obtained as an object but can be instantiated moment by moment. ACT uses a variety of exercises to help a client choose life directions in various domains (e.g., family, career, spirituality) while undermining verbal processes that might lead to choices based on avoidance, social compliance, or fusion (e.g., 'I should value X' or 'A good person would value Y' or 'My mother wants me to value Z'). In ACT, acceptance, diffusion, being present, and so on are not ends in themselves; rather they clear the path for a more vital, values consistent life. (p. 8)

Summary and Conclusions

This chapter has examined common challenges that both the therapist and the client may experience at different stages and phases of the therapeutic process. This has been achieved by referencing the work of Freeman and Dolan (2001) who modified the original construct of Prochaska and DiClemente's 'Stages of Change'. A key observation is: 'The change process is more of a spiral through the stages than a straight line. Each of the individual change states will, in the course of therapy, be revisited many times, often within the same session. The therapist must be aware of the potential for the spiral and accommodate the therapy to that possibility' (p. 231).

A final point to consider, with regard to the CBT practitioner's part in positive therapeutic change and maintenance, is the relevance and ongoing need for self-practice/self-reflection (SP/SR) Bennett-Levy et al. (2003). Results from their study suggested that 'SP/SR enhances the "professional artistry" of therapists, a finding consistent with literature suggesting that reflection is a key process in the development of therapist expertise' (p. 143).

References

Bennett-Levy, J., Lee, N., Travers, K., Pohlman, S. and Hamernik, E. (2003). 'Cognitive therapy from the inside: Enhancing therapist skills through practicing what we preach', *Behavioural and Cognitive Psychotherapy*, 31: 143–58.

DiGuiseppe, R. and Tafrate, R.C. (2007). *Understanding Anger Disorders.* New York: Oxford University Press.

Franklin, M.E., Riggs, D.S. and Pai, A. (2005). 'Obsessive-compulsive disorder', in M.M. Antony, D. Roth Ledley and R.G. Heimberg (eds), *Improving Outcomes and Preventing Relapse in Cognitive-Behavioral Therapy.* New York: Guilford Press.

Freeman, A. and Dolan, M. (2001). 'Revisiting Prochaska and DiClemente's Stage of Change Theory: An expansion and specification to aid in treatment planning and outcome evaluation', *Cognitive and Behavioral Practices*, 8: 224–34.

Freeman, A. and McCloskey, R.D. (2003). 'Impediments to effective psychotherapy', in R.L. Leahy (ed.), *Roadblocks in Cognitive-Behavioural Therapy: Transforming Challenges into Opportunities for Change.* New York: Guilford Press.

Grazebrook, K. and Garland, A. (2005). *What is CBT?* British Association for Behavioural and Cognitive Psychotherapies (BABCP) www.babcp.com (assessed 16 July 2010).

Hayes, S.C., Luoma, J.B., Bond, F.W., Masuda, A. and Lillis, J. (2006). 'Acceptance and commitment therapy: Model, process and outcomes', *Behaviour Research and Therapy*, 44: 1–25.

Hill, C.E. and Knox, S. (2009). 'Processing the therapeutic relationship', *Psychotherapy Research*, 19 (1): 13–19.

Leahy, R.L. (2001). *Overcoming Resistance in Cognitive Therapy.* New York: Guilford Press.

Leahy, R.L. (ed.) (2003). *Roadblocks in Cognitive-Behavioural Therapy: Transforming Challenges into Opportunities for Change.* New York: Guilford Press.

Ledley, D.R., Marx, B.P. and Heimberg, R.G. (2005). *Making Cognitive-Behavioural Therapy Work: Clinical Process for New Practitioners.* New York: Guilford Press.

Marks, I. (1997). 'Behaviour therapy for obsessive-compulsive disorder: A decade of progress', *Canadian Journal of Psychiatry*, 42: 1021–7.

Marlatt, G.A. and Gordon, J.R. (eds) (1985). *Relapse Prevention: Maintenance Strategies in the Treatment of Addictive Behavior.* New York: Guilford Press.

Marlatt, G.A., Parks, G.A. and Witkiewitz, K. (2002). 'Clinical guidelines for implementing relapse prevention therapy: A guideline', in *The Behavioral Health Recovery Management Project*, Seattle, WA: Addictive Behaviors Research Center. pp. 1–49.

Miller, S. and Rollnick, W.R. (1991). *Motivational Interviewing: Preparing People for Change.* New York: Guilford Press.

Parks, G.A., Anderson, B.K., and Marlatt, G.A. (2001) *Relapse Prevention Therapy in the Handbook of Alcohol Dependence and Problems.* Chichester: John Wiley & Sons, Ltd.

Prochaska, J.O. and DiClemente, C.C. (1983). 'Stages and processes of self-change in smoking: Towards an integrative model of change', *Journal of Consulting and Clinical Psychology*, 51: 390–5.

Roth Ledley, D. and Heimberg, R.G. (2005). 'Social anxiety disorder', in M.M. Antony, D. Roth Ledley and R.G. Heimberg (eds), *Improving Outcomes and Preventing Relapse in Cognitive-Behavioral Therapy*. New York: Guilford Press.

Rowa, K., Bieling, P.J. and Segal Z.V. (2005). 'Depression', in M.M. Antony, D. Roth Ledley and R.G. Heimberg (eds), *Improving Outcomes and Preventing Relapse in Cognitive-Behavioral Therapy*. New York: Guilford Press.

Schön, D.A. (1983). *The Reflective Practitioner: How Professionals Think in Action*. USA: Basic Books.

Smith, M.K. (2001). 'Donald Schön: Learning, Reflection and Change', *The Encyclopedia of Informal Education*, www.infed.org/thinkers/et-schon.htm (accessed 19 May 2011).

Tafrate, R.C. and Kassinove, H. (2003). 'Angry patients: Strategies for beginning treatment', in R.L. Leahy (ed.), *Roadblocks in Cognitive-Behavioural Therapy: Transforming Challenges into Opportunities for Change*. New York: Guilford Press.

Vittengl, J.R. Clark, L.A. and Jarrett, R.B. (2011). 'Moderators of continuation phase: Cognitive therapy's effect on relapse, reoccurrence, remission and recovery from depression', *Behaviour Therapy and Research*, 48 (6): 449–58.

Westra, H.A. and Phoenix, E. (2003). 'Motivational enhancement therapy in two cases of anxiety disorder: New responses to treatment refractoriness', *Clinical Case Studies*, October, 2 (4): 306–22.

PART FOUR

CBT: Specific Populations and Settings

SIXTEEN CBT with Children and Adolescents

TREVOR WITHERS

Introduction

Estimates vary, but research suggests that 20% of children aged 5–15 have a mental health problem in any given year, and about 10% will have a clinically recognisable mental illness at any one time. The environment into which children are born has a significant impact on the likelihood of them developing a mental illness. Children of lone parents are twice as likely to have a mental health problem as those living with two parents; children in reconstituted or large families (4 or 5 children) are one and a half times more likely to experience problems. Parental mental health status and poorly functioning families increase the likelihood of mental disorders in children. There are also links between childhood mental health problems and parental employment status, household income, social class, the type of accommodation in which children live and a number of other stressful life events (Meltzer et al., 2000).

During the last forty years Cognitive Behaviour Therapy (CBT) has become a popular and widely researched therapy for use with adults, and has become the treatment of choice for a wide range of disorders. This popularity is being replicated among therapists working with children and young people. CBT is increasingly applied to a wide variety of childhood psychological problems including phobias, anxiety disorders, depression, impulsivity and school refusal. CBT has now established itself as the therapy most strongly backed by research for most forms of child and adolescent psychiatric disorder, although there is still a shortage of CBT practitioners working in child and adolescent mental health services. Where therapists using CBT with children initially used models and techniques adapted from those used with adults, there is now a growing selection of literature and workbooks to assist the therapist to undertake more developmentally appropriate CBT. Materials such as 'Coping Cat' (Kendall, 2006), 'FRIENDS' (Barrett et al., 1999) and 'Think Good - Feel Good' (Stallard, 2002b), provide practical ideas in adapting CBT for children and adolescents. While the availability of these materials indicates an acceptance that children are not 'small adults', there is still a shortage of theoretical models which take account of child development.

Age-related Considerations

There are a range of skills that children (like adult CBT clients) need to acquire for the cognitive components of CBT to be accessed. Children need to be able to: recognise thoughts and identify particular cognitive biases, recognise a range of emotions and rate their intensity, make connections between thoughts and feelings and, ultimately, learn to challenge and manipulate thoughts in order to influence emotional responses. Traditional theories of cognitive development based on the work of Piaget would suggest that children between the ages of 7 and 11 (concrete operational), have not yet developed abstract reasoning skills and are therefore unlikely to be able to engage in the cognitive components of CBT. While the work of Piaget is still a major influence in the field of child development, there is evidence to suggest that children may develop some of the skills needed to engage with CBT at an earlier stage than Piaget's theory would suggest. The research of Quakley et al. (2003) would support current child development research which suggests that some, if not all, children are able to engage in abstract thinking much earlier. In a study comparing two groups of children (aged 7–8 and 10–11 years) they found that most children aged seven and older were able to distinguish between thoughts and behaviours. Most of the children in the younger age group were able to discriminate between thoughts and behaviour, while all of the older age group were also able to correctly make the distinction. While the task chosen does not demonstrate that children are able to benefit from the cognitive elements of a CBT intervention, it would suggest that children are able to demonstrate at least one of the skills required. More research would appear to be needed into auditing and assessing the skills required for CBT to be effective with younger children, e.g. identifying negative thoughts, grading emotions, challenging and manipulating thoughts, etc.

Flavell et al. (2001) suggest a three-stage developmental sequence in which children first learn to connect events and feelings e.g. bumping one's head may make us feel sad. The connection between thoughts and feelings occurs at the next stage when they discover that a memory of a past event can trigger the associated feeling. Finally, they are able to understand that thoughts alone, unrelated to any specific previous experience, can trigger an emotion. Their research suggests that children at age eight were far more aware than five year olds that a thought may, on its own, trigger an emotional response.

Systemic Issues

Children are part of a complex system in which a wide range of people have varying degrees of influence over their development while the children themselves have little or no control. Though such influences gradually expand to include peers, school teachers and others, early influence will come primarily from the family. While there is some evidence of a genetic contribution, there is significant evidence for a link between childhood mental health disorders and environmental factors. In a study of five year olds, Murray et al. (2001) observed significant differences between the children of depressed and nondepressed mothers during an experimentally manipulated card game. Children whose mothers were, or had been, depressed displayed higher rates of negative cognitions defined as 'spontaneous' expressions of hopelessness or low self-worth when they were losing. A number of research articles link the inappropriate expression of anger in children with aspects of parenting or parental modelling (Kerr & Schneider, 2008) and there is some evidence that, although there may be a vulnerability already present, controlling, over-intrusive parenting behaviours can increase the likelihood of anxiety in children (Rapee, 2001).

The evidence suggests that depressed, anxious, or conduct-related cognitions are evident at an early age. Children need to develop a range of skills to enable them to function well in adult life and are reliant on the adults in their environment to foster this development by modelling and encouraging these skills. Numerous studies support the link between parental emotional coping strategies and those of the child. As a result, interventions that target the child in isolation are often limited in effectiveness. While this is reflected in the growing number of treatment packages for a range of disorders which recommend parental involvement, the level and nature of this involvement is still a question of debate.

Adolescents may show a drive for independence and not wish their parents to be involved in the therapeutic process, or it may prove difficult in some cases to engage parents who are struggling to cope with problems of their own. Where parents are engaged in the process, this can be at a number of levels, either by supporting the process, acting as co-therapist or by taking part in therapy as a joint client. It may even be the case that direct work with the child is not necessary and that work with the parent alone may impact on the child.

Case Study 16.1

Supporting the process: Following an infection, Stephen had undergone a circumcision. His initial self-consciousness in toilets at school had developed into a phobia which prevented him from using public toilets altogether. Stephen was motivated to overcome his phobia before starting at sixth-form college. He felt that he would be unable to discuss his fears in front of his mother without feeling uncomfortable. He was, however, happy for his mother to be informed about the cognitive behavioural model and receive regular updates. Stephen was treated individually and successfully conquered his fears.

Case Study 16.2

Co-therapist: Fifteen-year-old Leah had been referred for treatment for Obsessive Compulsive Disorder, which had been prevalent for about three years. Parents both worked and Leah was offered individual sessions which were frequently cancelled. She made little progress in treating her OCD. At a meeting with Leah and her family it was suggested that her father bring her to sessions and sit in. Her father became familiar with the cognitive model for OCD and was then successfully able to support Leah.

Case Study 16.3

Co-client: Eight-year-old Jack suffered from separation anxiety. His father had left when he was three and contact had been intermittent at first, although it was now more regular. He became anxious whenever his mother left him, 'screaming and kicking'. Jack's mother, Samantha, reported a 'nervous breakdown' at age 20 and a history of panic attacks. At the time of Jack's referral she was taking antidepressant medication. She reported that she had become very protective towards him and acknowledged that this may have been a complicating factor. Jack's mother attended treatment with him. The sessions were planned to meet both of their needs – even to the extent of them completing the same homework tasks. Samantha was then given individual sessions to treat her panic attacks.

Case Study 16.4

Parent as client: Sophie suffered anxiety when faced with car journeys. She refused to travel on motorways or use public transport. She had been a passenger in the car when her mother, Susan, collided with a bus. Susan was extremely nervous about driving, would not travel on motorways, suffered panic attacks and – when she did drive – gripped the steering wheel tightly and travelled well below speed limits. Treatment was directed initially at Susan. No direct intervention was necessary with Sophie.

Assessment

Assessment is a key component of CBT with children and adolescents as it is with adults. It is important to assess the developmental readiness of the child to engage in the various elements of the treatment, as well as assessing the nature of the presenting difficulties. A comprehensive assessment may include information from multiple sources including parents, teachers and others. There are a number of decisions to be made prior to the assessment, including whether to conduct the initial interview with the child, the parents or both. While Nelson et al. (2006) recommend meeting with the entire family, there are a number of potential difficulties with this option. While it enables the therapist to observe familial interactions, it may become a delicate balancing act in retaining a neutral stance with all parties. Parents may talk for their children and the children themselves may be less open about their difficulties when parents are present, possibly resulting in the child becoming defensive. Any initial reticence may then be continued into the first stages of therapy. With older children the writer would favour giving them the choice of meeting alone or with parents initially, and the choice of whether or not parents will be present at future meetings. This helps to establish the therapeutic relationship

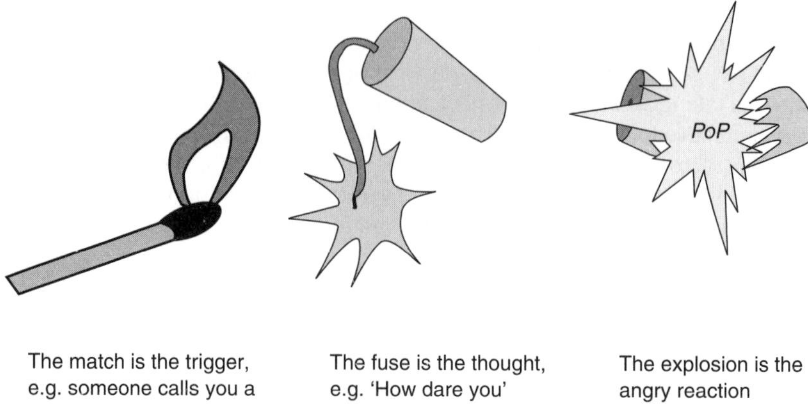

The match is the trigger, e.g. someone calls you a name

The fuse is the thought, e.g. 'How dare you'

The explosion is the angry reaction

Figure 16.1 The firework model

Source: Adapted from Novaco's model for anger arousal in Feindler, E. and Ecton, R. (1986). *Adolescent Anger Control: Cognitive Behavioral Techniques* (New York: Pergamon Press).

and encourages the child to take an active role in therapy as an equal partner from the beginning.

A linear Beckian formulation in CBT groups a range of external factors under the single heading 'Early Experiences', a number of models have also incorporated systemic factors, either for specific disorders (Fairburn et al., 2003) or for generic application (Dummett, 2006). These models may be useful and allow interventions to be tailored to the needs of young people and families. When working with younger children a simpler formulation may suffice.

There is a growing battery of self-reporting measures for the therapist to use and a variety of behavioural checklists. Children may not always be the best reporters of their own behaviour so behavioural observations may help to provide more information. Interviews with children can produce shrugs and one word answers, so a warm-up period of problem-free talk about a subject that the child feels comfortable talking about can help develop a therapeutic alliance. Adolescents may automatically respond to questions with 'Don't know' and this may have to be tackled. An interview with 15-year-old Chloe illustrates the point.

Therapist: Can you guess what I'm drawing?
Chloe: It looks like a wall.
Therapist: We all have a bit of a wall that we hide behind when a question is either too hard or we don't like the answer and that's fine. Can you see what I'm writing on the wall?

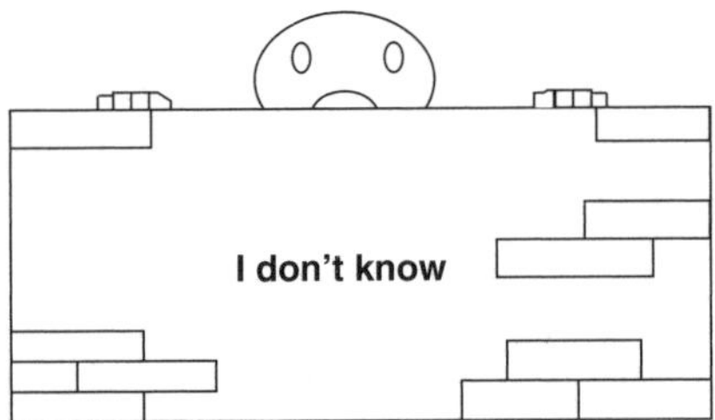

Figure 16.2 The 'I don't know' wall

Chloe: I don't know.

Therapist: I've noticed that when a question is either too hard or maybe you don't like the answer you say 'I don't know' immediately and duck back behind the wall. Do you think you could do me a favour?

Chloe: What's that?

Therapist: Well it could be me that's asked the wrong question so it would help me out if you waited ten seconds and thought about the question. Then you might still choose to go behind the wall and that's OK.

Adolescents may demonstrate self-centredness and a desire for independence that the therapist should acknowledge. They may choose to adopt a more passive listening role during sessions which will require more input from the therapist. While this is acceptable, the therapist should always encourage the child to become an active partner as therapy progresses.

Introducing the Model

A skills audit may be needed with young children to ensure that CBT is a developmentally appropriate intervention and it may be possible to rectify skill deficiencies in early sessions to prepare the child for treatment. Games are a useful way to prepare children for treatment and make sessions fun. A 'Think-Feel-Do' card sorting exercise can help to ensure that children are able to differentiate between thoughts, feelings and behaviours. Children are given a set of cards. Each card has a thought, feeling or behaviour on it. Children are then asked to sort them according to whether you would 'Think', 'Feel' or 'Do' the statement on the card. As an extension exercise they can be asked to pair up thoughts on the 'Think' cards that would create corresponding emotions on the 'Feel' cards.

A variation on 'noughts and crosses' can be used to help children distinguish between thoughts and facts. A series of statements are read to the child; e.g. 'Oranges are a fruit', or 'Fireworks are scary'. They are then asked to decide whether the statement is a fact or a thought. They then record it as an 'F' or a 'B' on the grid. This can lead to a discussion about how difficult it is to tell the difference and whether everyone would have the same thought. Some of the thoughts may be specific to the child, e.g. 'People will laugh at me' or 'I am going to get this wrong.'

Most children are familiar with thought bubbles and they can be used in a variety of ways.

Gary O'Reilly (O'Reilly, 2004) has devised an excellent resource for teaching children the concept of Negative Automatic Thoughts. He calls them gNATs who sting humans to produce Negative Automatic Thinking. He has used this idea to create a child-friendly 'Thought Diary' called a gNAT trap. He takes it further by introducing a variety of 'species' of gNAT such as 'The Over-Generalising gNAT', 'The Jumping to Conclusions gNAT' and 'The Predicting the Future gNAT'.

An extension of the gNAT trap requires the child to 'swot' the gNAT by identifying the species, looking for evidence and examining alternative ways to look at situations (see Figure 16.3). O'Reilly et al. (2009) have also developed a six-session computer game, David Gnatenborough's Island, to support the workbook.

There are a number of ways of introducing emotions to children. The DfES (Department for Education and Skills, 2005) publication 'Social and Emotional Aspects of Learning' has some excellent resources for teaching children and adolescents about emotions. A 'feelings fan' for children has some basic emotions displayed on the fingers of a fan so that younger children can select the face that best represents how they are feeling. An 'emotional barometer' for adolescents asks them to name an emotion and decide on its intensity. Other resources include 'Feeling Detective' posters and a selection of pictures of real people displaying a range of emotions. Children can be asked to identify the emotion, think of a possible situation when they felt like that and, if they are happy to do so, to describe that situation.

The writer favours a working model of an 'Emotions Thermometer' (see Figure 16.4).

Having made an 'Emotions Thermometer' it can be used in a variety of ways with either groups or individuals. With groups it can be used to challenge some of their beliefs. Give all members of the group a thermometer. Read out a situation which may lead to an emotional response (e.g. someone calls you a name). Ask them to rate their intensity of emotion on the thermometer and face it towards the group. For the student who rates a situation '10' it can be a powerful message to hear another student rate it a '2' and say that the comment could be ignored. With both individuals and groups it can be used to teach children an emotional vocabulary by writing words alongside the numbers, e.g. an anger scale may read: Calm,

Can you Capture a Pesky gNAT?

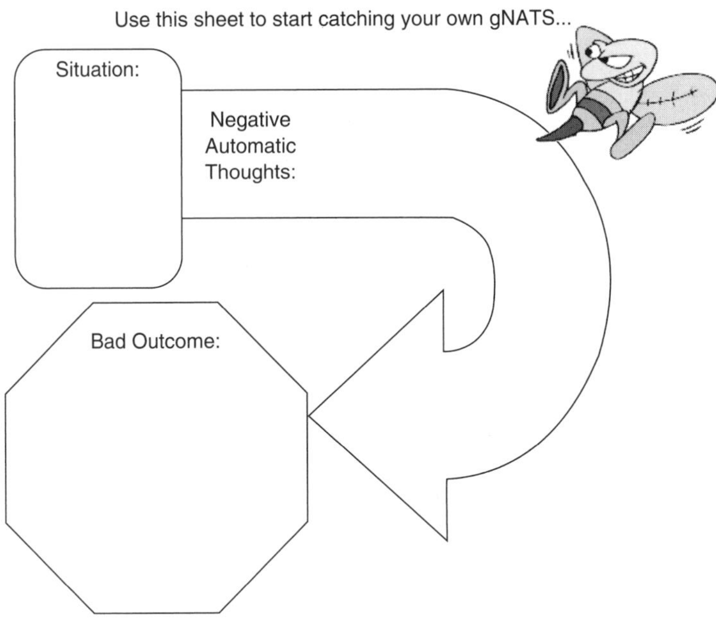

What species of gNAT have you captured? Is it on list or have you discovered a new one?

Figure 16.3 Can you capture a Pesky gNAT?

Printed with kind permission of Gary O'Reilly, School of Psychology, University College Dublin.

Irritable, Grumpy, Annoyed, Snappy, Cross etc. It is also possible to teach children that experiencing negative emotions can be healthy, for example:

Therapist: Just imagine that you've got an exam tomorrow morning and you want to do well. You're a bit nervous, probably about a 3 or 4 on the scale. What would you do tonight?

Jake: I'd probably do some last minute revision and get an early night.

Therapist: And what would you do tomorrow morning?

Jake: I might get up early and do some more revision and check my equipment for the exam.

To make an Emotions Thermometer

1. Print an A4 Emotions Thermometer as shown on card.

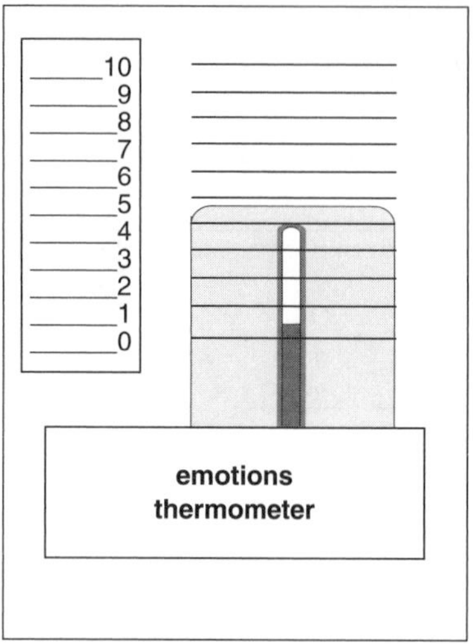

2. Lay it on top of another A4 sheet of card.
3. Laminate both sheets and cut off the top to make an envelope.
4. Cut out the reservoir and tube from the thermometer.
5. Laminate and cut an A4 'L'-shaped piece of card.

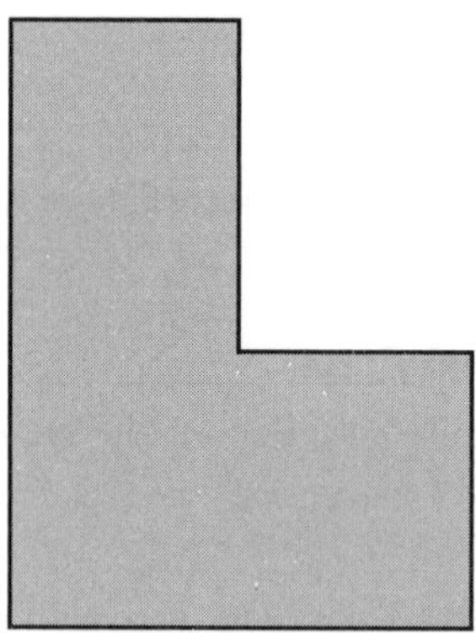

5. Insert the 'L' shaped card into the envelope/
6. Slide the 'L' shaped card up and down to display intensity of emotion.

Figure 16.4 To make an Emotions Thermometer.

Therapist: So doing those things would be good for you.
Jake: I guess so.
Therapist: Just imagine that your nervousness moved up the scale to be a 9 or 10. Now it's anxiety. You're panicking about this exam. What do you think would happen tonight when you tried to revise?

Jake: Well, I wouldn't be able to concentrate.
Therapist: And when you went to bed, what would happen?
Jake: I wouldn't be able to sleep.
Therapist: And tomorrow morning?
Jake: I'd feel tired.
Therapist: And in the exam?
Jake: I suppose that I wouldn't remember things.
Therapist: So do you think that feeling a 9 or 10 would be good for you?
Jake: I suppose not.
Therapist: So if you weren't a bit concerned you probably wouldn't bother to revise but if the emotion is too strong it can get in the way. Can you think of any other emotions that might be a problem if they get too strong?

Once children are able to identify thoughts and feelings, the next step is to teach them the connection between thoughts and feelings:

Therapist: So Jake, I just want you to imagine that you're in class tomorrow morning and the secretary comes in and tells the teacher that the Head wants to see you. How would you feel?
Jake: I'd be nervous.
Therapist: And why would you be nervous?
Jake: Because I'd probably be in trouble.
Therapist: And why would you think that?
Jake: Because I'm always in trouble.
Therapist: So if the assistant came to the door with a message for you to see the Head Teacher you would feel nervous?
Jake: Yes.
Therapist: Can you think of someone in your class who might not feel nervous?
Jake: Adam.
Therapist: And how might Adam feel?
Jake: Well, he wouldn't be bothered.
Therapist: Why not?
Jake: Well, he's never in trouble.
Therapist: So why would he think that the Head Teacher wanted to see him?
Jake: Probably to give him a sticker.
Therapist: So, even though the situation is the same you would both feel very differently about it. Why do you think that might be?
Jake: Well I suppose that we'd think different things about it.

By developing this idea the therapist can introduce Jake to the A-B-C model with 'A' being an activating event, 'B' being our beliefs and 'C' being our emotional consequence.

Recognising emotions may be difficult for adolescents as well as young children.

The psycho-educational element of CBT would include the recognition of the physiological effects of strong emotions. With children this might include a model of the human body, looking at the effects on the various parts of the body. It would also involve looking at possible functions of strong emotions. Situational triggers could be identified and recorded using a hassle log which records where they were, what happened, with whom, how they reacted and what happened afterwards to them and others. This can be extended to record thoughts, feelings, how well they managed a situation and possible alternative ways of reacting.

CBT Treatment for Children and Adolescents

Cognitive Behaviour Therapy has become an umbrella term for a variety of interventions (Stallard, 2002a), which can be applied either as an individual or group treatment. Children learn at a remarkable rate - soaking up knowledge - thus, much of CBT with children is psycho-educational and typically in a structured format. The treatment package for many young people may include a number of the following components.

Motivational Interviewing

Children may be extremely resistant to change. Externalising disorders especially may have a functional nature. Behaviour can serve to get adult interaction or access to a preferred activity. It can be used to avoid either a task or a situation and can be an easy way for a child to communicate. While a child who is anxious or depressed will usually accept the elimination of their disorder as a goal of treatment, the same may not be true of a child with anger difficulties. Motivational interviewing can be a useful part of a treatment package with many children. While adult clients will usually self-refer, children rarely self-refer whatever the disorder. Children may well be referred because of the impact that their behaviour has on others and may see little need for change themselves. Motivational interviewing may help to enlist desire for change. Techniques may include:

Active or reflective listening. The therapist reflects key words or phrases back to a child in order to build the therapeutic relationship and plant the seeds of change.

Positive restructuring. This involves looking for existing resources that the client may possess and may strengthen their sense of competence.

Cognitive restructuring. The theory behind cognitive restructuring suggests that faulty thinking is responsible for dysfunctional emotional states and the resulting behaviour. While cognitive behavioural theory distinguishes between cognitive distortion and cognitive deficiency (Kendall et al., 1990; Kendall, 1993), cognitive deficiencies in children may lead to cognitive distortions. Children view the world with limited life experience to interpret life events rationally; they may well attach extreme negative emotions to events which may be viewed differently in light of greater life experience.

Case Study 16.5

An example from the writer's own experience is of a 14-year-old boy who, when he was six, witnessed his father being violently sick as a result of food poisoning. His interpretation, based on his limited experience, was that this was a life-threatening event. His faulty thinking continued and, following an incident at secondary school, he developed emetophobia. Restructuring of his early interpretation was an important part of the intervention.

A 'catastrophe scale' is a useful way to encourage children and adolescents to put things into perspective. A 0–100% scale is drawn and the child is asked to rate how bad the event was that they found difficult. The student who was given a detention at school may rate the incident as 90% bad at the time and react accordingly. Asking them to think of a range of potential 'catastrophes' of varying degrees of seriousness (such as a car crash, a serious injury etc.) may lead to a re-evaluation of the initial incident. If the student still insists that the event was a catastrophe then an alternative approach may work.

Therapist: So you still think that being given a detention was that bad?
Ryan: Yes.
Therapist: What would happen if they made a school rule that you had to do a detention every night of the week? You've three more years at school, that's about six hundred detentions. In fact they're going to make you do Saturday morning detentions as well. How bad would that be?
Ryan: Awful. That would be a hundred.
Therapist: As bad as a car crash or a serious injury?
Ryan: Well, not far off.
Therapist: And what would you have to give up?

Ryan:	Well, I'd miss football training on Thursdays. And I play for a team on Saturday mornings so I'd miss that as well.
Therapist:	So imagine if we changed the rule and you only had to do a detention once a week. It's not even a Thursday, you even get Saturday mornings off. How much better would that be?
Ryan:	Well, quite a bit I guess.
Therapist:	Can you give me a percentage?
Ryan:	About forty.
Therapist:	But that's still about 120 detentions. What about if we reduced that further. How much would we have to cut the number of detentions to bring it down to 20%?
Ryan:	Maybe one a month.
Therapist:	So how bad would one detention really be?
Ryan:	I suppose one's not really that bad.

Problem-solving

A problem-solving approach encourages children to focus on and evaluate several possible solutions to a given problem. Most problem-solving approaches involve a stepped process:

- Describe the problem and set goals for the solution. Sometimes children can react to a situation and lose sight of long term goals. It may be necessary to break problems down into smaller ones.
- List the alternatives in terms of how well they will assist in the achievement of the ultimate goal, even those that are not helpful. It might be useful to grade them into a hierarchy of usefulness or rate them out of ten.
- Select and enact the best strategy from those identified.
- Evaluate the degree of success of the outcome and look at possible reasons.

Introducing children and adolescents to basic problem-solving enables them to generate their own solutions.

Assertiveness Training

Lack of assertiveness and an inability to communicate desires/needs (in a manner that maintains healthy relationships) can lead to interpersonal difficulties. Children may not have learnt the skills necessary for dealing effectively with situations involving conflict. There is a plethora of self-help materials on the market aimed at helping individuals become more assertive and better able to recognise and modify a variety of conflict response styles. Assertiveness training with children should be interactive using a range of activities: for example a card-sorting exercise which arranges a selection of words (e.g. mumble, shout, blame, threaten, negotiate, smile) into passive, aggressive and assertive response styles. Assertiveness is more than knowing the right words. It stems from a belief that all humans have basic rights and the recognition of our own rights as well as the rights of others. Children may have a schema about needing to appear 'strong or tough' and may lack a counterbalancing alternative schema, which isn't tantamount to 'losing face'. Assertiveness training may help to give them that alternative.

Case Study 16.6

Laura had been bullied while at junior school. Upon moving to secondary school she became friends with a group who were oppositional to authority and frequently in trouble at school. Laura gradually became more aggressive to students who were not in her social group. After fixed-term exclusion for a serious assault she agreed to attend therapy. Her assumption was that if she appeared strong then she would not be bullied again. Assertiveness training as part of the treatment enabled her to remain strong without resorting to aggression.

An important part of assertiveness training is the use of role-play to practise new skills during sessions. Creatively devising opportunities for rehearsal and practice between sessions is also essential.

Controlled Breathing or Relaxation Techniques

Breathing is a core element of relaxation yet many children do not use the lungs fully, which is more likely to encourage tension. The use of sporting models can demonstrate to children that breathing exercises can be helpful. Watching a footballer taking deep breaths before taking a penalty can help to 'sell' breathing exercises to most adolescents. Breathing out at a slower rate than breathing in can also encourage relaxation, breathing in for a count of three and breathing out for a count of five or, while walking, breathing in for two steps and breathing out for three.

Relaxation techniques can slow the heart rate and reduce tension thus leading to arousal reduction. This can create a calmer state of mind which better enables us to think more rationally and use cognitive techniques. Younger clients, especially in groups, may find closing their eyes threatening at first, thus creating more anxiety. This can be helped by simple exercises such as identifying sounds outside the room and then inside the room. This can progress to 'Sound Detectives' in which the therapist makes sounds (tearing paper, jangling keys, and clicking a pen) which the client then has to identify. Relaxation with younger children may involve them using more concrete examples such as animal imagery:

> Imagine that you're a monkey. Pull your shoulders as high as you possibly can, now let your shoulders drop and let your arms hang as low as you can.
>
> Now imagine that you're a swan. Lift your chin as high as possible and make your neck as long as possible.

This can move on to simple progressive relaxation (PR) scripts where different parts of the body are alternately tensed and then relaxed. This can be made more accessible for children by using examples such as squeezing the juice out of an orange or imagining an elephant standing on one's stomach. Visual imagery can enhance the relaxation process and is used in many sports. This may take the form of imagining oneself in a relaxing scene such as on a beach or thinking of something that makes them really happy such as stroking a rabbit. This can be developed to include stress inoculation training (Meichenbaum, 1985), in which, after the introduction of relaxation and other coping strategies such as self-talk, a stress-provoking situation from a personal hierarchy is imagined. Alternating between a relaxed state and a stressful situation can lead to a realistic or adaptive appraisal of problems and associate them with effective coping responses.

Self-control Training

Meichenbaum and Goodman (1971) found that the addition of explicit self-instructional training to modelling procedures significantly altered the attentional strategies of impulsive children and helped to facilitate behavioural change. This may start with a child describing what they are doing while tackling a simple task such as drawing a picture or writing a story. Initially they can be encouraged to think out loud, then in a whisper and then in silence. This can be extended to using self-talk while visualising an anxiety provoking situation and then using self-talk while taking part in role-play. Many children report that they 'go straight to ten' when faced with an anger-provoking situation. Adding 'self-talk' while visualising and role-playing progressively more intense anger-provoking scenes can lead to greater behavioural change.

Case Study 16.7

James found written work difficult. When given a written task he would react angrily. His anger was reinforced because it often led to him not having to complete the task. James was trained to self-talk when given a written task. 'What do I have to do?' 'It's OK to go slowly.' 'It's hard but not impossible.' 'I've done well today, everyone will be proud of me.' Teachers were instructed to set a small target of thirty words at the start of each lesson and praise on-task behaviour rather than quality of work. If James completed the task he would be rewarded. Rather than losing his entire fifteen minute break for failing to complete a task he would earn one minute for every two words completed.

Relapse Prevention

Typically this would be the focus of the final sessions of treatment and would take place once every other week. Relapse prevention would involve a review of progress during treatment, including the identification of specific actions and thoughts associated with treatment gains and setbacks. A relapse prevention plan would be developed that included identification of:

1. Possible warning signs of relapse.
2. Specific strategies to use in response to lapses and relapse.
3. Encouragement to continue strategies that the client has found useful during treatment.

Homework

Engaging in negotiated therapeutic tasks is an essential part of a CBT treatment package. This may include regular diaries, graded exposure, behavioural experiments or a range of other therapeutically relevant activities. The word 'homework' may well have negative connotations for some school age children and other terms such as 'practice' may be used.

Therapist: So if we're going to work effectively together it's important that we both do some work between sessions.

Laura: You mean like homework.

Therapist: I take it from the way that you said that, that you don't much care for homework.

Laura: Homework sucks.
Therapist: Well, I like to think of it more as practice. For example have you got any friends who play a musical instrument?
Laura: There's a boy in my class who plays the drums.
Therapist: And is he any good?
Laura: He's wicked.
Therapist: And how did he get to be good?
Laura: Well, he plays all the time.
Therapist: So he practises?
Laura: I see what you're getting at.
Therapist: Well, if he had a lesson every week and never practised he wouldn't make much progress would he?
Laura: I suppose not.
Therapist: But just a little bit of practice between lessons would make a huge difference.
Laura: I suppose.
Therapist: Well, this works the same way. There may be things that we do in sessions that it might help to practise, and that would help you to reach you goals faster. The same goes for me. I mean you wouldn't be impressed if I turned up to sessions without having done any preparation.

Discussion

This chapter has discussed the use of CBT for children and adolescents and the adaptations that need to be made for its effective use with children and adolescents. There is evidence that, when presented in a way that takes consideration of children's development, and tailors treatment interventions to the child's comprehension level, CBT can be an effective intervention.

In addition to the competencies required for working with adults, therapists working with children should have knowledge of a range of additional factors. The theoretical model of cognitive therapy with adults focuses mainly on cognitive distortions rather than cognitive deficits. When working with children, developmental experiences and patterns of attachment must be considered. There are a range of systemic factors, such as the influence of schools, families and peers, which need to be taken into account. The language used should be tailored appropriately and regard should be given to the learning style of the child. Children may find it difficult to sit and talk to an adult about thoughts and feelings, and kinaesthetic learners especially will need a variety of activities. Games and video clips to make a particular point can make sessions more interesting. Puppets can be introduced into role-play. Friedberg et al. (2004) have devised a feedback form for use with children. One of the questions asks them to rate how much fun they had during the session. Using imagination, CBT with children can be enjoyable as well as effective.

References

Barrett, P., Webster, H. and Turner, C. (1999). *The* FRIENDS *Group Leaders Manual for Children*. Brisbane: Australian Academic Press

DfES (2005). *Primary National Strategy, Enjoyment and Excellence: Social and Emotional Aspects of Learning*. Norwich: DfES Publications.

Dummett, N. (2006). 'Processes for systemic cognitive-behavioural therapy with children, young people and families', *Behavioural and Cognitive Psychotherapy*, 34 (2): 179–89.

Fairburn, C.G., Cooper, Z. and Shafran, R. (2003). 'Cognitive behaviour therapy for eating disorders: A "transdiagnostic" theory and treatment', *Behaviour Research and Therapy*, 41: 509–28.

Feindler, E. and Ecton, R. (1986). *Adolescent Anger Control: Cognitive Behavioural Techniques.* New York: Pergamon Press.

Flavell, H. Flavell, E.R. and Green F.L. (2001). 'Development of children's understanding of connections between thinking and feeling', *Psychological Science*, 12: 430–2.

Friedberg, R.D., Miller, R., Perymon, A., Bottoms, J. and Aatre, G. (2004). 'Using a session feedback form in cognitive therapy with children', *Journal of Rational-Emotive and Cognitive-Behavior Therapy*, 22 (3): 219–30.

Kendall, P.C. (1993). 'Cognitive-behavioral therapies with youth: Guiding theory, current status, and emerging developments', *Journal of Consulting and Clinical Psychology*, 61: 235–47.

Kendall, P.C. (2006). *The Coping Cat Workbook*, 2nd edn. Ardmore, PA: Workbook Publishing.

Kendall, P.C., Stark, K.D. and Adam T. (1990). 'Cognitive deficit or cognitive distortion in childhood depression', *Journal of Abnormal Child Psychology*, 18: 255–70.

Kerr, M.A. and Schneider, B.H. (2008). 'Anger expression in children and adolescents: A review of the empirical literature', *Clinical Psychology Review*, 28 (4): 559–77.

Meichenbaum, D. (1985). *Stress Inoculation Training*. New York: Pergamon.

Meichenbaum, D. and Goodman, J. (1971). 'Training impulsive children to talk to themselves: A means of developing self-control', *Journal of Abnormal Psychology*, 77 (2): 115–26.

Meltzer, H., Gatward, R., Goodman, R. and Ford, T. (2000). *Mental Health of Children and Adolescents in Great Britain*. London: The Stationery Office.

Murray, L., Woolgar, M., Cooper, P. and Hipwell, A. (2001). 'Cognitive vulnerability to depression in 5-year-old children of depressed mothers', *Journal of Child Psychology and Psychiatry*, 42: 891–9.

Nelson, M.W., Finch, A.J. and Cash Ghee, A. (2006). 'Anger management with children and adolescents: Cognitive-behavioural therapy', in P.C. Kendall (ed.), *Child and Adolescent Therapy: Cognitive-behavioral Procedures*. New York: The Guilford Press.

O'Reilly, G. (2004). *A Cognitive Behavioural Workbook for Children and Adolescents*. Unpublished manuscript. Available free from: www.juvenilementalhealthmatters.com

O'Reilly, G., Coyle, D. and McGlade, N. (2009). David Gnatenbough's Island: A Computerised CBT Game for Young People. Available online at: www.juvenilementalhealthmatters.com/Welcome.html (accessed 8 July 2011).

Quakley, S.S., Coker, S., Palmer, K. and Reynolds, S. (2003). 'Can children distinguish between thoughts and behaviours?', *Behaviour Research and Therapy*, 31: 159–68.

Rapee, R.M. (2001). 'The development of generalised anxiety', in M.W. Vasey and M.R. Dadds (eds), *The Developmental Psychopathology of Anxiety*. New York: Oxford University Press, pp. 481–503.

Southam-Gerow, M. and Kendall, P. (2000). 'Cognitive-Behaviour Therapy with youth: Advances, challenges, and future directions', *Clinical Psychology and Psychotherapy*, 7: 343–66.

Stallard, P. (2002a). 'Cognitive Behaviour Therapy with children and young people: A selective review of key issues', *Behavioural and Cognitive Psychotherapy*, 30: 297–309.

Stallard, P. (2002b). *Think Good – Feel Good: A Cognitive Behaviour Therapy Workbook for Children and Young People*. Chichester: John Wiley & Sons, Ltd.

Stationery Office (2000). *The Mental Health of Children and Adolescents in Great Britain*. London: The Stationery Office.

SEVENTEEN CBT with Older People

DICHELLE WONG AND KEN LAIDLAW

Introduction

CBT is a well-known form of psychotherapy with good evidence base for a variety of mental health conditions. Older people that experience depression, anxiety and other mental health problems often have coexisting complicating physical health problems, for example, acute illnesses like strokes resulting in long-term sequelae affecting their daily functioning; or chronic illnesses like arthritis, resulting in pain and poor mobility that also affect their functioning. A proportion of older people will also experience dementia.

Although there are additional challenges for a psychotherapist who is working with older people due to the coexisting physical health problems, research evidence shows that CBT can be applied with good effect for older people (Cuijpers et al., 2006; Laidlaw, 2010b; Pinquart & Sorensen, 2001).

In this chapter, we will discuss the evidence of CBT with older people and adaptations when used with older people. We will use case studies to illustrate CBT use with older people. We will make suggestions for therapists on how to prepare for working with older people and a discussion of computerised CBT.

Evidence for CBT with Older People

CBT for Depression and Anxiety

CBT with older people is a mainstream treatment approach for depression and anxiety in later life. It is particularly useful as an intervention because it is skills-enhancing, present-oriented, problem-focused, straightforward to use and effective (Laidlaw et al., 2003).

There are many systematic reviews and meta-analyses that show that CBT is an efficacious treatment for late life depression and more latterly for late life anxiety (Depression: Laidlaw, 2010b; Pinquart et al., 2006; Wilson et al., 2008 - Anxiety: Ayers et al., 2007; Hendriks et al., 2008; Wolitzky-Taylor et al., 2010). To very briefly summarise results of late life depression systematic reviews, it would appear that psychotherapy outcome is comparable in efficacy to medication both in terms of treatment outcome and in terms of drop-out. In addition, individual CBT appears to be superior to group-based CBT interventions. Also of note is that no single modality of psychotherapy is definitively superior to another. CBT has been the most systematically and extensively used psychotherapy for depression in later life and the consensus is that it is efficacious.

In the UK, two recent systematic evaluations of individual CBT for late life depression in primary care have published results with similar and complementary outcome (Laidlaw et al., 2008; Serfaty et al., 2009). In a study recruiting from primary care settings in Scotland, Laidlaw et al. (2008) randomly allocated participants to receive either CBT alone or treatment as usual (TAU) alone. TAU is standard treatment that older people would ordinarily receive in primary care, with no constraints upon standard practice and in this condition treatment was provided in the primary care clinic apart from one exception: access to structured psychotherapy. In the majority of cases participants in the TAU condition received antidepressants. In the CBT alone condition people received on average eight sessions. At the end of treatment and at six months follow-up evaluation, participants in both treatment arms reported benefits in levels of depression. However, there was a significant difference in outcome favouring the CBT treatment group for significantly lower Beck Hopelessness scores at six months follow-up after taking account of baseline scores between the groups. Unfortunately this study was very small and while all participants met diagnostic criteria for major depressive disorder, the levels of depression were mild; nonetheless this study remains one of the very few to compare the efficacy of psychotherapy alone with treatment usually offered in primary care and one of the very few studies that systematically measured CBT effectiveness as a treatment in a nonmedicated treatment group. This is important as many older people may not wish to receive antidepressant medication for depression or may have medical conditions that contraindicate use of antidepressants.

In the most recent RCT for late life depression, Serfaty et al. (2009) compared 'CBT plus TAU', versus 'talking control condition plus TAU' versus 'TAU alone'. In this well-conducted treatment trial, the design utilised a 'Talking control condition' that was designed as a nondirective, non-interventional supportive 'treatment', to control for the time and attention provided for the participants in standard psychological therapies. The talking control condition was designed to act much like an analogue for a placebo control condition and is a notable and welcome addition to treatment outcome research in late-life depression. When the conditions were compared, CBT participants on average achieved better treatment outcome compared to the talking control condition and TAU. Of those participants receiving CBT, 33% recorded a 50% or greater reduction in Beck Depression Inventory (BDI) scores in comparison with 23% and 21% respectively for those receiving TAU and talking control treatments. Serfaty et al. (2009) note that these results challenge the belief that depressed older people are lonely and simply need a listening ear as treatment as those in the talking control condition did less well compared to those participants in the more active CBT treatment. Thus it is evident from the work by Serfaty et al. (2009) that older people with depression benefit from active directive treatments such as CBT rather than just having someone to talk to. Talk is seldom going to be enough, behavioural change is often necessary to bring about a reduction in depression symptoms.

Adaptations to CBT with Older People

CBT should be given with the understanding of the wider picture of the older adult's life, taking into account his/her current social situation, physical and mental health problems. There are times when the problems that an older adult face cannot be altered. Often these may be health problems associated with ageing. However, what can be changed is the way the older adult perceives the strength by which he/she can cope with the problem. Instead of trying to remove the problem and feeling at a loss, there may be times where CBT can focus on helping the client use skills to cope with the problem, and to devise new ways to live with the problem.

Although older people may present with multiple health problems to the therapist, the primary aim of CBT is symptom reduction (Laidlaw et al., 2003). CBT is a time-limited, goal-orientated form of psychotherapy. Treatment should end once symptom reduction has been achieved and in practical terms CBT sessions often cease before full symptom reduction has been achieved once the individual has taken on board a new set of skills and strategies to manage their problems more optimally. This can be assessed objectively by the use of standardised rating scales before and towards the end of CBT.

CBT empowers individuals; it seeks to promote and encourage self-agency in the face of challenges and it adopts a nonpathologising stance in understanding a client's problems (Zeiss & Steffen, 1996). CBT can be a very attractive type of therapy for older people who often endorse strong cohort beliefs about personal independence and problem-solving (Laidlaw et al., 2004).

The Three Phase Approach of CBT

CBT often lasts for 16–20 sessions, with three distinct phases; early, middle and late (Gallagher-Thompson & Thompson, 2009). In the early phase of treatment, clients are socialised into the cognitive model and educated about the process of therapy and the nature of their illness (for example, depression or anxiety). The idiosyncratic appraisal of the client is important in how they manage challenges facing them. For example, in depression, there is a negativity bias where individuals have a tendency to overlook positive information, selectively and preferentially attending to negative stimuli instead (Clark et al., 1999). It is often helpful and reassuring to the client if the therapist agrees to review therapy goals and progress periodically throughout treatment. It is important to use Socratic questioning to allow a joint process of discovery where the destination and elements of the journey may be and should be unknown at the outset.

Older people are often keen to tell the therapist about their life experiences and all the health problems and social problems they face. Due to constraints of time during CBT sessions, it is advisable to try to keep the focus on the present ('here-and-now'), though allowing some exploration of past events (Laidlaw & McAlpine, 2008). A useful technique for the therapist to employ when understanding an individual's personal narrative over the course of their lifetime without getting overwhelmed with negative recall is to ask clients to construct a 'timeline' within therapy (Laidlaw, 2010a). This allows important events to be highlighted. The timeline should start from birth and go on until the date of therapy. The therapist should try to note down the client's strengths and resilience in difficult times throughout his/her life (Laidlaw, 2010a). These should be brought to the attention of the client, so as to help with empowering him/her to deal with other current stressors.

During the middle phase of CBT treatment, the focus is on identifying and modifying negative automatic thoughts. Examples of negative automatic cognitions in older people include, 'Old age is a terrible time', or 'All my problems are to do with my age', or 'I'm too old to change my ways now' (Laidlaw & Pachana, 2009). These cognitions may limit progress in therapy as problems are considered as being internal (an attribute of the individual, i.e. their age), global (all of their problems are because they are old) and stable (these problems, as they are to do with ageing, are with them for the rest of their life). These negative cognitions need to be addressed. This can be daunting and challenging for therapists who are inexperienced and not used to working with older people.

Behavioural experiments are discussed and completed as homework, in order to aid client self-discovery and promote symptom change. As many older people will have successfully met and dealt with adversity throughout their lives, CBT provides a means of rediscovering old skills and competences that have been forgotten by the client's mood-congruent biased processing of information (Laidlaw et al., 2003). Often a therapist may feel out of his/her depth due to the wealth of life experience a client has. Sometimes an older adult may question how CBT provided by a younger therapist can be helpful to him/her. One must bear in mind that the therapist is there to provide guidance on the rediscovery of existing skills instead of teaching clients new skills. A skilled CBT therapist will be able to do that regardless of their own age and life experience. The therapist can see himself/herself with the role of a coach rather than a professor when working with older people.

Older people should complete homework as part of CBT, after a collaborative discussion. If the homework task was not completed, the therapist should explore why it was not done. The homework tasks can be modified so the client feels able to do them. Homework is important since it allows the client to continue to embrace CBT when they are away from direct contact with the therapist.

As CBT is skills-enhancing, clients are taught self-monitoring skills to identify thoughts that are associated with negative mood and maladaptive behavioural response (Gallagher-Thompson & Thompson, 2009). Identifying and challenging negative automatic thoughts is termed cognitive restructuring and a common method of doing this is to use a dysfunctional thought record.

In the final phase of therapy, two main tasks remain to be accomplished. Firstly, the agreement of an appropriate termination point for therapy and secondly, drawing a relapse prevention plan. Prior to the termination of treatment, it can be helpful to engage the client in a review of what they have learned from therapy, listing what strategies have worked well. This can be completed as a homework task. At the end of treatment intermittent or booster sessions can be agreed upon in advance of discharge (Laidlaw et al., 2003).

Practical Details and Other Issues

Attending to practical details may enhance the experience of CBT for older people (Gallagher-Thompson & Thompson, 2009). A suitable environment is important. This includes a quiet room free from disruption so older people are able to focus and concentrate on the session. Disabled access may be required. Do check that the chairs are comfortable and not too low to cause difficulty for older people to get up from. If the older people have hearing impairment, the therapist should speak clearly and face the client when he/she is speaking. Older people may get tired and shorter sessions may be required. Older people may have other health appointments or be troubled by illness episodes affecting their attendance at CBT sessions. However, from experience, this does not result in poorer attendance compared to younger adults, if the therapist is prepared to be flexible in planning appointments.

Other issues that the therapist should be aware of in older people include the risk of suicide, alcohol or substance abuse. These should be discussed and raised early on in therapy. If there is an acute deterioration, the client may need to be referred onto other clinicians urgently to deal with the crisis if it is out of the area of expertise of the psychotherapist.

Preparing the Psychotherapist to Work with Older People

In addition to having CBT skills, it is very useful for the therapists to have an understanding of the symptoms of common physical health problems of older people and the consequences of having these conditions. Experience in old age health problems can be gained from medical textbooks or educational sessions, or by gaining experience directly from medical wards or clinics. It is often useful to be aware and mindful of the older people's cultural background and major historical events in the world during their lifetime.

Contrary to some people's beliefs that older people may be traditional and fixed in their ways of thinking, many older people take to CBT quickly and are able to make very good use of the CBT sessions and make adaptations to their lives. It is unhelpful to assume that older people's accounts will be drawn-out and verbose. A skilled CBT therapist should be able to guide the therapy sessions and help the client maintain his/her focus.

Although working with older people can be more challenging due to the complexity of their health and social problems, it can also be incredibly rewarding when clients make good progress.

As people are living longer, many more therapists are likely to come into contact with older people. The most important message to bear in mind here is that people are living longer but also in better health than any previous older generations and therefore therapists ought to examine their own potential age biases (Laidlaw & Pachana, 2009). The chronological age of clients reveals and predicts little and therapists ought to approach their clients and the problems they bring into the clinic with an open mind. It is worth remembering that older people are not a homogenous age grouping as there may be as many as four generations contained in that group. As people are living longer it will not be uncommon in future to work with older people who care for their parents and who still have caregiving responsibilities with younger generations too. As the baby boomer generation hits the age at which we consider people to enter later life expectations and demands for psychological therapies may increase and it may become important to consider theories of ageing rather than geriatrics to consider how we might wish to adapt CBT to enhance outcome (Laidlaw, 2010a). Increasingly therapists will be challenged to become much more knowledgeable and more effective about understanding ageing when working with older people in order to adequately meet the needs of this new generation of older people. In a recent paper Laidlaw (2010a) has outlined how negative internalised attitudes to ageing among older people may act as a stress-diathesis when older people develop age-related problems and outlines some strategies for challenging this. In the same paper, the consideration of wisdom as a concept that older people can identify with and use to recruit a sense of competence gained from challenging and/or traumatic growth experiences earlier in life points the way to consider potential adaptations that are more scientific and conceptual rather than merely procedural (see also Laidlaw & McAlpine, 2008). This is an exciting time to work with older people.

New Developments: CBT for Depression in Dementia and Computerised CBT

CBT in the Context of Dementia

In the first systematic application of CBT for people with dementia, Scholey and Woods (2003) reported a series of seven case studies exploring the potential benefits of CBT. In this pilot evaluation, cognitive impairments needn't necessarily provide major obstacles for the development of working alliances in therapy and in constructing effective individualised treatments. Results are mixed in this study as only two out of the seven participants record clinically significant change using standardised mood scales at the end of treatment although five out of seven did record reductions in mood scores over the course of treatment. What may be more important in this paper is that process issues are important in tracing out what may be helpful for other clinicians considering work with this population. This paper outlines how flexible CBT can be in addressing the idiosyncratic subjective experience of living with dementia. Receiving a diagnosis of dementia can be a potentially catastrophic experience, although, as Scholey and Woods (2003) point out, dementia can start before a diagnosis is received.

Adapting CBT for Those with Dementia

Inspiration for modifying CBT for people with dementia can be drawn from CBT used with people with other common age-related chronic comorbid conditions such as CBT for post-stroke depression (Laidlaw, 2008). Older people may have lived with dementia for a variable length of time before being diagnosed with this condition and therefore the client may have a number of preconceptions about how the condition will impact on their life. Often the individual with dementia will also have concerns about becoming a burden to their loved ones (Scholey & Woods, 2003).

Given the experiences of older people with dementia, CBT may be a particularly appropriate psychotherapy option because it is practical, skills-enhancing, and problem-focused. CBT aims to empower individuals to cope with the personal consequences of living with impairment and disability. The relative strengths of individuals are identified and practical suggestions for remaining active and oriented are emphasised in treatment. In dementia, symptoms of depression are characteristically the same as with people without dementia (Teri, 1994), and may include apathy, anhedonia and hopelessness about the future, thus increasing an individual's sense of passivity as they feel more isolated from loved ones and the world around them. In the application of CBT for older people with depression and anxiety in dementia the primary aim remains symptom reduction.

CBT also focuses on the identification and modification of erroneous cognitions. Although people living with dementia have to deal with realistic challenges, nonetheless individuals may still endorse unhelpful or erroneous cognition that can impact negatively on living with dementia. Thus the here-and-now orientation of CBT remains a potentially helpful stance when working with older people with dementia. While it may be understandable that people will have fears about the future, the reality is that the person with dementia will have more than enough problems and adjustments to contend with currently and this is an important focus for therapists (Laidlaw, 2010b). By making changes and accepting reality of some unwelcome limitations (such as memory failings etc.), the individual may find that paradoxically they are more in control of situations than previously.

A core element of CBT has always been that it is not the experiences per se but the meanings and perceptions that people adopt after experiences or in preparation to cope with experiences that determine how people feel, behave and importantly, *cope*. Thus when working with people with dementia it is their appraisal of their experiences that is important in understanding how well an individual copes with an event. CBT for chronic physical health conditions also provides a useful frame of reference when applying psychotherapy for people with dementia (Halford & Brown, 2009). Of note from this frame of reference is the need to examine an individual's illness-related beliefs and illness-behaviour. This concept may have profound implications in work with people with dementia. Older people's experience of illness may reflect memories of family members being disabled with conditions from many years ago. This is standard within work with older people and is considered cohort beliefs (Laidlaw et al., 2004). Older people may therefore experience illness within a historical context and their illness-beliefs may reflect this (Laidlaw & Pachana, 2009). Thus when working therapeutically with older people with dementia, it may be wise to understand their beliefs about this illness. The social impact of the illness may also need to be considered as the opinions and stereotypical views of those around the older person with dementia may need to be challenged in order to potentiate the active-nature of CBT interventions.

Computerised CBT with Older People

There is an increased awareness that as more older people live longer, there will likely be an increased demand for access to psychological treatments for older people. Computerised CBT (cCBT) offers a potential means of increasing access. There are an increasing number of packages available on the market although none so far have been designed with older people in mind. In a recent pilot evaluation Elsegood and Powell (2008) distributed a brief questionnaire about the use and acceptability of cCBT among 38 older people mental health service users. Although in qualitative analyses a number of negative themes were detected about use of computers, in the quantitative analyses almost half of the respondents with mild depression and anxiety expressed a willingness to use cCBT. This is a good result with a lot of potential for shaping up competence and confidence among older people using new media to deal with mild depression, especially when one considers that only 6 out of the 38 respondents had previously used a computer.

These results are intriguing and suggest that older people are more open to new approaches and methods than may be the cultural expectation. This suggests that older people are interested and invested in using new technologies as long as there is a pragmatic and practical use for these new media. Over the years there have been many misconceptions about older people and their openness to psychotherapy, especially CBT techniques like Socratic questioning and use of dysfunctional thought diaries (for review see Laidlaw et al., 2003) and cCBT with older people may be more difficult a concept for professionals than older people themselves if the results by Elsegood and Powell (2008) are confirmed in further studies and in trials of cCBT.

Case Study 17.1: Depression and anxiety

Jane is a 74-year-old lady with a history of postnatal depression. She was admitted to an old age psychiatry ward with severe anxiety and depression. Prior to admission, she showed depressive symptoms of low mood with suicidal thoughts and plans, anhedonia, poor sleep and poor appetite. She was frightened to leave her house and felt panicky whenever she tried to go out. She was also agitated when friends came to visit her at home. She viewed her situation as being so bad that death would be the only escape from her symptoms. Jane was so anxious and agitated on the hospital ward that benzodiazepine tablets (Lorazepam) had to be used for the short-term alleviation of her symptoms. Although this controlled Jane's symptoms temporarily, she became quite dependent on Lorazepam and thought that was the only way to help her. She was also prescribed an antidepressant.

Jane could not see how CBT would help her but was willing to try it. The Beck Anxiety Inventory (BAI) score was 46 before CBT was commenced, indicating a high-anxiety level consistent with her clinical state. Significant life events were identified to increase the understanding of her life situation. Negative automatic thoughts were identified with the use of a dysfunctional thought record. Jane described having panicky feelings such as 'butterflies in the stomach' and her 'heart racing away'. One of the negative thoughts she had was, 'My head is about to burst open and I will die.' The therapist looked at the evidence supporting the thoughts, and the evidence that does not support the thoughts. After a few sessions, Jane was able to come up with a more appropriate alternative thought, 'My head is not really going to burst open; it's just that I am imagining it.' Relaxation breathing techniques were taught and set as 'homework' tasks. A relaxation tape was also provided. Graded exposure was used to get Jane to take short walks outside the ward. Jane was reluctant to take walks initially but the therapist encouraged her and walked with her during the CBT sessions. They used breathing techniques while walking to control anxiety symptoms. By session 7, Jane felt that things had improved a lot. This was reflected in a reduction of the BAI score to 31.

Further CBT sessions focused on consolidating Jane's understanding in the relationship between physiological symptoms, thoughts, mood and behaviour.

Much time was spent devising a collaborative plan to tackle anxiety or panic symptoms should they arise again. The plan included five steps to cope with anxiety: (1) do relaxation breathing exercises; (2) go out for a walk to escape from stressors at home (for example, due to visitors); (3) listen to relaxation tape; (4) use the alternative thought that Jane was imagining the fear of her head bursting, and that it would not really happen; (5) take Lorazepam as the last resort if none of the previous steps had worked to relieve her symptoms.

After a total of 12 sessions, Jane was looking forward to going home. She had managed several successful days and nights at home. She had a few anxiety episodes at home but she managed to use the above four steps to control her symptoms. Jane felt in control of her symptoms and felt confident that she would be able to stop any anxiety/panic symptoms from escalating. She did not need to take any Lorazepam at home. In fact, she had not required it for the last three weeks of her seven-week hospital admission. Jane no longer felt suicidal. She was planning to take up swimming and was eager to go on a holiday with her husband. She had been out in a car trip with her husband successfully, and was able to sit with her friends at home. She was successfully discharged from hospital with follow-up at the out-patient clinic. Jane's BAI score was 6 at the last session, indicating very low level of anxiety, which was a marked improvement compared to the initial score of 45.

Case Study 17.2: Anxiety

May is a 66-year-old lady who has mild anxiety. She tends to worry about her family members and friends, and often catastrophises. She worries about all sorts of things that might go wrong. This prevented her from fully enjoying her retirement. May is independent in her activities of daily living and keeps well physically.

CBT sessions focused on exploring her strengths in coping with previous difficult situations, and cognitive restructuring to help her stop catastrophising. She had previously read a self-help CBT book, and was putting strategies she learnt from the book into use again. The therapist taught her some worry-management strategies.

CBT was completed within five sessions as her symptoms were mild, and she was thoughtful and engaged well with therapy.

Exercise

Imagine you have a client who is 87 years old. She is very anxious and preoccupied since she has developed urinary incontinence. She has a past psychiatric history of recurrent depression and early vascular dementia. She has a

(Continued)

(Continued)

medical history of hypertension, diabetes and heart attack. Her mother died from bladder cancer. The dose of antidepressant with anxiolytic effect is limited due to her medical health problems. Her psychiatrist has referred her to you for CBT to control anxiety symptoms in relation to urinary symptoms.

What other information would you like to know?
How would you prepare yourself before the CBT sessions?
How would you adapt CBT for her?
How would you explain to her what CBT is?
What problems might you face?
Who might you ask for help?

Reflection Points

- As people live longer there will be relatively large numbers of older people. How will therapists be able to meet the CBT needs for them?
- In what ways can therapists adapt CBT to make it more efficient, seeing that the demand for CBT will likely increase over time?
- What new problems and challenges will therapists face with the new and evolving cohorts of older people?
- How can therapists make use of the lifetime experiences of older people to reduce the levels of hopelessness and passivity in depression and anxiety?
- Can adversity be an opportunity for older people to make use of CBT to develop more positive coping strategies in life?

Conclusion

CBT is a practical and evidence-based intervention for older people. CBT can be successfully applied with minor adaptations. For those with coexisting health problems including dementia, CBT is skill-enhancing to help older people cope with their daily lives. The active problem-solving stance of CBT may mark this therapy out as useful for individuals who are trying to maintain optimal levels of function in the face of deterioration. As people live longer there will be relatively large numbers of older people who experience dementia or other chronic health problems. There may be more people in need of care or have the experience of providing care. There is a great need for access to efficacious psychological therapies for older people, and this need will likely increase over time.

Further Reading and Resource List

Gallagher-Thompson, D., Steffen, A. and Thompson, L.W. (2007). *Handbook of Behavioral and Cognitive Therapies with Older People*. New York: Springer.

Gallagher-Thompson, D. and Thompson, L.W. (2009). *Treating Late Life Depression: A Cognitive-Behavioral Therapy Approach. Therapist Guide*. Oxford: Oxford University Press.

Johnson, M.L., Bengston, V.L., Coleman, P.G. and Kirkwood, T.B.L. (2005). *The Cambridge Handbook of Age and Ageing*. Cambridge: Cambridge University Press.

Knight, B.G. (2004). *Psychotherapy with Older People*. Thousand Oaks, CA: Sage.

Laidlaw, K., Thompson, L.W., Siskin-Dick, L. and Gallagher-Thompson, D. (2003). *Cognitive Behavioural Therapy with Older People*. Chichester: John Wiley & Sons, Ltd.

Qualls, S.H. and Knight, B.G. (2006) *Psychotherapy for Depression in Older People*. Chichester: John Wiley & Sons, Ltd.

References

Ayers, C.R. Sorrell, J.T., Thorp, S.R. and Wetherell, J.L. (2007). 'Evidence-based psychological treatments for late life anxiety', *Psychology and Aging*, 22: 8–17.

Clark, D.A., Beck, A.T. and Alford, B.A. (1999). *Scientific Foundations of Cognitive Theory and Therapy Of Depression.* New York: John Wiley & Sons Inc.

Cuijpers, P., van Straten, A. and Smit, F. (2006). 'Psychological treatment of late life depression: A meta-analysis of randomized controlled trials', *International Journal of Geriatric Psychiatry*, 21: 1139–49.

Elsegood, K, and Powell, D. (2008). 'Computerised Cognitive-Behaviour Therapy (cCBT) and older people: A pilot study to determine factors that influence willingness to engage with cCBT', *Counselling and Psychotherapy Research*, 8: 189–92.

Gallagher-Thompson, D. and Thompson, L.W. (2009). *Treating Late Life Depression: A Cognitive-Behavioral Therapy Approach. Therapist Guide*. Oxford: Oxford University Press.

Halford, J. and Brown, T. (2009). 'Cognitive-Behaviour Therapy as an adjunctive treatment in chronic physical illness', *Advances in Psychiatric Treatment*, 15: 306–17.

Hendriks, G., Oude, R., Voshaar, G. et al. (2008). 'Cognitive-behavioural therapy for late-life anxiety disorder: A systematic review and meta-analysis', *Acta Psychiatrica Scandinavia*, 117: 403–11.

Laidlaw, K. (2008). 'Using CBT with older people with post-stroke depression', in Gallagher-Thompson, D., Steffen, A. and Thompson, L.W. (eds), *Handbook of Behavioral and Cognitive Therapies with Older People*. New York: John Wiley & Sons, Inc.

Laidlaw, K. (2010a). 'Are attitudes to ageing and wisdom enhancement legitimate targets for CBT for late life depression?', *Nordic Psychology*, 62 (2): 27–42.
Laidlaw, K. (2010b). 'CBT approaches in older adults – what the research tells us', *Healthcare Counselling and Psychotherapy Journal*, 10: 16–21.
Laidlaw, K., Davidson, K.M., Toner, H.L., Jackson, G., Clark, S., Law, J., Howley, M., Bowie, G. and Connery, H.A. (2008). 'Randomised controlled trial of cognitive behaviour therapy versus treatment as usual in the treatment of mild to moderate late life depression', *International Journal of Geriatric Psychiatry*, 23: 843–50.
Laidlaw, K. and McAlpine, S. (2008). 'Cognitive-Behaviour Therapy: How is it different with older people?', *Journal of Rational Emotive Cognitive Behaviour Therapy*, 26: 250–62.
Laidlaw, K. and Pachana, N. (2009). 'Aging, mental health and demographic change: psychotherapist challenges', *Professional Psychology: Research and Practice*, 40, 601–8.
Laidlaw, K., Thompson, L. and Gallagher-Thompson, D. (2004). 'Comprehensive conceptualisation of Cognitive Behaviour Therapy for late life depression', *Behavioural and Cognitive Psychotherapy*, 32: 1–8.
Laidlaw, K., Thompson, L.W., Siskin-Dick, L. and Gallagher-Thompson, D. (2003). *Cognitive Behavioural Therapy with Older People.* Chichester: John Wiley & Sons, Ltd.
Pinquart, M. Duberstein, P.R. and Lyness, J.M. (2006). 'Treatments for later-life depressive conditions: A meta-analytic comparison of pharmacotherapy and psychotherapy', *American Journal of Psychiatry*, 163: 1493–1501.
Pinquart, M. and Sorensen, S. (2001). 'How effective are psychotherapeutic and other psychosocial interventions with older people? A meta-analysis', *Journal of Mental Health and Aging*, 7: 207–43.
Scholey, K.A. and Woods, B.T. (2003). 'A series of brief cognitive therapy interventions with people experiencing both dementia and depression', *Clinical Psychology and Psychotherapy*, 10: 175–85.
Serfaty, M., Haworth, D., Blanchard, M., Buszewicz, M., Murad, S. and King, M. (2009). 'Clinical effectiveness of individual cognitive behavioral therapy for depressed people in primary care: A randomized controlled trial', *Archives of General Psychiatry*, 66: 1332–40.
Teri, L. (1994). 'Behavioral treatment of depression in patients with dementia', *Alzheimer Disease and Associated Disorders*, 8, Suppl. 3: 66–74.
Wilson, K., Mottram, P.G. and Vassilas, C.A. (2008) 'Psychotherapeutic treatments for older depressed people', *Cochrane Database of Systematic Reviews*, Issue 1, Art. No.: CD004853.DOI: 10.1002/14651858.CD0044853.pub2
Wolitzky-Taylor, K.B., Castriotta, N., Lenze, E.J., Stanley, M.A. and Craske, M.G. (2010) 'Anxiety disorders in older adults: A comprehensive review', *Depression and Anxiety*, 27 (2): 190–211.
Zeiss, A.M. and Steffen, A. (1996). 'Treatment issues with elderly clients', *Cognitive and Behavioral Practice.* 3: 371–89.

EIGHTEEN CBT for People with Intellectual and Developmental Disabilities

JOHN L. TAYLOR AND WILLIAM R. LINDSAY

Introduction

This chapter provides an overview of recent developments in the application of CBT for people with intellectual and developmental[1] disabilities (IDD) who experience mental health and emotional problems. The prevalence of mental health problems in this population and factors associated with the development of such difficulties are described. The historically poor response to such needs and recent developments in

[1]The term developmental disability refers to the definition given in the US Developmental Disabilities Assistance and Bill of Rights Act (1978) and is a broad concept covering the equivalent terms of intellectual disability, learning disability, and mental retardation. In addition to intellectual disability, the concept includes other conditions that do not necessarily involve significant sub-average intellectual functioning such as autism, epilepsy, and other neurological conditions.

the evidence base supporting the use of CBT with people with IDD are summarised. Finally, how people with IDD can be prepared for these interventions, and how the interventions can be adapted for people in this population are explored.

Mental Health Problems and People with IDD

As a group, people with IDD are more likely than those in the general population to experience living circumstances and life events associated with an increased risk of mental health problems, including birth trauma, stressful family circumstances, poverty, unemployment, stigmatisation, lack of self-determination, and a lack of meaningful friendships and intimate relationships (Martorell et al., 2009). People with IDD report experiencing stigma and negative beliefs about themselves and their social attractiveness (MacMahon & Jahoda, 2008). In addition, people with IDD may have fewer psychological resources available to cope effectively with stressful events, as well as poorer cognitive abilities including memory, problem-solving and planning skills (van den Hout et al., 2000).

Studies of mental health problems among people with IDD report large variations in prevalence depending on the methodology used, such as the nature and type of diagnostic assessment used, the location of the study sample (e.g. in-patient vs. generic community services), and the inclusion of challenging behaviour as a mental health problem or not (see Kerker et al., 2004 for a brief review).

Studies of populations of people with IDD using screening instruments to identify potential cases report rates of mental health problems (excluding challenging behaviour) of between 20% and 39% (see Table 18.1). This compares with approximate rates of between 16% and 25% for similar mental health problems in the general population (e.g. Meltzer et al., 1995). Although the overall rates of mental health problems among people with IDD appear to be broadly similar to those found in the general population, the profiles for different types of disorders seem to differ. In particular, the finding that rates for psychosis is higher among people with IDD is consistent across studies (e.g. Deb et al., 2001; Taylor et al., 2004). See Hatton and Taylor (2010) for a more detailed discussion of the prevalence of specific types of mental disorder (depression, anxiety, psychosis, dementia, substance misuse and anger) among people with IDD.

Case recognition is a crucial step in meeting the mental health needs of people with IDD (Moss et al., 1998). However, many people with IDD have mental health problems that are not detected and so remain

Table 18.1 Selected Studies of the Prevalence of Mental Health Problems Experienced by Adults with Intellectual and Developmental Disabilities using Screening Assessments

Study	N	Prevalence %	Sample (and Screening measure)
Taylor et al. (2004)	1,155	20	All adults with IDD known to services within a local authority county district, England, UK (PAS-ADD Checklist)*
Deb et al. (2001)	90	22	Random sample of adults with IDD on local social services case register, Wales, UK (Mini PAS-ADD)*
Roy et al. (1997)	127	33	Consecutive sample of adults with IDD from a social services register, England, UK (PAS-ADD Checklist)*
Reiss (1990)	205	39	Random selection of IDD community-based day programme users, USA (Reiss Screen)*
Iverson & Fox (1989)	165	36	Random sample of adult IDD service users, USA (PIMRA)*

*Key: (PAS-ADD Checklist) Psychopathology Assessment Schedule for Adults with Developmental Disability (Moss et al., 1998); (Mini PAS-ADD) Mini Psychopathology Assessment Schedule for Adults with Developmental Disability (Prosser et al., 1997); (Reiss Screen) Reiss Screen for Maladaptive Behavior (Reiss, 1988); (PIMRA) Psychopathology Instrument for Mentally Retarded Adults (Matson et al., 1984).

untreated. There are a number of reasons for this. Services for people with IDD and those for people with mental health problems are often separate and have distinct cultures leading to gaps in provision for people with IDD who also have mental health problems (Hassiotis et al., 2000).

Given the values base and ethos of their training, many staff supporting clients with IDD are likely to use a challenging behaviour rather than a mental health conceptual framework to understand problematic behaviour and thus may be antithetic to viewing a person's behaviour as indicative of a mental health problem rather than a form of 'challenging behaviour' (Costello, 2004).

A related issue is that of *diagnostic overshadowing* (Reiss et al., 1982), where carers and professionals misattribute signs of a mental health problem, such as social withdrawal as a result of feelings of depression, to an aspect of a person's intellectual disability, for example poor social skills. Although it is likely that there are overlaps in terms of causes and maintaining factors, the relationship between mental health problems and challenging behaviour in people with IDD is unclear (Emerson et al., 1999).

The assessment measures available to detect mental health problems among people with IDD are not well developed and often lack reliability and validity. However, work is underway concerning measures for a range of purposes and conditions (e.g. screening and detailed diagnostic assessments for multiple mental health problems, anxiety, depression, psychosis and trauma) using adapted and *de novo* measures that can be self- or informant-rated. Detailed information on a wide range of mental health measures for people with IDD is provided by Hatton and Taylor (2010).

An Overview of the Evidence for CBT for People with IDD

Reviews of Evidence Supporting CBT for People with IDD

There have been numerous (mainly narrative) reviews and commentaries that have considered the application of CBT to people with IDD who have mental health and emotional problems (see Taylor et al., 2008 for a synopsis of these publications). Prout and Nowak-Drabik (2003) reported on perhaps the most comprehensive review of psychotherapy for people with IDD. Using a clear definition of psychotherapy, they considered 92 studies published over a 30-year period. Twelve studies (13% of the total) were categorised as CBT-based interventions. Overall, these interventions were rated as being 'moderately' to 'significantly' effective or beneficial to clients receiving them. Exploratory analyses indicated that manual-guided individual treatments that were behaviourally orientated produced the most effective outcomes.

Gustafsson et al. (2009) surveyed systematic reviews that evaluated the effects of psychosocial interventions for adults with IDD who experienced mental health problems. They found 55 reviews that concerned the effectiveness of psychotherapy (mainly behavioural and cognitive-behavioural interventions) for adults with IDD published between 1969 and 2005. Only two reviews met the survey inclusion criteria. The results of these reviews showed that interventions based on cognitive-behavioural approaches appear to reduce aggression at the end of treatment, although the reviews included studies judged to be of low quality.

Willner (2005) critically reviewed psychotherapeutic interventions for people with IDD. He found that CBT interventions utilising cognitive skills training (e.g. self-management, self-monitoring, self instructional-training) show promise for a range of mental health and emotional control problems. Approaches focussing on cognitive distortions were considered to have only a very limited evidence base. Willner concluded that there is a 'wealth of evidence' (p. 82) from methodologically weak studies that psychological therapies (chiefly CBT) can benefit people with IDD with emotional problems for which there is no realistic alternative.

Evidence for Specific Mental Health and Behavioural Problems

Cognitive-behavioural interventions for people with IDD have been applied to five main areas: anger; anxiety; depression; psychosis; and offending behaviour.

Anger. More controlled intervention studies have been conducted concerning cognitive-behavioural interventions to reduce anger and related aggression in people with IDD than in any other clinical area (see Taylor & Novaco, 2005 for a review). A series of studies involving either wait-list or randomised control groups have demonstrated the effectiveness of cognitive-behavioural anger treatments in community settings (e.g. Willner et al., 2002) and more secure settings (e.g. Taylor et al., 2005).

Anxiety. Case studies and case series have demonstrated the effectiveness of cognitive and behavioural interventions in reducing anxiety among people with IDD (Dagnan & Jahoda, 2006); including behavioural interventions such as relaxation and anxiety management training (Lindsay et al., 1989) and Cognitive Behaviour Therapy (Lindsay et al., 1997).

Depression. There is a small number of case studies, case series and small trials evaluating CBT with people with mild/moderate IDD and depression (Jahoda et al., 2006) which indicate improvements in self-reported depressive symptoms and behaviour maintained at follow-up (e.g. McGillivray et al., 2008).

Psychosis. Quite limited evidence is available supporting psychosocial interventions for people with IDD and psychosis, with early case studies of behavioural treatments (Mace et al., 1988) and more recent case studies and case series of cognitive-behavioural treatments (e.g. Barrowcliff, 2008; Haddock et al., 2004) demonstrating both feasibility and the potential for improvements in outcomes.

Offending behaviour. Lindsay et al. (2004) have comprehensively covered the field of offending by people with IDD, with additional specific reviews of psychological interventions with offenders with learning disabilities (e.g. Lindsay & Taylor, 2005). Group and individual Cognitive Behaviour Therapy with sex offenders with IDD has shown considerable promise (see Lindsay, 2008), as has group cognitive-behavioural intervention for convicted fire-setters and arsonists (e.g. Taylor et al., 2002), and a pilot study reported improved coping skills in forensic IDD patients using a dialectical behaviour therapy (DBT) group intervention (Sakdalan et al., 2010).

Access to Therapy for People with IDD

Despite the vulnerability of people with IDD to mental health problems, historically there has been a general lack of interest in or regard for the needs of this client group (Stenfert Kroese, 1998). This, despite there being clear evidence that people in this population have higher levels of unmet need and receive less effective treatment, and despite the introduction of anti-discrimination legislation designed to break down these barriers (Michael, 2008). The *National Service Framework for Mental Health* (DoH, 1999) applies to all adults of working age, and was aimed to improving quality and tackling variations in access to care. People with IDD who experience mental health problems should be able to access services and receive the same treatment as others with reasonable modifications being made in accordance with relevant disability legislation.

In the past, therapists have been reluctant to offer individual psychotherapy to clients with IDD because this would require the development of close working relationships with people perceived to be unattractive because of their disabilities which make the therapeutic endeavour more demanding and the achievement of quick treatment gains more difficult. Bender (1993) used the term the 'the unoffered chair' to describe this 'therapeutic disdain' (p. 7). In addition, people with IDD may not be considered to have the cognitive abilities required to understand or benefit from CBT. There is, however, no evidence in the IDD field that deficits in particular cognitive abilities result in poorer outcomes, and studies involving children show that it is not necessary to have mature adult cognitive apparatus to benefit from CBT (Durlak et al., 1991).

A further reason for services and therapists failing to offer psychological therapy to people with IDD is, as can be seen above, a paucity of research to support its use with these clients. The lack of good quality research is in part due to difficulties in obtaining funding for research in this area. Another issue is clients' capacity to give valid consent to take part in clinical research. Although some people with IDD may not be able to comprehend all the elements necessary for participation in research (Arscott et al., 1998), there is evidence that research participants of average intellectual ability do not fully comprehend key aspects of treatment studies they have consented to take part in either (Featherstone & Donovan, 2002). Thus we risk discriminatory practices in excluding people with IDD from potentially beneficial or benign treatment outcome research based on erroneous assumptions about their capacity to consent compared with the general population.

Fortunately, there are some indications that the application of CBT with people with IDD is becoming more widely accepted. Around a third of British psychologists who responded to a survey on the use of psychotherapy with people with IDD reported using these approaches frequently (Nagel & Leiper, 1999). An edited book on CBT for people with IDD (Stenfert Kroese et al., 1997) and a special issue of the *Journal of Applied Research in Intellectual Disabilities* devoted to CBT (Willner & Hatton, 2006) point to increasing interest in the use of these therapeutic approaches with these clients, in the UK at least. Another positive indicator is that a recent special issue of *Behavioural and Cognitive Psychotherapy* – the official scientific journal of the *British Association for Behavioural and Cognitive Psychotherapies* (BABCP) – concerning developments in the theory and practice of CBT included a paper on applications for people with IDD (Taylor & Steel, 2008).

Adapting CBT for People with IDD

Assessment Issues

Successful CBT interventions are underpinned by good quality formulations, which in turn require reliable and valid assessment. Thus in considering CBT for people with IDD appropriate clinical assessment tools to aid treatment formulation and evaluate outcome need to be identified. Hatton and Taylor (2010) describe a number of measures that can be used to assess and evaluate mental health and emotional problems in this population. In general terms, it is important that clients can understand any assessment given to them. Since this client group is characterised by significant deficits in literary and comprehension skills, all assessments must be suitably adapted to simplify the language and concepts employed.

One solution to this problem is to read and explain the assessment items and response categories to respondents. This has two consequences. First, assessment will take much longer and it is not possible to give the client a series of questionnaires to take away and bring back completed to the next appointment. Second, because the assessor has to read the item and explain the responses, all assessments take the form of a structured interview. The respondents' reactions to questions, tangential comments and emotional responses are all available to the assessor as part of the assessment process. This is an added strength of conducting assessments with this client group in this manner and it provides information that can add to the richness of the assessment-formulation and treatment planning processes.

Finlay and Lyons (2001) reviewed the available literature on the assessment of emotion and other psychotherapeutic issues in people with IDD and concluded that there was ample evidence that suitably adapted assessments could be understood and used appropriately by this client group. However, as adaptations to content and administration of measures used with clients with IDD can be extensive then it is important that the psychometric properties of the instruments remain intact and that the integrity of the assessment process is not undermined or invalidated by the adaptations. These issues have been dealt with extensively elsewhere (e.g. Taylor & Novaco, 2005).

The Focus of Intervention – Cognitive Distortions and Deficits

Kendall (1985) distinguished between a *cognitive distortion* model as the basis of traditional CBT (e.g. Beck, 1976) which aims to identify and modify distortions in the content of thoughts, beliefs and attributions; and a *cognitive deficit* model as the basis of self-management interventions (e.g. Meichenbaum's (1977) self-instructional training) that focus on deficiencies in the processes by which information is acquired and processed. Cognitive deficit based self-management approaches are the most common type of cognitive interventions used with people with IDD, but these approaches have been criticised for their lack of generalisability across skills and settings, and their dependence on external cues (e.g. Willner, 2005).

One potential advantage of cognitive therapy based on Beck's (1976) approach, which aims to modify distorted evaluative beliefs, is that it endeavours to promote portable internalised control that facilitates generalisability across situations and settings (Taylor, 2005). Unfortunately, many interventions for people with IDD labelled as CBT have not included techniques aimed at identifying and modifying cognitive distortions. They have instead focused on cognitive deficit based approaches to developing clients' skills in self-monitoring and self-instruction (Beail, 2003).

This orthodoxy is now being challenged. Willner and Goodey (2006) describe how CBT can be modified in practice for clients with a range of significant cognitive impairments to take account of these deficits in such away that it is still effective in targeting the cognitive distortions that are central to the presenting problem. Also, there has now been a number of controlled studies of cognitive behavioural anger interventions that have explicitly incorporated cognitive content and restructuring treatment components and resulted in successful outcomes with people with IDD living in secure and community settings (e.g. Taylor et al., 2005; Willner et al., 2002). Further, Lindsay (1999) reported successful CBT adaptations that explicitly incorporated work on the content of cognitions underpinning and maintaining emotional difficulties with adults with IDD referred for a range of clinical problems including anxiety, depression and anger. Haddock et al. (2004) reported a case series of five people with mild intellectual disability and psychosis who improved on measures of psychotic symptoms and behaviour following adapted CBT that included a cognitive restructuring component. Using imagery rehearsal therapy, a technique that treats dream imagery as cognitive distortions, Willner (2004) and Stenfert Kroese and Thomas (2006) successfully treated a man and two women respectively who were experiencing post-abuse nightmares.

Therapy Process and Delivery Adaptations

While the evidence available suggests that treatment is most effective with people with IDD when it is set out in manual form (e.g. Prout & Nowak-Drabik, 2003), there has to be variation in the focus, pace and emphasis of the therapy delivered by different therapists working with different clients based on an analysis and formulation of their needs. CBT is, by nature, collaborative and interactive. Therapy, therefore, has to be delivered in a manner that reflects these dynamics. Thus, manualised interventions should be used to provide a framework within which therapists and clients can flexibly apply the therapeutic techniques described to meet the needs of individual patients. There is a clear distinction between *protocol-guided* and *protocol-driven* treatments - the latter tend to be applied rigidly, are not reflexive to needs of clients and lead to poorer outcomes when administered by skilled therapists.

It has been suggested that when working with clients with IDD therapy sessions are delivered at the rate of two sessions per week (Taylor & Novaco, 2005). A more intensive treatment schedule can offset some of the cognitive limitations of this client group which can result in problems with assimilation and recall of information from session to session. This in turn can enhance clients' motivation to remain engaged in treatment by maintaining momentum and preventing therapy drift.

The core components of CBT should be readily recognisable and well defined in interventions targeted at people with IDD. However, account the material used will need to be adapted to take into account the client's cognitive impairments and learning style. For example, a simplified cognitive model will need to be developed to enable clients with IDD to make sense of their emotional problems, share a common vocabulary, and collaborate in the formulation process. An attempt to produce a simple cognitive model of anger to support CBT with a patient with a history of serious aggression and violence towards others is shown in Figure 18.1. The linear model depicted in the boxes, reinforced by simple pictorial representations, allowed the therapist and client to set out on the left-hand side of the worksheet a starting formulation concerning this individual's experience of anger in terms of provocations, typical cognitive, emotional and behavioural responses to such stimuli, and the personal costs for this person. This can be used as a basis for discussing and agreeing the focus of the intervention at an individual level.

Another adaptation to CBT for people with IDD concerns the involvement of carers in the therapy process. This has been done to good effect in the cognitive-behavioural treatment of psychotic symptoms experienced by people with IDD (Haddock et al., 2004). Also, anger management interventions for adults living in community settings have routinely involved direct carers in group therapy sessions (e.g. Rose et al., 2005). In this study the involvement of carers had a significant positive impact on outcomes post-treatment, though this effect was not maintained at follow-up. In other instances carers have not been routinely involved in treatment sessions but have been asked to support the completion of homework tasks and diaries between sessions (Taylor et al., 2005).

Preparing Clients with IDD for CBT

Incorporating a Preparatory Phase

Many people with IDD and mental health problems have personal histories that create barriers to their engagement in trusting therapeutic relationships. Physical, emotional and sexual abuse, as well as repeated failures in human service settings and perceived rejection by important others are common experiences. Thus, a psycho-educational 'preparatory

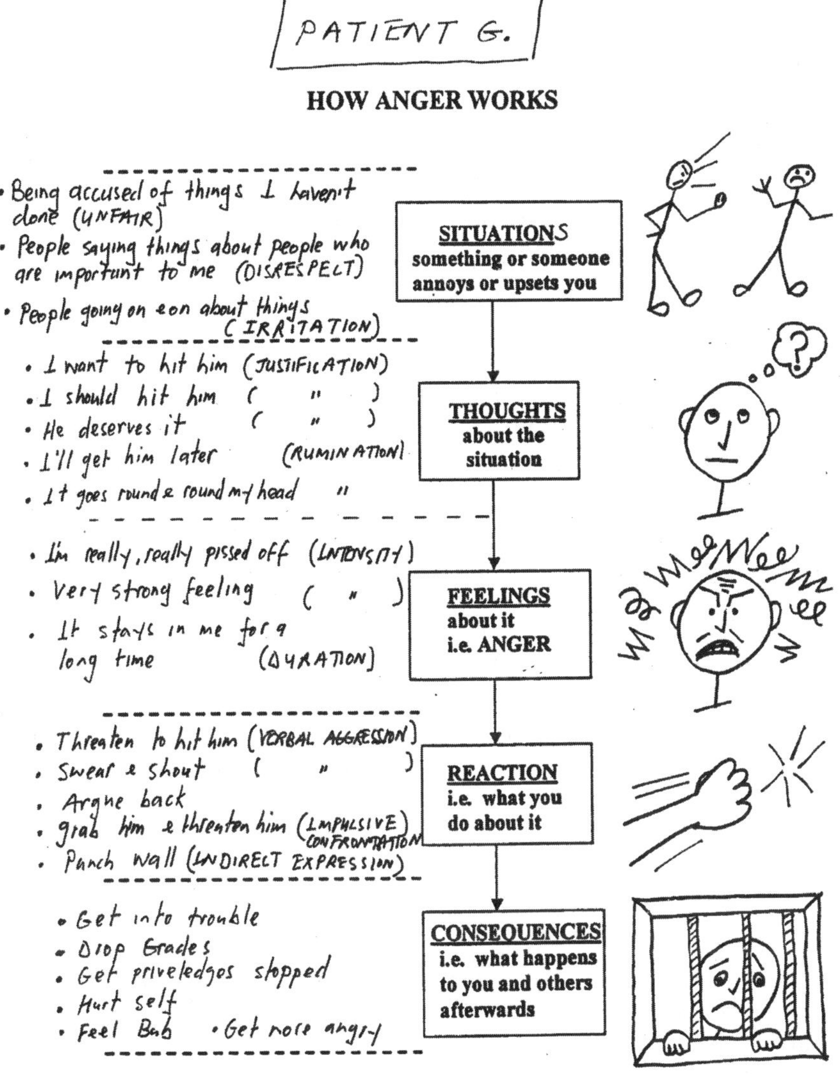

Figure 18.1 Simplified CBT model of anger

phase' can be helpful in helping to develop the skills and confidence required to successfully engage in and benefit from treatment, and to judge whether the individual can cope with the demands of treatment. Taylor and Novaco (2005) developed a six-session preparatory phase aimed at desensitising patients to any fears that they might have about embarking on intensive cognitive behavioural anger treatment. The goals of this phase of treatment were to: (a) give the client information on the nature and purpose of treatment; (b) encourage motivation to change unhelpful coping responses by identifying the costs of this behaviour; (c) develop some basic skills needed for successful treatment including self-disclosure, emotional awareness, self-monitoring and recording, and basic relaxation techniques; (d) foster trust and confidence in the therapist and the therapeutic process; and (e) emphasise the collaborative nature of the treatment that is aimed primarily at helping the client achieve better self-control.

Cognitive Skills Training

Despite their cognitive impairments there is experimental evidence that people with mild IDD can recognise emotions, label emotions, discriminate thoughts, feelings and behaviours, and link events and emotions (Taylor et al., 2008). However, it has been found that the majority of IDD participants were unable to successfully complete experimental tests of their ability to understand the mediating role of cognitions, particularly when the complexity of the task was increased (Oathamshaw & Haddock, 2006). On the other hand, Bruce et al. (2010) have demonstrated in a controlled study that this ability for cognitive mediation can be successfully trained and is generalisable to new material. Inclusion of a preparatory phase can enable an assessment of a client's cognitive skills deficits and then an opportunity for training to optimise their involvement in the treatment process.

Consent to Treatment

Unlike most non-IDD populations, people with IDD do not generally self-refer for help with their emotional and mental health problems. Family members, support workers or other professionals involved in their care, have usually identified those who present for treatment. Thus, it is incumbent on therapists to ensure every effort is made to seek valid consent to treatment (Sturmey & Gaubatz, 2002). Although some people with learning disabilities can understand the elements necessary for participation in treatment, many cannot (Arscott et al., 1999).

According to the Lord Chancellor's Department (1999) valid consent requires: (a) that clients are provided with sufficient accurate information concerning the treatment; (b) that they have capacity to make a decision about accepting treatment and to understand the consequences of the decision; and (c) that their decision to accept treatment is voluntary. Capacity involves the ability to comprehend information about the treatment, to be able to assimilate and recall the information, and to be able make a decision about accepting the treatment being offered (Wong et al., 1999).

Making information about treatment understandable and accessible to people with cognitive limitations is challenging for clinicians, but not insurmountable (Arscott et al., 1999). A psycho-educational preparatory phase has the added benefit of improving patients' understanding of the treatment process so that they are in a better position to give or withhold valid consent before moving in to the next phase of treatment.

Summary and Conclusions

While people with IDD are potentially more vulnerable than others to experiencing mental health problems, historically their needs have not been clearly identified, they have endured significant obstacles to accessing services, and the therapeutic community has eschewed them. Based on the emerging evidence concerning the effectiveness of psychological interventions, chiefly CBT, for the emotional problems experienced by these clients, this historical 'therapeutic disdain' is no longer justified.

Clients with mild IDD do have or can be trained to have the skills required to engage in the cognitive component of CBT. Although these skills appear to decline as receptive vocabulary decreases, it is not clear whether this is a function of the complexity of the experimental tasks involved or a real phenomenon and there are risks in extrapolating from failure on experimental cognitive tasks to an inability to engage with cognitive components of CBT in a therapeutic context (Taylor et al., 2008).

Clinical research has indicated that clients' responsiveness to the cognitive appraisal and restructuring components of CBT is not related to clients' IQ level in a linear way (Taylor et al., 2009). This and other potential moderators of treatment effectiveness, such as the routine inclusion of carers in treatment and therapist's training and experience, require further investigation.

Although the picture is gradually changing from one of professional indifference to one of increasing interest and concern, some basic issues concerning access to and delivery of mental health services for people with IDD have yet to be resolved. The DoH Improving Access to Psychological Therapies (IAPT) programme is focussed on the implementation of NICE guidelines for common mental health problems in England (www.iapt.nhs.uk). The *Learning Disabilities Positive Practice Guide* (DoH, 2009) states that IAPT services need to be flexible in providing effective psychological therapies for people with IDD. This might include offering materials in easy-to-understand formats, assessments, and NICE approved psychological interventions modified to meet the needs of people with IDD. However, it is currently not known and no data are being systematically collected to show whether or not people with IDD are able to access and benefit from these services. This would seem to be an appropriate and feasible next step in moving towards integrated services that take seriously the mental health needs of people with IDD.

References

Arscott, K., Dagnan, D. and Stenfert Kroese, B. (1998). 'Consent to psychological research by people with an intellectual disability', *Journal of Applied Research in Intellectual Disabilities*, 11: 77–83.

Arscott, K., Dagnan, D. and Stenfert Kroese, B. (1999). 'Assessing the ability of people with a learning disability to give informed consent to treatment', *Psychological Medicine*, 29: 1367–75.

Barrowcliff, A.L. (2008). 'Cognitive-behavioural therapy for command hallucinations and intellectual disability: a case study', *Journal of Applied Research in Intellectual Disabilities*, 21: 236–45.

Beail, N. (2003). 'What works for people with mental retardation? Critical commentary on cognitive-behavioural and psychodynamic psychotherapy research', *Mental Retardation*, 41: 468–72.

Beck, A.T. (1976). *Cognitive Therapy and the Emotional Disorders*. New York: International Universities Press.

Bender, M. (1993). 'The unoffered chair: the history of therapeutic disdain towards people with a learning difficulty', *Clinical Psychology Forum*, 54: 7–12.

Bruce, M., Collins, S., Langdon, P., Powlitch, S. and Reynolds, S. (2010). 'Does training improve understanding of core concepts in Cognitive Behaviour Therapy by people with intellectual disabilities? A randomized experiment', *British Journal of Clinical Psychology*, 49: 1–13.

Costello, H. (2004). *Does Training Carers Improve Outcome for Adults with Learning Disabilities and Mental Health Problems?* PhD thesis. London: King's College, University of London.

Dagnan, D. and Jahoda, A. (2006). 'Cognitive-behavioural intervention for people with intellectual disability and anxiety disorders', *Journal of Applied Research in Intellectual Disabilities*, 19: 91–7.

Deb, S., Thomas, M. and Bright, C. (2001). 'Mental disorder in adults with intellectual disability. I: Prevalence of functional psychiatric illness among a community-based population aged between 16 and 64 years', *Journal of Intellectual Disability Research*, 45: 495–505.

Department of Health (1999). *National Service Framework for Mental Health: Modern Standards and Service Models*. London: Department of Health.

Department of Health (2009). *Learning Disabilities Positive Practice Guide*. London: Department of Health.

Durlak, J., Fuhrman, T. and Lampman, C. (1991). 'Effectiveness of cognitive-behavior therapy for maladaptive children', *Psychological Bulletin*, 110: 204–14.

Emerson, E., Moss, S. and Kiernan, C. (1999). 'The relationship between challenging behaviour and psychiatric disorders in people with severe developmental disabilities', in N. Bouras (ed), *Psychiatric and Behavioural Disorders in Developmental Disabilities and Mental Retardation*. Cambridge: Cambridge University Press, pp. 38–48.

Featherstone, K. and Donovan, J. (2002). '"Why don't they just tell me straight, why allocate it?" The struggle to make sense of participating in a randomised controlled trial', *Social Science and Medicine*, 55: 709–19.

Finlay, W.M. and Lyons, E. (2001). 'Methodological issues in interviewing and using self-report questionnaires with people with mental retardation', *Psychological Assessment,* 13: 319–35.

Gustafsson, C., Ojehagen, A., Hansson, L., Dandlund, M., Nystrom, M., Glad, J. et al. (2009). 'Effects of psychosocial interventions for people with intellectual disabilities and mental health problems: a survey of systematic reviews', *Research on Social Work Practice*, 19: 281–90.

Haddock, G., Lobban, F. Hatton, C. and Carson, R. (2004). 'Cognitive-Behaviour Therapy for people with psychosis and mild intellectual disabilities: a case series', *Clinical Psychology and Psychotherapy*, 11: 282–98.

Hassiotis, A., Barron, P. and O'Hara, J. (2000). 'Mental health services for people with learning disabilities: a complete overhaul is needed with strong links to mainstream services', *British Medical Journal*, 321: 583–4.

Hatton, C. and Taylor, J.L. (2010). 'Promoting healthy lifestyles - mental health and illness', in G. Grant, P. Ramcharan, M. Flynn and M. Richardson (eds), *Learning Disability: A Life Cycle Approach to Valuing People*. 2nd edn. Maidenhead: Open University Press, pp. 381–408.

Iverson, J.C. and Fox, R.A. (1989). 'Prevalence of psychopathology among mentally retarded adults', *Research in Developmental Disabilities*, 10: 77–83.

Jahoda, A., Dagnan, D., Jarvie, P. and Kerr, W. (2006). 'Depression, social context and cognitive behavioural therapy for people who have intellectual disabilities', *Journal of Applied Research in Intellectual Disabilities*, 19: 81–9.

Kendall, P.C. (1985). 'Toward a cognitive-behavioral model of child psychopathology and a critique of related interventions', *Journal of Abnormal and Child Psychology*, 13: 357–72.

Kerker, B.D., Owens, P.L., Zigler, E. and Horwitz, S.M. (2004). 'Mental health disorders among individuals with mental retardation: Challenges to accurate prevalence estimates', *Public Health Reports*, 119: 409–17.

Lindsay, W.R. (1999). 'Cognitive therapy', *The Psychologist*, 12: 238–41.

Lindsay, W.R. (2008). *The Treatment of Sex Offenders with Intellectual Disability*. Chichester: John Wiley & Sons, Ltd.

Lindsay, W.R., Baty, F.J., Michie, A.M. and Richardson, I. (1989). 'A comparison of anxiety treatments with adults who have moderate and severe mental retardation', *Research in Developmental Disabilities*, 10: 129–40.

Lindsay, W.R., Neilson, C. and Lawrenson, H. (1997). 'Cognitive-Behaviour Therapy for anxiety in people with learning disabilities', in B. Stenfert Kroese, D. Dagnan and K. Loumidis (eds), *Cognitive-Behaviour Therapy for People with Learning Disabilities.* London: Routledge, pp. 124–40.

Lindsay, W.R. and Taylor, J.L. (2005). 'A selective review of research on offenders with developmental disabilities: Assessment and treatment', *Clinical Psychology and Psychotherapy*, 12: 201–14.

Lindsay, W.R., Taylor, J.L. and Sturmey, P. (eds) (2004). *Offenders with Developmental Disabilities.* Chichester: John Wiley & Sons, Ltd.

Lord Chancellor's Department (1999). *Making Decisions. The Government's Proposals for Making Decisions on Behalf of Mentally Incapacitated Adults.* London: The Stationery Office.

Mace, F.C., Webb, M.E., Sharkey, R.W., Mattson, D.M. and Rosen, H.S. (1988). 'Functional analysis and treatment of bizarre speech', *Journal of Behavior Therapy and Experimental Psychiatry*, 19: 289–96.

McGillivray, J.A., McCabe, M.P. and Kershaw, M.M. (2008). 'Depression in people with intellectual disability: an evaluation of a staff-administered treatment program', *Research in Developmental Disabilities*, 29: 524–36.

MacMahon, P. and Jahoda, A. (2008). 'Social comparison and depression: people with mild and moderate intellectual disabilities', *American Journal on Mental Retardation*, 113: 307–18.

Martorell, A., Tsakanikos, E., Pereda, A., Gutierrez-Recacha, P., Bouras, N. and Ayosu-Mateos, J.L. (2009). 'Mental health in adults with mild and moderate intellectual disabilities: the role of recent life events and traumatic experiences across the life span', *The Journal of Nervous and Mental Disease*, 197: 182–6.

Matson, J.L., Kazdin, A.E. and Senatore, V. (1984). 'Psychometric properties of the Psychopathology Instrument for Mentally Retarded Adults', *Applied Research in Mental Retardation*, 5: 881–9.

Meichenbaum, D. (1977). *Cognitive Behaviour Modification: An Integrative Account.* New York: Plenum.

Meltzer, H., Gill, B., Petticrew, M. and Hinds, K. (1995). *The Prevalence of Psychiatric Morbidity among Adults Living in Private Households: OPCS Survey of Psychiatric Morbidity in Great Britain, Report 1.* London: HMSO.

Michael, J. (2008). *Healthcare for All: Report of the Independent Inquiry into Access to Healthcare for People with Learning Disabilities.* www.iahpld.org.uk

Moss, S., Prosser, H., Costello, H., Simpson, N., Patel, P., Rowe, S., Turner, S. and Hatton, C. (1998). 'Reliability and validity of the PAS-ADD Checklist for detecting psychiatric disorders in adults with intellectual disability', *Journal of Intellectual Disability Research*, 42: 173–83.

Nagel, B. and Leiper, R. (1999). 'A national survey of psychotherapy with people with learning disabilities', *Clinical Psychology Forum,* 129: 14–18.

Oathamshaw, S.C. and Haddock, G. (2006). 'Do people with intellectual disabilities and psychosis have the cognitive skills required to undertake Cognitive Behaviour Therapy?', *Journal of Applied Research in Intellectual Disabilities*, 19: 35–46.

Prosser, H., Moss, S., Costello, H., Simpson, N. and Patel, P. (1997). *The Mini PAS-ADD: An Assessment Schedule for the Detection of Mental Health Needs in Adults with Learning Disability (Mental Retardation)*. Manchester: Hester Adrian Research Centre, University of Manchester.

Prosser, H., Moss, S., Costello, H., Simpson, N., Patel, P. and Rowe, S. (1998). 'Reliability and validity of the Mini PAS-ADD for assessing psychiatric disorders in adults with intellectual disability', *Journal of Intellectual Disability Research*, 42: 264–72.

Prout, R. and Nowak-Drabik, K.M. (2003). 'Psychotherapy with persons who have mental retardation: an evaluation of effectiveness', *American Journal on Mental Retardation*, 108: 82–93.

Reiss, S. (1988). 'The development of a screening measure for psychopathology in people with mental retardation', in E. Dibble and D. Gray (eds), *Assessment of Behavior Problems in Persons with Mental Retardation Living in the Community*. Rockville, MD: National Institute of Mental Health.

Reiss, S. (1990). 'Prevalence of dual diagnosis in community-based day programs in the Chicago metropolitan area', *American Journal on Mental Retardation*, 94: 578–85.

Reiss, S., Levitan, G.W. and McNally, R.J. (1982). 'Emotionally disturbed mentally retarded people: an underserved population', *American Psychologist*, 37: 361–7.

Rose, J., Loftus, M., Flint, B. and Carey, L. (2005). 'Factors associated with the efficacy of a group intervention for anger in people with intellectual disabilities', *British Journal of Clinical Psychology*, 44: 305–17.

Roy, A. Martin, D.M. and Wells, M.B. (1997). 'Health gain through screening – mental health: developing primary health care services for people with an intellectual disability', *Journal of Intellectual and Developmental Disability*, 22: 227–39.

Sakdalan, J.A., Shaw, J. and Collier, V. (2010). 'Staying in the here-and-now: a pilot study on the use of dialectical behaviour therapy group skills training for forensic clients with intellectual disability', *Journal of Intellectual Disability Research*, 54: 568–72.

Stenfert Kroese, B. (1998). 'Cognitive-behavioural therapy for people with learning disabilities', *Behavioural and Cognitive Psychotherapy*, 26: 315–22.

Stenfert Kroese, B., Dagnan, D. and Loumidis, K. (eds) (1997). *Cognitive-Behaviour Therapy for People with Learning Disabilities*. London: Routledge.

Stenfert Kroese, B. and Thomas, G. (2006). 'Treating chronic nightmares of sexual assault survivors with an intellectual disability – two descriptive case studies', *Journal of Applied Research in Intellectual Disabilities*, 19: 75–80.

Sturmey, P. and Gaubatz, M.D. (2002). *Clinical and Counselling Practice: A Case-guided Approach*. New York: Allyn & Bacon.

Taylor, J.L. (2005). 'In support of psychotherapy for people who have mental retardation', *Mental Retardation*, 43: 450–53.

Taylor, J.L., Hatton, C., Dixon, L. and Douglas, C. (2004). 'Screening for psychiatric symptoms: PAS-ADD Checklist norms for adults with intellectual disabilities', *Journal of Intellectual Disability Research*, 48: 37–41.

Taylor, J.L., Lindsay, W.R. and Willner, P. (2008). 'CBT for people with intellectual disabilities: emerging evidence, cognitive ability and IQ effects', *Behavioural and Cognitive Psychotherapy*, 36: 723–33.

Taylor, J.L. and Novaco, R.W. (2005). *Anger Treatment for People with Developmental Disabilities: A Theory, Evidence and Manual Based Approach*. Chichester: John Wiley & Sons, Ltd.

Taylor, J.L., Novaco, R.W., Gillmer, B.T., Robertson, A. and Thorne, I. (2005). 'Individual cognitive-behavioural anger treatment for people with mild-borderline intellectual disabilities and histories of aggression: a controlled trial', *British Journal of Clinical Psychology*, 44: 367–82.

Taylor, J.L., Novaco, R.W. and Johnson, L. (2009). 'Effects of intellectual functioning on cognitive behavioural anger treatment for adults with intellectual disabilities in secure settings'. *Advances in Mental Health and Learning Disabilities*, 3: 51–6.

Taylor, J.L. and Steel, C. (eds). (2008). 'Current theory and practice of cognitive and behavioural psychotherapies' [Special issue]. *Behavioural and Cognitive Psychotherapy*, 36: 639–786.

Taylor, J.L., Thorne, I., Robertson, A. and Avery, G. (2002). 'Evaluation of a group intervention for convicted arsonists with mild and borderline intellectual disabilities', *Criminal Behaviour and Mental Health*, 12: 282–93.

van den Hout, M., Arntz, A. and Merckelbach, H. (2000). 'Contributions of psychology to the understanding of psychiatric disorders', in M.G. Gelder, J.L. Lopez-Ibor Jr. and N.C. Andreasen (eds), *New Oxford Textbook of Psychiatry*. Oxford: Oxford University Press, pp. 277–92.

Willner, P. (2004). 'Brief cognitive therapy of nightmares and post-traumatic ruminations in a man with learning disabilities', *British Journal of Clinical Psychology*, 43: 459–64.

Willner, P. (2005). 'The effectiveness of psychotherapeutic interventions for people with learning disabilities: a critical overview', *Journal of Intellectual Disability Research*, 49: 73–85.

Willner, P. (2007). 'Cognitive behaviour therapy for people with learning disabilities: focus on anger', *Advances in Mental Health and Learning Disabilities*, 1: 14–21.

Willner, P. and Goodey, R. (2006). 'Interaction of cognitive distortions and cognitive deficits in the formulation and treatment of obsessive-compulsive behaviours in a woman with an intellectual disability', *Journal of Applied Research in Intellectual Disabilities*, 19: 67–73.

Willner, P. and Hatton, C. (eds) (2006). 'Cognitive Behavioural Therapy'. *Journal of Applied Research in Intellectual Disabilities*, special issue 19 (1).

Willner, P., Jones, J., Tams, R. and Green, G. (2002). 'A randomised control trial of the efficacy of a cognitive behavioural anger management group for clients with learning disabilities', *Journal of Applied Research in Intellectual Disabilities*, 15: 224–35.

Wong, J.G., Clare, I.C.H., Gunn, J. and Holland, A.J. (1999). 'Capacity to make health care decisions: It's importance in clinical practice', *Psychological Medicine*, 29: 437–46.

NINETEEN CBT in Health and Social Care Settings

MICHAEL J. SCOTT

The National Institute for Health and Clinical Excellence (NICE), is the arbiter of what should be regarded as evidence supported treatments in the UK. With regard to mental health, NICE has recommended diagnosis specific CBT protocols for depression (2004), panic disorder with and without agoraphobia and generalised anxiety disorder (2011), obsessive compulsive disorder (2005a), post-traumatic stress disorder (2005b) and computerised Cognitive Behaviour Therapy for depression and anxiety (2006). But despite these recommendations sufferers rarely receive an evidence supported CBT treatment and this has led to a Government initiative Improving Access to Psychological Therapies (IAPT, 2008). In this chapter the author looks at the shortcomings of the mental health delivery system and suggests improvements. The CBT therapist does not work in a vacuum in health settings; they may be influenced for good or ill either directly by their training, manager, supervisor or indirectly by the ethos of the organisation for which they work, the Consortium of Commisioning GPs and IAPT. In principle, at least, these sources of influence are supposed to facilitate the CBT therapist's implementation of the NICE guidelines. The second part of this chapter is devoted to shaping these influences. While the NICE guidelines are not intended to cover the practice of Social Services,

NICE asserts that they are relevant to the work of Social Services. Though the therapeutic role of social workers has steadily declined over the last thirty years, Social Services may have an advocacy role in helping to ensure that its service users are given an evidence-based treatment even though CBT therapists themselves are a rarity in such settings. The difficulties of discharging a therapeutic role in such settings are briefly described at the end of this chapter.

CBT in Routine Practice – Suboptimal

Driven by a concern that mental health practitioners only treated the tip of the iceberg of those with mental health problems, the British Government has funded the IAPT initiative and the training and employment of at least 3,600 new psychological therapists by 2011. While this is a welcome improvement in the provision, only about half of GP practices have been covered by the IAPT initiative. But at least the question of the quantity of CBT provision has begun to be addressed.

While CBT is of demonstrated efficacy in controlled trials (Butler et al., 2006) and effectiveness studies (e.g. Scott and Stradling, 1990), CBT as practised on the ground may be suboptimal. Studies by Westbrook and Kirk (2005) and Brown et al. (2011) of CBT conducted in routine practice found lower effect sizes for completers of treatment than found in controlled trials. Further the results were even more disappointing if the results from the dropouts from treatment were included, i.e if an intention to treat analyses was performed. These results are echoed by Oei and Boschen (2009) who examined the effectiveness of Group Cognitive Behaviour Therapy (GCBT) in a client population, 17.3% of whom were suffering from depression, 30.2% with panic disorder, 14% with generalised anxiety disorder and 8.4% post-traumatic stress disorder. Only 43% of individuals showed reliable change and 17% were 'recovered' from their anxiety symptoms. Oei and Boschen (2009) concluded that their mixed group treatment was less effective than a disorder specific treatment but was comparable to the individual CBT treatments of Westbrook and Kirk (2005).

While Oei and Boschen (2009) had a treatment manual there were no checks of fidelity to the manual. In both the Brown et al. (2011) and Westbrook and Kirk (2005) studies no treatment manual was used and thus there was no test of fidelity to an evidence-based treatment protocol. Further, in none of these studies was a standardised diagnostic interview used to establish diagnosis; Beck et al. (1962) have shown that non-standardised assessments have poor reliability, 32–54%.

Reliable diagnosis and fidelity to a treatment manual would appear to be prerequisites for the dissemination of an empirically supported treatment.

IAPT is clearly a major force for increasing the availability of psychological therapies, but arguably, its more difficult task is in ensuring the quality of those services. The initial evaluation of IAPT Services (Clark et al., 2009) was conducted using a psychometric test PHQ-9 (Kroenke et al., 2001) as yardstick, scores of 10 or above were regarded as a clinical case, and on this basis 55–56% of clients were classified as recovered when they left the service. But this should probably most properly be seen as just over half those treated 'moving towards recovery' as there was no assessment of diagnostic status and comparison with results of controlled trials was problematic. Clark et al. (2009) concluded 'NICE guidance varies between the different disorders covered by the IAPT initiative. In order to establish which guidance is relevant, a provisional diagnosis needs to be established for each patient on entry to the service.' This has been echoed more recently in the IAPT document (2010a): 'Provisional diagnoses are needed as specific treatments have been developed to assist people with particular symptom patterns and NICE guidelines are diagnosis based. We can therefore only ensure that patients receive the best treatments in line with NICE recommendations if provisional diagnoses have been obtained. Provisional diagnosis should not be viewed as a pejorative label. Many patients feel diagnosis is useful to reassure them that there are others with similar patterns and difficulties'.

Case Study 19.1

Maria had been involved in a serious car accident in which she thought she could have died. She was referred via her GP to a CBT therapist at the local hospital who took her through an Eye Movement Desensitisation Reprocessing Protocol with regards to the incident. Maria was very distressed at the procedure, her nightmares increased and memories of the incident were more vivid in the day. Over three sessions Maria was asked by the therapist to focus on traumatic details while watching the therapist move her finger across her field of vision. At the fourth session Maria told the therapist that she was fine now and did not need any more therapy and she was discharged. Maria was very fearful of referral to another CBT therapist for fear of having to go through the same procedure. However when the CBT therapist asked diagnostic questions about each of the symptoms of PTSD it was discovered that she had never suffered from PTSD at any time rather she had developed a simple phobia about driving and travelling as a passenger in a car. Maria had been needlessly re-traumatised and her phobia had been untreated because of a failure to make a reliable diagnosis.

What Can be Done?

Whether the number of psychological therapists will increase beyond 2011 is problematic given the current UK economic climate as the author writes (January 2011). Charities have just expressed concern at the possible closure of 150 Sure Start Centres. Rather than an increase in manpower/facilities the focus may well be on potentially more efficient modes of outreach, guided self-help, groups, computer-assisted therapy.

Health services are obliged to check fidelity to an evidence-based treatment protocol and implicitly this involves inter alia establishing the diagnostic status of a client. Social services are in a different position and may act more as advocates that a particular service user is given an evidence-based treatment, agencies funded by Social Services may, however, from time to time engage a CBT therapist but this seems to be on a very ad hoc basis. Scott (2009) has provided a simple way of ensuring the CBT therapist is using an evidence-based protocol by specifying therapeutic targets and treatment strategies using a SatNav for depression and each of the anxiety disorders. The SatNavs are part of a CBT Pocketbook in which the therapist is provided with diagnostic questions that directly access each of the DSM IV TR symptoms for depression and the anxiety disorders. An example of the depression part of the Pocketbook is shown in Table 19.1.

Table 19.1 Extract from CBT Pocketbook, from *Simply Effective Group Cognitive Behaviour Therapy* (Scott, 2011)

Table 19.1 Part 1

Depression

During the last 2 weeks have you been:

1. Sad, down or depressed most of the day nearly every day?
2. Have you lost interest or do you get less pleasure from the things you used to enjoy?
3. Have you been eating much less or much more?
4. Have you been having problems falling asleep, staying asleep or waking up too early of a morning?
5. Have you been fidgety, restless, unable to sit still or talking or moving more slowly than is normal for you?
6. Have you been tired all the time nearly every day?
7. Have you been bothered by feelings of worthlessness or guilt?
8. Have you had problems taking in what you are reading, watching/listening to or in making decisions about everyday things?
9. Have you been hurting or making plans for hurting yourself?

If the client answered 'yes' to five or more of the above (at least one of which has to be question 1 or 2) then it is likely that the client is suffering from depression.

Table 19.1 Part 2

Depression

Therapeutic Targets	Treatment Strategies
1. Depression about depression	Focus on responsibility for working on solutions and not on responsibility for problem.
2. Inactivity	Developing a broad investment portfolio, wide ranging modest investments.
3. Negative views of self, personal world and future	Challenging the validity, utility and authority by which these views are held. Use of MOOD chart.
4. Information processing biases	Highlighting personal biases and stepping around them using MOOD chart.
5. Over-valued roles	Valuing multiple roles, renegotiation of roles in social context.
6. Relapse prevention	Personally constructed self-help 'manual', utilising key points from therapy and drawing on self-help books and computer assisted material.

Case Study 19.2

Sean was diagnosed as suffering from depression; using the questions in Table 19.1 his symptoms were present at clinically significant level. With regard to his responses to the questions:

- Question 1: he was depressed and down most of the day at least half the days a month;
- Question 2: he had lost interest in his main pastime going to football matches and rarely interacted with his family;
- Question 4: he was waking at about 4 am for at least an hour;
- Question 7: he felt a complete failure;
- Question 8: he couldn't concentrate to read or perform his work as a joiner.

Treatment began by increasing his activity levels (Target 2), breaking work tasks into manageable doses, working only sequentially, with planned breaks between tasks. Sean was also introduced to the MOOD (Monitor Mood, Observe Thinking, Objective Thinking, Decide what to do and do it – strategies 3 and 4) chart, to generate better second thoughts than the overly negative first thoughts; then having sorted out his thinking moving on to activities by doing, thus avoiding depressive rumination.

(Continued)

(Continued)

However during the fifth treatment session the CBT therapist noted how persistent Sean's sense of failure was despite the MOOD chart; he felt at a loss, but glancing at the SatNav above, the therapist recalled that an over-valued role (target 5) was often an appropriate target in depression and proceeded to ask Sean what ultimately were the important roles. Sean said that at the end of the day all that mattered was whether his wife and two sons knew that he really cared and tried. By the next session there was a marked improvement in his mood.

Further examples of the use of the SatNavs are given in Scott (2009), together with examples of the interweaving of protocols for clients suffering from more than one disorder.

Those aspects of therapist competence that have been shown to best relate to outcome relate to structure and the setting and review of homework (Shaw et al., 1999; Strunk et al., 2010) and not non-structural items like guided discovery (Socratic questioning). Table 19.2 shows an extract from a therapist competence screen.

Shaping the Force Field in Which the CBT Therapist Operates

The day-to-day working of a CBT therapist will, inter alia, reflect their training, how they are managed and the supervision they receive. In Figure 19.1, the therapist is represented by the inner circle, the direct

Table 19.2 Extract from Therapist Competence Screen from *Simply Effective Cognitive Behaviour Therapy* (Scott, 2009)

4. Did the therapist negotiate a homework assignment that addressed the therapeutic target and integrated new learning from the session?

Yes	No	Unsure

5. Was there a review of homework?

Yes	No

CBT therapists can assist all by keeping a written copy of the homework given to clients (either a photocopy, carbon copy or using a Tablet PC to print out a copy for the client).

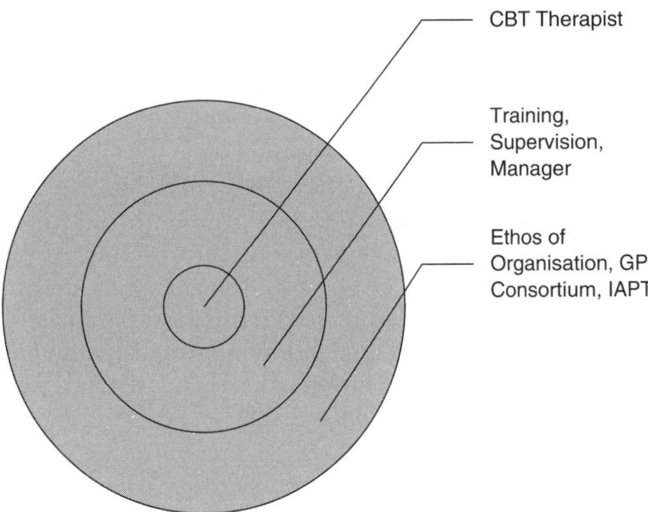

Figure 19.1 Force field in which the CBT therapist operates

forces acting on them are depicted by the second concentric circle. The outermost circle reflects the indirect forces acting on the CBT therapist, the ethos of the Organisation, the Commissioning GP Consortium and IAPT.

The ways in which each of these forces can be enhanced to ensure that the CBT therapist delivers evidence-supported treatment are described below.

Training and Supervision

The proper dissemination of empirically supported treatments requires adequate training and supervision. Unfortunately as yet we have only partial answers to 'What type of CBT training/supervision works with which students in which circumstances?' Intuitively the training needs of a CBT therapist working, say, in a secure unit with many personality disordered clients are likely to be different to those of the CBT therapist working with clients with depression and anxiety disorders in primary care. It may be that for some disorders teaching students a more prescriptive manualised approach is more cost-effective than for other disorders. Or it may be that some students learn better by the supervisor modelling an interaction with a client, inviting the supervisee to role-play a similar case and then giving feedback than by guided discovery. These are all empirical questions that await research. Perhaps the biggest danger is becoming a slave to tradition in teaching/supervising without reflecting that there are other possibilities. The current zeitgeist is to assess therapists in terms of a range of competences for each disorder and meta-competences but there is no simple way of measuring these competences and no indication that they relate to outcome. Again current training and supervision emphasises both the uniqueness of the individual and the need for problem formulation, but the latter has poor reliability (Kuyken et al., 2005) which may in turn lead to idiosyncratic formulations and a marginalising of manualised treatments. There is a danger that instead of having a balance of fidelity and flexibility, the latter is elevated.

Managers and Managerial Ethos

Health and Social Service Organisations (HSSOs) are Government funded and mandated to be as efficient as possible, and there is a constant drive to do more with the same. Managers are charged with achieving certain targets, e.g. a certain throughput of clients, in the event of those targets being met there is pressure to achieve the same with less resources. Therapists may become a victim of their own success. There is an inherent danger that managers pay more attention to the imposed target of say a GP consortium than the needs of the CBT therapist. At its worst managers are engaged in destructive testing, increasing the demands on therapists to breaking point, with therapists either going off sick or leaving. Just as the non-destructive testing of materials involves a proper assessment of the nature of the particular material before imposing loads, so too appropriate management involves properly gauging the resources of the CBT therapist and maximising the resource with appropriate supervision and training.

A business model has pervaded HSSOs for the last 20–30 years, bringing with it a focus on efficiency. But if mission statements are to be believed, this business ethos comes with a 'human face', ostensibly employees are to be regarded as the most important resource and the manager's door is always open. Such an apparently benign environment encourages the employee to seek managerial approval by meeting targets. But the constantly changing targets pose a threat to the employee's well-being, the unguarded CBT therapist may find his/her openness with a manager used as ammunition against him/her, as the latter is preoccupied with set targets.

Case Study 19.3

Paul has told his manager that most CBT practitioners involved in individual CBT (high-intensity) see 5–6 clients a day but his manager argues that some always fail to attend and eight would be more appropriate. He raised with his manager that he is currently suffering from sciatica and is having to stand for consultations but his manager replied, 'Don't give me problems just solutions.' Paul felt dismissed and raised the issue with his GP when he saw him for a review of his sciatica. The GP informed him that sciatica usually lasts about six weeks but can recur and that if his manager pushed him to the high target when he was suffering such an episode he would sign him off sick. Paul felt he would be letting his team down if he went off sick. The GP muttered expletives as he reminded Paul that both the health authority and his manager had to discharge their duties to clients, as well as he and his colleagues, and that the system only worked if all played their part. Less costly interventions such as groups are very attractive to managers and rightly so to a degree, but a therapist can come under pressure to include all-comers to a group and struggle to make the case that this is inappropriate; the best defence is to insist on evidence-supported treatment which with regard to group interventions is diagnosis specific (see Scott, 2011). Thus while many CBT therapists may shelter under the umbrella of a supportive manager, others cannot.

The CBT therapist may compound their stress if they perceive not meeting a particular target as evidence of their failure, i.e they personalise the situation. While openness and agreeableness are probably necessary components of being a CBT therapist, these traits may become liabilities when faced with a persistently unhelpful manager. The danger is that the therapist simply redoubles their efforts to explain themselves to the manager on the basis that if they are reasonable enough the latter will understand but this may result in just giving further ammunition to the manager. The only options left to the CBT therapists may be to work rather like an 'undercover policeman', restricting disclosure of information and/or engage in a collaborative effort to challenge the manager. But working as an 'undercover policeman' is likely to go against the grain for a great many CBT therapists, albeit that it is the only option left. Ethically the prime imperative is simply to give a fair day's work for what one is paid. Ultimately the CBT therapist may seek the advice of an employment lawyer.

The managerial ethos may be particularly problematic in a social care setting, in that managers may be reluctant to take children into care because of the cost involved and the CBT therapist may be made to feel that they are 'fussing' and not expert in such matters. At the other end of the age spectrum the elderly have been neglected by mental health specialists, indeed the initial IAPT focus was on those of working age, but in redressing this age discrimination the CBT therapist working with the elderly may be trying to discharge a therapeutic role but at the same time in a quandary about, say, unexplained bruising to an elderly client. The particular problems of working in a social care setting are briefly addressed at the end of this chapter.

GP Consortium

Historically clients have been referred to CBT therapists in the NHS via GPs, although most recently IAPT have also encouraged self-referral. Given the present Conservative–Liberal Democrats Coalition Government's commitment to ensuring that GPs have a pivotal role in the commissioning of services, it is likely that GPs will be even more heavily involved in referral to CBT therapists and in audit.

From a GP's perspective, any reduction in the number of their consultations a day will be welcomed, as many GPs see as many as 40 patients a day (and may be somewhat askance at the news that CBT therapists see five or six clients a day), so that any resource that caters for mental health problems is likely to be welcomed. Thus the initial response of GPs to commissioning is that it is an opportunity to reduce their workload and should be done as cheaply as possible to ensure the profitability of their own 'business'. There is a danger that GPs look to agencies who claim substantial throughput and are well marketed. But unless there is evidence of effectiveness CBT clients will soon be regulars at the GP surgery. It is imperative that GPs see the agencies that they wish to commission as competing not only on price but also on quality.

However, less than half of cases of depression are correctly identified in primary care, with more false positives, than either missed or identified cases (Mitchell et al., 2009) and those with anxiety disorders often remain undiagnosed and untreated (Stein, 2003), with, for example, 50% of cases of PTSD being missed (Zimmerman & Mattia, 1999); i.e if current assessment strategies (unstructured interview and occasional use of PHQ-9) continue most of those below the waterline will continue to drown. Further when a disorder is identified, clinicians tend to stop at the first identified disorder missing comorbidity (Zimmerman et al., 2008). The CBT therapist acting on the 'case' identified by the GP, is therefore in danger of offering inappropriate treatment. At first glance the distrust by probably most CBT therapists of the 'medical model' might provide salvation, but there is little evidence that generic CBT works - the CBT evidence base attests to the efficacy of disorder specific protocols. Dialogue between GPs and CBT therapists are likely to become fraught as the latter rely increasingly and exclusively on improvements on psychometric tests, whereas the medics' bottom line is likely to be what proportion of treated patients are no longer suffering from the particular condition at the end of treatment. Anecdotally, GPs are frustrated at the communications of CBT therapists, reading only the last paragraph of their reports to glean whether there is anything that the therapist wants them to do and unclear as to the diagnostic status of their patient.

GPs are unlikely to use structured interviews to better identify mental health problems, because of the time involved and fears of 'opening a can of worms'. However, GPs may use screening devices such as the Seven Minute Interview and the self-report version, The First Step Questionnaire Revised (Scott, 2011), which conducts a brief enquiry about all the common disorders and importantly asks after each disorder 'is this something with which you would like help?' and the patient answers 'yes', 'no' or 'don't know' (see Table 19.3).

Table 19.3 The First Step Questionnaire – Revised

1.	Yes	No	Don't know
During the past month have you often been bothered by feeling depressed or hopeless?			
During the past month have you often been been bothered by little interest or pleasure in doing things?			
Is this something with which you would like help?			
2.	Yes	No	Don't know
Do you have unexpected panic attacks, a sudden rush of intense fear or anxiety?			
Do you avoid situations in which the panic attacks might occur?			
Is this something with which you would like help?			
3.	Yes	No	Don't know
In your life, have you ever had any experience that was so frightening, horrible or upsetting that, in the past month, you			
i. Have had nightmares about it or thought about it when you did not want to?			

(Continued)

Table 19.3 (Continued)

ii. Tried hard not to think about it or went out of your way to avoid situations that reminded you of it?			
iii. Were constantly on guard, watchful, or easily startled?			
iv. Felt numb or detached from others, activities, or your surroundings?			
Is this something with which you would like help?			
4.	Yes	No	Don't know
Are you a worrier?			
Do you worry about everything?			
Has the worrying been excessive (more days than not) or uncontrollable in the last 6 months?			
Is this something with which you would like help?			
5.	Yes	No	Don't know
When you are or might be in the spotlight say in a group of people or eating/writing in front of others do you immediately get anxious or nervous?			
Do you avoid social situations out of a fear of embarrassing or humiliating yourself?			
Is this something with which you would like help?			
6.	Yes	No	Don't know
Do you wash or clean a lot?			
Do you check things a lot?			
Is there any thought that keeps bothering you that you would like to get rid of but can't?			
Do your daily activities take a long time to finish?			
Are you concerned about orderliness or symmetry?			
Is this something with which you would like help?			
7.	Yes	No	Don't know
Do you go on binges were you eat very large amounts of food in a short period?			
Do you do anything special, such as vomiting, go on a strict diet to prevent gaining weight from the binge?			
Is this something with which you would like help?			

Table 19.3 (Continued)

8.	Yes	No	Don't know
Have you felt you should cut down on your alcohol/drug?			
Have people got annoyed with you about your drinking/ drug taking?			
Have you felt guilty about your drinking/drug use?			
Do you drink/use drugs before midday?			
Is this something with which you would like help?			
9.	Yes	No	Don't know
Do you ever hear things other people don't hear, or see things they don't see?			
Do you ever feel like someone is spying on you or plotting to hurt you?			
Do you have any ideas that you don't like to talk about because you are afraid other people will think you are crazy?			
Is this something with which you would like help?			
10.	Yes	No	Don't know
Have there been times, lasting at least a few days when you were unusually high, talking a lot, sleeping little?			
Did others notice that there was something different about you?			
If you answered 'yes', what did they say?			
Is this something with which you would like help?			

This questionnaire is a first step in identifying what you might be suffering from and pointing you in the right direction. In answering each question just make your best guess; don't think about your response too much – there are no right or wrong answers.

The likelihood of GPs using such a screening device would be increased if they were reimbursed as they are for use of the PHQ-9 which relates to only one disorder and is not a comprehensive screening device.

GP consortia are likely to be attracted to the provision of low-intensity interventions, nonfacilitated self-help, guided bibliotherapy and guided computer therapy because of the cost savings involved. But the quantity and quality of the evidence supporting the low dose interventions is at present much less compelling than for high-intensity individual CBT or group CBT. Nevertheless NICE (2011) recommends low-intensity interventions as a first step in treating depression and the anxiety disorders, with the exception of obsessive compulsive disorder and post-traumatic stress disorder.

Ideally the low-intensity CBT therapist should offer clients a choice of treatment modality, involving an opportunity for the client to familiarise themselves with the material. However, there are shortcomings in the availability of materials, for example no guided computer therapy programme specifically for generalised anxiety disorder available in the UK. Further, the reading age of some materials may be problematic for some clients. In addition, the cost of books and computer-guided materials is rarely nonexistent. Scott (2011) has provided self-help survival manuals for depression and each of the anxiety disorders, which are just 12 pages long, and as many copies as necessary can be freely downloaded by the purchaser of the book. The manuals can be used as they stand for non-facilitated self-help or for guided bibliotherapy, in the latter the therapist after an initial face-to-face meeting with the client would cover the material of the manual (or manuals if the client had more than one disorder) over a six-week period, setting sections of the manual to be focused on and then having a 15–20 minute telephone conversation about how they had got on with the set material and the prescription of further material. It is, however, equally possible to conduct these exchanges over email. Email has been used by Carlbring et al. (2011) for communication with clients in their individually tailored internet-based treatment for anxiety disorders. All clients had a face-to-face diagnostic interview, on the basis of the diagnosis clients were assigned to one or more computer modules that covered social anxiety, generalised anxiety, panic disorder, agoraphobia/behavioural activation, applied relaxation and sleep. They also had a cognitive restructuring, introduction and relapse prevention modules, the latter two were included in all programmes. The programme was conducted over ten weeks and the tentative conclusion drawn was that tailoring internet-based therapy is feasible.

IAPT and Beyond

The likelihood is that the remit of IAPT services will be gradually extended beyond depression and the anxiety disorders, recent suggestions include providing services to those with long-term physical problems such as diabetes who have elevated risk of suffering from these disorders. Such extensions will, however, have training and resource implications. But there is a danger of IAPT overreaching itself; for example, the NICE guidelines recommend group CBT for mild/moderate depression but there is to the best of the author's knowledge no training provision for group work; generally speaking CBT courses do not see group work as part of basic training. Indeed there are a number of complications to providing group interventions including the preference of most clients for individual rather than group treatment given a free choice and how to address comorbidity in a group context. While these issues are addressed in Scott (2011), there is a dearth of opportunities for CBT practitioners to learn group work skills. CBT courses are generally much more geared up to teach individual CBT, in IAPT terms a high-intensity intervention.

Social Care Settings

Many of the clients of Social Services are at the severe mental illness end of the scale of difficulties suffering from psychoses and/or personality disorders. Unfortunately the evidence base for the effectiveness of CBT with these conditions is much less robust than for depression and the anxiety disorders. Matters are further complicated in that the therapist often cannot operate a therapeutic role in isolation; for example, a CBT therapist may be teaching child management skills but cannot be so seduced by the therapeutic role that they do not take seriously the 'odd' explanation for a child's bruising. The therapist has a protective role as well as a therapeutic one, even though the former may be limited to informing the social worker. Further the CBT therapist has to be aware of the limits of a therapeutic intervention. For example, in helping clients with a drug addiction who have the care of a small child, unless there is a very significant change in their behaviour within two to three months it is unlikely to ever happen and the child is at risk and this should be communicated to the social worker.

References

Beck, A.T., Ward, C.H., Mendelson, M., Mock, J.E. and Erbaugh, J.K. (1962). 'Reliability of psychiatrics diagnoses: A study of consistency of clinical judgements and ratings', *American Journal of Psychiatry*, 119: 351–7.

Brown, J., Slade, M., Beecham, J., Sellwood, K., Andiappan, M., Landau, S., Johnson, T. and Smith, R. (2011). 'Outcome, costs and patient engagement for group and individual CBT for depression: a naturalistic clinical study', *Behavioural and Cognitive Psychotherapy*, 39: 355–8.

Butler, A.C., Chapman, J.E., Forman, E.M. and Beck A.T. (2006). 'The empirical status of cognitive-behavioral therapy: A review of meta-analyses', *Clinical Psychology Review*, 26: 17–31.

Carlbring, P., Maurin, L. and Torngren, C. (2011). 'Individually-tailored, internet-based treatment for anxiety disorders: A randomised controlled trial', *Behaviour Research and Therapy*, 49: 18–24.

Clark, D.M., Layard, R., Smithies, R., Richards, D.A., Suckling, R. and Wright, B. (2009). 'Improving access to psychological therapy: Initial evaluation of two UK demonstration sites', *Behaviour Research and Therapy*, 47: 910–20.

IAPT (2008). IAPT Implementation Plan. National Guidelines for Regional Delivery - Improving Access to Psychological Therapies: *Implementation Plan: Curriculum for High-intensity Workers.* Department of Health Mental Health Programme.

IAPT (2010a). IAPT Data Handbook v 1.0. Department of Health Mental Health Programme.

IAPT (2010b). IAPT Data Handbook Appendices v 1.0. Department of Health Mental Health Programme.

Kroenke, K., Spitzer, R.L. and Williams, J.B. (2001). 'The PHQ-9: validity of a brief depression severity measure', *Journal of General and Internal Medicine*, 16: 606–13.

Kuyken, W., Fothergill, C.D., Musa, M. and Chadwick, P. (2005). 'The reliability and quality of cognitive case formulation', *Behaviour Research and Therapy*, 43: 1187–1201.

Mitchell, A.J., Vaze, A. and Rao, S. (2009). 'Clinical diagnosis of depression in primary care: a meta-analysis', *The Lancet*, 374: 606–19.

NICE (2004). *Depression: Management of Depression in Primary and Secondary Care* (Clinical Guide 23). London: National Institute for Clinical Excellence. www.nice.org

NICE (2005a). *Obsessive-compulsive Disorder: Core Interventions in the Treatment of Obsessive-compulsive Disorder and Body Dysmorphic Disorder* (Clinical Guideline 31). London: National Institute for Clinical Excellence. www.nice.org

NICE (2005b). *Post-traumatic Stress Disorder (PTSD): The Management of PTSD in Adults and Children in Primary and Secondary Care* (Clinical Guideline 26). London: National Institute for Clinical Excellence. www.nice.org

NICE (2006). *Computerized Cognitive Behaviour Therapy for Depression and Anxiety* (Technology Appraisal 97). London: National Institute for Clinical Excellence. www.nice.org

NICE (2011). *Generalised Anxiety Disorder and Panic Disorder (With or Without Agoraphobia), in Adults in Primary, Secondary and Community Care* (Clinical Guidance 113). London: National Institute for Clinical Excellence. www.nice.org

Oei, T.P.S. and Boschen, M.J. (2009) 'Clinical effectiveness of a cognitive behavioural group treatment program for anxiety disorders: A benchmark study', *Journal of Anxiety Disorders*, 23: 950–7.

Scott, M.J. (2009). *Simply Effective Cognitive Behaviour Therapy: A Guide for Practitioners*. London: Routledge.

Scott, M.J. (2011). *Simply Effective Group Cognitive Behaviour Therapy: A Guide for Practitioners*. London: Routledge.

Scott, M.J. and Stradling, S.G. (1990). 'Group cognitive therapy for depression produces clinically significant reliable change in community-based settings', *Behavioural Psychotherapy*, 18: 1–19.

Shaw, B.F., Elkin, I., Yamagughi, J., Olmsted, M., Vallis, T.M., Dobson, K.S., Lowery, A., Sotsky, S.M., Watkins, J.T. and Imber, S.D. (1999). 'Therapist competence ratings in relation to clinical outcome in cognitive therapy of depression', *Journal of Consulting and Clinical Psychology*, 67: 837–46.

Stein, M.B. (2003). 'Attending to anxiety disorders in primary care', *Journal of Clinical Psychiatry*, 64: 35–9.

Strunk, D.R., Brotman, M.A., DeRubeis, R.J. and Hollon, S.D. (2010). 'Therapist competence in cognitive therapy for depression: predicting subsequent symptom change', *Journal of Consulting and Clinical Psychology*, 78: 429–37.

Westbrook, D. and Kirk, J. (2005). 'The clinical effectiveness of Cognitive Behaviour Therapy: outcome for a large sample of adults treated in routine practice', *Behaviour Research and Therapy*, 43: 1243–61.

Young, J. and Beck, A.T. (1980). 'Cognitive therapy rating scale: rating manual'. Unpublished manuscript. Philadelphia: Centre for Cognitive Therapy, University of Pennsylvania.

Zimmerman, M. and Mattia, J.I. (1999). 'Is posttraumatic stress disorder underdiagnosed in routine clinical settings?', *Journal of Nervous and Mental Disease*, 187: 420–8.

Zimmerman, M., McGlinchey, J.B., Chelminski, I. and Young, D. (2008). 'Diagnostic co-morbidity in 2300 psychiatric out-patients presenting for treatment evaluated with a semi-structured diagnostic interview', *Psychological Medicine*, 38: 199–210.

TWENTY CBT in Criminal Justice Settings

KEVIN GOURNAY

Introduction

As with many other areas in mental health care, the use of Cognitive Behaviour Therapy (CBT) in Criminal Justice Settings (CJS) is increasing, both in the breadth of problems dealt with and in respect of the numbers of CJS based practitioners who are using a cognitive behavioural approach. At the same time, forensic mental health is itself an expanding area. This chapter will explore how CBT is used in the treatment of offenders and consider issues the CBT therapist may encounter when working with this population.

Accurate and comprehensive assessment of all (available) aspects of the offender's current life and developmental history are paramount in the endeavour to deliver effective CBT within CJS settings; most probably more so than in generic settings. From thorough assessment comes the fodder for sound holistic problem formulation and increased opportunity for incisive therapeutic interventions. Though the precise CBT strategies and techniques offered to clients within CJS settings may not differ wildly from those used in general psychiatric settings, understanding of how (and when) an individual may best receive them will be informed via stringent adherence to certain assessment guidelines. For this reason, in addition to necessary brevity, this chapter will give the bulk of focus to assessment considerations within CJS populations and less will be said about specific treatment interventions.

To begin, it is worth noting that cognitive behavioural approaches are used in a wide spectrum of CJS, from the Probation Service and Community Forensic Mental Heath Teams (CFMHT) through to settings of the highest possible security – for example the Dangerous and Severe Personality Disorder Units of High Secure Hospitals (HSH).

Hence, before discussing common problems encountered within the CJS and the role of CBT within the overall approach to treatment and management of offenders, contextual matters merit some discussion.

Context

Any practitioner wishing to work in CJS needs to be aware of a number of matters regarding context. First, the practitioner will be faced with difficulties not encountered in other settings. The person receiving CBT (as with any other individual) merits CBT that is provided to the highest level of skill, set within an appropriate evidence base and using a collaborative framework. However, some individuals present for treatment within various confines set down by the Criminal Justice System itself. Thus, for example, the practitioner may work in a custodial setting and encounter individuals who have received a custodial sentence or, as is common within Medium and High Secure Units, someone who initially received a custodial sentence to be served in prison who has now been transferred (under a section of the Mental Health Act) to receive treatment in a hospital setting. Such individuals may be under substantial pressure to undergo treatment so as to reduce the time that they spend in custody. Individuals who do not engage in treatment, particularly those who are detained under the Mental Health Act, are likely to remain in a custodial setting until a reasonable trial of treatment has been delivered. Therefore, the cognitive behaviour therapist always needs to be aware of the possibility that coercion is an important variable in the motivation to receive treatment. Some additional basic and common considerations for CBT therapists working within CJS include:

- Literacy issues: Individuals within the CJS are perhaps more likely to be wholly or partially illiterate than those in general practice arenas. Poor scholastic attendance, undiagnosed dyslexia or learning difficulties and parental neglect often contribute to failure to learn basic reading and writing skills. Verbal and visual methods of psychoeducation are therefore most appropriate with such individuals.
- Access to CBT 'tools of the trade': Therapists working in custodial settings may find that patients are not allowed basic writing equipment such as pencils for safety reasons. The ubiquitous CBT white

board may also be prohibited. The CBT therapist therefore needs to exercise creativity when delivering therapy with such restrictions in place.
- Limitations to behavioural homework tasks: Individuals within CJS may have limited opportunities to practise CBT strategies outside of sessions. This is particularly the case with those in prison or restricted special units. Again, creative and practical therapeutic exercises need to be devised.
- Alliance issues and boundary challenges: It may take longer to build a working alliance with an individual who has an entrenched mistrust and opposition to authority and professional figures. Additionally, the CBT therapist needs to be extremely aware of the potential for CJS patients to push professional boundaries and launch sometimes pointedly personal challenges.
- Peer influence within and without therapeutic sessions: Prison social structures are complex and can impede therapeutic advancements. CBT therapists need to be aware of peer pressure to act in certain ways and present a 'front'. For the CJS individual this is often seen as an essential strategy for survival. Therefore peer influences need to be carefully considered when devising treatment plans.
- Aggressive and intimidating behaviour: CBT therapists working in CJS may encounter aggression (and occasionally violence) from the individuals they treat. Risk assessment is highly important and personal safety risks should never be underestimated.
- Regular and context-specific supervision can do much to prepare the CBT therapist working within CJS for such treatment challenges.

In the assessment process, the practitioner has to consider the willingness, or otherwise, of the person receiving treatment. It might be argued that some people presenting for treatment are at a stage of either pre-contemplation or contemplation, concerning their desire to change behaviour and thinking. The stages of change have featured largely in the treatment of addictive behaviour for a number of years. The model that is often used is that of Prochaska and DiClemente (2005). This model describes the four stages of change a person goes through when attempting to alter habitual behaviour. The model is helpful insofar as it describes the four stages of the treatment process; i.e. pre-contemplation, contemplation, active engagement in treatment and finally maintaining changes made in behaviour and thinking. In CJS, it is quite common for people to present at the pre-contemplative or contemplative stage. Hence, while the practitioner may feel obliged to attempt to change behaviour, which may be at the very least antisocial in its nature and at its very worst life-threatening, he/she may also feel an ethical and moral obligation not to use coercion. Some CJS clients will always resist any changes to alter their thinking or behaviour, even if the consequences may mean indefinite incarceration. Other individuals may be genuinely ambivalent about change. Still others may actively seek new ways of thinking and behaving. Cognitive behavioural practitioners are therefore often in a very tricky situation and, perhaps more than in any other treatment setting, need to embed their work within a multidisciplinary framework, allowing for professional group case discussion and clinical supervision.

At this point it is worth commenting on some uncomfortable truths. While CBT has a long history of use within Criminal Justice settings, psychological treatments are often viewed with scepticism – and sometimes great disapproval. It must be remembered that behavioural procedures have, in the past, been used in ways that now would be considered unethical. One needs to remember that as recently as the 1970s electrical aversion therapy was in common usage to change 'undesired' or 'aberrant behaviours' such as homosexuality. Indeed this author recollects receiving training in the use of electrical and chemical aversion therapy. These therapies were used with participants, who had no acceptance whatsoever of the need to change and who received treatment only because they were contained in settings where they had no choice. These points need to be considered because, unfortunately, there is still a common misperception that cognitive behavioural approaches are used in a coercive context. Practitioners need to understand that although unethical practices are no longer used or condoned by any responsible body governing CBT, the fact remains that there is a substantial history. Therefore some members of the public, and indeed other professionals, might need some persuading that CBT in use today is fully collaborative in nature.

Types of Problems Encountered within Criminal Justice Settings

Before describing some of the psychological problems that are more specific to CJS, it is worth emphasising that, as with any population, general mental health problems are very prevalent. Regardless of the specific forensic context, individuals in community and custodial settings often present with depression, anxiety, phobic states, OCD, schizophrenia and other mental health problems, which may not be directly connected with offending behaviours. Prisons and probation services have a client population that, for a whole range of reasons not least those of social deprivation, are very vulnerable to common mental health problems.

In May 2008, the prison population was 82,682. Of great concern is the Prison Reform Trust Bromley briefings: (www.prisonreformtrust.org.uk/Search Results/tabid/41/Default.aspx? Search=bromley+briefings

> *Many prisoners have mental health problems. 72% of male and 70% of female sentenced prisoners suffer from two or more mental health disorders.* 20% of prisoners have four of the five major mental health disorders.
>
> *Neurotic and personality disorders are particularly prevalent – 40% of male and 63% of female sentenced prisoners have a neurotic disorder, over three times the level in the general population.* 64% of male and 50% of female sentenced prisoners have a personality disorder.
>
> *According to the NHS plan, around 5,000 prisoners at the time, between 5% and 8% of the population, have severe and enduring mental illnesses.*
>
> *A significant number of prisoners suffer from a psychotic disorder.* 7% of male and 14% of female sentenced prisoners have a psychotic disorder; 14 and 23 times the level in the general population. *10% of men and 30% of women have had previous psychiatric admission before they come into prison.*

The following mental health problems are most commonly linked to offending behaviour:

- Personality disorders; particularly of the antisocial variety, but often combined with other personality disorders, commonly Borderline and Narcissistic types.
- Anger and associated problems.
- Substance abuse and increasingly polysubstance abuse. Individuals may regularly take a wide range of substances; often the pattern of use depends on availability.
- Substance abuse and serious mental illness; this combination is usually referred to as a Dual Diagnosis.
- Sexual offending; the range of offences referred for psychological interventions commonly include rape and paedophilia.
- Post-traumatic stress disorder. It is quite common to see sexual offenders who have themselves suffered abuse and hence experience PTSD symptoms. Perpetrators of violent crimes may also suffer from PTSD caused by crimes committed.
- Compulsive behaviour. Individuals who engage in compulsive behaviours such as shoplifting and gambling are often in conflict with the law.

This chapter is too brief to describe assessment and treatment for each of the above listed problems. Individuals often present with more than one problem, problem categories often overlap and, within each of the categories listed, there is tremendous variation in presentation. Hence the assessment and treatment needs of individuals within a given category(ies) are tremendously diverse.

To an extent, mental disorders commonly present in primary care or outpatient settings can be approached in a somewhat standard way (taking into account individual variations). However, the problems that present in CJS generally are much more complex at every level. For example, an individual presenting in primary care with a specific phobia or obsessive rituals (regardless of the severity of such symptoms and their impact on the individual's life) may be more suited to a standard treatment protocol than the same individual within CJS. Because of the background psychological difficulties which have brought these individuals into conflict with society, treatment presents a much greater challenge.

Assessment and Formulation

Assessment processes for CBT in the CJS include a number of similarities to those used in primary care or outpatient settings. However, for several reasons, the assessment processes in CJS are somewhat different. For example, when conducting an assessment in a custodial setting, such as a prison or a secure ward in a hospital, clinicians have the advantage of being able to see the individual on several occasions and also rely on the observations of other professionals. Thus, nursing staff may be delegated observation tasks such as recording anxiety levels, the time taken for someone with obsessive rituals to complete daily activities, and so on.

Importantly the CBT clinician needs to consider assessment material made available from other sources - for example pre-sentence reports conducted by psychiatrists, social workers or probation officers. However, the clinician has a responsibility to check such sources of information for accuracy. In the author's experience, even information concerning the person's offence history from the Police National Computer may contain inaccuracies.

Formulation Considerations

The formulation of problem and treatment objectives is always a complex matter when working with offenders. Again, CBT therapists need to work closely with other colleagues. The CJS environment is unique and therapists need to make appropriate professional adjustments. Coercion issues need to be explicitly assessed and addressed within the therapeutic process. The practitioner often will work with individuals who are detained against their will, or who may be subject to a community order involving a mandatory requirement to attend therapy. One therefore needs to be very sensitive to the treatment obstacles inherent to working with a less willing client. The usual collaborative approach needs to be adopted to help ensure treatment objectives are met. It is here that the cognitive behavioural approach, with its emphasis on transparency and an active-directive style, may be very productive. Addressing explicitly with the client, that treatment is taking place within a coercive context and striving to establish a 'best working compromise' under the circumstances. Such explicit recognition often leads to a positive reaction on the part of the offender.

The therapist's duty to public protection also needs to be considered at all times. Over the course of therapy one might, for example, begin to understand and to some extent empathise with individuals who may have had numerous adverse life experiences. Through treatment offenders may reveal themselves to be suffering with very poor self-esteem and wracked with feelings of guilt or shame. Yet such individuals might still pose a serious risk to the public. Therefore, the practitioner understandably finds themselves to have 'mixed feelings.' This situation, common enough in the CJS, demands that the practitioner has access to plentiful and experienced supervision. Without such supervisory contact, therapists will often find themselves in great moral and ethical difficulties.

Prior to formulating a treatment plan, historical contextual factors and current presentation need to be assessed.

Family History

It is important to investigate all relevant family history, i.e. ages of parents and siblings, health issues, quality of familial relationships and the individual's attitude towards family members. It is also important to ascertain to what extent (if any) family provides – or has in the past provided – social support. In the case of bereavement and loss, it is important to explore the individual's reactions to that loss. Separation is also an important issue. One should establish whether there have been significant periods of separation from the family unit – for example, being taken into care. This is particularly relevant as a substantial proportion of offenders will have had very adverse experiences being in foster or institutional care.

Developmental History

A history of development, including factors such as birth injury is very important. The achievements of milestones, significant problems with behaviour or learning during childhood are key issues. Many people encountered in the CJS will present with important and problematic developmental issues, such as early physical, sexual or emotional abuse and severe neglect. In a number of cases abuse continues into adolescence and, sometimes, into early adulthood. A history of abuse is very common within offender populations.

Education

Obtaining an educational history, schools attended, examinations passed and so on, presents an opportunity to understand the offender's attitude to authority figures and peers. It is important to gather factual information regarding bullying, truanting, exclusion etc.

Of particular importance to CBT practitioners in CJS is the fact that 25% of young offenders are said to have reading skills below those of the average seven-year-old and 60% of the prison population is said to have difficulties in basic literacy skills (Clark & Dugdale, 2008). Offenders are often very guarded about their inability to read and write and the therapist needs to be sensitive to these problems. This author has personal experience of people dropping out of CBT because they were unable to complete diaries, or read the books provided as part of their therapy. The shame that such offenders feel about illiteracy often generalises to other areas of life; it is not uncommon for offenders to demonstrate global feelings of shame. Shame and its behavioural consequences can be addressed with CBT. However, practical issues such as support resolving skills deficits need equal attention.

Relationships

An understanding of the quality of the individual's relationships - past and present - needs to be obtained. Whether or not they have sustained meaningful relationships, the nature of such relationships, and attitudes to romantic partners and significant others are all topics that merit investigation.

Employment

The CBT therapist will often have access to reliable information concerning the individual's employment history yet it is essential to explore employment experiences. For example, discussing particular episodes in employment may reveal much about the individual's underpinning beliefs and attitudes to peers, responsibility, team participation, success/failure, and authority figures. Valuable information about an individual's ambitions, disappointments and future plans may also be gained.

Medical History

Some issues regarding medical history are particularly relevant – for example, brain injury or epilepsy, which may be linked to behavioural problems. In cases where there is a significant medical history, the CBT therapist should liaise with the appropriate clinician to obtain further information. It is not uncommon to find that individuals who present with temper problems have a history of brain injury and their temper outbursts may be caused by a range of factors, both organic and psychological.

Psychiatric History

Previous psychiatric history is important and there is a particular need to ask questions regarding the nature of interventions delivered and the person's attitude to past treatments. It is common to find that individuals within the CJS have experienced psychological interventions since childhood. It is essential to obtain as much information as possible about past psychiatric experiences since they carry obvious implications for future treatment. For example, the author has come across many individuals who have had a great deal of psychoanalytic therapy and therefore hold preconceptions about talking therapies generally. An entirely different therapeutic relationship may be anticipated and preparation for CBT collaboration is indicated. Often, individuals have had adverse experiences and their expectations of psychological treatments are negative (to say the least). Again, it is essential to explore these areas during initial assessment, so steps may be taken to pre-empt associated problems arising during therapy.

Substance Abuse

In the Bromley briefing (2008), the Prison Reform Trust noted that epidemiological studies show around 55% of those received into custody are problematic drug users. Additionally, four out of every ten prisoners reported using drugs at least once while in their current prison, a quarter had used in the past month and 16% in the past week. Cannabis and opiates were the drugs most often used. As for alcohol, nearly two-thirds of sentenced male prisoners (63%) and two-fifths of female sentenced prisoners (39%) admit to hazardous drinking, carrying the risk of physical or mental harm. Of these, about half have a severe alcohol dependency. For obvious reasons any assessment for CBT must include a very detailed substance abuse history.

Collateral Information

Collateral information may be obtained from reliable external sources (professional or familial) and aid in building a comprehensive formulation. Family members and friends are often particularly valuable in providing information about developmental issues and may have observed the individual's reaction to various significant life events. Sadly, however, many individuals in the CJS have lost contact with family members and have few, if any, close friends or confidants. Eventually, the practitioner will need to collate all available information, including of course that from the individual concerned, and cross-check for validity.

Current Presentation of Offending Behaviour and Associated Thoughts, Beliefs and Attitudes

The CBT practitioner needs access to a comprehensive list of offences. In the majority of settings information is available from the Police National Computer and considerable additional detail of offences may come via other documentation such as trial transcripts and depositions. This is particularly the case in medium and high secure settings, where the offences that have led to an individual's detention are of a serious nature.

The examination of each offence is often a time consuming activity. The CBT therapist may undertake this part of assessment in conjunction with others. However, even if – for example – a psychiatrist has documented detail of the forensic history, it is important for the practitioner to obtain for themselves the individual's account.

In order to formulate effective treatment approaches, offending behaviour and related thoughts, beliefs, attitudes need to be examined in detail. The cognitive behaviour therapist needs to assess offending behaviour within the context of background factors rather than in isolation.

Functional Analysis

Functional analysis is one of the essential and central parts of the assessment process. The functional analytic approach has been used for decades by practitioners. Originally, practitioners of behaviour therapy and behaviour modification used functional analysis. Behaviours are examined with consideration to relevant antecedents, i.e. factors that apparently trigger the behaviour. Next behavioural consequences are considered with particular emphasis on consequences perpetuating and reinforcing undesirable behaviour. Functional analysis is often described as an ABC approach (antecedents, behaviours and consequences). In the past three decades, the functional analytic framework has been extended to incorporate cognitive processes. Thus, when considering antecedents (A), triggers include thoughts, memories and/or the presence of particular images. Similarly, B now stands for behaviours and beliefs. Finally, C now refers to a much wider range of consequences including a range of cognitive variables. Therefore, one needs to obtain an account, from the individual, of all of the possible antecedents to the offence. In turn, one then needs to obtain the widest possible account of consequences.

Decision Chain

An additional framework used which augments a functional analytic approach (particularly with sexual offences) is the Decision Chain (Ward et al., 1995). The Decision Chain framework helps the practitioner to identify choices made along the pathway to offending and how each choice is informed by thoughts and beliefs. For example, choices may involve a consideration of the risks of being apprehended or dysfunctional beliefs about a child's willingness to engage in sexual activity. The practitioner needs to carefully understand the thought processes leading up to the offence, so as to identify dysfunctional beliefs and attitudes that may become the target of cognitive behavioural interventions. This leads to the next section of this chapter.

Pathway Models

In sexual offending particularly, the pathways conceptual model is very helpful in assessing the causation of offending behaviour (Beech & Ward, 2004). The pathways are as follows.

Intimacy Deficits Pathway

In this pathway individuals have normal sexual drives and attitudes, but they undergo temporary changes in their attitudes and thinking, particularly when a preferred sexual partner is not available. It is not uncommon to see individuals with normal, adult sexual interests who, in the absence of an appropriate consenting sexual partner, are indiscriminate in their choice and may involve underage children in sexual activity. Any decision to engage in such inappropriate and illegal behaviour may, of course, be underpinned by more general personality disorder, characterised by a callous lack of concern for others.

Deviant Sexual Scripts Pathway

In this pathway individuals demonstrate defective learning processes and can develop very dysfunctional thinking and abnormal beliefs about relationships and sexual activities. The assessment process may be particularly difficult because of the need to understand how such abnormal schemas have evolved. A common example is those who engage in sexual activities with children. During assessment, the offender often expresses beliefs that the child wished to engage in such a relationship and was therefore a willing and equal partner. Such individuals may also profess that a love affair existed, citing age as an unnecessary barrier. The CBT practitioner needs to be prepared to hear accounts that are alien, particularly from sadistic sex offenders, who have rationalised their actions as justifiable.

Emotional Dysregulation Pathway

Individuals in this pathway are characterised by holding relatively normal sexual beliefs and attitudes, but are unable to restrict or contain sexual arousal. Such individuals are therefore indiscriminate in finding a sexual outlet. Once more, these individuals often have pervasive personality disorders, characterised by callous unconcern for others.

Distorted Cognitions Pathway

These individuals exhibit deviant sexual behaviour within the context of also exhibiting a wide range of other antisocial and criminal behaviours. In this pathway, beliefs and attitudes are typically profoundly dysfunctional and all pervasive.

Obviously, this typology has its limitations, but it is helpful for the practitioner to use these pathways as a method of examining various hypotheses about causation from a cognitive perspective.

Assessment of Behaviours Directly and Indirectly Linked to Offending

One helpful way of beginning this assessment process is to consider individuals from the point of view of their social (interpersonal) skills. The clinical interview itself allows the therapist to assess deficits and excesses directly. For example, important social skills such as eye contact, posture, voice tone and volume can be observed in vivo. A mixture of clinical interviewing and the use of valid and reliable measures of change (see below) are essential. Interpersonal skills often feature as treatment targets with individuals who have committed sexual or violent offences. When formulating a treatment approach, it is essential to incorporate treatment strategies linking both cognitive and behavioural elements.

Assessment of Physiological Factors

Physiological factors are of obvious importance in violent and sexual offences. A clinical interview is extremely helpful in observing an individual's state of physiological arousal. It is also important to explicitly ask the individual for information about sexual arousal and one needs to explicitly enquire of intimate matters, such as frequency of masturbation.

Assessment of Thoughts, Beliefs and Attitudes

Information about thoughts, beliefs and attitudes is obtained by taking a background history and using a functional analytic framework. However, it is also necessary to investigate the following topics to gain a more complete picture:

Pro-offending Attitudes

Space does not permit detailed consideration of how pro-offending attitudes can be assessed. However, it is worth noting that this is probably the most challenging issue for therapists. Perhaps the most important advice to be given is that pro-offending attitudes need to be considered over time and, in addition to the clinical interview, it is important to use valid and reliable assessment methods and measures of change. The use of collateral information is also very important. All human beings justify and rationalise their behaviour and it is thus important to understand how offending behaviour is justified and rationalised. The offender will, like any other client, hold underlying schemas that need to be considered at assessment. This is similar to how a CBT practitioner in primary care may explore, for example, the effects of holding more common and less malignant beliefs about incurring disapproval from others. Examples of schemas underpinning offending behaviours might include beliefs that children are not harmed by sexual contact with adults or attitudes like 'anyone who looks at me the wrong way has earned himself a good hiding, nobody disrespects me'.

Victim Empathy

This is far from a straightforward area, since empathy, or the lack of it, may be quite selective and may only apply to the victim involved in the specific offence (Fernandes et al., 1999). The practitioner will need to examine empathy to others more generally and this might be simply effected by engaging the individual in discussions about people who might be suffering from painful terminal illnesses, or victims of crimes other than those perpetrated by the particular offender. Exploring this area one will often uncover what, at first sight, are rather incompatible, empathic feelings. On many occasions the author has seen individuals who have engaged, apparently without concern, in quite sadistic behaviours yet also feel very strongly about the abuse of animals. In some cases being confirmed vegetarians because of animal welfare issues. It is also not uncommon to see people who appear to have a lack of concern for their victims but, on the other hand, take 'the moral high ground' over such matters as MPs expenses. The CJS often requires individuals to show remorse for their crimes. This is particularly noteworthy in the Parole Board processes. However, obtaining a true picture of the individual's empathy and remorse is often very difficult.

Self-esteem

Many offenders have low self-esteem and esteem factors are often important components in the causal offence pathway. Some offenders will state quite clearly: 'I'm rubbish. It doesn't matter what happens to me.' These common beliefs tragically underpin offending behaviours and are clearly self-destructive. Some individuals may put themselves into the position of being caught so that they may be punished. Other manifestations of poor self-esteem are seen in child sex offences. Perpetrators may feel more comfortable in the company of children and only in such situations can they feel that they are adequate.

Anger, Aggression and Violence

Anger, aggression and violence are important topics for assessment and they may present as primary or secondary problems. Once more, it is important to assess these topics using a functional analytic framework. Again, certain underlying schemas such as a lack of victim empathy are important to explore. It is also important to explore psychological factors that consistently correlate with violent offending, such as a poor impulse control or 'over-controlling' attitudes.

Measures – Assessment and Change

A cornerstone of CBT is the use of valid and reliable measures. Such measures may be used at assessment – for example, compiling a list of anxiety symptoms and their intensity. Measures should be repeated during and after the therapy process so as to determine the effect of treatment. As in CBT more generally, a number of measures of assessment and change should be used to build an objective picture of the individual and to examine where therapy has and has not been beneficial. For example, in the case of an anxiety disorder, one might observe that on measures of change an individual engages in much less avoidance. However, when using an intensity measure, one might find that the client experiences the same level of distress as at the beginning of treatment. Such a picture, where one measure shows improvement and one shows no improvement should therefore lead the therapist to the conclusion that the therapeutic process is incomplete. In such a case, if one was to terminate therapy at this point, the individual would probably revert to the previous pattern of avoidance behaviour.

With respect to offending behaviour, one cannot overemphasise the need to be over- rather than under-inclusive in the use of measures. That said, the therapist should select measures relevant to a particular individual's problems and not - as is unfortunately the case in some institutions - subject every individual to the same set of numerous measures, many of which may be completely inapplicable.

The scope of this chapter does not extend to detailed discussion of specific diagnostic measures, such as those used to assess personality and risk. However, it is worth emphasising the need for CBT practitioners to become familiar with such measures. The entire team needs to be involved in obtaining the most comprehensive picture possible and the CBT practitioner's role in case management needs to include a repeated measures approach, to enable and ensure a meaningful contribution to the client's treatment. Ongoing reassessments are important from the point of view of rehabilitation and also within the legal framework within which the therapist will operate. For example, the Mental Health Act Review Tribunal or the Parole Board will be very interested in the individual's response to therapy and in the valid and reliable measures of change used. Such bodies will rely on this valuable information when considering an offender's release, transfer, or continued detention.

Example of Measures

- Attitude - Schema Questionnaire (Young & Brown, 2003)
- Self-esteem - Multidimensional Self Esteem Inventory (O'Brien & Epstein, 1983)
- Problem-solving - Social Problem Solving Inventory (D'Zurilla et al., 2002)

- Victim empathy - Victim Distortions Scale (Beckett & Fisher, 1994)
- Sexual attitudes - Hanson Sex Attitudes Questionnaire (Hanson et al., 1994)
- Children and sex - Cognitive Distortions Scale (Beckett, 1987)

Many of these measures are used in treatment programmes within the UK Prison Service and, in particular, throughout the Sex Offender Treatment Programme, which is now run across more than 25 English and Welsh prisons.

Treatment Approaches

Over the past decade or so, there has been an expansion of the use of cognitive behavioural methods across the entire CJS. While this is to be welcomed, particularly as offenders are now provided with evidence-based treatment, expansion means that treatment demands outstrip resources. The supply and demand problem within the CJS is much greater than in the ordinary primary care or outpatient settings. To some extent, the needs of the CJS population have been met by the development of group treatments. Nevertheless, one cannot overemphasise the resource problem that exists in the CJS and, although the literature clearly shows major advances in the development of effective psychological treatments, the numbers of individuals who are able to receive CBT of a reasonable quality will, sadly, remain very small for years to come.

Community Treatment Approaches

For offenders subject to community treatment, CBT and other psychological interventions are usually delivered in probation or community mental health team settings. Depending on the severity of the individual's offending behaviour, they may be allocated to a Community Forensic Mental Health Team, where there are more resources. In community settings, CBT practitioners often find themselves experiencing treatment challenges. Clients are less immediately observable than in a prison or hospital and therapeutic contact is more limited. Communication with other professionals involved in a client's care plan is also more difficult and sporadic than in an institutional setting. However, the need for effective teamwork cannot be overemphasised. CBT practitioners need to recognise that their therapeutic interventions are an important part of the overall treatment and rehabilitation process.

Anger Management Approaches Used in Community Settings

Most local community mental health teams (CMHTs) and probation services offer anger management training, usually delivered in group formats. The range of violent offender profiles is wide and it is impossible, in a chapter of this length, to provide a detailed account of each and every type of offence. Within domestic violence, for example, presentations vary widely from people with generalised anger management problems, to those who only exhibit anger and violence within the context of a specific relationship. In the latter case, offenders may present with pathological jealousy or sexual dysfunction. Such problems will need individual, rather than group treatment approaches.

In the past, anger management problems have been treated within a behavioural framework, emphasising a functional analytic approach to identifying specific obvious (external) cues and triggers, then teaching the individual to deal with these in a more socially acceptable way. A corollary of this is training in appropriate assertive, rather than aggressive, interpersonal skills. However, increasingly, advances in cognitive therapy have led to the incorporation of schema based treatments with an emphasis on modifying cognitive distortions and dysfunctional thinking.

Substance Abuse Programmes

Substance abuse programmes offered by community facilities emphasise two specific components: drugs/alcohol/health education and harm reduction interventions (or goals of abstinence). Increasingly, CBT protocols for substance misuse are used in residential rehabilitation units, replacing (or adding to) the traditional 12-step model. Most treatment programmes will also use the Cycle of Change Model (Prochaska & DiClemente, 2005) to target attitudes and behaviours associated with substance misuse. Both CBT and the cycle of change model emphasise the need for individuals to develop functional attitudes and beliefs towards their substance abuse. This is achieved by working in a collaborative fashion, exploring the 'pros and cons' of various elements of their using behaviour, attitudes, beliefs and overall thinking. Barriers to change are also targeted, for example, those posed by the individual's peer group. The individual may say, 'All my friends drink; if I don't drink I won't have any friends.' Such attitudes are then explored and challenged appropriately. Once the individual has decided to abstain from their substance (or substances) of choice, therapy focuses on maintaining abstinence and avoiding relapse through the development of new coping strategies. This obviously involves the modification of existing high-risk behaviours. For example, some newly abstinent individuals, will continue to visit pubs on a frequent basis; putting an unnecessary amount of temptation in their path. Often individuals need to learn an entirely new way of socialising and living generally. Abstinence necessarily involves significant behavioural change, which needs to be supported throughout the therapeutic process. To facilitate sustained abstinence, it is essential for the individual to be well supported in continuing with positive behavioural and cognitive changes. Although such support is a feature of CBT treatment, an external support network is also very important. Programmes such as Alcoholics Anonymous (AA) are highly accessible and provide valuable support to many recovering individuals outside the therapy room.

Alternatively, substance abuse programmes may emphasise harm reduction as a compromise to abstinence. In the case of alcohol this may involve 'controlled drinking'. The literature now makes it clear that controlled drinking may be an option for some individuals. (However for many people with longstanding, severe alcohol problems, abstinence is often the only meaningful solution.) In the case of other substances, CBT practitioners may need to reach an uneasy compromise with the individual concerned. For example, with cannabis and heroin users, who may not be willing or able to completely abstain. The emphasis therefore is on harm reduction. Many community-based services offer needle exchange programmes. Some CBT therapists may be uneasy about harm minimisation approaches and the advice in such cases is to perhaps either avoid working with this population or to undergo further addiction specific training.

Inpatient and Custodial Approaches

Sex Offender Treatment Programmes are now in operation across the UK and, commendably, many of the programmes now offer literally hundreds of treatment hours organised into blocks. Typically, sex offender treatment programmes take place over 12–18 months and comprehensive reassessment procedures have become commonplace throughout treatment initiatives. While enormous sums of money have been put in place to support these programmes, and several evaluations have been conducted, the effectiveness of sex offender treatment programmes is still a very controversial issue. For a comprehensive account of such controversy, the reader is referred to an excellent chapter by Lockmuller et al. (2009).

Conclusion

This chapter has provided an overview of cognitive behavioural approaches within the criminal justice system. It is perhaps salutary to note that more than 40,000 18–20 year olds were found guilty of an indictable offence in 2008. In the United States, 6% of the population have been in prison. And perhaps of greater concern, 100,000 children aged 10–17 were found guilty of (or cautioned for) indictable offences in 2008. Half of these offences were committed by children aged 15 or under. Put these statistics together with the rising prison population of 90,000 in 2010, and one begins to understand some of the challenges involved in rehabilitation. Many of those in prison suffer disadvantage in almost every aspect of their lives. Many have wide-ranging psychological problems. Indeed, some of the statistics provided above (especially those that demonstrate the extent of mental health problems in prisons) indicate an urgent need for more treatment resources. This chapter has outlined enormous potential for CBT in this population. However, because of the depth and complexity of the psychological problems in CJS, it has only been possible to outline specific approaches. Any practitioner wishing to learn more about the area will be pleased to know that there are now a number of very useful publications. *The Journal of Forensic Psychiatry and Psychology* publishes regular articles of interest to the CBT practitioner. Similarly *The International Journal of Forensic Mental Health* provides a range of articles. The British Association for Behavioural and Cognitive Psychotherapy (BABCP), the main CBT organisation in the UK, runs workshops that are applicable in forensic settings. Finally, for an excellent overview of forensic mental health, the reader is referred to Soothill et al. (2008).

References

Beckett, R. (1987). *The Children and Sex Questionnaire*. Oxford: Roxford Clinic, Littlemore.

Beckett, R. and Fisher, D. (1994). *Assessing Victim Empathy: Community Based Treatment for Sex Offenders and Evaluation of Seven Treatment Programmes*. Home Office Occasional Report. London: Home Office.

Beech, A., and Ward, T. (2004). 'The integration of aetiology and risk in sexual offenders: A theoretical framework', *Aggression and Violent Behaviour*, 10: 31–63.

Clark, C. and Dugdale, G. (2008) *Literacy Changes Lives: The Role of Literacy in Offending Behaviour*. London: National Literacy Trust. Available at www.literacytrust.org.uk/assets/0000/0422/Literacy_changes_lives_prisons.pdf (accessed September 2011).

D'Zurilla, T., Nezu, A. and Maydeu-Olivares, A. (2002). *Social Problem Solving Inventory* (Revised). North Tonawanda, New York: Multi Health Systems.

Fernandes, Y., Marshall, W., Lightbody, S. and O'Sullivan, C. (1999). 'The Child Molester Empathy Measure', *Sexual Abuse: A Journal of Research and Treatment*, 11: 17–31.

Hanson, R., Gizzarrelli, R. and Scott, H. (1994). 'The attitudes of incest offenders: Sexual entitlement and acceptance with children'. *Criminal Justice and Behaviour,* 21: 187–202.

Lockmuller, M., Beech, A. and Fisher, D. (2009). 'Sexual offenders with mental health problems: Epidemiology, assessment and treatment', in K. Soothill, P. Rogers and M. Dolan (eds), *Handbook of Forensic Mental Health*. Devon: Willan Publishing, Chapter 18.

O'Brien, E. and Epstein, S. (1983). *The Multidimentional Self-Esteem Inventory*. Odessa, Florida: Psychological Assessment Resources.

Prochaska, J.O. and DiClemente, C.C. (2005). 'The transtheoretical approach', in J.C. Norcross and M.R. Goldfried (eds), *Handbook of Psychotherapy Integration* (2nd edn). New York: Oxford University Press, pp. 147–171.

Soothill, K., Rogers, P. and Dolan, M. (eds) (2008). *Handbook of Forensic Mental Health*. Devon: Willan Publishing,

Ward, T., Louden, K., Hudson, S. and Marshall, W. (1995). 'A descriptive model of the offence chain in child molesters', *Journal of Interpersonal Violence*, 10: 453–478.

Young, J. and Brown, G. (2003). *Schema Questionnaire (YSQ–L2).* New York: Cognitive Therapy Center of New York.

TWENTY ONE CBT in Private Practice

GLADEANA MCMAHON

Introduction

As Cognitive Behaviour Therapy (CBT) continues to grow in popularity, more CBT therapists are being trained than ever before. The introduction in the UK of the Improving Access to Psychological Therapies (IAPT) scheme has rapidly increased the number of therapists recruited and trained to offer CBT since October 2008. Additionally, the number of medical practitioners, psychiatrists, nurses and mental health practitioners who use CBT, together with nonmedical specialists such as counsellors, counselling and clinical psychologists, social workers and stress management practitioners add up to more CBT on offer, in a variety of clinical and nonclinical settings, than ever before.

Many CBT therapists consider setting up in full-time private practice (sometimes called independent practice) at some point in their career. In 2009, a Special Interest Group (SIG) for those in private practice was set up by the British Association for Behavioural and Cognitive Psychotherapies (BABCP, www.babp.com), the largest professional body for those practising a range of cognitive, behavioural and cognitive behavioural therapies in the UK. Within a matter of months the first training event was hosted and the SIG attracted 151 therapists who were then listed in its first referral directory. This new development reflects the growing interest of cognitive behavioural therapists from all backgrounds in pursuing private practice. Most therapists start by running a part-time private practice alongside full-time employment and many choose to continue to operate this dual system. Doing so allows the individual to enjoy the financial security of full-time employment alongside the flexibility and additional income generated by seeing a few clients privately on a weekly basis. Regardless of whether a therapist wishes to operate a full or part-time private practice it is important s/he is aware of the range of skills required to ensure financial success and sound ethical practice.

As in many professions, there are always conflicts between personal needs, professional ethics and the achievement of acceptable living standards for the therapist (McMahon et al., 2005).

In private practice, the therapist has to take sole responsibility for building and sustaining a credible and acceptable professional reputation. Self-employment means accepting an element of inherent risk. This holds true whether the individual is running a shop, setting up as a self-employed accountant or as a self-employed Cognitive Behavioural Therapist. There are three main risks associated with operating any type of business which also relate to a therapist entering into private practice (McMahon, 1994).

1. Acceptable Risks

This type of business risk refers to situations where the individual decides on a course of action based on his or her analysis of a particular situation. For example, an individual may have been building up his or her private practice alongside full-time employment. There comes a point when the individual has to decide whether to limit the growth of his or her private practice and remain in full-time employment or leave full-time employment to become fully self-employed. Although the therapist may have undertaken an analysis of client numbers and the growth of client referrals, there is no guarantee that client referrals will continue at the current rate. However, the individual feels confident that the referral rate will remain consistent based on the evidence available. S/he therefore decides to embark on full-time private practice.

2. Unacceptable Risks

These are business risks that carry too great a chance of damage to the business or to the individual him/herself. For example, a therapist working on his/her own decides not to accept a particular client referral as s/he believes there may be unacceptable safety risks associated with doing so. In this case the therapist decides that s/he does not have the same protection or back-up available as when working within a medical setting and that personal safety is paramount. The rationale being that, were the CBT therapist to treat such a high risk client and be subsequently assaulted, s/he would be unable to generate an income during an unavoidable recovery period.

3. Risks You Have to Take

There are some risks an individual has to take to ensure the success of any business. In the case of a newly self-employed Cognitive Behavioural Therapist, taking on several clients at a reduced fee entails financial pressure to see more clients than may be professionally desirable. This can often intensify the individual therapist's stress levels. The therapist may understand that s/he should limit the number of clients being seen (and therefore raise his or her fees) but equally fears a drop in client numbers. In order to safeguard fitness to practise and ensure the provision of quality service to clients, s/he concludes that there is no choice but to reduce the number of clients and increase fees. Failing to reach this decision may lead to therapist exhaustion which, in turn, may result in poor client care or therapist illness. Both possibilities would impact negatively on the therapist's fee generating capacity and professional reputation. As professional reputation and word of mouth recommendation translate into future referrals, it is not in the interest of the therapist or his/her practice to avoid the risk of limiting client numbers by increasing fees.

This chapter now explores three additional aspects associated with setting up and running a successful private practice. Part I covers the business requirements that CBT therapists need to consider in order to ensure financial success. Part II considers professional issues associated with CBT private practice. Finally, Part III considers the personal impact of running a private practice on the individual CBT therapist.

Part I Business Requirements

An aspect that many CBT therapists fail to realise is that setting up a private practice is no different to setting up as a self-employed plumber, electrician or management consultant. The business skills required for any type of self-employment tend to be the same regardless of the type of work itself. Whether a plumber or cognitive behavioural therapist, if an individual does not take care of the business requirements common to all businesses it is unlikely that he or she will survive financially (Tyson & Schell, 2008).

Why Do Private Practices Fail?

There are a number of reasons why businesses fail and the same apply to private practice (McMahon, 1994; Weitz, 2006): Many of the issues mentioned below will be expanded upon later in this chapter under their appropriate heading.

1. The Original Idea was Not Well Thought Through

Therapists may not have thought about what is actually involved in running a successful private practice. While the therapist may have the relevant professional skills, s/he may not consider basic business facets such as: how to secure clients, financial outlays involved in running a business and the importance of location.

2. Insufficient Income

If a CBT therapist embarking on private practice fails to complete the neccessary financial planning required to address all the costs associated with running a business (e.g. tax, room rental, marketing costs etc.) or fails to consider ongoing professinal requirement costs (e.g. supervision, professional indemnity insurance) s/he may have an insufficient profit margin to provide a practical monthly income.

3. Insufficient Working Capital

Setting up a business involves some type of investment and this investment needs to be made upfront, before any fees are collected. In some instances therapists may be overly optimistic about how quickly their client base will grow. This can lead to a situation where, although the client base is growing, it is not growing quickly enough to meet the outgoings required. In this scenario, the therapist does not have sufficient working capital to fund the period of time between setting up in private practice and earning a full-time income from it.

4. Insufficient Financial Control

Running a private practice requires the therapist to maintain monthly accounts and to have robust accounting systems in place. Although monies may be coming in, if the therapist does not have the basic bookkeeping skills required s/he may find it difficult to keep adequate track of income and expenditure and this can lead to problems, especially when tax bills that may not have been anticipated for fall due. In addition, the therapist will find it advantageous to register with the majority of private medical insurers (PMI's) so clients with private cover can be referred. However, this also means invoicing, delayed payment and adherance to various PMI financial rules. Therapists also need to consider the financial implications of developing administrative systems for dealing with nonpayment generally. This aspect is explored more fully later in this chapter.

5. Insufficient Skills

The CBT therapist in private practice needs to be very clear about the types of clients and psychological problems s/he is trained and experienced to work with. Otherwise it may be tempting to take on any referral. The therapist may then find themselves struggling to offer an adequately professional service. Cognitive behavioural therapists are likely to be familiar with the various CBT protocols for specific psychiatric disorders through their previous full-time employment and training. However, once a therapist moves into private practice it is important that mechanisms are in place to keep abreast of new developments in client treatment and care. This can be achieved by regular attendance at appropriate Continued Professional Development (CPD) events held by professional bodies such as the BABCP and by receiving up-dates from the National Institute of Clinical Excellence (NICE, www.nice.org.uk).

In CBT private practice, attention also needs to be given to building good relationships with psychiatrists, medical practitioners and other referral sources. It is these individuals as much as any local advertising that will provide vital client referrals. Whereas a GP may simply make an initial referral and require no further contact, most psychiatrists require regular progress reports. Building a good reputation involves conveying confidence in your professional abilities to potential referral sources.

6. Lack of Motivation and Energy

The private CBT therapist has to be self-motivated as s/he is the person who orchestrates everything from basic administration, finances, marketing, CPD to delivering effective client care. The therapist also sets his/her own working hours. Without adequate drive and self-discipline, tasks essential to promoting success may be neglected. Regular CBT supervision and CPD activities eat into practice time. It is not always easy to find a suitably qualified CBT supervisor locally. Allowances may need to be made for travel time. Good practice dictates that supervision is essential. The British Association for Behavioural and Cognitive Psychotherapies (BABCP), requires evidence of ongoing supervision as a criterion for accreditation and re-accreditation.

It is normal practice for CBT therapists to bring audio recordings of client work to supervision. 'In vivo' supervision methods allow both therapist and supervisor to accurately identify clinical strengths and target areas for development. CBT therapists are required to obtain written permission from clients prior to presenting a session in supervision.

7. Overworking

In a bid to make their business a success, some therapists end up working far too many hours. Overworking can lead to burnout, poor client care and ulimately failure of the business. Guidelines recommending clinical and supervision hours ratios often are subject to change. It is helpful to regularly refer to the BABCP for guidance.

8. Family Pressures

If a therapist decides to work from home s/he may not have fully taken into account the needs of those s/he lives with or the impact family members can have on client work. For example, young children can be hard to keep quiet and other family members may find being restricted in their normal household behaviours during therapy hours difficult. There are also a range of risks relating to client and therapist security and household insurance to be considered that will be addressed later in this chapter.

9. Wrong Location

Location is often the key to success. A therapist may live in an area where there is much need for CBT services but where the population does not have the financial resources to pay for private therapy. Alternatively, the therapist may live too far away for most clients to reasonably make the journey. Additional factors relating to room rental and office location are addressed in Part II of this chapter.

10. Bad Luck

Being a self-employed CBT therapist means that if the therapist has an accident or becomes ill, income stops. Moreover, changes in legislation or professional expectations may mean the therapist finds him/herself unable to capitalise on their skills as s/he may not meet the current criteria laid down to practise. For example, statutory regulation and the introduction of protected titles means the therapist may find that s/he does not meet the specified criteria and is therefore unable to trade as normal and this would inevitably have an impact on the monies the therapist could expect to earn from their practice.

The Personal Characteristics of a Successful Business Person

There are a number of personal characteristics associated with successful business persons and these also hold true for cognitive behavioural therapists setting up in private practice (Caird, 1993).

The therapist needs to have the drive and determination to succeed. S/he alone is the business and is responsible for the many tasks involved in running it, i.e. administration, financial control, marketing, record-keeping and actual client care (Grodzki, 2000). Therapists also need to creatively compose basic information about their practice. For example, as the efficacy of CBT is now widely accepted by the general public, promotional materials explaining clearly what CBT can offer will help generate referrals.

An ability to objectively assess what is working and what is not is also essential. For example, the number of referrals from a therapy referral website may not justify the cost of subscription. Attention to detail, the ability to plan and organise also play a part in running a successful practice.

1. Setting Up the Business

Before embarking on private practice it is useful to get as much advice as possible about the issues involved and to identify any skill deficits that may require development. It can be useful to talk to other therapists who are already established in private practice since much can be learned from their experiences. Most high street banks have business advisers and produce a range of materials such as CDs on topics relevant to setting up a private business. Therapists are likely to need an accountant for auditing and taxation purposes. Accountants offer professional advice about how best to set up the financial administration systems (Hedges & Walkley, 2006). There are also government-funded initiatives such as Business Link. Many libraries, local authorities and adult education centres also offer a range of useful information.

2. The Type of Practice

One of the first decisions made early in the planning phase is whether to set up a full- or part-time private practice. Many individuals begin by seeing a few clients in the evenings or at weekends yet maintain full-time employment. Doing so minimises the early financial risks involved in embarking on self-employment. This also allows the therapist to consider whether continued private practice is a viable option and affords time to establish the essential administrative and financial infrastructure. Alternatively, some therapists will secure part-time employment to generate a certain amount of guaranteed monthly income while devoting the bulk of their time to private practice.

3. Financial Matters

A basic understanding of financial planning is fundamental to successful private practice. For example: budgeting, financial forecasting, financial analysis (understanding concepts of profit and loss) and financial control (the facility to pay tax and VAT where applicable (Gail &, Walker, 2009)). Arguably, one of the most crucial aspects of running a practice is deciding on a fee structure. This depends partly on how much profit the therapist needs to cover business expenses and allow for personal income. For example, a therapist working 45 weeks of the year, seeing 12 clients a week at £50 per client session, would be earning £27,000 per annum. A fee of £80 per client session generates an annual income of £43,200. The therapist needs to be realistic about the income needed to cover all business costs as well as personal living expenses. Legitimate business expenditure is tax deductable and this is where having an accountant can be of significant assistance. S/he will identify tax-deductible expenditures.

4. Marketing

How best to attract clients to the service is an important consideration. Market research in relation to the client population sought and where clients with financial resources to fund private therapy are located, needs to take place. The therapist also needs to understand the concept of professional networking. Knowing how to set about promoting the private practice to potential referral sources is imperative (Schenck, 2005). Keeping information sheets brief and to the point while providing enough detail about the therapist's professional background, experience and the type of services on offer is attractive to potential referral sources.The Internet is a growing resource (e.g. personal websites to attract clients, social networking groups to market services and online therapy directories etc.) (Safko & Brake, 2009). If the therapist offers more than one service then consideration needs to be given as to how to promote each service. For example, promoting clinical supervision or training is quite different to promoting therapy services. Information for the general public needs to be 'jargon free' since the average person may not understand clinical terminology. However, when promoting CBT supervision services the target client group will expect to be treated as a peer professional.

5. Premises

The therapist will also need to consider the type of premises from which s/he will operate. Working from home is more economical but may not be feasible if a dedicated room is not available to provide a professional setting. Issues regarding personal safety also require attention in any treatment setting. Many therapists in private practice turn down clients with severe anger management or mental health challenges where violence could ensue, recognising that working alone poses too great a personal risk. Renting suitable rooms in a health centre or the like reduces personal safety risks and ensures professional ambience but does increase financial overheads.

6. Insurance

There are a number of factors associated with insurance cover over and above the therapist having his or her own professional indemnity insurance. For example, if a therapist works from home then s/he would have to check their existing home contents insurance policy, as this may not cover the use of any part of the premises for business purposes. Issues of public liability come into play as clients visiting home premises may have an accident such as falling down the stairs for which the private practitioner may be liable (Whitely, 2002).

Reflection Points

- How many qualities of a successful business person do you possess and which ones do you need to develop?
- What factors associated with failing practices need you be aware of?
- What type of help would be most useful to you and where can you find it?
- How clear are you about all the financial considerations of setting up a practice?
- What types of marketing will be most helpful to you?
- What type of location might you be working from?
- How will you ensure you have the right insurance cover?

Part II Professional Considerations

In addition to the business considerations listed above, there are a number of professional aspects that need to be thought through when setting up as a cognitive behavioural therapist in private practice. These include the following.

1. Legal Requirements

When accepting money for a service such as providing CBT therapy in private practice, a number of laws aimed at protecting the consumer become activated (Bryan, 2009). If a therapist works in a paid or voluntary capacity then the employer provides protection if claims are brought. However, it remains the therapist's responsibility to act with 'due care'. When a therapist works in private practice the law presumes that s/he is working in a professional capacity with the relevant skills required to do so. If a claim is made it will be made against the individual (Jenkins, 2002).

Therapists stress the confidential nature of their services to clients. The exemptions usually cited are 'danger to self or others', child welfare and terrorist threat. However, in reality, no one, bar a solicitor or barrister, has the right to total confidentiality (Bond, 2000). A therapist may be subpoenaed for reasons including court action and professional misconduct. It is therefore important to be aware of what information may be required and ensure relevant administration and note-taking systems are in place. Courts of law may ask to see sessional notes together with any associated materials including tapes, questionnaires and letters (Palmer, 2002).

Private therapists also need to be aware of their responsibilities under the 2003 Data Protection Act (Harris & Carnes, 2009). The Data Protection Registrar is usually very helpful and provides information designed to make the process as simple as possible. Once registered a small annual renewal fee is required (www.dataprotection.gov.uk).

The private CBT practitioner needs to safely store client information and consider what would happen to confidential material in the event of his/her death. Computers that store client data need to be password protected; hard copies of client information require safe storage in a lockable filing cabinet. It is prudent to ask a colleague to act as your professional executor showing him/her where all your client data is stored. Additionally, it is helpful to write down all information related to client care and alert the executor as to where such a letter is stored. Petruska Clarkson first used the term 'Counselling Executor' when highlighting this issue (Taynor & Clarkson, 1992). The counselling contract will be seen externally as a set of terms and conditions (Sills, 1997). By stating fee levels, payment terms, cancellation policy and confidentiality limitations, this acts as a legal document; a standard 'client information sheet' (given to all clients before meeting for an initial assessment) and a signed 'client details form' (which holds basic contact details), prevents later claims that the client was unaware of terms and conditions. See Figure 21.1.

A therapist may find that a client owes money for sessions, although this is unlikely if fees are paid at the end of each client session. In such cases copies of all correspondence requesting payment of outstanding fees should be retained. Depending on the sum involved, the therapist may wish to seek payment via the Small Claims Court which deals with claims under £10,000 (Spadaccini, 2007). It is therefore useful if the final correspondence sent to a client asking for outstanding monies states quite clearly that if payment is not received, the matter will be taken to

My signature below confirms that I have read and understood the information detailed in the Client Information Sheet supplied to me and that I agree to abide by the terms and conditions outlined therein. In addition, I also give my permission for contact to be made with the appropriate external agencies if my therapist believes I am either a danger to myself or to others.

Signed:

Date:

Figure 21.1 Client terms and conditions acceptance statement

the Small Claims Court. Sending a recorded or registered letter ensures that there is a record of receipt of this communication.

2. Professional Bodies and Registration

Most cognitive behavioural therapists belong to a professional body and some will belong to more than one. Membership with professional and accrediting bodies keeps the therapist 'up to date' and also demonstrates commitment to continued professional development. Many professional bodies use terms such as Accreditation, Registration or Chartership to identify practitioners who have undertaken additional forms of competence evaluation. There has also been a move in the UK towards statutory regulation via the Health Professions Council (HPC) www.hpc-uk.org – an independent regulator. In 2009 a register of Practitioner Psychologists was set up and a number of titles were given protected status thereby legally only allowing those formally registered with the HPC to use such titles to practise. Practitioner Psychologist, Registered Psychologist, Clinical Psychologist, Counselling Psychologist, Educational Psychologist, Forensic Psychologist, Health Psychologist, Occupational Psychologist and Sport and Exercise Psychologist are the titles included. The term Psychologist itself was not protected. Therefore, CBT therapists, who are also psychologists, will benefit from registering with the HPC. A three-year grandparenting scheme exists for professionals who have been practising under one of the protected titles but whose original training route may not quite fit the standard model. Although this scheme currently only caters for psychologists, there are future plans to include other therapeutic professions such as counselling and psychotherapy. If such plans reach fruition, then CBT therapists with a core profession in counselling and/or psychotherapy are likely to be affected.

3. Professional Administration

Aspects such as notetaking, client documentation and all written communications fall under the heading of 'professional administration'. As mentioned earlier, these aspects need to be considered in the light of the therapist's legal obligations. Client notes need to be securely stored for a minimum of seven years (Bond, 2000). When completing work with a client, the therapist may wish to print off hard copies of all emails sent to, or received from, the client or use a variety of electronic data storage systems to keep these for the required period. The predominant reason that client notes are retained is to facilitate a smooth return to treatment at a later date. In addition, should the client take legal action against the therapist concerned then these notes would act in the therapist's defense. It is also possible that the client makes a legal case against a third party and instructs his/her solicitor to contact the therapist to gain a relevant report.

4. Supervision and Medical/Psychiatric Back-up

Unlike working within an organisational or agency setting where there are normally opportunities for peer supervision, client discussions and time to discuss client care with colleagues, such opportunities do not exist in private practice. Working alone means that the therapist, rather than the employing organisation, is responsible for arranging requisite supervision arrangements (Syme, 1994).

A number of professional bodies specify the amount of supervision a therapist is expected to receive. For example, the British Association for Counselling and Psychotherapy (BACP) require one and a half hours per month for an accredited therapist and the British Association for Behavioural and Cognitive Psychotherapies (BABCP) require one hour per month. In addition, some bodies such as the BABCP require a live presentation element as part of the supervision process for example, providing audio recordings of therapy sessions. Many therapists arrange regular individual supervision while others may opt for co-supervision, group supervision, peer supervision or a mixture of all of these (Hawkins & Shoet, 2007).

Supervision provides a degree of protection for the therapist and the client. Supervision not only provides support, but also an independent assessment of the quality of clinical work (Jenkins, 2002). If a therapist's competence is questioned by a client, his or her supervisor may be called upon to provide independent witness as to how the therapist handled the case in question (Milne, 2009).

Therapists will occasionally need to access medical and/or psychiatric backup for particular clients. It is therefore important that the therapist is able to assess individual client need and is familiar with the services available locally. For example, a therapist may believe that a depressed client also requires medication. In such cases the therapist may refer the individual back to his/her GP having written a letter outlining his/her concerns and including assessment tools outcomes, such as the Beck Depression Inventory. Using the Client Information Sheet to outline 'duty of care' (stating when confidentiality will be breeched and under what circumstances) makes it more straightforward for the CBT therapist to consult an external agency/professional when therapeutically indicated.

5. Personal security

For therapists who choose to work from home or privately rented offices, personal safety is a crucial consideration. For example, clients with a history of violence may be more prudently treated in a populated and protected setting (McMahon et al., 2005). In private practice it can be difficult to vet clients before an initial assessment as the only contact the therapist may have with the individual is an email or perhaps a telephone call. Carrying out a risk assessment prior to the first meeting (by phone or email) is advisable. If the therapist is in any doubt, s/he can take steps to refer the individual for a psychiatrict assessment.

Reflection Points

- How comfortable/familiar are you with the professional accountability issues you need to consider when setting up a private practice?
- What additional research do you need to undertake in order to adequately understand legal requirements affecting private practice?
- What systems will you need to put into place regarding your professional administration?
- What medical/psychiatric backup do you require and where/how will you get it?
- What action do you need to take to ensure that personal security issues (for both yourself and your clients) are catered for?

Part III The Personal Impact of Private Practice

As stated at the beginning of this chapter, an aspect of running a successful private practice is the personal impact on the therapist.

Over the years many CBT therapists have cited six key reasons for considering setting up in private practice (McMahon, 1994; McMahon et al., 2005), these being:

- a desire for independence;
- seeking an additional income;
- being bored or fed up with current position;
- disliking the restrictions of an individual's current post;
- a desire for more flexible working hours;
- a need for new challenges.

While all of the above can be met through private practice, there are a number of downsides to entertain as well. For example, a therapist may attain independence, but do so at the cost of isolation and worry about financial security. The self-employed therapist may alleviate boredom, avoid the restrictions of working to agency rules and gain new challenges but equally find themselves working harder than before and at unsociable times (early mornings, late evenings and at weekends). This can have an impact on the therapist's personal life as s/he may feel compelled to work at less desireable times. Some therapists may also find it a challenge to switch off from work, especially when seeing clients at home.

Personal Stamina and Determination

Consideration needs to be given to how the therapist will cope under the pressure of hard work, sporadic income and minimal support (due to working independently). To most CBT therapists, understanding stamina as behavioural, physical and psychological in nature is no surprise. Successful action leads to motivation which, in turn, stimulates the mind and energises the body. However, when having to work hard though not necessarily achieving a high income, getting no positive feedback from colleagues, plus performing additional duties - stamina may be harder to sustain. It is therefore important that the self-employed therapist gives attention to self-care and time management regimes.

The Stresses of Private Practice

Psychotherapists have had a long history of private practice (Syme, 1994). While therapists of other theoretical orientations have been operating private practices for many years, CBT therapists are relatively new to this way of working and therefore may not be as aware of the number of stressors that private therapists are likely to encounter. These are as follows (McMahon et al., 2005):

- financial stress - irregular income, business overheads, cash flow difficulties and lack of holiday and sick pay;
- environmental stress - if practising from home: noise, unexpected visitors, and no receptionist; if practising in a health centre or renting a room: the room being used by others, external noise, unsuitable furniture and decoration;
- increase in competition from other therapists;
- unsociable hours, e.g. evening work;
- working in isolation;
- lack of administrative support;
- clash of values, e.g. taking fee-paying clients and turning away those who cannot afford the fee.

Individuals successful in private practice find this way of working suits their personalities and manage to overcome the financial difficulties setting up a business initially involves. Many therapists fail to realise the profundity of the aspects outlined above until confronted by them. It can be helpful to discuss such issues with an experienced colleague who runs a successful private practice.

Managing Personal Energy, Expectations and Workload

Many newly self-employed CBT therapists underestimate the number of unpaid working hours required to support their fee paying work. Sustaining a private CBT practice means time is required for emails, letter writing, marketing, telephone calls, face-to-face meetings, invoicing, note-taking, record-keeping, stationery ordering, computer maintenance, research, CPD courses, supervision and completing tax returns etc. It is therefore important that these are factored into a workplan to avoid overload and burnout (Weitz, 2006).

Retirement

When a therapist moves into private practice s/he also becomes responsible for his/her own personal retirement plan. Issues such as pensions come into play. One of the upsides of being a CBT therapist in private practice is that (providing the therapist keeps up to date on clinical developments and is physically, emotionally and psychologically able), s/he can continue working part-time for as long as desired. However, concerns about financial security post retirement can be emotionally and psychologically taxing. These financial challenges are best addressed early on, to ensure a realistic retirement plan is in place (Larimore et al., 2009).

Reflection Points

- How will you maintain your personal stamina and determination?
- How will you ensure that you use your time effectively and take into account your personal energy levels?
- What future planning do you need to put in place to cater for your retirement?

Conclusion

This chapter has attempted to cover the main issues involved with setting up in private practice as a CBT therapist. The implications of running a business, combined with the professional and personal demands associated with self-employment, all merit careful consideration. Private practice can be a rewarding and profitable occupation. However, as with copious other types of independent professional practice, it requires careful, educated thought to reap maximum profit and avoid unwelcome pitfalls.

References

Bond, T. (2000). *Standards and Ethics for Counselling in Action*. London: Sage.

Bryan, D. (2009). *Straightforward Guide to the Rights of the Consumer*. Brighton: Straightforward Publishing.

Caird, S. (1993). 'What do psychological tests suggest about entrepreneurs?', *Journal of Managerial Psychology*, 8 (6): 11–20.

Gail, J. and Walker, P. (2009). *Self-Employed Tax Solutions: Quick, Simple, Money-Saving, Audit-Proof Tax and Recordkeeping Basics for the Independent Professional*. Guilford: Globe Pecout Press.

Grodzki, L. (2000). *Building Your Ideal Private Practice: A Guide for Therapists and Other Healing Professionals*. London: W.W. Norton.

Harris, B. and Carnes, A. (2009). *Disciplinary and Regulatory Proceedings*. Bristol: Jordan Publishing.

Hawkins, P. and Shoet, R. (2007). *Supervision in the Helping Professions*. Buckingham: Open University Press.

Hedges, R. and Walkley, R. (2006). *Bookkeeping Made Easy*. London: Lawpack Publishing Ltd.

Jenkins, P. (2002). *Legal Issues in Counselling and Psychotherapy*. London: Sage.

Larimore, T., Lindauer, M., Ferri, R., Dogu, L.F. and Bogle, J.C. (2009). *The Bogleheads' Guide to Retirement Planning*. London: John Wiley & Sons, Ltd.

McMahon, G. (1994). *Setting Up Your Own Private Practice*. Cambridge: NEC.

McMahon, G., Palmer, S. and Wilding C. (2005). *Successful Skills of Private Practice*. London: Routledge Brunner.

Milne, D. (2009). *Evidence-based Clinical Supervision: Principles and Practice*. London: Wiley-Blackwell.

Palmer, S. (2002). 'Confidentiality: a case study', in P. Jenkins (ed.), *Legal Issues in Counselling and Psychotherapy*. London: Sage.

Safko, L. and Brake, D.K. (2009). *The Social Media Bible: Tactics, Tools, and Strategies for Business Success*. London: John Wiley & Sons, Ltd.

Schenck, B.F. (2005). *Small Business Marketing for Dummies: Updated to Cover the Latest Low-cost, High-impact Strategies.* London: John Wiley & Sons, Ltd.

Sills, C. (ed.) (1997). *Contracts in Counselling*. London: Sage.

Spadaccini, M. (2007). *Small Claims Court Guidebook*. Irvine: Entrepreneur Press.

Syme, G. (1994). *Counselling in Independent Practice*. Buckingham: Open University Press.

Taynor, B. and Clarkson, P. (1992). 'What happens if a psychotherapist dies?', *Counselling*, 3 (1): 23–4.

Tyson, E. and Schell, J. (2008). *Small Business for Dummies*. London: John Wiley & Sons, Ltd.

Weitz, P. (2006). *Setting Up and Maintaining an Effective Practice.* London: Karnac Books.

Whitely, J. (2002). *Going for Self-employment: How to Set Up and Run Your Own Business*. Oxford: How to Books Ltd.

Further Resources

Data Protection Registrar
Wycliffe House
Water Lane
Wilmslow
Cheshire
SK9 5AF
Tel: 01625 545 745 (enquiries)
www.dataprotection.gov.uk

British Association for Behavioural and Cognitive Psychotherapies (BABCP)
Victoria Buildings
9-13 Silver Street
Bury
BL9 0EU
Tel: 0161 797 4484 Email: babcp@babcp.com
www.babcp.com

British Association for Counselling & Psychotherapy
BACP House
15 St John's Business Park
Lutterworth LE17 4HB
Tel: 01455 883300
www.bacp.co.uk

PART FIVE

CBT: Professional Issues

TWENTY TWO Ethical Principles for CBT Practitioners

TIM BOND AND WINDY DRYDEN

Therapists carry considerable responsibility for the effectiveness and good reputation of their practice. As professionals, we are expected to make reasonable and informed decisions in the best interests of our clients that meet the standards relevant to our practice. This requires three elements in professional practice, namely:

- a theoretical basis for the work that has been applied and tested by rigorous research and professional opinion;
- the exercise of reasonable care in therapeutic practice that meets professional standards;
- a commitment to values and ethics by which practitioners can test, reinforce and be accountable for their commitment to the good of their clients.

In its current state of development, Cognitive Behaviour Therapy (CBT) is arguably one of the most highly developed therapeutic approaches concerning the scientific basis of its theory accompanied by a robust set of standards for practice. However, it may be relatively less developed in its professional ethics. For instance, core texts for CBT practitioners that contain passages of sufficient length about 'values', 'ethics' or 'ethical problem-solving' are just beginning to appear (e.g. Hope, 2010). Professional bodies are similarly inattentive to ethics. The Association for Behavioral and Cognitive Therapies (ABCT) in North America defers to the American Psychological Association (APA) in matters of ethics. The British Association for Behavioural and Cognitive Psychotherapies (BABCP) published standards which almost exclusively concern standards of conduct without really setting out the ethical basis for these standards. In this chapter we will seek to adjust the balance and argue that professional practice is enhanced by developing ethical awareness to the equivalent high scientific standards that inform CBT theory and practice.

Ethics: The Missing Step Between Values and Standards in CBT?

Values lie at the heart of what motivates most practitioners to undertake the work they do in the caring professions and is reflected back in the esteem with which the public regards the profession. Psychological therapists typically explain their values in terms of promoting human well-being and relieving distress (Mahrer, 1967). Each therapy is distinctive in how it develops the application of these values around particular therapeutic insights. When behavioural and cognitive approaches merged to form CBT during the 1950s, their shared commitment to science formed the basis for joining together. This commitment has remained core to what it means to be a cognitive behaviour therapist. This enthusiasm for empirically based therapy informed by scientific evidence is immediately apparent in any of the key texts. This is a therapy that is proud of its scientific origins and one that values science over therapeutic assertion based on the beliefs of founding figures or the individual untested reflections of practitioners. ABCT captures this zeal for science in its vision and values:

> *Vision*: The application of science to the prevention and treatment of behavioural and emotional problems.
>
> *Values*: We value inquiry based on the scientific method to understand and ameliorate human suffering ... (DiGiuseppe et al., 2008)

This enthusiasm and valuing of scientific methods is shared by BABCP on this side of the Atlantic. It is this value-base with its emphasis on providing scientifically based therapy that has undoubtedly given CBT an advantage over other approaches when competing for public or commercial funding of services or influencing public policy over the talking therapies. Before we turn to the well-established ethical principles in scientifically informed professions, we want to address a more fundamental issue. Why do ethics matter? What are the problems that ethics address?

Why Ethics Matter

Ethics are concerned with resolving the unavoidable ambiguity and complexity of situations encountered by people that cannot be fully resolved by science alone. For example, what should a therapist do when a client suggests that a therapeutic solution based on good science is inappropriate to that client's particular circumstances or values? The therapist is faced with a dilemma. Should the therapist attempt to insist on or even attempt to impose a scientifically validated treatment against the client's wishes? This is an ethical rather than a scientific problem. Contemporary ethical standards emphasise the adult client's right to give free and informed consent to any treatment. This prohibits any attempt to coerce a client into receiving therapy regardless of how scientifically justified the therapy might be. This in turn opens the possibility of new levels of complexity. How far ought a therapist to compromise the science in order to negotiate a therapeutic approach that is acceptable to the client? When is it appropriate to offer a scientifically validated therapy on a 'take it or leave it' basis so that the client is faced with a stark choice between accepting therapy on fixed terms or leaving without any therapy? These are ethical questions about the relationship between therapy and social values.

The Problems that Ethics Address

Ethics can be represented in different formats and voices and from different perspectives and these are much debated within moral philosophy and applied ethics. In this chapter, we are going to bypass these debates by accepting the current position in health care which is that the most practical and effective way of addressing ethical issues is by presenting ethics as a set of principles. Ethical principles combine values and a commitment to action that can be used to inform different responses to ethical dilemmas and problems. In the latter half of the twentieth century four principles have predominated in the application of science to human problems, particularly in therapeutic settings:

- respect for autonomy;
- ethical commitment to doing good;
- avoiding harm;
- justice.

These are the principles developed in biomedical ethics (Beauchamp & Childress, 2008) and now used to inform the social value judgements in the development of the authoritative National Institute for Clinical Excellence guidance (NICE, 2005) that is so influential in determining what treatments are funded from general taxation and how treatments ought to be delivered. We will consider these principles first before considering whether the characteristics of the talking therapies require the addition of a further two principles:

- being trustworthy;
- therapist self-respect.

Principle 1: Respect for Autonomy

Respect for a client's autonomy means respecting that person's right to be self-governing. It puts the client in charge of making decisions that relate to themself. This principle requires that the therapist prioritises the client's right to be self-governing over what the therapist believes is best for the client. One of the most basic ways of demonstrating respect for client autonomy is to be attentive to seeking the client's consent to the terms on which therapy is being offered. In some therapies, consent can be little more than a momentary formality in which someone is asked do they agree to a specific treatment before the treatment commences. This minimalist approach to consent has been much criticised and, as a result, the consent process has been elaborated to require that consent must be both freely given and based on being adequately informed of any potential benefits and any risks. It has also been questioned whether someone can give full and free consent in one set of circumstances at the beginning of therapy that is adequate for all future eventualities in a course of treatment. In other words, does valid consent require periodically checking whether consent is still being offered by the client on the original understanding or do new conditions apply? These concerns and ethical debates in health care have largely been addressed in CBT through the principle of collaboration which is at the core of CBT practice from its earliest origins (Beck et al., 1979). The principle of collaboration extends consent from a discrete activity at the beginning of therapy to something that is attended to throughout the therapy as the basis for building a good client-therapist relationship by:

- careful listening to get a real sense of how it is to be the client;
- taking time to set a shared agenda;
- making it clear that feedback is welcome;
- carefully establishing the client's goals for treatment. (Westbrook et al., 2007).

Confidentiality is perhaps one of the foremost concerns for clients and counsellors alike. It provides essential protection to the client's autonomy by putting them firmly in control of what, if anything, is communicated about their counselling to others. However, confidentiality seldom involves absolute secrecy. It is about the protection and management of personally sensitive information in ways that keep the trust of the client. Protected disclosures to other therapists in order to ensure that the client receives the best possible care through consultations with colleagues and supervisors are usually acceptable to clients who will readily give consent. Disclosures to other services, perhaps to make referrals, may be more problematic. The principle that adults are generally entitled to refuse any treatment is long established in English law. The situation with children and young people is more complex and depends on whether the young person is assessed by the therapist as having sufficient maturity, intelligence and understanding to appreciate the implications of a confidential relationship, particularly where the young person does not want parents or responsible adults informed. This is a complex area of law (Bond, 2010; Bond & Mitchels, 2008), but the collaborative approach with young people (Verduyn et al., 2009) creates a foundation upon which to build in order to meet the legal requirements.

A good therapeutic relationship requires mutual accountability between client and therapist. However, there may be other stakeholders in the therapy to whom the counsellor is accountable. For example, the counselling agency, clinical supervisors, the person paying for the counselling where this is not the client, tutors and assessors for trainee counsellors, auditors of services, colleagues and line managers may all have legitimate reasons for wanting to know about aspects of the counselling. One of the ethically best ways of protecting client autonomy is to ensure that clients are adequately informed about anyone to whom the counsellor expects to be accountable and what type of information is likely to be disclosed. This information should be provided prior to the client's consent to therapy and therefore accepted as part of the consent.

Principle 2: Ethical Commitment to Doing Good

If the core values of CBT are understanding and easing human suffering, it follows that 'doing good' is understood in these terms. For example, depression and anxiety are unpleasant psychological states to experience and typically limit someone's opportunity to live life fully. To be able to alleviate these types of human suffering is not only desirable for the individual and their families but also improvement in mental health has further benefits for society including improving productivity and economic performance in the workplace. Most psychological therapists of all types share a commitment to easing psychological suffering but vary in the way they seek to demonstrate that they achieve these aims. Some therapists base their claims on their autobiographical experience about what has helped them faced with problems similar to their clients. Many claim professional experience of what has helped their clients. However, the most authoritative claims are those based on systematic empirical studies that satisfy the demands of scientific rigour. These claims are by no means exclusive to CBT (Cooper, 2008) but the compatibility of CBT with scientific values has undoubtedly made it one of the most scientifically studied therapies. This places CBT in a particularly favourable position in demonstrating that its good intent to alleviate suffering is actually achieved within the conditions of particular studies. CBT is currently better placed than many other approaches to provide clinically credible answers to the critical questions about how effective this approach to therapy is and how this is known. It is therefore unsurprising that CBT is prominent and usually foremost in NICE Guidance about recommended treatments for depression and anxiety with computerised programmes to assist milder forms of these conditions. Provided that someone is correctly assessed and the therapy properly delivered, a cognitive behaviour therapist is well placed to satisfy the ethical principle of doing good (beneficence) in ways that are quantifiable and scientifically demonstrable. Other approaches are joining CBT in demonstrating their effectiveness as further research is undertaken but currently CBT leads the field in being able to claim scientific support for its effectiveness and beneficial outcomes for many common psychological conditions.

One of the common concerns of new clients is how long do I need to be in therapy? Frequently, they are hoping for an answer that indicates the shortest time possible to achieve particular benefits. Clients invest time, travel, may pay fees and face the opportunity cost in being prevented from doing something else when attending for appointments. For most clients, the shortest route to their preferred outcomes, especially rapid relief of emotional pain or distress, is highly desirable.

Similarly, service providers may be hoping to maximise the effectiveness of therapy in the shortest possible time in order to increase throughput and control costs, often for ethically desirable aims related to distributive justice - see below. All these pressures may encourage the therapist towards exaggerating what can be achieved in the shortest possible time. However, there are considerable risks in giving in to these pressures. If clients fail to achieve overambitious improvements they may lose confidence in their therapy. More seriously, they may lose hope in their ability to recover or come to believe that they are in some way more seriously unwell than is really the case. Creating realistic expectations about what is possible avoids these pitfalls and creates a foundation of mutual expectations which are most likely to achieve the good outcomes that both therapist and client hope for.

Principle 3: Avoiding Harm

In medicine, there has been a longstanding concern to avoid doing harm even if it is not possible to improve someone's health. This imperative is sometimes summarised as 'first, do no harm' or is more technically referred to as the principle of nonmaleficence. In CBT some 'harms' are more easily avoided than others.

The deliberate abuse and exploitation of clients is widely forbidden across all therapeutic approaches. Therapists who use their role and expectation that they are trustworthy as a platform for grooming clients in preparation for sexual abuse or exploitation cause considerable harm to clients. The clients who may be most vulnerable to such therapists are those who have been socialised to exploitation by earlier experiences of abuse, particularly in childhood. These are the same clients who may also suffer the greatest harm in terms of guilt, inappropriate sense of responsibility, ambivalence and identity confusion. Financial exploitation can have similarly serious effects. When therapy is unjustifiably extended to increase the financial income of the therapist, clients are receiving very confusing messages about their state of psychological health and their capacity for managing this for themselves. Exploitation usually involves creating a false sense of dependency on the therapist to mask sexual or financial duplicity. This false sense of dependency often prevents clients from complaining or reporting therapists for sexual and financial exploitation This means that therapists as a profession need to be vigilant in pre-empting such behaviour in other therapists by initiating appropriate investigations and disciplinary processes where there is a reasonable suspicion of serious malpractice.

Doing harm is not always intentional. It may be the result of mistakes made in good faith or unknowingly due to the therapist's ignorance. The only people who do not make mistakes are those who do not do anything (although this in itself may be a mistake!). It is possible that the most effective therapists are those who are sensitive to the impact of their interventions, recognise a mistake or substandard intervention promptly, and can adjust the next intervention to counteract any adverse effect. In this way mistakes are transitory and become prompts for more effective interventions. However, some mistakes may become harmful if they are allowed to persist and shape the therapeutic process. Errors in assessment tend to be more likely to persist in ways that damage clients because of the foundational role of assessment in negotiating a treatment plan with a client. Plausible errors in assessment can be particularly persistent and hard to identify and rectify.

For example, I (TB) remember working with a client who was apparently troubled by depression in response to difficult relationships with a teenage son. There occurred a sequence of activating events, sometimes on a daily basis. Her beliefs that a good mother ought to be able to prevent such clashes of will contributed to her feeling frustrated, deskilled and increasingly doubting her competence in other areas of her life, particularly at work. My initial assessment was that some greater insight into the developmental phases of adolescence and individuation presented in a client friendly way might help her to form new beliefs and insights that could support reinterpretation of the activating events and the emotional consequences. We both considered this plausible and worked accordingly, but the sense of losing her ability persisted and worsened. As the sessions progressed, she started to refer to worsening headaches that had not featured to any great extent in our early work together. When these were accompanied by dizziness, we agreed that medical rather than psychological assessment seemed increasingly urgent.

It was the successful treatment for a benign brain tumour that made the critical change for this client, although she thought the therapy had helped her to begin re-evaluating her expectations of herself as a mother of teenage children. We were fortunate that a plausible psychological assessment did not obscure the need for a physiological one. As psychological therapists, we use plausible psychological assessments that are frequently helpful but in the knowledge that they are work in progress rather than definitive. We expect that a first assessment may need to be adjusted as new information is revealed. Adjustments to the original assessment prevent a plausible but inaccurate or incomplete assessment determining future treatment. This is where a collaborative way of working helps clients to play their part in challenging and refining initial assessments. Collaboration helps to transform plausible therapeutic hypotheses into effective therapy.

Errors in knowledge or skills are obvious sources of harm or may involve an avoidable delay in easing a client's distress. However, as most therapy involves a therapist working alone with a therapeutically inexperienced client in private, it is quite possible for errors to go unnoticed. Therapists working in pairs, as in conjoint couple therapy or co-facilitating groups have opportunities for direct observation of each other and discussion that may identify and provide remedies for such errors that are not available to a therapist working alone. The solo therapist is faced with the conundrum of how can I know what I do not know or incorrectly believe to be good practice? This is where good supervision or case discussions with experienced colleagues can be so valuable in testing out ideas and practice. Practice also changes over time especially in a research-led therapeutic approach. Being out of date is another source of potential error for which the best remedies are setting aside time for regularly reading relevant journals and investigating internet sources. Periodic training and updating as a form of continuing professional development is a characteristic of most health work and a requirement of reputable professional bodies.

If helping to establish an appropriate expectation about what a client can realistically hope for is beneficial, it follows that the opposite may become a source of harm. Therapists who are over confident in their own effectiveness or the effectiveness of their therapeutic methods may create false expectations and collude with clients' demoralisation and growing belief that they are somehow responsible for their failure to progress with something that apparently works so well with others. It is hard to find the right balance between being purposeful and optimistic in ways that inspire realistic hope in clients and being too cautious in what is promised that the client is reluctant to engage with therapy. This is particularly hard for novice therapists or therapists applying techniques for a first time. Nonetheless, helping to create appropriate expectations that support therapeutic engagement are an ethical imperative that helps to protect against harm to clients and support the achievement of good.

Principle 4: Justice

One of the major challenges facing most services providing psychological therapies, especially those that have established good reputations among potential clients or sources of referral, is the way demand outstrips the capacity to provide a service. This creates major ethical challenges which have been traditionally managed by holding people on waiting lists until a vacancy occurs. The ever-extending waiting list is the clearest sign of a problem about how to distribute the available services fairly. Should the available services be apportioned equally between clients regardless of need, typically by an entitlement to a fixed maximum of sessions, or should they be allocated according to need, perhaps determined by an initial assessment? Managers concerned about the allocation of scarce resources and growing waiting lists have frequently resorted to limiting the number of sessions available to clients in order to increase throughput. The developmental work that informed the establishment of Improving Access to Psychological Therapies (IAPT) has provided a bigger range of choices in how to achieve distributive justice. The combination of affordable and widely available computerisation has offered alternative methods of providing therapy as partial or almost total alternatives to face to face therapies, particularly for people who either prefer computerised methods of communication such as email or are willing to work through computer-based programs such as 'Beating the Blues' for mild to moderate depression or 'FearFighter' for the management of panic or phobia. As the gradation of the severity of psychological illness has become better established, it has also become possible to match the level of need against the level of intervention required in more sophisticated ways. IAPT has pioneered large-scale stepped psychological therapy provision, particularly CBT, in ways that match levels of need against low- or high-intensity interventions. The ethical basis of this approach is to protect clients' interests by offering the least intrusive form of therapy in terms of demands placed on clients in order to receive therapy (and correspondingly the most efficient use of resources by the therapist) with the most effective method of delivery. Systematic data collection within IAPT should make it possible to determine how services can be delivered more effectively in ways that meet client needs and inform the efficient use of available resources. Greater efficiency is going to be increasingly important as all public services in the UK face some of the biggest cuts in funding in recent times.

The issue of what is fair to clients concerning the availability of services confronts therapists in all sorts of ways. Sometimes it is the manager imposing restrictions on the number of sessions a service can resource. However, it can arise in ways that are more directly within the control of the therapist. For example, why are we more willing to increase the number of sessions with one client than another? Whose needs are being met? For what therapeutic purpose are the sessions being extended? When we have asked ourselves these questions, we have sometimes caught ourselves wanting more time to relish seeing the 'hard won' success story or the opportunity to observe the longer-term implications of particular interventions. Awareness of distributive justice challenges us to justify such extensions against the lost opportunities for therapy with other clients and to question the balance between therapist and client-based choices. Some trainee therapists are required to demonstrate competence through case studies of both short or time-limited therapy and more open-ended therapy of longer duration. How should a trainee decide which client to offer the extended therapy to? How should the trainee engage with the issues of distributive justice between clients and the implications for the client offered longer-term therapy? These are all primarily questions of distributive justice but also involve other ethical principles. Is more therapy invariably good?

Inequalities across society add to the ethical challenges in resource distribution. It is well established that people in socially deprived communities may have as little as 50 years of good quality life in comparison to the additional 20 years enjoyed by people in more privileged circumstances. Inequality is also a major factor in poor mental health. Mental illness is strongly associated with poverty, having less education, unemployment and being economically inactive. What is less clear is whether poor mental health causes poverty or is the consequence of poverty. On any view of the epidemiology of mental illness there are wider social challenges concerning justice which extend beyond the rationing of therapy within particular services. These challenges extend to the availability of psychological help and prevention of mental illness within society and particularly for those most at risk of mental illness due to inequality. There is a strong ethical imperative to address inequalities that damage health, although people may disagree politically over the best ways of achieving this.

The Case for Two Additional Principles: 'Being Trustworthy' and 'Therapist Self-Respect'

The four principles that we have discussed so far in this chapter have been widely adopted as sufficient in healthcare. However, the case for a further two principles in psychological therapies has been advocated since the early 1990s. Thompson (1990) argued for the addition of two principles that he called 'fidelity' and the 'therapist's self-interest'. These principles were adopted by the British Association for Counselling and Psychotherapy in 2002 and reiterated in the latest version of their *Ethical Framework for Good Practice in Counselling and Psychotherapy* (2010) as the principles of 'Being Trustworthy' and 'Therapist Self-respect'. The latter incorporates 'fostering the practitioner's self-knowledge and care for self'. As both are relevant to CBT, it is worth setting out the reasons for the consideration of these additional principles.

Principle 5: Being Trustworthy

When clients are asked what they what in a therapist, their answer will usually include reference to someone they can trust. Being able to trust someone takes on added significance if clients are feeling vulnerable or have low confidence in their ability to solve a troublesome or persistent problem. What clients require of their therapists to be regarded as trustworthy varies between individuals. For some, it is about the therapist using her expertise to serve the best interests or well-being of the client. For others, it is primarily about the honouring of promises, keeping confidences, or being respectful of clients and their values. For many 'being trustworthy' involves more than one ethical commitment. Where clients come from a highly individualised cultural background such as the dominant English-speaking cultures in North America and Western Europe there may be relatively little difference between a principle of respect for autonomy and being trustworthy. Respecting someone's right to self-government is understood as respecting the individual client's wishes and working within the terms of their consent.

However, reliance on a principle of autonomy as a primary ethical principle can be problematic in a number of ways. Firstly, it may encourage an overreliance on client consent as a way of resolving ethical issues. There are some issues that consent cannot resolve totally. Even when a therapist has been conscientious in providing the client with adequate information about the proposed therapy, its benefits and risks, there remains a power differential in favour of the therapist by virtue of being the expert in comparison to the relative powerlessness of the client as the person seeking help. Attentiveness to obtaining a client's consent helps to redress the power imbalance. Informed consent that is freely given is an ethical advance, but the therapist remains responsible for providing the services to which the client has consented to a reasonable standard of care and competence. Clients may not have the expertise to know what their reasonable expectations ought to be. Often consent is given on the basis of hypothetical situations which have not yet been encountered and, if such a situation were to arise, the client may experience it very differently from how they viewed it when they gave their consent. For example, an ethically conscientious therapist will often retain the right to breach confidentiality in order to protect the client from serious self-harm or harm to others. Yet when such situations are encountered, some clients are surprised by the strength of their feelings and become extremely worried about the consequences of their initial consent. This has led some therapists to question consent as a single act by the client and to think of obtaining consent as an iterative process that has to be revisited periodically as a client's experience, understanding and circumstances change. The emphasis on a sustained collaboration between therapist and client goes a long way to resolving this concern in CBT.

The second way in which an overemphasis on respect for client autonomy can be counterproductive arises where the client's state of dependence on others or cultural identity requires a more relational understanding of the client's capacity for consent and the range of choices open to a client. Approximately two-thirds of the world's population live in social systems where the primary unit of ethical identity is the family, possibly an extended family or tribe. The sense of self as an individual may be secondary or even nonexistent. Some clients may be helped where the therapist is both understanding of collective identity and willing to vary practice in order to negotiate a consent that is meaningful to a client by involving other family members or community leaders. For example, many therapists working in highly individualised cultures are accustomed to judging how best to involve family members, especially an adult with parental responsibility in therapeutic decisions concerning young people. Similar adjustments may be required in order to be trustworthy to some clients from traditional communities with a strong sense of collective identity. Being trustworthy with some clients may also require attention to gender and perhaps ensuring that a male therapist does not work with female clients without a chaperone present, or that female therapists are available. No matter how ethically a therapist behaves towards a particular client, some clients may be vulnerable to damage to their reputation within their own community unless the required propriety or etiquette is followed. The social harm to the client may counteract or even exceed the benefits of any therapy.

The use of homework between sessions in CBT can raise issues of trust to an extent not encountered in therapy without formal homework. Trust is mutual. It requires both parties to honour promises made to the other. As homework typically is undertaken unobserved by the therapist, the therapist trusts the client to undertake what they have promised to attempt and to report honestly what occurred. Conversely, the client trusts that the therapist will only suggest homework that has reasonable prospects of being beneficial and certainly not harmful. For example, a client may rely on the therapist to know what is legally or culturally acceptable and assume that this has been taken into account in deciding what homework to suggest unless this has been explicitly discussed. When working with young people on the threshold of adulthood, finding appropriate homework can be particularly challenging as the legal age at which someone can have sex, leave home, consume alcohol, smoke tobacco, and drive are not necessarily consistent with each other or obviously rational and can change periodically.

No matter how carefully a therapist plans their implementation of therapy, the unexpected can happen. For example, a therapist working with a client who suffers from claustrophobia, a fear of confined spaces, in particular using lifts, may be working progressively through a programme of desensitisation to the point where the therapist accompanies a client in a lift. Being trustworthy would require the therapist to avoid lifts that are known to be unreliable or vulnerable to getting stuck. However, no therapist can totally exclude the possibility of freak events such as a power cut causing a usually reliable lift to get stuck temporarily between floors. The client might reasonably expect that the therapist would be particularly supportive and attentive to the client's needs in such circumstances and, if possible, turn misadventure to therapeutic gain. The principle of avoiding harm encourages the therapist to provide adequate safeguards and remedies for unavoidable harm in ways very similar to an ethical commitment to being trustworthy. Being trustworthy directs attention beyond the technical assessment of harm to considering the relational dimension of what it means to be trustworthy to a particular client. This relational dimension can easily be overlooked if therapy is thought of solely in terms of protecting client autonomy without adequate attention to the personal dynamics.

Principle 6: Therapist Self-Respect

A principle of self-respect is particularly relevant to psychological therapy because the therapist is the medium through which the therapy is delivered typically without any intervening medical instruments or medicine. The personal well-being of the therapist is important to the client and ought to be factored in when looking at the ethical nature of psychological therapies. There is a case for arguing that self-respect ought to be an ethical factor in all health-related therapy but the thresholds may be lower in methods that rely on interpersonal interaction as the primary or sole mode of delivering the intervention. When Thompson (1990) proposed the introduction of a principle of self-interest he argued that identifying the therapist's preferences in how ethical dilemmas are resolved ought to be explicitly considered in any ethical problem-solving that takes these into account alongside the interests of the client in determining what is ethically right. Thompson was concerned that if these interests are left out of consideration then the proposed solution will be based on partial consideration of the factors at work and the self-interest of the therapist may be disproportionately and thus inappropriately influential at a subconscious level. In the UK, these concerns may be better understood in terms of the therapist's self-respect in order to provide the motivation and resilience to undertake the challenges of providing therapy. An important aspect of self-respect which also supports the client's interests is having given careful thought to:

a What can you promise, particularly to clients with a reasonable prospect of being able to fulfil that promise?
b How can you present your level of expertise appropriately in ways that match your professional and personal integrity?
c What professional and personal support will be required to ensure that you provide a service to a reasonable standard or care and competence?
d How should you communicate your strengths and limitations to clients?

Having presented and discussed the six ethical principles, we will outline a sequence of steps for ethical problem-solving which include using these principles to inform ethical problem-solving in practice.

An Example of Ethical Problem-solving

One of the ethical dilemmas which may be encountered in CBT concerns deciding when it is ethical to depart from a therapeutic manual. A therapeutic approach based on empirical research supported by claims to efficiency is particularly suitable to being set out in therapeutic manuals designed to inform the actions of the therapist. Where 'manualisation' is a support to good therapy, the use of a manual of procedures and processes is ethically unproblematic. However, at what point is it acceptable to depart from a manual and on what grounds might such a departure be considered ethically justifiable?

Case Study 22.1

Tony is seeking help with what he knows is an irrational fear of insects, especially spiders, which is disrupting his personal life but has taken on new urgency because he has been offered the opportunity to take a leading role in a series of wild life films starting in a few weeks time. He is a man in his mid-twenties with a promising potential career in television. He reports that

(Continued)

(Continued)

he is physically fit, regularly competes in endurance sports and has no known illnesses. He has approached the only available service in his locality. The therapist is required by her employers to offer therapy as set out in a manual. The manual recommends a programme of desensitisation for phobias spread over a longer period of time than Tony is prepared to wait for. Instead he asks to be treated more intensively by 'flooding'. He understands that this will involve intense and potentially overwhelming exposure to insects in order to increase his tolerance of less significant exposures to spiders. He has negotiated access to a range of insects including some in large numbers but wants therapeutic guidance and support to implement the 'flooding' technique. The manual makes reference to 'flooding' as 'an outdated and less effective approach to treating phobias than a phased programme of desensitisation'. It cautions that flooding is potentially more prone to medical complications as a result of the high levels of stress associated with an intense and sustained exposure to the fear objects until the person feels reassured and at ease with the source of the fear.

Would a therapist be ethical in offering the therapy that Tony requests especially as it means departing from the approach recommended by the manual? We will consider this example against a sequence of steps for ethical problem-solving that one of us (TB) has set out in more detail elsewhere (Bond, 2010).

Step 1: Produce a Brief Description of the Problem or Dilemma

The therapist produced the description provided above as a way of testing her appreciation of the issues involved. After a brief period of reflection she added a series of further questions for herself:

1 How ought I to balance the client's wishes against the guidance of the manual?
2 How competent am I to deliver 'flooding' (which after further research seems technically less demanding than desensitisation)? Do I think I could resolve any psychological trauma which might occur if flooding proves ineffective?
3 What medical safeguards ought to be in place?
4 How can I test my client's commitment to his chosen therapy and willingness to take the associated risks?

5 Do I have any ethical or legal constraints that would prevent me offering this treatment if the balance of all other ethical considerations were favourable?
6 What do I want to do and how does this fit with the ethical analysis?

Step 2: Whose Dilemma Is It Anyway?

This step is recommended as a way of clarifying where responsibility rests for resolving the dilemma. In this case the client appears willing to take responsibility for his choice of therapy and has some appreciation of the risks involved but considers these acceptable because of time constraints. The therapist carries the ethical dilemma of deciding whether the client's wishes are sufficient to override the guidance of the manual and whether she considers herself capable of delivering the preferred therapy in ways beneficial to the client and with the minimum risk of harm. She decides that responsibility can be apportioned between them but, as presented, the therapist carries the major responsibility in determining whether she is willing to provide the requested therapy in the way requested and for carrying out the therapy if she agrees to proceed.

Step 3: Consider All Available Ethical Principles and Guidelines

She analyses the dilemma against all six ethical principles although she elides being trustworthy and respecting the client's autonomy as largely coinciding in this case.

Respect For Autonomy and Being Trustworthy

The client's wishes are known and he has taken steps to make these possible by securing access to insects and determining the time constraints. In order to be trustworthy, the therapist decides that she needs to give realistic assessments of the likelihood of success and the risks.

Doing Good

The professional literature suggests that flooding has been successful in a number of cases but that the empirical evidence is more limited than for other types of treatment for phobias. The therapist needs to weigh these reservations against other factors in favour of flooding. The client's sense of purpose and motivation to succeed are significant positive factors in favour of the likelihood of success that might be less present in more ambivalent clients seeking relief from phobias. The rewards of employment might be valuable reinforcement of any success.

Causing Least Harm

She notes that the manual does not expressly forbid flooding as a technique but takes a cautionary view of effectiveness and safety. After careful reflection she considers that she would want to schedule three sessions in the available time with at least two follow-up sessions after the new employment has commenced either to build on any success or to monitor its ineffectiveness and provide remedial therapy if required. With regard to safety she would insist on a medical check-up by a practitioner informed about the proposed treatment and insist on simultaneous monitoring of cardiovascular functions by a trained nurse or sports coach with resuscitation skills for the flooding phase of treatment. After discussion with colleagues she decided to have an initial session in which she assesses the client's level of phobia by a phased introduction to objects of fear so that she is better informed about his likely reactions. She wanted to test his suitability as well as whether she considered herself competent to work with client with a technique that was one of the less familiar techniques to her, although related to interventions with which she was both familiar and competent. She considers that the proposed therapy is a difference of degree rather than kind from her usual ways of working. Nonetheless, she wanted to take the change seriously. She decides that using flooding will depend on her assessment, the client's affirmation of his consent at the end of this assessment and on him consenting again at the beginning of the flooding session. She will also seek additional clinical supervision for this case, if she decides to proceed.

Justice

She considers the proposed service will be more resource-intensive than the agency's usual way of working and that subject to agency approval the client may be asked to make an additional contribution to the costs in order to ensure fairness between clients.

Self-Respect

As a therapist she values the support of the manual and generally works within its framework when this is beneficial to clients. She is an experienced therapist with phobias and has successfully modified treatment plans in response to clients' needs or wishes in the past. She enjoys the challenge of judicious deviation to the benefit of clients but not at any price or for its own sake. She expects to have to justify her decisions to an employer who is increasingly respectful of her clinical judgment. She is reluctant to risk this growing respect frivolously. She wants to discuss with her manager her preferred approach to the treatment plan for Tony. She will only proceed if she can elicit adequate agency support or at least their acquiescence. For her, self-respect requires both working effectively with clients and within her agency.

Step 4: Identify All Possible Courses of Action

Her thinking was clearly pointing towards offering the client a form of treatment that she had modified to take account of her ethical analysis. In order to make sure that she was considering all possible actions, she asked what is she authorised to do? This question provided an opportunity to decide the parameters of her choice and might well exclude some possible courses of action. She considered what other legal and policy requirements ought to be taken into account. Before making a final decision she had decided to check that her employer would support her working in the proposed way with the safeguards envisaged. She also decided to double check for any further guidance issued by NICE, her professional body and in recent publications.

As a final check, she considered three options:

- Refusing flooding as a potential therapy and insisting on the manual's recommended desensitisation programme.
- Modifying the requested treatment to fit more closely with her usual approaches with additional safeguards against identifiable risks.
- Responding to the client's request for flooding without any additional conditions other than his informed consent.

Step 5: Select the Best Course of Action

She tested her choice for the second option as a compromise between the recommendations of the manual and the client's preferences against three criteria:

- Universality
  - What course of action would she recommend to others?
  - How would she respond to her proposed course of action if it were followed by someone else?
- Publicity
  - Could the chosen course of action be explained to other CBT therapists?
  - Would she be willing to have her proposed course of action and rationale exposed to scrutiny in a public forum, for example, or in the press or on television/radio?
- Justice
  - Would she do the same for other clients in a similar situation?
  - Would she do the same for a client who is well known or influential?

After careful consideration and discussion with her line manager and her supervisor she decided to offer a modified version of the requested treatment that she considered had sufficient safeguards for the client and was closest to her known range of competence and experience.

Step 6: Evaluate the Outcome

A great deal will depend on the clinical outcome for the client. This case study is fictitious, but is loosely based on real events that I (TB) was fortunate enough to observe. The outcome of events that I observed (if typical – and they may not be) would suggest that some beneficial effects may result but probably not the secure eradication of the phobia to the level that the client hoped for. Further treatments may be required that may be developed in collaboration with a motivated client who wants to participate actively in shaping his therapy.

Part of the accountability for favourable and especially unfavourable outcomes will depend on the adequacy of recording the decision-making process in the case notes in ways that take account of both therapeutic and ethical considerations. Ethical and therapeutic judgements are seldom mutually exclusive. Rather, as this example illustrates, therapeutic and ethical considerations help to inform each other and maximise the contribution of therapy.

Summary

In this chapter, we have noted CBT's commitment to scientific enquiry, but have argued that a number of ethical principles need to be considered in addition to the scientific status of particular interventions. In particular we discussed six ethical principles:

- respect for autonomy;
- ethical commitment to doing good;
- avoiding harm;
- justice;
- being trustworthy;
- therapist self-respect.

We also outlined a sequence of steps for ethical problem-solving which included using the above principles to inform ethical problem-solving in practice. We hope that the ethical framework outlined in this chapter will stimulate further debate concerning the role of ethics in CBT practice.

References

Beauchamp, T.L. and Childress, J.F. (2008). *Principles of Biomedical Ethics*, 6th edn. New York: Oxford University Press.

Beck, A.T., Rush, A.J., Shaw, B.F. and Emery, G. (1979). *Cognitive Therapy of Depression.* New York: Guilford Press.

Bond, T. (2010). *Standards and Ethics for Counselling in Action*, 3rd edn. London: Sage.

Bond, T. and Mitchels, B. (2008). *Confidentiality and Record Keeping: Recording Confidences*. London: Sage.

British Association for Counselling and Psychotherapy (BACP) (2010). *Ethical Framework for Good Practice in Counselling and Psychotherapy.* Lutterworth: BACP.

Cooper, M. (2008). *Essential Research Findings in Counselling and Psychotherapy: The Facts are Friendly*. London: Sage.

DiGiuseppe, R., Albano, A.M. and Eimer, M.J. (2008). 'ABCT 2007 Strategic Planning Retreat', *The Behavior Therapist*, 31 (3): 1–7.

Hope, T. (2010). 'Ethics', in M. Mueller, H. Kennerley, F. McManus and D. Westbrook (eds), *Oxford Guide to Surviving as a CBT Therapist*. Oxford: Oxford University Press.

Mahrer, A. (ed.) (1967). *The Goals of Psychotherapy*. Englewood Cliffs, NJ: Prentice-Hall.

NICE (2005). *Social Value Judgements: Principles for the Development of NICE Guidance*, 2nd edn. London: National Institute for Clinical Excellence. www.nice.org.uk

Thompson, A. (1990). *A Guide to Ethical Practice in Psychotherapy*. New York: John Wiley & Sons, Inc.

Verduyn, C., Rogers, J. and Wood, A. (2009). *Depression: Cognitive Behaviour Therapy with Children and Young People*. Hove: Routledge.

Westbrook, D., Kennerley, H. and Kirk, J. (2007). *An Introduction to Cognitive Behaviour Therapy: Skills and Applications*. London: Sage.

TWENTY THREE Therapist Development and Self-care in CBT

RHENA BRANCH

This chapter explores some of the key areas involved in therapist self-care. Many of the issues discussed apply to therapists of any orientation although the chapter is aimed at Cognitive Behaviour Therapists (CBT) in particular. How we look after our own mental, emotional and physical health as therapists is a subject often neglected (or given only a cursory mention) on the majority of training courses. This may be due to an underlying assumption that, as mental health practitioners, psychotherapists are by default well-rounded, highly resilient and stable individuals. The CBT therapist especially may be hailed as an expert in rationality and therefore virtually impervious to emotional disturbance caused by faulty thinking. It would be a fine thing indeed if these two assumptions were invariably proved correct. In reality of course, all psychotherapists are *human beings* and therefore *not* immune to the same types of difficulties that befall their patients (Geller et al., 2005).

Many psychotherapeutic traditions (such as psychoanalysis) require students to undergo personal therapy throughout training. Personal therapy may help ensure that budding psychotherapists 'sort out their own issues' prior to treating others (Scott & Hawk, 1986), though it offers no such guarantee. CBT training courses typically place far less emphasis on personal therapy and more on the effective use of supervision. Perhaps there is a role for both within CBT training and professional practice. Placing trainees in the patient's chair may increase their understanding and appreciation of the patient experience. The sense behind experiencing therapy one's self when one is planning to become a qualified therapist, is rather stark. Considering that most individuals will at some point in their lives experience *some* form of mental health problem (either clinical or subclinical), it seems ludicrously optimistic to assume that psychotherapists will not. However ironically, stigmas within the mental health professions still exist and many mental health professionals are reluctant to seek help for their own psychological problems.

In addition to seeking treatment when needed, there is the issue of general physical and emotional 'upkeep'. Because CBT therapists are focused on helping others, it can be easy to overlook the need to care for yourself while striving to develop your career. Avoiding 'burn-out' is aided by frank self-reflection on one's limitations both professional and personal. Taking stock of your current level of skill and experience then adjusting your expectations of what you can achieve or 'take on' professionally – is a habit best started early. Personal life also affects professional performance and this holds true for CBT professional at all levels of experience. Recognising when you are diminished through personal crisis, and making adjustments to your workload accordingly, is integral to avoiding burn-out.

Novice CBT therapists are perhaps more likely to experience vicarious trauma and job related stress than seasoned colleagues. Generally resilience increases with experience and confidence. However, experienced therapists may become complacent about self-care for this very reason. The negative effects of working long hours with complex cases, isolation and the pressure of external professional commitments may be less obvious or profoundly experienced. Nevertheless, they will take their toll on any psychotherapist regardless of experience level. Hence, self-care necessitates deliberate and conscious action. Paying due attention to overall self-care as an ongoing endeavour helps maintain professional competency and promotes job satisfaction. Some of the crucial aspects of CBT practice that may suffer due to therapist stress or burn-out include:

- attention to detail (in general and perhaps particularly during assessment);
- patience and tolerance when dealing with patients;
- attending to the therapeutic alliance;
- keeping abreast of theoretical and clinical advancements (research, articles etc.);

- truly collaborative practice (socratic questioning and psycho-education);
- creative and imaginative use of interventions and homework assignments;
- session to session continuity (due to impaired concentration and memory, lack of time to review case notes etc.).

Many CBT practitioners will work in private practice at some point during their career, either full- or part-time. With the growing popularity and recognition of CBT efficacy, however, therapists find themselves working within a range of settings. Schools, prisons, corporate organisations, specialist treatment units, hospitals, GP surgeries and other multidisciplinary settings all play host to CBT job opportunities. The advice and information offered in this chapter may be easier to follow if you are self-employed and therefore to some extent master of your own workload. You can, however, tailor the information provided here to meet your own professional circumstances and even introduce key concepts to your line manager or in-house supervisor.

Keeping Your Practice Healthy and Hygienic

The terms 'healthy' and 'hygienic' (as used here) refer to CBT practice that complies with the guidelines set by organising bodies such as the British Association of Cognitive and Behavioural Psychotherapies (BABCP). Guidelines for ethical practice, amount/frequency of supervision, CPD hours and confidentiality for example, are devised to ensure patients receive a high standard of care. Correspondingly, adherence to practice guidelines also contributes to therapist well-being for reasons already stated in the chapter introduction. Key issues involved in maintaining ethical and responsible practice are as follows.

Realistic and Manageable Caseload

There are no hard and fast rules about how extensive a caseload should be and many CBT practitioners will regularly see five or more patients during an eight-hour day. Newly qualified therapists often go from placement scenarios where the norm may be three to four clients per week, straight into paid positions where the expectation is to see as many or more clients each day. The transition can be arduous. Novice therapists may be reluctant to decline new referrals out of eagerness to show willingness and capability. Seasoned CBT therapists may also overload themselves because referrers expect they can 'handle it', and they feel compelled to live up to this expectation. Financial factors can also contribute to an overly heavy caseload for those working privately. Though you may think you are able to provide a top-notch service despite working long hours, your clients may disagree. It is nigh on impossible to remain sharp and interested when working long hours for a protracted period.

As part of professional development, CBT therapists will often choose to specialise in specific disorders. Although patients are individuals with varied personalities, histories and current life circumstances, psychiatric disorders are more predictable. To exemplify, it can become monotonous and taxing treating back-to-back OCD (obsessive-compulsive disorder) sufferers all day. Some variation in presenting problems may help break up the working day and stretch your therapeutic skills. It is possible to both specialise *and* treat general psychiatric disorders, though it may require a deliberate decision to do so. Centres and hospitals devoted to treating specific conditions and client populations afford less opportunity to vary your caseload. However, you may be able to vary your therapeutic duties by, for example, leading groups as well as doing one-to-one work.

Complex cases such as Axis II disorders are often very rewarding to work with, but they can also be challenging and tiring. A client base dominated by complex cases may deplete a therapist's resources more quickly than a varied and less severely disordered patient population. If you are working exclusively with high risk, complex and severely disordered patients then adequate supervision and peer support is doubly important.

Sufficient and Suitable Supervision

Supervision is essential for CBT therapists at every level of experience. It provides a useful forum for discussing difficult cases, gaining support, honing skills, safeguarding theoretically consistent practice and exploring your own beliefs and reactions to patients. CBT supervision usually takes place face-to-face and this mode is certainly most recommended for novice therapists. Seasoned therapists will occasionally have telephone supervision or even use email from time to time. CBT remains somewhat unique with respect to supervision in that audio recordings of actual sessions are considered essential. In-vivo supervision techniques lend transparency to practice and provide invaluable information to supervisors. Even the most conscientious supervisee may forget, misinterpret or overlook vital aspects of their work when relying on verbal case presentation alone.

It is important to choose a supervisor that is accredited or has evidence of being qualified to supervise (course certificate etc.). Often course tutors are well placed to recommend a CBT supervisor post training. The majority of work places will provide in-house supervision though in a number of cases, therapists will find this is either insufficient or unsuitable. If your workplace is unable to offer you CBT supervision you may need to make external arrangements for yourself. In some cases you may also be expected to fund extra supervision.

Chapter 24 is devoted to the subject of CBT supervision and thus repetition will be avoided here.

Continued Professional Development (CPD)

CPD is not only essential to meet accreditation and re-accreditation requirements, it also provides opportunity to add more strings to your therapeutic bow. The more knowledgeable you are about CBT theoretical advancements, research outcomes and clinical applications, the more confident you are likely to feel as a practitioner. Regular attendance at CBT conferences and pre-seminar workshops can help you to adopt new skills and ideas, which will ultimately enhance your practice. Providing training, workshops and participating in case presentations or academic seminars can also increase your sense of mastery. The BABCP requires accredited therapists to accrue 30 hours of CPD each year. CPD hours should ideally include a mixture of training provision, research, attending workshops or conferences and self-learning.

External Professional Commitments

In the interest of developing as a therapist and progressing your career, you are likely to take on a number of projects outside of your core practice. For example, you may become involved in a research project, write a book, join a special interest group (SIG) via the BABCP, present at conferences, teach or engage in further specialist training. While extra professional projects may further your career and keep you stimulated, they also take up time. Most of the projects mentioned will take place outside of your normal working hours, therefore be realistic about how much you can commit to without sacrificing all your leisure time.

Peer Support and Interaction

As a CBT therapist, you will often be working in isolation. You may only emerge from your office for a few minutes between clients during an eight-hour day. Depending on where you work, you may have time for a quick chat with the centre receptionist or perhaps catch up with a colleague over a hasty cup of coffee. On busy days though, you may only have time to make fleeting eye contact with a co-professional. In private practice, you may not see another nonpatient soul until you leave work for home in the evening. The author recently had a conversation with a colleague (also in private practice), agreeing to meet regularly for lunch since we were both getting 'stir crazy'. Even having a ten-minute telephone conversation with someone who is not a client may give your brain a much-needed break. Try to schedule breaks into your day that coincide with those of friends or colleagues. Making time to catch up with other therapists also provides an opportunity for informal peer supervision, as you will almost invariably end up discussing cases.

'Burn-Out' and Vicarious Trauma

Adequate supervision can do much to curtail therapist burn-out and vicarious trauma (Freudenberger & Richelson, 1980). It is incumbent upon the supervisee, however, to be honest and descriptive about her difficulties in supervision. It may be uncomfortable to admit to lack of clinical expertise with a specific client population for example, or that your work load is too heavy for your level of experience. Bear in mind, however, that supervisee failure to disclose is probably one of the main contributing factors to therapist burn-out.

Because CBT therapists are men and women, not machines, some client material will inevitably 'get under your skin'. Even the most experienced and skilled CBT practitioners will sometimes find it hard to leave certain client material in the counselling room, either because it resonates with them personally or because it is simply disturbing. Talking your personal reactions to client problems through with your supervisor and/or colleagues can help you detach from the material and deal with it more effectively in session. Do not mistakenly conclude that you are not entitled to be affected by client information because you are a qualified CBT practitioner.

Suicidal patients necessitate thorough risk assessment and in some cases extra sessions. The vast majority of CBT therapists will encounter a suicidal patient within the first year of practice. Most, within a few years of qualifying, will treat at least one client who has attempted suicide prior to, during or after CBT treatment. Many others will lose a patient to a successful suicide attempt at some point during their careers. Such is the nature of the business.

Suicidal ideation requires the CBT therapist to follow steps to reduce risk, carefully document interventions and inform other professionals as appropriate. Suicidal patients flummox many novice therapists and the weight of professional responsibility can hang heavily upon their shoulders. It is imperative that you seek guidance regarding procedures for suicidal patients and discuss concerns with your supervisor and/or clinical lead without hesitation. When you find yourself distressed and worried about a suicide case of any kind, do discuss your feelings with your supervisor openly. Just having someone clarify where your professional responsibility legitimately begins and ends can help you to regain perspective.

Ethics and Therapeutic Boundaries

The code of ethics that pertains to CBT practitioners is largely the same as those that apply to other therapeutic traditions and psychologists. Ethical guidelines for CBT can be found on the BABCP website. It is worth reviewing the ethics code every so often as a reminder of where your responsibility lies. Chapter 22 deals with values and ethics in more depth.

As a rule, keeping all therapist–client contact within the confines of the therapeutic hour is advisable (with the exception of booking appointments). In general it is easier to slacken boundaries once treatment is underway than to tighten them. You may appropriately introduce controlled and planned between-session telephone contact when doing exposure work for example. Or a client may email between sessions to fill you in on how an assignment went or to request clarification on how to execute a homework task. Ultimately between-session contact should be at your discretion. Exceptions may include genuine client crisis, although CBT is not especially a crisis intervention and clients may be better directed towards community crisis teams or even psychiatric A and E units.

CBT therapists working in multidisciplinary settings have more boundary issues to juggle. You may be providing individual therapy and also running groups, covering reception or attending ward rounds etc. Playing more than one role within a workplace can confuse boundaries for your client who may not understand that the hospital corridor is not the place for therapy. You therefore need to be clear in your own mind about professional boundaries and able to communicate these clearly to your clients.

Rules and procedures pertaining to client confidentiality will also vary somewhat depending on the professional setting. If you are unsure of the rules in your workplace be sure to ask for clarification early on. Multidisciplinary practice and confidentiality is discussed in Chapter 11.

Summary of Points

- Keep your caseload lighter when you are newly qualified. As you gain experience you will be able to incrementally increase your number of clients. Psychiatry is, to an extent, seasonal. If you are busier at certain times of the year, remember to titrate your referral intake once the busy period has passed. Be open with your managers and supervisor about feeling overwhelmed before you hit crisis point.
- Err on the side of 'too much' supervision rather than too little. Choose your supervisor carefully to ensure that she can provide the specialist knowledge you may need and overall clinical expertise. Prepare for supervision in advance. Decide which cases you want to present, compile any paperwork and cue your audio recording to the point in the session where you want feedback.
- Choose CPD activities carefully and be selective about which extra professional commitments you take on. Fortunately several professional projects such as research and writing will double as CPD hours. Decide what areas of CBT you want (or need) to learn more about and choose corresponding workshops or seminars.
- Schedule in times to meet with other CBT professionals to keep yourself stimulated and to minimise isolation. Involvement in SIGs may give you some interaction although these groups tend to meet only a few times each year. Peer supervision is a good way of getting extra support and a chance to regularly meet up with your colleagues.
- Be honest with your managers, supervisor and *yourself* about your limitations. Seek out extra training and supervision if you are having difficulty treating specific disorders or working with particular client populations. Discuss your personal reactions to client material with your supervisor.
- Remember that providing CBT treatment is a *job* and you have the right (as well as the obligation) to maintain professional boundaries.

Keeping Your Instrument in Good Condition

As a CBT therapist, you are your instrument. Keeping yourself physically and emotionally healthy is part and parcel of being a 'good' CBT therapist. Responsible and conscientious mental health professionals will monitor themselves and be alert to signs that they may be temporarily unfit to practise. The following are areas of personal self-care which, if neglected, can impact on professional performance:

Self-Evaluation and Reflection

Examining your own beliefs, automatic thoughts, inferences and behavioural tendencies related to your overall practice and individual client cases is part of self-care/professional development. Reflection and self-evaluation are typically emphasised during training but are too frequently neglected post qualification. Allocate time for reflecting on your interventions and evaluating your skill treating specific types of problems/patients. Keeping a written record of your reflections in a designated notebook allows you to review and chart progress. You can then take your notebook to supervision rather than relying upon your memory. What you actually do as a CBT therapist is rarely (if ever) witnessed by anyone other than yourself and your client. Hence the CBT position on in-vivo supervision methods. Even with supervision on actual recorded sessions, therapists have to rely on themselves for validation and constructive criticism to a great extent.

Your supervisor may use competency forms with you, instead of seeing these measures as a test view them as a valuable opportunity to grow and develop as a CBT therapist.

Throughout your career it is important to keep mindful of your therapeutic successes as well as your failures (Norcross & Guy, 2007). In case conferences and supervision, we tend to spend much time focusing on therapeutic impasse and failures, investigating where we went wrong, what we missed and how we can learn from the experience. More rarely do we dissect a highly successful case and try to determine exactly what went right. Potentially there is much to learn from both types of retrospective investigation.

Values and Interests

People tend to feel more contented and fulfilled when living in line with their personal values. For example, if you value family life yet spend every weekend catching up on paperwork, then your values are not being reflected through action. Acting in opposition to your core values undermines self-esteem as it creates a rift between your sense of identity and your constructed reality. Over time your personal happiness will suffer and eventually your work performance and job satisfaction. Take stock of your personal values and make plans to consistently demonstrate them through specific action. That may mean making moderations to your broad professional routine and even your daily schedule.

Nurture interests outside of CBT and psychology generally. There is more to life than work and your brain will thank you for realising this point. Engaging in a sport, social activity or hobby is absorbing and forces your attention away from work and onto whatever it is you are doing. Relaxation generally follows.

Time Off

Running a private practice means that when you aren't working, you don't get paid. Without even noticing, you may begin to take fewer days off for illness and book shorter holidays. Being employed by a hospital or centre usually gives you sick pay and a set amount of annual leave. However, with a heavy workload and other professionals buzzing around you, taking leave may be easier said than done. Often annual leave ends up being lumped in towards the end of the year as an afterthought. Also taking time off for illness may not seem like an option unless you are completely unable to drag yourself into work. Taking time to fully recover from periods of illness is important to avoid burnout. You also may as well keep your germs at home instead of infecting colleagues and ultimately having to cover for them.

Work can also leak into your evenings and weekends if you allow it to. Everybody needs time off from work in order to recharge the old batteries and keep performing well. Try to earmark at least half of your weekends and evenings for relaxation, socialising and attending to domestic duties. To ensure that you get a truly work-free holiday with no emails, calls or emergencies leave a voicemail/'out of office' email response, stating that you are on leave and redirecting callers to another professional who has agreed to cover for you during your absence.

Lifestyle Management

Do you practise what you preach? How often do you advocate that your clients: exercise more, eat better, take holidays, organise themselves, stop procrastinating, drink less alcohol, challenge negative thoughts, be self-compassionate, note their successes, leave work on time, reinvest time in hobbies, socialise more, spend time with family, go to bed earlier or get up earlier – to list but a few possibilities? As a CBT therapist, the answer is probably: a lot. Can you honestly say that you take your own advice on board more often than not? The author was fortunate to work under an excellent manager/supervisor in her early training. When this manager would hear the staff griping about work and personal issues, her stock response would always be 'What would you tell your client to do?' This simple question invariably shut everyone in the office up. It is the kind of question that we CBT therapists (and mental health professionals in general) perhaps ask ourselves too rarely. We presumably have faith in our ability to deliver sound constructive advice; it stands to reason that we should follow our own instructions to solve our own difficulties.

Despite being mental health professionals, CBT therapists (like other human beings) may fail to act in their own best interests (Dryden, 1995). Reflect on your own lifestyle and ask yourself if you are expecting your clients (or supervisees) to do things that you are either neglecting or are not prepared to do yourself. Taking charge of your own lifestyle will probably make it easier to 'sell' the concept to clients.

Figure 23.1 shows different areas that typically comprise an individual's life. Depending on age and circumstances, some areas may be more developed than others. In the interest of maintaining a balanced lifestyle, approximately equal attention will be given to each area. Work or family,

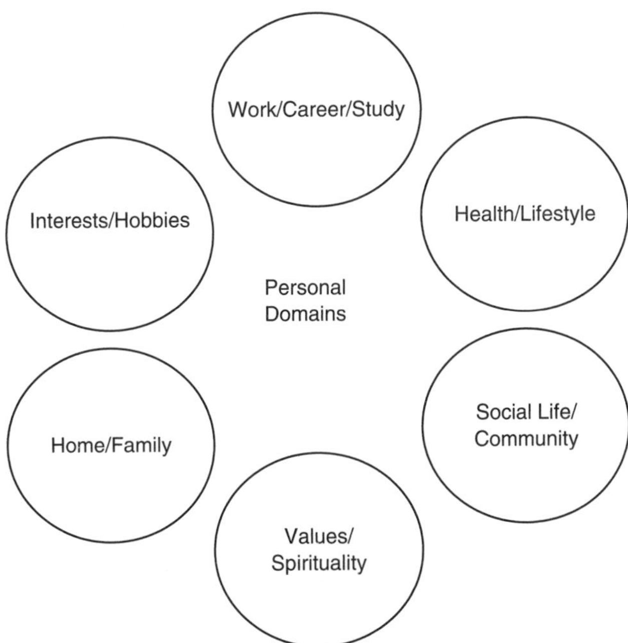

Figure 23.1 Typical domains which comprise an individual's experience

for example, may take priority for a period; however, ideally all areas will be given an adequate amount of consideration on the average.

Personal Therapy and Medication

During training, personal therapy can help foster appreciation of the client experience. It allows trainees to observe therapy in action and be on the receiving end of many of the interventions that they will employ themselves in future (Norcross, 2005). CBT trainees in CBT therapy will face their own belief systems, thinking biases and dysfunctional behaviours. Without doubt personal therapy can be a very valuable learning experience and perhaps should be given more importance on CBT courses than it currently receives.

Entering therapy to deal with personal crisis or psychological and emotional problems can be a difficult pill for mental health professionals to swallow. Perhaps it seems a bit like taking coal to Newcastle. Obstructing beliefs such as: 'I should be able to sort myself out', 'People in my profession are not meant to suffer psychologically' or 'There's nothing anyone else can tell me that I don't already know' and 'How can I expect my clients and colleagues to respect me if I enter treatment?' can come into play. Realistically of course, it is immensely difficult to remain objective when in the throes of emotional distress. Getting a professional perspective can be illuminating and even humbling. The author has (as have many other CBT therapists without doubt) been privileged to treat psychoanalysts, consultant psychiatrists, clinical psychologists, psychiatric nurses and fellow CBT therapists over the years. Almost without exception, they have expressed sentiments along the lines of those cited above (usually in the first session). In short, we who uphold the virtues of therapy employ a double standard when it comes to our own mental health. CBT is often said to be guiltier of this double standard than other therapeutic traditions – although the assertion is based mainly on conjecture.

Medication can prove an even greater bone of contention for many therapists: 'Who? Me? In therapy, on medication? With *my* reputation?' Of course there are plenty of therapists who do not find personal therapy or medication an issue at all. Some professionals have long-standing psychiatric conditions that are under control due to medication and regular therapy. They perhaps came to terms with the reality of their psychological make up and essential interventions well before they began training as therapists themselves.

The gist of the message offered here is thus: if it can happen to your patients, it can happen to you. Refusing to get therapeutic help or take appropriate psychiatric medication because of pride and/or shame is as ridiculous as a medical doctor refusing to take antibiotics for an infection (or a dentist refusing to let another dentist perform his root canal).

CBT therapists who seek treatment may want to see another CBT therapist so both parties are singing from the same hymn sheet so to speak. While this makes logical sense, be wary of then turning the session into peer supervision or a forum for theoretical discussion. Also take stock of your competitive professional beliefs and possible demands to impress. You may know of someone suitable or follow a recommendation. Receiving treatment from someone you know of professionally may inspire your confidence, but it may also impede frank and undefended disclosure. For these reasons a CBT therapist may opt for treatment from a therapist of a different orientation. However, seeing a therapist from a too vastly divergent theoretical background may result in a 'locking of horns' if your understanding of psychological concepts is fundamentally incompatible and no common ground can be established. Consider these points carefully and if your chosen therapist transpires to be unsuitable, explain and move on.

Reflection Points

- Do I reflect on my practice and evaluate my own performance regularly? Also, do I allow myself to confront my own beliefs about (and reactions to) client material as well as certain clients? Do I take my findings to supervision?
- Am I allowing work and professional commitments to supercede my personal values? Do I allot time to indulge in my recreational interests outside of work?
- Do I take enough time off each year to fully relax and forget about work (as opposed to taking the 'bus driver's holiday')? If I am ill, do I give myself adequate time away from work to recover?
- Does my lifestyle reflect a reasonable 'work–life' balance? Do I practise the healthy behaviours that I urge my patients to adopt?
- If I recognised the need to enter personal therapy, would I be prepared to do so? Would I consider taking psychiatric medication if my GP or therapist suggested it?

The following case studies illustrate the importance of continued self-care from trainee/novice to expert status. Though fictional, these examples include the kinds of issues and difficulties observed through providing supervision.

Case Study 23.1

Tilda is a CBT therapist working full-time in a private psychiatric hospital. She completed her formal training last year and has been working to make up the hours needed for accreditation. Tilda does an average of eight hours group work per week and provides individual CBT for 13 in-patients. The hospital has a reputation for treating post-traumatic stress disorder (PTSD) and Tilda therefore has several patients who have been involved in accidents or been victims of violent assault on her caseload. Despite being an avid reader of relevant CBT literature, Tilda feels out of her depth when attempting to treat PTSD. She finds it hard to listen to her patients' stories without experiencing emotional distress; she's also unsure of the treatment protocol. Tilda often goes home feeling upset and unable to clear her mind of work-related material; she even has dreams of providing therapy. Because she is eager to prove herself a capable CBT therapist and fulfil accreditation criteria, Tilda is reluctant to discuss her difficulties with her supervisor. She observes her fellow therapists who appear to take it all in their stride, and feels pathetic and useless by comparison.

Tilda's self-care interventions

After a particularly gruelling day, Tilda sat down with a notebook and honestly recorded how she was feeling about work. She then compiled a list of things she thought would help her overcome her difficulties. Despite being anxious, Tilda took her concerns to supervision and subsequently arranged a three-way meeting with her supervisor and manager. After explaining her difficulties she read them her list of proposed changes:

- Fewer PTSD referrals.
- Extra training on PTSD treatment protocol.
- An additional hour of supervision every fortnight until she became more adept at treating PTSD cases.

Happily her suggestions were agreed with and actioned. Tilda also took personal responsibility for her own part in her distress and resolved to make the following changes:

- Resist comparing myself negatively to CBT colleagues with greater expertise with PTSD and/or more experience generally.
- Arrange to meet up with friends from my course (who are also at my level of experience) and share how I've been feeling at work.
- Go for a run after work to de-stress.
- Keep lines of communication open with my manager and supervisor (not just leave it up to them to approach me).

Case Study 23.2

Margo is an experienced psychiatric nurse who retrained as a CBT therapist three years ago. Because of her years of experience working with mental health, Margo assumed that she would find the transition from nurse to therapist straightforward. She was somewhat surprised to find that her new role as a CBT therapist demanded so much of her mental attention and time. Whereas Margo was accustomed to shift work, she now has to manage her own diary and arrange her own CPD and supervision. Margo hasn't taken more than four days off consecutively since she began her private practice three years ago. Next month her four-year-old son is due to have a serious operation to correct a problem with his heart. Margo wants to be with her son but feels terribly guilty about abandoning her clients by taking time off. She also worries about lost income and whether referrers will stop sending her new clients if she is off work for an extended period. Margo tells herself that she will be fit to return to work in a week's time since her husband and mother will happily care for her son.

Margo's self-care interventions

Margo discussed her concerns about taking time off to be with her son post-operation in supervision. Her supervisor challenged Margo about repeatedly reassuring herself that a week off would be fine and that her son wouldn't suffer as a result of her returning to full-time work. 'Who are you trying to convince, me or yourself?' she asked. 'Do you really think you'll be giving your clients the best possible service when you're preoccupied with worries about your son?' After some frank discussion, Margo's supervisor made the following suggestions:

- Let referrers know this week that you will be off work for personal reasons next month.
- Take a minimum of three weeks off to be with your son, as the doctors seem to be suggesting is advisable.
- Make a stepped return to work, starting part-time (or three-quarters time) depending on your husband and mother's childcare availability.

The supervisor also urged Margo to remember that loss of earnings during times of personal crisis is inevitable in private practice; never taking time off is simply not realistic. She suggested that Margo weigh up the financial cost of employing someone to do her administration duties versus the potential pay off in quality of life. Following the discussion with her supervisor, Margo also decided to consider the following actions to alleviate her work stress in the longer-term:

(Continued)

(Continued)

- Engage in self-reflection more consistently. Take time to write down my demands about 'being there' for my clients and needing to 'fix them'. Address these in supervision.
- Schedule in holidays and breaks several months in advance so I don't end up not taking any time off at all.
- Enter personal therapy to address my anxiety about my son's future health prospects.

Case Study 23.3

Raj has been a CBT therapist for 15 years. He is well respected and liked by patients, students and colleagues alike. Raj is renowned for his ability to maintain a busy private practice, present at conferences, teach part-time at university level and keep a smile on his face. Recently Raj has been experiencing headaches, loss of energy and feels anxious on waking. His family complains that he is never able to spend time with them due to a paper he must write or marking he must complete. Raj knows that he's missing out on family life and leisure activities he previously enjoyed. He is less enthusiastic about work generally and notes that his mood is subdued with a background of anxiety. Though he is concerned that he may be depressed, Raj refuses to stop and take stock of his multiple work commitments and the effect they may be having on his mental health. After all, he has a reputation to maintain and people rely on him. It would be awful to let his patients and students down. He can't imagine exposing weakness to his colleagues.

Raj's self-care interventions

After listening to his wife's perspective on Raj's overall mood and degree of family involvement, he found his depressive symptoms harder to ignore. One day a colleague and friend spoke to Raj confidentially, expressing concerns that he may be suffering from overwork since he did not 'seem himself' lately. Although Raj felt mortified that his depression had become obvious to other professionals, it pushed him to confront the issue. He spoke to his supervisor and together they agreed upon the following course of action:

- Cut down on all nonessential professional projects and activities for the foreseeable future.
- Enter personal therapy to treat his depression *and* help him overcome his shame about being depressed in the first place.
- Speak to his GP about antidepressant medication.

- Use the time gained through relinquishing extra professional duties to re-engage with his family.
- Start golfing again and reading for pleasure.

These case examples, by dint of being fictional, provide some fairly ideal solutions to less than ideal situations. In reality, your supervisors and managers may be less superlatively informed and understanding. The onus to come up with, and implement solutions, may land more squarely on your shoulders than depicted here.

Conclusion

This chapter has aimed to underscore the importance of servicing your therapeutic engine on an on-going basis. Therapist self-care facilitates and complements professional development. A common misconception is that in order to progress your career everything else in your life must suffer. In actuality, a content and healthy person more readily yields a productive and competent professional.

This chapter has also striven to normalise the phenomenon of 'therapist as patient'. Accepting that there may be times when you are not fit to practise due to either physical or emotional reasons (or both), rather than being a 'weakness', indicates a responsible and mature practitioner. Ultimately, what is good for the goose is good for the gander.

Good self-care practices are best bedded down early on in your career; start as you mean to go on. Attention to your own mental and physical well being combined with remedial action can do much to curtail vicarious trauma and therapist burn-out. Seasoned practitioners, who may have allowed some of the subjects covered in this chapter to slip, may do well to reinstate a self-care regime. As CBT therapists we owe it to our patients *and ourselves* to keep the therapeutic machine in good running order throughout our careers. Therapist self-care helps ensure high standards of professional care and long-term job satisfaction.

Bibliography

Dryden, W. (ed.). (1995). *The Stresses of Counselling in Action*. London: Sage.
Freudenberger, H.J. and Richelson, G. (1980). *Burn Out: How to Beat the High Cost of Success*. New York: Bantam.

Geller, J.D., Norcross, J.C. and Orlinsky, D.E. (eds) (2005). *The Psychotherapist's Own Psychotherapy: Patient and Clinical Perspectives*. New York: Oxford University Press.

Norcross, J.C. (2005). 'The psychotherapist's own psychotherapy: Educating and developing psychologists', *American Psychologist*, 60: 840–50.

Norcross, J.C. and Guy, J.D. (2007). *Leaving It at the Office: A Guide to Psychotherapist Self-care*. New York: Guilford Press.

Scott, C.D. and Hawk, J. (1986). *Heal Thyself: The Health of Health Care Professionals*. New York: Brunner/Mazel.

TWENTY FOUR Supervision of CBT Therapists

RHENA BRANCH AND WINDY DRYDEN

Introduction

Clinical supervision is an essential and central component of both CBT training and professional practice post-qualification. Ideally, CBT trainees and experienced practitioners alike will place considerable importance on ensuring that they receive an adequate amount of high quality supervision appropriately pitched to their level of training and experience. The purpose and benefit of clinical supervision will be discussed in the early part of this chapter.

Regrettably, it is sometimes the case that supervision is viewed merely as a 'box-ticking' exercise to meet accreditation criteria or to pacify employers. Supervision may also be considered a necessary evil – where little is actually learnt and time is spent defending one's professional ego. Additionally, it is not entirely uncommon for students to anxiously attend course related supervision, believing that they must prove their competency to tutors, course supervisors and classmates. The reasons for dissatisfaction with (and/or avoidance of) supervision include both supervisee and supervisor factors. Clinical settings and organisational issues such as funding and availability can also come into play. In short, there exists a hotbed of potential factors that may render supervision less than helpful, spoil the enjoyment and stimulation of supervision and/or lead one to avoid it as much as possible. This chapter will highlight common factors that confound appropriate, useful and enriching supervision experiences and suggest ways of addressing these factors.

Issues regarding supervisory contracts, costs, regularity, method and setting of clinical supervision will also be discussed. Finally, the chapter will discuss assessment tools and techniques used in CBT supervision to chart progress or evaluate therapist competency.

Why is CBT Supervision Important?

Emphasis on the importance of clinical supervision is by no means unique to CBT. Supervision is held to be important by most every therapeutic tradition, new and old (Bernard & Goodyear, 2004). The style and method of supervision will in most cases reflect that of the therapy itself. For example, psychoanalytical supervision may attend to issues of transference and counter-transference between supervisor and supervisee, in addition to exploring similar dynamics between therapist and client. CBT supervision, in contrast, tends to consider therapist–client (and supervisee–supervisor) relational dynamics in terms of schemata, which is in keeping with the theory. Moreover, CBT supervisors are likely to take an active-directive approach and expect supervisees to arrive well prepared for supervision (Liese & Beck, 1992). In general, CBT supervision is a transparent focused arena, promoting skills refinement (including conceptualisation and intervention) and overall professional development. Therefore, less supervisory emphasis is given to experiential and investigative processes than is perhaps found in other therapeutic orientations.

CBT is scientific, evidence-based and can broadly be described as 'formulaic' in the sense that disorder-specific treatment protocols are employed. Hence, much of individual supervision with newly qualified practitioners will include:

- core skills development (including disorder-specific protocol adherence);
- guidance with initial assessments and fine-tuning case formulations;
- evaluating the timeliness and appropriateness of specific interventions;
- reviewing negotiated homework assignments;
- feedback regarding therapeutic style and alliance issues;
- the opportunity to learn from the experience and expertise of a seasoned practitioner;
- space to 'offload' or vent clinical frustration and discuss alliance ruptures;

- guidance and support with difficult or complex cases (including risk assessment and professionally responsible action);
- regular assessment of overall clinical development with remedial action outlined as needed;
- advice and guidance about continued professional development (CPD);
- a reminder to consider issues of diversity when working with a broad clientele (see Chapter 9).

For the more experienced CBT practitioner, individual supervision will become progressively more peer-based than expert-novice based. The benefits of continued supervision for seasoned professionals are not to be underestimated. These include:

- a stimulating environment to discuss and explore theoretical advancements;
- reduced risk of 'burn-out' and reduced negative effects of working in isolation;
- feedback and ideas for overcoming obstacles with resistant clients;
- support in working with complex cases, heavy workloads and adjacent professional responsibilities;
- promotion of creativity and diversity with regard to clinical interventions;
- help to ensure good practice and curtail complacency.

In addition to the above points, supervision can also encourage ongoing reflective practice and frank nondefensive discussion of clinical strengths and weaknesses (see Chapter 23).

As mental health professionals, CBT therapists have a duty of care to their clients. Supervision helps to regulate practice in so far as clinicians are monitored regarding their adherence to evidence-based treatment protocols (NICE guidelines for example), theoretical consistency in practice and the overall quality of the CBT they provide. Supervision also helps to ensure ethical boundaries are maintained and professional conduct is rigorously upheld.

Modes of CBT Supervision

There are different ways of receiving CBT supervision and of providing the material to be supervised. Each mode has its own strengths and limitations. Which method of supervision is best recommended will often depend on the supervisee's level of experience.

Individual (one-to-one) Supervision

This traditional scenario involves the CBT therapist finding a suitable supervisor and paying an hourly fee for intensive one-to-one supervision (or having this fee paid for). This mode of supervision is suitable for CBT practitioners of all levels.

Paired (or shared) Supervision

Here two or perhaps three therapists (trainee or qualified) will attend supervision in a shared capacity with a single supervisor. This mode can make supervision more affordable and give supervisees the additional bonus of learning from one another while still getting a fair amount of individual attention.

Group Supervision

The majority of training courses provide group supervision. There may be as many as 8–10 students in a supervision group, however, each session will last up to three hours. Feedback is likely to focus mainly on skills development, the translation of theory into practice, case conceptualisation and treatment planning. Many trainees seek extra individual supervision to supplement their course learning. Other settings such as hospitals and specialist clinics will often offer group supervision but expect employed therapists to secure their own additional one-to-one supervision externally.

Peer Supervision

As the name suggests, this mode of supervision involves CBT peers or colleagues meeting for mutual supervision. Peer supervision can take place in groups or in pairs. The salient point is that supervision is reciprocal rather than one-way. Typically, CBT therapists will be of a similar level of experience so that each member benefits equally. Peer supervision is recommended for qualified and seasoned therapists rather than novices or trainees. While peer supervision carries its benefits such as being affordable, convenient and informal, it does not necessarily provide expert guidance or formal professional monitoring. For these reasons, peer supervision is often best used as an adjunct to individual supervision.

Remote Supervision

Supervision can be done remotely via email, over the phone or through the post (e.g. Dryden, 1983) – in some cases all three methods may be used. Obviously remote supervision is less than ideal since feedback is less immediate. Telephone supervision relies on verbal report on the part of the supervisee unless an audio recording has been previously sent to the remote supervisor. However, in cases where there are no suitable CBT supervisors in the geographical area, remote supervision may be the only option. Ideally this mode of supervision should be supplemented by group and/or peer supervision. Therapists who rely heavily on remote supervision are advised to make the journey to see their supervisor face-to-face as often as is feasible. It is also strongly advised that audio recordings are regularly used in addition to verbal reporting. CBT therapists most typically will use remote supervision to gain expert advice from a respected supervisor in another country or city as a supplement to their usual face-to-face supervision. Remote supervision is probably most successful when the supervisee's work is already known to the supervisor, for example from a previous job or training course.

Video and Audio Recordings

Most CBT supervisors will expect supervisees to present an audio recording of sessions at least 50% of the time. This ensures that clinical practice is sufficiently monitored for competence and professionalism. It also provides the supervisee with the chance to listen objectively to themselves in action and notice aspects of practice that may have gone unnoticed during the live session. Supervisors will often point out technical errors, alliance issues and assessment omissions (to list but a few examples) while reviewing a recorded session. Opportunities for such spontaneous feedback can be limited when the supervisory mode used is case presentation or verbal report – since both rely heavily on the supervisee's accurate account of treatment. In addition to highlighting errors, audio recordings allow supervisors to point out their supervisee's clinical strengths. Visual recordings offer the supervisor and supervisee additional information such as facial expression and body movement that can enrich supervision. Although clients may be initially reluctant to consent to sessions being recorded, often when the purpose behind recording sessions is explained, they readily become accustomed to a discreet recording device.

Case Discussion

Case discussion may involve a formal, very detailed and comprehensive presentation of a single client or less formal verbal reports on one or more clients. When formally presenting a case for supervision, it is important to include as much relevant information as possible. The aim is to provide the supervisor(s) with a clear treatment overview from the point of referral and assessment through to the present. Therefore previous psychiatric treatment, early developmental issues, historically significant events, medication history and familial/significant relationships past and present are all relevant. Comprehensive problem formulation and the rationale informing specific interventions must be included. Any measures/forms used, such as risk assessments or the Beck's Depression Inventory (BDI), should be included and referred to when discussing therapeutic progress. Additional information and reports from other medical professionals involved in the client's care also merit inclusion. Plans for future CBT sessions (in the case of ongoing treatment) should be thought out in advance and presented for constructive feedback. Case notes may also be included during case presentation within multidisciplinary settings, however, patient confidentiality must be appropriately upheld (see Chapter 22).

Less formal verbal reporting is typically more present focused and less detailed than full case presentation. Supervisees, at all levels of expertise, rely heavily on verbal report in supervision. Realistically, CBT therapists carrying heavy caseloads will simply not have the luxury of time to present audio recordings of every patient. It is important therefore that CBT supervisees strive to be as accurate as possible when using verbal report in supervision. Reviewing case notes prior to supervision can help promote such accuracy. Listening to earlier audio recordings (even if they are not going to be presented in supervision) can also help therapists to provide accurate accounts of treatment. In complex cases, it is strongly advised that therapists do not rely exclusively on verbal report.

Direct Observation

A supervisor sitting in on actual CBT sessions is relatively uncommon. This is in part due to confidentiality issues, patient comfort and the impact it may have on the client's confidence in their therapist. A client may lose faith in a therapist's ability to help them if they see a more senior practitioner monitoring the session. Also, most clients expect to be treated by one therapist and may feel uncomfortable if they are suddenly faced by two. A secondary consideration is the effect direct observation may have on the supervisee. Anxiety may come into play and impair concentration, creativity and possibly harm the therapeutic alliance. In cases where a two-way mirror with audio feed is used to observe live therapy sessions, the element of intrusion is reduced.

Indirect Observation

In some settings such as clinics and hospitals, the supervisor may observe informal interaction between the CBT supervisee and client. Observing the manner in which the CBT therapist greets the client in reception, for example, may provide some limited information about the quality of the alliance. Or there may be some chance to observe informal therapeutic interaction during a ward round. Alternatively, a supervisor may sit in on group treatment led by the supervisee. This type of observation can provide useful information about the supervisee's CBT skills and theoretical knowledge and may be experienced as less intrusive by clients than direct observation within a one-to-one session. Since direct observation is problematic due to its potentially negative impact on the recipient of treatment, visual recordings (such as DVD or video) make an excellent substitute.

Selecting a CBT Supervisor

Finding a supervisor who meets the needs of your current level of experience and is accessible, affordable and with whom you have a sound working relationship is ideal. In reality, the search for an ideal supervisor may not be wholly straightforward. The more experienced the supervisor, the more likely it is that he/she will be busy and expensive. Some CBT supervisors will offer reduced rates to trainees and newly qualified therapists; however, many will charge the same fee for clinical supervision as they do for CBT treatment. Because supervision is a requirement for accreditation and re-accreditation (not to mention essential to professionally responsible and ethical practice), it helps to view supervision as an unavoidable business expense. The amount of supervision needed will depend on the weight of your caseload. More supervision is needed when you are seeing many clients each week and treating complex presentations. Equally, novice therapists are likely to need more regular supervision than seasoned therapists. The exact amount of supervision required is not clearly specified by BABCP guidelines - although an hour and a half per month is generally considered the minimum.

It may be helpful to consider the following points when organising CBT supervision.

Ensure that Your Supervisor is Qualified to Supervise

CBT supervisors are often accredited via the BABCP. However, the supervisor and trainer accreditation process is relatively new, thus many eligible clinicians may not yet be on the register. Look for accredited CBT therapists with a minimum of 3–5 years' post-qualification practice and some form of supervision training or experience.

Follow Recommendations

Course tutors, employers and colleagues may be able to suggest a tried and tested CBT supervisor. Respected experienced colleagues may also be willing to provide supervision themselves, so it pays to ask. Specialists working with certain disorders or authors of books and research articles may also provide ad hoc supervision when approached.

Look for a Supervisor with the Appropriate Level and Area of Experience

If you find yourself working in a residential addictions unit for example, or a specialist eating disorders centre, it makes sense to look for a CBT supervisor with expert knowledge of these disorders. Moreover, you will probably need a supervisor who is equally or more experienced than yourself.

Strive for Variety

Although it may be tempting to stick to a supervisor with whom you are comfortable, seeking out extra clinical input is useful. A lot can be learnt from supervisors working within specific settings and with certain client populations. Getting more than one opinion and perspective is always a good idea. Seeking more than one source of supervisory input helps avoid falling into the 'comfort trap' – where you may be assured that you will not be overly challenged or clinically stretched. Varied supervision, including more than one individual supervisor and group or peer supervision, can help safeguard good practice by keeping CBT therapists on their 'clinical toes'.

Be Mindful of the Supervision Relationship

Ideally your CBT supervisor will clearly have your professional interest and the best interest of your clients at heart. Your supervisor will ideally be respectful, forthcoming, attentive and interested. If supervision seems to be overly critical or unhelpfully dominated by the supervisor's own opinions for example, consider a change.

Supervision Contracts

Supervision contracts are often pre-devised forms that are signed by both supervisee and supervisor. Generally contracts will clarify the frequency of supervision, methods used, goals and information about fees. What the supervisor expects from supervisees in terms of preparation and case presentation may also be included. Space may also be included for recording supervisee expectations regarding input from the supervisor (Townend, 2004). Sometimes the terms of supervision are outlined less formally via mutual verbal agreement. Whether a written contract is used or not will probably depend on the supervisor in question.

However, supervisees are within their rights to request a formal supervision contract if that is their preference. One of the benefits of contracts is that they elicit supervision expectations from all involved parties - this is true of individual, shared/paired, group and individual modes. If verbal agreement is used in lieu of formal contracting, it remains important to ascertain the core purpose of supervision from the outset. For example, trainees may want their supervision to focus on skills acquisition, novices may be more interested in continued professional development and experienced therapists may require emphasis on research outcomes, theoretical advancements and associated practical application. Moreover, peer supervision may include all of the elements mentioned. In all likelihood, the core purpose of supervision will change and evolve over time. Therefore it is worth regularly reviewing and updating supervision contracts/expectations whether formal or informal.

Preparation for Supervision

For supervision to be useful, supervisees need to decide what they want to focus on in each session prior to arrival. If an audio or visual recording is being presented, it should be cued to the point in the session that the supervisee has a specific question about. Any additional material such as assessment forms, completed ABC formulations, medication information or even written client homework should also be brought along to supervision. Supervisee questions should be well thought out and articulated to give the supervisor the best chance of providing useful specific guidance. Supervision sessions may be recorded for review purposes later or notes can also be taken. Typically both supervisee and supervisor will keep a written record of sessions. Keeping a supervision log is also necessary for accreditation and re-accreditation purposes.

Additional preparatory considerations for supervisees include the following.

Being Prepared to Risk Presenting 'Less Good' Clinical Work as well as Successful Treatment Samples

There is much to be learned through making clinical errors. A balanced representation of the 'good' and the 'bad' lends a more comprehensive picture of supervisee competency. Skills deficits and knowledge limitations can only be addressed when they are exposed through supervision.

Continuity of Material Presented

If feedback is given on a single CBT session, the same client should be re-presented at a later stage of treatment to demonstrate that supervisory comments have been implemented. This provides opportunity for supervisees to ensure they have understood and properly attended to critical instruction. Indeed, it is sensible to present session recordings of at least one client from beginning, middle and end treatment stages. Doing so affords supervision of the entire CBT treatment 'sequence' from assessment to relapse prevention.

Attention to Beliefs and Attitudes about Supervision

CBT supervisees will benefit from using their theoretical understanding of CBT to challenge and correct their own dysfunctional thinking. Supervision is intended to be an ongoing educational, developmental and supportive professional forum. Perfectionistic tendencies, dire need for approval, inability to receive constructive criticism and impatience – by way of example, can all pose obstacles to the smooth running of supervision.

Factors that can Confound useful CBT Supervision

As mentioned in the introduction, supervisor, supervisee and supervisory settings can all contribute factors, which may interrupt the smooth running of clinical supervision.

Organisational/Setting Factors

Different organisations may put more or less emphasis on clinical supervision. Certain community-based settings may not provide any supervision at all due to lack of funding, time or space and a member of staff qualified to supervise. Hospital and medical clinics may also have a limited budget for supervision. Hence, only group supervision may be offered and in some cases this may only take place fortnightly or even monthly. In many settings, supervision is the first thing to be pushed onto the back burner when both funds and work time get tight. If regular individual supervision is provided in the workplace, there is often still no guarantee that the person acting as supervisor is a fully qualified and accredited CBT clinician. In such circumstances as those cited above, it is incumbent upon the CBT therapist to arrange appropriate external supervision to meet with BABCP regulations.

Reflection Points

- Are you getting CBT specific supervision in your workplace and is the person providing your supervision accredited (or eligible to be accredited) as a CBT supervisor by the BABCP?
- Are you prepared to take professional responsibility for arranging (and paying for) sufficient high quality supervision outside your workplace if necessary?
- Do you consistently keep supervision a high professional priority despite varying attitudes in your workplace?

Supervisee Factors

One of the more common supervisee factors confounding useful supervision is a dread of being found 'incompetent' and an overarching intolerance to criticism. Therapists (novice and expert alike) may conceal doubts, errors, gaps in knowledge and skills deficits for fear of 'showing themselves up'. Additionally, they may become immediately defensive (or disproportionately despairing) at the first whiff of negative feedback, however constructively it is delivered. Inability to make good use of sound supervisory feedback obviously impedes the individual CBT therapist's development; however, it also destabilises the one-to-one supervisory relationship and can wreak havoc on group supervision dynamics. Supervisees experiencing difficulties accepting criticism or alternative clinical suggestions would do well to investigate their own dysfunctional thinking. Bear in mind that supervision is intended to improve and enhance CBT practice – as well as to monitor clinical competence. No freshly qualified CBT therapist can possibly be expected to know every treatment protocol for every disorder nor to acquire an overnight encyclopedic knowledge of every possible CBT intervention. Indeed, not even the most experienced therapist can legitimately claim to 'know it all'. A willingness to learn, take responsible risks and filter the 'feedback wheat from the chaff' is essential to a good supervision experience.

Another confounding supervisee factor is lack of preparation for supervision; a section on this precedes so repetition will be avoided here. However, the importance of clarifying supervision goals and expectations bears repeating. Supervision contracts are sometimes used and can help maintain focus. Recording supervisory comments and corrective suggestions also helps to ensure that feedback is put into practice and can be later reviewed.

Reflection Points

- Do you hold unhelpful beliefs about needing to prove your skills and knowledge that lead you to react defensively to criticism?
- Do you have unrealistic professional expectations for yourself that lead you to feel discouraged by critical feedback?
- Do you take personal responsibility for your attitudes, which may be impairing your supervision experience, and are you prepared to challenge them?
- Do you prepare for supervision in advance and put feedback into practice?

Supervisor Factors

Senior CBT clinicians may be accredited or qualified supervisors but lack teaching skills. Supervision with trainee and novice therapists usually includes a large educational component. If a supervisor is unable to pitch supervision at a level suitable for a junior CBT therapist supervisee(s), the whole experience can be frustrating and unhelpful for all parties concerned. Theoretical points need to be made clearly relevant to the supervisee and accompanied with advice on how to implement them in practice. Ideally supervision will leave supervisees better equipped to treat their patients effectively; not result in further confusion. Even the most skilled CBT clinician, teeming with experience, may not make a suitable supervisor if he or she is unable to disseminate knowledge in an accessible manner.

Professional egos can also complicate supervision within group, peer or individual formats. Supervisors with a dire need to be respected, held in reverence or constantly be 'right' can result in tedious, or even damaging, supervision experiences. Such supervisors may be overly critical and/or dismissive of more junior therapists in group or individual supervision. Within peer supervision formats, they may react defensively or peevishly when their ideas are questioned. More than one overly inflated professional ego in a supervision group can lead to competitive behaviour, which is rarely helpful to other members. Alternatively, supervisors may be under-confident in their own knowledge and abilities as clinicians, and therefore take an overly passive stance with supervisees, thus failing to provide authoritative guidance when most needed.

The supervisor factors discussed above may be avoided, or highlighted and addressed, through competency-based assessment of supervisory practice. Many CBT supervisors will have their supervisory work overseen by a senior CBT supervisor either during training or at various points throughout their supervision 'career' (Townend, 2008). Supervision of supervisors is increasingly seen as an important part of maintaining professional standards.

Reflection Points

- Does your supervisor give highly relevant, clear and useable feedback?
- Does your supervisor appear to take your questions and ideas seriously?
- Do you have confidence in your supervisor's CBT expertise? If not, why not?
- Does your supervisor challenge and stretch you without being harshly critical?
- Above all, do you find supervision supportive and helpful?

The following fictional case studies outline possible problematic supervision situations and suggestions for resolution:

Case study 24.1: Gail – fear of criticism (supervision scenario 1)

Gail is a newly qualified CBT therapist entering her first year of practice. She recently started working in a private psychiatric hospital with several well-respected consultant psychiatrists and experienced CBT therapists. Gail sees clients individually and runs two disorder-specific CBT groups (social anxiety and depression). Gail gets one hour of individual supervision each fortnight from a senior CBT therapist on the team and weekly group supervision with the entire therapy team. A consultant psychiatrist also trained in CBT leads group supervision. Gail believes that she needs to prove her competency and so has been careful to present recordings of her better sessions in individual supervision. Her supervisor seems pleased with her work but secretly Gail feels out of her depth with many of her more complicated clients. She dreads each supervision session in case her work is criticised. Due to her professional insecurity, Gail also tends to keep quiet during group supervision and only offers opinions that she is certain won't be challenged. Gail's individual supervisor is due to sit in on one of her group sessions in the next month and she is extremely anxious about making some grave clinical error.

Suggestions for Gail

Firstly, Gail needs to work on overcoming her fear of making errors and incurring criticism. Until she accepts that critical feedback is an essential part of professional growth, Gail will continue to loathe asking for support with difficult cases and will curtail her own learning. Moreover, Gail will perpetuate her high levels of anxiety which is neither conducive to clinical development nor effective CBT practice. Secondly, Gail needs to communicate more honestly and effectively with her supervisor(s) and team members. This may involve talking to her individual supervisor about her anxiety over being monitored running a group session. Her supervisor may offer some reassurance about the ultimate purpose of monitoring, prepare Gail for what to expect and normalise the process. Gail may also produce recordings of more difficult sessions in supervision and ask for specific advice. Additional steps Gail can take may include:

- speaking up during group supervision, asking questions and offering her opinions more freely;
- arranging additional disorder-specific training;
- seeking external supervision to supplement that which is provided through work;
- talking with colleagues about her cases informally and thereby obtaining the benefit of their experience.

Responsibilities of Gail's individual supervisor

Ideally Gail's supervisor will spot her tentativeness to offer her opinions or ideas during group supervision and sense her unease about having her work individually supervised. Her supervisor may be advised to normalise concerns over competency and errors when one is a novice CBT therapist. Additionally, her supervisor should highlight and address, any undue defensiveness that he witnesses from Gail in response to legitimate criticism. Gail's supervisor ought to temper criticism (and be mindful of the manner in which it is delivered) to avoid Gail feeling professionally threatened - without, however, pandering to her demand to be seen as competent. A mutual agreement to confront (rather than disguise) knowledge and skill deficits also ought to be proposed by Gail's supervisor. Gail's supervisor may also advise on further training and set Gail some homework, such as taking the risk of asking questions during group supervision.

Case study 24.2: Victor - the experienced supervisee (supervision scenario 2)

Victor is a chartered psychologist and qualified CBT therapist with over ten years of experience under his belt. Victor is an accredited CBT supervisor himself, has been involved in several research projects over the years and has authored many psychology books. Victor does some NHS work and runs his own private practice. Victor finds that during NHS-based group supervision other CBT therapists rarely, if ever, challenge him. Even his individual supervisor, an experienced practitioner herself, rarely disagrees with his formulations or interventions. As a result, Victor is under stimulated and fears that he is losing objectivity about his clinical practice. Victor concludes that his reputation and experience can be intimidating to less seasoned therapists. He also wonders if his manner in supervision fails to invite comments.

Suggestions for Victor

Victor may consider directly encouraging his NHS colleagues to give him more feedback. He may need to check how receptive and approachable he appears, making a few modifications to his demeanour if necessary. He may also start up his own peer supervision group comprising other experienced CBT therapists whom he knows will not be intimidated by his experience. Additionally, Victor may benefit from regular individual supervision with an even more experienced CBT supervisor than the one he currently sees.

(Continued)

(Continued)

Responsibilities of Victor's individual supervisor

Victor's supervisor ideally ought to discuss openly with him any stagnancy she notes developing in their supervision sessions; she could suggest that he bring in more complex cases for discussion. Victor may have some ideas himself, about how she can provide a more stimulating and challenging supervisory experience. She also needs to be aware of her own input; perhaps she has become complacent, assuming that she has little of value to offer Victor given his advanced experience. Ultimately, Victor's supervisor may realise that a change is needed and suggest that he see a different supervisor for a period of time. Finally, when discussing Victor's experience of peer supervision, she should sensitively point out any aspects of his demeanour that may be alienating others.

Competency-based Measures of Therapist Behaviour used in CBT Supervision

Given CBT's emphasis on observable and measurable phenomena, it is not surprising that a number of competency-based measures of therapist behaviour have been devised and refined. While these measures have been devised to ensure quality of therapist interventions in research studies and are used in the training of CBT therapists, they can and are used in supervision.

The Revised Cognitive Therapy Scale (CTS-R)[1]

The most well-known and widely used of these measures is the12-item Revised Cognitive Therapy Scale – CTS-R (Blackburn et al., 2001) which assesses competency in the delivery of Beck's approach to Cognitive Therapy. This scale measures general therapist skill (agenda-setting and adherence, feedback, collaboration, pacing and efficient use of time and interpersonal effectiveness) as well as specific skill in cognitive therapy (eliciting appropriate emotional expression, eliciting key cognitions, eliciting behaviours, guided discovery, conceptual integration

[1]While we will focus on the CTS-R scale here we note that a similar scale has recently been published detailing and measuring similar competencies in REBT (Dryden, et. al, 2010).

which covers how the cognitive therapy rationale is explained as well as how case formulations are presented and application of change methods and homework setting) and has satisfactory reliability and validity. Each item is scored using a 0–6 point Likert scale corresponding to an adaptation of the Dreyfus (1989) model of competence where six levels of competence are outlined (incompetence, novice, advanced beginner, competent, proficient, and expert).

The CTS-R can be used in supervision to rate a supervisee's overall performance on an audio-recording of a therapy session or to focus on specific skill such as homework setting. The way that the scoring is structured means that benchmarks are available for supervisees at developing levels of training. Thus, for example, supervisors using the scale are encouraged to have appropriate expectations of novice and more highly trained therapists. In addition, supervisees can set realistic expectations of their own performance as they progress in their training.

Sudak et al. (2003) mention a number of other scales that can be adapted for use in supervision.

The Cognitive Therapy Formulation Scale (CFRS)

This scale was developed by the Academy of Cognitive Therapy (1998) as a method of assessing a therapist clinician's ability to conceptualise a case based on the CBT model and to plan treatment. Ratings on the CFRS are made in three main areas: Case History (2 items), Case Formulation (5 items), and Treatment Plan and Course of Therapy (5 items). Each item is rated on a 3-point scale (0 = not present, 1 = present but inadequate, 2 = present and adequate). The Academy of Cognitive Therapy criterion for a passing score on the CFRS is 20 out of 24 total possible points.

The Cognitive Therapy Awareness Scale (CTAS)

This scale was original designed as a method of measuring the acquisition of basic knowledge of cognitive therapy concepts and methods in patients who are being treated with this approach (Wright et al., 2002). However, it can also be used in supervision to gauge changes in knowledge associated with participation in cognitive therapy courses. The CTAS is comprised of 40 true/false questions on topics such as 'definitions of automatic thoughts and schemas; description of thought records, activity schedules, and other commonly used treatment methods; and identification of maladaptive thinking in case illustrations' (Sudak et al., 2003). The maximum score on the CTAS is 40. A score of about 20 would be expected if one knew nothing about cognitive therapy.

Core

In addition to these scales, in the UK the Centre for Outcomes Research and Effectiveness (CORE) have produced a number of CBT competency-based documents that can be used in both CBT training and supervision (www.ucl.ac.uk/clinical-psychology/CORE/CBT_Framework.htm#Map).

It also has published a 'Competencies Framework for Supervision' that can be adapted for use by CBT supervisors (www.ucl.ac.uk/clinical-psychology/CORE/supervision_framework.htm).

This group's work is ongoing and both CBT supervisors and therapists are advised to keep abreast of its developments.

Becoming a CBT Supervisor

There is now a BABCP accreditation process for CBT supervisors and trainers. Requirements include a minimum of three years since initial accreditation as a CBT practitioner; some recognised training in CBT specific supervision and evidence of related experience. Information about BABCP recognised supervision training courses can be found on the website. As with delivering CBT treatment, delivering CBT supervision requires practice. Simply being a competent therapist does not automatically render one a skilled CBT supervisor (Townend, 2008). If you are serious about becoming a qualified CBT supervisor, it can be useful to volunteer your time to a recognised CBT course and 'shadow' an experienced supervisor. 'Shadowing' involves observing a more senior supervisor in action and eventually taking on a more active supervisory role yourself (while being monitored and supported by the senior supervisor). Additionally, you may begin by supervising trainees and recording your sessions to then be supervised by a seasoned CBT supervisor. This 'supervision of supervision practice' is akin to trainee teachers being monitored and evaluated by experienced teachers. Most CBT supervision courses will expect students to provide audio and visual recordings of actual supervision sessions as part of assessment.

Providing CBT supervision can be rewarding and a mutual learning experience. Critically assessing other therapists' clinical work can help keep CBT theory and treatment protocols fresh in the supervisor's mind and encourage critical reflection on one's own practice (see Chapter 23). Supervising can also provide variety to clinical work.

Conclusion

Regular supervision is an important element of continuing professional development for CBT practitioners, at every stage of training and experience. Though specific supervision needs are likely to change over time, the general need for ongoing supervision is a constant throughout one's CBT career. Supervision aims to ensure responsible and professional practice as well as much needed support and objectivity about one's clinical proficiency. Moreover, and not least importantly by any means, supervision helps protect the best interests of treatment recipients, ensuring that all patients receive high quality CBT in both private and public settings.

Regular and appropriate supervision can also help curtail therapist isolation (see Chapter 23) and encourage inter-therapist communication, ultimately (and ideally) leading to shared knowledge and theoretical advancements in CBT.

Summary

1 Supervision is a professional requirement for all CBT therapists at any level of training and experience.
2 Regular supervision needs to be evidenced for BABCP accreditation purposes.
3 Supervision contracts can be useful to clarify supervisor/supervisee goals and expectations.
4 It is important to select a CBT supervisor who is qualified to supervise, sufficiently experienced to meet your professional development needs and with whom you can establish a sound working alliance.
5 A proportion of CBT supervision should include 'in-vivo' methods such as audio or visual recordings of actual sessions.
6 Trainee and novice CBT therapists should not rely solely on peer, group or remote supervision formats.
7 Several factors (supervisor, supervisee and organisational) can confound the effectiveness of supervision and thus should be given due consideration.

8 Individual face-to-face supervision may be supplemented by peer or group supervision and can lend depth and variety to the whole experience.
9 Competency-based supervision is particularly stressed in CBT and there are a variety of scales to help supervisors and therapists monitor and improve the latter's competencies.

References

Academy of Cognitive Therapy (1998). *Cognitive Case Formulation and Rating Scale.* Available on Academy of Cognitive Therapy Website (http://academyofct.org).

Bernard, J.M. and Goodyear, R.K. (2004). *Fundamentals of Clinical Supervision.* Boston: Pearson.

Blackburn, I-M., James, I.A., Milne, D.L., Baker, C., Standart, S., Garland, A. and Reichelt, F.K. (2001). 'The revised cognitive therapy scale (CTS-R): Psychometric properties', *Behavioural and Cognitive Psychotherapy,* 29: 431–46.

Dreyfus, H.L. (1989). 'The Dreyfus model of skill acquisition', in J. Burke (ed.), *Competency-based Education and Training.* London: Falmer Press.

Dryden, W. (1983). 'Audiotape supervision by mail: A rational-emotive perspective', *British Journal of Cognitive Psychotherapy,* 1 (1): 57–64.

Dryden, W., Beal, D., Jones, J. and Trower, P. (2010). 'The REBT competency scale for clinical and research applications', *Journal of Rational-Emotive and Cognitive-Behavior Therapy,* 28: 165–216.

Liese, B.S. and Beck, J.S. (1992). 'Cognitive therapy supervision', in C.E. Watkins (ed.), *Handbook of Psychotherapy Supervision.* Hove: Wiley.

Sudak, D.M., Beck, J.S. and Wright, J. (2003). 'Cognitive behavioral therapy: A blueprint for attaining and assessing psychiatry resident competency', *Academic Psychiatry,* 27: 154–9.

Townend, M. (2004). 'Supervision contracts in cognitive behavioural psychotherapy', *BABCP*: Supervision Supplement. August, 1–4.

Townend, M. (2008). 'Clinical supervision in cognitive behavioural psychotherapy: Development of a model through grounded theory'. *Journal of Psychiatric and Mental Health Nursing,* 15: 328–39.

Wright J.H., Wright A.S., Salmon P., Beck A.T., Kuykendall J., Goldsmith L.J. and Zickel M.B. (2002). 'Development and initial testing of a multimedia program for computer-assisted cognitive therapy', *American Journal of Psychotherapy,* 56: 76–86.

TWENTY FIVE Getting the Most from your CBT Training

GEOFF BAXTER

Having recently completed an MSc in Rational-Emotive and Cognitive Behaviour Therapy (RECBT) at Goldsmiths, University of London, I hope to offer some of my experiences to the reader considering embarking on a similar course of study.

Training courses will differ depending on the level of qualification offered and teaching methods used. However, there are likely to be several elements in common on most CBT training courses such as: group supervision, research modules and placement requirements. This chapter discusses these key areas and offers basic guidance on choosing a suitable course in the first instance.

Rewarding and successful study is greatly facilitated by preparation and forethought. Knowing what to expect from a course, and what is likely to be expected from students, can enhance your enjoyment of study and potentially improve your end results. Suggestions for pre-study preparation, such as additional reading, are therefore offered here.

Drawing on my own experiences as a CBT trainee and student, I offer some tips about using CBT principles in your own life and within the CBT 'classroom'. Managing relationships with your fellow students, supervisors and tutors can be important and offer a chance to put your learning into personal practice.

Finally, continued professional development and career pathways post-qualification are also explored.

Preparation for Training

Why choose CBT? Once you have decided to train in CBT it is good to consider your reasons for doing so.

- Is it for personal development, career development or both?
- Where do you see yourself in 1 year, 5 years, 10 years?
- What type and level of training do you need?
- Is CBT training a requirement for your current job?
- Are you in private practice or do you plan to set up in private practice?
- Would you like a salaried job?

The above considerations will have an impact on the type of course you ultimately choose. Furthermore, how much time and money you are willing to commit to training plus the level of qualification you wish to obtain will influence your career choice. If you have a general interest in CBT then perhaps a workshop or seminar will be enough to give you the information you need. You may then consider a certificate or diploma course if your appetite for further study has been whetted. If you are already a counsellor or psychotherapist from another tradition a certificate or diploma course will give you the basics of CBT, which you may then incorporate into your own practice. If you are intending to practise exclusively as a CBT therapist, Masters Degree level courses will not only provide you with the best all round training in CBT but also the qualifications required for accreditation (which will be discussed in more detail later in this chapter). The British Association for Behavioural and Cognitive Psychotherapies (BABCP) is the leading CBT organisation in the UK and is a useful resource if you are considering training in CBT. Their website also has a list of training courses: www.babcp.com/Training/Training.aspx

Once you have identified the level at which you intend to study, you may also wish to consider which specific type of CBT approach you would like to study. The broad term 'CBT' encompasses many 'third wave' CBT developments including more classic approaches such as Aaron Beck's CT and Albert Ellis's REBT. A full discussion of the various types of CBT is beyond the scope of this chapter but for further information see Chapter 3.

Investigating thoroughly course requirements in terms of hours of study, assessed coursework, admission prerequisites (and fees) is strongly recommended prior to application. If, for example, you choose to study on an MSc course, this may take two years to complete and while you may only be required to attend lectures one day a week, studying at this level requires a considerable time commitment. Most MSc courses expect you to practise the theory you learn with real clients in a placement and to document each session thoroughly. Research essays and a final dissertation are also typically part of MSc level training. You will also be required to attend supervision and possibly individual therapy by your placement.

You will also be required to complete assignments for your course and will be required to read extensively, both in preparation for your lectures and also in preparation for treating your clients. As is apparent, in addition to actual lecture room hours, considerable time commitment is unavoidable. The expense of buying books, attending supervision, travelling to your course and placement - not to mention loss of earnings through study - also merit careful contemplation. If you are unable or unwilling to commit to training at this level, consider another type of course or postpone higher-level training until your circumstances allow you to make the commitment.

It is also essential to realise your own limitations and the other commitments in your life. As a therapist, self-care is very important and you should refer to Chapter 23 in this book for further information. Remember, you will be encouraging your clients to look after their physical and mental health and it stands to reason that you practise what you preach in this regard. If you are working full-time then it will be very difficult to complete a Master's level course and you may need to consider making some adjustments to your working hours. Similarly if you have family commitments then some changes may need to be made in order to allow you to focus on your training. Remember that you will be required to complete a lot of work between classes of your own accord. It is very unlikely that anyone will be checking homework and so you are cheating yourself of a valuable element of your training if you do not complete the required reading and assignments between lectures.

At this point it is useful to consider in more detail the purpose of your training course. The high level of commitment required can be daunting - keep motivated by reminding yourself of what you will gain from training. You can use a simple goal-setting exercise to help clarify training goals and the steps required to reach them.

1 State your goal as a positive statement. Be specific at this point about exactly what you would like to achieve and set a realistic time frame.
2 Write your goal down.

3 List the potential benefits of achieving your goal.
4 List the potential costs involved in achieving your goal.
5 Define the starting point.
6 Ascertain possible obstacles and strategies for overcoming them.
7 Identify extra information you need and where to source such information.
8 Identify other people who may be able to support you. This can be in the form of practical help from family and friends, an employer who is willing to allow you flexible working hours as you study, or an experienced CBT therapist who can offer advice and share their experience of training.
9 Set smaller goals along the way. A large-scale goal can be daunting and so it is useful to break it down into manageable steps. Again, be specific about what you want to achieve and when you want to achieve it. Be realistic. Be clear about what is possible in the timescale you have set and in the context of other commitments in your life. Set performance goals, not solely outcome goals. Ensure that the goals you set are within your control.
10 Plan. Following the steps outlined will ensure a structured approach to achieving your goal.

Once you have identified your goals and selected a course of study it is worth considering what you can do by way of preparation. Most CBT courses at postgraduate level expect high standards of academic writing; if you are returning to study after a long absence, it is useful to begin reading relevant material as early as possible before the course begins. Academic material is often written in a particular style and it is useful to refamiliarise yourself with this before you attend your first lecture. You also may need to complete a preliminary course in basic CBT or general counselling prior to admission on a postgraduate course, depending on your academic history.

Starting Your Training

Typically your course will cover CBT theory thoroughly before you are required to put your learning into practice with clients. At this stage it is a good idea to remain focused on the specific theory you are learning. It is likely that you will be presented with a lot of extra, related information. You may be tempted to try to absorb everything at once but doing so can be overwhelming and confusing. Remain focused on the learning requirements for each stage of your training. There will be time to read more widely once you have consolidated your core learning.

CBT courses often comprise a diverse group of individuals, from different professional backgrounds and this too can be a rich environment in which to learn. Again, the temptation can be to read too much when in the midst of a group of people with different interests, areas of expertise and therapeutic backgrounds. My advice is to make note of areas of interest and recommended reading but stick closely to the reading that is relevant to your course. Note any interesting or new techniques, theories, authors, or books and return to this list once you have time to do so. If you buy reading material on every subject of interest you will end up spending a fortune on books you don't have the time to read. Consider only buying new books once you have read what you already have, unless you need specific information for a client.

At this level of study punctuality and attendance are extremely important. As has already been mentioned, you will learn a large amount of theory in a relatively short period and will then be putting this theory into practice with real clients. Each class is only presented once and so there is only one opportunity to learn each element of theory. If you miss the start of a lecture or even miss a whole class you will find it very difficult to catch up.

It can be useful to familiarise yourself with the technical jargon that is used in CBT prior to studying. Various strands of CBT use different terms to refer to the same (or similar) concepts. There are also words used in general English language that have a very specific definition in the context of CBT, such as: rational, logical, beliefs, inferences, interpretation, prediction etc. It is important that you have a clear understanding of CBT terminology early on in your training to avoid confusion. From the outset of training, it is a good idea to be disciplined in your use of language and to use terms that are consistent with the theory that you are learning. In particular, CBT stresses the importance of emotional responsibility, meaning: we are largely responsible for our emotions due to our perception of a situation or event and the beliefs we hold about (or meaning we attach to) given events. Therefore we avoid phrases that imply an event-emotion causal relationship such as 'how does that make you feel' and discourage the client from phrases such as 'he made me angry' and 'she really hurt my feelings.' Being consistent with your language in day-to-day life will help you do the same in clinical practice.

Individuals enter CBT training from a variety of backgrounds thus it is likely that you will have had some previous training in counselling or psychotherapy. Avoid being defensive of previous training you have received, especially when confronted by fundamental theoretical differences between your previous training and CBT. It will hinder your training if you adhere to previous contradictory principles and are not committed to the theory you are learning. This is not to say that other forms of therapy are inherently wrong, simply to state that you have chosen to study CBT and in order to complete your training and graduate, it is necessary to demonstrate that you are putting the principles learned into practice with clients.

As your training course may contain a large number of individuals from various backgrounds there is every chance there will be some students with whom you disagree or simply dislike. As part of your study it is likely that there will be an element of role-playing and group tasks that you will be required to take part in. In order to become accustomed to working with a diverse group I would encourage you to choose people to work with that will challenge you rather than those that you feel most comfortable with. Do not align yourself too closely with one person or faction and try to develop relationships with all members of the class, especially those you do not initially connect with. You will not always be able to be so selective with your clients - so take the opportunity to develop the skills to relate effectively with a diverse group of individuals while you are studying.

There are some key elements of CBT that will differ fundamentally to other therapies you may have studied and it is useful to discuss these briefly:

- Use of questions - in CBT you will use questions in order to get information, assess your client's problems and check their understanding of theory you are presenting.
- Active/directive style - as a CBT therapist you will be much more involved in the process of therapy and will direct the client towards solutions to their problems in a way that may be unfamiliar to those trained in other therapies.
- Assessment - you will learn how to assess your client's problems according to the ABC model. This will mean clearly identifying the emotion your client experiences and the perceptions and beliefs that lead to this emotional response.
- Homework and behavioural assignments - CBT theory places a great deal of emphasis on the importance of the work that the client does between sessions. This homework can be in the form of written exercises, reading assignments, or behavioural assignments where the client will put what she has learned in the session into practice.

CBT Yourself

While you are studying CBT it is a good idea to try to put the techniques you are learning into practice in your own life. Try to identify your own unhelpful rules, beliefs and attitudes and see if you can come up with more helpful alternatives. CBT encourages you to take responsibility for your own emotions and the influence of your thinking and behaviour. You may experience strong unhealthy emotions in relation to studying itself. Look at the following examples and see if you can identify beliefs or behaviours that may thwart your studies, and formulate healthier alternatives.

Mary is anxious about whether or not she is going to pass the course. She procrastinates and avoids studying. She believes:

- I must pass.
- I couldn't stand it if I failed.

Steve is anxious about speaking in public or answering questions in front of the class. He withdraws from other students, isolates himself and does not interact with his classmates. Steve believes:

- I have to get it right and they'll think I'm a fool if I make a mistake.
- It would be unbearable if I got a question wrong.

Sue is angry with one of her classmates because he is always making comments to show how clever he is (at least that's her perception).

She tries to get her classmates to agree with her opinion of him and believes:

- he absolutely should not be so arrogant;
- he is a complete idiot for showing off in this way.

Pete is envious of those he perceives are doing better than him on the course. He disparages the achievements of others and tries to convince himself he doesn't care about results. He believes:

- they absolutely should not be doing better than me;
- it's terrible to be doing badly;
- I'm not bothered about the results anyway.

Can you see how the students' behaviour and thinking would influence their emotions? See if you can identify alternative ways of thinking and behaving that would be more helpful, and more conducive to learning.

You can also put CBT theory into practice in your personal and professional life. Are you feeling under stress at work or at home? Are you arguing more with your friends or family? Are you impatient? Do you get road rage? Are you struggling to juggle studying with home life and work? Avoid rigid rule based thinking and try to hold flexible preferences about what you would like to achieve. Learn to develop high frustration tolerance (HFT) (Dryden & Branch, 2008). Be patient and remember you are learning a lot of new information. Think of other skills you have mastered in the past, whether it was learning to drive, playing a sport or musical instrument - remind yourself that it took time to gradually absorb new information and put it into practice. Develop HFT with others and try not to impose your own values and expectations on them. This will protect you from becoming unhelpfully angry or allowing frustration to get the better of you.

Have a look at the following case study.

Case Study 25.1

Sally started CBT training in pursuit of a career change after being a nurse for ten years. She had been working part-time while her three children were growing up and her youngest child had just started school allowing her a few extra hours each day. Sally started the course with the belief that she could fit it easily into her life since she only needed to attend college one day a week. However, she soon realised that she had underestimated the amount of work required between lectures and had not been prepared for the commitment required. She found herself trying to do everything she was doing before, including looking after her family and going to work, on top of her college work. Despite offers of help from her husband, friends and family she believed that it was her responsibility to look after her home and family. She also believed that others were interfering and they thought she couldn't handle it when they offered to help. As a result Sally found it difficult to concentrate when she did find time to study and her college work suffered as a result. She also felt tired all the time and lost her temper with her children and husband more often.

See if you can identify the beliefs Sally held and the effect of these beliefs on her emotions and behaviour. Formulate alternatives and see what Sally could do differently that would allow her to get the most from her CBT training and incorporate it more smoothly into her life.

Placement

A key element of your training will involve putting the theory you learn in class into practice with clients. You will therefore need to find a placement and there are a number of considerations to bear in mind when choosing a placement. My first piece of advice would be to start looking for a placement as soon as possible as there is likely to be competition for places. Your chosen course will have specific requirements for your placement and it is worth trying to ascertain such requirements as far in advance as possible as they will influence the type of placement you pursue.

Your course tutors may be able to provide some guidance on finding placements but here are some ideas to get you started:

- NHS placements. Contact local GP surgeries and Community Mental Health Teams (CMHT). Your success at this level will vary according to where you are geographically as different primary care trusts (PCTs) will have different mental health provisions and different policies regarding trainee therapists.
- Mental health charities such as MIND or SANE. There is also a list of mental health charities on the website www.charitiesdirectory.com that you can contact.
- Alcohol or addiction organisations.
- School and university counselling services.
- Previous trainees. An organisation may be more likely to take a trainee on if they have had a good experience working with a previous student from your course.

Once you have secured a placement there are some further points to bear in mind. Firstly, consider the number of therapeutic hours you are required to complete for your course and whether or not your placement can provide them. Discuss what you require from your placement before you commit to volunteering your time. For example if you are working at a university counselling service you should be aware of the length of academic holidays when you are calculating the number of client hours you need. You should also consider the number of clients that will fail to attend your sessions, as it is inevitable that some clients will not show up for therapy. This is a particular issue in drug and alcohol treatment since there is evidence of higher therapy dropout rates in the treatment of substance misuse (Craig, 1985).

Someone at your placement will be required to take overall clinical responsibility for your clients while you are training and this may be a GP, psychologist, psychiatrist, or lead therapist. Having this person in place ensures that you are supported in your placement and this individual should also be responsible for referring appropriate clients to you. It is important that you are not faced with highly disturbed clients while you are still familiarising yourself with new techniques. On the other hand you do not want to be working with a client base that does not challenge you in any way. Also consider the diversity of the demographic you are working with. Ideally your placement will be able to provide you with a range of clients in terms of age, culture, gender, and presenting problem. If you are working in settings such as education, substance misuse, or bereavement counselling, the diversity of client problems you see will be more limited.

As well as criteria your course requires from your placement, the placement may have specific requirements for trainee volunteers. For example, you may be required to be in personal therapy for the duration of your placement and there may be supervision requirements above and beyond those of your course. You may be required to attend non-CBT specific group supervision. These possible placement factors will clearly have implications in terms of cost and time and therefore should be borne in mind when selecting an appropriate placement. There is a strong possibility that your placement supervisor will not be CBT trained and so may have opinions about therapy that will be at odds with your CBT principles. Try to be flexible and open to other opinions but remain focused on the principles of CBT. Be aware that your course will require you to provide examples of pure CBT practice during supervision.

Your placement may also have specific requirements for the type of CBT therapy you deliver and you should ensure this is not at odds with your course learning. Even if a placement offers CBT therapy, they may require you to practise a particular CBT approach. For example, if you are studying REBT your placement may require you to practise Beckian CT, which could be problematic when it comes to your course supervision. Ensure that you can practise the techniques that you are learning in your training at your selected placement.

By the time you start your placement you will hopefully be more comfortable with CBT theory and be able to start putting it into practice. Be bold and try out new techniques and interventions as you learn them, even if you get it wrong you will learn from your mistakes. Course supervision will help you hone your skills and work towards your client's best interest. You may be tempted to continue using elements of CBT that you are most comfortable with or resort to using interventions from previous training in another orientation, but doing so will have an adverse effect on your acquisition of CBT skills. Read relevant protocol-based literature relating to the specific diagnoses of your clients. Take the advice of your tutors and CBT supervisor(s) regarding recommended reading.

Supervision

Once you start seeing clients at your placement the supervision element of training becomes paramount. Supervision (during and post training) comes in a variety of forms (see Chapter 24). The majority of training course supervision will be in groups. Thus you get the benefit not only of your own supervisory feedback but also a chance to learn from that of others. Placement supervision may be individual, involve group sessions, or – in some cases – both. However, as previously mentioned, this may not be CBT specific supervision and may therefore be of limited use to your learning. Your training supervision will support you with difficult cases but be largely focused on your delivery of the techniques you are learning. It is therefore recommended that you arrange additional external individual CBT supervision to support you in your training – even though doing so will involve further commitment from you. A list of accredited supervisors can be found on the BABCP website (www.babcp.com) or you can ask your course tutors to recommend external supervisors.

When you start supervision your supervisor may draw up a contract. If they do not, it is worth defining your respective roles and tasks in supervision. Ascertain their expectations of you, state what you would like from them, and review your respective roles as supervision proceeds. Your supervisor may require you to bring recordings of sessions and it is generally a good idea to tape sessions so you can review your own progress and learn from your mistakes. For example, you may think that you presented an element of theory particularly well in session but on reviewing the recording realise that the client barely spoke and there is no evidence that he understood you. So what seemed like a theoretically good session could actually be therapeutically poor. Recording sessions will help you identify your own strengths and weaknesses. If you do record sessions, ensure that you obtain your client's written consent and if you record sessions on a digital voice recorder (DVR) be aware of data protection issues. Ensure that the data is stored securely and that you delete sessions when you no longer need them.

Ensure that you are prepared for each supervision session. If you are bringing a recording ensure that it is cued to the section you want supervised and prepare specific questions that you want answered. Also consider the material that you bring to supervision. You may be tempted to bring only your best work to supervision in order to impress your tutors or do well in your course but this is a pointless exercise as you will not receive supervision that will aid your development as a CBT therapist nor will you learn from your mistakes. On the other hand do not bring a session that you know to be of low quality and that does not demonstrate the use of CBT since equally little will be learned from a poor-quality session. Remain consistent with CBT theory and bring sessions that you genuinely need supervised. Be aware of the number of sessions you are required to bring to supervision and do not assume that you will have an appropriate session if you see clients the day before supervision. Your session may not be suitable for supervision and there is no guarantee your client will even attend the session.

View supervision as another opportunity to examine your own beliefs and behaviours and be aware of the attitude that you bring to supervision. For example, you may be receiving CBT training after a great deal of experience in another form of psychotherapy or counselling and it is even possible that you will have been a therapist for longer than your CBT supervisor. But remember that your supervisor will be experienced in specific CBT theory. Remain open-minded and try to take criticism as an opportunity to hone your skills. Of course, you should not take your supervisor's comments unquestioningly; after all they are just the opinion of one individual. If you do not understand or agree with feedback you should express your opinions and enter into a healthy discussion with your supervisor. Once again be aware of your own beliefs in this situation. Do you feel threatened by their criticism? Are you overly concerned with the opinions of your peers? Are you unsure of your own skills as a CBT therapist? See if you can identify and challenge your own unhealthy beliefs.

Have a look at the following case study and see if you can answer the questions that follow:

Case Study 25.2

John was 55 years old and had been a person-centred counsellor for nearly 20 years when he decided to enter CBT training. He had been reading a lot about CBT and was encouraged to get CBT training by the counselling service he worked for. However, John was committed to his chosen therapeutic discipline and was fed up hearing about CBT and the research that supported its effectiveness. He therefore entered training because he thought he needed to rather than because he really believed in CBT. On top of all that, he was faced with a CBT supervisor, 25 years his junior, giving him advice on how he should conduct a therapy session. John thought he knew best and was doing what he believed was best for his client, whether or not it was consistent with CBT. When criticised he became angry and defended the interventions he used. He resented the comments of this young supervisor and felt that his ability as a therapist was being undermined in front of a group of his peers.

What beliefs do you think John held? How do you think the remainder of his training went for him? What could John have thought and done differently to enable him to get the most from his CBT training?

Research

Studying or conducting research will be a requirement of an MSc level course and may form part of other training courses. It is therefore important to develop an understanding of how to read and interpret research studies and journal articles. Psychological research is written in a specific style and it is very useful to understand the terminology and learn to interpret data. At this stage you may need some help if you have not studied psychological research before. Your course will provide training in this area if it is required.

Many journal articles can be accessed online:

- Cambridge Journals: http://journals.cambridge.org/
- Springerlink: www.springerlink.com/
- University of London Research Libraries: http://catalogue.ulrls.lon.ac.uk/

Many of these resources will require a subscription but you may have access through your college or university. You may also decide to join the BABCP while you are studying and so will receive their journal. As before, it is very useful to have a basic understanding of the work you will be studying before attending lectures. Obtain the recommended reading and come prepared with relevant questions. For further information on counselling research see Heppner et al. (2008) or Houser (2009).

In the course of your studies you may be required to conduct your own research project. You will receive guidance on this if it is part of your course but once again it is good to do some preparation. If you have a particular area of interest you can begin to study literature that is relevant to that subject. You will find that research papers often identify areas that would benefit from further study and this may give you some ideas for your own research. If you do not conduct your own research you will most likely be required to write a dissertation examining the literature on a specific area of psychological research. Again, you will find it useful to consider possible subjects well in advance and to select an area that interests you or in which you have some prior experience. For further guidance on conducting and reporting research see Findlay (2003) or Tilley (1999).

Putting CBT into Practice

When you have completed your training you will find that the skills you have acquired and techniques you have learned will serve you well in treating many different client groups and disorders. According to the National Institute for Health and Clinical Excellence (NICE) guidelines, CBT is the recommended treatment for many disorders including depression and anxiety. There is a large body of evidence that supports the use of CBT in the treatment of many common psychiatric disorders including: obsessive compulsive disorder (OCD); body dysmorphic disorder (BDD); social phobia; and substance misuse. CBT can also be used successfully with relationship and interpersonal problems.

Use the CBT skills you have acquired to help your clients understand their unhelpful thought patterns and behaviours and to formulate functional alternatives. You can then help them to put these new patterns into practice by completing behavioural exercises. CBT can assist your clients in overcoming their psychological problems and give them skills that better equip them to cope with life experiences more generally in the future.

Next Steps

Although you may only be considering studying CBT, or be at an early stage in your training, it is worth looking at which further steps you may take once you have finished your course. Hopefully you will have considered career development prior to embarking on a course of study. If you have done so, you will have a clear idea about you career goals (if indeed studying CBT is a professional development step for you) and your next steps at this stage will be dictated by these goals. You may decide to set up or develop your own private practice, work in a hospital setting, or a combination of both. If you are looking for a salaried position you can register on the NHS job website (www.jobs.nhs.uk) or other general jobsites (www.indeed.com); the BABCP also has a job page (www.babcp.com/Advertising/Jobs/Jobs.aspx).

If you are pursuing a career as a CBT therapist, it is becoming increasingly essential to be accredited with the BABCP. They have a database of CBT therapists and accreditation is a requirement for some CBT jobs and looks likely to become more important in the coming years. Further accreditation information can be obtained on the BABCP website and the steps you need to take, depending on your previous training and experience, are outlined.

Once you have completed your course you may also consider further training. This may be in the form of workshops, seminars, conferences, or short courses that will not necessarily require the same high level of commitment as the course you have just completed. CPD is excellent for your growth as a CBT therapist and is a requirement of re-accreditation. Once again the BABCP is a good source of information about further training.

As you have been treating clients, you will hopefully have been reading more about CBT protocols for specific diagnoses. If, as suggested, you noted areas of interest while studying you can take this opportunity to expand your knowledge in these areas. As well as reading disorder specific information and CBT protocols you may consider expanding your knowledge of diagnostic criteria and for this purpose you should consult diagnostic manuals such the Diagnostic and Statistical Manual of Mental Disorders (DSM-IV; APA, 1994) or International Classification of Diseases (ICD-10, 2007). It is also useful to have some understanding of the medication your clients may be taking. For information on medication obtain a copy of the British National Formulary (BNF; Joint Formulary Committee, 2010). You may become interested in other areas of CBT such as 'third wave' CBT including Acceptance and Commitment Therapy (ACT); Dialectical Behaviour Therapy (DBT); and Mindfulness Based Cognitive Therapy (MBCT); or you may decide to further your education and become a supervisor or teacher of CBT. Hopefully you will see your CBT training as the beginning of a new chapter in your personal and professional development.

Conclusion

This chapter has been written based on my personal experience of studying CBT and includes much of the excellent advice, support, and supervision I received during my training. It contains information that was useful to me while I was studying and I hope that you will find this chapter helpful if you decide to study CBT.

Let's recap on a few of the main points covered in this chapter.

- Preparing for training
  - Choose an appropriate CBT training course
  - Set goals for your career
- Starting your training
  - Read relevant material
  - Commit to studying CBT
- CBT yourself
  - Apply CBT principles to your personal and professional life
  - Learn how your beliefs influence your emotions and behaviour
- Placement
  - Find an appropriate placement
  - Ensure your placement meets your needs

- Supervision
  - Prepare for supervision
  - Aim to get the most from supervision
- Research
  - Read and interpret research papers
  - Identify an area of interest to study
- Putting CBT into practise
- Next steps
  - Consider what to do with your CBT training
  - Focus on career development
  - Investigate further training

References

American Psychiatric Association (1994). *Diagnostic and Statistical Manual of Mental Disorders*, 4th edn. Washington, DC: American Psychiatric Association.

Craig, R.J. (1985). 'Reducing the treatment drop out rate in drug abuse programs', *Journal of Substance Abuse Treatment*, 2 (4): 209–19.

Dryden, W. and Branch, R. (2008). *The Fundamentals of Rational Emotive Behaviour Therapy: A Training Handbook*. Chichester: John Wiley & Sons, Ltd.

Findlay, B. (2003). *How to Write Psychology: Laboratory Reports and Essays*, 3rd edn. Frenchs Forest, NSW: Prentice Hall.

Heppner, P.P., Wampold, B.E. and Kivlighan, D.M. (2008). *Research Design in Counselling*, 3rd edn. Belmont: Brooks/Cole.

Houser, R. (2009). *Counselling and Educational Research: Evaluation and Application*, 2nd edn. Thousand Oaks, CA: Sage.

International Classification of Diseases 10th revision (ICD-10) (2007). www.who.int/classifications/icd/en/

Joint Formulary Committee (2010). *British National Formulary*, 60th edn. London: British Medical Association and Royal Pharmaceutical Society.

Tilley, A.J. (1999). *An Introduction to Research Methodology and Report Writing in Psychology*. Brisbane: Pineapple Press.

TWENTY SIX Reflective and Self-evaluative Practice in CBT

BEVERLY HAARHOFF AND PAUL FARRAND

Introduction

Reflective practice is an integrated process whereby the psychotherapist reflects on therapeutic methods, the client's response to methods, and the therapist's contribution to the therapy process (Sperry, 2010). Given the role it has in increasing the therapist's self-knowledge and understanding it has become regarded as central to the development and maintenance of psychotherapeutic competence in the talking therapies (Sperry, 2010). Indeed such importance has been highlighted by Sigmund Freud (1937/1857: 246): 'Where, and how is the poor wretch to acquire the ideal qualifications which he will need for his profession? The answer is in the analysis of himself with which the preparation for his future activity begins.'

This chapter highlights the emerging importance of reflective and self-evaluative practice in Cognitive Behaviour Therapy (CBT). Recent advances in CBT are outlined reflecting changing attitudes and perceptions regarding the role of self-reflective practice in contemporary CBT. The Declarative Procedural Reflective model for psychotherapeutic skill acquisition is presented as providing a rationale for the inclusion of self-reflective practice in CBT training and ongoing professional development. Self-practice (SP: practising CBT techniques on self)/ Self-reflection (SR: reflecting on this process) is proposed as a method to improve self-reflective capacity in a number of important ways, incorporating some of the benefits of personal therapy such as 'learning by doing' in a manner more compatible with the empirical focus of CBT (Bennett-Levy, 2006). A number of examples of SP/SR, derived primarily from CBT training, are provided. However, most CBT training programmes are filled by mental health professionals who are already working in the mental health field making the examples of SP/ SR applicable to practitioners in training and ongoing professional practice. It should be noted that reflective and self-evaluative practice are an important aspect of clinical supervision, and as some of the examples of SP/SR included in this chapter show, SP/SR can be usefully integrated with the CBT supervision process; however, a number of other methods promoting self-reflection and self-evaluation are also utilised in the supervision of CBT therapists (see Chapter 24). The chapter will conclude with some of the difficulties and solutions associated with SP/SR.

Self-reflective Practice and Personal Therapy in CBT

A major longitudinal cross-sectional study tracking the professional development of one hundred psychotherapists and counsellors over 15 years concluded that continuous self-reflection is necessary for learning, professional development, and competence at all levels of experience, and that if self-reflection did not take place 'stagnation' and 'deterioration' are likely to occur (Rønnestad & Skovholt, 2003). Additionally the authors noted that personal life experience of therapists' influences professional functioning, and that problematic developmental experiences can affect professional development adversely. However, negative effects can be mediated by the practitioner's openness to personal therapy and self-reflection.

In personal therapy (PT), the clinician attends therapy in the same way as a client would. PT is conceived as a forum in which the psychotherapist is able to 'learn by doing', acquiring psychotherapy skill through observing a more experienced psychotherapist, and simultaneously gaining self-knowledge, thus insuring against personal 'blind spots' which could potentially interfere with therapy progress. Psychotherapies advocating PT emphasise the psychotherapist's personal growth and self-understanding with self-reflection crucial in realising this aim. Large numbers of practitioners from all models of psychotherapy report that they have attended PT and found it professionally and personally helpful (Norcross, 2005). Given that a primary aim in undertaking PT is to obtain an increased understanding of the psychotherapy model utilised by the practitioner, traditionally PT is provided by therapists practising in the same model.

Conversely, CBT practitioners often seek their PT from therapists practising in other insight orientated, experientially based models (Laireiter & Willutzski, 2005) and therefore, are not availing themselves of the opportunity to 'learn by doing'. One could speculate that a reason for this trend is that CBT is perceived as an empirical, present orientated, problem focussed therapy and not as a forum in which to achieve personal growth. In addition CBT focussed professional organisations have not endorsed the inclusion of PT as a mandatory requirement for accreditation as a Cognitive Behaviour Therapist in English speaking countries. Reasons include lack of objective evidence supporting positive effects on the development of therapists or clinical outcomes, and confidence in the strength of CBT interventions and targeted treatment protocols as paramount in effecting therapeutic change (Wampold, 2001).

Advances and Changes in CBT

Traditionally CBT has emphasised specific factors associated with the evidence-based interventions themselves over common factors related to the therapeutic relationship. While developing competency in the specific factors has taken prominence the common factors have been relegated to being perceived as positive background for the application of specific CBT interventions (Burns, 1989). Consequently personal growth and self-understanding have been considered less important than training the CBT practitioner to deliver the appropriate structured, evidence-based CBT protocols. A consequence of this stance has been the lack of a consistent pathway or model facilitating the development of self-reflective, self-evaluative capacity of CBT practitioners.

Since the early nineties, however, the scope of CBT has expanded and treatment protocols for a wide range of diagnostic presentations including chronic and complex diagnoses such as the Personality Disorders have been developed (Hollon & Beck, 2004). Clients diagnosed as suffering from a personality disorder frequently present with chronic interpersonal problems which impact negatively on the therapeutic alliance. As a result, common factors associated with the therapeutic relationship are now being recognised as increasingly important. CBT practitioners have therefore begun to focus on the therapeutic relationship as foreground rather than background, characterising it as a 'laboratory' where the client can experiment with new ways of negotiating interpersonal difficulties (Leahy, 2001; Rudd & Joiner, 1997). Recognising the importance of the therapist's contribution to the interpersonal therapeutic dyad has resulted in CBT theorists and practitioners calling for a greater emphasis on self-reflection in training and continuing professional practice: 'Self-reflection is no luxury but a necessary component of therapeutic practice and accordingly it should be regarded as a criterion of quality therapeutic practice in CBT' (Laireiter & Willutzski, 2005: 48).

The Declarative Procedural Reflective Model

The Declarative Procedural Reflective (DPR) model of therapist skill acquisition (Bennett-Levy, 2006) provides a template to address the increased focus within CBT upon self-reflection (Grant et al., 2010), providing a strong rationale for the inclusion of reflective practice as a key component in CBT. The DPR model proposes three interacting information processing systems, namely the Declarative, Procedural and Reflective systems.

The Declarative System: 'What do I know?'

The Declarative system processes factual or 'book-knowledge' obtained through didactic methods such as listening to lectures, and consists of interpersonal knowledge (what makes a good therapeutic relationship), conceptual knowledge (understanding the three levels of thought, namely automatic thoughts, underlying assumptions and core beliefs) and technical knowledge (what are the most common thought processing errors). Translating Declarative knowledge to competent clinical practice requires the Procedural system.

The Procedural System: 'How and When should I Use My Book-knowledge in Clinical Practice?'

Procedural knowledge consists of a set of 'when?/ then?' rules and relies on interpersonal skills, and 'self-knowledge'. Objectivity in interpersonal relationships is difficult for therapists and clients (Leahy, 2001) and if the therapist lacks self-awareness the therapeutic relationship can be compromised which can interfere with CBT.

Procedural knowledge is difficult to teach directly, as it accumulates over time, and is, to some degree, reliant on experience and innate interpersonal ability. Consequently it is felt to differentiate experienced and expert clinicians from novices (Dobson & Shaw, 1993). According to the DPR model, the Procedural system can be enhanced by self-reflective skills activated by the reflective information processing system, helping clinicians 'discern in what context, under what conditions, and with what people, particular strategies may be useful' (Bennett-Levy, 2006: 60).

The Reflective System: 'What is the Best Way to Apply My Knowledge?'

The Reflective system is described as the 'engine' driving the other two systems. It holds no permanent knowledge, and only comes into play under certain 'attention getting' conditions such as noticing a problem, often precipitated by a rupture in the therapeutic relationship. When this happens, the Reflective system helps the clinician solve the problem by gaining perspective on past, present and future experiences. Facilitating the capacity for self-reflection is therefore important in managing the unexpected twists and turns which occur in psychotherapy. It is proposed that the Reflective system can be strengthened by exposing trainees to practising CBT interventions on themselves and reflecting on the process. CBT training should therefore create opportunities for trainees to enhance self-reflective ability. Self-practice/self reflection (SP/SR) has been proposed as an approach to help achieve this aim (Bennett-Levy, 2006).

Applying SP/SR in CBT Training and Practice

The Role of Self-practice/Self-reflection

Self-practice (SP) refers to practising CBT techniques and interventions on self as therapist, and self-reflection to reflecting, verbally or in writing, on this process. Several studies have shown SP/SR helpful in promoting therapeutic understanding, therapist skill, and changes in therapist self confidence (Bennett-Levy et al., 2001; Haarhoff & Stenhouse, 2004; Haarhoff, 2008; Sutton et al., 2007). Therapeutic understanding includes appreciating the CBT model in greater depth, recognising CBT as an effective tool for personal change, a greater understanding of what it is like to be a client (empathy), and the difficulties involved in psychological change. Theoretical understanding of the CBT model, self-awareness, improved utilisation of CBT interventions and quality of CBT case conceptualisation have been favourably influenced by SP/SR (Haarhoff, 2008).

Several advantages have been proposed concerning the use of SP/SR within CBT training programmes. The approach is compatible with the principles and structure of CBT and can be targeted at learning to use specific CBT interventions (Bennett-Levy et al., 2001; Haarhoff & Stenhouse, 2004), or more general core competencies such as CBT case conceptualisation (Haarhoff, 2008). Furthermore, standardisation can be achieved in that variability of model and therapist in personal therapy can be eliminated, and finally the impact of SP/SR on therapist skill can be monitored and evaluated in a manner more compatible with the empiricism characteristic of CBT.

Methods to Support SP/SR

Given the advantages that can arise when SP/SR is adopted it is perhaps unsurprising that the approach has now become common in CBT training programmes within the United Kingdom, New Zealand and Australia. In the examples below, some methods used to support SP/SR within training programmes from across these countries are highlighted.

SP/SR Workbooks

Designed to consolidate therapeutic understanding and improve competency, self-administered SP/SR workbooks are used within coursework or supervision to target different levels of competence from low-intensity CBT interventions through to complex competencies such as case conceptualisation. Typically, SP/SR workbooks lead the trainee through a series of SP CBT exercises which mirror CBT protocols such as the treatment for depression and specific anxiety disorders, target competencies such as CBT case conceptualisation, or specific interventions such as the thought record. SP exercises are alternated with SR questions which guide and structure the self-reflective process. To progress through a SP/SR workbook trainees are required to use their own experience and this is most often in the form of a personal problem related to current experience, causing a moderate amount of emotional distress. The trainee is then guided systematically through commonly used techniques such as mood monitoring, using the activity schedule, functional analysis, the thought record, behavioural experiments and core belief worksheets. Experiential and emotionally focussed techniques such as imagery exercises can be included to facilitate access to deeper levels of thought. In the example below an SP/SR exercise directs a trainee to consider their strengths and reflect on this.

Exercise

Conduct a 'talent search' for your *strengths*. Strengths are personal attributes such as problem-solving skills, humour, intelligence, and creativity.

- List your strengths in different areas of your life
- How could your strengths help with your problem?
- Redraw the five-part model incorporating your strengths

Examples of SR questions:

'What was it like reflecting on your strengths?'

'Actually really, really helpful. Once I wrote down my strengths in the areas you suggested I could immediately see a solution to the problem. I'd love to know if this was the case for others.'

'Does it change the way you think about the identified problem?'

'Yes. I actually have a lot more I can do about it than I thought, and the five-part model highlighted that my thinking had made a big difference. I cue-carded my new thoughts for future reference.'

Other examples of SR questions are: 'Comment on how it felt to process your thoughts in this way?', 'Did you experience any difficulties?', 'What did you learn about yourself?', or 'Did you notice any themes which might relate to your underlying beliefs?'

Overall, trainees exposed to SP/SR workbooks report finding the experience helpful in a number of relevant ways previously described. Trainees report that it was the act of 'doing' or experiencing the CBT interventions through SP/SR using their personal material, which enabled them to gain a deeper understanding of and confidence in CBT.

Trainees can work through the SP/SR workbooks independently, in pairs, or groups. Feedback from trainees consistently supports the view that groups or pairs are preferable to individual work, recognising the importance of the therapist's role. SP/SR workbooks can also be used in supervision and personal CBT. In addition to targeted SP/SR workbooks, self-help CBT workbooks can be used in conjunction with a series of guiding SR questions.

SR Blogs

While the SP/SR workbook supports trainees when engaging in the SP of CBT techniques this does not necessarily result in trainees undertaking SR however. Consequently some training courses have also ensured that equal weight is given to promoting the act of reflection and that SR is well planned and supported (Farrand et al., 2010). To promote and support SR, web-based blogs, a space on a website set aside to enable people to interact and comment around a chosen topic, have been incorporated within the training programme itself. Within this approach individual SP/SR blogs are created to support personal reflections for each of the CBT techniques included within the SP/SR workbook. Trainees are asked to undertake SP on each of the CBT techniques and then to provide a SR on the appropriate blog by a specific deadline. Ground rules specified that blog postings would be under the name of the contributing trainee and it was stressed that reflections should contain no confidential patient information or personal information that the trainee would not wish to share. Differences between providing self-reflections within this context and within PT were therefore emphasised.

Several benefits associated with using blogs to support SR were identified (Farrand et al., 2010). Trainees reported being more engaged with the SR process, in part due to the lack of anonymity regarding blog posting providing a certain amount of instrumental encouragement to post reflections by the deadline. However, also having the opportunity to read others' self-reflections helped to establish the value of the SP/SR process and hence motivated continued engagement. A further interesting benefit of the use of blogs to support SR was with respect to the quality of the reflections provided. When posted on the SR blog each reflection became available for other trainees to read, and indeed reflect upon. This provided all trainees with the opportunity to familiarise themselves with a variety of different reflective styles which enabled them to challenge and adapt their own reflective style. Monitoring of the blog postings by members of the course team who highlighted particularly good self-reflections also aided this process. The success of SP/SR blogging has resulted in the approach being adopted by many university-based CBT training programmes across England as part of the Improving Access to Psychological Therapies programme (Richards & Suckling, 2009). With respect to training in low-intensity CBT in particular, SP/SR blogging provides a link between the formal university-based training in the low-intensity CBT techniques and the trainees' personal development of competence.

Self-reflective Journals and Learning Logs

A number of universities in the United Kingdom encourage students to use reflective learning journals or learning logs to document and reflect on personal and professional development with the explicit goal of increasing self-awareness. At the University of Derby this is a course requirement for the CBT Certificate, Diploma, and Master of Science programmes (Sutton et al., 2007). The instruction contained in the handbook is that students 'make explicit, explore and examine the learning experiences which influence their schematic representations of themselves, others and the worlds in which they live'.

Benefits arising from the use of the learning log identified have included increased empathy for the clients, 'deeper understanding', improved self-awareness and the release of cathartic expression (Sutton et al., 2007). However, lack of clarity around expectations of the exercise, lack of structure, and support systems surrounding the use of the log, coupled with the fairly open-ended instructions were reported as problematic by the students who participated. The authors concluded that the self-reflective component of the course was probably not given the structure and attention it required. It would therefore appear that the greater structure and direction inherent in the SP/SR workbook format is more conducive to facilitating self-reflection in CBT. Journals and logs however have their place and are frequently used in other professions for the development of competence. The fact that there is less structure can facilitate a greater depth of self-discovery at times.

Applications of SP/SR

SP/SR has been applied within CBT training programmes to help improve therapeutic understanding, CBT case conceptualisation, therapist skill, and changes in therapist self awareness and self confidence. The utility of SP/SR for improving therapeutic competence is gaining support and the following goals have been identified: (1) educational goals such as understanding the CBT model in depth and more effective management of self, and the therapeutic relationship; (2) preventative goals such as reducing potential negative effects of the therapist and reducing burnout through the development of skills such as self-monitoring, self-esteem, interpersonal sensitivity, and social assertiveness; (3) the acquisition of specific CBT skills, learning to conduct CBT, and experiencing CBT as a client to increase the awareness of process; and (4) didactic goals such as learning CBT techniques and models and seeing how CBT works in 'real-life' (Laireiter & Willutzski, 2005). Some of the areas in which SP/SR has been applied are highlighted below.

Targeting the Therapist in the Therapeutic Relationship in CBT

The therapeutic relationship is increasingly seen as the vehicle through which alternative more adaptive patterns of relating can be explored. Relevant psychoanalytic concepts such as countertransference, and resistance have recently been reconceptualised to fit more comfortably with the fundamental principles of CBT (Rudd & Joiner, 1997). In a nutshell, the psychoanalytic notion of 'unconscious projection' is rejected, and countertransference is defined as the therapists' cognitive, emotional, and behavioural reactions to the client which are conscious and accessible to the clinician, if the ability to self-reflect and self-observe is developed (Leahy, 2001). Resistance is characterised as therapy interfering behaviour which can be tackled in an overt manner using strategies such as functional analysis. Leahy warns that ignoring countertransference results in negative therapy interfering consequences such as technique avoidance, guilt or fear over patient anger, feelings of inferiority, the inability to set limits, overextending the therapy hour, inhibitions regarding the discussion of sexual matters, and anger at the client.

Understanding countertransference requires the trainee to be aware of her belief system in CBT terms and consequently identify 'self' and 'therapist-schema', underlying assumptions, and compensatory behaviours within the context of specific triggering situations with particular clients or issues (procedural knowledge).

A number of SP/SR exercises can be employed to facilitate deeper self-understanding. Trainees can complete and score schema questionnaires which also identify underlying assumptions and compensatory behaviours (see www.schematherapy.com). Completing the questionnaires can provide learning experiences for trainees beyond discovering their own underlying beliefs. In the example below a trainee discovered that completing self-report measures can be time consuming, challenging, and confronting for some clients. Reflecting on this process he wrote:

> I ask my clients to fill out these questionnaires as a matter of course. Now I realise they are very challenging to the person and there is a temptation to be less truthful about the answers because of the emotional pain of being exposed as how I really am. Last week an older client refused to fill out the Young Schema Questionnaire. She was very anxious and became angry because looking at the questions made her feel anxious ...We negotiated to look at the schema questionnaire later.

In this instance personal confrontation with his schema resulted in an avoidant response. Reflecting on his own process meant being able to empathically understand the client's response, and adapt and accommodate her reaction in his therapy plan (Haarhoff, 2008).

'Therapist-schema', characterised as less pervasive and unconditional and triggered in certain therapy related contexts, can be identified using the Therapists' Schema Questionnaire (Leahy, 2001). The measure consists of 46 assumptions which represent 14 of the most common therapist-schema and can be utilised in specific contexts where a therapist is experiencing problems with a client. This could be done in the supervision hour or in a group where different schema can be discussed. Trainees commonly experience 'demanding standards', 'excessive self-sacrifice' and 'special superior person' therapist-schema (Haarhoff, 2006). Ellis (2002) distinguishes a number of common irrational beliefs held by therapists for example 'I absolutely must be successful with practically all of my clients all of the time' which are similar to the therapist schema identified above. Ellis suggests a number of cognitive, emotive and behavioural techniques to deal with what he calls 'Your most difficult client - you (*the therapist*)'. It is helpful for trainees to be made aware of the implications of common therapist-schema such as 'Demanding Standards' which signals a somewhat obsessive, perfectionist and controlling approach to therapy and an expectation that there is a 'right way' to do things; a schema which can lead to frustration and insecurity when the therapy process becomes ambiguous or something unexpected happens. Resulting compensatory behaviours can be making too many demands on the client, and overemphasising structure. Group SR can normalise such therapist schema and behavioural experiments can be designed to test alternative more constructive perspectives.

Examining the Therapist's Belief System

Another useful conceptual framework is the Therapist Belief System (TBS: Rudd & Joiner, 1997). The TBS provides a framework for identifying common therapist beliefs about self, the client, and the course of treatment, the emotions that these beliefs might trigger, and typical behavioural responses. Proposed as an interactive system, client beliefs about the therapist, self and the course of treatment are also identified. For example, the therapist, might perceive the client as 'hostile aggressor', 'helpless victim', or 'collaborator'. Each of these beliefs would result in a different emotional and behavioural reaction from the therapist. For instance, perceiving the client as a 'helpless victim' might lead to a depressed or anxious response, resulting in over cautious or excessively nurturing behaviour which could result in the therapist avoiding appropriate treatment interventions because of beliefs about the client's vulnerability.

Conceptual taxonomies such as the TBS provide trainees and practitioners with a useful CBT framework to reflect on their own responses in the therapeutic relationship. A framework such as this helps the clinician develop the awareness that a strongly felt emotional response often has an underlying cognition and will frequently result in a compensatory behaviour if it is not 'observed' through self-reflection. It is important to point out to trainees that positive emotional responses to clients also need to be monitored. For example, if the client feels like a 'friend' the therapist should reflect on what consequences this may have for the therapeutic relationship.

The case study below shows how therapist schema can interfere with targeting CBT interventions.

Case Study 26.1: Jane

Jane had an intense anxious reaction when contemplating setting homework involving a behavioural experiment to target her client's long-standing social avoidance. After completing a thought record (SP), 'I will look silly' emerged as the 'hot' thought. The downward arrow technique uncovered the assumption 'If I try something new I should always get it right', together with seeking frequent reassurance from 'experts' and avoiding something new in therapy, as compensatory behaviours. Completing the Therapist Schema Questionnaire with this client in mind, Jane identified 'demanding standards' as a therapist schema. She also recognised her catastrophic view of the consequence of tolerating any degree of ambiguity in therapy. The combination of SP/SR led to an exploration in supervision regarding the advantages and disadvantages of her beliefs and resulting behaviour. She planned a behavioural experiment which involved testing a more optimistic view of her client's resilience and took the risk of assigning exposure homework without being certain of the outcome. Increased awareness of her belief system generalised to other situations where Jane consciously increased her tolerance of ambiguity and making the odd mistake, and resisted continually seeking reassurance from her supervisor and re-evaluated her 'demanding standards' therapist schema.

(adapted from Haarhoff & Kazantzis, 2007)

Sociocultural Factors Influencing CBT Practice

Sociocultural factors such as ethnicity, socio-economic status, spiritual beliefs, gender and sexual identity can influence the course of therapy in positive and negative ways. This is true of the therapist's and the client's cultural identity which can often operate out of immediate awareness. Trainees can be encouraged to reflect on the implications of their cultural identity or bias, in groups where discussion and comparisons can occur, or in the context of the SP/SR workbook where specific SR questions can be posed. The majority of training programmes in the United Kingdom have a wide variety of cultural identities represented. Cultural beliefs can be identified and the implications for CBT considered, and where appropriate challenged, in the group situation. Many cultures have prohibitions concerning the appropriateness of some aspects of CBT such as structuring time, following an agenda, taking an active role in directing the session, and setting homework tasks. Ethical differences in the right to privacy, confidentiality, sexuality and gender differences are all important areas for self-reflection in the context of cultural influences. The following SP/SR example demonstrates how a trainee's culture impacted on CBT for depression.

Case Study 26.2: Nisha

Nisha reported difficulties getting her client, a depressed older woman, to complete the thought record for homework. She attributed the difficulties to the client, whom she described as overwhelmed by depression and unable to cope. Reflecting that she had rushed through assigning homework, presenting the task in a flippant and self-depreciating manner, she completed a thought record (SP) identifying her 'hot thought' as 'She's older than me – it's uncomfortable telling her what to do' and recognised her cultural identity as a salient maintaining factor. As a Fijian Indian, her family of origin emphasised respect for elders, and there were rules preventing her expressing opinions or contradicting elders. She experienced the thought that it was

(Continued)

(Continued)

'improper and disrespectful' to ask the client to complete homework in the face of even the mildest ambivalence or reluctance. Working mainly with children, she had little experience with adults. Her SP/SR, however, had a ripple effect and she was able to identify that her cultural prohibitions prevented her from being appropriately assertive with the parents of the children she usually worked with. SP/SR enabled her to design a behavioural experiment and explore the reasons for her client's failure to complete the thought record, discovering that her client suffered from arthritis making writing difficult. As a result Nisha provided her client with a computerised template making the task more comfortable.

(adapted from Haarhoff & Kazantzis, 2007)

SP/SR Difficulties

SP/SR can be challenging and emotionally confronting for trainees and CBT practitioners, giving rise to strong negative emotions in a minority of trainees (Bennett-Levy et al., 2001; Haarhoff, 2008). CBT is perceived as a pragmatic, problem focussed, present orientated, relatively short-term, model and trainees can be 'taken by surprise' by the personal impact of the interventions, particularly when underlying assumptions and schema are triggered. Working independently through a structured workbook can induce feelings of vulnerability and it is important to provide support in this context. However, even in the context of support, given through supervision or co-therapy, anxieties concerning the implications of self-disclosure may arise. Depending on idiosyncratic schema, trainees can experience fears around being judged and found wanting, and if emotionally avoidant, will shy away from the process. SP/SR can also be perceived as time consuming and 'yet another hurdle to jump' in what are often demanding courses. For these reasons there may be a reluctance to participate in SP/SR as part of training.

Solutions

It is important to provide a clear rationale explaining why SP/SR is essential for professional development as a CBT practitioner. To legitimise the approach training programmes are advised to introduce the

DPR model highlighting the central role self-reflective practice has with respect to competency development. A workshop is a useful forum to introduce the benefits of SP/SR, expose trainees to different views, allow for discussion concerning the advantages and disadvantages, provide a forum to voice concerns, and advise trainees of supports available. It is also recommended that regular times are scheduled to meet with trainees completing structured SP/SR as part of their training. Practice in tackling SP/SR exercises can also occur within the structure of a workshop. The literature indicates that trainees benefit from a situation where they are able to share the results of their SP/SR with their peer group and this can be done in small groups or group supervision. Where there are practical difficulties in meeting the internet can be utilised in the form of blogs, interactive chat rooms, or Skype. Worries about self-disclosure can be overcome by providing a clear distinction between sharing content and process and advising trainees that it is the process which is therapeutically relevant. A degree of self-disclosure should be modelled and normalised by supervisors and trainers. If self-reflective journals are used, once again trainees should have a clear rationale as to why this is important and a degree of structure to guide them. Concerns about time can be allayed by structuring time for SP/SR within the course framework. It is recommended that where there is past, or current psychological trauma, there should be extra support in the form of traditional PT.

Conclusions

There is considerable theoretical support provided by the DPR model for the inclusion of self-reflective practice in the training and accreditation of CBT practitioners in the United Kingdom. A growing number of qualitative studies have established SP/SR as helpful in acquiring, consolidating, and improving CBT competency. Qualitative studies relying on the self-report of clinicians exposed to forms of self-reflective practice in CBT report predominantly positive outcomes in both the professional and the personal domain, and one quantitative study showed a significant improvement in the quality of written CBT case conceptualisations (Haarhoff, 2008). SP/SR as a model facilitating self-reflective practice in a manner compatible with the principles of CBT, shows considerable promise, and it is anticipated that more quantitative data supporting its utility both for the practitioner and in terms of therapeutic outcome will be available in the near future.

Summary

1 Self-reflective practice is central in developing and maintaining CBT competency.
2 The DPR model of psychotherapist skill acquisition provides a strong rationale for developing the self-reflective information processing system as a means to improving the declarative and procedural knowledge systems.
3 SP/SR is compatible with the principles and practice of CBT and shows promise as a pathway towards developing reflective capacity in CBT practitioners.

Activities

1 Develop a CBT self-conceptualisation. Choose an underlying assumption linked to a problematic behaviour and devise a behavioural experiment to strengthen a new, more helpful assumption. What did you learn about yourself? What implications does your experience have for your clinical practice?
2 Consider completing and scoring schema questionnaires found at www.schematherapy.com

Further Reading

Bennett-Levy, J. and Thwaites, R. (2007). 'Self and self-reflection in the therapeutic relationship: A conceptual map and practical strategies for training, supervision, and self-supervision of interpersonal skills', in P. Gilbert and R. Leahy (eds), *The Therapeutic Relationship in the Cognitive Behavioral Psychotherapies*. London: Routledge, pp. 255–81.

Ellis, A. (2002). *Overcoming Resistance: A Rational Emotive Behaviour Therapy Integrated Approach.* New York: Springer, Chapter 13, pp. 204–14.

References

Bennett-Levy, J. (2006). 'Therapist skills: A cognitive model for their acquisition and refinement', *Cognitive and Behavioural Psychotherapy*, 34: 57–78.

Bennett-Levy, J., Turner, F., Beaty, T., Smith, M., Paterson, B. and Farmer, S. (2001). 'The value of self-practice of cognitive therapy techniques and self-reflection in the training of cognitive therapists', *Behavioural and Cognitive Psychotherapy*, 29: 203–20.

Burns, D. (1989). *The Feeling Good Handbook*. New York: William Morrow.

Dobson, K. and Shaw, B. (1993). 'The training of cognitive therapists: What have we learned from treatment manuals', *Psychotherapy*, 30: 573–7.

Ellis, A. (2002). *Overcoming Resistance: A Rational Emotive Behaviour Therapy Integrated Approach*. New York: Springer.

Farrand, P., Perry, J. and Linsley, S. (2010). 'Enhancing self-practice/self-reflection (SP/SR) approach to cognitive behaviour training through the use of reflective blogs', *Behavioural and Cognitive Psychotherapy*, 38: 473–83.

Freud, S. (1937/1857). 'Analysis terminable and interminable', in J. Strachey (ed.), *The Complete Psychological Works of Sigmund Freud*. London: Hogarth Press, pp. 216–53.

Grant, A., Townend, M., Mills, J. and Cockx, A. (2010). *Assessment and Case Formulation in Cognitive Behavioural Therapy*. Thousand Oaks, CA: Sage.

Haarhoff, B. (2006). 'The importance of identifying and understanding therapist schema in cognitive therapy training and supervision', *New Zealand Journal of Psychology*, 35: 126–31.

Haarhoff, B. (2008). 'The map, the navigator, and the explorer evaluating the content and quality of CBT case conceptualizations and the role of self-practice/self-reflection as a training intervention'. Unpublished doctoral dissertation. Massey University, Auckland, New Zealand.

Haarhoff, B. and Kazantzis, N. (2007). 'How to supervise the use of homework in cognitive behavior therapy', *Cognitive and Behavioral Practice*, 14: 325–32.

Haarhoff, B. and Stenhouse, L. (2004). '"Practice makes perfect": Practicing Cognitive Behaviour Therapy techniques and training', *New Zealand Clinical Psychologist*, 4: 26–30.

Hollon, S. and Beck, A. (2004) 'Cognitive and cognitive-behavioural therapies', in M.J. Lambert (ed.), *Garfield and Bergins' Handbook of Psychotherapy and Behaviour Change and Empirical Analysis*, 5th edn. New York: John Wiley & Sons, Inc., pp. 447–92.

Laireiter, A. and Willutzski, U. (2005). 'Personal therapy in cognitive-behavioural therapy: Tradition and current practice', in J. Gellor, J. Norcross and D. Orlinsky (eds), *The Psychotherapists' Own Psychotherapy: Patient and Clinician Perspectives.* Oxford: Oxford University Press, pp. 41–51.

Leahy, R. (2001). *Overcoming Resistance in Cognitive Therapy*. New York: Guilford Press.

Norcross, J. (2005). 'The psychotherapist's own psychotherapy: Educating and developing psychologists', *American Psychologist*, 60: 840–50.

Padesky, C. (1996). 'Developing cognitive therapy competency: Teaching and supervision models', in P. Salkovskis (ed.), *Frontiers of Cognitive Therapy*. New York: Guilford Press, pp. 266–92.

Richards, D.A. and Suckling, R. (2009). 'Improving access to psychological therapies: Phase IV Prospective cohort study', *British Journal of Clinical Psychology*, 48: 377–96.

Rønnestad, M. and Skovholt, T. (2003). 'The journey of the counselor and therapist: Research findings and perspectives on professional development'. *Journal of Career Development*, 30: 5–44.

Rudd, M. and Joiner, T. (1997). 'Counter transference and the therapeutic relationship: A cognitive perspective', *Journal of Cognitive Psychotherapy*, 11: 231–49.

Sperry, L. (2010). *Core Competencies in Counseling and Psychotherapy Becoming a Highly Competent and Effective Therapist*. New York: Routledge.

Sutton, L., Townend, M. and Wright, J. (2007). 'The experiences of reflective learning journals by cognitive behavioural psychotherapy students', *Reflective Practice*, 8: 387–404.

Wampold, B. (2001). *The Great Psychotherapy Debate*. Mahwah, NJ: Lawrence Erlbaum Associates.

Index